Child Abuse

Third Edition

Christina Lyon LLB, FRSA, Solicitor
The Queen Victoria Professor of Law
The University of Liverpool

With contributions by

Cathy Cobley
Cardiff University

Stephanie Petrie
The University of Liverpool

Caroline Reid Barrister
14 Gray's Inn Square

Family Law

2003

Published by Family Law
an imprint of Jordan Publishing Limited
21 St Thomas Street
Bristol BS1 6JS

British Library Cataloguing-in-Publication Data

A catalogue record for this book is available
from the British Library.

ISBN 0 85308 576 5

Typeset by Jordan Publishing Limited
Printed by MPG Books Limited, Bodmin, Cornwall

DEDICATION

This book is dedicated to Adrian Lyon without whose support, love and encouragement it could not have been completed, and of course to our children Sasha and David Lyon.

FOREWORD

The protection of children from abuse is one of the most important features of our justice system. This book, which is now being published in its third edition, brings together in a thoughtful and comprehensive form a review of the relevant law and practice. In preparing this volume the writers have undertaken a very detailed revision and rewriting exercise, and have produced an up-to-date manual for practitioners across all disciplines.

This volume reflects the enormous changes in the landscape of child protection which have taken place over the last decade. This edition incorporates all the major recent reforms of laws relevant to child care, both civil and criminal. It takes into account the far-reaching impact of new legal developments such as the Human Rights Act 1998, as well as the impact of social developments in the new millennium.

Readers will find in the first chapters of the book a useful explanation of the socio-legal context of national and international child protection. In the following chapters, forms of, and issues surrounding, child abuse are discussed. The range of available civil and criminal proceedings are explored and their mechanisms detailed. A separate chapter is given to the important issues involved in inter-agency co-operation. This issue is highlighted in the final chapter, which touches on the outcomes of the Laming Inquiry. A new chapter has been devoted to the complex area of evidence in child abuse cases. The chapter on contact gives a careful survey of the difficult issues involved where children are in various types of care.

This book adopts an informative, cross-disciplinary approach. In my view it is essential reading for all those practising in this field, whether as judges, lawyers, guardians, social workers, education or health professionals.

Dame Elizabeth Butler-Sloss, DBE

February 2003

PREFACE

Child Abuse is making its appearance as a third edition, but I would like to take this opportunity to emphasise, as I am sure will be obvious to those familiar with both the first and second editions of this text, that I, together with my new collaborators – Stephanie Petrie of the Department of Sociology, Social Work and Social Policy at the University of Liverpool; Cathy Cobley from the Cardiff Law School and Caroline Reid, Barrister, of 14 Gray's Inn Square, London – have undertaken a radical restructuring and a complete rewriting of the book. This has been necessitated by major reforms of the civil law relevant to children encompassing: a number of amendments to the Children Act 1989, including as we went to press late major amendments to the Adoption and Children Act 2002, the enactment of the Human Rights Act 1998 incorporating the European Convention on Human Rights, the enactment of the Protection of Children Act 1999, the Care Standards Act 2000 and the Children (Leaving Care) Act 2000. In addition, there have been a whole series of major reforms to the Criminal Justice System effected by a number of criminal justice measures throughout the 1990s including the Criminal Justice Act 1991, the Crime and Disorder Act 1998, the Youth Justice and Criminal Evidence Act 1999, and into the new millennium: the Criminal Justice and Courts Services Act 2000, and the Powers of Criminal Courts Sentencing Act 2000. Sadly, in mid-2001 my former co-author, Dr (now Professor) Peter de Cruz of Staffordshire University, had to drop out because of other commitments, but my publisher and I believe that the fresh and new perspectives contributed by my current colleagues will add to the appeal of the text. Thus, in this new work, I have been solely responsible for writing Chapters 1, 2, 4, 5, 6, 7, 10, 11, 12, whilst Stephanie Petrie wrote Chapter 3: Issues in child abuse; Caroline Reid wrote Chapter 8 on Evidence and procedure in civil child abuse cases, which thus for the first time gets an entire chapter to itself; and Cathy Cobley was responsible for Chapter 9 on Criminal proceedings, which gets a much needed expansion and expert treatment.

Whilst it was hoped that the Home Office Sex Offences Review would have completed its work in time for legislation to have been on the statute book by the date of completing this book, such was not the case. Although the consultation period on the Review closed on 31 March 2001, there was still no legislation in contemplation even by the summer of 2002. In this area, therefore, Cathy has had to try to anticipate the changes that might be effected possibly in 2003 in response to the consultation on *Setting the Boundaries: Reforming the Law on Sex Offences* (Home Office Steering Group, 2000). In addition, the Family Court Welfare Service, the panels of guardians ad litem and reporting officers and those members of the Official Solicitor's department working on children's cases, had their work merged as a result of the Criminal Justice and Courts Services Act 2000 to form the new Children and Family Courts Advisory and Support Service (CAFCASS), which has now been operating, although with a rather troubled first 18 months, since April 2001.

The new amendments to the Family Proceedings Rules 1991, the Rules of Court setting out the duties of the Family Court reporters/advisers, reporting officers and children's guardians were produced in the summer of 2001. It is now clear that, at least in child protection proceedings, the support given to children and the functions and duties previously performed by guardians ad litem on guardian ad litem panels continue to be performed by the newly named children's guardians within CAFCASS and little, if any, amendment at all apart from a change in nomenclature has been needed in the public law area to the relevant court rules. Further rules will, however, have to be produced for the new powers of CAFCASS officers to refer a child's position to the courts under the new s 26(2C) of the CA 1989.

More major changes have occurred in the private law area and, where relevant, these too are dealt with in this book. At the time of going to press, the Adoption and Children Act 2002 was undergoing further late major amendments and in the main body of the text I have tried to incorporate at final proof stage the changes which received legislative assent. Officials from the Lord Chancellor's Department have indicated, however, that it is likely to be 2003–2004 before any such new legislation could be implemented.

Once again, as was the case with the increase in volume from the first edition to the second edition, the third edition is now some 400 pages and two chapters longer than the second edition. The many changes to the law and the hugely increased numbers of decisions, which have been made since the second edition was written in 1993, have, of course, necessitated such an increase.

In writing the book *de novo* as it were, both I and my colleagues have, however, endeavoured to respond to a large number of constructive criticisms and suggestions made by students, judicial and academic colleagues, and those in a wide variety of professions including: social work, psychiatry, psychology, paediatrics, education, law, health and welfare, as well as to criticisms and suggestions made by various reviewers of the second edition. As a result, therefore, I have again reorganised the structure of the book in order, it is hoped, to make it more coherent and comprehensible.

I would like to acknowledge the help of the following people for expressing views or giving information on matters contained in these pages: Patrick Crawley, Training and Development Officer, Nottingham Social Services;

Mr Melvyn Barker, Team Leader, Child Protection in the Schools Directorate of the DFES; Dr Jane Wynne, formerly of the Clarendon Wing, Leeds General Hospital; Professor Helen Carty, Professor of Paediatric Radiology at the University of Liverpool; Professor Chris Jones, Professor of Sociology, Social Policy and Social Work at the University of Liverpool; Chief Inspector Steve Kelly, Merseyside Police; Jessica Gardener, Adviser on Medical Ethics to both the Medical Ethics Committee of the British Medical Association and the Conduct Health and Standards Division of the General Medical Council; Mr Justice Mark Hedley, the former Acting Family Liaison Judge at the Queen Elizabeth II Law Courts, Liverpool; His Honour Judge Adrian Lyon, Manchester Law Courts; Ernest Ryder, QC, TD, Barrister at Law; Sue Ashton, Panel Manager, Liverpool and Sefton Guardian ad Litem Panel; and, finally, to the many students on the University of Liverpool's Diploma and MA courses in Children, Policy, Practice and the Law, and in Social Work, on the MSc in Forensic Psychology and Community Paediatrics as well as students on the LLB and LLM Child Law courses.

Most important of all, I acknowledge with extreme gratitude the life-saving assistance provided by Miss Freda Mainwaring, who typed up the manuscript, and who has been with the book in both previous editions. It simply would not have appeared without her assistance.

The publishers, Jordans, have borne with extreme fortitude and patience, the various delays caused by my constant requests for more time in order to take into account the provisions of two Adoption and Children Bills, since the first fell with the general election of 2001, but more especially to take on board the task of writing three chapters I had never anticipated having to write. Martin West has been with the book all the way through, Gary Hill very ably picked up the reins after the departure of Stephen Honey and saw the book through to publication, whilst Richard Hudson was an invaluable source of ideas on new authors for two and-a-half of the Chapters previously written by Peter de Cruz. The two-and-a-half then became three! I therefore owe an enormous debt of thanks to all of them. In some ways these various hurdles enabled us to incorporate the implications of a huge number of important decisions as well as unexpected implementations of statutory provisions. For example, the implementation of the special measures provisions in Part II of the Youth Justice and Criminal Evidence Act 1999, was effected almost without warning on 24 July 2002. The recommendations of the UN Monitoring Committee, of the *Safeguarding Children* Joint Inspectorates Report, relevant provisions of the Adoption and Children Act 2002, noting references only to the Court of Appeal's decisions in *Re B* [2002] EWCA Civ 752, [2002] 2 FLR 1133 and *Re O and N* [2002] EWCA Civ 1271, [2002] 2 FLR 1167, excepted we ultimately agreed, therefore, on a final cut-off date of 31 August 2002.

The Laming Report on the Inquiry into the Death of Victoria Climbie (see *www.victoria-climbie-inquiry.org.uk/report*) published on 28 January 2003, as this book was going to press, concluded that: 'the current legislative framework is fundamentally sound but the gap is in its implementation'. Whilst the 108 recommendations (some of which it has been possible to include in this book) include the reduction in the amount of guidance issued to those involved in child protection, this will take time and may not ultimately prove possible. In the meantime, however, my publishers, my colleagues and I hope that this book may fill some of the gaps for the sake of the children.

Professor Christina M. Lyon,
Liverpool,
October 2002 and January 2003

CONTENTS

TABLE OF CASES

References are to paragraph numbers.

TABLE OF STATUTES

References are to paragraph numbers.

TABLE OF STATUTORY INSTRUMENTS

References are to paragraph numbers.

TABLE OF CIRCULARS, GUIDANCE AND OTHER OFFICIAL PUBLICATIONS

References are to paragraph numbers.

TABLE OF CONVENTIONS AND FOREIGN ENACTMENTS

References are to paragraph numbers.

FOREIGN ENACTMENTS

TABLE OF ABBREVIATIONS

ACPC	Area Child Protection Committee
ACPO	Association of Chief Police Officers
BMA	British Medical Association
CA 1989	Children Act 1989
CAFCASS	Children and Family Courts Advisory and Support Service
CAPO 1991	Children (Allocation of Proceedings) Order 1991
CCETSW	Central Council for Social Work Education and Training
CDA 1998	Crime and Disorder Act 1998
CICA	Criminal Injuries Compensation Authority
CJA 1967	Criminal Justice Act 1967
CJA 1988	Criminal Justice Act 1988
CJA 1991	Criminal Justice Act 1991
CJCSA 2000	Criminal Justice and Court Services Act 2000
CJPOA 1994	Criminal Justice and Public Order Act 1994
CPIA 1996	Criminal Procedure and Investigations Act 1996
CPR 1998	Civil Procedure Rules 1998
CPS	Crown Prosecution Service
CPU	Child Protection Unit
CSA	child sexual abuse
CSA 2000	Care Standards Act 2000
CYPA 1933	Children and Young Persons Act 1933
CYPA 1969	Children and Young Persons Act 1969
CYPU	Children and Young People's Unit
DfEE	Department for Education and Employment
DFES	Department for Education and Skills
DOH	Department of Health
ECHR	European Convention on Human Rights
FPC(CA 1989)R 1991	Family Proceedings Courts (Children Act 1989) Rules 1991
FPR 1991	Family Proceedings Rules 1991
GAL	guardian ad litem
GMC	General Medical Council
GSCC	General Social Care Council
HRA 1998	Human Rights Act 1998
ICA 1960	Indecency with Children Act 1960
ISP	Internet Service Provider
LEA	local education authority
LGA 1974	Local Government Act 1974
LCD	Lord Chancellor's Department
MAP	Management Action Plan
MAPPA	Multi-Agency Public Protection Arrangements
MAPPP	Multi-Agency Public Protection Panel
MSBP	Munchausen Syndrome by Proxy
NCSC	National Care Standards Commission

OAPA 1861	Offences Against the Person Act 1861
NHSCCA 1990	National Health Service and Community Care Act 1990
PACE	Police and Criminal Evidence Act 1984
PCA 1999	Protection of Children Act 1999
PCC(S)A 2000	Powers of Criminal Courts (Sentencing) Act 2000
RP(C)R 1991	Representations Procedure (Children) Regulations 1991
SCIE	Social Care Institute for Excellence
SIDS	Sudden Infant Death Syndrome
SOA 1956	Sexual Offences Act 1956
SOA 1967	Sexual Offences Act 1967
SOA 1997	Sex Offenders Act 1997
SO(A)A 2000	Sexual Offences (Amendment) Act 2000
UNCRC	United Nations Convention on the Rights of the Child 1989
YJCEA 1999	Youth Justice and Criminal Evidence Act 1999
YOI	Young Offender Institutions
YOT	Youth Offending Team

CHAPTER 1

INTRODUCTION: THE NATIONAL AND INTERNATIONAL LEGAL AND SOCIAL POLICY CONTEXT

'Children should be aware of their daily rights so that they can decide whether they are being abused or not.'

'The most important and difficult view to accept is the notion that children have the right to be regarded as equal. It would be impossible to cease to call the children one has physically given life to anything other than "mine" as we do, but the notion of one person belonging to another not only flatly contradicts the notion of human equality, but also offers a feeling of being at liberty to personally control the use of this particular possession as one does of inanimate possessions. One of the most important tasks we need to undertake if we are to halt child abuse is to educate people into an understanding that humans cannot be owned by others and that physically producing and nurturing a child concerns no more rights of authority than one holds over any other human being. What it does, I think, do, is impose upon parents a duty to nurture in a manner that is respectful towards children's rights to be treated as a fellow human. This then has societal indications. If we expect people to manage children carefully then we need to make it possible for them to do so. This suggests that we need to make it possible for adults to function in a society that offers basic material well-being as a right, that provides education for parenthood, help, guidance and practical support. ... One way we may start the process of change is to initiate a nation-wide discussion as to the difference between our behaviour towards adults and our behaviour towards children.' (Both quotations taken from *Childhood Matters, Report of the National Commission of Inquiry into the Prevention of Child Abuse* (1996) vol 2: Background Papers, at p 129.)

The United Nations Convention on the Rights of the Child 1989

Background

1.1 The United Nations Convention on the Rights of the Child 1989 (UNCRC) adopted by the UN General Assembly on 20 November 1989 is the

---

Note: References in the text have been abbreviated using the author/date system. Full publishing details are included in the Bibliography at p **673**. Full details of Circulars, Guidance and other Official Publications are included in the tables at p **lv**.

world's most ratified Convention with the USA and Somalia being the only countries not to have ratified it. It is also taken extremely seriously by all the ratifying countries. The vast majority comply with the very stringent reporting requirements to the UNCRC Monitoring Committee laid down to ensure compliance with its terms (see Articles 43 and 44). See the UNCRC website (www.unhchr.ch/) for publication of each nation's Reports to the Monitoring Committee and for reports of the special sessions of the Committee to which each country sends government representatives to answer questions and criticisms relating to their latest Reports. The UNCRC makes reference in its preamble to, and builds extensively upon, the skeleton of children's rights laid down under earlier versions of the Convention, for example the Geneva Declaration on the Rights of the Child 1924 and the UN Declaration of the Rights of the Child 1959, as well as complementing other relevant UN human rights documents such as the International Covenant on Civil and Political Rights 1966 and the International Covenant on Economic, Social and Cultural Rights 1966. (For a detailed account of the earlier Conventions and an in-depth consideration of the UNCRC and other relevant International covenants, see van Beuren (1995).)

Relevant Articles of the UNCRC (3, 6, 9, 12 19, 32–36, 37, 39 and 40)

1.2   The UK government was an early signatory to the UNCRC and went on to ratify the Convention on 16 December 1991. In the UK, however, ratification of such an international Convention does not mean that it is automatically incorporated into UK law. For this to occur, a further Act of Parliament is required to provide that the Convention or treaty should take direct effect in the courts and that the rights provided by such a Convention or treaty can be relied upon in those courts. This has *not* occurred in relation to the UNCRC and the Convention is *not* part of UK law. Despite that fact, the UK government has nevertheless indicated through its Reports to the UN Monitoring Committee (see the UK's *First Report to the UN Monitoring Committee* (Department of Health (DOH), The Stationery Office, 1994) and see the UK's *Second Report to the UN Monitoring Committee* (DOH, The Stationery Office, 1999)) that it does regard itself as bound by the demands of the Convention. In the child protection field, the UK government has further emphasised the increasing importance and relevance to its thinking of the UNCRC by according it first place within the description of the relevant 'Legislative Framework' in its most recent *Guidance* document issued in relation to child protection (see *Safeguarding Children in Whom Illness is Fabricated or Induced* (DOH, Home Office, DFES, Welsh Assembly, 2002), at para 1.12, directing attention specifically to Articles 3, 9, 19, 37 and 39). In relation to the *Framework for the Assessment of Children in Need and their Families* (DOH, 2000), at p viii and *Working Together to Safeguard Children* (DOH, 1999), at p viii, the first statements relating to 'The Status and Content' of both pieces of *Guidance* are that the *Guidance* 'reflects the principles contained within the

United Nations Convention on the Rights of the Child'. All of these documents of guidance thus make the critical assumption that everyone working in the child protection field is thoroughly conversant with those principles and with the relevant Articles of the Convention. It is certainly the case that the courts in England, Wales and Scotland have also increasingly made reference to Articles of the UNCRC when reaching decisions concerning children and their families (see, for example, *Re S* [2001] 2 FLR 776 (Articles 19 and 37); *R on the application of P v Secretary of State for the Home Department* [2001] 2 FLR 383 (Articles 3, 5, 9 and 18); *Re L, V, M and H* [2000] 2 FLR 334 (Article 9(3)); *Re T* [2000] 2 FLR 192 (Article 12); *Re J* [2000] 1 FLR 571 (Article 24); *Re P* [1999] 2 FLR 573 (Articles 3 and 14); *Re C* [1999] 2 FLR 1004 (Articles 5, 6 and 24); *R v Central Criminal Court ex parte S* [1999] 1 FLR 480 (Articles 3 and 40); *Re P* [1998] 1 FLR 624 (Articles 3 and 14); *Re A* [1998] 1 FLR 354 (Article 9); and *Re R* [1993] 2 FLR 762 (Article 9)). The rights contained within the Articles of the UNCRC may thus be seen perhaps as the 'aspirant' or 'gold' standard to which the UK government, its courts and all of its sevices to children including social services, health, education and housing must aspire.

1.3   Thus, throughout the length and breadth of the UK all local authorities, health authorities and health service trusts, education departments and all non-governmental organisations working with children have signed up to and indicate that they regard themselves as bound by the principles contained within the Convention. Whilst at the time of the *First Report to the UN Monitoring Committee* few if any children had actually heard of the UNCRC or of the rights which it purported to give them, it was hoped that by the time of the UK's *Second Report* this situation would have improved. The government itself was forced to acknowledge, however, in the opening chapter that although attempts had been made to involve children in the closing stages on the consultation of the report, there was little awareness generally within the body of children themselves that they had any of the rights which they had been given under such an important document as the UNCRC. All of the agencies and organisations which work in the sphere of child protection are part of the grouping which signed up to observing the principles contained within the UNCRC and applying these in their everyday work. It may not be the case that all children know of their rights under the UNCRC, but all of the professionals working to protect children should be aware that they are themselves bound by the provisions of the Convention and that these should therefore be applied in all of their everyday work. Given the importance, identified in the quotations above, which children and other survivors of child abuse have put on the notion of children's rights and parental responsibilities, it is perhaps scandalous that the principles contained within the UNCRC are not more widely known and understood by both parents and children within the UK.

1.4 Given its importance, however, the relevant provisions of the UNCRC which may be applicable in the context of child protection will now be considered, bearing in mind that, as set out above, this is the gold standard to which we in our professional practice should be seeking to aspire. The Articles of the UNCRC which are of specific relevance in the sphere of child protection include Articles 3, 6, 9, 12, 19, 32–36, 37, 39 and 40.

1.5 Article 3(2) provides that:

> 'State Parties undertake to ensure the child such protection and care as is necessary for his or her well-being, taking into account the rights and duties of his or her parents or others with parental responsibility, and to this end, shall take all appropriate legislative and administrative measures.'

Article 6(1) provides that: 'every child has the inherent right to life', and goes on in Article 6(2) to state that it is the State's obligation to 'ensure to the maximum extent possible the survival and development of the child'. (It should be noted that upon signature the UK declared that it interprets the Convention as applicable only following a live birth.)

Article 9 provides that:

> 'States shall ensure that a child shall not be separated from his or her parents against their will, except when competent authorities subject to judicial review determine, in accordance with applicable law and procedures, that such separation is necessary for the best interests of the child.'

It goes on to provide that:

> 'such determination may be necessary in a particular case such as one involving abuse or neglect of the child by the parents.'

Article 12(1) actually provides that:

> 'States shall assure to the child who is capable of forming his or her own views the right to express those views freely in all matters affecting the child, the views of the child being given due weight in accordance with the age and maturity of the child.'

Article 12(2) critically goes on to provide that:

> 'for this purpose, the child shall in particular be provided the opportunity to be heard in any judicial and administrative proceedings affecting the child, either directly, or through a representative or an appropriate body, in a manner consistent with the procedural rules of national law.'

Article 19 is the Article which most people would recognise as conferring rights upon children to protection from abuse and neglect. Thus Article 19(1) provides that States shall:

> 'take all appropriate legislative, administrative, social and educational measures to protect the child from all forms of physical or mental violence, injury or abuse, neglect or negligent treatment, maltreatment or exploitation including sexual abuse whilst in the care of parents or others responsible for their care.'

It is clear that the community of nations drawing up the provisions to be included in the UNCRC were firmly of the view that prevention should be a clear goal in the area of protection of children from abuse and neglect. Thus, Article 19(2) provides that:

> 'Such protective measures should, as appropriate, include effective procedures for the establishment of social programmes to provide necessary support for the child and those who have the care of the child, as well as for other forms of prevention and for identification, reporting, referral, investigation, treatment and follow up of instances of child maltreatment, and, as appropriate, for judicial involvement.'

1.6   Other Articles of the UNCRC go on to provide for the protection of children in very specific situations. Thus, in Article 32, States are required to:

> 'recognise the right of the child to be protected from economic exploitation and to be protected from engaging in work which constitutes a threat to their health, education or development,'

and States are required to:

> 'take the appropriate legislative, administrative, social and educational measures to ensure the implementation of the Article, in particular setting minimum ages for employment and regulating the conditions of such employment.'

Article 33 provides for the child's 'right to protection from the illicit use of narcotic drugs and psychotropic substances' and also provides for the State's obligation to prevent the use of children in the illicit production and trafficking of such substances'. In Article 34 the UNCRC provides for the child's right:

> 'to protection from sexual exploitation and sexual abuse including the inducement or coercion of a child to engage in any unlawful sexual activity, the exploitative use of children in prostitution or other unlawful sexual practices and the exploitative use of children in pornographic performances and materials.'

Article 35 provides for the State's obligation 'to make every effort to prevent the sale, trafficking and abduction of children' and in Article 36, the Convention, in an effort to catch all potential forms of exploitation of the child, provides that 'States have an obligation to protect the child against all other forms of exploitation prejudicial to any aspects of the child's welfare'. Article 40 recognises the right of children alleged or recognised as having committed a criminal offence under the laws of their governing jurisdictions to respect for their human rights and, in particular, to benefit from all aspects of the due process of law, including legal or other assistance in preparing and presenting their defence. The Article provides for the principle that recourse to judicial proceedings should be avoided wherever possible (Article 40(3)(b)). Critically, for the purposes of the scope of this work, in Article 40(4) it asserts as a right that:

> 'a variety of dispositions, such as care, guidance and supervision orders; counselling; probation; foster care; educational and vocational training programmes and other alternatives to institutional care shall be available to ensure that all children are dealt with in a manner appropriate to their well-being and proportionate both to their circumstances and the offence.'

1.7   Finally in this area, one must consider Article 37(a) of the UNCRC which in its first sentence provides that States parties shall ensure that 'No child should be subjected to torture or other cruel, inhuman or degrading treatment or punishment'. This provision, of course, echoes Article 3 of the European Convention on Human Rights (ECHR), as implemented by the Human Rights Act 1998 (HRA 1998) (see para **1.21**).

1.8   In addition to the Articles of the UNCRC which require States to ensure that they take all the appropriate preventive and protective measures, the UNCRC crucially goes on to provide in Article 39 that:

> 'States parties shall take all appropriate measures to promote physical and psychological recovery and social reintegration of a child victim of: any form of neglect, exploitation, or abuse; torture or any other form of cruel, inhuman or degrading treatment or punishment; or armed conflicts. Such recovery and reintegration shall take place in an environment which fosters the health, self-respect and dignity of the child.'

Commentary on policy and legislative responses to the UNCRC

1.9   Much of the UK government's *First Report to the UN Monitoring Committee* (see para **1.2**) was taken up with an account of the Children Act 1989 (CA 1989), as implemented in October 1991 in England and Wales. A far more systematic evaluation of the state of children's rights at that time in the UK was then undertaken by a huge group of non-governmental organisations and was submitted to the UN Monitoring Committee by the Children's Rights Development Unit (see *UK Agenda for Children* (CRDU, 1994)), which threw the inadequacy of the official Government Report into sharp relief, more especially when it came under the detailed consideration of the Monitoring Committee at its hearings in January 1995. The strong view put forward by the Conservative government at that stage was that the CA 1989 represented the sort of measures referred to in Article 3(2) that governments should take 'to ensure the child such protection and care as was necessary for his or her well-being taking into account the rights of those with parental responsibility'. The government also argued in that document that compliance with the provisions of Article 6 requiring that States recognise that every child has a right to life and to ensure to the maximum extent possible the survival and development of the child were to be found not only in the provisions of the CA 1989 but also in the various duties imposed on health authorities. This was a view repeated in the *Second Report* although the new Labour government was anxious to promote the large number of programmes intended to supplement the provisions in the legislation (see Chapter 7). Nevertheless, as is acknowledged in *Learning from Past Experience – A Review of Serious Case Reviews* (DOH, 2002) (ie those cases where a child has died or suffers serious injury as a result of abuse or neglect; for more detail see para **6.91**), and as has emerged from the findings of the Victoria Climbie Inquiry, the imposition of such duties on a range of agencies (including, in Victoria's case, housing, police, social services and the NHS in several London boroughs) will not necessarily ensure that children will not die or suffer serious abuse at the hands of their parents or carers. *Learning from Past Experience* is the first of an ongoing series of national overview studies of serious case reviews, but it demonstrates, even from the limited sample of 40 cases, that there was a wide range of diversity apparent in terms of the prior involvement of the child and family with welfare agencies. Thus, apparently, some were virtually unknown to anyone, others were long-standing cases, often with parents being known since the time of their own childhood. In only six out of the 40 cases studied had there been enduring concerns about risks of harm to the child. The child's right to live with his parents as guaranteed in Article 9, is, according to the government in the *Second Report* (see Chapter 7), met by the provisions of the CA 1989 in England and Wales, as well as the adoption legislation, which prevent removal of the child from his family against that family's wishes only where it can be justified by reference to the paramountcy of the child's welfare, and by the corresponding statutory provisions in Scotland and Northern Ireland. The child's right to contact with his family as provided for in Article 9(3), unless again this is proved to be contrary to the child's welfare, is further met by the relevant provisions of the CA 1989 as interpreted by the courts. The importance of Article 12(1) (which asserts the right of the child to express an opinion and to have that opinion taken into account in any matter or procedure affecting the child) in informing government thinking is implicit in much of the guidance issued in the child protection field and is a constant theme in the *Quality Protects* programme. In addition, its influence was very apparent in the principles underlying the formation of the Children's Fund and in the publication in November 2001 of the document *Learning to Listen – Core Principles on the Involvement and Engagement of Children and Young People* by the

Children and Young People's Unit (CYPU) (see para **1.11**). All government departments have been required to produce action plans to implement the principles and these are being published on the CYPU website. The demands of Article 12(2) in requiring that the child be heard in judicial or administrative proceedings concerning them are met in the rules, made pursuant to the CA 1989, applying to child protection proceedings in England and Wales, providing that children are, of course, parties to such proceedings and benefit from the unique dual sytem of representation by both a solicitor and an officer of the Children and Family Courts Advisory and Support Service (CAFCASS). (See Chapters 7 and 8, and for comment on the problems experienced by the new CAFCASS service see Chapter **12**.) The government has further argued that the CA 1989 represented compliance with the demands of Article 19(1) and (2). Much was therefore made of the CA 1989 but, of course, this only applied in England and Wales whereas Scotland and Northern Ireland were to wait a further 6 years before relevant new child protection statutes were passed for both those jurisdictions (see Children (Northern Ireland) Order 1995, SI 1995/755 and the Children (Scotland) Act 1995). Despite criticism made of that *First Report*, the government continued in its *Second Report* to see the CA 1989 as providing the appropriate response to the demands of Articles 19 and 39. Thus, the *Second Report* states that:

> 'The Government is firmly committed to ensuring that all children within the community are safeguarded and protected from abuse. The Children Act 1989 was designed to promote appropriate and decisive action to protect children from abuse and neglect' (at para 7.7.1).

1.10   Clearly, much more is needed if the government is to try to claim compliance through its various agencies with the demands of Article 19 and certainly of Article 39, but it does have to be acknowledged that the Labour government, in its now one-and-a-half terms in office, has embarked on an enormous number of programmes and policies intended to provide better and more effective safeguards in the protection of children. The government points out that the issuing of the new guidance *Working Together to Safeguard Children* in 1999 provides a solid foundation for inter-agency co-operation in child protection work and that real improvements have been made in tackling serious cases of abuse (*Second Report*, para 7.7.2). The government also states that, at that stage, the proposed new *Framework for Assessment of Children and their Families* (actually published in its final form by the DOH in 2000) is a framework which has been developed for use by a range of workers and represents the needs-led assessment of children and their families. It emphasises that the *Framework for Assessment* focuses on:

> 'Assessing the needs of the children and the capacity of parents and family members to meet those needs in both the short term and long term. It will be underpinned by the latest knowledge of the impact that domestic violence, alcohol

and drug misuse, mental health and sex offending can have on child development' (*Second Report*, para 7.7.6).

1.11   It is still then the case that the government relies on the CA 1989 and various other documents of guidance issued pursuant to that Act to satisfy the demands placed upon it by the UNCRC. It does, however, acknowledge the problems faced by children being looked after within the care system and repeats several of the recommendations from the *Children's Safeguards Review* (DOH, 1997) and states that further action will be needed in this area in order to respond appropriately to the recommendations of the Utting Report (see also *The Government's Response to the Children's Safeguard Review* (Cm 4105, The Stationery Office, 1998)). As an immediate response to the *Safeguards Review*, the government reported in the *Second Report* that a Ministerial Task Force on Children's Safeguards would manage the government's response and monitor the overall programme of action whilst at the same time noting that some of the proposals could not be taken forward until there was time in the legislative programme.

1.12   Since the publication of the *Second Report* (in August 1999), relevant time has, however, been found and, as a direct result of the Utting Report (*People Like Us*), the Care Standards Act 2000 (CSA 2000), the Children Leaving Care Act 2000 and the Children (Leaving Care) Regulations 2001 have now been enacted, and further changes have also been incorporated in the Adoption and Children Act 2002, which was enacted as this book was going to press. Other relevant legislation includes: the Carers and Disabled Children Act 2000 implemented on 1 April 2001, which gave parents of disabled children and 16- and 17-year-old disabled young people greater choice and flexibilty in how they receive services by introducing direct payments (see Chapter 6); and the Special Educational Needs and Disability Act 2001, which strengthens the right of children with specific educational needs to be educated in mainstream schools and since September 2002 protects them from discrimination on grounds of their disability in their access to education. A revised *Special Educational Needs: Code of Practice* was also issued in 2001 (DfES, 2001). The government has not only engaged in a raft of legislation since the *Second Report* but it has also launched a whole series of funded policy initiatives to better protect children to whom local authorities owe responsibilities under the expansive provisions of the CA 1989. For children served by social services departments a set of 11 Objectives with asssociated performance indicators was published in 1999 under the title *The Government's Objectives for Children's Social Services* (DOH, 1999) and the latest *Children Act Report 2001* (DOH, 2002) is stuctured around those 11 objectives and updates information on the volume and effectiveness of services for children in need under each objective. The linked *Quality Protects* programme, originally a 5-year £885 million programme to transform services and outcomes for children in need including looked-after children, disabled children and children in need of protection, was also launched in 1999 with the aim of improving the governance, management and delivery of children's services. The DOH maintains that *Quality Protects* has already been shown to have improved outcomes for children (*Children Act Report 2001* (DOH, July 2002), at para 5). On 28 February 2001, the Secretary of State for Health announced the intention to produce a National Service Framework for Children, which it is intended will produce national standards across the NHS (including maternity services) and social services. The Children's Taskforce set up after the publication of the NHS plan is overseeing the development of the Framework, with six external working groups taking this work of developing the standards forward. On 20 March 2002, a major review of placement choice and fostering services entitled *Choice Protects* was launched by the Minister of State for Health. The review is intended to focus on helping councils commission and deliver effective placements and services for looked after children, with special empahsis on foster care. It will also carefully consider the issues putting pressure on the fostering services which are being increasingly relied upon to provide family-based care for the increasing volume of care being provided by councils. Also in 2002, the government announced its intention of integrating performance monitoring and the Quality Protects Management Action Plans (MAPs), which have been one of the key mechanisms within the *Quality Protects* programme. The DOH acknowledged that the overall performance monitoring of councils has developed significantly and that children's services needed to be mainstreamed within performance monitoring, thus it confirmed that the MAPs submitted by councils in January 2002 would be the last and that in future information on children's services will be fully integrated into the 2003–04 Position Statements (*Children Act Report 2001* (DOH, 2002), at para 5). Other improvements were noted in the *Second Report*, including the provision of additional finance to improve services to children in need and those in local authority care, and the government introduced a Children's Special Services Grant totalling £375 million over 3 years. It was the case that when the UK's Report was considered by the UN Monitoring Committee in October 2002 the government reported, many of us would say, *at last*, it is recognition of the need to take an overall, cross-departmental view of children and young people in the way that policy is formulated which found expression in the establishment of the office of the CYPU in late 2000, administratively based in the DfES, but supported by staff from many departments. It has a Minister for Children and Young People directly responsible, and the Unit is accountable to a Cabinet Committee. Its role is to administer the Children's Fund, designed to extend preventive services for children aged 5–13 and to contribute to a local preventive strategy across agencies. The Fund is now in place in two-thirds of the country and will be rolled out across England by 2004. Funding has recently been extended to those programmes which commenced in 2002 and should have completed work by 2004 to enable them to continue with their work until at least 2006. The Fund emphasises the importance of involving children, young people and their families in the design and delivery of services and the importance of what works for children as well as recognising the significant role the voluntary and community sectors can play in enhancing local preventive services. The *Second Report* had also made an announcement of further provision of money into a Children's Special Fund, although it is not entirely clear whether this was simply a re-announcement of monies previously made available under the Children's Special Services Grant (see *Second Report*, para 7.8.5), but as can be seen from the announcements of a range of other programmes, the UK government has provided a masssive injection of resource into a whole range of preventive approaches. Whilst so much money can be found for short-term programmes, there remains a long-standing but now heightened concern over the chronic under-funding of one of the most critical resources in providing an effective system of child protection – the social work profession (see Chapter **12**).

Preventive social and educational measures

1.13 Unfortunately, as many survivors of abuse testified to the National Commission of Inquiry into the Prevention of Child Abuse and Neglect (*Childhood Matters* (The Stationery Office, 1996), vol 2), the type of systems of prevention envisaged in Article 19(1) of the UNCRC, in the taking of appropriate social and educational measures and as set out in Article 19(2), the establishment of social programmes to provide necessary support for the child, have not been provided. The government has failed to appreciate the necessity for establishing clear programmes to enable children to identify when they are being subjected to abuse in whatever form (see, particularly, *Childhood Matters*, vol 2, pp 127–131). Various respondents set out their feelings about the importance of education for children in order to protect them from any form of abuse. Thus different respondents stated:

> 'There should be early use in schools of appropriate information, starting at nursery age. Including father/mother stories as abusers, not confining the abuser to stranger, uncle, babysitter. Each school should have a Child Protection Policy.'

> 'Looking back, I do think that had I been told that this should not happen it would have perhaps given me the confidence to speak out, or otherwise to try and defend myself. I had concluded that abuse happened to everyone. I was also unsure myself what it was or whether I was being abused. … It is peculiar that my mother made efforts to educate us and protect us (two brothers and myself) from abuse from strangers when she thought we might be at risk but could not face up to the fact that we were being abused by our step-father in our own house. My mother never taught me anatomical words or stand-ins for them. I think it is very important to do this – I didn't know as a young child how to tell what happened to me because I didn't know I had a vagina and a boy/man had a penis, so how could I explain what someone had done.'

'School is the main source of any child's life and they should play a bigger role in trying to educate kids against child abuse and what to do.'

'I believe child abuse should be discussed in schools from an early age. If it was, maybe I would have realised when I was little, what was wrong and why I preferred my fantasy life. If child abuse is discussed as sex education these days in primary schools, surely that cannot be a bad thing? It would give the child an opportunity to say "My home life is like that and it upsets me"; "I'm frightened of my dad"; "Is he wrong, or am I naughty?"; I would never have thought of asking for help, although I know I desperately needed it.'

1.14   The whole notion of educating children about the issue of abuse is surprisingly absent from the *Second Report* which, where it does look at the issue of education, does so in the context of Circulars 10/95 and 11/95, issued as guidance to those working in schools telling them how to deal with statements made by children and young people about abuse either within the home context (Circular 10/95) or where a complaint is made about a member of staff (Circular 11/95). It can therefore scarcely be said that the current legal provisions in England and Wales cater satisfactorily for the demands of the UNCRC, and in particular, it should be stated that they totally fail to give children the relevant education in order to enable them to protect themselves from any such abuse. A classic example of this was provided in early 2002 by the investigation conducted by the BBC 2 *Newsnight* team into the child sexual abuse scandal on the Woodchurch Estate in the Wirral Metropolitan Borough area. It transpired that criminal prosecutions were being pursued in a number of families where the fathers had been found to have sexually abused their daughters from an early age, seeing it as their right to initiate their female offspring into sexual activity. When a number of the girls, who were now much older, were interviewed and asked why they had not reported the situation when they were younger, they replied that they had not known that their situation was anything out of the ordinary and they thought this sort of thing went on in in all families and was part of the process of growing up. The government must seriously address the demands of Article 19(2) and must make sure that we introduce appropriate sex education into all our educational establishments including nurseries and SureStart provision at the earliest opportunity. As the quotations above indicate, survivors of such familial abuse see it as a breach of their rights and a failure of government responsibilty to protect children that such critical information is not provided to children from a very young age.

Employment of children and drug abuse as abuse of children

1.15   A very considerable amount of space within the *Second Report* is taken up with the issues raised in Articles 32–36 (see *Second Report*, chapter 10, pp 161–168). The government's record on the demands of Articles 32–36 is rightly highlighted in chapter 10 of the *Second Report*. The government emphasises its lifting of its Reservation, originally entered upon ratification, to Article 32, the obligation to protect children in employment, and indicates the extent of protection now provided to children aged under 18 in the labour market in the UK (see para **10.68**). It highlights in the *Second Report* its response to the demands of Article 33 contained in its programme, outlined in *Tackling Drugs Together* (Cm 2846, DOH, 1995), which sets out a strategy for dealing with the problems of drug abuse by young people and the establishment of 106 Drug Action Teams. The government points out that it recognises:

> 'That the drug problem cannot be tackled in isolation. It is linked to other socio-economic issues and needs to be tackled in conjunction with social exclusion and regeneration initiatives. Drugs affect individuals in communities. The strategy aims to tackle both the supply of, and demand for drugs through a detailed programme of action, supported by research' (*Second Report*, para 10.1.10).

1.16 The government goes on to highlight that the DOH and the Health Education Authority began their National Drug Prevention Campaign in 1995 and that this has continued within schools in order to try and reduce the abuse of children represented by the problems of drug abuse. Similar education initiatives have been adopted in all parts of the UK and the former Drug Action Teams have now been developed into Drug and Alcohol Action Teams so that the government is seen to be tackling wider problems of both drug and alcohol abuse. In addition, in April 1998, the government published a 10-year national strategy to tackle drugs misuse, *Tackling Drugs To Build a Better Britain* (Home Office, 1998). It set out four over-arching aims:

- to help young people resist drug abuse in order to achieve their full potential in society;
- to protect our communities from drug-related anti-social and criminal behaviour;
- to enable people with drug problems to overcome them and live healthy and crime-free lives; and
- to stifle the availability of illegal drugs on our streets.

Particular emphasis is given in the strategy document to targeting interventions at younger age groups and vulnerable people most at risk of becoming involved in problematic drug misuse. Vulnerable young people include those who have been abused or are involved in prostitution. The second *Annual Report and National Plan*, published in July 2000, makes specific reference to a programme of in-depth studies of drug misuse amongst vulnerable groups such as children in care, children of drug or alcohol misusing parents, homeless children, children excluded from school or truants, and children in contact with the criminal justice or mental health systems. The *Anti-Drugs Co-ordinator's First Annual Report and National Plan* published in May 1999 set down quite challenging targets, the key performance target in relation to young people being the reduction by 25 per cent in the proportion of young people under 25 reporting the usage of Class A drugs by 2005 and by 50 per cent in total by 2008. In addition, the Prevention Working Group of the government's Advisory Council on the Misuse of Drugs is part-way through an enquiry into the children of problem drug users, which will also cover issues such as the effects of drug misuse during pregnancy and an assessment of the relevant child protection legislation. Its report is due out in early 2003.

Child prostitution as a form of child abuse

1.17 One of the major criticisms made by the UN Monitoring Committee of the *First Report* was the failure on the part of government guidance to consider properly the position of children caught up in prostitution. It was suggested that the UK was actually in breach of the requirements under Article 34 to protect child prostitutes from sexual exploitation and abuse in that relevant child protection guidance did not actually include children in this position. Major steps forward have been taken since the *First Report* in 1994 such that the UK government now recognises that there is widespread concern that children involved in prostitution have previously been inappropriately regarded as consenting adults both by the police and others involved in child protection work. The *Second Report* states, at para 10.5.2, that the UK government's aim is to prevent and deter children from entering or staying in prostitution and that the government now believes that the best way forward is a multi-agency approach with children's welfare as the prime concern. As a result of the government taking very seriously the criticisms which had been made in 1995 by the UN Monitoring Committee, the Home Office and the DOH issued in December 1998 joint guidance for consultation on children involved in prostitution and final authoritative guidance through a local authority circular has now been issued. This emphasises that the whole issue of child prostitution is one of child protection and that police and social services should therefore work very closely together in order to comply most effectively with the demands of Article 34 (see *Guidance on Safeguarding Children Involved in Prostitution: Supplementary Guidance to Working Together to Safeguard Children*, 22 May 2000). This supplementary guidance which is discussed in more detail in Chapter 6 has been issued jointly by the DOH, the Home Office, the DfEE and the National Assembly for Wales and states:

> 'that it is for all agencies and professionals who may work with children where there are concerns that they are involved in prostitution, and reflects the joint responsibility for safeguarding and promoting the welfare of children involved in prostitution.'

The guidance was also distributed separately to the police under a Home Office Circular (see *Supplementary Guidance*, 22 May 2000). In the summer of

2001 the government commissioned work to review how this *Guidance* was being implemented across the country and its impact, and the report of that review is expected in 2002 or 2003 (see Part 1 of the *Children Act Report 2001* (DOH, 2002), at para 5). In addition, in seeking to respond to the UN Monitoring Committee's earlier trenchant criticims of its failure in this area, the DOH in England, together with the Welsh Assembly, the Northern Ireland Office and the Scottish Executive, have come together to hold a UK confernce and have published a joint *National Plan for Safeguarding Children from Commercial Sexual Exploitation* (2001), which it is intended will be developed on a year-by-year basis to ensure that it remains up to date and continues to focus on priorities for action (see para **1.11**). The *National Plan* declares that its aim is to 'combat UK-based and international sexual exploitation of children, with particular emphasis on commercial aspects' (see para **1.6**). The *National Plan* does not therefore cover sexual abuse *within the family*, unless linked to commercial exploitation. The *National Plan* formed an important part of the UK government's preparations for the Second World Congress on the Commercial Sexual Exploitation of Children which took place in Yokahama in Japan in December 2001, and a website on the Yokahama conference and further progress in this area is now being maintained by the ASEM Resource Centre at the Centre for Europe's Children in the University of Glasgow.

Other exploitative abuse of children caught up in child abduction, sale and trafficking

1.18   With regard to the problems of child abduction, sale and trafficking, which are the subject of the right conferred by Article 35, when the government issued the *Second Report,* and even later into 2001, it was anticipated that the main area of concern was the sale and trafficking of children for the purposes of sexual exploitation (see Somerset (2001)) and see also *Second Report* at para 10.58). Increasingly in 2002, however, it has become apparent that there are real concerns over the trafficking of children, particularly from the African continent, for purposes of providing child labour in the homes of alleged 'carers', some of whom may even be extended family members. The government will clearly need to take steps to protect children caught up in such practices which would amount to a clear breach of the rights of children protected not only under Article 35, but also Article 36. Article 37(1), as has been noted, echoes the demands of Article 3 of the ECHR, and, since that Convention has the force of law within the UK, the requirements of Article 40(4). The clear intention of this part of this Article is that children who commit offences should not then find themselves in a system which may in itself be abusive and disregard key issues relating to child protection, which, if practised in other settings, might provide grounds for the compulsory removal of the child.

The UK government's view of the UNCRC

1.19 It should thus be acknowledged that whilst it cannot be said that the UNCRC has the binding force of law within the UK, the response of the UK government in both legislative and policy terms clearly indicates that it regards its obligations under the Convention extremely seriously. It is therefore the case that all those who practise within the child protection field must be aware of the imperative imposed by the government upon all agencies working in the child protection sphere to observe the rights set out in the UNCRC. It is interesting to note that at various points where the government acknowledges that domestic legal provisions may not adequately protect the child then it suggests that reliance should be placed on the demands of the UNCRC itself (see, for example, *Second Report*, para 9.24). Far from the UNCRC being seen as an unattainable gold standard, it is clear that the government now views the standards set out in the UNCRC and the rights, which it so critically gives to children, as rights which we should all be seeking to protect and to safeguard wherever we work in the child protection system. The UK's compliance with the demands of Article 39 in providing for the physical and psychological recovery and social re-integration of any child victims seems in the *Second Report* (see paras 10.18.1–10.18.9) to focus entirely on improvements made to the procedures relating to child witnesses appearing in court (see further, Chapter **9**) and no mention whatsoever is made the issues of the therapeutic treatments and recovery and offer of services which should be made to children in such circumstances. Reference could have been made here to the importance of child protection plans drawn up under *Working Together to Safeguard Children* (DOH, 1999) but the very serious issues raised by a detailed consideration of Article 39 and the experiences of those who responded to the National Commission of Inquiry into the Prevention of Child Abuse and Neglect would all tend to suggest that this critical area of appropriately planned therapy, rehabilitation and re-integration is, again, *not* one which is properly addressed today within the child protection system of England and Wales (see *Childhood Matters* (The Stationery Office, 1996) vol 2, at pp 84–103).

The response of the UN Monitoring Committee to the Second Report

1.20 The *Second Report* of the UK was considered by the UN Monitoring Committeee on 19 September 2002. The Monitoring Committee, through its Pre-sessional Working Group had submitted to the UK a list of some 13 issues upon which it wanted further written information before 19 September arising from its preliminary consideration of the *Report* on 10–14 June 2002, and a list of some 16 major issues which the Committee intends to take up during dialogue with the UK represevatives (see www.unhchr.ch/tbs/doc.nsf). Those matters relating to child protection on which the Committee wanted further written information included:

- the total amount being spent on child protection including, for example,
  - amounts being spent on foster and institutional care; and
  - the monitoring taking place in the different devolved regions and at the level of local authorities, including receiving and addressing individual complaints of violations of child rights at those levels.

The child protection issues to be raised in the dialogue include:

- information about the implementation in practice (ie in court decisions) and in decisions by administrative bodies, in developing national and local policies on children's issues of the general principles of the Convention including the best interests of the child (Article 3) the right to life and survival and development of the child, (Article 6) and the right of the child to be heard (Article 12);
- the investigation of child death;
- abuse and neglect of children including sexual abuse within the family and domestic violence;
- the use of corporal punishment in families, schools, care and other institutions; and
- the problem of bullying and abuse by teachers in schools.

The UK government responded to all these various concerns by filing, on 30 August 2002, a 106-page response updating the UNCRC on developments since 1999 and trying to address the areas of concern, which were the subject of more detailed attention on 19 September 2002. The fact that the current government responded in such detailed terms to the concerns of the Monitoring Committee is indicative of a sea change in central government attitudes to the Convention and its response makes clear, as never before, its belief in the Convention's core principles and the rights which it accords to children. Thus, at page 101, it is declared that 'the Government fully recognises its obligations under the CRC and is committed to ensuring that it complies with them' (www.unhchr.ch.tbs/doc.nsf).

European Convention on Human Rights and the Human Rights Act 1998

The impact of the Human Rights Act 1998 and the relevant Articles of the European Convention on Human Rights

1.21 When the CA 1989 was first introduced into the House of Lords by the then Lord Chancellor, Lord Mackay of Clashfern, it was described as 'the most comprehensive and far reaching reform of child law which has come before Parliament in living memory'. This has certainly turned out to be the case, not only with that Act but also with the comparable provisions for Scotland and Northern Ireland. Nevertheless, if that was an apt description of the CA 1989, it applies even more to the implications of the enactment of the HRA 1998, implemented across the whole of the UK since 2 October 2000, providing as it does for a very considerable number of the Articles of the ECHR to have direct effect in English law. The HRA 1998 extends to all UK citizens the right to rely upon the ECHR in any proceedings which come before any UK courts, tribunals or quasi-judicial bodies, and further requires all public authorities including health authorities and social services departments as well as the police to act in accordance with the rights conferred by the ECHR. (In both Scotland and Wales, the Convention took direct effect earlier under the relevant provisions of the Scotland Act 1998 and the Government of Wales Act 1998.) Interestingly, the UK government in its *Second Report* to the UN Monitoring Committee identified the introduction of the human rights legislation as conferrring crucial additional support and protection of children's rights within the UK (see *Second Report*, at paras 5.1.1– 5.1.7).

1.22 Various Articles of the ECHR have assumed critical importance in child protection cases. These include:

Article 2   'everyone's right to life shall be protected by law';

Article 3   'no one shall be subjected to torture, or to inhuman or degrading treatment or punishment';

Article 4   'no one shall be held in slavery or servitude', or required to perform forced or compulsory labour except in certain very limited situations such as work done by prisoners, those in the military, or work which forms part of normal civic obligations;

Article 5   'everyone has the right to liberty and security of person' except in certain clearly defined circumstances;

Article 6   'everyone is entitled to a fair and public hearing within a reasonable time by an independent and impartial tribunal established by law of any determination of an individual's civil rights and obligations or of any criminal charge against him';

Article 8   'everyone has the right to respect for his private and family life, his home and his correspondence' (Article 8(1)) and further that 'there shall be no interference by a public authority with the exercise of this right except such as is in accordance with the law and is necessary in a democratic society in the interests of national security, public safety or the economic well being of the country, for the prevention of this order or crime, for the protection of health or morals, or for the protection of the rights and freedoms of others' (Article 8(2));

Article 9   'the right to freedom of thought, conscience and religion; which includes the freedom to change one's religion or belief and freedom, either alone or in community with others and in public or private, to manifest one's religion or belief in worship, teaching, practice and observance', such rights being subject to the same limitations as those governing the right to respect to private and family life;

Article 10   'everyone has the right to freedom of expression. This right shall include freedom to receive and impart information and ideas without interference by public authority and regardless of frontiers', such rights being subject to the same limitations as those in Article 8(2) with the additional limitations for the purposes of protection of the reputation of others, for preventing the disclosure of information received in confidence, or for maintaining the authority and impartiality of the judiciary.

Article 14   'the enjoyment of the rights and freedoms set forth in this convention shall be secured without discrimination on any grounds such as sex, colour, language, religion, political or other opinion, national or social origin, association with a national minority, property, birth or *other status*' (emphasis added). (This right can be characterised as being parasitic on at least one other right protected by the Convention since it has to be asserted that discrimination has been practised in relation to the enjoyment of a particular right protected under at least one of the other Articles of the Convention.)

1.23   As can be seen from a very brief perusal of just a few of the Articles, which may be relevant to the issue of child protection, the implication of the guaranteeing of these rights by means of the implementation of the HRA 1998 means that any agencies involved in the sphere of child protection must now ensure that their actions do not breach the fundamental rights secured to citizens, including, it must be emphasised, all children, under the ECHR as implemented by the HRA 1998. Since, for example, *Working Together to Safeguard Children* simply notes in its Preface that the guidance has been drawn up particularly with the requirements of both Articles 6 and 8 in mind but makes no further detailed reference to the demands of the ECHR, it is quite clear that all those working in the Child Protection arena must familiarise themselves with the *Core Guidance*, issued by the Home Office on the obligations of public authorities under the HRA 1998. (See *A New Era of Rights and Responsibilities – Core Guidance for Public Authorities – Human Rights Comes to Life* (Human Rights Task Force Secretariat, Human Rights Unit, Home Office, 2000) which is available at www.homeoffice.gov.uk/hract). The HRA 1998 provides by s 1 that only certain Articles of the ECHR are to take direct effect within UK law; these are Articles 2–12 and 14, Articles 1–3 of the First Protocol and Articles 1 and 2 of the Sixth Protocol, as read with Articles 16–18 (see HRA 1998, s 1(1) and Sch 1).

Compatibility of legislation with the Human Rights Act 1998

1.24   Section 3 of the HRA 1998 provides that all primary and secondary legislation (whenever enacted) must, so far as it is possible to do so, be read and given effect in such a way as to make it compatible with the Convention rights. Section 6(1) goes on to provide that it is unlawful for a public authority to act in a way which is incompatible with a Convention right, and thus the clear imperative derived from both s 3 and s 6 is that all public authorities, including social services, health, education and the police as well as the courts must perform their duties and exercise their powers in a way which is compatible with the Convention rights.

1.25   In those situations where it is impossible to do so, then the courts must resolve the situation and if it is impossible for the courts to read the legislation so as to make it compatible with the ECHR then the High Court, or any court above the High Court, is able to make a declaration of incompatibility (HRA 1998, s 4). Where such a declaration is being considered by the court, then the Minister from the relevant government department concerned with the sphere of operation of the legislation is entitled, on being given notice of the proceedings, to be joined as a party in order to see whether this will assist the court. (See, for an example, *R on the application of J v Enfield London Borough Council (Secretary of State for Health as Intervener)* [2002] 2 FLR 1, where it was helpfully pointed out by the government department that although s 17 of the CA 1989 did not require local authorities to provide financial assistance to secure housing, there was no gap in legislation which prevented the authority from giving lawful effect to the claimant's HRA 1998 rights since authories had power under s 2 of the Local Government Act 2000 to provide such assistance.) The requirement that the courts must attempt to interpret legislation so as to uphold the Convention rights is essentially a new 'rule of construction' which must now be applied by the courts to previous as well as to current and future legislation. Since the courts are not bound by previous decisions or interpretations as to the meaning of a particular legislative provision, the courts are given authority to establish a new body of case-law to take into account the Convention rights. Such a step will certainly have a major impact upon the law of precedent (the practice in common law countries of courts following the previous decisions of higher courts according to the position of the higher court in the hierarchy or courts). This, in itself, could have a substantial and very wide-reaching effect on the system of law as practised in the English courts.

1.26   Where a declaration of incompatibility is issued ruling that a piece of legislation cannot be read in such a way as to make it compliant with Convention rights then the HRA 1998 provides the government with a procedure whereby a signal is given that the law needs to be changed and s 10 of and Sch 2 to the HRA 1998 provide a fast-track procedure for the government to follow in order to amend the legislation. Until any such legislation is changed, however, the obligation is to apply the legislation as laid down, albeit that this involves potential breaches of human rights. Section 6(1) of the HRA 1998 makes it unlawful for a public authority to act in a way which is incompatible with the Convention rights except where either:

(a) it could not have acted any differently as a result of there being incompatible primary legislation; or
(b) where the relevant primary or subordinate legislation could not be read or given effect to, so as to make it compatible with Convention rights and the authority was acting so as to give effect to or enforce those provisions.

1.27 It is important to understand what is comprehended by the term 'public authority'. Since no express definition is provided in the HRA 1998 one must turn to the *Core Guidance* where, at para 92, it is suggested that this is likely to include: government departments; local authorities; the NHS; police, prison and immigration officers; public prosecutors; courts and tribunals; non-departmental public bodies; and any person exercising a public function. In the child protection field, therefore, the definition of public authority will clearly include all local authority departments and, most particularly, social services and also any bodies which fulfil obligations or provide services on behalf of a local authority. As a result of s 6(1), therefore, where a public authority, including a court, acts in a way which is incompatible with a Convention right then it will be a breach of the Convention rights. It is quite apparent that such rights take precedence over the interpretation previously given to legislative provisions by the courts in this country. In the child protection arena, therefore, all professionals will have to consider and test out whether current case-law and practice, as well as relevant guidance issued by such departments as the DOH, are compatible with the relevant Convention rights. If not, then previous precedent and practice will have to give way to an interpretation which is compatible with Convention rights.

Asserting Convention rights

1.28 Section 7 of the HRA 1998 goes on to provide that a person who claims that a public authority has acted or proposes to act in a way which is unlawful because it is incompatible with that individual's Convention rights, may either bring proceedings against the authority under the HRA 1998 in the appropriate court or tribunal or, instead, rely on the Convention rights in any legal proceedings, although in both situations the individual must be or would be a victim of the unlawful act. Since the HRA 1998 came into force, all individuals have therefore been able to allege breaches of their Convention rights in the UK courts at all levels. It was assumed that the vast majority of Convention breaches would be alleged during the course of ordinary proceedings under the provisions of s 7(1)(b), although if such proceedings are not available, then under s 7(10) it is possible for individuals to commence a case under the Act relying on a breach of the Convention rights alone. The court or tribunal in which such a free-standing application could be taken has not been determined by any rules which it was originally anticipated would be made by the Lord Chancellor and the Secretary of State. The *Core Guidance* does indicate that where such proceedings are taken then they must be commenced within one year or less of the act complained of, although the court can allow the individual to bring proceedings after a longer period if it thinks this is fair in the circumstances (see *Core Guidance*, at para 87). The vast majority of cases in which Convention points have been argued since the implementation of the HRA 1998 have been those where the isssues have been raised in the course of other proceedings. A number of applications for judicial review have, however, relied heavily on the potential breaches of human rights under the Convention, and there have been a small number of free-standing applications (see para **1.29**). In the absence of court rules, the President of the Family Division, in the case of *C v Bury Metropolitan Borough Council* [2002] 2 FLR 868 indicated that human rights challenges to care plans should be heard in the Family Division of the High Court and where possible by judges with experience of sitting in the administrative court. Where the court finds that a public authority has breached an individual's Convention rights, the court is able to award whatever remedy is open to it and it sees as just and appropriate (HRA 1998, s 8(1)). The Act makes it clear (s 8(2)), as does the *Core Guidance* (para 89), that the court could make an award of damages provided it has the power to do so and the *Core Guidance* further sets out that where the court does set damages it will take into account the Strasbourg norm which means the normal levels of damages set by the European Court in Strasbourg, which 'tend to be modest' (para 89).

1.29 Generally speaking, in the child protection arena it will usually be the case that Convention points will be taken in the course of proceedings as identified under s 7(1)(b) and that, generally, the Convention rights will be used to support the relevant party's legal case rather than by way of seeking a specific remedy for violation of a Convention right, although on this see *Re S (Minors), Re W (Minors)* [2002] UKHL 10, [2002] 1 FLR 815. In the case of *Re M* [2001] 2 FLR 1300, the parents involved commenced free-standing applications pursuant to ss 6, 7, and 8 of the HRA 1998. In that case a local authority had reviewed its care plan for a child in its care at a permanency planning meeting without giving the father or mother the opportunity to be present and without hearing from them. The conclusion of the meeting was that there was no prospect of successful placement with either of the parents and that if placement with the maternal grandmother was not a viable option then the authority would place the child for adoption. The parents claimed that the way in which the local authority had reached its conclusion at the meeting was incompatible with the parents' right to respect for their private and family life under Article 8(1) of the ECHR, that the authority's decision was accordingly unlawful under s 6(1) of the HRA 1998, and further that the combined effects of ss 6, 7 and 8 of the Act required that the current plans of the local authority should be reviewed and sanctioned by the court. Both parents also applied under s 39 of the CA 1989 for discharge of the care orders. Holman J in the High Court held that the way in which the local authority had reached its decision did *not* comply with Article 8(1) of the ECHR and s 6(1) of the HRA 1998. Since the combined effect of the Article and the section required the court to consider whether, having regard to the circumstances of the case and the serious nature of the decision to be taken, the parents had been involved in the decision-making process to a degree sufficient to provide them with the proper protection of their interests, in the very specific circumstances of this case the process as a whole had not involved the parents as required and thus the authority had acted unlawfully. The authority's decision was ordered to be quashed (see further, Chapter **11**). With respect to the parents' claim for review of the authority's plans, Holman J held that the proposed change was such a *fundamental* change of plan that, in such circumstances, the legality of the authority's actions could be examined by the court in free-standing proceedings under the HRA 1998. The court then had power under s 8(1) to grant any relief or remedy, or to make an order, whilst ensuring that any extension of function was used sparingly and not for the perpetuation of adversarial issues. Holman J gave directions for a full hearing to take place of the review issue in the case as well as the specific applications for discharge of the care orders. Holman's decision in this case was upheld and cited with approval by the House of Lords in *Re S; Re W* [2002] 1 FLR 815, at p 828. Other commentators have indicated that where a specific remedy for a violation is requested, the family courts will be restricted to their statutory powers and, in the case of the High Court, its inherent jurisdiction, and thus it has been suggested that an alternative remedy could be given by way of declaratory relief (see *Butterworths Family Law Service: The Human Rights Act 1998 – A Special Bulletin for Family Lawyers*, at para 2.32).

1.30　Section 2 of the HRA 1998 makes it clear that UK courts and tribunals must, however, take into account the relevant Convention case-law when determining any question which arises in connection with a Convention right. The words 'take into account' suggest only that such case-law should be used as guidance and does not operate as a system of binding precedent. Heather Swindells et al have pointed out that in assessing the weight to be given to Convention case-law, the following matters should be borne in mind.

—　The ECHR is a 'living instrument' which evolves to meet changing social circumstances and, therefore, Convention case-law places less reliance upon established precedent than domestic law. In general, this means that older decisions are less reliable as a guide.

—　Decisions of the European Court have greater weight and admissibility than any relevant decisions of the Commission issued before the demise of the Commission on 31 October 1998.

– Decisions generally turn upon whether an individual's rights have been infringed in the particular circumstances, although some general principles may be discerned from them.

– The European Court allows 'a margin of appreciation' to national authorities which varies according to the particular point in issue. By way of example, a wide margin of appreciation has been permitted to national authorities in assessing the necessity of taking children into care, whereas a strict scrutiny has been applied to the restrictions placed by those authorities on parental rights of access to children (see Swindells et al, (2000)).

1.31 Where one wants to consider the body of previous Convention case-law which might apply then the easiest means of accessing the decisions of the European Court based in Strasbourg and the previous determinations of the now defunct Commission is via the internet given that, with the exception of lawyers, most people will not be able to access copies of the *Human Rights Reports*. (See *www.echr.coe.int* (for the Court) and *www. DHCOMMHR.COE.FR* (for the Commission).)

1.32 The *Core Guidance* points out that the principal aim of the ECHR was to protect individuals against arbitrary interference by the State and that therefore the Convention establishes 'vertical' duties between the individual and the State. The European Court has, however, stated for example, in relation to Article 8, that 'Article 8 does not merely compel the state to abstain from such interference; in addition to this primarily negative undertaking, there may be positive obligations inherent in an effective "respect for family life" ' (see *Marckx v Belgium* 2 EHRR 330, at para 31; and *X and Y v The Netherlands* 8 EHRR 235). Such positive obligations may also include an obligation upon the State to protect a private individual's Convention right against breach by other private individuals (see *Hokkanen v Finland* 19 EHRR 139, [1996] 1 FLR 289). Thus, as the *Core Guidance* puts it, the ECHR also had a 'horizontal' effect by imposing upon the State positive duties to protect the Convention rights of private individuals against interference from other private individuals, and thus gave the State a role in regulating disputes between private individuals which involve any of the Convention rights. Such an approach is reinforced by s 6 of the HRA 1998, which provides that it is unlawful for a court as a public authority to act in any way which is incompatible with a Convention right. This, therefore, means that courts not only have the duty of acting compatibly with the Convention in cases involving other public authorities but also in developing the case-law in disputes between private individuals. In any situation in which the court becomes seized of any matter with regard to family proceedings being taken before it, then the Court itself has to apply the relevant Convention rights to see whether there has been a breach and thus the Convention is given a 'horizontal' effect by the HRA 1998 in any private proceedings taking place between individual family members.

Principle of proportionality

1.33 One further principle of particular importance when considering the impact of the ECHR is the 'principle of proportionality'. The *Core Guidance* defines this as a crucial concept and explains it as meaning that 'any interference with a Convention right must be proportionate to the intended objective'. The *Core Guidance* states that this means that even if the particular policy or action which interferes with a convention right is aimed at pursuing a legitimate aim (for example the protection of the health or rights and freedoms of others for the prevention of crime), this will not justify the interference if the means used to achieve the aim are excessive in the circumstances. Any interference with a Convention right should therefore be carefully designed to meet the objective in question and must not be arbitrary or unfair. As the *Guidance* puts it 'you must not use a sledgehammer to crack a nut'. Thus, even taking into account all the objectives laid down in a particular Article in a given case, an interference may still not be justified because the impact on the individual or the group is too severe. A good example of the operation of this principle in the child protection field can be seen in the case of *Re C and B (Care Order: Future Harm)* [2001] 1 FLR 611. This case was actually decided some 6 months before the implementation of the HRA 1998, but reveals the determination of the Court of Appeal in care cases to uphold very firmly the principles of the ECHR. In this case two older children of the family were taken into care in 1996 under orders based on actual harm to the emotional and intellectual development of the elder child and the likelihood of such harm to the younger child. Although the parents were capable of commitment and stability, they had both experienced difficult childhoods, the mother had suffered a mental breakdown and both found it hard to accept the care order and abide by the restrictions and limitations which had been placed on contact. An experienced independent social worker then reported on the third child, aged 10 months, and an interim care order was made on the basis that there was a likelihood he would suffer significant harm in the future even though all the evidence indicated he was currently doing very well. The mother then gave birth to her fourth child, an emergency protection order was made the same day, and both younger children were placed with the same foster parents. The county court judge made care orders in respect of the two younger children, gave permission for the local authority to refuse contact betweeen the parents and all four children, and imposed a 2-year prohibition on any application by the parents for contact or to discharge the care orders without permission of the court. The parents appealed and the Court of Appeal, whilst confirming the orders on the two older children, allowed the appeal in relation to the two younger children. The Court of Appeal found that although there had been no immediate harm to the two younger children there had been evidence which had entitled the judge to find a real possibility of future harm. Bearing in mind the demands of Article 8 of the ECHR that intervention must be proportionate to the legitimate aim of the protection of the children, and that in this case where there were no long-standing problems of the sort which interfere with the capacity to provide adequate parenting, the local authority could have taken time to explore other options. The Court of Appeal emphasised that the principle of proportionality must be that the local authority works to support and eventually reunite the family unless the risks are so high that the child's welfare requires alternative care.

1.34 The implementation of the HRA 1998, incorporating as it does many of the key articles of the ECHR, means that a whole new vista has been opened up to the courts in terms of developing a UK-based human rights jurisprudence. Although the UK courts are required by the HRA 1998 to take into account the Strasbourg cases in interpreting the Convention rights, the interpretation of those rights within the UK courts was said by the *Core Guidance* to be likely to develop its own momentum quickly. At the time of writing, it had become apparent that the impact of the incorporation of the ECHR into the HRA 1998 in the field of families, their children, and the laws affecting them had indeed been considerable. By the summer of 2002, cases reported since 1995 in the *Family Law Reports* involving consideration by the English courts of the application of relevant Articles of the ECHR numbered at least 175, of which more than 100 had come before the courts since the implementation of the HRA 1998 on 2 October 2000. The importance of these cases in the interpretation of the law on child protection will be identified and discussed at the relevant sections of this book, although the principle that the Convention is a living instrument and not to be bound by any system of precedent must be borne in mind when considering the decisions of the courts in England and Wales (see para **1.33**). It was quite clear from the *Core Guidance* that it was anticipated that the effect in areas of law involving children and families would be very substantial indeed, but few could have predicted the energy and enthusiasm of both family and children's lawyers in arguing the principles of the Convention nor of the courts in applying them. (For particularly cogent examples of this see the Court of Appeal cases of *Re A (Contact: Separate Representation)* [2001] 1 FLR 715 and of *Re W and B; Re W* [2001] 2 FLR 582 (later *Re S; Re W* [2002] UKHL 10, [2002] 1 FLR 815). For a fully argued and detailed analysis of the implications of this important decision, see Tolson (2002).)

1.35 The procedure with regard to the declaration of incompatibility has already been noted but it is also the case that all future primary legislation made since the coming into force of the HRA 1998 requires a written statement of compatibility issued by the relevant government Minister that particular legislation does not in his or her view breach any of the Convention rights. This important step has been taken in relation to the Adoption and Children Act 2002, which makes a number of important amendments to the CA 1989. The general view of the family judiciary both before and since implementation of the HRA 1998 was that the CA 1989 itself had been drawn up in compliance with the demands of the ECHR, but this has not prevented senior members of the judiciary from attempting to make improvements to the Act in accordance with the spirit of the Convention (see, for example, the reasoning of Hale and Thorpe LJJ in *Re W and B; Re W* [2001] 2 FLR 582. See for further analysis of the decisions in the Court of Appeal and the House of Lords, Tolson (2002).)

Conclusion

1.36 There is no doubt that the implementation of the HRA 1998 has opened up the possibility of even greater protection being extended to children within our society. In January 2002 the government also established a Joint Select Committeee on Human Rights, which thus far has taken evidence from the Lord Chancellor, the Home Secretary, the Human Rights Commissioner Mary Robinson, and the Minister of State at the Cabinet Office and on 10 June 2002 it became the first parliamentary Committee to take evidence from children as young as 10 on their view of children's rights in the UK. The Chair of the Committee, Jean Croston MP, acknowledged that 'debate on human rights rarely extends to children'. She stated that the Committee would be looking at whether the current equality provisions lead to unmet need, and she stated that it seemed 'right to look at children and the way in which they perceive their own rights'. She went on to state that the children's evidence 'will be used to help the Committee with its inquiry into whether the the UK needs a Human Rights Commission'. The Committee, she said, had invited six children, three from London and three from the regions, to give evidence on the case for a Commissioner for Children's Rights (see Chapter **11**). She also emphasised that the Committee was 'keen to comply with Article 12 of the UNCRC, in listening to and taking account of what children say'. James Sweeney, one of the six young people to give evidence on 10 June, welcomed the opportunity to speak to the Committee, saying:

> 'I think it will give young people a chance to say what they want for once. This might bring us closer to something we have been campaigning for for the last twelve months: getting a Children's Rights Commissioner for England.'

The children's session before the Committee was part of an on-going thematic inquiry into children's rights involving a whole range of evidence sessions from leading figures in social services, education, health and children's non-governmental organisations (see www.parliament.uk/commons/selcom/hrhome.htm). The incorporation of the ECHR and the increasing seriousness with which the Labour government is treating the rights conferred on children by the UNCRC is encouraging for all of us working in the child protection field. Whilst we cannot be complacent, for there is still much to be done (see Chapter **12**) there now appears to be much more room for hope than was previously the case.

1.37 As this book was going to press, the report of Lord Laming's Inquiry into the death of Victoria Climbie was published (28 January 2003). As was noted in the Preface, Lord Laming concluded that 'the current legislative framework is fundamentally sound but that the gap was in its implementation' (Press Conference, 28 January 2003). The Secretary of State for Health, Alan Milburn, took 'little comfort from that' stating that 'sound legislative policy and guidance is frankly useless unless we can be sure that it is implemented effectively and consistently' (Press Release, DOH 2003/038). In all, Lord Laming made some 108 recommendations which will be briefly discussed at the end of the final chapter, including, critically, the establishment of a Children's Rights Commissioner for England, heading a national agency for children and families to ensure that local services meet national standards for child protection and implement reforms. The Secretary of State, whilst refusing to acknowledge the case for such a move, nevertheless made some ambitious commitments on behalf of the government, including: additional inspections of services in North London; the infusion of extra resources into both health and social services; the improvement of training for all agencies in child protection with a particular focus on inter-agency working; the complete revision and reduction of all *local* child protection guidance into new shorter, clearer, *national* guidance; consideration to be given to the condensation of the current 15 national child protection guidance documents into a single document; the publication of a checklist of the basic elements of good professional practice in child protection for police, social services and health; increased inspections of all agencies by the relevant Government Inspectorates, with increased powers to intervene earlier and more effectively; and, finally, the breaking down of barriers to working together by removing them through the creation of (the previously announced) Children's Trusts. Sadly, no acknowledgement was given by the Secretary of State to the vital necessity of implementing the UNCRC directly into UK law so that its principles might pervade the consciousness of everyone – adults and children alike – as well as our institutions and agencies, so that the 'rights' of children like Victoria to protection could be more securely guaranteed. Indeed, the failure to acknowledge the case made by Lord Laming for a Children's Rights Commissioner seems to belie the strength of the government's real commitment to children's rights in England.

CHAPTER 2

FORMS OF CHILD ABUSE

'Agreed definitions of child abuse are important for two reasons. The first is to establish a general framework within which policies designed to prevent child abuse can be developed and assessed. The second is to provide a set of technical definitions for identifying actions or circumstances which are taken to be abusive to children. These technical definitions are needed for statutory, legal, statistical, procedural and research purposes.' (*Childhood Matters, Report of the National Commission of Inquiry into the Prevention of Child Abuse* (The Stationery Office, 1996), vol 1, para 1.1.)

'The range and the extent of the unkindness, cruelty, violence and wrongdoing to which children are subjected is shocking ... Instances of gross or sadistic abuse are acutely distressing but so also is the extent to which children's lives are impoverished by lack of affection or care, by intrusive sexual contacts, relentless verbal abuse, ongoing physical assault, and constant fear.' (*Childhood Matters*, at para 1.7.)

'In some ways our system helps to support abuse. Children are not always brought up to value themselves. They are forced to be pliant and people pleasers, instead of encouraging them to speak up if things are bothering them ... They are not taught how to listen to and value their inner feelings.' (Letter to the Commission, *Childhood Matters*, at para 3.5.)

'What is the thing you would most like to change about grown ups? ... "Make them listen to what you are saying and to make them think that children are just the same as adults, just younger and smaller".' (10-year-old girl in Commission Questionnaire, *Childhood Matters*, para 3.7.)

Introduction

2.1   The above quotations serve to highlight a range of different problems associated with the phenomenon of child abuse in today's society. As the first quotation emphasises, agreed definitions of child abuse are important both in order to establish a framework within which polices designed to prevent child abuse can be developed and assessed, and also in order to provide a set of technical definitions which will enable a wide range of professionals coming into contact with children to identify a range of actions or circumstances which may be potentially abusive to children. The second quotation, taken from ChildLine's submissions to the National Commission of Inquiry into the Prevention of Child Abuse, reveals the range and type of abuse to which children may be subject which include both acts of commission as well as acts of omission. The third quotation, again taken from the National Commission Report, reveals the concerns which a number of commentators share with the child quoted in the fourth extract – that children, by virtue of their very position in society which mirrors their position in their families, are the objects of power wielded over them by a range of adults in positions of authority, from their parents through to their schoolteachers.

2.2	Reference should be made here to Freeman (2001), at p 3; Lyon (2000); and also Newell (2001). All three of these writers argue very powerfully that the lack of equality of rights accorded to children, particularly in relation to corporal punishment of children by their parents, entails the perpetuation of the notion of property rights over one's child. They all argue forcefully that the denial of recognition of the child's right to bodily integrity as being equal to that possessed by adults is a serious and grave breach of children's human rights. As Freeman points out, 'children's rights – or their absence – are very much a key to the understanding of child abuse and neglect. Children without rights are by that very fact vulnerable' (op cit, at p 3). (See also Lyon 2000). As we understand more about the vulnerability of all individulas, but in particular that of children who lack the physical maturity to assert their rights, so it must be appreciated that the categories of 'child abuse' never seem to close.

2.3	Whilst the maltreatment of children has been on the national agenda now for at least 118 years, ever since the foundation of the London Society for the Prevention of Cruelty to Children in 1884, there is no hard evidence that acts of child abuse have multiplied. What has happened, however, is that public and social awareness of the problem has dramatically increased; closer monitoring of children within their families or within the institutional setting and more effective reporting of incidents now occurs as a result of greater professional recognition of its existence and this heightens social unwillingness to tolerate any forms of child abuse. From the mid-1960s to the mid- to late-1980s, the focus on child abuse tended to be concentrated within the nuclear family and not on acts of abuse perpetrated by strangers or professional carers. From the late 1980s onwards, however, information began emerging which suggested that abuse of children in children's homes and special schools had been taking place, in some cases for between 10 and 20 years. (See *The Pindown Experience and the Protection of Children: the Report of the Staffordshire Child Care Inquiry* (1991) (The Pindown Report); *The Leicestershire Inquiry 1992* (The Kirkwood Report) (Leicestershire Social Services, 1993) and *Lost in Care: Report of the Tribunal of Inquiry into the Abuse of Children in Care in the former County Council areas of Gwynedd and Clwyd since 1974* (The Stationery Office, 2000) discussed in Chapter 3.)

2.4   A wide range of guidance documents now exist to assist professionals in the recognition of what may be encompassed within the notion of child abuse. Such guidance emphasises that child abuse can include physical harm and neglect, social harm, sexual abuse and emotional harm, but the view of victims themselves is that professionals do not fully understand what constitutes child abuse. Thus, Wattam and Woodward concluded from their study of the letters from victims of child abuse that whilst many included the more conventional descriptive terms (ie sexual, physical and emotional abuse and neglect), they also addressed a broader range of potentially harmful actions such as bullying, the deliberate subjection of a child to danger, and lack of concern for children's rights. Wattam and Woodward revealed that many victims place greater emphasis on the longer-term emotional consequences of abuse than on the immediate effect of physical injury or assault. The victims also linked abuse to its impact on personal relationships within the family, partly defined by what sense the child made of what was happening to him or her. In other words, the victim's definition of child abuse related not only to the abuse itself, but also to its context and its longer-term impact on the individual and the family concerned. That indeed was to be a key component of the wide definition of abuse eventually proposed by the National Commission of Inquiry into the Prevention of Child Abuse (see Wattam and Woodward (1996)).

2.5   That the definitions and perceptions of child abuse held by people who wrote of their own experiences did not relate to the definitions provided in legislation and in government guidance, clearly troubled the authors of the National Commission Report. The Report points out that the importance that these survivors attached to the emotional impact of abuse is not accurately reflected in the numbers of child protection registrations. The letters sent in to the Commission demonstrated that, in terms of defining abuse, greatest weight was generally given to the views of professionals. These letters showed how 'official definitions' excluded certain forms of abuse that could have damaging consequences. It is a measure of the impact which the National Commission Report had, that, whilst in 1996 the Commission reported that 'for example, the emotional impact on the children who witnessed violence, was mentioned many times but was not acknowledged in official definitions, this issue has now received much more attention is included within official government guidance' (see *Working Together to Safeguard Children* (DOH, 1999), at para 2.21) and the definition of harm in the CA 1989 has been amended to include it (CA 1989, s 31(9) as amended by the Adoption and Children Act 2002). In addition, *Working Together to Safeguard Children* now acknowledges other forms of potential abuse including the effects of social exclusion (see para 2.20); the mental illness or a parent or carer (see paras 2.22 and 2.23); and drug or alcohol misuse by a parent or carer (see para 2.24). To some extent therefore it would appear that the differences in perception between professionals and victims have now at last been addressed in law, policy and in professional practice.

2.6 In writing the previous edition of this book in 1993, reference was made to the cases which had been described by the media as instances of ritual or satanic abuse. Nowadays, less hysterical terminology is used and 'organised or multiple abuse' is defined in relevant DOH guidance (see *Working Together to Safeguard Children*, op cit, at paras 6.24–6.26). As *Working Together to Safeguard Children* also points out, the available UK evidence on the extent of abuse among disabled children suggests that disabled children are at increased risk of abuse, and that the presence of multiple disabilities appears to increase the risk of both abuse and neglect (see para 6.27). The 1999 version of *Working Together to Safeguard Children* thus builds on this research evidence and identifies a number of factors which may make disabled children especially vulnerable to abuse, and advises upon a number of measures intended to promote a higher level of awareness of the risks for such children (see paras 6.27–6.30).

2.7 Other types of abuse to which the 1999 version of *Working Together to Safeguard Children* draws attention include the involvement of children in prostitution and other forms of commercial sexual exploitation. Following on from the pioneering work of Nottinghamshire Social Services, together with the Nottinghamshire Police and with pioneering reports by the Children's Society (see Lee and O'Brien (1995)), *Working Together to Safeguard Children* now advises that such children should be treated primarily as the victims of abuse and that their needs require careful assessment. *Working Together to Safeguard Children* points out that the problem of children involved in prostitution is often hidden from view and that Area Child Protection Committees (ACPCs) should actively enquire into the extent to which there is a local problem, and should not assume that it is not a local issue. The prosecution of child victims of such sexual exploitation is now specifically discouraged and, instead, in addition to providing a much greater range of support services to such children, advice to social services and the police now emphasises the investigation and prosecution of those who coerce, exploit and abuse children (see *Working Together to Safeguard Children*, para 6.44). Recognition of the complex nature of situations which will involve children at risk of a whole range of abuse being perpetrated not just by adult clients but also by those who may be managing their engaging in prostitution, has led to the production of a separate volume of guidance as a Supplement to *Working Together* (see *Guidance on Safeguarding Children Involved in Prostitution* (DOH, 2000)).

2.8 Governments and parents across all continents have begun at the start of the new millennium to become extremely concerned about the use of the internet in the distribution of child pornography. There is now recognition that adults are using the internet to try to establish contact with children with a view to 'grooming' them for inappropriate or abusive relationships. Use of internet 'chat rooms' in which abusive adults make appointments to meet up with children came to the fore with a number of high-profile cases being reported in the media in England in the summer of 2000. Arrests followed throughout 2001 and 2002 of a range of individuals who held positions of responsibility in society including teachers, social workers and even police officers working on high-profile children's cases who were found to be involved with child pornography rings on the internet (see further, Chapter **9**).

2.9   The problem of female genital mutilation continues to cause significant concern amongst health and social welfare professionals. *Working Together to Safeguard Children* emphasises that the Prohibition of Female Circumcision Act 1985 makes female circumcision, excision or infibulation an offence except on specific physical and mental health grounds. *Working Together to Safeguard Children* points out that available medical evidence indicates that female genital mutilation causes harm to those who experience it and that a local authority may exercise its powers under s 47 of the CA 1989 (to conduct child abuse investigations) if it has reason to believe that any child is likely to be or has been the subject of female genital mutilation. The guidance goes on to emphasise that local agencies should be alert to the possibility of female circumcision among the ethnic minority communities known to practise it. In local areas where there are communities or individuals who traditionally practice female genital mutilation, then *Working Together to Safeguard Children* advises that ACPC policy guidance should focus on a preventive strategy involving community education.

2.10   The importance of the approach of the community as a whole to problems of child abuse is a very important one and the absolute necessity of educating adults is of primary importance in working to reduce the current levels of child abuse within our society. Adult members of society have a critical role to perform in the prevention of child abuse. Thus, as Gerrilyn Smith has argued, 'our prevention programmes should be aimed first at the adults who surround children in their day-to-day lives: parents, extended family members, child minders, nursery workers and teachers *among others*'. Smith observes that the *Bulger* case demonstrated that 'we, as a community of adults, are reluctant to take responsibility for protecting other people's children. Hence protectiveness has become increasingly professionalised and more removed from the natural network that surrounds children where it would be most effective' (Smith, (1996)), at pp 77–79). How we as adults conceive of abuse, as informed by the array of research evidence and guidance, is therefore critical. Of equal importance, however, must be our acknowledgement that children deserve recognition of their absolute right to bodily and mental integrity (see Chapter **1** on Article 19 of the UNCRC).

Definitional issues

2.11   As the National Commission of Inquiry into the Prevention of Child Abuse pointed out in 1996, and such is still the case, there is some uncertainty or, in some instances, disagreement amongst professionals and the public over what constitutes child abuse. The National Commission decided therefore to adopt a deliberately broad definition of child abuse for the purposes of their report. Thus, the Commission defined child abuse as consisting of 'anything which individuals, institutions or processes do or fail to do which directly or indirectly harms children or damages their prospects of safe and healthy development into adulthood' (see *Childhood Matters*, at para 1.4). The Commission acknowledged that this broad definition was designed to ensure that the promotion of safe and healthy development of children is the primary aim of all policies affecting them and to stress that institutions and processes can be quite as abusive as individuals to any particular child. To that extent, therefore, this definition requires policymakers to consider broad social and economic issues which run far wider than the particular needs of children but which, nevertheless, profoundly affect them. The Commission emphasised that the adoption of a broad definition of abuse is also intended to encourage everyone to consider how all aspects of their behaviour affect children and was further intended to reflect the principles set down in the UNCRC (see Chapter **1**). When the Commission report was first published in 1996, the then Conservative Minister of Health criticised the definition adopted as being far too wide. It is interesting to note, however, that official guidance on protecting vulnerable adults from abuse, published under the new Labour government and anticipating the implementation of the HRA 1998, defines abuse in a similarly broad way, and the further clarification provided could usefully be adapted for a range of situations involving children and young people (see *No Secrets – Guidance on Developing and Implementing Multi-agency Policies and Procedures to Protect Vulnerable Adults from Abuse* (DOH, 2000). Thus at para 2.5 of the document, abuse is defined as 'a violation of an individual's human and civil rights by any other person or persons'. This is immediately expanded upon to provide that: 'Abuse may consist of a single act or repeated acts. It may be physical, verbal or psychological, it may be an act of neglect or an omission to act, or it may occur when a vulnerable person is persuaded to enter into a financial or sexual transaction to which he or she has not consented or cannot consent'. Abuse can occur in any relationship and may result in significant harm to or exploitation of, the person subjected to it (see *No Secrets*, at para 2.6). The National Commission acknowledged that their broad definition was derived from that of Gil (see Gil (1970)). Gil, writing in 1975, however, proposed a definition which points up the very critical issue of abuse encompassing commissions and omissions, which deprive children of equal rights and liberties, now of course adopted by the government in its guidance on the protection of vulnerable adults (see *No Secrets*, at para 2.6). Thus, Gil wrote that:

'any act of commission or omission by individuals, institutions or society as a whole, and any conditions resulting from any such acts or inaction, which deprive children of equal rights and liberties, and/or interfere with their optimal development, constitute by definition abusive or neglectful acts or conditions' (see Gil (1975), at p 346)).

2.12 This is also reminiscent of the working definition proposed by Dr Alan Gilmour, former Director of the NSPCC in 1988. Thus, Dr Gilmour was of the view that: 'Child abuse occurs when any avoidable act, or avoidable failure to act, adversely affects the physical, mental or emotional wellbeing of a child' (see Gilmour, (1988), at p 11). Gilmour went on to define an 'avoidable act' as something which had happened which need not have happened, but which need not have been deliberate, such as shaking a child in anger which causes a brain haemorrhage (pp 11–12). The concept of avoidable harm was one with which lawyers and social workers were familiar as being included within former care grounds contained in s 1(2) of the Children and Young Persons Act 1969 (CYPA 1969) which were repealed by the CA 1989 and replaced with the concept of 'significant harm' (see further on this, Chapters **4** and **5**). The CA 1989 which covers England and Wales, the Children (Northern Ireland) Order 1995 and the Children (Scotland) Act 1995, all use the concept of 'significant harm' to ground investigations and potential civil legal proceedings in circumstances where children may have been or have been abused. Thus, all the principal UK jurisdictions provide that harm is defined as follows (although it should be noted that the CA 1989, applicable to England and Wales, has been amended by the Adoption and Children Act 2002 as shown in *italics* to reflect increasing awareness of the impact of domestic violence upon children and young people):

> '"harm" means ill-treatment or the impairment of health or development; *including, for example, impairment suffered from seeing or hearing the ill-treatment of another*;
> "development" means physical, intellectual, emotional, social or behavioural development;
> "health" means physical or mental health;
> "ill-treatment" includes sexual abuse and forms of ill-treatment which are not physical.'

2.13 'Significant' is not in itself defined and thus is seen by the courts as bearing its ordinary everyday meaning (see comments of Sir Stephen Brown P in *Newham London Borough Council v A.G.* [1993] 1 FLR 281) but the legislation does go on to provide that:

> 'where the question of whether harm suffered by a child is significant turns on the child's health or development, his health or development shall be compared with that which could reasonably be expected of a similar child.'

2.14 Other definitions provided in the respective pieces of legislation which are seen as being important to the issue of child abuse include the definition of a child 'in need'. Thus, all three pieces of legislation define a child as being 'in need' if:

(a)   he is unlikely to achieve or maintain, or have the opportunity of having or maintaining, a reasonable standard of health or development without the provision for him of services by the local authority;

(b)   his health or development is likely to be significantly impaired or further impaired, without the provision of such services; or

(c)   he is disabled.

The Children (Scotland) Act 1995 provides a fourth criterion which is not to be found in the English, Welsh or Northern Irish legislation: that 'the child is affected adversely by the disability of another family member'.

2.15 The link between the two concepts of a child being 'in need' and a child 'suffering significant harm' are clear and there is a duty imposed upon local authorities to prevent the need for bringing child protection proceedings by making available the provision of such services as are appropriate provided by the local authority or some other agency on its behalf (see CA 1989, Sch 1, para 7). The civil provisions enacted in each of the jurisdictions in 1989 and 1995 did, however, break the links between the civil and criminal law previously linked by s 1 of the CYPA 1969 and s 1 of the Children and Young Persons Act 1933 (CYPA 1933). Section 1 of the CYPA 1933 (and its comparable provisions in Scotland and Northern Ireland) laid down the criminal liability of those providing care for children under the age of 16. Thus s 1(1) provides that:

> 'any person who is at least 16 years old, and has responsibility for any child or young person under that age, and who wilfully causes or procures that child to suffer assault, ill treatment, neglect, abandonment, or exposure in a manner such as to cause the child unnecessary suffering or injury to health, including injury to or loss of sight, or hearing or limb, or organ of the body and any mental derangement, will be liable to criminal prosecution.'

2.16 Several of the grounds listed under s 1(1) of the CYPA 1933 formed grounds for the making of a care order under s 1(2) of the CYPA 1969. There is now, however, no such link between s 31 of the CA 1989 and s 1 of the CYPA 1933. This section is analysed in detail in Chapter **7** but it is interesting to note that criminal law expands upon the issues to be taken into consideration when considering the five different types of abusive behaviour which are encompassed within the criminal law provision. The types of ill-treatment which are covered are: assault, although a special exemption for parents administering reasonable chastisement to their children confers upon them a defence which may be raised to any charge of assault made against them (see further, para **2.63** *et seq*); ill-treatment; neglect; abandonment; and exposure. Despite the severance of the link between the civil and criminal law provisions, it is interesting to note that all of the five categories of criminal offence are covered in the guidance issued by the DOH in relation to the determination of whether a child is suffering or likely to suffer from significant harm (see *Working Together to Safeguard Children*, at chapters 2 and 6).

2.17   It can be seen, therefore, from a consideration of both the civil and criminal law that neither provides any meaningful definition as to the type of conduct which the courts in this country will deem to constitute 'child abuse' sufficient to justify either the removal of the child from his family or other care setting in civil proceedings, or the criminal prosecution of the child's parents, others having parental responsibility for the child or any others who are looking after the child. As the author pointed out in *Childhood Matters*, op cit (at pp 290–293), none of the five types of abuse identified in s 1(1) of the CYPA 1933 (as amended by the CA 1989) is defined in the statute. All the types of treatment identified under s 1 have therefore had to be defined and explained by case-law in the courts (see further, Chapter **9**). Whilst the term 'child abuse' is one that is widely used in England by ordinary members of the public, the media and even official government publications, it is not a phrase which is actually to be found in either English criminal or civil law provisions governing what may be deemed to be potentially abusive behaviour towards children.

2.18   In its *First Report to the United Nations Monitoring Committee* in 1994 the UK government claimed that the CA 1989 ensured that children were protected from *all* forms of abuse and neglect as delineated in Article 19 of the UNCRC (see Chapter **1**). That report could certainly be criticised for taking an over-Anglocentric view of the benefits of such legislation, since at the time Scotland and Northern Ireland had yet to have measures enacted comparable to the CA 1989. It was also apparent that English law did not in fact provide protection against *all* forms of physical violence, injury or abuse while in the care of parents or legal guardians, since parents, legal guardians or anyone else having responsibility for the care of a child aged under 16 is, as s 1(7) of the CYPA 1933 provides, allowed to engage in reasonable physical chastisement of the child. Whilst it is apparent that 'reasonable physical chastisement' exercised by a parent, guardian or other person with the care of the child will not constitute ill-treatment, the question which was left hanging in the air as a result of the European Court's decision in *A v UK* [1998] 2 FLR 959, and in the absence of the government's response to *Protecting Children, Supporting Parents* (Consultation Paper on the Reform of Corporal Punishment of Children by their Parents) (DOH, 2000) was what constitutes 'reasonable' physical chastisement? In the case of *A v UK*, the European Court found that the step-father's treatment of his step-son in beating him on the legs with a garden cane such as to draw blood was not 'reasonable chatisement' and that UK law in failing to define for parents what was meant by the term 'reasonable', failed to provide adequate protection of the child's right under Article 3 to be free from inhuman and degrading treatment or punishment. (For a full discussion of the problems raised by the decision in *A v UK* and the government's failure to respond appropriately, see Lyon (2000).) The step-parent of the child A in *A v UK* was actually acquitted in the English court of an offence under s 1 of the CYPA 1933 since the jury found his conduct in inflicting punishment on his step-son by beating him with a garden cane so as to leave wounds requiring hospital attention to be 'reasonable' on the direction of the judge. The step-parent was thus acquitted of any criminal offence albeit that the then Health Minister, Paul Boateng, in his press statement released on hearing the initial determination of the Commission, indicated that the step-father's actions had been plainly abusive, and further, when responding to the final decision of the European Court, stated that parents know the difference between a 'loving smack' and 'a beating'. Whilst the government in England has announced (19 November 2001) that it will not introduce legislation in response to the European Court's ruling, chiefly as a result of the public's response to the Consultation process (see para **2.68**), the Scottish Executive has introduced proposed legislation to outlaw all forms of corporal punishment of children under 3 and 16 or over, and the use of any implements whatsoever in the corporal punishment of children. The Welsh Assembly has yet to announce its intentions after the publication of the responses in Wales (19 November 2001). The Northern Irish Executive is engaging in further consultation on the issue. In the absence of new legislative guidance from the government in England, the English courts were forced to step in to fill the obvious lacuna in the law arising out of the incompatibility of the defence of reasonable chastisement with the demands of the ECHR. In *R v H* [2001] 2 FLR 431, CA, the Court of Appeal indicated that since there had been no legislation on the subject, although the consultation period had closed 13 months previously, future directions to juries on the defence of 'reasonable chastisement' must henceforward be in very detailed terms and contain supplementary directions in order to comply with the demands of the ECHR and the ruling of the European Court in *A v UK*. The Court stated that in future the jury should be directed in detailed terms as to factors relevant to whether the chastisement in question was reasonable and moderate; and a judge should direct the jury considering the matter of reasonableness or otherwise of such chastisement that they must consider the following:

(a)   the nature and context of the defendant's behaviour;
(b)   the duration of that behaviour;
(c)   the physical and mental consequences in respect of that child;
(d)   the age and personal characteristics of the child;
(e)   the reasons given by the defendant for administering the punishment.

The Court went on to stress that to give such directions was not to involve a judge in breach of his obligations under statute or the ECHR, and that such an incremental development of the common law was wholly appropriate. Indeed, the Court was honest enough to indicate that a number of the directions, which it was prompted to give in 2001, were even foreshadowed within the 1860 case of *R v Hopley*, from which the defence of 'reasonable chastisement' as now employed by defendants in relation to allegations of any type of assault or ill-treatment of a child, was first derived. The Court of Appeal thus implied (as was first pointed out in Lyon (2000)) that *Hopley* could have been used much more effectively to protect children if it had been properly interpreted and applied by the judiciary.

The failure to lay down standards

2.19   One of the major difficulties in trying to comprehend how the concept of child abuse may be understood in England lies in the failure, even in the CA 1989, to lay down standards of care which children in this jurisdiction can expect from their parents. The English provisions apply also to Wales and to Northern Ireland through the Children (Northern Ireland) Order 1995, which adopts the same definitions as the CA 1989. Scottish law, by contrast, does provide greater guidance. The CA 1989 defines 'parental responsibility' as 'all the rights, duties, power and responsibilities and authority which by law a parent of a child has in relation to the child and his property' (CA 1989, s 3(1) and Children (Northern Ireland) Order 1995, Art 6(1)). Nothing further is said in either piece of legislation to define *what these are*, or *how* they should be exercised. The Act, nevertheless, provides as has already been noted, local authority social services departments or the NSPCC with the power to intervene in families to remove children where it can be shown that 'the child is suffering or is likely to suffer significant harm' and that this is 'attributable to a lack of *reasonable* parental care' or 'the child is beyond parental control' (see CA 1989, s 31). The definition of 'significant' and what may be encompassed within the terms harm, ill-treatment and impairment of health and development have already been noted but again, the definition of 'significant' can scarcely be said to give any sort of guidance to parents, in that the characteristics of a 'similar child' are not given and, more critically, 'reasonable', 'abuse', 'ill-treatment', and 'impairment' are not further defined. Thus, as well as creating clear difficulties for the courts, the legislation fails to give authoritative guidance as to the standard of care expected from both parents and carers or to guide those who may have to intervene in families in order to protect children.

2.20   The CA 1989 fails to lay down standards of care which children in this jurisdiction can expect from their parents, nor does it exist to guide or educate parents themselves. In this sense it also fails to comply with the provisions of Art 18(2) of the UNCRC which states that 'State Parties shall render appropriate assistance to parents and legal guardians in the performance of their child rearing responsibilities'. No clearly defined positive duty, in relation to the care which parents should exercise in bringing up their children, is laid down in the legislation, and there is a complete absence of any further statutory guidelines comparable to those which exist in Scotland (see ss 1 and 2 of the Children (Scotland) Act 1995). It is therefore the case that a negative but ill-defined issue takes precedence, and emphasis is laid on the fact that both civil child protection proceedings and criminal proceedings may be instituted based on vague, ambiguous and ill-defined provisions.

2.21 Use of the term 'significant' in relation to the harm suffered by the child, is, as has been noted above, defined by reference to a comparison of the child's health and development with that of a 'similar' child. This again necessarily imports into the concept of child abuse some notion of comparative and evaluative judgments on the part of professionals coming into contact with the family, who have to determine, in accordance with these notions, whether it can be said that, *significant harm* has occurred to the child. In addition, the provision of s 31 of the CA 1989 expects them again to draw on their own notions of 'what care it would be reasonable to expect a parent to give to a child'. The professionals are thus expected to draw on their own professional knowledge and their personal experiences of the health and development of similar children, as well as their view as to what constitutes 'reasonable care'. The definition of 'significant' can scarcely be said to give any guidance at all to parents, particularly those who have no other children, any more than it does to professionals, some of whom may be young, without children and recently qualified and who may lack any very great experience or knowledge in relation to the health and development and the reasonable care of 'normal children'.

2.22 The lack of guidance given to all those who must interpret the various phrases in the CA 1989 may then give rise to problems. It should also be noted that the provisions relating to 'significant harm' do not again comply with the demands of Article 19(1) of the UNCRC since that Article is unequivocal in stating that appropriate measures must be taken to protect the child from *all forms of abuse* and does not qualify this in any way with regard to the degree of harm (see Chapter 1). The CA 1989 demands, however, that the harm must be 'significant' and the difficulties attendant upon establishing this are well illustrated by the struggles which the courts have had in interpreting this phrase (see Chapters 4 and 7). Considerable attention has focused on the notion of 'significant harm' by social work, psychiatric and medical commentators (see, for example, Adcock and White (1998)), but little critical comment has developed on the issue of the measurement of significance, how this related to Article 19(1) of the UNCRC and how parents, guardians or other carers are to be enabled to make some sense of the standard of care which is expected from them under this piece of legislation.

2.23 Given that the definition of harm contained within the civil law of England is somewhat problematical for professionals to interpret, let alone parents, it is not surprising that official government departments, charged with the task of overseeing the well-being of children, have successively determined that further guidance is necessary in order to elucidate this area for all the professionals who might be working together on suspected cases of child abuse. Thus the Home Office, the DOH, the Department of Education, and the Welsh Office have on two separate occasions (1988 and 1991) issued guidance which contained detailed consideration of what may be understood to constitute 'child abuse'. The third version of this guidance, issued for use by the DOH, Home Office and the then DfEE, in England only, is entitled *Working Together to Safeguard Children*. It is a very significant document in that it consolidates previous guidance procedures for the protection of children from abuse and recommends developments aimed at making these even more effective. The document takes into account the requirements of the CA 1989, lessons learned from a succession of enquiry reports, lessons learned from national surveys such as that of the National Commission and the NSPCC, as well as drawing on examples of good practice provided by a number of agencies. Virtually identical guidance exists for Wales as approved with the same title by the Welsh Assembly in 2000. Similar guidance exists for Scotland entitled *Protecting Children, A Shared Responsibility: Guidance on Inter-Agency Cooperation* (The Scottish Office, 1998), and Northern Ireland entitled *Cooperating to Protect Children: Guidance Dealing with Inter-Professional and Inter-Agency Cooperation in Child Protection* (DHSS NI, 1996).

Working Together to Safeguard Children: the inter-agency guidance

2.24 The 1999 version of *Working Together to Safeguard Children*, together with its two Supplements, *Safeguarding Children involved in Prostitution* (22 May 2000) and *Safeguarding Children in Whom Illness is Fabricated or Induced* (30 August 2002) has, like its predecessors, become a 'working bible' on inter-agency co-operation in the field of child protection. This guidance and its supplements must now be read together with the *Framework for the Assessment of Children in Need and their Families* (DOH, DfEE, Home Office, 2000) and the *Practice Guidance on the Assessment Framework* (DOH, 2000). (A separate *Framework of Assessment* document under the same title, as approved by the Welsh Assembly, exists for Wales (2001). It should be noted, however, that the two Supplementary Guidance documents on *Fabricated Illness* and *Child Prostitution* (see above) have both been adopted entirely by the Welsh Assembly.) As the *Framework for Assessment* points out (at para 1.22), knowledge of the assessment framework will be of use to all professionals when they are contributing to assessment of children in need, *including* when they are undertaking or contributing to assessments as part of their responsibilities for safeguarding children under *Working Together to Safeguard Children* and its supplementary guidance.

2.25   *Working Together to Safeguard Children* gives a general indication of what is understood by the concept of abuse and neglect and then goes on to give much more detailed definitions of the various categories of abuse which are provided as a precondition for entry of a child's name on the local child protection register (see *Working Together to Safeguard Children*, chapter 2, at paras 2.3–2.15). The principal purpose of the register is to make agencies and professionals aware of those children who are judged to be at continuing risk of significant harm and in need of active safeguarding (see *Working Together to Safeguard Children*, at para 5.100 and see further on this, Chapters **4** and **5**).

2.26   In considering what is meant by abuse and neglect, *Working Together to Safeguard Children* states that:

> 'Somebody may abuse or neglect a child by inflicting harm, or by failing to act to prevent harm. Children may be abused in a family or in an institutional or community setting; by those known to them or, more rarely, by a stranger' (at para 2.3).

According to para 5.101 of *Working Together to Safeguard Children*, children should be registered on the child protection register under one or more of the categories of physical, emotional, or sexual abuse or neglect and these various categories of abuse or neglect are further defined in chapter 2 of *Working Together to Safeguard Children*, which considerably expands within the chapter on further potential sources of abuse constituted by a range of circumstances or family situations in which children may find themselves. Chapter 6 of *Working Together to Safeguard Children* further provides definitions of other forms of abuse additional to those set out in chapter 2 and includes: abuse by children and young people, abuse of disabled children, the issues of abuse of children involved in prostitution, the problems of child pornography and the internet, the problem of children and families who go missing, and the difficult issue of female genital mutilation. The various categories expanded upon in chapter 6 are of course manifestations of the other types of abuse referred to and defined more strictly in chapter 2.

2.27   These definitions provided in chapter 2 of *Working Together to Safeguard Children* (and in the cases of children in whom illness is fabricated or induced or those who may be involved in child prostitution, further expanded upon in the Supplementary Guidance on those subjects (see para **2.24**)) are reproduced in many local authority child protection procedure guidelines and are set out below.

'Physical Abuse

2.4   Physical abuse may involve hitting, shaking, throwing, poisoning, burning or scalding, drowning, suffocating, or otherwise causing physical harm to a child. Physical harm may also be caused when a parent or carer feigns the symptoms of, or deliberately causes ill health to a child whom they are looking after. This situation is commonly described using terms such as factitious illness by proxy or Munchausen syndrome by proxy.

Emotional Abuse

2.5   Emotional abuse is the persistent emotional ill-treatment of a child such as to cause severe and persistent adverse effects on the child's emotional development. It may involve conveying to children that they are worthless or unloved, inadequate or valued only insofar as they meet the needs of another person. It may feature age or developmentally inappropriate expectations being imposed on children. It may involve causing children frequently to feel frightened or in danger or the exploitation or corruption of children. Some level of emotional abuse is involved in all types of ill-treatment of a child, though it may occur alone.

Sexual Abuse

2.6   Sexual abuse involves forcing or enticing a child or young person to take part in sexual activities, whether or not the child is aware of what is happening. The activities may involved physical contact, including penetrative (e.g. rape or buggery) or non-penetrative acts. They may include non-contact activities, such as involving children in looking at, or in the production of pornographic material or watching sexual activities, or encouraging children to behave in sexually inappropriate ways.

Neglect

2.7   Neglect is the persistent failure to meet a child's basic physical and/or psychological needs, likely to result in the serious impairment of the child's health or development. It may involve a parent or carer failing to provide adequate food, shelter and clothing, failing to protect a child from physical harm or danger, or the failure to ensure access to appropriate medical care or treatment. It may also include neglect of, or unresponsiveness to, a child's basic emotional needs.'

2.28   Before going on to explain how these various categories of abuse link in to the concept of 'significant harm', the guidance next goes on to consider the impact of abuse and neglect upon children pointing out that the sustained abuse or neglect of children physically, emotionally or sexually can have major long-term effects on all aspects of a child's health, development and well-being. The notions of 'health', 'development' and what these may cover are contained in the provisions of s 31(9) of the CA 1989, which set out an expanded definition of what is encompassed within the phrase 'significant harm' provided in s 31(2)(a) of the CA 1989. The guidance sets out at paras 2.8–2.15 the different ways in which the various forms of abuse and neglect identified at paras 2.4–2.7 (see above) can impact upon the child. Much of the guidance provided has been informed by a whole variety of research studies (see *Child Protection: Messages from Research* (HMSO, 1995); Harris-Hendricks and Newman (1998), at pp 33–58; Cleaver, Unell and Aldgate (1999) and *The Children Act Now: Messages from Research* (DOH, 2001)), and by the experience of a wide range of childcare professionals and close critical scrutiny of current working practice (see Adcock and White (1998)). Amongst the adverse impacts which *Working Together to Safeguard Children* identifies, considerable attention focuses on the damaging effects of abuse in childhood extending well into adulthood. Sustained abuse will undoubtedly have a deep impact on the child's self-image and self-esteem and on his or her future life. Difficulties arising from such childhood experiences will extend into adulthood and may well lead to difficulties in forming or sustaining close relationships, establishing oneself in the workforce, and to extra difficulties in developing the attitudes and skills needed to become future effective parents.

2.29 The document further emphasises that it is not only the stressful events of abuse, which may have an impact, but also the context in which they take place and that it is the interaction between a number of factors which serve to increase the likelihood or level of actual significant harm. The guidance acknowledges that for every child and family there may be factors which aggravate the harm caused to the child and others which protect against harm. Relevant factors will include the individual child's means of coping and adapting, support from a family and social network, and the impact of any intervention. The effects on the child may also be influenced by the quality of the family environment at the time of abuse and subsequent life events. The guidance points out that a very important issue, which is sometimes overlooked, is that the way in which professionals respond to the child and the family could have a significant bearing on subsequent outcomes.

2.30 The guidance identifies particular impacts which may occur as a result of the different types of abuse. Thus it notes that physical abuse can lead directly to neurological damage, physical injuries, disability or, at the extreme, death. Harm may be caused to children both by the abuse itself and by the abuse taking place in the wider family or in an institutional context of conflict and aggression. Physical abuse, it points out, has been linked to aggressive behaviour in children, emotional and behavioural problems, and educational difficulties. As far as emotional abuse is concerned, *Working Together to Safeguard Children* emphasises that there is increasing evidence of the adverse long-term consequences for children's development where they have been subject to sustained emotional abuse. Emotional abuse has an important impact on a developing child's mental health, behaviour and self-esteem. It can be especially damaging in infancy. The document stresses that underlying emotional abuse may be as important, if not more so, than any more visible forms of abuse in terms of its impact on the child. Domestic violence, adult mental health problems and parental substance misuse may be features in families where children are exposed to such abuse.

2.31 The guidance indicates that disturbed behaviour including self-harm, inappropriate sexualised behaviour, sadness, depression and a loss of self-esteem have all been linked to sexual abuse. The adverse effects of sexual abuse may well endure long into adulthood and the severity of impact on a child is believed to increase the longer the abuse continues, the more extensive the abuse, and the older the child. A number of features of sexual abuse have also been linked with severity of impact, including the extent of premeditation, the degree of threat and coercion, sadism and bizarre or unusual elements. A child's ability to cope with the experience of sexual abuse, once recognised or disclosed, is strengthened by the support of a non-abusive adult carer who believes the child, helps the child understand the abuse and is able to offer help and protection. Whilst the guidance indicates that a proportion of adults who sexually abuse children have themselves been sexually abused as children and may also have been exposed as children to domestic violence and discontinuity of care, it would, however, be quite wrong to suggest that most children who are abused will inevitably go on to become abusers themselves.

2.32 As far as neglect is concerned, the guidance states that severe neglect of young children is associated with major impairment of growth and intellectual development and that persistent neglect can lead to serious impairment of health or development, and long-term difficulties with social functioning, relationships and educational progress. (All of these problems were found to exist in a very acute form in all of the five children whose problems formed the basis of the application to the European Court in the case of *Z v UK* [2001] 2 FLR 612.) As is pointed out in the guidance, neglect can also result, in extreme cases, in death. (For a further detailed discussion of neglect see paras **2.124–2.138**).

2.33 *Working Together to Safeguard Children* does not expressly acknowledge that these definitions are not included explicitly within the concept of 'significant harm', but it continues immediately to identify that any one or more of these various definitions of abuse and neglect will be of relevance in determining whether the threshold has been crossed to justify compulsory intervention in family life in the best interests of children. Thus the guidance acknowledges that there are no absolute criteria on which to rely when judging what constitutes 'significant harm'. In trying to judge what might constitute 'significant harm' the guidance advises that consideration of the severity of ill-treatment and thus as to whether it is 'significant' or not, may include 'the degree and the extent of physical harm, the duration and frequency of abuse and neglect and the extent of premeditation, degree of threat and coercion, sadism, and bizarre or unusual elements in child sexual abuse' (*Working Together to Safeguard Children*, at para 2.17). As the guidance points out, each of these elements has been associated with more severe effects on the child, and/or relatively greater difficulty in helping the child overcome the adverse impact of the ill-treatment. It stresses that sometimes, a single traumatic event may constitute 'significant harm', for example a violent assault, suffocation or poisoning. More often, it suggests, 'significant harm' is a compilation of significant events, both acute and long-standing, which interrupt, change or damage the child's physical and psychological development. It points out further that some children live in family and social circumstances where their health and development are neglected, and that for them, it is the corrosiveness of long-term emotional, physical or sexual abuse that causes impairment to the extent of constituting 'significant harm'. It emphasises that in each case it is necessary to consider any ill-treatment which a child may have suffered alongside the family's strengths and supports (*Working Together to Safeguard Children*, at paras 2.16–2.18).

2.34 Whilst acknowledging that this last point is important, it is suggested here that one must always be aware of the risks posed to the children in leaving them where they are and, in particular, whether it is consistent with their welfare so to do. This must more especially be so since the decision of the European Court in *Z v UK* [2001] 2 FLR 612. From the account of the facts of the case it would appear that too much attention focused on the issue of supporting the adult members of the family and insufficient attention focused on the severe neglect and different forms of abuse suffered by the children. *Working Together to Safeguard Children* acknowledges at para 2.26 that the child's safety and welfare are paramount but nevertheless puts it in such a way as to appear to give equal prominence to the potentially abusing adults; again in the light of *Z v UK* and the attitude of the Court of Appeal in *Re L, V, M and H* [2000] 2 FLR 334, such prominence might be difficult to defend. Thus *Working Together to Safeguard Children* states at para 2.26 that, whilst recognising that the child's safety and welfare are paramount, professionals must give due consideration to the needs of all family members. The chapter does, however, end by emphasising that the *Framework for the Assessment of Children in Need and their Families* provides the foundation for a systematic assessment of children and families and, therefore, that careful assessment of the child's position should be undertaken.

2.35 Chapter 6 of *Working Together to Safeguard Children* identifies, as has been noted above, other different potential sources of stress for children and families which may in turn leave children open to abuse or neglect. These include social exclusion, domestic violence, the mental illness of a parent or carer and drug and alcohol misuse by parents and carers.

2.36 Further definitions of other types of abuse which may come under the headings identified in *Working Together to Safeguard Children*, at chapter 2 are also provided in chapter 6 of that document. Considerable attention therefore focuses on problems of children living away from home in both institutional and foster care (drawing on the lessons learned from *Caring for Children Away from Home – Messages from Research* (DOH, 1998), the problems of peer abuse and bullying (a particularly worrying feature for children locked up in secure penal settings (see especially, Goldson (2002)), 'race and racism'. All of these will present various aspects of the types of abuse identified in chapter 2 of *Working Together to Safeguard Children* but it is significant that much greater attention is focused in the 1999 edition on the problems which children may experience both from their peers and other members of the community when considering issues of peer abuse, bullying and racism.

2.37 Other groups of children who may be at risk of suffering the different forms of abuse identified in chapter 2 of *Working Together* have also been considered above, but chapter 6 of the document sets out the detailed guidelines on issues which should be considered in relation to:

— the potential abuse of disabled children;
— abuse by children and young people generally;
— children living in situations of domestic violence;
— children involved in prostitution (although here reference should also be made to the Supplementary Guidance to Working Together, *Safeguarding Children Involved in Prostitution* (2002);
— children who may be approached via the internet (see further, Chapter **9**);
— the problem of children and families who go missing; and
— the vexed problem of female genital mutilation.

2.38 Chapter 6 of *Working Together to Safeguard Children* contains a further definition of abuse which should be considered here. Thus at paras 6.24–6.25 of that document, a definition of organised or multiple abuse is provided:

'6.24 Organised or multiple abuse may be defined as abuse involving one or more abuser and a number of related or non-related abused children and young people. The abusers concerned may be acting in concert to abuse children, sometimes acting in isolation or may be using an institutional framework or position of authority to recruit children for abuse.

6.25 Organised and multiple abuse occur both as part of a network of abuse across a family or community, and within institutions such as residential homes or schools. Such abuse is profoundly traumatic for the children who become involved. Its investigation is time consuming and demanding work requiring specialist skills from both police and social work staff. Some investigations become extremely complex because of the number of places and people involved, and the time scale over which abuse is alleged to have occurred. The complexity is heightened where, as in historical cases, the alleged victims are no longer living in the situations where the incidents occurred or where the alleged perpetrators are also no longer linked to the setting or employment roles.'

2.39 The problem of organised or multiple abuse has prompted a wide range of police investigations as well as institutional inquiries. The problems associated with allegations of organised or multiple abuse will be examined in more detail in Chapter **3**.

2.40 The definitions provided in *Working Together to Safeguard Children* are clearly important to guide both child protection investigations and potential registrations on the child protection register (see Chapter **5** for further detail on this) as well as to inform the development of a shared professional understanding as to what may constitute *significant harm* for the purposes of the taking of legal proceedings. As well as being thoroughly conversant with the principles of *Working Together to Safeguard Children*, and the two pieces of Supplementary Guidance, practitioners in the child protection field must also now be familiar with the *Framework for the Assessment of Children in Need and their Families*, which as *Working Together to Safeguard Children* emphasises 'can inform contributions by all agencies and disciplines when assessing children about whom there are child safety concerns' (see *Working Together to Safeguard Children*, at paras 5.13, 5.33, and for further discussion on this, see Chapters **3**, **5** and **6**).

The Scottish approach

2.41 The Scottish Office guidance *Protecting Children: A Shared Responsibility: Guidance on Inter-Agency Co-operation* (1998) deals with the definitions rather differently from the approach adopted in *Working Together to Safeguard Children*. Thus, in Annex C the document amplifies the bare descriptions of the categories of abuse for registration which have been outlined in Part 3. The Scottish Office guidance first of all provides a general definition of abuse, not to be found in the guidance documents for England and Wales. Thus, under the heading 'General Definition of Abuse' the document provides that:

'children may be in need of protection where their basic needs are not being met, in a manner appropriate to their stage of development, and they will be at risk from avoidable acts of commission or omission on the part of their parent(s), sibling(s) or other relative(s) or a carer (i.e. the person(s) while not a parent who has actual custody of a child)' (*Protecting Children: A Shared Responsibility*, Annex C, at para 2).

2.42 The Scottish Office guidance expands upon this definition in the following paragraph, and provides that:

'to define an act or omission as abusive and/or presenting future risk for the purpose of registration, a number of elements must be taken into account. These include demonstrable or predictable harm to the child which must have been avoidable because of action or inaction by the parent or other carer' (Annex C, para 3).

2.43 The Scottish Office guidance continues to set out definitions of different types of abuse which can then be used for the purposes of entering the child's name on the Child Protection Register. The document points out that although these are presented as discrete definitions, in practice there may be overlaps between the categories and although registration should take place under one main category of abuse for the purpose of individual case management, the document indicates that a case conference may identify a combination of abuse categories which the child protection plan will need to address (see further, Chapter **5**). The definitions set out under different headings are different from those provided in *Working Together to Safeguard Children* and there is a further additional definition provided in the Scottish Office guidance of 'non-organic failure to thrive'. The guidance sets out the following definitions:

'Physical injury

Actual or attempted physical injury to a child, including the administration of toxic substances, where there is knowledge, or reasonable suspicion, that the injury was inflicted or knowingly not prevented.

Sexual abuse

Any child may be deemed to have been sexually abused when any person(s), by design or neglect, exploits the child, directly or indirectly, in any activity intended to lead to the sexual arousal or other forms of gratification of that person or any other person(s) including organised networks. This definition holds whether or not there has been genital contact and whether or not the child is said to have initiated, or consented to, the behaviour.

Non-organic failure to thrive

Children who significantly fail to reach normal growth and developmental milestones (i.e. physical growth, weight, motor, social and intellectual development) where physical and genetic reasons have been medically eliminated and a diagnosis of non-organic failure to thrive has been established.

Emotional abuse

Failure to provide for the child's basic emotional needs such as to have a severe effect on the behaviour and development of the child.

Physical neglect

This occurs when a child's essential needs are not met and this is likely to cause impairment to physical health and development. Such needs include food, clothing, cleanliness, shelter and warmth. A lack of appropriate care, including deprivation of access to health care, may result in persistent or severe exposure, through negligence to circumstances which endanger the child' (Annex C, para 4).

2.44 Whilst the Scottish Office guidance provides a definition of non-organic failure to thrive, which is not contained within *Working Together to Safeguard Children*, the Scottish Office guidance also looks at neglect in purely physical terms under the heading of 'physical neglect'. *Working Together to Safeguard Children* defines neglect as a persistent failure to meet children's basic physical and/or psychological needs, whereas the Scottish Office guidance subsumes the failure to provide for the child's basic emotional needs under the heading of 'emotional abuse'. It is interesting to note that the 1998 document *Protecting Children: A Shared Responsibility* appears to differ quite markedly from the 1989 Scottish Office guidance *Effective Intervention: Child Abuse – Guidance on Co-operation in Scotland* (1989), where there was a much greater emphasis on the development of local definitions by local Area Review Committees. Thus the 1989 guidance stated that local agreements or definitions should take account of existing guidance which sets out the general categories of abuse which at that point were identified as being: physical injury; physical neglect; failure to thrive; and children at risk of abuse. The 1989 guidance further stated that definitions should be developed of sexual abuse and emotional abuse, which it acknowledged several Area Review Committees had already done and advised that in agreeing definitions of sexual abuse and emotional abuse, Area Review Committees might find it helpful to note the formulations provided in that guidance (see *Effective Intervention: Child Abuse*, at paras 2.6 and 2.7). Note that the previous Area Review Committees have now been replaced by the Child Protection Committees (as referred to in *Protecting Children: A Shared Responsibility*, at para 1.6).

2.45 *Protecting Children: A Shared Responsibility* has been further expanded upon in the document under the same name issued as *Guidance for Health Professionals in Scotland* in September 1999. That document, in its 'Glossary of Terms and Definitions' adopts the general definition of abuse contained in the 1998 guidance but then goes on to point out that whilst the term 'significant harm' has not been defined in the Children (Scotland) Act 1995, in medical usage the term is used to encompass the extent of immediate and long-term damage resulting from any forms of abuse and neglect. The term 'significant harm' highlights the need to consider not only the degree of impairment/ injury at presentation, be it physical (including growth), sexual or emotional, but also the degree of long-term impairment/disability, be that physical, intellectual, emotional, social or behavioural, which is likely to result. The *Guidance for Health Professionals* goes on to give examples of what should be considered in terms of both immediate and long-term damage resulting from some examples of abuse. Thus, it states, that considering the degree of 'significant harm' in a shaken baby would include the severity of the presenting illness, indicated to some degree by the level of medical intervention required and the long-term sequelae such as cerebral palsy, seizures and visual impairment. It goes on to state that evaluating 'significant harm' in sexual abuse would include not only genital injury but any accompanying physical injury, the possibility of sexually transmitted disease or pregnancy and short/long-term psychological or psychiatric sequelae. It further advises that in considering the degree of 'significant harm', both ill-treatment and impairment and impact on long-term functioning, require consideration (see 'Glossary of Terms and Definitions', at p 4).

2.46 The various definitions of child abuse provided in the different volumes of guidance issued in the jurisdictions of the UK do not claim to be exhaustive, for as the Scottish Office guidance points out, new forms of child abuse may evolve over time and understanding as to what types of behaviour or combination of family circumstances might prove abusive to children is inevitably influenced by the gathering of evidence from research studies, experiences of professionals, families and children and the critical scrutiny of practice. That such an approach has been adopted can clearly been seen from a comparison of the different guidance documents which have been issued over the years since 1988. A comparison even between the 1991 and 1999 documents issued by the DOH for England and Wales in 1991, and England only in 1999, reveal the very considerable extent to which lessons have been learned from a plethora of research studies, some of which have been done under the auspices of the DOH but also from many other studies and published works. Such documents are of immense value to all the professionals who may come into contact with the different issues posed by problems of child protection. Both *Working Together to Safeguard Children* and *The Framework for the Assessment of Children in Need and their Families*, and their companion documents in Scotland and Northern Ireland, have been productive of very considerable amounts of training for all the professionals involved. Despite the importance of the guidance documents and the training which has been provided on them, it still appears to be the case that professionals involved in working on child protection cases may be ignorant of the guidance and have been untouched by extensive training programmes. This was one of the shocking features to emerge in relation to two of the social workers in the Victoria Climbie case, who had to admit that they were not aware of *Working Together to Safeguard Children* nor had they received relevant training on the guidance. This then prompted Victoria's father to comment, in an interview with the BBC, that he could not understand how someone employed as a social worker could not read, a damning indictment of the employment of someone as a child protection worker who was both unfamiliar with, and untrained in, the detail of these critical documents. The volumes of guidance and the relevant training provided upon them, however, only serve to accentuate the comparable lack of guidance and lack of training provided to parents and carers of children within the UK as a whole.

2.47 Since it is acknowledged within the various documents of guidance that it is not possible to define in detail all the various categories of abuse and that professionals should draw widely upon research, experience and other published works it is proposed to examine in more detail here the different types of abuse which the various documents have identified.

Physical abuse: non-accidental abuse including incidence

2.48   In its most extreme form, physical abuse will result in the death of a
child and in the potential prosecution and conviction of the child's parents for
homicide. (For details of offences and criminal processes, see further at
Chapter **9**.) The NSPCC has argued very strongly in both editions of *Out of
Sight* (1999 and 2001) that we have lost sight of the children who are killed by
abuse and neglect. The NSPCC points out that deaths which command the
most attention tend to be those in which a child is killed by a stranger,
although on average fewer than 10 children die in this way each year. Its
reports highlight the fact that children killed by abuse and neglect, with few
exceptions, receive little attention in the media and that is why they published
the second edition of *Out of Sight* in order to draw attention to the sizeable
number of children who suffer this most extreme form of cruelty – being
killed as a result of abuse and neglect. They point out that currently one to
two children are known to die in this way each week, although the NSPCC
believes that the true number is likely to be significantly higher and that many
such deaths still go unreported, uninvestigated and unnoticed (see further,
A Wilczynski (1994)), at pp 61–66). Most people, including professionals
working within the child protection system, are always surprised by the scale
of the figures set out in the NSPCC reports and most members of the public
simply cannot accept that this level of child homicide within a child's family
occurs within our society.

2.49   The NSPCC's report *Out of Sight* was accompanied by a further report
on *Reporting Child Deaths: The Role of the Media* produced for the NSPCC by the
Glasgow Media Group. This report covered a series of cases since 1980 in
which children had died as a result of abuse by their parents or step-parents.
The group considered 15 selected cases of child death on BBC Network
News, ITN and then coverage in *The Times*, *The Sunday Times*, the *Mirror* and
the *Sunday Mirror*. This study demonstrated that there had been quite a
dramatic decline in the coverage of child deaths from the 1980s through to the
end of 2000, a pattern which was replicated in all media in their sample of
cases. One of the journalists who gave evidence to the report team, David
Brindle of the *Guardian*, pointed up both an explanation as to why such deaths
are not as newsworthy as those when a child is murdered by a stranger as well
as indicating a possible explanation for non-acceptance of the problem by
members of the public. Thus he stated that:

> 'People are not comfortable with the reality of the fact that ... overwhelmingly
> most abuse, most homicides are committed by family' (see *Reporting Child Deaths:
> the Role of the Media* (NSPCC, 2001), at p 12).

Brindle went on to state that:

'Tabloids, particularly those that present themselves as strong supporters of the family, do not want to flag up that what goes on inside families is not always very nice. It much more suits their view of the world to write about risks from paedophiles than about the reality that children are much more likely to be abused by their own family' (at p 15).

2.50 Whilst the NSPCC has put the figure at approximately one or two child deaths per week, Reder and Duncan from their most recent research put the figure at closer to 200 per year which would equate to between 3 and 4 deaths per week (see Reder and Duncan, (1999)) which as Fitzgerald comments 'provide a stark contrast to the six or seven child deaths each year of children killed by strangers'; or as he puts it 'a child is thirty times more likely to be killed by a family member or carer than by a stranger' (see J Fitzgerald 'Lessons from the Past – Experience of Inquiries and Reviews' in *Out of Sight* (NSPCC, 2001), at pp 92–93). Since the beginning of 2000, the DOH has been keeping a statistical record of these kinds of child deaths but as yet no figures are available, not even in the recently published *Learning from Past Experience – A Review of Serious Case Reviews* (2002). That review does, however, state that the DOH has recently introduced an enhanced computerised database of deaths or serious injuries of children where there are child protection concerns. This database records details of the incident, the child and the family, any criminal proceedings and whether or not a serious case review has been conducted into the incident. The new database was launched in April 2002. Data is being entered by DOH staff on the basis of notifications received from local authorities but there is no public access to the database although it is available to assist agencies in the identification of cases where there have been serious reviews for future reference (at p 2).

2.51 The type of physical abuse which may result in the death of the child is exemplified in the Laming Report and in the various reports reproduced in *Out of Sight* at Appendix 1 (at pp 117–149). Previous editions of this work have examined the physical abuse leading to death in cases such as Maria Colwell, Jasmine Beckford, Tyra Henry, Heide Koseda and Kimberly Carlile, thus details given here will concentrate on later cases from 1995 onwards.

2.52 In 1995 at the age of just 17 weeks, Anthony Thomas died from unknown causes but was later found by a post-mortem examination to have seven fractures to his legs. The baby had been found dead in his pram by his father at their home in Berkshire. Although initially Anthony was thought to have died from Sudden Infant Death Syndrome (SIDS), after the leg fractures were detected, caused by a 'violent grip, twist and pull action' according to the pathologist, bruising to the head and evidence that he had also suffered lack of oxygen was found (*Daily Telegraph*, 18 August 1995 reproduced in *Out of Sight*, at p 138).

2.53   On 5 November 1996, the *Northern Echo* reported the circumstances leading to the death of Darren Leegleaves. Six-week-old Darren had been shaken and squeezed to death by his father aged 21, and had suffered a fractured skull, bleeding in the head and broken ribs. The father denied murder but admitted manslaughter stating that he had picked up the baby and pushed his feet to his shoulders. He had then repeatedly thrown him into his carry-cot. The mother also admitted cruelty because she did not seek help for the baby sooner as the ambulance was called the day after the attack (see *Out of Sight*, at p 141). *The Times* reported on 17 December 1997 the circumstances surrounding the death of Sarah Adams, who had died at the age of 18 months, with severe brain injuries. She had bruises and bites all over her body. Her mother Lavinia Adams, 32, who had learning difficulties, and her boyfriend, John Sherrington, 33, could not be charged with murder because the Crown Prosecutor was unable to say which of them was responsible for the fatal injuries. The couple, from Surrey, initially denied child cruelty but changed their pleas to guilty after a tape recording made by Sherrington was played to the court, which revealed that while he squeezed Sarah in a leg lock until she cried in severe distress and pain, her mother made little effort to intervene, and talked about her shopping list and the washing up. A neighbour, who was a nurse, saw Sarah and described her as 'like a rag doll' – limp and glassy-eyed and staring vacantly with purple bruises all over her face. The neighbour told the couple to take the child to the hospital immediately but they waited 24 hours and went on a shopping trip before calling an ambulance.

2.54   On 25 July 1998, the *Daily Mirror* reported that Jordan Sullivan, who had been born 6 weeks premature, had been battered to death by his mother's boyfriend, Dean John, when only 8 weeks old. His liver had been split in two and he had numerous broken ribs. John was convicted of murder at Cardiff Crown Court and sentenced to life imprisonment (see *Out of Sight*, at p 145).

2.55   The same paper on 16 January 1999 reported the death of Kate Carman who had died, aged 10 weeks, with 35 broken bones. Her skull had been fractured twice, almost all her ribs were broken, both arms and one leg had fractures and she had brain damage. She died as the result of a ruptured liver after being hit and her parents blamed each other for the death with Sarah Carman, the mother, receiving 4 years' imprisonment and her husband, Kevin, 3½ years (see *Out of Sight*, at p 146).

2.56   On 17 June 2000, the *Birmingham Post* reported the death of 8-week-old Bradley George, who had been murdered by his father, Christopher Rees, in October 1999. The paper reported that Rees had a history of violence towards Bradley's mother, Samantha George, during the course of their relationship such that even after their separation, Rees continually sought contact with her. On the night in question, Rees, in a drunken frenzy, broke down the front door of her home, broke into the bedroom, snatched Bradley off a 10-year-old girl who was also staying in the house, and proceeded to use his son as a club to batter Samantha. In addition to the heavy blows that Bradley sustained when he struck his mother, Rees also swung his son around causing his head to strike the bedroom walls before throwing him to the floor. Bradley died from multiple injuries, including fractures to his skull and lower legs. Christopher Rees was found guilty of murder and sentenced to life imprisonment (see *Out of Sight*, at p 147).

2.57 Whilst there are as yet no published figures from the DOH in respect of child deaths (see para **2.50**), statistics from the Home Office reveal that for the year 1998–1999 there were some 90 homicides of children under the age of 16. Forty-two of these homicides were against children under the age of one, 23 against children between the ages of one and 5 years and 25 against children aged between 5 and 16 years (see *Criminal Statistics England and Wales 1999* (HMSO, 2000)).

2.58 Serious assaults falling short of homicide are not broken down by reference to the age of the victim and thus there is no way of telling what the prevalence of such offences are as perpetrated against children. Such offences would include various offences under the Offences Against the Person Act 1861, such as s 18 (causing grievous bodily harm), s 20 (malicious wounding) and s 47 (assault occasioning actual bodily harm). (The details of these offences are dealt with in Chapter **9**.) The only offence which is characterised by reference to the fact that it is perpetrated against children generally is that to be found under s 1 of the CYPA 1933. This offence is classified in the statistics as 'cruelty to or neglect of children' and for the year 1999 the number of notifiable offences were 2,631. The statistics, however, do not break this down any further so there is no way of knowing which of the five constituent offences in s 1 of the CYPA 1933 were actually the subject of these notifiable offences.

2.59 A rather clearer picture, perhaps, of the prevalence of physical abuse emerges from the statistics compiled by the DOH in relation to registration of children on local Child Protection Registers. Annual returns are made by local authorities of the numbers on such registers and the child's name will be placed under one of the categories described in more detail above, thus for England and Wales under the categories of physical abuse, sexual abuse, emotional abuse and neglect. These statistics indicate that overall the number of children on the Registers has declined from 45,300 in 1991 to 26,800 for the year ending 31 March 2001 (*Children Act Report 2001* (DOH, 2002) at para 2.2) and the figures also reveal that the numbers of children being registered under the categories of physical and sexual abuse are decreasing, whilst those under emotional abuse and neglect are increasing both in actual numbers and as a proportion of all registrations. As a proportion of all registrations, physical abuse has dropped from around 40 per cent to 34 per

cent and numerically from 11,500 to 9,900 (*The Children Act Report 1995–1999*
(DOH, 2000) at fig 3.1. These figures were not further updated nor any
additional details given in the *Children Act Report 2001*). As has been noted
above in relation to the definition of physical abuse provided by the DOH
and also from the types of injuries suffered by those children who ultimately
died, physical abuse will cover a very wide range of actions including forcing
children's limbs back on themselves, punching, kicking, throwing the child
against a wall, burning the child with cigarettes, biting, shaking, beating a child
into unconsciousness and severe fracturing of all limbs of the body.

2.60   It would be impossible to set out a full list of the range of actions
which have been encompassed in the notion of physical abuse upon children
and society has moved horrifyingly further on from the notion of the 'battered
child syndrome' first introduced into the public consciousness by the work of
Kempe, Silverman, Steele, Drogemuller and Silver (1962), at pp 17–24).
Kempe himself was the first to acknowledge that he had not 'discovered' this
syndrome since it had first been described in 1868 by Ambroise Tardieu, a
professor of legal medicine in Paris. Relying on autopsy findings, Tardieu had
described 32 children battered or burned to death and in the same year, Athol
Johnson at the Hospital for Sick Children in London called attention to the
frequency of repeated fractures in children which he attributed at the time to
rickets. As Kempe pointed out, it was later realised that almost every case
Johnson described was, in fact, an abused child and official London records
reveal that of the 3,926 children under 5 years of age who died by accident or
violence in 1870, 202 deaths were attributed to manslaughter; 95 to neglect; 18
to exposure to cold – all effectively due, comments Kempe, to child abuse
(see Kempe and Kempe (1978)).

2.61   It was not until 1946, Kempe explained, that John Caffey reported his
original observations regarding the unexplained association of subdural
haematoma and abnormal x-ray changes in long bones. Soon thereafter,
Caffey and Silverman clearly defined their traumatic nature (seeCaffey and
Silverman (1953)) and in 1955 Woolley and Evans published a paper entitled
'Significance of Skeletal Lesions in Infants resembling those of Traumatic
Origin' (see Woolley and Evans (1955), at pp 158 and 539). In 1961 Henry
Kempe arranged for an inter-disciplinary presentation at the Annual Meeting
of the American Academic of Paediatrics on the subject of the battered child
syndrome and their resulting comprehensive description of the syndrome was
published in the *Journal of the American Medical Association* (as detailed in
para **2.61**). Their presentation dealt with paediatric, psychiatric, radiological
and legal concepts, as well as providing the earliest incidence figures on child
abuse for the United States. Since 1962, literally thousands of articles,
hundreds of books, academic and practitioner journals and research studies
have added very considerably to the understanding of the whole subject of

child abuse and neglect and particularly of the manifestations of physical abuse.

2.62 It should be noted that the DOH definition of physical abuse includes the word 'hitting' and this inevitably raises the issue of the link between physical punishment and physical abuse of children. This relationship has for some time been regarded as problematic, although research has suggested that physical abuse is more likely to occur in families with a culture of violence, including regular use of physical punishment (see Cleaver, Wattam and Cawson (1998) and for much greater detail on this, see Lyon (2000)).

2.63 In the Bridge Inquiry Report into the death of Sukina, one of the major issues of concern was the types of punishment inflicted on the child by her father. On one occasion the child had been unwell at nursery school but when a teacher suggested she should go home Sukina had stated that she did not want to because 'my daddy will beat up on me'. Various other punishments inflicted injuries upon Sukina, which caused professionals concern, but the father was always able to explain away the marks. Social workers had queried the hitting of Sukina on the hands with a ruler repeatedly but had seen these measures as a harsh but not excessive form of physical punishment. The events culminated on 6 December 1988 when Sukina's father murdered his daughter in quite horrific circumstances. The incident began with the father asking Sukina and her sister to spell their names which they would not or could not do. When the request was repeated, both girls still did not respond and the father hit Sukina on the hand with a ruler repeatedly asking her to spell her name. Sukina still did not do so, but the younger sister then spelled out her name. Sukina continued to refuse and the attack by the father then escalated. Sukina was beaten first with a ruler then with a short length of rigid plastic tubing and finally with a length of kettle flex which had the kettle attachment on one end but not the three-pin plug. At least 50 blows were inflicted upon Sukina interspersed with repeated demands that she spelled her name. Sukina, at one stage, when she was too weak to stand, tried to crawl out of the room to the stairs asking her father to stop hitting her. Sukina's mother tried to intervene but was herself assaulted causing injuries to her face which required a hospital examination. The attack on Sukina, however, continued until she was barely conscious, at which point she was taken, by her parents, to the bathroom and placed in a bath of warm water in an attempt to revive her. At one point whilst lying in the bath, Sukina tried to lift herself from the lying position but was unable to do so. As she slipped into unconsciousness, Sukina told her father she was sorry. Although an ambulance was called, Sukina was already dead on arrival at the hospital. Sukina's father was convicted of murder and received a mandatory life sentence and a 6-month concurrent sentence for assaulting his wife (see *Sukina: An Evaluation Report of the Circumstances Leading to her Death* (The Bridge Child Care Consultancy Service, 1991)).

2.64 Whilst no one would suggest that every physical punishment of a child descends into this sort of physical abuse and ultimately death, many commentators are extremely concerned at the message which the legitimation of corporal punishment by their parents gives out not only to children but also to parents. As was pointed out earlier, the denial of equal protection of children under the law in respect of the various offences of assault is an affront to their status as people. Children, by virtue of their very vulnerability, should have at least equal rights to those of adults and not lesser rights. The defence of reasonable chastisement which is available to parents charged with any form of physical assault on their child is an affront to the child's human dignity and a very poor reflection of the type of society in which we live.

2.65 As a result of the European Court's decision in *A v UK* [2000] 1 FLR 266, the government in the UK was forced into announcing a review of the defence of reasonable chastisement. The jurisdictions within the UK have held their own separate consultation processes or, as in the case of Northern Ireland, are about to embark on a consultation process. In England, the government's consultation paper *Protecting Children – Supporting Parents* (DOH, 2000) assumed that parents would not agree to the removal of the defence of reasonable chastisement and thus sought views as to how the defence of reasonable chastisement could be clarified so that parents would appreciate what was and what was not 'reasonable punishment'. The questions posed by the DOH in England appeared almost surreal when one realised that this was the department concerned with the health and protection of children which was asking the general population whether there should be additional guidelines describing those circumstances of a case which might be relevant when determining whether punishment was reasonable or not. The circumstances which had been determined by the European Court to be relevant in determining whether treatment constituted inhuman and degrading treatment included: the nature and context of the treatment; its duration; its physical and mental effects; and, in some instances, the sex, age and state of health of the victim. The Court of Appeal (Criminal Division) by May 2001 could not wait any longer for the government to come to some sort of conclusion about the definition of 'reasonable chastisement' and thus in the case of *R v H* [2001] 2 FLR 431 required that judges hearing assault cases against parents should direct the jury as to what might be considered reasonable punishment in the light of the basic requirements set down by the European Court (see para **2.18** for a more detailed discussion of this issue and the case-law.)

2.66 The government in England went on to ask the public whether there were any forms of physical punishment which could never be capable of being defended as 'reasonable', specifically asking whether physical punishment which causes or is likely to cause injury to the head including injuries to the brain, eyes and ears should never be defended as reasonable. In addition, they asked the public whether physical punishment using implements should also be outlawed. Both these questions add to the utterly surreal feelings which one has in aligning these notions with the idea of protecting children. The government's own survey, the results of which were published in *Protecting Children – Supporting Parents*, had revealed that the vast majority of people who had been consulted had indicated that punishment which left a red mark or bruising was unreasonable (96 per cent and over 99 per cent respectively), parents should not be allowed to use implements like canes, sticks, belts or slippers on children aged over 7 (89 per cent), on children aged under 7 but over 5 (93 per cent) and on children aged under 2 (97 per cent). Overwhelmingly the vast majority of respondents to the government's own survey felt that only punishment which leaves no mark at all on the child could be deemed to be 'reasonable' (see *Protecting Children – Supporting Parents* (DOH, 2000), at pp 20–22).

2.67 Consultation on the English proposals closed on 21 April 2000, and the results of that consultation were finally published on the DOH website (www.doh.gov.uk) on 19 November 2001. The government received over 830 responses to the Consultation in England, of which nearly a third represented the views of professional organisations, statutory bodies or groups, whilst the largest number of responses, over 500, came from individuals of whom approximately one-third made explicit the fact that religious convictions had strongly influenced their views. Apparently the Consultation document:

> 'evoked strong reactions and, whilst some welcomed the decision not to ban physical punishment of children, there was little overall support for the alternative proposals made. For some these went too far, for others they fell well short of what is needed to protect children. Opinions were generally polarised between those who supported physical punishment of children and those who wanted it banned completely' (para 13).

Professional and voluntary bodies which work with children, health, education and social services groups were strongly and virtually unanimously of the view that physical punishment of children should be banned and there should be no defence of reasonable chastisement (para 14), whilst the public reaction was mixed with the majority of the individual responses received supporting physical punishment and the retention to varying degrees of the defence of reasonable chastisement. According to the report, a particular feature of the individual responses was the number strongly influenced by religious convictions that led those respondents to believe it was their duty as loving and responsible parents physically to punish their children in particular circumstances. At the end of the report the government indicated that as a result of the Consultation exercise it felt there was little support from the public for legislative reform of the right to physically punish children (para 76) and that its approach is to avoid heavy-handed intrusion into family life and instead that it should put in place policies which are supportive of families, offer encouragement and make help available to parents (para 71). The report also stated (at paras 73–75) that the guidance issued by the Court of Appeal in *R v H* [2001] 2 FLR 431 (see para **2.18**) was sufficient to provide the protection guaranteed by Article 3 of the ECHR and that the ruling given there on the directions to be given to juries in future cases effected a 'wholly appropriate incremental development of the common law defence of reasonable chastisement' (para 75). The fact that the government preferred to follow the views of a vociferous, very religious but incredibly small section of the public over the considered, well-researched views of 350 of the very groups and organisations charged with the tasks of child protection is intensely worrying. The denial of children's rights to their bodily integrity represented by the retention of the defence of 'reasonable chastisement' is one which should be abhorrent to all those with concerns about child protection. For any who believe that a government, which has signed up to the principles of the UNCRC (see Chapter **1**), must abide by those principles, the publication of documents such as *Protecting Children – Supporting Parents* and the *Report on the Responses to the Consultation on Physical Punishment of Children* must seem both shocking and a denial of those basic human rights. (For a further much more detailed discussion on this see Lyon (2000).)

2.68 As the NSPCC report *Child Maltreatment in the United Kingdom – A Study of the Prevalence of Child Abuse and Neglect* (2000) notes:

> 'whilst previous research suggests that physical abuse is more likely to occur in families where there is regular use of physical punishment and there is a clear statistical relationship between the greater use of physical punishment to respondents in social classes D and E, and a similar greater frequency of physical abuse, other relationships were not so clear cut. In particular, the data appeared to reveal a divide between the families where children were hit with implements or often hit to a level which caused lasting pain, bruising or other injury and those where occasional slaps occurred which rarely or never had lasting effects. There was no substantial bridging group in which smacking was regular but not severe which the NSPCC report would have expected to find if escalation were a common phenomenon' (at p 97).

2.69 The NSPCC report notes that in general it seems that parents either hit children rarely and lightly or they did it to cause serious hurt. They quote from the Newson and Newson survey in 1970 (Newson and Newson (1970)) who had concluded that 'we would tentatively suggest that those mothers who smack most frequently are also likely to smack hardest' (p 448) and the NSPCC report comments that this seems as true today as it was 30 years ago. The report goes on to indicate that qualitative studies which describe the process of escalation into more frequent or more serious smacking may, however, provide an explanation. Newson and Newson (1970) and Leach (1999)) describe the way in which parents became aware that they were coming to use more and more physical punishment which was damaging their relationship with their child, and ineffective in improving the child's behaviour. The report comments that this may be the point at which parents having fundamentally close relationships with their child call a halt to their own use of physical punishment and may represent a qualitative difference between parents able to enter into their child's feelings or distress and those who cannot do so, or whose own anger takes precedence over the child's needs.

2.70 The NSPCC also reported that stereotypes of physical punishment and physical abuse were also challenged by their survey (see *Child Maltreatment in the United Kingdom*, at p 97). Thus they found that the stereotype of more physical abuse being carried out by men, especially fathers or step-fathers, was on their survey untrue. Their respondents had indicated that violent treatment was more likely to be meted out by mothers (49 per cent) although fathers were responsible for 40 per cent. Step-parents were rarely mentioned. In relation to the stereotype that physical punishment was likely to escalate into abuse, the study found that this was questionable with, as indicated above, a qualitative difference between the use of occasional slaps and smacks with an open hand (which was experienced by over 70 per cent of the sample), and violent treatment by parents rated seriously abusive because it caused injury or regularly had lasting physical effects (experienced by 7 per cent). Very few respondents (3 per cent) experienced regular smacking without bruising or other lasting effects, suggesting an abrupt change between the two modes of treatment rather than a 'slide'. With regards to the stereotype that physical abuse is more common in manual workers' families, the survey revealed that this was probably true. Although the socio-economic data available had limitations, there was a markedly greater use of violence towards respondents in social grades D and E and they were more likely to be rated by researchers and to rate themselves as having been abused. Finally, as to the stereotype that boys were more often victims of physical abuse than girls were, this again was found to be untrue. More female respondents (8 per cent) were rated as seriously abused by parents than were males (6 per cent) although males were more likely to be rated as experiencing intermediate or intermittent abuse (15 per cent) than females were (12 per cent).

2.71 Despite the qualitative differences pointed up by the survey of the literature and by the analysis of the responses, the NSPCC report emphasises that noting these qualitative differences does not undermine the earlier point that there is a continuum along which acceptable and unacceptable treatment of children moves into abuse, and the earlier material on physical punishment and violent treatment shows gradation in seriousness at both ends of the continuum. The report goes on to state that, 'nor does it mean that parents using violence do not love their children, are unable to change or could not use help in modifying their behaviour or developing greater understanding of their children', but the report also states that it does have implications for the form of help needed to safeguard children in these circumstances. It is submitted here that the best form of help which could be given would be to provide children with equal protection and rights to bodily integrity under the law so that there can be no question of professionals having to give guidance on what may or may not be deemed to be 'reasonable chastisement'.

Children in whom illness is fabricated or induced or Munchausen Syndrome by Proxy and its incidence

2.72   This is being considered at this point because under the DOH definition provided in *Working Together to Safeguard Children,* this was included in the category of physical abuse (at para 2.4 and see above). Apart from the brief description given in *Working Together to Safeguard Children* there is no further expansion upon this elsewhere in that document because it was always the intention to consult widely on the production of a separate volume of guidance and this process has now been completed. The new guidance, issued on 30 August 2002, adopts different terminology to that used in *Working Together to Safeguard Children*. where the description appeared under the heading Munchausen Syndrome by Proxy (MSBP), whereas the new guidance is entitled *Safeguarding Children in Whom Illness is Fabricated or Induced* (DOH, Home Office, DfES, Welsh Assembly, 2002) also available on the department's website at www.doh.gov.uk/qualityprotects). The purpose of the new guidance is to provide a national framework within which agencies and professionals at local level draw up and agree upon their own more detailed ways of working together where illness may be being fabricated or induced in a child by a carer who has parenting responsibilities for him. It is addressed to those who work in health, education, the police, social services, probation and others whose work brings them into contact with children and families and thus is relevant to those who work in the statutory, voluntary and independent sectors. The guidance emphasises that it is intended that ACPCs and local child protection procedures should incorporate this guidance and its references to covert video surveillance rather than having separate guidance on fabricated or induced illness in children (para 1.2). In the legal framework part of the guidance it is noted that the Regulation of Investigatory Powers Act 2000 is of particular significance. The main purpose of that Act is to ensure that investigatory powers are used in accordance with human rights. These powers include the use of covert video surveillance in the course of specific operation and Part II and Sch 1 set down a system of authorisations for the use of surveillance. The guidance then suggests that where there is any potential for the use of covert video surveillance the police should be informed and, within the multi-agency team, take the lead on co-ordinating such action, which should be in accordance with local ACPC procedures. It emphasises (para 1.22) that where there is any doubt about the use of covert video surveillance legal advice should be taken.

2.73 The guidance itself notes at para 1.3 that the fabrication of illness in children by a carer is referred to by a number of different terms, the most commonly used being MSBP (Meadow, 1977), Factitious Illness by Proxy (Bools, 1996; Jones and Bools (1999)) or Illness Induction Syndrome (Gray et al, 1995). In the USA, the term Paediatric Condition Falsification has been adopted by the American Professional Society on the Abuse of Children (APSAC). This terminolgy is also used by some as if it were a psychiatric diagnosis. The American Psychiatric Association's Diagnostic and Statistical Manual (DSM-IV) has proposed using the term Factitious Disorder by Proxy for a psychiatric diagnosis applicable to the fabricator (para 1.3). The guidance is anxious to emphasise that differences of opinion over terminology may result in a loss of focus on the child and that the department's reason for adopting the description of the 'fabrication or induction of illness in a child' rather than using a particular term is intended to keep the primary focus of all professional activity on the child's safety and welfare. It goes on to state that 'if as a result of a carer's behaviour there is concern that the child is or is likely to suffer significant harm then this guidance should be followed' and warns that the key issue is not what term to use to describe this type of abuse, but the impact of fabricated or induced illness on the child's health and development, and consideration of how best to safeguard the child's welfare (para 1.4). This guidance suggests that there are three main ways of the carer fabricating or inducing illness in a child, which are not mutually exclusive:

— fabrication of signs and symptoms, which may include fabrication of past medical history;
— fabrication of signs and symptoms and falsification of hospital charts and records, and specimens of bodily fluids. This may also include falsification of letters and documents;
— induction of illness by a variety of means (para 1.5).

2.74 The guidance emphasises that carers exhibit a range of behaviours when they believe that their child is ill and thus a key professional task is to distinguish between the over-anxious carer who may be responding in a reasonable way to a very sick child and those who exhibit abnormal behaviour (see paras 3.1–3.3). Such abnormal behaviour in a carer can be present in one or both carers and often involves passive compliance of the child (see para 2.20). Such carer behaviour may of course constitute ill-treatment under s 31(9) of the CA 1989. The guidance then sets out a list of behaviours which can be associated with fabricating or inducing illness in a child but stresses that it is not an exhaustive list and should be interpreted with an awareness of cultural behaviours and practices which can be mistakenly construed as abnormal behaviours:

— deliberately inducing symptoms in children by administering medication or other substances, or by means of intentional suffocation;

- interfering with treatments by overdosing, not administering them, or interfering with medical equipment such as infusion lines;
- claiming the child has symptoms which are unverifiable unless observed directly such as pain, frequency of passing urine, vomiting or fits. These claims result in unnecessary investigations and treatments which may cause secondary physical problems;
- exaggerating symptoms, causing professionals to undertake investigations and treatments which may be invasive, are unnecessary and are therefore harmful and possibly dangerous;
- obtaining specialist treatments or equipment for children who do not require them;
- alleging psychological illness in a child.

The guidance also emphasises that the majority of cases of fabricated or induced illness are confirmed in a hospital setting because either medical findings or their absence provide evidence of this type of abuse. In drawing out lessons from research and experience, the guidance advises that following identification of fabricated or induced illness in a child by a carer, the way in which the case is managed will have a major impact on the developmental outcomes for the child, as will the extent to which the parents have acknowleged some responsibility for fabricating or inducing illness in their child (para 2.39).

2.75 Guidance given to healthcare professionals in Scotland, however (see *Protecting Children: A Shared Responsibility*), gives somewhat different guidance on the syndrome. The Scottish Office guidance defines MSBP, or induced illness syndrome, as significant harm which is caused to a child by the actions of a parent or other carer who deliberately fabricates symptoms and/or signs of illness or induces actual illness in a child, which would not otherwise be present. It goes on to state that the actions may be as a result of omission or commission and includes such behaviour as:

- deliberate poisoning;
- deliberate burning or other damage to the skin to induce symptoms;
- deliberate suffocation to induce symptoms;
- removal of/or tampering with necessary equipment;
- introducing foreign material to tests or other behaviour which causes damaging and unnecessary tests to be performed on the child;
- deliberate inducing of fits in the child;
- active withholding of food and/or fluids.

2.76 The Scottish Office guidance further states that on the extremely rare occasions when MSBP is strongly suspected, it may be considered necessary and justified for the future health and safety of the child to consider the use of covert video surveillance. The document stresses, however, that the use of covert video surveillance is contentious, and that an inter-agency protocol must be in place, agreed by the local Child Protection Committee and the Trust Ethical Committee, before such use is contemplated. Similar advice on the use of such surveillance has been issued by the DOH for England and Wales (see *Safeguarding Children in Whom Illness is Fabricated or Induced* (DOH, 2002), at paras 1.21 and 1.22).

2.77 There are no separate figures on the potential abuse of children in whom illness is fabricated or induced in the information provided by the DOH in the *Children Act Report 2001* (DOH, 2002), the *Children Act Report 1995–1999* (DOH, 2000) or in *Children and Young People on Child Protection Registers Year Ending 31 March 1999, England* (DOH, 1999). In Maclure's 2-year study to determine the epidemiology of fabricated or induced illness, data from 128 confirmed cases notified to the British Paediatric Association Surveillance Unit between September 1992 and August 1994 was analysed (Maclure, Davis, Meadow and Sibert (1996)). Based on this data, the researchers estimated the combined annual incidence of these forms of abuse in children in the UK to be at least 0.5 per 100,000 and for children under one year at least 2.8 per 100,000. The authors calculated that 'in a hypothetical district of one million inhabitants therefore the expected incidence would be approximately one child per year' (at p 58). This study showed that reported rates of fabricated or induced illness varied greatly between different health service regions and the researchers suggested it was under-reported nationally. Their findings also suggested that paediatricians considered that at the time of their study the identification had to be virtually certain before a child protection conference was convened and thus a number of cases might be unrecorded because of the absence of irrefutable evidence in situations where the level of concern about harm to the child is extremely high. It was also suggested that the cases may present in ways which result in unnecessary medical interventions, for example where symptoms are verbally reported to surgeons who then carry out operations without questioning the basis of the information. Consequently, the guidance advises that the estimate of one child per million head of population is likely to be an under-estimate (at para 2.4). International research findings suggest that up to 10 per cent of these children die and about 50 per cent experience long-term morbidity. In the Maclure study it was found that 8 out of 128 (6 per cent) of children died as a direct result of this type of abuse. A further 15 (12 per cent) required intensive care and an additional 45 (35 per cent) suffered major physical illness, again as as result of this type of abuse. The way in which a child's circumstances are managed will impact on their outcomes, but the lives of some who present at hospital in a life-threatening situation, for example having been poisoned, might not be capable of being saved.

2.78 Professor David, in an extremely informative and comrehensible article which makes an excellent introduction to the subject for those who might not be familiar with the various forms of the condition as described in the new Departmental guidance (*Safeguarding Children in Whom Illness is Fabricated or Induced*), has recently pointed out, in common with the Departmental guidance (see David (2001)) that few diagnostic labels have caused as much confusion as MSBP. As he explains, the term MSBP is used to describe two related types of child abuse. In one variety a parent, most commonly the mother, fabricates an account of illness in a child, for example reporting that the child is having fits or passing blood in the urine. The child is taken to doctors, and if the story is sufficiently convincing for the doctors to be duped, then the child may be exposed to a multitude of tests, treatment and even surgery, all of which are entirely needless. The abuse is in fact inflicted upon the child by the doctors who in turn have been deceived by the parent. In the other variety, the parent, most often the mother, directly procures illness in the child, for example by covertly poisoning the child with drugs, or by suffocating the child so as to produce mysterious attacks of unconsciousness. The end result is the same, namely deception of doctors leading to tests and treatment, all of which would, of course, have been entirely unnecessary had the parent not interfered with the child. David points out that, in a partially successful attempt to avoid the confusing and emotive term of MSBP, some have preferred the diagnostic label of 'fictitious illness abuse' and whereas both terms are used in the guidance set out in *Working Together to Safeguard Children* (see para **2.41**), the guidance in *Safeguarding Children in Whom Illness is Fabricated or Induced* is much more circumspect in relation to terminology (see paras 1.3 and 1.4). David emphasises that perhaps the most important concept is that the diagnostic label applies to the child and not to the perpetrator.

2.79 Munchausen Syndrome was first described in adult medical literature by R Asher, a general physician, in 1951 (see Asher (1951)). In 1977, Dr R Meadow reported the facts of two cases in which children had been subjected to innumerable hospitalisations and medical tests because their mother had either falsified the history of the illness or induced illness in the child (see Meadow (1997)). Meadow adopted the term MSBP to describe this form of non-accidental injury because of its reminiscence to the adult Munchausen Syndrome. David points out that although presentations of MSBP are numerous, there are common features that include the following.

– The child's illness is either falsified or procured by a parent or carer of the child.
– The child's persistent presentation for medical assessment and care usually results in multiple medical procedures.
– The perpetrator denies any knowledge of the cause of the child's illness.
– Acute signs and symptoms of the illness abate when the child is separated from the perpetrator (p 445).

2.80 David acknowledges that although the prevalence of the disorder in all its forms is unknown, and it is an unusual manifestation of child abuse, nevertheless it is thought to be much more common than is reported in the medical literature. He further points out that infants and young children are the most common victims of MSBP but school age children and even adolescents are at risk. He also indicates that in cases involving older children and adolescents, the child often gets drawn into the illness-fabricating behaviour, either by validating the mother's claims or by colluding with the mother to produce illness. In addition, older children may independently display behaviour more typical of the adult Munchausen patient (at p 446).

2.81 David continues, in this extremely informative article, to set out the various medical problems which will be presented but emphasises that the creativity of MSBP parents in their attempts to deceive physicians can be remarkable, and new variations continue to be described (at p 446). He goes on to describe the various types of problems in some detail and these include the following. Haematuria, which is the presence of blood in the urine indicating a possibility of serious underlying kidney disorder, always warrants medical investigation but in MSBP it is fabricated by adding blood to the urine thus involving the serious consequences of major invasive tests inflicted on the child (at p 446 and see also Meadow (1992)). Reports of vomiting may be fabricated, or alternatively the parent may induce genuine vomiting; reports of diarrhoea may also be fabricated by directly adding water to stool samples or induced by the mother administering laxative drugs to the child. Epileptic convulsions may be invented by a parent, or might include fits caused by partial suffocation with a pillow (at p 446 and see also R Meadow, 'Factitious Epilepsy' (1984) 2 *Lancet* 25–28). Suffocation may induce recurrent attacks of apnoea (the stopping of breathing) in infants, and David states that Sudden Infant Death Syndrome (SIDS) may be caused by deliberate suffocation by a parent. Studies both in the UK and the USA using covert video surveillance have demonstrated that there are a group of infants whose repeated attacks of apnoea are the result of deliberate suffocation, which can be done with a hand over the mouth and nose, or by covering the mouth and nose with a pillow or with cling film, but David points out that a classic pattern of events is for a child to suffer from multiple attacks before succumbing to a final fatal episode. There may be drowsiness and attacks of coma, which may be due to a parent giving a child sedative drugs which David states can be correctly diagnosed by testing the urine or blood to reveal the presence of sedative drugs which have not been prescribed for the child.

2.82 Poisoning, where children present with over ventilation due to salicylate poisoning, and poisoning of children with salt, which is an exceptionally dangerous type of poisoning since, as David indicates, most people are unaware that only very small quantities of salt (eg a teaspoon) can be sufficient to cause a child's death. Other poisons used against children include ipecac, rat poison, alcohol, glutethimide, propoxyphene hydrochloride, insulin, diazepam, caustic soda, pepper and barbiturates (at p 447 and see also Rogers et al (1976)). An unexplained fever in a child having an intravenous infusion may be traced to parents introducing infected substances into treatment equipment (at p 448). Intolerance to food and food additives is, as David points out, in practical terms undoubtedly the most difficult category to deal with. This is partly because of the large number of unorthodox private allergy specialists, who David states will readily diagnose non-existent entities such as allergy to North Sea gas or diesel fumes, the end result being a child who does not leave the home because of the risk from diesel fumes and does not attend school because of the risk of gas central heating. The parent in such a case is supported by an array of medical practitioners willing to attest that the child is allergic to everything under the sun, and David comments that some of the most gross forms of abuse fall into this category. There may be deliberate fabrication of skin disease; David describing in one case how a mother created skin lesions which required multiple surgical excisions, and the child missed school for 16 months and required four skin grafts. Finally, the most recently described variety of MSBP is false allegations of child abuse in which the parent, almost always the mother, not only invents the story but may also go as far as to teach the child to substantiate allegations of abuse (see p 448 and see Meadow (1993)).

2.83 David goes on to describe the perpetrators of MSBP, who are most often mothers, and says that what all perpetrators share since they can be of either sex, married or single, intelligent or unintelligent, friendly or abrasive, rich or poor, is a lack of empathy for the child. Schreier and Libow postulate that the child means less to the parent as a person than as an object to be manipulated. David notes that although a number of psychiatric disorders have been described in MSBP mothers, perpetrators of MSBP are generally not psychotic and he notes that many perpetrators have normal findings on psychological tests and that some mothers are potentially treatable, an aspect of the condition reviewed by K Bluglass (see Bluglass (1997) also cited in the DOH guidance). As David further notes, in trying to understand MSBP, it is helpful to see the condition as part of a spectrum of parental behaviour, from the one extreme of complete neglect to the other extreme of procuring symptoms (at p 449).

2.84 David highlights the very difficult problems associated with the diagnosis of MSBP but even when suggesting that nine different features should be considered when attempting to diagnose the condition, he still urges very great caution, since as he says 'there are few families in which one or more of the conditions do not apply'. In addition to the nine features which he identifies, he further states that other features have been described as being suggestive of MSBP including 'parents who are unusually calm for the severity of the illness', 'parents who are unusually knowledgeable about illness and its repercussions' and 'parents who fit in contentedly with ward life and attention from staff'. As David states, there is no objective or controlled data to support these assertions, and it must be appreciated that many normal, caring parents fit into these categories. If calmness by parents, he states, is to be regarded as sinister and suspicious, then many parents must be regarded with suspicion. In concluding his very informative and helpful review of MSBP, David emphasises that it is important 'to remember that it takes two people to have a case of MSBP – a parent who invents or procures symptoms and a doctor who is fooled' (at p 451). David points out that hitherto most interest has been focused on the parent perpetrator, but there needs to be some interest in the behaviour of doctors. He emphasises that 'the keys to the early detection of factitious illness are attention to detail during history taking, a questioning approach and corroboration of the history. Precision', he stresses 'is essential in the history taking – exactly who saw what, when and where? It is vital', he says, 'to remember that just because an illness is unexplained does not mean that it must have a sinister cause' (at p 451).

2.85 As an introduction to the subject and indeed to the guidance issued by the DOH, David's article is, as has been pointed out above, extremely useful and informative and for those who seek more information on the subject apart from the various articles referred to above, there is now available an extremely useful work by Mary Eminson, Consultant Child and Adolescent Psychiatrist with the Royal Bolton Hospitals NHS Trust and RJ Postlethwaite, Consultant Paediatric Nephrologist at the Manchester Children's Hospital NHS Trust (Eminson and Postlewaite, 2000), which is quoted from extensively in the new government guidance, *Safeguarding Children in Whom Illness is Fabricated or Induced* (DOH, 2002) particularly in Chapter 3).

2.86 Whilst there are no separate recorded figures for MSBP in relation to the Civil Child Protection Register Statistics, it must be pointed out that there are also no detailed figures in the criminal statistics, although the behaviour characterised by parents or other carers who subject children to MSBP will be included in the notifiable offences of cruelty to children and in more serious cases of homicide. Examples are the case of the nurse Beverley Allitt at Grantham and Kesteven General Hospital in 1991 and the case of the death of Christopher Lloyd on 1 March 1997 after being poisoned with salt by his mother. Over the course of the previous 10 days, while her husband had been at work, Caroline Lloyd gave her son fizzy drinks containing salt up to six times a day which made him suffer fits of vomiting, diarrhoea and stomach cramps. The mother said at her trial that she never wanted the child to die but the salt tired him and made him sleep, enabling her to get some rest. The mother was diagnosed as suffering from MSBP and jailed for life after admitting cruelty to a child and manslaughter on the grounds of diminished responsibility (the *Guardian*, 18 June 1997).

Emotional abuse and its incidence

2.87   The definition of emotional abuse, as defined by the DOH in *Working Together to Safeguard Children*, features examples of the way in which persistent emotional ill-treatment of a child may have severe and persistent adverse effects on the child's emotional development and the form the abuse may take (see *Working Together to Safeguard Children*, at para 2.5). *Working Together to Safeguard Children* goes on at para 2.12 to state that there is increasing evidence of the adverse long-term consequences for children's development where they have been subjected to sustained emotional abuse. Emotional abuse has an important impact on a developing child's mental health, behaviour and self-esteem. It can be especially damaging in infancy. Underlying emotional abuse may be as important, if not more so, than other more visible forms of abuse in terms of its impact on the child. *Working Together to Safeguard Children* further notes that domestic violence, adult mental health problems and parental substance abuse may be features in families where children are exposed to such abuse.

2.88   Emotional abuse was first introduced as a criterion for inclusion on child abuse registers in 1980 (*Child Abuse: Central Register Systems*, LASSL (80)4, HN 80(20) (DOH, 1980)). Since then, guidance on the assessment and protection of children has stressed the child's emotional and development needs as much as physical needs and, as *Working Together to Safeguard Children* points out, some level of emotional abuse is involved in all types of ill-treatment of a child although it may occur alone. As far as the incidence of emotional abuse is concerned, whilst it comes within the categories of offences which may be charged under the Offences Against the Person Act 1861 (OAPA 1861) and also within the notifiable offence of cruelty to children, there are no separate criminal statistics indicating prosecution of parents or other carers for emotional abuse. The principal source of statistical information, therefore, is that issued by the DOH in relation to children who are placed on Child Protection Registers. As the *Children Act Report 1995–1999* notes, the figures reveal that emotional abuse is increasing both in terms of actual numbers and as a proportion of all registrations. Thus the figures reveal that registrations for emotional abuse have gone up from just over 4,000 in 1994 to 5,200 in 1998 (see *Children Act Report 1995–1999*, at fig 3.1). The DOH further notes that the increasing number of registrations under the category of emotional abuse may be related to local authorities being clearer in their understanding of the impact of emotional abuse on children's health and development, and that they may be using both this category and the category of neglect, instead of the 'grave concern' category, the use of which was no longer recommended in 1991; however, the DOH admits the picture is clearly complex.

2.89   Of considerable concern is that the DOH comments that a recent inspection found continuing staff uncertainties in the assessment and identification of emotional abuse which, the DOH comments, suggests that emotional abuse is under-identified and therefore would be under-represented on Child Protection Registers. Recent reports have emphasised the fact that emotional abuse is the least studied of all forms of child maltreatment, and the area in which reliable prevalent data is almost non-existent (see *Child Maltreatment in the United Kingdom: A Study of the Prevalence of Child Abuse and Neglect* (NSPCC, 2000), at p 54). The report emphasises that the state of knowledge in relation to emotional abuse is considerably less advanced than for physical or sexual abuse and that there is a lack of a consensual paradigm within which it has been studied. This is said to be partly to do with the innate difficulties of definition, measurement and proof, which affect both research and practice. The report points out that social workers and other professionals feel less confident that they can reach a conclusion and prove a case for abuse when the suffering is emotional than when it is physical or sexual (at p 54). Although the figures for registration of children suffering from emotional abuse have increased, this is still the smallest category officially recorded in child protection statistics throughout the UK, and this has also been found to be the case in the USA and in Australia (see Tomison and Tucci (1997)).

2.90 The NSPCC reports that studies which have attempted to assess and categorise emotional abuse use various different terms: emotional abuse, emotional maltreatment, psychological abuse or maltreatment, psychological attack, emotional or psychological neglect. There is further confusion, it reports, over the boundaries between emotional abuse and neglect, with behaviour such as rejection and responsiveness and violence between parents sometimes being classified as one and sometimes the other (*Child Maltreatment in the United Kingdom*, at p 54). Doyle (1997), at p 334 notes that 'unlike physical and sexual abuse, where omissions are paramount, and physical neglect where omissions are pre-eminent, in emotional abuse, omission and commission are inextricably fused'.

2.91 The problems in providing a definitive classification of emotional abuse stem from the very wide range of potential behaviour which may be classified as abusive, together with the possibility of considering omissions as well as commissions, but it is also critical to appreciate that because emotional abuse targets the child's individual vulnerability, this will change with the child's development and the changing external world experienced by the child. Thus, what will isolate, frighten or humiliate a 4-year-old and a 14-year-old are likely to be very different, while increasing links with the world outside the family both create new vulnerabilities and offer escape from a punitive or uncaring atmosphere at home (see Iwaniec (1997), at p 371). The NSPCC report (at appendix 2) demonstrates a huge range of behaviour which can be described as emotional abuse and furthermore encompass the additional issues to which the DOH guidance now makes reference (see *Working Together to Safeguard*

Children at para 2.12). In addition, the DOH guidance further identifies the potential issues of child abuse involving emotional abuse in chapter 6 where it identifies bullying by other children, abuse of disabled children and again makes reference to domestic violence in considering potential examples of emotional abuse.

2.92 As the NSPCC report revealed, there have literally been dozens of studies concentrating on different types of behaviour which can be included within the notion of emotional abuse (see *Child Maltreatment in the United Kingdom*, appendix 1, pp 122–127). Thus the types of behaviour engaged in included: refusal/failure to show affection; abandonment/leaving home; excluding the child from family activities/treats; refusing approaches or affection from a child; belittling the child's achievements; insulting the child, for example calling the child demeaning names such as 'dummy', 'stupid', 'monster', 'evil'; scapegoating or favouring siblings; humiliating; subjecting to excessive criticism; infantilising (treating as younger than the child's actual age); expelling from the family; threatening with extreme punishments; creating a climate of unpredictable threats; creating unmeetable expectations/punishing when not met; teasing and making frightening threats of monsters and bogies; inconsistent demands; frequent raging at the child, threats of public humiliation and ridicule; threats of loss of love; being psychologically unavailable to the child; not responding to the child; exhibiting coolness and lack of affection; not speaking to the child; not protecting the child from siblings or from bullying by other children; no interest in the child's school or adolescent progress; preventing the child's social relations; leaving the child unattended for several hours; denying others access to the child; punishing the child's approaches to others; withdrawing the child from school or other activities; encouraging anti-social and deviant behaviour; encouraging aggression; encouraging sexual precocity/exposing to pornography; inducing into prostitution; encouraging drug and alcohol abuse; refusal to allow treatment for emotional/behavioural problems; role reversal where the child takes over the parent's responsibilities and supports the parent; domination of the child; constantly changing carers and leaving the child mostly in the care of older children.

2.93 This is but some of the emotionally abusive conduct which may be engaged in and which has been subject to studies across Denmark, the USA and the UK. The studies used were those of Christensen in Denmark in 1983, Garbarino, Guttman and Seeley in the USA in 1986, Burnett in the USA in 1993, Sedlak and Broadhurst in the USA in 1996, Hart, Bingelli and Brassard in the USA in 1998; and the studies of Boyle in the UK in 1997 and Bifulco and Moran in the UK in 1998. The NSPCC categorises the types of behaviour into the dimensions of emotional abuse originally identified by Garbarino, Guttman and Seeley in 1986 (see Garbarina, Guttman and Seeley (1986)). The five dimensions of emotional abuse identified by them were: rejecting;

terrorising; ignoring; isolating and corrupting the child. These dimensions could not, however, encompass all types of emotional abuse such as, for example, domestic violence which might affect the child but does not target the child. Hart, Germain and Brassard added the dimension of degrading and denying emotional responsiveness (see Brassard, Germain and Hart (1987)), at pp 3–24).

2.94 Bifulco and Moran (1998) further examined the link between child abuse and mental illness. Qualitative material from over 800 interviews, noting down histories, was categorised to describe the women's experience of childhood abuse and provided a graphic and comprehensive understanding of the complexity of emotional abuse. The case examples provided by Bifulco and Moran indicate that hurtful behaviour which is calculated by parents or others is experienced differently from that which results from such factors as poverty, stress or illness of the parents. Their studies describe some incredible examples of the lengths to which abusers would go to cause emotional distress to children including the father who forced his young daughter to watch while he killed, cooked and ate her pet rabbit; the mother who told her children that they were being sent to a 'bad girls' home and made them sit on stools to wait to be collected by the policeman, while their father was secretly sent out to ring the front door bell as if calling to collect them. As Bifulco and Moran's case studies illustrate, it is almost impossible to define all the different varieties of emotional abuse which can be perpetrated by human beings upon each other.

2.95 In order to be fully aware of the range and types of behaviour which children may experience as emotional abuse, there is no substitute for reading the various studies detailed in appendix 1 of the NSPCC report and the experiences and reactions of survivors of such abuse contained within the Report of the National Commission of Inquiry into the Prevention of Child Abuse and Neglect (see respectively, *Child Maltreatment in the United Kingdom*, at pp 122–127, and *Childhood Matters: Report of the National Commission of Inquiry into the Prevention of Child Abuse* (The Stationery Office, 1996), vol 2, especially chapters 3 and 4).

Bullying, as a form of child abuse and its incidence

2.96 Whilst *Working Together to Safeguard Children* highlights a range of issues which have come increasingly to the attention of all agencies as affecting children's emotional health such as the witnessing of domestic violence, the mental health problems of parents or living with substance abuse engaged in by parents, one of the most interesting features of the NSPCC report (*Child Maltreatment in the United Kingdom*) was its conclusion that the most common source of distress to children is bullying and discrimination by other young people, suffered by more than four out of 10 of its respondents. Such bullying was mostly verbal but there was also a substantial amount of physical attack (p 95). Much of the bullying apparently was focused on physical or social characteristics over which the children had no control, attacks which were likely to challenge fundamentally their self-confidence and self-esteem. Whilst the NSPCC report states that theirs was not a study of bullying 'per se', material on bullying was included in order to complete the picture of possible abuse and enable examination of the relationship between bullying, discrimination and abuse in the family and the community. The NSPCC report concluded that their findings on levels of bullying were quite similar to those of other recent studies, and as such reinforced previous evidence of the extent to which it is a common and miserable experience for so many children and young people. The results, it stated, represent a serious cause for worry about development and management of relationships between young people, in settings where they meet in groups, particularly in schools (p 95). As to other institutional settings in which bullying can be seen as a form of child abuse by other childen, which may have even more damaging effects, we need to consider very carefully the position of children and young people in secure and penal settings. Goldson's descriptions of the bullying which he found to be endemic in both secure accommodation and young offender institutions are extremely chilling and should sound warning bells to all those responsible for their adminisration but should also raise questions as to the location of responsibility for the inspection of such establishments from the child protection perspective if we are to continue with the process of locking children up (see Goldson (2002)). In addition, the former Chief Inspector of Prisons has described penal and secure accommodation settings for children and young people as institutionalised abuse.

2.97 In *Working Together to Safeguard Children*, bullying is not separately identified as abuse in the chapter dealing with definitions (see chapter 2) but is identified as a problem to which schools should pay attention in the chapter considering roles and responsibilities of different agencies (see chapter 3) and is considered separately in chapter 6 which deals with child protection in specific circumstances (at para 6.8). It provides a useful definition of bullying to which all those engaged in child protection should have careful regard especially in the light of the NSPCC's findings that bullying is the main cause of distress to children and young people. *Working Together to Safeguard Children* defines bullying as 'deliberately hurtful behaviour, usually repeated over a period of time, where it is difficult for those bullied to defend themselves. It can take many forms but the three main types are physical (eg hitting, kicking, theft), verbal (eg racist or homophobic remarks, threats, name calling) and emotional (eg isolating an individual from the activities and social acceptance of their peer group)'. *Working Together to Safeguard Children* further acknowledges that 'the damage inflicted by bullying can frequently be underestimated. It can cause considerable distress to children, to the extent that it affects their health and development or, at the extreme, causes them "significant harm" (including self harm)'. Such bullying and discrimination does not only come about as a result of bullying by other children but also bullying by adults. Whilst four out of 10 children had experienced bullying and discrimination by other children, one in 10 reported having experienced this from adults. Both bullying by children and bullying by adults most commonly occurred in schools, 94 per cent of those cases involving bullying by children and 71 per cent of those reporting bullying by adults (see *Child Maltreatment in the United Kingdom* at chapter 4 generally). All schools are now required by the Department for Education to have in place anti-bullying strategies (see Circular 10/95), and *Working Together to Safeguard Children* notes that all settings in which children are provided with services or are living away from home should have in place rigorously enforced anti-bullying strategies (at para 6.8).

2.98 To the definition of bullying provided by *Working Together to Safeguard Children* may be added the definition provided by Besag in 1989 (see Besag (1989)). Thus he defines bullying in terms of three components: it must occur over time, rather than being a single aggressive act; it involves an imbalance of power, the powerful attack the powerless; and it can be psychological, verbal or physical in nature. Arora and Thompson noted that children and young people included all these elements in their own descriptions of bullying behaviour (see Arora and Thompson (1987)).

2.99 Whilst the prevalence rates revealed by the NSPCC report are high, other studies also show that children of all ages are subject to bullying, although there is evidence that younger children experience higher rates (see Central Statistical Office, *Social Focus on Children* (HMSO, 1994); Creighton and Russell (1995); and Balding (1998)). Very worryingly, however, Ghate and Daniels (see Ghate, and Daniels (1997)) found that more than half of a national sample of 998 children aged between 8 and 15 years worried sometimes or often about being bullied at school, and that younger children worried most. The NSPCC's conclusions as to the results of their findings and the findings of other studies indicate a number of questions about the way in which we socialise young people in groups, manage their contacts with each other and educate them into expected behaviour with peers. The results of these studies further illustrate the central importance of 'anti-bullying' strategies to reduce the harm suffered by many children in schools and other youth settings, and also of a constructive education programme for the young on sexual relationships, since this was another area in which bullying or power abuse tactics had been identified (see *Child Maltreatment in the United Kingdom*, at p 95). Other recent studies have considered the psychological disturbance not only to victims of bullying but also to the perpetrators and have also considered the issue of the persistence of bullying (see Kumpulainen, Rasanen and Henttonen (1999) at pp 1253–1262).

2.100 Bullying has now been recognised by a wide range of health professionals as being potentially extremely damaging to children (see Dawkins (1995); and Dawkins and Hill (1995), at pp 103–122). Whilst both *Working Together to Safeguard Children* and Circulars issued by the Department for Education stress the importance of the adoption of anti-bullying strategies which should, in the words of the DOH, be 'rigorously enforced', more attention needs to be focused on the different strategies which may reduce bullying and the constructive steps which institutions can follow in order to achieve this. Constructive advice which can be followed by both schools and children's homes can be found in a further study published in 1999 (see Katz (1999)). Thus, this advises that the following steps could be taken: time should be made for effective listening to children and young people; a sense of belonging and mutual respect should be encouraged; each person should feel safe and valued; people should be taught how to manage conflict and deal with anger; there should be recognition that how you feel will affect how you learn and how you react in different environments; the stigma of asking for help should be removed; and young people's perception of the institutional atmosphere in which they are being educated or living should also be closely monitored.

2.101 Given the much greater recognition which all the different departments involved with children and young people now attach to the problem of bullying it is to be hoped that all professionals involved in child protection, most particularly social services and the police, will, in the light of the potential damage which it causes, and its current prevalence, now accord it a much higher level of attention than it has been accorded in the past.

Child sexual abuse and its incidence

2.102 As was the case with the category of emotional abuse, sexual abuse is described in outline at para 2.6 of *Working Together to Safeguard Children* and then later on in that chapter there are descriptions of other types of behaviour which may be caused by sexual abuse of a child (see *Working Together to Safeguard Children*, at para 2.13). Thus the guidance indicates that disturbed behaviour including self-harm, inappropriate sexualised behaviour, sadness, depression and a loss of self-esteem, have all been linked to sexual abuse. The guidance goes on to comment that its adverse effects may endure into adulthood and that the severity of the impact on a child is believed to increase the longer the abuse continues, the more extensive the abuse, and the older the child. It notes that a number of features of sexual abuse have also been linked with severity of impact, including the extent of premeditation, the degree of threat and coercion, sadism, and bizarre or unusual elements. A child's ability to cope with the experience of sexual abuse, once recognised or disclosed, is strengthened by the support of a non-abusive adult carer who believes the child, helps the child understand, and is able to offer help and protection. *Working Together to Safeguard Children* also goes on to point out that a proportion of adults who sexually abuse children have themselves been sexually abused as children. They may also have been exposed as children to domestic violence and discontinuity of care, although the guidance notes that it would be quite wrong to suggest that most of the children who are abused will inevitably go on to become abusers themselves (see *Working Together to Safeguard Children*, at para 2.14).

2.103 Elsewhere in the document, the DOH advises that children involved in prostitution and other forms of commercial sexual exploitation should be treated primarily as the victims of abuse, and it advises that their needs require careful assessment. The guidance further states that such children are likely to be in need of welfare services and, in many cases, protection under the CA 1989. It points out that the problem is often hidden from view and that ACPCs should actively enquire into the extent to which there is a local problem, and should not assume that it is not a local issue (see *Working Together to Safeguard Children*, at para 6.43). Further types of child sexual abuse dealt with in chapter 6 of *Working Together to Safeguard Children* include the problem of child pornography and the internet. The guidance points out that adults are now using the internet to try to establish contact with children with a view to 'grooming' them for inappropriate or abusive relationships. The guidance advises that when somebody is discovered to have placed child pornography on the internet, or access child pornography, the police should normally consider whether that individual might also be involved in the active abuse of children. It advises that, in particular, the individual's access to children should be established within the family and employment contexts and in other settings (eg work with children as a volunteer) and that if there are particular concerns about one or more specific children, there may be a need to carry out CA 1989, s 47 enquiries in respect of those children (see *Working Together to Safeguard Children*, paras 647–649; and Chapter **1**).

2.104 As far as criminal provisions are concerned, the modern legislation concerning sexual abuse started in the UK with the Incest Act 1906 but it was not until the broadcasting of BBC's *Child Watch* in 1986 (which reportedly attracted 16.5 million viewers), and the Cleveland Child Sexual Abuse Enquiry following the events in Cleveland in 1987 (see E Butler-Sloss, *Report of the Enquiry into Child Abuse in Cleveland* (HMSO, 1988)) that awareness of the severity and extent of child sexual abuse as encompassing more than incest was publicly considered and discussed within the UK. The Cleveland Enquiry prompted the DOH and others to invest in a range of research studies intended to consider the definition and measurement of child sexual abuse and the effectiveness of child protection measures to safeguard children.

2.105 There have been a considerable number of studies which have now been completed on the problem, usually concentrating on abuse of children by adults, but there are a number which demonstrate that children evidence considerable experience of sexual play (see Lamb and Coakley (1993); Smith and Grocke (1995)), and that they display a wide variety of sexual behaviours). Determining, therefore, where the line should be drawn between normal sexual play between children and adolescents and what has become referred to as 'peer abuse' has proved difficult. In his review of the literature, practices and procedures associated with young people who sexually abuse, Martin Calder has stated that awareness of this problem lags behind that of the USA and cites a number of obstacles to recognition including: viewing sexualised behaviour as experimentation, a fear of labelling and stigmatisation, a mistaken view that peer abuse is less serious or harmful than abuse by adults and the relatively low level of reporting (see Calder (1997)). Whilst the 1992 National Children's Home Report highlighted for the first time the problem of children and young people who sexually abuse other children in England and Wales (see *The Report of the Committee of Enquiry into Children and Young People who Sexually Abuse other Children* (NCH, 1992)) there was considerable surprise in the press when the NSPCC report, *Child Maltreatment in the United Kingdom*, was published in late 2000. The report revealed much higher levels of sexual abuse particularly between siblings than had previously been thought to be the case (see *Child Maltreatment in the United Kingdom*, at chapter 8 generally). Nevertheless, the report urges considerable caution with respect to the figures which it obtained, especially in relation to sexual acts involving family members, because of the small size of the sample used (see p 80 and table 41).

2.106 The NSPCC report further took into account the concerns emerging from their review of a whole range of previous studies on sexual abuse, by building in dimensions for age and informed consent, rather than focusing exclusively on the legal age of consent to sexual activity or on the respondents' own assessment of consent. Because opinions differed over the appropriate age gap for consensual sex, although there was general agreement that no sexual behaviour was acceptable between pre-teen children and those much older or adults, respondents were separated into two groups in order to assess sexual activities undertaken by consent with an older person. The NSPCC report therefore notes that sexual behaviour towards the respondent in their study was characterised by the researchers as 'sexual abuse' in the following circumstances:

- if the other person was a parent or carer (by definition more than 5 years older);
- if the relevant behaviour occurred against the respondent's wishes; or
- if consensual sexual acts involved a person other than a parent who was 5 or more years older when the child was aged 12 or under.

2.107 The team identified a 'borderline' group which was defined where teenagers aged 13–15 had sexual experiences with someone aged 5 or more years older and stated that this was with their full consent. The report points out that this is currently illegal when it involves vaginal or anal intercourse and notes that it raises many questions about young people's capacity for informed consent and it could be considered exploitative behaviour by the older person, whilst including a variety of circumstances in which public opinion might differ on what was acceptable or culpable, and therefore the team undertook further analysis to throw light on the respective prevalence levels. In this study, consensual activities between age peers were not rated as abuse, although again some of these would have been illegal (*Child Maltreatment in the United Kingdom*, at p 83). The team further notes that the definitions which were thus used were based on research evidence of the likely harmful effect of the abuse, which is known to be affected by the relationship to the abuser and the involvement of physical contact. Abuse was further classified into abuse involving physical contact which was again further broken down into whether the contact involved touching genital or other private parts of the body; and other physical contact such as sexual hugging and kissing. A non-contact category was also used including exposure of sexual organs or other private parts of the body, voyeurism and use in the production of pornography.

2.108 In 1984, Ruth and Henry Kempe listed nine categories of sexual abuse which it might be useful to set out here in order to assist those who might be called upon to interpret certain behaviour as constituting sexual abuse (see Kempe and Kempe (1984)). These categories have not increased in number despite the passage of years since, for example, the exhibition of child pornographic material on the internet is covered by their eighth category. The categories listed by Kempe and Kempe include:

(1) *Incest*: any physical sexual activity between family members, which it is suggested should be interpreted as broadly as possible to include step-relations, unrelated siblings connected through previous marriages who are living together as a unit, grandparents and uncles and aunts who are living together permanently with the child. (For the legal definition of incest in English law see Chapter **9**.)

(2) *Paedophilia*: the preference of an adult for pre-pubertal children as the means of achieving sexual excitement. The range of activity may include any of the forms of sexual abuse.

(3) *Exhibitionism (indecent exposure)*: this involves the exposure of the genitals by an adult male to girls, boys and women. The exhibitionist seeks to experience sexual excitement from the encounter and masturbation as well as exposure may take place.

(4) *Molestation*: this includes forms of indecent behaviour including touching, fondling, kissing the child, especially in the breast or genital areas, engaging in masturbation of the child or urging the child to fondle or masturbate the adult. These activities may lead to mutual masturbation or to oral-genital contact. The limits are not clearly demarcated.

(5) *Sexual intercourse*: this includes intercourse with a child of either sex including oral genital contact, anal genital contact, or penile vaginal intercourse. Kempe and Kempe emphasise that 'this may occur without physical violence through seduction, persuasion, bribes, use of authority or threats'.

(6) *Rape*: this includes sexual intercourse or attempted intercourse without the consent of the victim.

(7) *Sexual sadism*: this includes inflicting bodily injury on another as a means of obtaining sexual excitement.

(8) *Child pornography*: this includes arranging, photographing by still, video film production or any other means any material involving minors in sexual acts, including other children, adults or animals, regardless of consent given by the child's parents or guardian and the distribution of such material in any form with or without profit and the exhibition of such material, with or without profit. (For the offences which may be committed in such circumstances, see Chapter **9**.)

(9) *Child prostitution*: this includes involving children in sexual acts for profit and, generally, with frequently changing partners.

2.109 Using these various definitions, therefore, the prevalence of sexual abuse reported by this study was hoped to have produced the most reliable prevalence statistics to date available in the UK. Using the team's definitions, the report found that 1 per cent of the sample had been abused by parents or carers, almost all of this abuse involving physical contact, and 3 per cent had been abused by other relatives, with 2 per cent contact and 1 per cent non-contact. Abuse by other named people was the most common form of abuse, with 11 per cent of the sample having this experience, 8 per cent involving physical contact and 3 per cent non-contact. Abuse by strangers or someone just met had affected 4 per cent of the sample, 2 per cent contact and 2 per cent non-contact (*Child Maltreatment in the United Kingdom*, at p 89).

2.110 The findings on sexual abuse from this study supported those figures obtained from official sources and also those obtained from previous research, with girls far more likely to experience all forms of sexual abuse. The study found that most abusers were male, although a large minority of cases of abuse of boys involved female abusers. Sexual abuse against adults is most often perpetrated by men on women and this study found that the same was true for children and young people (at p 94).

2.111 What emerges most clearly from this study is the difficulty of reaching a commonly agreed definition from which the researchers were able to work and the same problem has beset those engaged in reform of the law relating to sexual offences, particularly when one is dealing with peer abuse or where differences in ages between the parties might be quite small, ie between one and 2 years. Nevertheless, a range of abusive activities found by such studies as that conducted by the NSPCC are covered by various criminal offences, which are dealt with in detail in Chapter **9**. When looking at the incidence of sexual abuse, therefore, one has to bear in mind that the criminal statistics will reveal only those persons who have been charged and convicted of such offences and because of massive under-reporting to the police in this area cannot be said to be a reliable guide as to prevalence.

2.112 The criminal statistics for the period 1989–1999 reveal a steady decline in almost all of the types of offences specifically referable to the age of the child but also in other offences such as incest. Thus offences of incest have fallen from 471 in 1989 to 139 in 1999; offences of unlawful sexual intercourse with a girl under 13, from 300 offences in 1989 to 153 in 1999; and unlawful sexual intercourse with a girl under 16 from 2,471 in 1989 to 1,133 in 1999.

2.113 In 1999, changes occurred to the way in which the Home Office recorded certain offences and thus there is far more detail available about the perpetration of sexual offences against those under the age of 16 in the sense that there are details on cautions, prosecutions and convictions, but there is an absence of some detail in relation to the numbers under the category of notifiable offences. Additional information obtainable from these particular Home Office statistics reveals the presence of figures reported of the offence of gross indecency with girls aged under 14 rising from 871 in 1988 to 1,365 in 1999, and although there is other data presented in these statistics they do not record the number of notifiable offences as such but produce simply the figures on cautions, prosecutions and convictions. The figures on prosecutions and convictions reveal that prosecutions for all types of age-specific offences on girls have declined quite dramatically, whilst figures for such offences as gross indecency with boys aged 14 and under appear to have remained fairly static with the figure being 103 prosecutions in 1988 and 105 prosecutions in 1999. Prosecutions for taking and making indecent photographs or pseudo-photographs of children have resulted in a considerable rise in prosecutions from 32 in 1988 to 175 in 1999 and the same is true of prosecutions for cases of possession of an indecent photograph or pseudo-photograph of a child which have risen in the magistrates' courts from one in 1988 to 163 in 1999 (see generally, tables 1–4 of the Criminal Statistics in England and Wales 1998 and 1999, reproduced in *Home Office Criminal Statistics Unit Bulletin 2001*).

2.114 As with all other forms of child abuse, the only other statistical indicator is that derived from the numbers of registrations of children on the Child Abuse Register under the category of sexual abuse. These figures reveal a steady year-on-year decrease for figures entered on 31 March each year for those actually on the Child Protection Register at that point in each year, for total numbers. The figures for sexual abuse alone reveal a slightly decreasing picture of entries under this category falling from 4,900 in 1996 to 3,600 in 2000. The numbers of those entered in the mixed abuse categories including sexual abuse have remained static in all three of the mixed categories of neglect, physical injury and sexual abuse, 300 in 1996 and 300 in 2000; in the category of neglect and sexual abuse 400 in 1996 up to 600 in 2000; and in the category of physical injury and sexual abuse 600 in 1996 and 600 in 2000. Thus the only category of mixed abuse which has showed an increase is that of neglect and sexual abuse which appeared to reach a peak in 1999 of 700 cases falling back to 600 in 2000.

2.115 Clearly, these figures do not match up with the levels of reports of sexual abuse in such studies as that completed by the NSPCC and it is felt by researchers that this category, in particular, is one which is seriously under-represented both in criminal statistics and statistics relating to the Child Protection Register. In *Child Maltreatment in the United Kingdom*, the authors noted in their recommendations that there is reason for great concern in the low level of reporting of abuse, particularly of sexual abuse, and the fact that respondents did not approach professional services. It states that young people often seem to have been afraid to approach members of their families and other adults, fearing that they would not be believed or that they would be taken away from home. The report further states that under-reporting of sexual offences has been known to be a problem for adults, and strategies have been developed to address this, and the report recommends strongly that similar strategic approaches are needed for children and young people and indeed states that 'urgent attention is needed in providing forms of help with sexual abuse which can be easily and confidentially accessed by young people' (at p 104).

2.116 Despite this recommendation, it should be noted that the research done by Jones and Ramchandanai (see Jones and Ramchandanai (1999)) indicated that a large number of children remain vulnerable despite professional intervention. In their study, half of all children seen were considered vulnerable to further abuse 3 months after referral, with nearly one in five considered definitely unsafe one year after referral. In common with other studies, they found that large numbers of children who had been sexually abused were neither offered nor received therapeutic help. The study revealed that there was a strong association between getting therapeutic help and improved behaviour but only 20 per cent of the sexually abused children in one study were offered any form of psychological help or counselling, whereas in another one-half of those not getting treatment were still depressed some 3 months later. Jones and Ramchandanai further found in their survey that sexual abuse had a very high impact on the families as a whole. Parents, who had to cope with their children's distress as well as with their own distress and guilt feelings, had not had their needs met and in one study 75 per cent of parents were in poor psychological health at 3 months after the diagnosis, although this tended to improve over time. Finally, as has been noted above, there appeared to be a relatively low proportion of cases in all the studies where there had been a successful criminal conviction which often led to the abused child feeling badly let down when hopes had been raised by professionals and other family members. The survey also found that failure to prosecute an abuser who was a family outsider was associated with a poor outcome for both the child, who often became very depressed, and his or her parent who remained unengaged.

2.117 Again, as has been noted above, child sexual abuse is now recognised as covering the problem of child prostitution. Various measures including Home Office guidance to police and social services as well as specific guidance in *Working Together to Safeguard Children* has now ensured that all services are aware of the problems and are on the lookout for the difficulties faced by those children who may be caught up in prostitution. In 1999 the Children's Society published a report revealing results which were distressingly similar to those which they had revealed a decade earlier in their report *Young Runaways* (see Newman (1989)). The latest report entitled *One Way Street* (Children's Society (1999)) reveals disturbing facts about the age of involvement of children in prostitution, their experience of conflict within their own families, the fact that a large number had been in local authority care, that a large number were runaways and that a considerable percentage had begun using drugs after becoming involved in prostitution. The report revealed that the youngest children in the survey had become involved in prostitution aged 11, and 48 per cent were involved in prostitution before they were 14, with 64 per cent becoming involved before they could legally consent to sex. For 42 per cent, their first sexual experience was one of sexual abuse, 26 per cent of them saying that this had occurred before they were aged 10. For 8 per cent, prostitution was their first sexual experience; 72 per cent revealed that they had experienced conflict or abuse in their family while 48 per cent also revealed that they experienced violence committed upon them by their partners, pimps or punters.

2.118 The outlook for those children who had been in care seemed to get worse rather than better, with 66 per cent of those questioned aged under 18 having been in care whilst only 33 per cent of those over 25 had been in care. The younger group of 'looked after' children had also been involved in prostitution at a younger age, with over half of them becoming involved before the age of 14. Over 75 per cent of those who had run away from care became involved in prostitution before the age of 14. Of the whole group surveyed by the Children's Society in 1999, 60 per cent of them had run away, with one-third becoming involved in prostitution whilst on the run and in order to survive. The statistics for drug use were exceptionally high amongst this group of children with over 50 per cent using hard drugs such as heroin, crack and/or amphetamines. In the two age groups, drug use was far higher in those under 25, with over 75 per cent of them having used drugs before becoming involved in prostitution, but out of the whole sample 65 per cent had resorted to hard drugs after becoming involved in prostitution.

2.119 The survey completed on behalf of the Children's Society was concluded in early 1999 and, arguably, the more enlightened policies now instituted by the Home Office, together with the DOH through their *Guidance to Police and Social Services*, would not have had time to take effect since the draft only appeared in late 1998 and was not fully operational until towards the end of 1999. Where this sort of policy had been enforced for some time, however, as in Nottinghamshire, then the experience there has been a reduction in the numbers of child prostitutes. That guidance, previously issued to police and social services, has now been supplemented by the issuing of inter-agency guidance entitled *Safeguarding Children Involved in Child Prostitution* (DOH, Home Office, DfES, Welsh Assembly, 2000) which is described as supplementary guidance to *Working Together to Safeguard Children*. This puts the procedures and approaches agreed under the earlier guidance into a more comprehensive and structured framework within the overall umbrella of *Working Together to Safeguard Children*. It again emphasises that the child involved in prostitution is to be seen to be just as much a victim of child abuse as the child abused within the family or any other setting, and that the primary law enforcement effort must be against abusers and coercers who break the law and who should be called to account for their abusive behaviour (para 2.5). The principal aim of those working with the children must be to protect them from further abuse and to support them out of prostitution. Since the research has indicated that factors particularly associated with child prostitution include either running away from residential care or the financial problems associated with leaving care, the government has also announced very determined efforts to try and improve the experiences of children who are looked after, both to reduce the numbers of those who might to seek to run away and also to improve the position of young people when leaving care (see *Quality Protects: Educational Attainment of those Children in Care* (2000) and see also the CSA 2000 and the Children (Leaving Care) Act 2000).

2.120 As with all forms of child abuse, most particularly with regard to child sexual abuse, a key issue for those involved in responding both to the NSPCC Report *Child Maltreatment in the United Kingdom* and to *Childhood Matters* in 1996, was that of education. In the National Commission survey, respondents viewed education as being the most important way of preventing child sexual abuse. The Commission points out (at p 127) that very many of those who had been under the age of 11 when the abuse began pointed to the need for education on abuse from a relatively young age. Thus one respondent indicated that early use in schools of appropriate information, starting at nursery age and not confining the notion of abuse to strangers but also to include family members, was critically important (at p 127). Others indicated the importance and value of education in helping them to have had the confidence to speak out, and others felt that school, being the main source of information in any child's life, should play a much bigger role in trying to educate children about child abuse and what to do. One respondent stated: 'I believe child abuse should be discussed in schools from an early age. If it was, maybe I would have realised when I was little, what was wrong and why I preferred my fantasy life'. Surely child abuse should be discussed in sex education these days in primary schools, surely that cannot be a bad thing? It would give the child an opportunity to say 'my home life is like that and it upsets me'; 'I'm frightened of my dad'; 'is he wrong or am I naughty?'. 'I would never have thought of asking for help, although I know I desperately needed it'.

2.121 The lack of education on issues such as child sexual abuse becomes of increasing significance when one realises that so many people only begin to understand what was wrong in their lives when they become adults and realise that sexual abuse of children by members of their family, by their peers or by people known to them is not something which is normal and is something which should be reported either to the relevant authorities or to a trusted adult as soon as it occurs. The failures of our education system in this regard are dramatically pointed up by the responses of people to the National Commission report and also to the NSPCC report in 2000.

Neglect and its incidence

2.122 Stevenson has pointed out that 'neglect is not a unitary concept but an administrative category covering a range of behaviours which are characterised by the omission of care' (see Stevenson (1988)). Linking all the types of behaviour which may be encompassed within the description of neglect is the notion of an absence of parental care. To attract the attention of the authorities, neglect of a child will usually have to be persistent or severe or may stem from a failure to protect a child from exposure to any kind of danger, including cold or starvation, or an extreme failure to carry out important aspects relating to the care of the child, which result in significant impairment of the child's health or development, including non-organic failure to thrive. Whilst this last item ranks as a separate category for registration in Scotland, within England and Wales it is encompassed by the notion of neglect. The responsibility for providing nurture and physical care of a child as well as protecting them from various dangers and providing them with appropriate medical care is attributed to parents or those with parental responsibility. The notion of providing appropriate nurture includes not only adequacy of nutrition, warmth and clothing, but also the provision of basic hygiene, ensuring that the child attends school, appropriate supervision of children within the home and levels of cleanliness within the home. Neglect has also been treated in some studies as encompassing the notion of abandonment of children, often within the home for several days (see Christenson (1996)). It should be noted as a matter of interest that this last survey covered 1,031 health nurses dealing with children out in the community.

2.123 As far as criminal offences of neglect are concerned, the criminal statistics for England and Wales do not break down the constituent offence of neglect as incorporated within the general notion of s 1 of the CYPA 1933. Thus the offences appear as offences under s 1 and there has been a noticeable and quite dramatic increase in the number of prosecutions of persons charged with cruelty or neglect of children, rising from 228 in 1988 to 839 in 1999. The number of notifiable offences for 1999 were 2,631 which resulted in 331 cautions, 839 prosecutions and 469 convictions.

2.124 As far as the Child Protection Register statistics are concerned, neglect forms the single highest category for registration of children on Child Protection Registers in England and Wales accounting for 10,100 registrations for neglect alone, constituting 35 per cent of all child protection registrations. Neglect is also additionally found in three other mixed categories of abuse (see *Registrations to Child Protection Registers During the Years Ending 31 March 1996– 2000 by Category of Abuse* (DOH, 2000), at table 1.6). As well as focusing on parental behaviour in not caring for their children, the NSPCC report *Child Maltreatment in the United Kingdom* noted that a separate but related issue is where children assume responsibility for the care of their parents or running of the home, rather than being able to rely on parents caring for them. It notes that this may arise in very varied circumstances, ranging from parents' illness or disability to parents with social or emotional problems of their own which take priority in their life either temporarily or long term. Bifulco and Moran (see para **2.96**) describe 'role reversal' in which daughters took over parental responsibilities, often as a result of a parent's death, illness, alcoholism or inability to cope. They identify the overlap between role reversal and neglect, commenting that role reversal 'rarely occurred without parental neglect and between one-third and one-half of those with neglect were found to have role reversal' (at p 37). Dearden and Becker (see Dearden and Becker (2000)) described the ways in which children matured and acquired practical skills through having carer responsibilities for parents who were sick, disabled, or had alcohol or drug problems, but they also pointed up that those gains were far outweighed by the educational and social deficits which the children experienced. They demonstrated that young carers were likely to experience serious poverty, reduced employment opportunities on leaving school and social exclusion (at p 81).

2.125 Two separate cases may serve to illustrate a number of the problems associated with cases of child neglect. The first which hit the news headlines is the case of Paul (see *Paul – Death through Neglect* (Bridge Child Care

Consultancy Service, 1995)) and the second is that of the case of *Z v UK* [2001] 2 FLR 612, both of which reveal tales of horrifying and dreadful neglect of children, in the former case leading to the child's death and in the latter leading to the children's major psychological and emotional health problems.

2.126 As the report on Paul, *Death through Neglect*, comments:

> 'more than any single form of abuse, the detection and diagnosis of neglect is dependent on establishing the importance and collation of sometimes small, apparently undramatic single pieces of factual information which, when seen together are of considerable significance. Information relating to these signs is likely to be spread throughout the community of child care professionals, and the implications for multi-disciplinary working are immense. Some of that information may be hard fact, whilst some of it may be more in the nature of expressing a concern' (at para 33).

2.127 Some attention has already been focused on the issues of emotional abuse, but under the category of neglect it is important to appreciate that both physical and emotional neglect can be included. Thus, various studies have indicated that babies and children who are physically and emotionally neglected are at high risk of suffering from a range of problems including: severe disturbances in emotional attachment; failure to thrive which can lead to poor growth, developmental delay and, in an extreme form, death; gross under-stimulation; language delays; conduct disorder; very poor educational performance; severe nappy rash and other skin infections; recurrent and persistent minor infections. As Clausen and Crittenden have concluded, 'severity of physical neglect was correlated with psychological maltreatment specifically with cognitive and social/emotional neglect. Children who experience neglect in one domain were, therefore, very likely neglected in other domains as well' (see Clausen and Crittenden (1991)).

2.128 Paul died on Sunday 7 March 1993. The Bridge report indicates that he had lain in urine-soaked bedding and clothes for a considerable number of days. Photographs taken after his death showed burns over most of his body derived from the urine staining plus septicaemia with septic lesions at the ends of his fingers and toes. In addition he was suffering from severe pneumonia. The Bridge report states that it is impossible to imagine the level of suffering that this little boy experienced as death slowly occurred (at paras 36 and 37). In February 1994, Paul's father was convicted of manslaughter, plus cruelty by neglect to three other children, and sentenced to 7 years' imprisonment. Paul's mother was also convicted of manslaughter but placed on probation for 3 years.

2.129 A great deal of information existed on the files of the different agencies dealing with the children in Paul's family which disclose serious concerns about gross neglect in respect of all of the children. The detail presented in chapter 3 of the report dealing with the history of the case runs to some 135 pages documenting the innumerable occasions on which the family either referred itself or was referred to a number of services. That case history chart leaves one in no doubt that the children within Paul's family all suffered gross emotional abuse and physical neglect throughout their childhood, yet this was not the perception held by most of the professionals dealing with the family at the time. The Bridge report notes (at para 81) that the view frequently repeated was of children who were 'dirty, smelly, but happy' but this is at odds with the factual contents of the case history chart. Again, when reading through these details there are many comments of incidents relating to the seven children in Paul's family which provide clear indicators of the neglect that the children were suffering but yet which were missed by the various agencies involved. The Bridge report comments (at para 89) that this suggests to them that no one who was dealing with the children in the family ever got to grips with the detailed history and the developmental issues that were unfolding in relation to each of the children over the 15 months. The Bridge report's conclusion in relation to the performance of all the agencies involved in this case were that issues such as lack of specialisation, lack of adequate professional supervision, consultation and support reduced the ability of each agency to recognise the reality of life in Paul's family (at para 393). Nevertheless, it is important to appreciate that social services have the lead responsibility in relation to child protection and the Bridge report heightens the importance of one person having the critical overall review of care involving a child or children in any particular family.

2.130 As with many other reports into child deaths which have been made over the last 45 years, the report on the death of Paul is clear that its importance lies in the lessons which can be learned for the guidance of future professional practice when dealing with families like those of Paul. The Bridge report is clear that Paul's parents, irrespective of any help which might have been given (and the report concludes that the services offered to Paul and his family were inadequate) could not effectively care for their children. It is noted that Paul's parents had accepted no responsibility for his death and indeed talked of having further children once Paul's father was released from prison (at para 378). The Bridge report therefore concluded that children living with these parents would, at the very least, be in constant danger of severe emotional abuse and neglect (at para 379). The conclusion of the Bridge report that the services offered to Paul and his family were inadequate was based on the identification that the services offered over 15 years on an inter-agency basis had been based on the false premiss that the children were safe, whereas the report concluded that they lived in an unsafe environment.

2.131 One of the most telling conclusions of the Bridge report is the identification of the challenge, noted above in relation to other abuse categories, that all professionals working in the child protection field should seek an accurate balance between developing a partnership with parents and not losing sight of the need to make services child-centred. The Bridge report recommended that the main areas of change in professional practice should be about ensuring: the accurate collation and sharing of historical information about the family; the seeking of the views of the children throughout the management case and *listening to their comments*; the accurate identification of the developmental needs of children; an awareness of the fact that neglected or abused children are attached to their parents and may deny or minimise their problems; and the identification of recognising neglect caused by the parents' inability to care for children. The Bridge report in its conclusions constantly emphasises the critical importance of requiring all professionals working with children and their families, their managers, policy makers and politicians, to make sure that 'the child is the focus of their work and to ensure that the child's views and needs are at the forefront of all decision making'. Paul died a horrible and lonely death aged 15 months and the Bridge report concludes with the cautionary words that 'none of us engaged in work with children can guarantee the safety of youngsters like Paul but if their needs are the focus of our work, we can reduce risk and maybe, just maybe, Paul's death may not have been in vain' (at paras 418–419).

2.132 The expressed hope in the last chapter of the Bridge report was that the report would assist agencies to build on developments in respect of services to children and families in ways which would reduce the risk of significant harm and that the report would both inform and assist the wider debate which needs to occur about the prevention of significant harm through neglect; and also that the demonstration in the report of the existence of neglect not solely related to poverty removed the myth that children did not die of neglect in 1994.

2.133 Whilst the neglect and ultimate death of Paul was occurring in the 15 months prior to March 1993, a group of five children were experiencing appalling physical and emotional neglect at the hands of their parents in Bedfordshire. But both the cases of Victoria Climbie and *Z v UK* [2001] 2 FLR 612 point up a problem which has been identified in successive child abuse inquiry reports, but which has never given rise to the acknowledgement that the system itself, in failing to protect children suffering neglect at the hands of their parents or carers could also be seen to be guilty of neglect itself. Whilst iatrogenic abuse (this means abuse by the very system which it has been intended should protect the individual from abuse) has been recognised, certainly since the Cleveland controversy in 1987, iatrogenic neglect (neglect by the very system intended to protect the individual from neglect) is a new concept. The children in the case of Z were subject to such appalling neglect including starvation, living in filthy conditions at home and sleeping on urine-soaked mattresses in faeces smeared bedrooms, together with a range of health problems associated with parental neglect, that the consultant child psychiatrist, Dr Dora Black, who saw the children in January 1993, was appalled. Her view was that the three older children in the family were all showing signs of psychological disturbance, all five children had been deprived of affection and physical care and she described their experiences as 'to put it bluntly, horrific' and stated that the case was the worst case of neglect as well as emotional abuse that she had seen in her professional career. It was her stated opinion that social services had 'leaned over backwards to avoid putting these children on the Child Protection Register and had delayed too long in taking any action leaving at least three of the children with serious psychological disturbance as a result'. In other words the system itself was guilty of neglect.

2.134 The delays in this case in taking any specific action in relation to the children covered nearly 5 years from October 1987 when the children were first referred to social services to October 1992, when the local authority decided to seek care orders in respect of the children. Throughout that period various meetings had been held between workers in different agencies, and discussions had taken place as to whether the children should be placed on the Child Protection Register. A decision was made not to place the children on the Child Protection Register and although the three elder children were accommodated voluntarily for short periods in 1991 and 1992 the children were not placed on the Child Protection Register finally until 22 June 1992 when they were entered under the categories of neglect and emotional abuse. Throughout this period of 5 years, concerns had been expressed about various of the children presenting in a starving condition, stealing food from dustbins and being very dirty, unkempt and smelly and the eldest child's head-teacher had voiced considerable concerns over the mother's care of the children in particular in relation to Z's role in the home and the mothering role which she played. She was apparently required to clean windows smeared with faeces belonging to her siblings and when the children were finally removed into care she stated that she did not want to live with her siblings and she did not like having to look after them all the time.

2.135 As has been noted earlier, the European Court was in no doubt that the neglect and abuse suffered by the children reached the threshold of inhuman and degrading treatment required to constitute a breach of Article 3 of the ECHR (see Chaper 1) and, whilst acknowledging the difficult and sensitive decisions facing social services and the important countervailing principle of respecting and preserving family life, as contained in Article 8(1) of the ECHR, this case left them in no doubt as to the failure of the system in protecting the children from serious long-term neglect and abuse.

2.136 Looking at the details of the case of *Z v UK*, there is absolutely no doubt that the same lessons which were drawn by the Bridge Child Care

Consultancy in relation to the death of Paul were also to be found in this case. Bedfordshire Social Services has indicated that it has taken steps to reform all of its current child protection procedures in order to try to ensure that such neglect by those in the system does not occur again. The decision of the European Court is, however, important in principle because it does recognise not only that the children were subject to neglect by their parents but that the social services' failure to act to intervene to protect them from inhuman and degrading treatment was in itself a form of neglect. The sum of money awarded to the children in the case of Z, namely the sum of £350,000 plus the payment of all legal costs and expenses, was one of the largest sums ever awarded by the European Court and indicative of the seriousness with which the court viewed the neglect of the children by the system in allowing them to be subject to such inhuman and degrading treatment or punishment. It was found by the European Court that the children in the case of Z would all suffer very considerable problems as they grew into adulthood including psychological and general mental health problems, inability to cope with the demand of employment, and inability to form relationships of any depth. Two of the children had been adopted but two others had repeatedly experienced problems in attempted family placements and were growing up in children's homes. The payment of such a large sum of damages also reflected the fact that there was a recognition by the European Court that the children had been denied the opportunity of experiencing and benefiting from normal loving and nurturing family life. It is to be hoped that not only Bedfordshire Social Services but all agencies working in the child protection field, together with the courts, keep the focus which the Bridge report identified as being of critical importance in the case of Paul, and that is the need to keep the focus on the child at all times.

System abuse

2.137 The issue of system neglect has just been discussed in relation to the problem of neglect of children, and within that, reference was made to the problem of iatrogenic abuse (where the system which is intended to protect the child actually results in greater abuse of the child). In *Childhood Matters*, it was emphasised that one form of abuse which requires greater recognition and more precise definition was that of 'system abuse'. This category of child abuse will not be found in official government guidance such as *Working Together to Safeguard Children*, however, that guidance is stated very clearly to be based on the evidence derived from research studies, experience and practice and thus implicit acknowledgement can be found throughout its pages of the fact that misuse of, or failure to use, recommended practices and procedures may result in the system itself abusing children and young people. This was more particularly to be found in *Child Protection: Message from Research* (DOH, 1995) but also in more recent studies completed on behalf of the DOH. It is also a very important message contained within the pages of the *Framework for the Assessment of Children in Need and their Families* (DOH et al, 2000).

2.138 The definition recommended by the National Commission in *Childhood Matters*, however, was as follows:

'System abuse may be said to occur whenever the operation of legislation, officially sanctioned procedures or operational practices within systems or institutions is avoidably damaging to children and their families' (at para 1.15).

2.139 The report goes on to identify that system abuse in its opinion, occurs where:

'(i)   children's needs are not recognised or understood and so they are not considered specifically and separately from those of adults, for example, as witnesses or victims in the criminal justice system, or as children of parents in receipt of punitive or harsh treatment in the penal, refugee or asylum systems;

(ii)   services are unavailable because they do not exist, are inadequate, with restrictive criteria for access, or inaccessible through lack of information, location or through insensitivity to race, culture or gender;

(iii)   services are so poorly organised, managed, monitored or resourced that they permit unskilled and unsafe environments in day, residential and family care settings; they permit repressive and abusive regimes to develop; and they do not detect and deal with abusive individuals who infiltrate organisations and services for children;

(iv)   services for children with emotional and behavioural disorders are so poorly defined and co-ordinated that organisations can avoid or shift responsibilities on to others or define problems so narrowly that the proposed "solution" is inadequate and partial;

(v)   there are unnecessarily intrusive procedures or practices which undermine children or their families' (at para 1.16).

2.140 This is an extremely wide definition of system abuse but one in relation to which there have been improvements since these problems were identified by the National Commission very valuably in 1996. Thus, as a result of *Speaking Up for Justice* (Home Office, 1998) and the reforms enacted by the Youth Justice and Criminal Evidence Act 1999 (YJCEA 1999) (see further, Chapter **9**), improvements have now been made for children as both witnesses and victims within the criminal justice system including, in particular, most recently the directions on provision of therapy for child witnesses (see Home Office, 2001 and further, Chapter **9**). Concern still remains, however, with regard to children of parents within the penal system and very considerable attention has focused in 2001 on the children of those seeking refuge or asylum in the UK.

2.141 Major issues remain with regard to the lack of availability and accessibility to services caused by insensitivity to issues of race, culture and gender and considerably more attention needs to be focused on these issues in the future.

2.142 Reports on abuse of children in day-care, residential and family care settings have continued to surface throughout the 1990s and into the new millennium (see Chapter **3**). Wide-scale police investigations of abusive regimes in children's homes all over the country have continued under the auspices of Operation Care and major attempts have been made to identify individuals working in organised networks or on their own who have infiltrated organisations and services for children. A wider range of criminal measures have now been enacted to try to ensure that registers are kept which may be accessed by any prospective employer or voluntary organisation seeking to employ those who might seek to access children through employment or voluntary work (see further, Chapter **9**). The position of the increasing number of children and young people locked up in penal or secure accommodation provision has also begun to receive greater attention. Thus, in 1997, the Report of Her Majesty's Inspector of Prisons highlighted the fact that such increases in numbers 'were unacceptable in a civilised society' and that such settings were a form of 'institutionalised child abuse' (*Young prisoners: A Thematic Review by HM Inspectorate of Prisons for England and Wales*, (HMSO, 1997) at p 11. Goldson (2002) exemplifies the misery which such setttings can induce in young people when he describes two incidents which left an indelible impression upon him. The first occurred when he arrived early one Saturday morning at a Young Offender Institution to do some interviewing. A 16-year-old boy had been foung hanging in his bedroom the previous evening. Goldson recounts, 'When I arrived the child who had been moved to the local hospital was clinging to life with the help of a respirator. By mid-day he was dead. If ever it can be "just another prison suicide", it is far more than that when you come so close' (at p 8). The second incident occurred when sharing sandwiches and lunchtime banter with a group of staff and children in a Secure Unit while 'unbeknown to us, another child, a young girl alone in her bedroom, was cutting away at her wrists'.

2.143 The problems inherent in the approach to corporal punishment have already been discussed above, as well as highlighting the fact that the Department charged with protecting and safeguarding children is advocating the continued existence of the legitimacy of assault on children (see para **2.63**).

Conclusion

2.144 The definition of child abuse in all its many forms and how these definitions are then operationalised is clearly critical to any system which has at its core the prevention of child abuse. The different definitions of child abuse derived from legislation, government guidance, research studies and published works have revealed a wide range of informative source material.

The critical importance of appreciating the lack of shared understanding between individuals who have been abused and the professionals and policy-makers has also been emphasised. There is now much greater awareness as a result of listening to victims, through reading their letters and including them on research studies, that child abuse has to be considered not only in relation to the abuse which is perpetrated upon the child at any time, but also in relation to its much longer-term impact on the individuals who suffer from such abuse. It has also been seen how official definitions of child abuse have changed enormously over the years and now encompass a wide range of behaviours which have not previously been acknowledged in official definitions. Much of this change, including the most recent amendment to the definition of harm with regard to the effects of witnessing domestic violence, effected by the Adoption and Children Act 2002, has come about as a result of pressure from victims and organisations working on behalf of victims as well as by learning the lessons from a whole host of research studies and from official enquiry reports.

CHAPTER 3

ISSUES IN CHILD ABUSE

'[I]t is acknowledged that the rights and views of children about professional interventions and about the impact of abusive events are easily disregarded or marginalized by parents and the state' (Farmer and Bushel (1999), at p 85).

'[T]he ambivalent social attitudes and values surrounding children – for example, that they are the property of adults but that they are also entitled to protection, or that they are individuals but must also do what adults demand of them – may be contributory factors to all forms of abuse, seen as a destructive manifestation of adults' power over children' (Frosh (2002), at p 71).

'Ultimately, the protection of vulnerable children must become the concern of us all and the focus should be on all children who are significantly harmed, not only on extreme cases. ... The public needs to understand these issues and participate in the debate about how best to tackle them. Policy makers need to take a clear lead in order to ensure that the needs of vulnerable children and their families are made a priority' (NSPCC (2001a), at p 15).

Introduction

3.1 The identification of 'the battered child' syndrome by Henry Kempe and his associates in 1962 (see para **2.61** for a detailed discussion and see Corby (2000)) and the death of the child, Maria Colwell, and subsequent child abuse inquiry (*Report of the Committee of Inquiry into the Care and Supervision Provided in Relation to Maria Colwell* (DHSS, 1974)) provided the impetus for the significantly increased importance of child abuse in UK childcare practices and, later, policies from the mid-1970s onwards. While child abuse was clearly not a new phenomenon that only emerged in the late twentieth century, Kempe's work did mark the first time systematic medical research was undertaken. This research revealed the prevalence and aetiology of the physical abuse of children by their carers in complex, affluent societies. During the subsequent decades, comprehensive research added much to the public and professional understanding of many forms of child abuse (see Chapter **2** generally and Browne (2002), at pp 50–70). However, perceptions of appropriate parenting behaviour and culpability for harms done to children change as social attitudes and socio-economic conditions change (Petrie and

Corby (2002), at pp 387–402). These changes in perception reflect the complexities inherent in the concept of child abuse, which is not simply a criminal act or medical problem but a social construction (Parton 2002), at pp 11–28).

3.2   Child abuse can be conceptualised as a spectrum of behaviours with, of course, the most severe acts of child harm being unacceptable at any time. However, at the other end of the spectrum, the acceptability of child-rearing practices change from one period to another, as clearly demonstrated by the present conflicting attitudes towards corporal punishment which will be discussed later. Many similar contested issues are currently facing childcare professionals and affect the way in which children's needs for protection are understood and legislation and policy are interpreted and applied. Furthermore, in recent decades, the organisation and management of welfare has undergone the most significant change in philosophy and structure since the establishment of the Welfare State in 1948 (Jones and Novak (1999)). These structural changes have also affected services for vulnerable children and will be discussed in greater detail in the last section of this chapter. For those working to protect children from child abuse the social and professional context is now highly fragmented and even contradictory.

3.3   Current policy has been greatly influenced by research showing that most families drawn into formal child abuse assessment processes received no further action or services (*Child Protection: Messages From Research* (DOH, 1995)). Occurring, as they have, alongside research revealing the enormous rise in child poverty in the UK during the 1980s and 1990s, discussed later in this chapter, these findings have been highly influential leading to a number of government initiatives that have followed under the policy theme of 're-focusing'. The intention of this policy theme is to require local authorities to refocus resources towards family support in the community and away from unnecessary, resource-heavy, child abuse investigations. The *Quality Protects* (*Quality Protects Circular: Transforming Children's Services* LAC(98)28 (DOH, 1998)) initiative, which includes substantial funding programmes for community-based services, and the new *Framework for the Assessment of Children in Need and their Families* (DOH, DfEE, Home Office, 2000), are part of the refocusing strategy and fundamentally affect child abuse services.

3.4   However, there are potential dangers in attempting to deal with the ravages of harm suffered by children as a result of poverty by using a system originally designed to identify those most at risk of abuse caused by their parents or carers. This chapter will argue there are indications that current policy may be failing to meet the needs of poor children and failing to protect those children most at risk of abuse. The first section will consider differing notions of 'child' and how these influence public and professional responses to child sexual abuse (CSA), physical abuse and neglect. The importance of child development and attachment theories when working with vulnerable children, whatever the dominant social context, will be examined and also ways in which the child's perspective can be identified and understood. The second section will examine the notion of 'family' and its changing structure. The importance of 'family' in child abuse policy will be examined in relation to the growth and impact of child poverty in the UK and the correlation between poverty and child abuse investigations before several critical family practice and preventive service issues are considered. The last section will focus on organisational and management issues and implications. Although the legal definition of child abuse is 'significant harm' (CA 1989, Pt IV, s 31 and see paras **2.13** and **2.21**) the terms child abuse and child harm will be used to identify all situations where children's health and development are avoidably impaired even where the legal conditions may not be met.

3.5   It is hoped that an exploration of the current context will assist child-care professionals in the task they have of understanding and managing child abuse policy and practice developments in the interests of children.

The child

3.6   Children are defined in our society primarily as non-adults, by what they are not allowed to do or by what is not allowed to happen to them at certain ages. The law defines many parameters of the lives of children, their care, education, employment, sexual activity, and so on. However, the dividing line between childhood and adulthood is difficult to identify as the acquisition of adult rights happens gradually. Rites of passage, marking a socially recognised transition from childhood to adulthood, such as the tradition of being given the 'key of the door' at the age of 21, have become unimportant. Since many adult rights are now acquired at 18 the 'age of majority' is a concept that no longer has utility.

3.7   Childhood, therefore, is not simply a biological state but is a social construction (Aries (1962)). Throughout history the way in which children have been understood and treated has varied, although adults in families and wider social institutions have always had power over the young. The variations in adult perceptions and expectations of children are formed by the prevailing cultural and socio-economic contexts and have little to do with observable differences in children's development or behaviour. Social attitudes to same-sex relationships, for example, have changed enormously in only four decades. Sex between men was a criminal act until 1967. In 2000 the age of consent for gay young men and women was fixed at 16 years in recognition of their right to be treated in the same way as their peers in female/male couple relationships. Social attitudes changed and moral concern about the impact on young people of removing legal prohibitions to same sex relations diminished.

Child sexual abuse

3.8   Issues of sexual behaviour and defining and responding to CSA have been important aspects of child protection practice in recent decades. From the 1980s onwards the sexual behaviour of adults towards children and young people became a major area of concern and the stories of survivors of CSA have been very influential in revealing the impact of such experiences from a child's perspective.

> 'Samantha's mother died when she was very young and her father ... began to abuse her when she was 4. When she was little he covered her head and top half with a blanket and interfered with her vagina. By the age of 10 it was regular sexual intercourse and thereafter it included buggery and oral intercourse. "He made me say that I enjoyed it, that I wanted it ... I thought any adult would not believe me ... I did not know what would happen ... I loved my father so much ... but I was confused, didn't understand. I wanted it to stop. I hated that part of it so much"' ('Samantha' in *Report of the Inquiry into Child Abuse in Cleveland 1987* (1988) cited in Hoggett 1991, at p 571).

3.9   However, the Cleveland and Orkney inquiries (*Report of the Inquiry into Child Abuse in Cleveland 1987* (HMSO, 1988); *Report of the Inquiry into the Removal of Children from Orkney in February 1991* (HMSO, 1992)) showed that the precipitate removal of children from their families can also be abusive and is not always necessary to keep them safe. Many children want abuse to stop but do not necessarily want their families to be broken up. Sometimes the conditions they experience after removal from their family can also be considered abusive which will be outlined later.

3.10   Although a small percentage of CSA perpetrators are women, most are male (and the aetiology of CSA by women and men appears to be different (Frosh (2002), at pp 71–88). Araji and Finkelhor (1986), at pp 89–118), reviewing the major theories of causality, suggest that CSA by men occurs as a result of the interplay of a number of factors rather than a single causal trigger. Their model of causality suggests that a combination of gratifying adult emotional needs by sexual arousal to children together with the failure of disinhibitors, such as the social mores that prohibit adult/child sex in our society, create the conditions in which CSA may occur. The challenge is therefore not so much in identifying *individuals* at risk to children but *individuals in situations*. Protecting children from CSA is complex. Removing the child is sometimes not the answer, particularly if the consequences mean major losses for her/him too. As will be discussed later in this chapter, a large part of a child's well-being is rooted in the quality and consistency of his or her attachment relationship(s) and moving to any new carer inevitably means major emotional upheaval for any child. Keeping children safe from CSA requires a sea-change in social and cultural attitudes towards children as well as action in relation to individual children.

'Sexually abusive behaviour arises out of a particular cultural milieu in which sex is something done *to* another and in which children are available for exploitation. It is linked with, but not specific to, the experiences of abuse suffered by some who go on to abuse others, and it may be strongly connected with dynamics of power and powerlessness, and fears of intimacy and dependency' (Frosh, op cit, at p 85).

3.11 Currently, it is the sexual behaviour of children and young people themselves that has generated interest and debate. This is focused not only on consensual sexual activity, driven by adult concern about the rates of teenage pregnancy and increasing rates of sexually transmitted diseases, but on coercive sexual behaviour by young people. Although men perpetrate most CSA, a high proportion of male perpetrators are adolescent, aged between 16 and 21 (Corby (2000)). Research shows that many juvenile offenders, including juvenile sex offenders, have a past history of physical and/or sexual abuse (Frosh (2002), at pp 71–88). Juvenile sex offenders are also likely to abuse much younger, usually female, children (average age 8.9 years) and the abuse is more likely to involve threats, physical injury and penetration (Manocha and Mezey (1998)).

3.12 However, sexual abuse by young people is quite different from sexual learning between peers that characterises the development of many children. Adults sometimes find it difficult to differentiate situations that are abusive from those that are not, failing to comprehend abuse in some circumstances yet over-reacting in others. This is due in part to an inability to listen to children and be guided by their experiences, wishes, feelings, verbal and non-verbal communication including developmental patterns and play – the child's own medium. A further difficulty occurs when the focus is not on the child and his or her unique circumstances but on defining situations according to criteria that are inevitably influenced by contemporary social mores and sexual attitudes. The following example demonstrates just how far attitudes have changed towards the sexuality of young people with learning impairments since 1987. Their right to the same sort of relationships, including parenting, as their abled peers is more acceptable in the current climate than it was 20 years ago.

'One widely publicized case was that of "Jeanette" a 17-year-old girl with Down's Syndrome who was sterilized without her own consent following hearings in the Appeal Court and the House of Lords in 1987, in response to requests from the local authority and her mother. Jeanette was said to have a "mental age" of five or six. However, such "mental ages" are often based on cognitive skills rather than emotional capacities, or even emotional potential. It is significant that in Jeanette's case what had precipitated the action by her mother and the local authority was the fact that Jeanette was showing signs of sexual awareness and sexual drive "with a risk of pregnancy" … revealing, perhaps emotional maturity far beyond that of a 6-year-old' (Williams (1992), at p 155.

3.13 It is unlikely that such an intervention by a local authority and judgment by a court would result today. As Lord Denning MR commented in *Hewer v Bryant* [1970] 1 QB 357, 'the common law can, and should keep pace with the times'. Legislative change and interpretation is often driven by changes in social attitudes.

Physical abuse

3.14 Physical abuse is another issue where changing perceptions affect the way in which some actions are defined as abusive and others are not. The violent behaviour of the young causes major social concern and has led to a plethora of measures designed to curb and control them. However, there is overwhelming evidence to show that many interventions designed to control the behaviour of children and young people have exposed large numbers of them to serious and continuous abuse. Children and young people may find the distinction between legitimate violence and unlawful violence towards them confusing. It may seem as though adults in society are judged by different standards to those applied to children and young people. Significant numbers of children placed in penal and 'care' institutions have been subject to regimes that have been 'neglectful and brutalising' (Butler (2002), at pp 172–185). In the UK, greater numbers of young people, particularly young males, than in any comparable country, are incarcerated in penal institutions where abuse and serious bullying are commonplace (Goldson (1999); Children's Society, (2002)). Residential care, provided or paid for by the State for children unable to live with their families, has also permitted the abuse of children on a large and sometimes organised scale (*The Pindown Experience and the Protection of Children: The Report of the Staffordshire Child Care Inquiry 1991* (Staffordshire County Council, 1991); *People Like Us: The Report of the Review of the Safeguards for Children Living Away from Home* (the Utting Report) (DOH, Welsh Office, 1997); *The Leicestershire Inquiry 1992* (Leicestershire County Council, 1993); and *Lost in Care* (The Report of the Waterhouse Inquiry into the Abuse of Children in North Wales (2000)).

3.15 The new juvenile justice system has been designed to be offence-focused rather than child-centred (*National Standards for Youth Justice* (2000)) despite the correlation referred to above between juvenile offending and childhood abuse. The aim of the youth justice system is to prevent offending by children and young people. Agencies have to work towards the following six objectives:

- '– The swift administration of justice so that every young person accused of breaking the law has the matter resolved without delay.
- – Confronting young offenders with the consequences of their offending, for themselves and their families, their victims and the community and helping them develop a sense of justice.

- Intervention that tackles the particular factors that put the young person at risk of offending.
- Punishment proportionate to the seriousness and persistence of the offending and which strengthens protective factors.
- Encouraging reparation to victims by young offenders.
- Reinforcing the responsibilities of parents.'

(*National Standards for Youth Justice* (2000), at p 1.)

3.16 There is nothing within the standards that directly acknowledges the likely abusive history of many young offenders themselves or promotes intervention towards these crucial emotional and social problems. It is difficult to understand how a juvenile sex offender, for example, could be helped to acknowledge and deal with their abusive proclivities, given everything that is now known about CSA perpetrators, following the schedule outlined in the standards.

3.17 Another aspect of violence towards children that is topical yet contested is corporal punishment. Although some aspects of parental violence are universally accepted as abusive, corporal punishment is still considered legitimate and even necessary by some. At the beginning of the twentieth century corporal punishment, both at home and in school, was socially acceptable. In fact the popular view was 'spare the rod and spoil the child'. However, although violence by children and young people is punished severely, corporal punishment is still permitted by parents and other adults acting in *loco parentis*. Currently there is a strong lobby for legislation banning the corporal punishment of children on the grounds that it is abusive (NSPCC (2001)) and see Lyon (2000) with Scotland likely to be the first country in the UK to ban smacking (the *Guardian*, 7 September 2001). (For a detailed discussion of this see paras **2.18** and **2.66–2.68**.) Yet there is increasing concern about the behaviour of children and young people in school and the lack of sanctions including corporal punishment available to teachers.

3.18 Schools appear to be rejecting increasing numbers of their pupils because of behaviour problems, leaving them unsupervised, particularly if their parents are following government exhortations to enter the labour market to escape poverty. A report by the Social Exclusion Unit in 1998 revealed an alarming upward trend in school exclusion rates. They rose to 13,500 by 1996–1997 from 3,000 in 1990–1991. Exclusions among primary school children, although a small percentage of the whole, increased by 18 per cent in 1995–1996 (Social Exclusion Unit, *Truancy and School Exclusion Report* (1998)). Children with special needs and African-Caribbean children are six times more likely to be excluded and children in care 10 times more likely. The report commented that substantial research revealed a high level of tension and even conflict between white teachers and black pupils, suggestive of racism. It has been shown that social class, living in areas with high levels of social deprivation and race are the correlative characteristics of excluded children. High levels of exclusion from school and significant academic under-achievement continue for black children compared to their white peers and government is to establish a special task force to tackle this problem (BBC News, 'Task force to help black pupils', 16 March 2002). Attempts have been made to ensure school-age children in trouble with the law are kept under surveillance at all times. Electronic 'tagging' programmes for children as young as 10 have beeen piloted in order to confine them to their homes to keep them out of trouble.

3.19 Child abuse and youth justice policies highlight the polarised perceptions of children in current policy. On the one hand, children and young people are seen as passive victims who need protection and on the other they are considered dangerous and in need of control. In truth, many vulnerable children can simultaneously experience abuse and be abusive themselves. It has been shown that pro-social behaviour is eminently trainable and that empathy and respect for others inhibit violence (Gilbert (1995), at pp 352–389). As far as children and young people are concerned, they cannot be expected to acquire and maintain these social behaviours if they are not also treated empathically and respectfully by adults.

Neglect

3.20 Children can suffer in other ways. Living without adequate food, shelter, clothing, protection and love denies children the very building blocks of development. Even if a child survives such experiences and grows into adulthood there may be irreversible effects on their growth and development. (See also the discussion on this at paras **2.124–2.138** as well as Hanks and Stratton (2002), at pp 89–113.) As can be seen every day in the media, many children in the world are denied these basics:

> 'Neglect of children is one of the most obvious aspects of maltreatment where not only the caregivers of the children are responsible, but where the issue has to be widened to include society as a whole and a global view has to be adopted' (Hanks and Stratton, op cit, at p 105).

3.21 The issue, in a wealthy country such as the UK, is the extent to which care-givers are to be held culpable for the unmet needs of their children and how far the prevailing socio-economic circumstances restrict their ability to meet those needs. This will be discussed in greater detail in the next section of this chapter.

3.22 Some welfare policies and practices, such as those relating to homeless families, expose children to conditions that undermine their health and development but are not recognised as 'abusive'. As a society we are prepared to allow children to suffer because their parents have failed in some way to be socially acceptable or are rejected because of 'difference'. The children of parents considered 'intentionally homeless' (Housing Act 1996, s 191) endure long periods in accommodation that is highly unsuitable and detrimental to their health and development:

'When mum and I arrived at the first hostel we stayed at, I remember thinking this was not home. It was a big dirty place with blocked toilets, and filthy carpets littered with rotten sweets. We were treated like neglected animals; simply ignored. I felt like I wanted to punch someone really hard in the face. I kept asking myself why are we treated so badly? ... Back at the hostel I became frightened to leave the building, even with my mum. At night I was frightened that someone would break into our room – it wasn't that secure. There were regular break-ins and lots of families staying there had things stolen ... when I see homeless people I can't look at them, because I think about my own experience and I just want to cry. I think where are these people going to end up?' (Kimberley Denny, aged 9, in *Community Care* 13 December 2001 – 9 January 2002, at p 24).

Recent changes to legislation (Homelessness Act 2002) place requirements upon local authorities to be more proactive in identifying, tracking and responding to homelessness in their locality. This is to be achieved through the publication of periodic homelessness reviews and associated strategies designed to reduce the problem, particularly among the young. However, without significant change in social attitudes to the homeless such strategies are unlikely to produce desired outcomes.

3.23 The plight of children whose parents are asylum-seekers or who are unaccompanied refugees is also pitiful. Violence and abuse are endemic in many hostels and camps set up for the dispossessed:

'Eustace de Sousa, Manchester Council's principal manager for asylum seekers and the lead for the North West Consortium for Asylum Seekers, says: "People are increasingly concerned about young people dispersed by other authorities into the Greater Manchester area." Agencies contracted to ensure children are linked into health and education services often fail to do so, he maintains. "In general, our experience of private providers has been a very poor one." Concerns in the Manchester area were highlighted recently when an armed gang ram-raided a block of flats in Salford, causing the 50 teenage asylum seekers in residence to flee in terror. Salford council, unhappy with the community implications of playing host to large groups of asylum seeking children, claims it was not told about the teenagers by Kent, which had placed them' (the *Guardian*, 9 January 2002).

Today, local authorities are responsible for some 6,000 children fleeing conflict in the Middle East, Africa and Eastern Europe (the *Guardian*, 9 January 2002).

3.24 Against this background of changing social attitudes, socio-economic factors and professional priorities, it is crucial to remain focused on the individual child and their unique circumstances when making decisions about their welfare. Contradictory standards of childcare and parenting behaviour mean that failure to focus on the individual child can either leave children unprotected or, by removing them unnecessarily from their family, subject them to institutional abuse – and in all too many instances actual abuse in institutions. It is possible, however, to identify the lived experience of any child whatever the context. There are three main ways in which children show how their welfare in any situation is being affected. These are their development, attachment behaviour, and verbal and non-verbal communication.

Child development

3.25 Child development measures in this country have been a major part of child-health monitoring for many decades. Health visitors (and for older children school nurses) are the professionals usually engaged in this surveillance and whose training includes most about children's optimal development (Rouse (2002), at pp 305–318). In comparison, social workers to date receive comparatively little training in child development. It has been argued that this habituates social workers to the 'abnormal' leading to an inappropriate tolerance of some appalling and damaging conditions in which children have lived (*Child Abuse. A Study of Inquiry Reports 1980–1989* (DOH, 1991)). Child development checklists are recommended by the DOH for social workers to use during assessments. These include the checklists based on the work of Mary Sheridan (*Assessing Children in Need and their Families: Practice Guidance* (DOH, 2000)). One of the critiques of many of the measures of child development, however, is that they have been developed in complex, affluent societies and are culturally specific. For example, identifying the point at which a child uses a spoon (*Assessing Children in Need and their Families: Practice Guidance*, at p 25) does not take account of the many cultures that have specific eating rules associated with the use of fingers and/or bread. Similarly children with a physical and/or learning impairment may develop at a different rate yet still acquire most major skills. The checklist of developmental tasks contained in government guidance (*Framework for the Assessment of Children in Need and their Families* (DOH, DfEE, Home Office, 2000), at p 3) identifies academic achievement as a suitable measure of development for children in middle childhood. As cited earlier, however, government research has consistently revealed that black children under-achieve academically due to racism endemic in the education system, not due to their own developmental incapacity.

3.26 Children do not develop uniformly or at the same rate throughout their childhood. What is very clear, however, is that developmental achievements, once acquired, are not lost unless the child experiences some difficulty. This may be organic, as in the case of illness, or emotional, such as a reaction to the birth of a sibling, or indicative of some form of child harm. The child's own developmental pattern, if closely monitored, will reveal whether difficulties are resolved, as the child will return to earlier developmental achievements and resume optimal growth, or whether the issues are chronic and long term.

3.27 Careful monitoring of any child experiencing a change of carer (from home to substitute care or vice versa), before, during and after placement, is one of the most revealing sources of information about a child's well-being. Any consideration of child abuse should draw on past as well as current information about a child's developmental profile. In recent years, routine child-health monitoring in some localities has been less comprehensive than in the past because of the disruptive impact of restructuring in the National Health Service and shortage of some key professionals such as Health Visitors. This issue will be discussed further in the next section of this chapter. Once concerns have been identified, child development monitoring becomes even more important and social workers and health visitors and other childcare workers are critical to the compilation of comprehensive and accurate data. Child development information does not become more accurate if gathered more frequently. Many of the measures, such as head circumference, only reveal patterns over long periods of time. What is crucial, however, is that there are no gaps in this information, particularly if a child moves from placement to placement. Without consistent assessment it will be difficult to identify the circumstances where a child's development first became concerning and the data will be less useful for evidential purposes.

Attachment

3.28 Attachment assessments are also very valuable aids to decision-making and attachment theory underpins the new *Framework for the Assessment of Children in Need and their Families* (DOH, DfEE, Home Office, 2000). In everyday language attachment means being fond of or loving someone, however attachment theory refers to a specific kind of relationship for a child which is essential for optimal development in childhood and psychological well-being in adulthood. Bowlby (1951), drawing on the work of animal behaviourists, drew the correlation between poor care in infancy and psychiatric ill-health in later life. His early work was criticised because of the concentration on 'maternal' care and the limits to the notion of 'bonding' between mother and baby. It was argued that women were thus held primarily responsible for the development of their children and fathers were excluded. However, Bowlby continued to develop his theories until his death. He acknowledged that the gender of the carer was unimportant, it was the consistency and quality of this primary early relationship that was critical.

3.29 His close colleague Mary Ainsworth undertook cross-cultural empirical work leading to an attachment assessment framework commonly used today by child psychologists, social workers and other childcare professionals (Howe, Brandon, Hinings and Schofield (1999)). One of the values of attachment theory, supporting its use in societies where family forms and cultures are diverse such as the UK, is that the observable attachment relationship types appear in all societies and cultures, although to different degrees. There are a number of ways of identifying the quality, and indeed existence, of a child's attachment relationship(s) and checklists proposed by Vera Fahlberg (see Fahlberg (1994)) which are commonly used by social workers, although the same caveat in relation to cultural specificity mentioned earlier with regard to developmental checklists, needs to be borne in mind.

3.30 The most damaging experience for a child is to be without attachment – either because that kind of relationship was never available or because the child experienced many changes of care-giver in their early years. In the former instance it is crucial the absence of an attachment relationship is identified as soon as possible to ensure good quality compensatory care can provide her or him with this critical emotional connection. Frequent moves from one carer to the other, as in the latter case, can be associated with changes of placement initiated by professionals. There appear to be two main reasons for this: either a placement breaks down because it was unsupported or inappropriate for the child, or a social worker, responding to the organisational definitions of placement type, decides the child is wrongly placed. For example, moving a child from short-term to long-term foster care may occur simply because of agency policy rather than responding to the quality of the relationship developed between carer and child:

> 'The [Children] Act reflects contemporary developments in psychological thinking about the importance of attachment relationships, and a recognition ... of the harmful effects on children of separation from their families. However, greater awareness ... of the deficiencies of the state as parent and the complexity of relationships between children, their birth parents and foster families led to the promulgation of "inclusive" and "task-centred" models of foster care, reflected in the shift of nomenclature from foster "parenting" to foster "caring". These approaches may, however, be in danger of minimizing both the attachment needs of many children and young people within the foster placement and the parenting role which is appropriate in many placements' (Wilson and Petrie (1998)).

3.31 Research shows that removing a child from an attachment relationship is always a loss for a child and produces reactions similar to the grief adults experience when bereaved. Children do not have the capacity to remain emotionally available to one attachment figure after another (Fahlberg (1994)).

3.32 The challenge in child protection is how to respond to those situations where child harm is feared or has taken place and where the child has some observable attachment relationship. In some instances this may be to the person who has abused them. Simply removing the child may not ensure the child's overall well-being is being promoted. Failure to remove the child may condemn them to a short life of pain and suffering. Gathering information from children themselves on all these matters is the cornerstone of good practice, not simply out of respect for children but because the more accurate the understanding of the child's perspective the more likely the resulting decisions will promote their welfare. Treating children respectfully also demonstrates the social behaviour children are urged to adopt towards others.

3.33 Although development and attachment have already been discussed, this does not imply that children should be passive subjects of assessment processes. No physical contact, examination or assessment of a child, however young, should take place without their meaningful participation and to the degree they wish. There are many ways that the non-verbal communication of small children can assist adults understand their needs and respond to these respectfully (David and Appell (2001)). Whatever assessments are taking place, ways of sharing the purpose and processes of these and creating as many choices for children as possible are essential.

Communicating with children

3.34 Guardians ad litem (now referred to as children's guardians) have been pioneers in developing ways of communicating with children of all ages. Guardians ad litem were only included in public law proceedings in 1984 despite their use in adoption proceedings since the Adoption Act of 1958. However, there had been a strong lobby for the appointment of independent social workers for children since the first major child abuse inquiry into the death of Maria Colwell in 1974 (Head 2002). One important part of the work of a guardian ad litem is understanding and interpreting a child's wishes and feelings:

> 'Most Gals have developed a wide repertoire of games, stories and toys to engage younger children and a variety of techniques to explore the feelings and views of older children. Some children, although young, can offer a sophisticated account of their history and family members as well as clear wishes of their own, whilst others can do little more than indicate where their feelings are very raw, or where they are strongly attracted to a particular person. Often children's behaviour is a more powerful indicator of their feelings than what they actually say' (Head (2002), at p 364).

3.35 Many childcare professionals now use these methods and approaches as a way of understanding the child's world and supporting their participation in decisions affecting their future. Such work developed because it was recognised that traditional interviews and statements did not enable children to explain their experiences meaningfully as they were denied their own communication medium of play. Controversy arose when interviews with children using play, particularly using sexually explicit dolls, were used for evidential purposes. The Criminal Justice Act 1991 permitted a child witness, in certain circumstances, to give their evidence-in-chief by means of a video-recorded interview. The *Memorandum of Good Practice* (*Memorandum of Good Practice on Videorecorded Interviews with Child Witnesses for Criminal Proceedings* (DOH, 1992)) set out a 'step-wise' approach to such interviews with a view to their admissibility in criminal proceedings. This has now been updated and the YCEA 1999 sets out a range of special measures. New guidance in relation to video interviews and supporting child and other vulnerable witnesses is contained in *Achieving the Best Evidence in Criminal Proceedings: Guidance for Vulnerable or Intimidated Witnesses, Including Children* (DOH, 2002 (see paras **9.183–9.188**)). If there are difficulties in obtaining sufficiently cogent evidence from a child through the use of these interviews, compliance with the Cleveland report guidelines, which stress the unacceptability of repeated interviews of children for evidential purposes, becomes critical. It is important that any interaction with vulnerable children is therapeutic, that is no further harm must be caused to the child and any intervention in place to assist the child deal with the consequences of abuse, should not be undermined (Furniss (1991)). Inevitably, if the immediate interests of the child are put first, criminal convictions may be more difficult to secure. Being able to understand accurately the child's position, however, does not mean abdicating the responsibility for making decisions about the child's welfare and placing the full weight on the shoulders of the child.

The family

3.36 The 'family' is the cornerstone of all current policy relating to child abuse, child protection and social exclusion:

> 'This government is committed to ensuring that we support families, especially in their parenting role, so as to give children the best start of life. We are committed to supporting families when they seek help, and before they reach crisis point, and to making the best use of scarce public resources' (Paul Boateng as Parliamentary Under-Secretary of State for Health cited in Parton (2002), at p 23).

3.37 One of the key principles of the CA 1989 is that, for the most part, unless it can be proved otherwise, a child is best cared for in her or his own family, with (ideally) both parents playing a full part in the child's upbringing and without resort to legal proceedings. The preferred family form, underpinning current policy, is the 'traditional' one of married female/male parents and children living in a single household (Burden, Cooper and Petrie (2000)). The notion of the 'traditional' family is one that is firmly embedded in welfare. It underpinned the Beveridgean Welfare State, which was founded on the assumption of a single income household with the male as breadwinner purchasing, through social insurance, State-provided 'cradle to the grave' services (Williams (1995)). Welfare in the 'mixed economy', a form of welfare organisation that has gradually replaced Welfare State provision since the NHS and Community Care Act 1990 (NHSCCA 1990), also relies on the 'traditional' family but this time as a first-line service-provider with State services being reserved for those without families or whose families are 'failing' to care for their own members. It has been argued that policies such as 'care in the community' initiated by the NHS and Community Care Act 1990 rely not on family care but on the unpaid labour of women (Langan (1995), at pp 67–91). The amount of care provided by children and young people within the family for disabled, ill or troubled parents is also causing concern (Deardon and Becker (2000)). However, both major parties identify the 'traditional' family as the most suitable family form for rearing children and promoting their welfare (Burden, Cooper and Petrie (2000)).

Changing family structure

3.38 Family structure has changed greatly since the end of the Second World War. Primarily this has been due to the increasing number of divorces, remarriages and cohabitations leading to what are commonly known as reconstituted or blended families, that is the remarriage or cohabitation of adults with children forming two families of step- and sometimes half-siblings. Another factor, however, has been the growing number of children living in 'lone' parent, usually lone mother, households (Ford and Millar (1998)). These changes have been identified by some commentators as indications of the demise of the 'family' and a major cause of social dysfunction. A welfare system that was too generous was held culpable for the downward trend in 'traditional' families:

> 'By 1994 rightwing attacks on welfare as a cause of "family" decline and the rise in social instability were ferocious. A report issued by the Adam Smith Institute called for a phased withdrawal of state responsibility for welfare on the grounds it was undermining the "family". Dr. David Marsland, one of the authors of the report, argued that state welfare "is rapidly destroying the family ... and thereby crippling children for life more reliably than "dark satanic mills" ' (the *Guardian*, 28 February 1994, cited in Burden Cooper and Petrie (2000), at p 250).

3.39 However, others have argued that changes in couple relationships and family groups are inevitable reflections of changes in the wider society:

> 'We are witnessing a renewed emphasis on the family as the one institution which *should not* change, even though it is taken for granted that everything else around the family is changing radically' (Smart (1997), at p 302 – original emphasis).

Possible reasons for changes in couple relationships, critical to the changes to family structures, are many. The remarriage rate in the seventeenth century was similar to that of today but made possible by death not divorce (James and Wilson (1986)). In more affluent societies, where the life expectancy of adults continues far beyond the maturation of family children, marriage as a permanent social institution may bring fewer benefits. Longer life expectancy, better health and greater equality between the sexes, combined with high expectations of inter-personal satisfaction within couple relationships suggests individuals are unlikely to remain in conflictful marriages if other choices are available to them.

3.40 Whilst research suggests that children who experience divorce are adversely affected, this correlates with the level of inter-personal conflict between the parents rather than the ending of the marriage (Rodgers and Pryor (1998)). In other words, it is not so much the parting of parents that adversely affects children but the degree of parental conflict before and after separation. Long-term adverse consequences are associated with subsequent conflict and poverty affecting many lone parent households (Ford and Millar (1998)). Social attitudes and responses to divorce can also have a negative impact on children. Non-traditional family forms, no longer a minority, are often identified in welfare policies and in practice as a family type that is second-rate and undesirable (Dominelli (1997)). This is particularly so for lone-mother households, especially black lone mothers, which attract a great deal of social disapproval (Song and Edwards (1997)). What is clear, however, is that unlike the notion of 'family' in policies, the ways in which parents and children live together are changing:

> 'The rise in lone parenthood has been one of the most striking demographic and social trends of the last 25 to 30 years. The growing social acceptance of a separation of sex, marriage and parenthood has created a situation in which lone parenthood is increasingly coming to be seen as another stage in the family life cycle, rather than as an aberration from "normal" family patterns. Not just in the UK, but throughout the western industrialised countries, much more diverse patterns of family structure are developing with more complex ties of family love, support, exchange, duty and obligation' (Ford and Millar (1997), at Box 1).

It is not surprising if welfare policies outlined earlier are at variance with family experience, that children living in non-traditional families absorb messages of social difference and undesirability – 'social exclusion'.

3.41 The adverse affects of parental conflict on children can occur outside situations of divorce or separation. Evidence shows there is a strong correlation between male violence in the home and child abuse (Hester and Pearson (1999)). Power differentials within the family have emerged time and time again in research and child abuse inquiries as important factors in the failure to protect a child suffering significant harm because of the reluctance of professionals to engage with a parent/carer who is violent, abusive and frightening:

'The Tyra Henry inquiry makes the point – it may sound absurd to talk now about involving Andrew Neil in planning for Tyra's well-being. The true starting point was not that he was a violent young man who had if possible to be kept away from Tyra. It was that he was Tyra Henry's father and, when not in custody, the regular boyfriend and near neighbour of Tyra's mother … [instead] the task … was invidiously left to Claudette and Beatrice Henry of warning Andrew Neil off ' (*Child Abuse. A Study of Inquiry Reports 1980–1989* (DOH, 1991), at p 82).

3.42 In order to work openly and effectively, social workers need the safety net of effective management and functioning organisations. Placing child abuse concerns on the agenda with potentially dangerous parents/carers requires planning around such issues as personnel, timing and venue and may have resource implications. As will be discussed later, organisational and managerial dysfunction has been a common factor in many of the child abuse inquiries where dangerous individuals were left unchallenged with dire consequences for the child.

The 'family' and poverty

3.43 The correlation between State intervention into families where children are suspected of suffering significant harm and poverty has been recognised by government (*Child Protection: Messages From Research*). The socio-economic context for families with children has deteriorated significantly since the first neo-liberal government headed by Margaret Thatcher in 1979. In the UK, the 1980s and 1990s saw a dramatic increase in poverty, particularly child poverty. By 1996 one-third of the total child population (over 4.3m children) were living in households with below half-average income compared with just 10 per cent of children in 1968 (Gregg, Harkness and Machin (2000)). Perhaps social concern with child abuse does not reflect social concern for children suffering avoidable harm but an unwillingness to take collective responsibility for harms done to children by parents or through poverty. Blame must be apportioned to an individual carer and/or professional. In other words there is social outrage over acts committed by parents or care-givers but no recognition of the harm done to children on a large scale as a result of social and welfare policies which have failed to ameliorate the savage impact of poverty on children.

3.44 However, the current government states its intention of reducing the impact of poverty, re-cast as social exclusion, on children:

'[T]he government is developing major strategies to tackle the root causes of poverty and social exclusion and to respond to the serious and multi-faceted problems for children and their families which these can create, particularly in the poorest areas. These strategies also aim to encourage and promote preventive and early intervention approaches to help reduce the scale and difficulty of such problems and tackle them before they become entrenched' (*Studies Informing the*

Framework for the Assessment of Children in Need and their Families (DOH, 2000), at
p 1).

3.45   Yet the social context in which these strategies are being developed is
very different from that at the height of welfare State provision. Since the
advent of the neo-liberals in 1979, and as policy of all subsequent
governments, there has been a move away from universal services of right,
with a high level of collective responsibility for all children through the
provision of free long-term services such as school meals and milk (Pratt
(1997)), at pp 196–213; Burden, Cooper and Petrie (2000)). Although the
welfare State was critiqued by the Left and the Right for failing to deliver truly
universal services on the one hand and cost effective welfare on the other
(Williams (1995)), there is ample evidence to show that the health and
development of poor children in the UK has been adversely affected by
increased deprivation that has arisen as the welfare State has declined
(Burden, Cooper and Petrie (2000)). The emphasis in the current mixed
economy of welfare is on individual responsibility and the State preventing
'welfare dependency' by targeting those with greatest needs and offering
mainly short-term services. As will be discussed later in this chapter, this may
have adverse consequences for children at risk of abuse.

3.46   Significant funding programmes through the *Quality Protects* (1998)
initiative have been made available by government to locality-based
'partnerships', between agencies in both sectors, statutory and independent, to
provide services aimed at poor parents and families. *Sure Start*, a cross-
departmental initiative to improve the health and welfare of children aged
under 4 and their families provides a range of services individualised to
localities that are available for children at risk of abuse, amongst others, in the
community. The expected outcomes are clearly identified.

> '– Gains in emotional and cognitive development for the child, and improved
>   parent–child relationships.
> – Improvements in health related indicators such as child physical development
>   and maternal health.
> – Improvements in educational process and outcomes for the child.
> – Increased economic self-sufficiency, initially for the parents and later for the
>   child through greater labour force participation, higher income and lower
>   welfare usage.
> – Reductions in criminality and teenage pregnancy.'

(Glass (1999), at p 262.)

The targets for *Sure Start* are very ambitious considering the piecemeal nature
of the services on offer, discussed more fully below.

The 'family' in practice

3.47   Changes to the way in which a 'child in need' (CA 1989, Pt III, s 17) is to be assessed have also been introduced by the government. The CA 1989 introduced the category of 'child in need' (to include those at risk of abuse) as the passport to state services. *Framework for the Assessment of Children in Need and their Families* (DOH, DfEE, Home Office, 2000), known as the *Lilac Book*, replaces the assessment framework previously issued (*Protecting Children. A Guide for Social Workers Undertaking a Comprehensive Assessment* (DOH, 1988)) (known as the *Orange Book*). Whilst the *Orange Book* focused on assessing risk to a child the *Lilac Book* has a wider purpose. The *Lilac Book* stresses the importance of identifying economic and environmental factors and that assessment should consider all 'children in need' not just children at risk of abuse. Professionals are directed to understand child abuse from a systemic perspective and such an ecological approach, as identified by Finkelhor et al (1986) in relation to child sexual abuse, is supported by most research (Sidebotham (2001)). However, the *Lilac Book* acknowledges that investigating whether or not a child has suffered or is at risk of suffering 'significant harm' (CA 1989, s 47) may take a different form, as recommended by *Working Together to Safeguard Children* (1999), and may be conducted simultaneously with the initial and/or core assessments outlined in the *Lilac Book*.

3.48   Although the guidance stresses the assessment framework should not be used as a checklist, the complexity of activities that may be conducted simultaneously (see the flow-chart in *Framework for the Assessment of Children in Need and Their Families*, op cit, at p 35), in the context of staff shortages and resource constraints discussed later, raises concerns that some children at risk may well be overlooked in a plethora of form-filling. For example, currently the 'Looked After Children' (LAC) forms require a minimum of 38 pages to be completed for each child within 5 days of coming into care. Whilst the desire to ensure all vulnerable children receive resources and services is laudable there is danger in conflating a number of variables into a simple causal relationship (Freeman (1999)). Recognising the 'last straw' contribution of economic pressure does not mean all poor parents do and affluent parents do not abuse their children. Professionals have at their disposal substantial research on aspects of child abuse and, as many inquiries have shown, children killed by their parents/carers are often known to child abuse agencies.

'The publication of *Messages from Research* by the Department of Health in 1995 was seen by many as representing a national policy shift in child protection towards more support for families and less intervention. What is needed is a balance between meeting needs and providing protection. In reality, the vast majority of families who are referred to social services are in need of help to parent their children and only a small minority of families should be categorised as dangerous. However, if the move towards supporting families rather than assessing risks goes too far, and if warning signs are consequently missed or ignored, the result for the child will be devastating' (Fitzgerald (2001), at p 93).

3.49 The 'family' is not only the cornerstone of policy but is also identified as the key change agent in child protection practice. Professionals are directed to work in 'partnership' with parents and other family members to promote the well-being of the child.

3.50 Partnership is a word that does not occur in statute and although it is referred to frequently in guidance, it is not defined (Petrie and Corby (2002), at pp 387–402). It has been argued that partnership implies some degree of power-sharing and that this is most difficult to achieve in the context of statutory child abuse interventions. One way of working openly with adult family members is through Family Group Conferences. Developed in New Zealand these are meetings where all members of the wider family, including the child, meet together with professionals to develop appropriate child protection plans. Research has shown (Marsh and Crow (1998)) that their limited use in the UK, despite acknowledgement in *Working Together to Safeguard Children* of their usefulness in some circumstances, is due to the reluctance of social workers to engage in the process:

> 'It seems that despite the rhetoric of refocusing, Social Workers found it difficult to relinquish the policing aspect of their role' (Bell (2002), at p 301).

This is perhaps hardly surprising considering the level of blame placed on individual social workers by the media and the public, despite the evidence in many child abuse inquiries of organisational dysfunction which will be discussed later (*Child Abuse. A Study of Inquiry Reports 1980–1989* (DOH, 1991)).

3.51 However, what constitutes a child's family? The individuals identified in law as forming a child's primary biological family may or may not be those adults with whom the child has a primary attachment relationship. Grandparents, step-parents, siblings, other family members, long-term partners, family friends and so on may all be very significant to the child and, in some instances, may have a stronger attachment relationship than the child's biological parents (Broad (2001)). Although the legal framework requires the identification and promotion of contact with the child's 'significant others', it is the perceptions of professional adults involved that are likely to be highly influential in the priority given to some relationships rather than others. Even if a child's attachment figure(s) and biological parents are the same there may still be difficulties maintaining attachment relationships for the child under the current contact arrangements.

3.52 Since the implementation of the CA 1989, local authorities have been required to 'promote contact' (CA 1989, Pt II, s 8) between the child and her or his parents or those with parental responsibility, rather than merely allow access as required under previous legislation. The change in nomenclature is important as it indicates that local authorities have to be proactive in maintaining attachment relationships for children and, as has been discussed earlier, these are critical to a child's optimal development. (For a detailed discussion, see Chapter **10** generally.) Contact between a child and her or his 'family' during court proceedings or when a child is subject to a care order (CA 1989, Pt IV, s 31) may well be supervised and observations of these meetings used for evidential purposes. Promoting contact has become a resource-heavy activity for local authorities. In the current climate of staff shortages and resource constraints, discussed below, contact can be supervised by unqualified, inexperienced workers with little knowledge or training in attachment assessments. Contact venues and content are sometimes unable to support purposeful child/parent interaction. Keeping children safe from alleged abusive parents/carers can often simply mean keeping them in view at all times. Such meetings can become solely time spent together without purpose and existing attachment relationships may weaken. In these circumstances, options for children, certainly in the longer term, may close down or be 'set up to fail'. Nothing of benefit to a child should ever be removed before something as good as or better is in place. Children do not have the capacity to stay on the 'back-burner' emotionally until the resources they need are prioritised.

The 'family' and preventive services: children's day care

3.53   Research shows that places in day care purchased by the State are used mainly for children at risk of 'significant harm' and both families and professionals identify children's day care as an extremely important support service. Day care is a common service for young children offered as part of a child protection plan (Statham, Dillon and Moss (2001)). Ideally, day care offers parents much-needed relief and informal advice on parenting skills from someone who knows their child well. The child should benefit from consistent care and stimulation and a trusting relationship with another adult. Day care should also ensure their development is carefully monitored. However, from the point of view of children there are a number of problems because professionals focus primarily on adult needs and places are often allocated on a short-term basis only:

> 'The objectives for children often took the form of expecting them to benefit from improvement in their parents' situation, rather than of seeing the provision of day care services as a way of promoting children's development and well-being' (Statham, Dillon and Moss (2001), at p 103).

3.54   As soon as family circumstances improve, places are withdrawn.

'They'll only pay for emergency [sic] and as soon as they think the family are climbing up the ladder a little bit then they stop the child coming' (Novak, Owen, Petrie and Sennett (1997), at p 14).

If circumstances deteriorate and a further placement is offered this is often with a different day-care provider because they are rarely paid to keep a place available for a child. Day-care providers are, in the main, women working in their own homes for very low rates of pay. In 1997 this was between £1.20 and £3.50 per hour per child (Statham, et al (2001)). Expecting such poorly resourced providers to undertake additional (usually) unpaid tasks associated with child protection, such as case conference attendance, and also to purchase training and supervision seems unreasonable. The child, however, whose well-being is supposed to be at the centre of child protection planning, receives fragmented and episodic services with little opportunity to develop consistent relationships (Novak, Owen, Petrie and Sennett (1997); Statham, Dillon and Moss (2001)). Furthermore it is difficult to monitor the ongoing development of such children since they will be potentially cared for by a number of different people during the course of any child protection plan. Day care is so expensive, the highest in Europe according to recent research by the Daycare Trust (the *Guardian*, 6 February 2002), that parents find the cost a tremendous burden whatever their circumstances, whatever financial assistance is received (Craig, Elliott-White, Kelsey and Petrie (1999)). The availability of this key support service is often, sadly, too little, too late.

3.55 During the last 20 years, it is clear that many families have been thrust into desperate economic situations the pressure of which may lead to child abuse. However, initially offering all assessed families preventive services, such as children's day care, based on this causal understanding discards the comprehensive child abuse research available to professionals. Child abuse of all kinds can be conceptualised as a spectrum. At one end are practices that are acceptable in some periods but not others, in the middle are the types of situational abuses that are unlikely to be repeated if appropriate services are available, even though harm to the child may be significant, and at the other end are the types of abusive acts that are sadistic and continuous. Research has shown that the most severely abused children suffer multiple abuse (*Child Abuse. A Study of Inquiry Reports 1980–1989* (DOH, 1991)). Families where children are living in the greatest harm may seem, initially, to be like most others:

'[Professionals have to] differentiate between those parents who, because of pressures of life, from time to time hit out at their children and those where the abuse is of a sadistic and continuous nature ... At the time these two kinds of families may not appear very differently from one another' (Bridge Child Care Consultancy Service (1991), at p 2).

Child abuse inquiries have highlighted many tragedies where focusing primarily on adult needs has abandoned children to serious harm and even death.

Organisations and management

3.56 The ability to protect children from abuse depends not only on the skills of individual workers but also on the effectiveness of the management and organisational structures of the agencies involved. Child abuse inquiries have consistently identified management issues as significant factors in the failure to protect those children who have died appallingly at the hands of their carers (*Child Abuse. A Study of Inquiry Reports 1980–1989* (HMSO, 1991)). Issues identified included unqualified and poorly supervised staff, a high turnover of staff, low morale, inadequate resources and the impact of organisational restructuring. Organisational dysfunction was identified by the Kimberley Carlile Inquiry (1987) as one reason for the failure of the health visiting service to respond to Kimberley's multiple bruises and scars, which were, according to the report, evident to the casual observer. Kimberley, aged 4½, died from a blow to her temple caused by her step-father and the report states it was clear she had been tortured and starved for many weeks before her death.

> '[T]he last six months of Kimberley's life unfortunately coincided with the delayed effect of the reorganisation of [the] National Health service in 1982. Case-loads of health visitors were heavy. The turnover of staff was high, and morale low. Inevitably, development of an effective service became stultified at a time when the number of child abuse cases calling for health visiting action was increasing' (Kimberley Carlile Inquiry, p 121 cited in *Child Abuse. A Study of Inquiry Reports 1980–1989* (DOH, 1991), at p 26).

3.57 Organisational and management failure have been identified as significant factors in many child abuse inquiries, and appears to be evident in the most recent inquiry into the death of Victoria Climbie (the *Guardian*, 4 December 2001). The change in recent decades from the welfare State to the mixed economy of welfare has, it can be argued, exacerbated the structural problems of child abuse agencies, particularly local authority social services departments.

The mixed economy of welfare

3.58 Social service departments of local authorities, charged in law with lead responsibility for the child abuse services, have changed their organisational culture and structure in the last decade. The impetus for this sea-change in public sector management was ideologically motivated and politically driven and was based on the theoretical premise that free markets deliver cost effective services that meet the demands of consumers. This was proposed initially by the neo-liberals under Margaret Thatcher and is now also the policy of New Labour (Burden, Cooper and Petrie (2000)). The change from welfare State provision to the mixed economy of welfare has been the most significant philosophical and organisational shift in welfare distribution since the establishment of the welfare State in 1948 (Jones and Novak (1999)). The mixed economy of welfare, which began with the NHSCCA 1990, has had far-reaching consequences for children's services, particularly child protection services.

3.59   Although the CA 1989 did not require the same changes in local authority structures or provision as were required by the NHSCCA 1990, the two Acts were designed to be 'consistent and complementary' (Stace and Tunstill (1990), at p 1). Adult services were required to separate the management of service assessment and service provision. In the decade since the implementation of both Acts it is evident that many local authorities have restructured their children's services to mirror those of adult services with a commissioning (purchasing) arm and providing arm (Petrie (1995)). For those authorities that have organised their children's services along purchaser/provider lines, each element is managed entirely separately until directorate level. Child protection services, for example, have often been placed in the commissioning arm and services such as fostering and residential care in the providing arm (Petrie and Wilson (1999)).

3.60   For children this inevitably means that those responsible for working with them during investigation and assessments are unlikely to be the same workers as those who will be responsible for permanency planning, whether that is to return to their family or to some form of substitute care. Although in previous structures there may well have been a change of worker if the child required long-term services, line-management would have remained the same. Currently managers within the same authority, working within devolved budgets and expected to meet performance targets, may be in active competition for resources to provide services for the same child albeit at a later stage of their care history. Welfare policy is also reducing the power of social services departments within local authorities. Some authorities are bringing together services such as housing, education and social services into one larger department. Single social services departments in local authorities have to compete for scarce resources with other hard-pressed departments such as education. The emerging statements given to the Victoria Climbie Inquiry suggest that organisational dysfunction and internal competition for resources were factors in the failure of agencies to protect this 8-year-old from abuse and death (the *Guardian*, 4 December 2001).

3.61   All child abuse inquiries have addressed the process of inter-agency collaboration. The DOH in *The Framework for the Assessment of Children in Need and their Families* clarifies why attention needs to be given to the way in which agencies such as health, social services, education, the police and independent sector work together:

> 'An important underlying principle of the approach to assessment in the Guidance, therefore, is that it is based on a [sic] inter-agency model in which it is not just social services departments which are the assessors and providers of services' (at p 14).

3.62 The NHSCCA 1990 required local authorities to spend a proportion of their budget for elders in the independent sector. The CA 1989 did not impose the same budgetary constraints on local authorities but directed them to 'enable' the provision of services by 'others' (Part III, s 17(5)(a)). As a result local authority direct provision for all service-user groups is reducing. Services such as residential care for children and specialist services such as child sexual abuse risk assessments and fostering schemes are being increasingly provided by the voluntary and commercial sectors (Petrie and Wilson (1999)). Some services, such as children's day care, have always been mainly provided by the commercial sector as has been outlined earlier (Novak, Owen, Petrie and Sennett (1997)). The growth in independent sector provision and reduction in local authority provision has increased the size and complexity of the multi-agency network and suggests inter-agency collaboration will become even more difficult to achieve. Differences in organisational culture, if not resolved, can undermine effective multi-agency work (see Laming Report, 2003).

3.63 In the Cleveland Inquiry (HMSO, 1988), for example, the primary issue was that agencies failed to work together and decisions were not child-centred. Many children had been abused and had been overlooked for some time because of the failure of statutory agencies to develop a joint approach to protecting children from child sexual abuse. The difference in organisational cultures between the police on the one hand and social services and the health authority on the other led to the most chaotic and damaging response to these children (Campbell (1988)). Currently, many of the government funding programmes for key preventive services such as *Sure Start* rely on agencies and workers who may have little specialist knowledge or experience of child abuse and will be offered little in the way of ongoing training or support. These agencies and providers are rarely funded to undertake the range of activities, such as attendance at case conferences, which involvement in child protection requires (Novak, Owen, Petrie and Sennett (1997)). There is some evidence to show, drawing on the experience of the independent welfare sector in the USA, that the mixed economy approach increases the administrative burden on small independent sector organisations to the detriment of their service provision (Gutch (1992); Hedley and Davis Smith (1994)).

3.64 The increase in the number and range of providing agencies has other possible adverse consequences for children. The purchase of services by a local authority from an independent sector organisation is a form of contracting. However, contracting within children's services has barely been recognised as such and children's services managers have had a great deal less preparation and training in contracting out than their counterparts in adult services (Petrie (1995)), and even then there is evidence to show that welfare contracts are problematical (Flynn and Hurley (1993)).

3.65 As far as placements for children are concerned, some local authority managers rely on the fact that provision is registered and inspected, as required by the Children Act 1989, to ensure suitability (Petrie (1995)). However, it is the provision that is registered and inspected to ensure minimum standards not the suitability of that placement for a particular child. Shortage of placements means that children, especially those with challenging behaviour, can be placed many miles from home. In the current climate of restricted local authority resources, the level of pre-placement selection and post-placement monitoring often barely meets statutory requirements and sometimes fails to meet those:

> 'Financial difficulties and overworked staff caused Brent council's child protection services to "unravel" in the months before child abuse victim Victoria Climbie was referred to it … The tight budget and necessary staff reorganisation left a department that was under "acute stress" and struggling to cope with the workload … Complex cases were not being allocated to experienced workers and there was inadequate training for locum social workers. Full-time staff were working long hours for little recognition and there was virtually no human resources department' (the *Guardian*, 18 October 2001).

3.66 Free market theory is based on the interplay of supply and demand. It is expected that provision will arise where there is none to meet unfilled demand and provision will fail if it does not meet the expectations of the consumer. It has been argued that the application of such theory to welfare is flawed (Le Grand (1990)) because markets are not true markets but 'quasi-markets': that is, the consumer (client, service-user) rarely has purchasing power particularly in children's services. The local authority may be purchasing services on behalf of a child and/or family who are not willing customers at all, especially when intervention by the State is compulsory. Despite the requirement for consultation with service users and involvement in service development and delivery it seems that families involved in child protection processes rarely feel they have much choice or control in the services they receive and therefore they are not experienced as helpful (Petrie and James (1995), at pp 313–333).

3.67 The organisational changes brought about by the advent of welfare markets have fundamentally changed the role of the welfare professional too. It has been argued that legislation requiring changes to local authority structures and role was politically motivated by a desire to reduce the power of local government and professionals:

'This complex of bureaucratic, professional and political power was identified by the new right in the 1970s as a major stumbling block to a radical reconstruction of the state and its role in British society. It is this which underpins the intensity of the attacks on all three modes of power represented by the welfare state. "Arrogant" professionals were arraigned alongside "inflexible" bureaucrats and "interfering" politicians as preventing efficient, effective and economic public services' (Newman and Clarke (1995), at p 23).

3.68 This perspective, arguably shared by New Labour, has led to the growth of the welfare manager at the expense, perhaps, of the welfare professional. Both left and right of the political spectrum have argued that professionals in health and welfare services have pursued self-interest at the expense of the consumer. Furthermore, professionals have held a great deal of power that has been difficult to challenge. Yet a recent DOH publication acknowledges that ultimately it is professional judgement that safeguards children:

'[D]espite increasing sophistication in the design and evaluation of risk assessment tools, the variables for assessing children in the context of their families are so complex that professional judgement underpinned by theory and research still remains the cornerstone of best practice (*Studies Informing the Framework for the Assessment of Children in Need and their Families* (DOH, 2000), at p 12).

3.69 Although the welfare manager may well be better placed than the welfare professional to support effective practice, it is also clear that safeguarding children's welfare is complex and depends on the judgement of self-confident and competent practitioners who are able to respond to the needs of the individual child.

3.70 The NHSCCA 1990 and the CA 1989 contained requirements for the greater transparency and accountability of local authorities in terms of their policy priorities and resource distribution. In addition government policy under New Labour has established a framework of performance criteria and related indicators for children's services that local authorities are now required to meet. The traditional management of professionals, with supervision being a reflective and supportive forum, has given way to management by performance indicators. Performance indicators are derived from the patterns observable at a macro level, for example projections that populations of a similar size and composition are likely to have a similar percentage of children suffering significant harm. However, as indicated earlier, there are dangers in confusing correlations with causalities. In any local authority area there may well be localised patterns of child harm that do not fit the expected average, for example the discovery of paedophile rings or murderers such as the West parents (Fitzgerald (2001), at pp 92–93).

3.71   Local authorities are judged and in part are allocated resources on the basis of the statistics contained in their MAPs. The DOH expects to see statistical evidence of outcomes for children as a result of the broader-based approach to 'children in need' recommended in policy. There are some indications that the current policy framework militates against competent professionals pursuing the interests of individual children as local authorities attempt to meet their performance targets with serious staffing and resource shortages. During the early stages of the Climbie Inquiry it was alleged by a senior social worker, since suspended, that the cases of children in his authority were closed immediately before a Social Services Inspectorate visit so the departmental statistics appeared more favourable (the *Guardian*, 9 October 2001).

3.72   This development has been called 'abstract management' (Townley, (2001)) carrying with it dangers that those involved lose sight of the true purpose of their activities:

> 'An abstract management system is where system wide controls take the place of a practitioner or self-control of quality. From an embodied practical evaluation that relates purpose, values and administrative systems, a bureaucratized system takes over the regulation of actions. And subtly the basis for identification with quality control changes. Accountability, the assurance that something is managed well … becomes transformed into audit' (at p 304).

3.73   Currently there is a national shortage of qualified social workers estimated at 40,000 (the *Guardian*, 30 March 2001). Plans are in place to increase their training to 3 years from 2003, to require programmes to work within a prescribed national curriculum, and to increase the number of trained social workers. Two new bodies, replacing the Central Council for Social Work Education and Training (CCETSW), have been established to regulate and oversee standards. These are the General Social Care Council (GSCC) and the Social Care Institute for Excellence (SCIE). Workers will be registered through a system similar to the present one for nurses administered by the GSCC from 2003. In addition to registration, social workers will be required to undertake mandatory post-qualifying training. In some local authorities this will link to promotion and appointment to specialist posts such as those working with child abuse. However, as indicated previously, many smaller agencies are now providing the services which children at risk of abuse and their families are likely to use. It remains to be seen whether these agencies will be able to afford to employ and support through post-qualifying training qualified social workers or train existing staff to the standard needed.

3.74 It is possible that in relation to child protection the UK will end up with a model similar to that in parts of the USA where the state provides surveillance and compulsory intervention services and specialist therapeutic services are provided by the voluntary sector, on a fairly hit and miss basis, for those who are unable to pay and by the commercial sector for those who can. In effect, a differential service for children based on their parents' socio-economic status.

Summary

3.75 Child protection has been a major part of policies and services for children during the last three decades. Comprehensive research during the same period has revealed a great deal about the manifestations and aetiology of many forms of child abuse in complex affluent societies. However, the notion of 'child' embedded in policies is constructed in part by socio-economic and cultural factors. The 'child' in policy varies from the passive victim of child abuse to the dangerous perpetrator of crime. Neither stereotype offers a helpful insight into the experiences of vulnerable children. Currently, harm perpetrated on children resulting from welfare policies, such as the situations of children who are homeless or asylum-seekers, causes less social concern than harm done to children by their care-givers. However, the well-being of any child can be ascertained if their individual perspective is identified through appropriate, respectful communication and comprehensive identification of their own patterns of development and attachment relationships.

3.76 Recent childcare policy has been influenced by government research showing many poor families were caught up in child abuse investigations inappropriately and received no services. Combined with concerns about harms suffered by children because of poverty this led to major changes in the assessment framework and service programmes for 'children in need' including children at risk of abuse. These initiatives have been designed to help local authorities 'refocus' resources to ensure more families in the community receive support. The context in which these changes are taking place is the 'market economy' of welfare. Legislation requires the role of local authorities as service-providers to diminish and their role in enabling provision of services by others to increase. As far as child abuse services are concerned this has increased the size and complexity of the multi-agency network and some agencies, by reason of funding, size and staffing levels and/or training, may not be able to recognise and respond appropriately to early indicators of child abuse. There are also signs that some local authority child protection services are failing because of structural, managerial and staffing pressures. The fragmentation of child abuse services and organisational pressures within the statutory sector may mean the extensive body of knowledge on the aetiology of all forms of child abuse may be dissipated. The inevitable consequence is that some children will be left unprotected.

Conclusion

3.77 At a time when the law for children is arguably the most child-centred it has ever been, the context for children has become less so. Combining intervention to reduce poverty, which affects many children, with systems designed to identify a small minority of children abused by their parents/carers, may mean all children are badly served. As has been outlined earlier, during the latter half of the twentieth century there has been a rise in non-traditional family forms including 'lone' parent families and 'blended' families. There has also been an enormous rise in poverty during the same period affecting children and their families, particularly non-traditional families, most severely. Current government policy promotes paid work as the way out of poverty for children and their parents. However, research has shown that economic and social pressure can lead to situational abuse of children if parents become overwhelmed with the many demands placed upon them. Supportive services, such as children's day care, are expensive for parents to purchase for themselves and if purchased by the State on their behalf are often short-term. Reducing child abuse occurring from situational stress requires a higher level of collective social responsibility and investment in all children than is currently promoted through policy. Parents and carers need free, good quality, comprehensive childcare services available merely because they have children and requiring no other assessment than that.

3.78 Children who are at greatest risk of abuse because of the pathological and continuous actions or omissions of their parents/carers must be identified as early as possible by anyone involved with children. This implies a higher level of vigilance from society as a whole (see Chapter **12**). Comprehensive knowledge about serious child abuse and its indicators must be accessible to a wider range of childcare agencies and workers than ever before. This implies an acceptance of a greater level of responsibility and engagement. For childcare agencies in general there are implications for increased training and supervision of staff. Issues of accountability will need to be negotiated as will the degree of risk society is prepared to accept. However, the investigation and assessment of child abuse requires knowledgeable, competent and confident professionals supported by a clear social mandate founded upon more benign attitudes towards children and young people. Making individual workers and agencies scapegoats for avoidable child harm, when the prevailing social climate for children is so hostile, cannot discharge collective responsibility.

CHAPTER 4

THE LEGAL FRAMEWORK

'The key message which the Government wishes to promote is a new emphasis on looking more widely at the needs of most vulnerable children and families in communities. Many of the families who find themselves caught up in the child protection system suffer from multiple disadvantages. They need help at an earlier stage to tackle their problems before parenting difficulties escalate into crisis or abuse. Assessment of the needs of children and families will be key to providing better targeted support ... However, the Government recognises that an effective child protection system will continue to be needed to deal with cases of abuse or neglect. There is commitment to reinforcing the best elements of the existing child protection system and no intention of destabilising those elements which work well' (*The Children Act Report 1995–1999* (DOH, 1999), at paras 3.10–3.11).

Introduction

4.1   It must be remembered that the provisions of the CA 1989, with their emphasis on partnership with parents to provide support for children in need, were enacted in November 1989 against the backdrop of the newly drawn UNCRC supported by the UK government, and in the context of increasing numbers of cases in the childcare arena being taken to the European Court in Strasbourg by dissatisfied parents or other family members. Increasingly, in the 1980s and 1990s, such family members relied on arguments put before the European Court that their basic human rights, as protected by the ECHR, had been breached as a result of deficiencies within the UK legal provisions. As was indicated in Chapter **1**, the implementation of the HRA 1998 on 2 October 2000, providing as it does that UK citizens can now rely on certain ECHR rights in UK court proceedings, means that special attention must now focus on the Articles of the ECHR of potential relevance in the fields of family support and family protection, and the ever increasing number of cases relying on breaches of such Articles under the ECHR, being reported in the *Family Law Reports* (now in excess of 175, see para **1.31**).

4.2   Whilst the UNCRC is, as was pointed out in Chapter **1**, the aspirant gold standard with which all States should seek to comply, the relevant ECHR Articles, as implemented by the HRA 1998, must be complied with by local authorities and all those acting on their behalf who work with children in need and their families. The importance in this field of the principles contained in the UNCRC and the ECHR is emphasised, as was pointed out in paras **1.2** and **1.31**, in the Preface to *Working Together to Safeguard Children: A Guide to Inter-Agency Working to Safeguard and Promote the Welfare of Children* (DOH, 1999), and in *Framework for the Assessment of Children in Need and their Families* (DOH, 2000), at p viii). Again, as was pointed out at para **1.2**, it should be noted that the latest pieces of guidance to emerge from the DOH put even greater emphasis on the UNCRC, as well as the ECHR, being considered to be part of the relevant legal framework in child protection (see particularly para 1.12 of *Safeguarding Children in Whom illness is Fabricated or Induced* (DOH, Welsh Assembly, 30 August 2002). Further, *Working Together to Safeguard Children* advises that its guidance takes account particularly of Articles 6 and 8 of the ECHR. These are worth setting out here since the DOH indicates that it has drawn up its guidance with these Articles in mind and also of course because all professionals working within this field must be aware of the precise details of both Articles 6 and 8. (For the importance of these and other Articles, see critically the judgment of the European Court in *Z v UK* [2001] 2 FLR 612.)

'*Article 6: Right to a fair trial*

1. In the determination of his civil rights and obligations or of any criminal charge against him, everyone is entitled to a fair and public hearing within a reasonable time by an independent and impartial tribunal established by law. Judgement shall be pronounced publicly but the press and public may be excluded from all or part of the trial in the interest of morals, public order or national security in a democratic society, where the interest of juveniles or the protection of the private life of the parties so require, or to the extent strictly necessary in the opinion of the court in special circumstances where publicity would prejudice the interests of justice.

2. Everyone charged with a criminal offence shall be presumed innocent until proved guilty according to law.

3. Everyone charged with a criminal offence has the following minimum rights:

(a)   to be informed promptly, in a language which he understands and in detail of the nature and cause of the accusation against him;

(b)   to have adequate time and facilities for the preparation of his defence;

(c)   to defend himself in person or through legal assistance of his own choosing, or if he has not sufficient means to pay for legal assistance, to be given it free where the interests of justice so require;

(d)   to examine or have examined witnesses against him and to obtain the attendance and examination of witnesses on his behalf under the same conditions as witnesses against him;

(e)   to have the free assistance of an interpreter if he cannot understand or speak the language used in court.

Article 8: Right to respect for private and family life

1. Everyone has the right to respect for his private and family life, his home and his correspondence.

2. There shall be no interference by a public authority with the exercise of his right except such as is in accordance with the law and is necessary in a democratic society in the interests of national security, public safety or the economic well-being of the country, for the prevention of disorder or crime, for the protection of health or morals, or for the protection of the rights and freedoms of others.'

4.3 *Working Together to Safeguard Children* further emphasises that the guidance takes account of other relevant legislation at the time of its publication, but 'is particularly informed by the requirements of the CA 1989 which provides a comprehensive framework for the care and protection of children'. As well as considering both the impact of the influential UNCRC and the now directly applicable relevant Articles of the ECHR, this chapter will examine the broad legal framework within which the provision of support to children in need as a result of the risk of abuse and the protection of actually or potentially abused children may be sought. Consideration will be given first to those measures which will allow those in personal social services for children to comply with the first of the eleven comprehensive and outcome-focused objectives laid down with the launch of the *Quality Protects* programme in September 1998 and as slightly amended and added to in November 1998 in the Social Services White Paper, *Modernising Social Services* (see *Quality Protects* (DOH, September 1998)) and *Modernising Social Services* (DOH, 1998).

4.4 The first of the eleven objectives is 'To ensure that children are securely attached to carers capable of providing safe and effective care for the duration of childhood'. In order to facilitate the provision of such safe and effective care by parents and families, consideration should be given to the provisions in the CA 1989, to safeguard and promote the welfare of children within the area of a local authority who are in need, and this chapter will therefore look in detail at the provisions in Pt III of the CA 1989. Given that relevant effective support systems may, however, fail, this chapter will also go on to consider those provisions which give social workers, NSPCC officers and, on occasions, police officers, the power to react to information concerning possible child abuse, to conduct investigations, to consider initiating emergency procedures, and to proceed in conjunction with other agencies (see Chapter **6**) in pursuing proceedings, whether these be criminal (see Chapter **9**) or civil proceedings (see Chapter **7**). The chapter will then, briefly, set out the position with regard to appeals (see further, Chapter **7**) and the making of complaints or representations, see further, Chapter **11**). These detailed legal provisions are designed to comply with the second of the comprehensive and outcome-focused objectives set down in the *Quality Protects* programme referred to above: 'To ensure that children are protected from emotional, physical, sexual abuse and neglect (significant harm)'.

4.5   It must be emphasised that provision of support through Pt III of the CA 1989 is intended to protect children. It will still, however, be the case that many children will suffer from emotional, physical, sexual abuse and neglect and then those working within the legal framework must step in to use the relevant legal provisions in order to prevent the continuing perpetration of the particular acts of abuse or neglect.

4.6   As such, this chapter will effectively constitute an outline overview of much of the remainder of this book, but it is also intended to describe the courts in which, if it is decided to proceed with formal legal action, such actions may be pursued. In doing so, it will again be necessary to consider the impact of Articles 6 and 8 of the ECHR. Finally, the position of the child who is made the subject of a care order is considered, since it is important to understand the local authority's statutory responsibilities towards children in their care. This is also of critical importance when one might be asked to consider the position of children abused whilst in the care of a local authority (see *People Like Us: Report of the Review of the Safeguards for Children Living Away from Home* (the Utting Report) (DOH, 1997); *Caring For Children Away From Home – Messages from Research* (DOH, 1998); and *Lost in Care: Report of the Tribunal on Enquiry into the Abuse of Children in Care in the Former County Council Areas of Gwynedd and Clwyd Since 1974* (the Waterhouse Report) (The Stationery Office, 2000)). In recognition of the fact that such abuse has indeed occurred, and pursuant to the various Inquiry Reports, the Government enacted the CSA 2000, to provide for a new, more rigorous and independent system of regulating and inspecting residential care settings generally, and has also published important new guidance entitled *Children's Homes – National Minimum Standards – Children's Homes Regulations* (DOH, 2002) (www.doh.gov.uk/nsc) (see also para **4.69**). Residential settings are not, however, the only locations in which potential abuse of children, being looked after by the care system, might flourish. It can also occur within foster placements also and the Government launched a major new Consultation in March 2002 entitled *Choice Protects* (see Chapter **1** and para **4.69**) which aims to look at improving the safeguards offered to children in foster families and other settings. In April 2002, the Government published *Fostering Services – National Minimum – Fostering Services Regulations* (DOH, 2002) in furtherance of this aim. In an effort to provide for some continuity and support in the lives of children, who may have been abused in any setting including their own families, and more generally for any child, who has formerly been looked after by a local authority or other organisation pursuant to the provisions of the CA 1989, the Government has also enacted the Children (Leaving Care) Act 2000, which is discussed briefly at para **4.80**.

The identification and support of children at risk of abuse

4.7 As *Working Together to Safeguard Children* puts it (see para 1.9): 'Effective measures to safeguard children should not been seen in isolation from the wider range of support and services available to meet the needs of children and families'. The guidance goes on to point out that:

> 'Many of the families, who become the subject of child protection concerns, suffer from multiple disadvantages. Providing services and support to children and families under stress may strengthen the capacity of parents to respond to the needs of their children before problems develop into abuse, and that child protection enquiries may reveal significant unmet needs for support and services among children and families.'

4.8 The provisions of Pt III of the CA 1989, taken together with Sch 2 to the Act, contain a list of wide-ranging duties, powers and responsibilities placed upon local authority social services departments in order to respond to the need to provide a whole variety of different support services.

4.9 Local authority social services departments are placed under a very wide duty by s 17 of the CA 1989 to safeguard and promote the welfare of children within their area who are in need; and, so far as is consistent with that duty, to promote the upbringing of such children by their families by providing a range and level of services appropriate to those children's needs. Pursuant to that, s 17(2) of the CA 1989 goes on to provide that for the purpose of facilitating the discharge of their general duties under s 17, local authorities must have specific regard to their duties and powers set out in the CA 1989, Sch 2, Pt I.

4.10 Under the CA 1989, Sch 2, Pt I, para 1, a duty is imposed upon local authorities to take reasonable steps to identify the extent to which there are children in need within their area and it is further provided that local authorities must publish information about services provided by them and by voluntary organisations, pursuant to their duties under Pt III of the CA 1989 and must take such steps as are reasonably practicable to ensure that those who might benefit from the services receive the information relevant to them.

4.11 A new para 1A was inserted into Sch 2, Pt I and took effect on 1 April 1996. This additional duty required all local authorities to review their provision of services under different parts of Pt III before 31 March 1997 and having regard to that review also to prepare and to publish a plan for the provision of services under Pt III. Such planning was supposed to take place in consultation with other agencies in order to lay the foundations for the development of services across agency boundaries. Study of the planning process both by the Social Services Inspectorate (*Partners in Planning* (DOH, 1998)) and the National Children's Bureau (*Children's Services Plans Analysing*

Need: Reallocating Resources (1998)) revealed that: local authorities were beginning to consider how the whole authority could improve the lot of children by lifting discussion above traditional agency boundaries; involving other agencies was difficult; users were seldom involved in the planning process; ethnic minority groups were under-recognised; and changing the type or range of services provided was a slow process. According to the *Children Act Report 1995–1999*, at para 1.8, the rapid development of a wide-ranging planning requirement, the recognition of the need for more coherence as a result of the work of the Social Exclusion Unit, and the clear requirements of better management information in response to the Health Select Committee's *Second Report on Children Looked After by Local Authorities* have led to a commitment to strengthen the planning process so as to increase its corporate and inter-agency effectiveness, and a drive to improve the use of management information through the *Quality Protects* programme.

4.12 As a result, therefore, both of the amendments to the CA 1989 and in response to the *Quality Protects* programme, local authority social services departments all over the country have published Children's Services Plans and Management Action Plans with regards to the provision of services to children in need. They have also now published a wide variety of information leaflets setting out details of those whom they regard as being 'in need' and what services are available to support the families of those children in need. In many of these leaflets, a high profile is given to the local authority's duty to safeguard children and it is made clear that children in need of protection will be given high priority for the provision of services. At this point, the definition of a 'child in need' as provided for in the CA 1989, s 17 will be considered.

4.13 Section 17 provides that it is the general duty of every local authority to safeguard and promote the welfare of children within their area who are 'in need' and 'so far as is consistent with that duty, to promote the upbringing of such children by their families, by providing a range and level of services appropriate to those children's needs'. Schedule 2, Pt I, para 1 requires the local authority to take reasonable steps to identify the extent to which there are children in need within their area, for whom they must make the plans for the delivery of services just described. Section 17(10) provides that for these purposes a child shall be taken to be in need if:

'(a) he is unlikely to achieve or maintain, or to have the opportunity of achieving or maintaining a reasonable standard of health or development without the provision for him of services by a local authority under this Part;

(b) his health or development is likely to be significantly impaired, or further impaired, without the provision for him of such services; or

(c) he is disabled',

and 'family' in relation to such a child, includes any person who has parental responsibility for the child and any other person with whom he has been living.

4.14 Section 17(11) goes on to define what is meant by the term 'disabled' in s 17(10). Thus it provides that 'a child is disabled if he is blind, deaf or dumb or suffers from mental disorder of any kind or is substantially or permanently handicapped by illness, injury or congenital deformity or such other disability as may be prescribed' and the subsection continues with provisions which correspond to those contained in s 31(9) of the CA 1989, which define what is meant by 'harm' for the purposes of care or supervision order proceedings. Thus both for the purposes of defining a 'child in need' in s 17(10) and (11) and for the purposes of s 31(9), 'development' means physical, intellectual, emotional, social or behavioural development; and 'health' means physical or mental health. The fact that there is a linkage between these two sets of provisions is no accident since, as has been noted, there is a very strong duty placed upon the local authority to safeguard children. This has been further reinforced and emphasised by the second objective in the *Quality Protects* programme and also in the *Children Act Report 1995–1999*, at paras 1.18 and 1.20.

4.15 The CA 1989 itself provided reinforcement of the safeguarding approach set out in s 17(1) in that para 4 of Sch 2 provided that local authorities must take reasonable steps, through the provision of services under Pt III of the Act, to prevent children within their area suffering ill-treatment or neglect. Further reinforcement of the local authority's duty to safeguard is provided by Sch 2, para 7, which requires local authorities to take reasonable steps designed to reduce the need to bring care or supervision order proceedings with respect to children in their area. As if to emphasise the point that children who abuse are, potentially, equally to be viewed as children in need as those children who are abused, the local authority is also required to take reasonable steps designed to reduce the need to bring criminal proceedings against children within its area and to take reasonable steps designed to encourage children within its area not to commit criminal offences (CA 1989, Sch 2, para 7(a) and (b)).

4.16 The methods by which local authorities establish which children require safeguarding services will depend upon the measures laid down for inter-agency collaboration in the identification process by local ACPCs pursuant to the guidance provided in *Working Together to Safeguard Children*, paras 1.10, 1.11:

> 'Promoting children's well being and safeguarding them from significant harm depends crucially upon effective information sharing, collaboration and understanding between agencies and professionals. Constructive relationships between individual workers need to be supported by a strong lead from elected or appointed authority members, and the commitment of these officers. At the strategic level, agencies and professionals need to work in partnership with each

other and with service users, to plan comprehensive and co-ordinated children's services. Individual children, especially some of the most vulnerable children and those at greater risk of social exclusion will need co-ordinated help from health, education, social services and quite possibly the voluntary sector and other agencies, including the Youth Justice Services. For those children who are suffering, or at risk of suffering significant harm, joint working is essential to safeguard the children and – where necessary – to help bring to justice the perpetrators of crimes against children' (paras 1.10–1.13).

4.17   As well as acknowledging that good practice calls for effective co-operation between different agencies and professionals working with parents and carers in order to achieve what is in the best interest of the children, the DOH, the DfEE and the Home Office have combined to produce the very important guidance on the *Framework for the Assessment of Children in Need and their Families* (April 2000) (Welsh Assembly, 2001). Through its emphasis on joint integrated working and planning, it is clear that central government is determined that local government should take very seriously its duty to safeguard the welfare of children in need within its area. This has now been taken even further with the announcement made in September 2002 by John Denham, the Minister for Young People that new local plans were to be put in place across England to support all children and young people at risk. The Minister stated that:

'Too many children fail to achieve their full potential and face involvement in crime, poor health, early unwanted pregnancies, substance misuse, or under-achievement in education, because we fail to stop the emerging risks or to intervene early enough to co-ordiante the support necessary. We know that factors such as poverty, failure at school, family problems or anti-social behaviour can each be possible indicators of future problems. Yet all the research and front-line experience studied in the *Cross Cutting Review of Children at Risk for the 2002 Spending Review* shows that we can do more to harness the contribution of mainstream services for education, social care, health, and criminal justice to support children during difficult periods in their lives. We will therefore be asking Local Authority Chief Executives to take the lead to ensure that all those responsible for relevant services are involved in agreeing a local preventative strategy, setting out their contributions to improving services for all children at risk. We expect health bodies, the police, the probation service, youth offending teams and the voluntary sector to be involved in the strategy. The development of local strategies will be supported by Government Offices and the inspectorates who, where necessary, will work with the local partners on ensuring that an effective strategy is in place.'

In many local authority areas, responsibilty for delivering on this new preventive strategy has landed straight into the laps of social services directors and their assistants, ironically at a time when the Joint Inspectorate report *Safeguarding Children* (DOH, 14 October 2002) (www.doh.gov.uk/ssi/childrensafeguardsjoint/html) has identified that a significant number of such services and their staff cannot deleiver on existing social services preventative duties laid down under the CA 1989 and are engaging in high risk work only. This report identifies (see Chapter **12**) areas of the service under acute stress and strain as a result of a shortage of human as well as economic resource so that one wonders how a service which is not currently performing its own preventative role can or should be coordinating a local strategy, thus putting even more strain on the scarce available resource. The Minister stated that 'essential parts of the strategy will be effective systems to identify children and families needing support, to exchange information between agencies and track the progress through agency referrals'. Yet all of this already exists. What is lacking is the personnel to deliver on the existing systems and strategies to engage in the information exchange arrangements and, most crucially, to engage in the necessary preventative work as required by the CA 1989. As well as requiring the establishment of this 'new' effective preventative strategy, the Minister confirmed that, as announced in the Treasury White Paper on the Spending Review published in July 2002, the Government also intends to pilot new organisational models for managing children's services known as Children's Trusts. Thus, instead of ensuring that the current systems are properly resourced and operating according to the plethora of central guidance we are now going to divert crucial attention away from that to the creation of new management tool. When will governments realise that it is not more or different management techniques that are needed but people to do the work on the ground? How much money and time which could have been spent on providing the much needed support for the mainstream services to children and their families is going to be wasted on designing and piloting the new Children's Trusts? It is not surprising that a certain amount of the critical support work for children and families is now being provided by short-term projects supported by such schemes as 'Sure Start' and the 'Children's Fund'. These are not mainstream services, however, and staff are often untrained and have short-term appointments. Crucially, this approach also means that some of the very rewarding work, which social workers could once engage in to make them feel as though they were making the difference they had wanted to make by choosing a career in social work, has now gone elsewhere and they are left with in the words of one of the social workers interviewed by Chris Jones, 'firefighting' (see further, Chapter **12**).

4.18　Other prevention measures can also be identified within the now amended provisions of the CA 1989. These include the provision in s 17(3) that any service provided by an authority in the exercise of its functions may be provided for the family of a particular child in need or *for any member of his family*, if it is provided with a view to safeguarding or promoting the child's welfare. It is important to realise that where an abused child is suffering at the hands of a family member, whether this is a parent, an older sibling or some other relative living in the family (see *Child Maltreatment in the United Kingdom* (NSPCC, 2000)), it may be the case that the local authority will seek to provide services to those family members in order to attempt to safeguard the child who has been abused.

4.19 Where it is felt desirable that an abusing member of the family should move out of the family home but the grounds may not be such as to satisfy those provided for in the new s 44A or s 38A, the provisions of Sch 2, para 5 could be used to encourage an alleged perpetrator to move out of the premises and to provide accommodation for him or her. This will demand the co-operation of the perpetrator and where one is considering the case of child perpetrators, who may well have been abused themselves, it may be more appropriate to consider the provision of accommodation under s 20 of the CA 1989, together with other necessary services such as psychiatric, psychological or social work assessment. The use of both the provision of accommodation under s 20 and other support services for such children will, of course, depend upon the level of co-operative partnership achieved between parents and workers. The results of many research studies brought together in *Child Protection: Messages from Research* (DOH, 1995) emphasise the critical importance of good partnership-style relationships between professionals and families in helping to bring about the best possible outcomes for children. In those situations where the risk presented to the child is such that the court has been prepared to issue an exclusion order under the provisions of the CA 1989, ss 44A or 38A or in those situations where police action has resulted in the removal of either an adult or child perpetrator, the necessity to use the provisions of s 20 or Sch 2, para 5 will be removed, either by the making of the exclusion order or, alternatively, by the imposition of bail conditions in respect of an adult perpetrator or in a remand to local authority accommodation in the case of a child perpetrator.

4.20 Given that the overriding philosophy in the CA 1989, and in successive documents of guidance and government support programmes, is that children are best brought up by their families, the provision of services under s 17 and Sch 2, as supplemented by the *Quality Protects* objective in order to prevent children suffering from or perpetrating abuse, is clearly the most desirable policy. The duty to safeguard and the powers and duties provided pursuant to it are examined in greater detail in Chapter 5 and are generally referred to as 'preventive statutory measures'. The main problem with regard to the achievement of the goal of prevention is that it depends upon available resources which, for a period of some 10 years following the implementation of the CA 1989, continued to be felt to be in very short supply. Despite sums of money being made available under such programmes as *Quality Protects*, and much more recently through the new Children's Fund administered by the Minister for Young People, concerns persist that the relevant financial resources, which should have been made available when the CA 1989 was first implemented in October 1991, have still not materialised.

4.21   The whole idea behind these preventive measures contained in the Act and highlighted in *Working Together to Safeguard Children*, whether these result in services being provided by local authorities, social services, health, education or voluntary organisations, is to improve the lot of families under stress so that the potential for child abuse is diminished, if not totally eroded. Whilst recognising that there are many factors which contribute to stress in families, such as: social exclusion; domestic violence; the mental illness of a parent or carer and drugs and alcohol misuse by a parent or carer; the DOH's own *Child Protection: Messages from Research* (1995) also revealed extremely important stress factors emerging as a result of the operation of child protection processes themselves. Thus, some important themes emerged about the operation of child protection processes, which revealed an insufficient focus on outcomes for the child and the lack of appropriate investment in sufficient time and resources across all relevant agencies in planning and implementing intervention to safeguard and promote the welfare of children at continuing risk of significant harm. In *Working Together to Safeguard Children*, therefore, it is recommended that professionals should be aiming for good long-term outcomes in terms of health, development and educational achievement for children about whom there are child protection concerns (at para 2.26). The guidance also usefully points out that many families feel that revealing their problems will lead to punitive reactions by service providers. It thus recommends that professionals should promote a positive but realistic image of services to encourage and enable people to gain access to the help and advice they need. The guidance points out that families need information on how to gain access to services and what to expect if and when they approach services for help. It is quite clear that the thrust of *Child Protection: Messages from Research* and the guidance set out in *Working Together to Safeguard Children* (chapter 2) is that in those cases where negative issues are focused upon too soon or too narrowly then much less positive outcomes for the children were the result. Again, however, *Working Together to Safeguard Children* is based upon the notion that it is possible to provide all children who might be in need with the relevant preventive services. Whilst it has to be admitted in the words of the old adage that 'prevention is better than cure', nevertheless it also has to be recognised that those working in social services face a very wide range of problems associated with inadequate resources being made available to them, not the least of which is the inadequacy of the number of social workers (see Chapter 12).

The identification and investigation of suspected child abuse

4.22   Under the CA 1989, s 47, a local authority is under a duty to investigate whenever it is provided with information which may suggest that a child living or found within its area is suffering, or is likely to suffer, significant harm or where it is informed that a child is the subject of an emergency protection order or is in police protection. Where information is passed on to the

NSPCC, a local authority may also undertake appropriate enquiries and investigations (see s 44(1)(c) and s 31(9) generally). To undertake such investigations the local authority is required to consult with a range of other agencies to enable it to decide what action it should take to safeguard or promote the child's welfare. The local authority social services may also request other agencies to assist them in such enquiries with investigations. As *Working Together to Safeguard Children* points out, the *Framework for the Assessment of Children in Need and their Families* is equally relevant in these circumstances as a structured framework for collecting, drawing together and analysing available information about a child and family. It will help provide sound evidence on which to base often difficult professional judgements about whether to intervene to safeguard a child and promote his or her welfare and, if so, how best to do so and with what intended outcomes (*Working Together to Safeguard Children*, at para 5.22). These various processes are described in further detail in Chapters 5 and 6.

Consideration of legal action

4.23 Where any situation involves an immediate threat to the life of a child or the possibility of serious immediate harm, then any of the agencies with statutory child protection powers, ie the local authority, the police and the NSPCC, should act quickly in order immediately to safeguard the child. Emergency action such as the use of CA 1989, s 44 emergency protection orders or s 46 police powers may be necessary as soon as any information is received or at any stage of involvement with children and families. As *Working Together to Safeguard Children* notes, however, the need for emergency action may become apparent only over time as more is learned about the circumstances of a child or children. It is also critically important to appreciate that if any agency is considering taking emergency action, it should always consider whether action is also necessary to protect other children in the same household (eg older or younger brothers or sisters), in the household of an alleged perpetrator, or elsewhere (see *Working Together to Safeguard Children*, at para 5.23). If it is felt necessary to take planned emergency action then this would normally only proceed after emergency strategy discussions between social services, the police and any other appropriate agencies. In those circumstances, where emergency action has had to be taken by the one agency without such a strategy discussion, then this should be held as soon as possible thereafter in order properly to provide and plan for the next steps to be taken in relation to the child or children at the centre of concerns. Such strategy discussions may also arise where there have been services provided by a range of agencies or by one in particular and concerns about significant harm occurring to the child emerge as a result of services being provided to the family. In such circumstances the criteria for initiating s 47 enquiries are met and the *Framework for the Assessment of Children in Need and their Families* states that the following questions should be addressed.

- What are the needs of the child?
- Are the parents able to respond appropriately to the child's needs?
- Is the child being adequately safeguarded from significant harm, and are the parents able to promote the child's health and development?
- Is action required to safeguard and promote the child's welfare?

4.24 At this stage of the process of initial assessment, the relevant professionals should be speaking to the child (according to age and understanding) and family members as appropriate; drawing together and analysing available information from a range of sources (including existing records); and obtaining relevant information from professionals and others in contact with the child and family. All relevant information (including historical information) should be taken into account from seeing and speaking (see *Working Together to Safeguard Children*, at para 5.14).

4.25 Where an initial assessment has taken place, then social services need to determine whether further steps should be taken and according to *Working Together to Safeguard Children*, the family, the original referrer and other professionals and services involved in the assessment should as far as possible be told what action will be taken consistent with respecting the confidentiality of the child and the family concerned and also so as not to jeopardise further action in respect of child protection concerns, which may also of course include police investigations (*Working Together to Safeguard Children*, at para 5.17).

4.26 Where the initial assessment has revealed that further legal steps under CA 1989, Pt IV or Pt V are not required, but instead that services should be provided under the legal provisions set out in Pt III, then the clear conclusion is that no suggested actual or likely significant harm has occurred to the child and that services can therefore be provided under Pt III. In such circumstances the *Framework for the Assessment of Children in Need and their Families* lays downs a framework (at paras 3.11–3.12 and 3.15–3.19) for the core assessment of a child's health and development, and the parents' ability to respond to their child's needs. Such a core assessment should provide a reliable evidential base upon which to base professional judgements as to which services would be most beneficial to a child and his or her family, and where such is the case, on the types of service which are most likely to bring about the best outcome for the child in the family. *Working Together to Safeguard Children* provides detailed guidance with regard to the suggestion that Family Group Conferences could be an effective vehicle for taking forward work in such cases (paras 7.13–7.18).

4.27 Following on from any relevant strategy discussions, s 47 enquiries and police investigations, as well as any relevant emergency action, the various agencies involved with the child and the family may, after sharing all the relevant information, conclude that the child is not at risk of further significant harm, which may be because the perpetrator of the abuse has permanently left the family home or that the parents and other family members are ready and able to co-operate together to ensure that the child will not be at any future risk. Nevertheless, careful consideration should be given to the need of the child or children for therapy, and any relevant family services plan would need to be informed by the findings of the core assessment. Any resulting plan should set out the responsibilities of the various parties including the service providers and should also seek to provide for any necessary action to be followed if adherence to the plan is not continued. As with any plan of this nature, a timetable should be set for the purposes of considering the progress made against the relevant intended outcomes.

4.28 Where at the conclusion of the s 47 enquiries, which may run concurrently with police investigations concerning potential crimes arising out of the same facts, and at the conclusion of the core assessment, it is the view that a child has suffered significant harm, or is at risk of being likely to so suffer, then the social services department should convene a child protection conference (see *Working Together to Safeguard Children*, at para 5.52). The principal purpose of the child protection conference is to gather together those professionals who have been most closely involved with the child and the family throughout the relevant investigations and assessments, together with the family themselves, in order to assess all the relevant information, and to determine on a plan as to how best to safeguard the child and promote his or her welfare. This is considered in further detail in Chapter **5**. As well as assessing all the relevant information, including the parents' ability to look after their child, and making judgements about the possibility of the child suffering further significant harm, its function is also to decide on further relevant steps, which may be needed in order to ensure the protection of the child. Where the conference concludes that a child is at continuing risk of significant harm, then the initial child protection conference needs to consider whether it is going to exercise its only decision-making power which is the decision to place the child on the local Child Protection Register and then in conjunction with this to formulate a child protection plan or, alternatively, if the circumstances require it, to consider whether or not to recommend to social services that further legal action may be required under Pt V of the CA 1989 (the taking of emergency protection orders or child assessment orders) or, alternatively, whether the situation is such that the conference will be recommending the pursuit of care or supervision order proceedings under the provisions of the CA 1989, Pt IV.

4.29 Where the child protection conference exercises its power to place a child on the local Child Protection Register, it is required by *Working Together to Safeguard Children* to agree also on the terms of a formal child protection plan.

It is considered to be the role of the initial child protection conference to formulate the outline child protection plan in as much detail as is possible. Where the decision is taken that the child should be registered and a protection plan provided, the Chair of the child protection conference should then determine the category of abuse against which the child's name should be registered. The importance of this is that the category used on registration, namely physical, emotional, sexual abuse or neglect, will indicate to those consulting the register at any later stage what were the primary concerns at the time of initial registration of the child. It should be noted here that the Chair of the child protection conference must be careful to ensure compliance with the provisions of Article 6 of the ECHR in the way in which the conference deals with the parents or with any adult who the conference may be considering placing on the adult section of the Child Protection Register (for more detail on this, see Chapter 11). The importance of the plan lies in the fact that mere registration alone confers no protection on the child of itself and what is needed is an agreement by all the relevant agencies concerned, together with the family, that they should work in partnership to ensure that the child will be safeguarded from any future harm. *Working Together to Safeguard Children* lays down therefore that the specific tasks to be included in the plan relate to such issues as the appointment of a key worker, the identification of the core group of professionals and family members, the laying down of timetables for meetings of the group and outlining a child protection plan, especially identifying what needs to change in order to safeguard the child.

4.30 Where the child protection conference has agreed on registration then, as indicated above, it must provide for the appointment of a key worker. The key worker must be a social worker from either the social services department or the NSPCC (see *Working Together to Safeguard Children*, at para 5.75). Without such a key worker who is responsible for ensuring that the outlined child protection plan is developed in a more detailed inter-agency plan, putting the child's name on the Child Protection Register would be a fruitless exercise and *Working Together to Safeguard Children* emphasises that 'each child placed on the Child Protection Register should have a named key worker'. The key worker has a range of responsibilities including that of ensuring the development of the outline plan into a more detailed inter-agency plan; the completion of the core assessment of the child and the family; the fulfilment of the role of lead worker for the inter-agency work with the child and the family; the co-ordination of the various contributions to the plan; and the reviewing of progress against the objectives set out in the plan. The role of the core group, referred to above, in further developing the child protection plan is critical and as *Working Together to Safeguard Children* emphasises, core groups are an important forum for working with parents, wider family members, and children of sufficient age and understanding. The guidance points out that:

'it can often be difficult for parents to agree to a child protection plan within the confines of a formal conference. Their agreement may be forged later when details of the plan are worked out in the core group. Sometimes there may be conflicts of interest between family members who have a relevant interest in the work of the core group. The child's best interest should always have precedence over the interest of other family members' (para 5.78).

4.31 Within 3 months of the initial child protection conference, a first child protection review conference should be held and then further reviews should be conducted at regular intervals of not more than 6 months apart for as long as the child's name continues to be on the Child Protection Register. Figures released by Health Minister, John Hutton, in the week beginning 12 October 2000 relating to the second annual performance assessment framework, revealed that only 19 per cent of local authorities reviewed all necessary cases in the year 1999. The Health Minister conceded that staff shortages in social services departments could be a significant factor in the failure of 80 per cent of the 150 local authorities to review all child protection cases. It appears, however, that the Minister insisted that social services directors were told to meet the 6-monthly review of all 'at-risk' children despite the pressures on their departments. He stated that 'we are saying to social services directors that we have got to focus on this'. Given the appalling shortages it is perhaps surprising that central government appears not to realise, yet again, the catastrophic gap in the available resources for such work, not purely in financial but also in human resource terms (see further, Chapter **12**).

4.32 Whilst the decision to register a child and formulate a child protection plan is a formal process, it is nevertheless the case that in the same way as with more informal social work involvement and provision of services, where things go wrong or emergencies intervene, consideration will have to be given to more formal legal action. In certain cases, the recommendation of the child protection conference may be that formal court action is immediately required.

Criminal proceedings

4.33 Where a child has been abused the police, who will have been involved at every stage of the investigation, assessment and child protection conference process, may wish to consider bringing criminal proceedings in the criminal courts. (For much greater detail on this, see Chapter **9**.) The suspected abuser will have to have been charged, consideration given to bail or to remand in custody or local authority accommodation in the case of a child perpetrator, and the case handed over to the Crown Prosecution Service (CPS). The onus will be on the CPS to determine whether there is sufficient evidence to take the case forward and whether it is in the public interest to do so. (See *Code for Crown Prosecutors* (CPS), June 1994, Pt 6.)

4.34 In addition, it must be remembered that the CPS will wish to satisfy itself that there is evidence sufficient to suggest that a jury is likely to be satisfied, beyond reasonable doubt, that the person charged has committed the offence. In order to satisfy itself that evidence of sufficient quality is available to go before a jury in any particular case, the CPS will wish to look at the video-recordings of the testimony and cross-examination of any child witnesses compiled in accordance with the provisions of the Criminal Justice Acts 1988–1991, as further amended by the Criminal Justice and Public Order Act 1994 (CJPOA 1999), and the provisions in the YJCEA 1999, Pt 2 (implemented 24 July 2002). (See also the new Guidance for Interviewing Children, *Achieving the Best Evidence in Criminal Proceedings: Guidance for Vulnerable or Intimidated Witnesses, Including Children* (DOH, National Assembly for Wales, 17 July 2002) which replaces the former *Memorandum of Good Practice on Video Recorded Interviews with Child Witnesses for Criminal Proceedings* (DOH, 1992) and the Crown Court (Amendment) Rules 1992.) (For more detail on this, see Chapter **9**.) The newly published Guidance takes on board many of the relevant and justified criticisms which were made of the old version of the *Memorandum* (see *Interviewing Child Witnesses under the Memorandum of Good Practice: A Research Review* (Home Office, 1999)).

4.35 Where a child is to give evidence by means of participation in the proceedings through a live television link (Criminal Justice Act 1988 (CJA 1988), s 32), the CPS may wish to determine whether the child is likely to be able to withstand cross-examination in such difficult cases. A number of preparation programmes for child witnesses are now in place run by the Victims Support Unit and other groups and these have clearly played a key part in prompting the CPS to feel more confident that a child may be able to endure the court process and be able to give evidence without breaking down.

4.36 The CPS, as a result of viewing the pre-recorded interview and pre-recorded cross-examination, or as a result of considering the nature of the evidence to be given by the child, may have very considerable concerns about proceeding with the case. It is for this reason that there may be occasions (which might be frustrating to individual police officers) where the CPS decides that, while the evidence gathered may be sufficient to justify the taking of civil care proceedings in respect of the child (where a lesser burden of proof has to be satisfied), it is nevertheless insufficient to justify the continuation of criminal proceedings. It should be noted that the reason it may be possible to pursue civil proceedings is that the conditions precedent for the taking of care proceedings do not look to the guilt of any one particular named individual, but rather to the fact that a child has suffered or is likely to suffer significant harm and that this is due to or likely to be due to the inadequacy of the care or control offered to the child in whichever setting the abuse has occurred. (See especially on this *Lancashire County Council v B*

[2000] 1 FLR 583, HL.) Care proceedings, therefore, are not in that sense focused upon the 'guilt' of particular individuals.

4.37 In addition, the CPS must also have regard to the status of the witnesses. Thus, if the only evidence available is that of a small child, uncorroborated by any other material evidence or witness, then, despite the fact that there is a good quality video-recording of the child's testimony which could be put before the court, the CPS may, nevertheless, be reluctant to recommend that a criminal case should be taken any further. (This is further explained in Chapter **9**.) Thus, even where someone has originally been charged with a criminal offence, whether it is a child or an adult, that charge ultimately may not be proceeded with on the direction of the CPS. Indeed, it may even have been the case that it was the police who were initially involved in the case, with an incident attracting police attention, resulting in the removal of the child victim temporarily to a police station under police powers of protection provided by the CA 1989, s 46. The police would then notify the social services (provided they are available for contact) that they were holding the child with regard to the likelihood of an offence having been committed against the child and that the child was to be examined by a police surgeon. (This is considered in more detail in Chapter **5**.)

4.38 The position with regard to criminal proceedings is examined in much greater detail in Chapter **9**, together with the role of the child as a witness in such proceedings. Also considered is the somewhat rarer situation where the child is himself the perpetrator of abuse and is over the age of 10. (See *Child Maltreatment in the United Kingdom: A Report by the NSPCC* (November 2000).) In addition, guidelines on sentencing will be examined in some detail in Chapter **9**.

Civil proceedings

4.39 The CA 1989, s 31(9), gives local authorities and authorised persons (currently only the NSPCC) power to intervene at an early stage where they believe it is necessary to do so or where an initial child protection conference has indicated that steps requiring court proceedings should be initiated. Thus, the CA 1989 provides for: intervention where there are merely suspicions that a child might be being ill-treated or is failing to develop properly and some form of assessment is required to establish whether or not this is the case (s 43, child assessment orders); emergency powers to remove children from their homes if certain criteria are satisfied (s 44, emergency protection orders); and gives the police the right to exercise the powers of police protection which do not require court authorisation (police powers of protection). In addition, where the court is satisfied that on making an emergency protection order under s 44, a child will nevertheless be safeguarded in his or her own home provided an exclusion requirement is attached to such an order, then under new provisions inserted into the CA 1989 by the Family Law Act 1996, the court can make such an exclusion order. In addition, a recovery order is provided to protect children who may have been abducted or run away from any place where they were being looked after while subject to a care or emergency protection order, or where they were in police protection (CA 1989, s 50). Moreover, provision is made for refuges for children at risk of harm (s 51) and a system of certification exempting those who run such a refuge from liability to prosecution for certain offences is also laid down (s 51(1) and (2)). Members of the public concerned about the actuality or potentiality of abuse to children with whom they are involved in some way have the ability to invoke the relevant provisions dealing with emergency protection (s 44(1)(a)), although most will be happier to inform relevant agencies such as the police, social services or the NSPCC and to see them take the appropriate action.

4.40 The opportunity presented by the reform of the substantive law as a result of the CA 1989 was also used to reform the civil jurisdiction of the courts dealing with children's cases (CA 1989, s 92 and Sch 11), the law on evidence in civil cases involving children (s 96) and the law governing procedure in all civil cases involving children (ss 93 (as amended by various successive pieces of legislation), 95 and 100). In addition, the Family Proceedings Rules 1991 (FPR 1991), SI 1991/1247, and the Family Proceedings Courts (Children Act 1989) Rules 1991 (FPC(CA 1989)R 1991, SI 1991/1395, as successively amended, have also effected radical reform of all the court processes and uniform sets of court forms to be used in all applications have vastly simplified formerly complex procedural documentation. (For further detail on this, see Chapter **8**.)

4.41 Where, therefore (and this will be considered in much more detail in Chapter **5**), there is reasonable cause to believe that the child is likely to suffer significant harm if either the child is not removed to accommodation provided by or on behalf of the applicant, or does not remain in the place in which he is then being accommodated, any person may make an application for an emergency protection order. Such an application is made pursuant to s 44(1)(a) of the CA 1989, and may be made without notice being given to the other side (ie without the other parties being present) to a single magistrate (see CA 1989, Sch 11, para 3(1)(a)). Such 'without notice' applications for emergency protection orders may also be made by any of the relevant child protection agencies using the provisions of s 44(1)(a). Local authority social services and the NSPCC are given additional rights to apply for orders under s 44 in cases of emergency. Thus, in the case of an application made by a local authority, s 44(1)(b) provides that where enquiries are being made with respect to the child in pursuance of an investigation, and those enquires are being frustrated by access to the child being unreasonably refused to a person authorised to seek access, and the applicant's social worker has reasonable cause to believe that access to the child is required as a matter of urgency, the court may make an emergency protection order authorising the removal of the child to accommodation provided by social services or the child's detention in the place in which he is being accommodated. Almost identical provision is made with respect to officers employed by the NSPCC (s 44(1)(c)).

4.42 It should be noted, however, that careful consideration now needs to be given to the granting of such orders without notice to the other side. It may be argued that the making of such orders without the presence of the other party offends against the fair trial provisions of Article 6 of the ECHR as implemented by the HRA 1998. In addition, it might be argued that such an intervention constitutes an interference with an individual's right to private home and family life as guaranteed by Article 8 of the ECHR. This may, however, be countered by arguing that such imperative action to remove a child may be necessary in order to protect the child's health or to protect the child's rights and freedoms to be free from abuse, thus relying on the provisions of Article 8(2). *Core Guidance* issued by the Home Office, however, recommends that those working in public authorities should also be aware of the principle of proportionality, which it translates into the notion that 'one should not take a sledgehammer to crack a nut' (see *Core Guidance: Human Rights Comes to Life* (Home Office, 1999), at para 73). What this means is that henceforward local authority social services or the NSPCC should be very careful first to consider whether there is actually any necessity to pursue an emergency protection order rather than some other alternative approach, which may then offend less against the principles of Articles 6 and 8 respectively.

4.43 Given that the provisions in relation to emergency protection orders were moulded in the way that they were as a direct result of the Cleveland Report (see *Report of the Inquiry into Child Abuse in Cleveland 1987* (HMSO, 1998), at para 16.15), it was specifically provided that: emergency protection orders should last for only 8 days (CA 1989, s 45(1)), with a provision for an extension in exceptional circumstances of 7 days (s 45(5)); there should be a right of challenge after 72 hours (s 45(8) and (9)) for parents and children and others who were providing care immediately before removal; if contact is to be anything other than what may be presumed to be reasonable (s 44(13)) specific court directions should be sought (s 44(6)(a)); and, finally, where it is proposed that the child be subject to medical, psychiatric or other assessments, specific directions of the court must be sought (s 44(6)(b)). It is further anticipated in relation to these provisions that there might be an objection to the restrictions on the right of challenge to the making of an emergency protection order. Thus, currently, there is no right of challenge until after the expiry of the period of 72 hours and it is suggested that this might offend against the principle of equal 'rights of access' to the courts encompassed within the notion of the right to a fair and public hearing enshrined in Article 6 (see Swindells, Neaves, Cushner and Skilbeck (1999), at paras 8.43–8.54.)

4.44 Applications in respect of emergency protection orders may be made out of hours to a single magistrate, possibly at his home following contact being made first with the duty clerk, but may, of course, be made during court time to a full bench of magistrates sitting in the family proceedings court (in which all family proceedings take place at magistrates' court level). Under the relevant orders issued by the Lord Chancellor, public law applications must generally be commenced in the Family Proceedings Court (see Children (Allocation of Proceedings) Order 1991 (CAPO 1991), SI 1991/1677, art 2) but provided that the relevant criteria are satisfied, such cases may, once they are beyond the emergency order stage, be transferred upon application to a district judge, a county court care centre or even the High Court (art 18(3)). Even where an application is made without notice to the other side to a single magistrate at home out of court hours, provision is made, under the CA 1989, s 41(6), for the court to appoint a CAFCASS officer at this early stage and, where the court believes a child should have a solicitor, the court may appoint one (s 41(3)).

4.45 Where there are merely concerns or suspicions that a child is suffering or likely to suffer significant harm, the local authority or the NSPCC may seek an order, usually from the family proceedings court, known as a child assessment order (CA 1989, s 43). Before granting such an order, the court must be satisfied that the applicant has reasonable cause to suspect that: (1) the child is suffering or is likely to suffer significant harm; (2) an assessment of the state of the child's health or development or of the way in which he has been treated is required to enable the applicant to determine whether or not the child is suffering or is likely to suffer significant harm; and (3) it is unlikely that such an assessment will be made, or be satisfactory, in the absence of a child assessment order. Since an application for such an order is likely to be a planned response to concerns, court rules provide that the application must be made on notice and this underlines the fact that the order should not be made in emergency (see FPC(CA 1989)R 1991, SI 1991/1395, r 4(1)). The child assessment order must specify the date by which the assessment is to begin, and it has effect for such period, not exceeding 7 days, beginning with that date as may be specified in the order (s 43(5)).

4.46 It should be noted that in relation to proceedings for a child assessment order, the court is required, by the CA 1989, s 41(1) and (2) as amended, to appoint a CAFCASS officer for the child unless satisfied that it is not necessary to do so in order to safeguard the child's interests. Figures available from the *Children Act Report 1995–1999* (DOH, 1999) appear to indicate that guardians ad litem, and since April 2001 CAFCASS officers, are appointed in the vast majority of public law proceedings in the various levels of courts (see *Children Act Report 1995–1999*, table 10.2, paras 10.11–10.19).

4.47 It should be pointed out that where evidence of abuse arises in certain situations, the local authority may have the power simply to remove the child rather than be required to go to court to obtain an order to do so. This will be the case where the child is being 'looked after' pursuant to the CA 1989, s 20, or pursuant to a care order made under s 31, and concerns about the child have developed as a result of care in a particular children's home or other residential placement, or where the child is being cared for by foster parents or indeed even when being cared for by their own parents or other family members, whilst on a care order .

4.48 Concerns about child abuse may also surface in the course of any family proceedings brought in the family proceedings court, the county court or the High Court. In such family proceedings, which may encompass applications for any of the s 8 orders under the CA 1989 or any applications for exclusion orders or personal protection orders under Pt IV of the Family Law Act 1996, a CAFCASS officer may have been requested to investigate the children's circumstances and may have returned to court indicating that there was a degree of concern about the possibility of the children having suffered or being likely to suffer 'significant harm'. In such circumstances, s 37 of the CA 1989 provides the court with the power to direct the local authority to undertake an investigation of the child's circumstances where it appears to the court that it may be appropriate for a care or supervision order to be made. Where the court gives such a direction under s 37, the local authority is required, when undertaking the investigation, to consider whether it should apply for a care order or a supervision order with respect to the child (s 37(2) generally). (See *Re H (A Minor) (Section 37 Direction)* [1993] 2 FLR 541; and *Re CE (Section 37 Direction)* [1995] 1 FLR 26.)

4.49 Where the local authority decides that there are grounds for the institution of care or supervision order proceedings as a result of the s 37 investigation, then those proceedings may be commenced in the same level of court as the original family proceedings. It should be noticed that whilst all magistrates' courts are of equal standing under the CA 1989, the jurisdiction of county courts has been classified according to the nature of the case being brought. Thus, county courts have been classified into divorce county courts, family hearing centres and care centres by the CAPO 1991, art 2 as amended. The judges who can hear proceedings in designated trial centres, and the types of proceedings to which they are restricted, are provided in the various Family Proceedings (Allocation to Judiciary) Directions issued by the Lord Chancellor from time to time. Where an application for a care or supervision order or any associated orders arises from a direction to conduct an investigation made by the High Court or county court under the s 37 of the CA 1989, then, provided that court is a county court care centre, the application can be made there (SI 1991/1677, art 3(2)(a)), or in such care centre as the court which directed the investigation may order (SI 1991/1677, art 3(2)(b)). Where a s 37 direction is made by the High Court, it has jurisdiction to proceed to hear the application for the care or supervision order made by the local authority.

4.50 Where concern over actual or potential abuse has not escalated suddenly, consideration may be given instead to initiating care proceedings by way of issuing an application for a care or supervision order in the family proceedings court. (For further detailed guidance on this, see Chapters **7** and **8**.) Such action may also be taken following on from an emergency protection order including one accompanied by a s 44A exclusion order, the exercise of police powers of protection, the result of a s 37 investigation or the obtaining of evidence pursuant to an assessment done under the provision of a child assessment order made under s 43. An application is made by filling in the relevant form (see Form CHA 19) but since it is unlikely that all parties will be ready to proceed to a full hearing on the first occasion, an order is actually issued in the form of an interim care or interim supervision order for such period as is determined by the court under the provision of s 38 (see Form CHA 27). It should be remembered that care proceedings are civil proceedings and that the standard of proof required is proof on the balance of probabilities. However, where the allegation is an extremely serious one, the House of Lords has determined in *Re H and R* [1996] 1 FLR 80 that the evidence required to satisfy the court that there is a real possibility of harm to a child must be even stronger. The basic message of this case, somewhat controversially therefore, was that the more serious the allegations made in respect of past events then the stronger the evidence would need to be to establish that it had actually occurred and that there was therefore a greater likelihood of the harm being repeated. Thus, under the terms of s 31 of the CA 1989 in general terms, the applicant will be required to 'prove on the balance of probability' that the particular child concerned is suffering, or is likely to suffer, significant harm and that the harm or the likelihood of the harm is attributable to:

(1) the care given to the child or likely to be given to him if the order were not made not being what it would be reasonable to expect a parent to give to him; or
(2) the child being beyond parental control.

4.51 It should be noted that the grounds provide for a care or supervision order to be made, not only where it can be established that significant harm has actually taken place, but where there is also a fear that significant harm may occur in the future. In considering whether or not to make an order, the court can look not only at the care actually being given to the child, but look to the care which is likely to be given to the child if the order was not made, and set that against the standard of care which it would be *reasonable* to expect a parent to give to a child.

4.52 Thus, in *Lancashire County Council v B* [2000] 1 FLR 583, it was held that these threshold conditions could be satisfied when there was no more than a possibility that parents, rather than one of the other carers, were responsible for inflicting the injuries which the child had suffered. It was emphasised that the court had to be satisfied that harm suffered by the child was attributable to 'the care given to the child'. The House of Lords determined that that phrase referred primarily to the care given by the parent or parents or other primary carers, but where care was shared the phrase was apt to embrace the care given by any of the carers. This interpretation, according to the House of Lords, was necessary to allow the court to intervene to protect the child who was clearly at risk, even though it was not possible to identify the source of the risk. Nevertheless, the House of Lords emphasised that it by no means followed that because the threshold conditions had been satisfied, the court would go on to make a care order, and when considering cases of this type, judges should keep firmly in mind, in exercise of their discretionary powers, that the parents had not been shown to be responsible for the child's injuries. The steps taken so far in this case of making a care order in respect of the child who had been the subject of shared care between the parents and the child minder, had been those reasonably necessary to pursue the legitimate aim of protecting the child from further injury, which was, emphasised the court, an exception to the guarantee for respect for private and family life contained within Article 8 of the ECHR. (See also *Re B* [2002] EWCA Civ 752, [2002] 2 FLR 1133 and *Re O and N* [2002] EWCA Civ 1271, [2002] 2 FLR 1167.)

4.53 The grounds set out in the CA 1989, s 31(1) do not, of course, mention the word 'abuse' but instead look to whether the child is suffering or likely to suffer 'significant harm'. Harm is further defined in s 31(9) and (10) of the CA 1989 and will be considered in more detail in Chapters **5** and **7**.

4.54 In addition to satisfying the grounds laid down in the CA 1989, s 31(2), the court is required when making any orders at all under the Act with respect to a child, to be satisfied that making an order is better for the child than making no order at all (s 1(5)). It may also be of the view, perhaps as a result of a report made by an officer of CAFCASS acting as the child's guardian, that the making of a full care or supervision order, or indeed an interim care or supervision order, would actually be the wrong order to make. Where a decision has to be made *whether to make* any of the orders provided for in Pt IV of the CA 1989, then the provisions of s 1(4) come into effect. This enables the court to decide whether to make one of a range of orders which are available under the CA 1989, including the making, where relevant, of any of the s 8 orders which could be made in conjunction with a supervision order.

(See the judgment of Ward J in *Re C* [1993] 1 FLR 664.) Thus, the local authority may have applied for a care order in respect of a child and the CAFCASS officer's report may recommend the making of a residence order in favour of grandparents or other relatives combined with a supervision order to the local authority, as well as the making of other s 8 orders in respect of the parents, such as a contact order in favour of the mother and a prohibited steps order in respect of the father, thus preventing the father from having contact with the child. Where the local authority or the court considers that contact should be supervised in any way, then this might be done by means of using a s 16 family assistance order (see the comments of Booth J in *Leeds City Council v C* [1993] 1 FLR 269).

4.55 The requirement in s 1(5) that the court be satisfied 'that making an order is better for the child than making no order at all', has been characterised by some as the 'no order principle'. Given the confusion which this shorthand nomenclature has caused (see *S v R (Minors) (No Order Principle)* [1993] Fam Law 42), the authors prefer the use of the term 'the positive advantage principle'. In order to prove to the court's satisfaction that there is to be some positive advantage derived from the making, in particular, of a care or supervision order, the local authority is now expected to submit its plan for the future care of the child (s 31A(1)), which must be kept constantly under review during the proceedings (see s 31A(2)), before the court will proceed to the making of a care order (for further detail on this, see Chapter 7). Where the court is proposing to make a care order, the local authority should, under the provisions of CA 1989, s 34(11), further submit to the court the arrangements which are being proposed for the child to have contact with members of his or her family. This is now particularly important in the light of Article 8 of the ECHR as implemented by the HRA 1998. It should be noted that since the thrust of the decisions of the European Court has been that State removal of children from their families will be done generally on the basis of such removal only being temporary and that rehabilitation with the family will be the goal in the vast majority of cases, the courts will now be expected to scrutinise such contact plans very carefully (see *Hokkanen v Finland* [1996] 1 FLR 289). Where the local authority is proposing to the court that there should be no contact, or the family or child do not agree with the arrangements being proposed, an application will have to be made to the court to determine issues of contact under the provisions of s 34, and, again, this will raise issues with regard to the protection of Article 8 (ECHR) rights. This will be considered in much greater detail in Chapter **10**.

4.56 Both in proceedings for care and supervision orders or in any contact proceedings, the child is a party to the proceedings under the relevant rules of court and the court is required to appoint an officer of the service for the child, who since 1 April 2001 has been drawn from the ranks of the officers of CAFCASS, where one has not earlier been appointed. An early appointment of an officer may have been made, for example in proceedings for an emergency protection order or a child assessment order and, where those proceedings are being continued, either the officer or the court must further consider whether an appointment of a solicitor for the child should also be made (s 41). This unique system of the dual representation of the child by a solicitor representing what the child wants (where he is capable of giving such instructions) and of the CAFCASS officer representing what is in the child's best interests, has gained considerable strength from the statutory provisions in the CA 1989 and the relevant rules of court. (See CA 1989, s 41, the FPR 1991, as amended, and the FPC(CA 1989)R 1991, as amended.) The success of the service provided now by officers of the service in care and supervision order proceedings as well as in s 25 (secure accommodation order) proceedings, linked with the service, which has already been provided in adoption proceedings, led to considerable pressure being put on the government around the time of the enactment of the Family Law Act 1996 and meant that provision was made in s 64 of that Act for the Lord Chancellor to be able to make provision for a widening of the principle of separate representation to include children in other specified proceedings. So far, this provision has not been implemented but the landmark decision of the President of the Family Division in *Re A* [2001] 2 FLR 715 means that there should be an increase in the numbers of children who are represented in such proceedings, pending any decision by the Lord Chancellor to implement s 64.

4.57 Whereas in most situations the making of a care or supervision order will be sufficient to guarantee the protection of the child suffering or at risk of suffering 'significant harm', there may be situations in which the local authority will need additional protection for the child, or specific guidance in relation to some aspect of the care of the child. Where this is necessary, and where it is not possible by any other means, including the use of the provisions of the CA 1989, to acquire such protection, the local authority may have to resort to the inherent jurisdiction of the High Court to obtain the relevant orders. Since a local authority, which has a child in its care, is unable to use the provisions of s 8 to obtain a prohibited steps order or a specific issues order (see CA 1989, s 9(1)), then the local authority would have to apply to the High Court to be given leave to make an application for an order providing relevant protection under s 100 in order to enable continuation of protection which might previously have been provided under the provisions of s 38(A) (exclusion order attached to an interim care or supervision order) or to extend any protection granted under s 44(A) (exclusion order attached to an emergency protection order). Generally, however, such protection as would be granted by a s 44(A) exclusion order would, if necessary, usually have been continued already by means of attaching such an order to the relevant interim orders and thus the jurisdiction under s 100 would need to be exercised to continue this during the operation of a full care or supervision order (see further, Chapter **8**).

4.58   The High Court may only grant leave where it is satisfied that the result which the authority wishes to achieve could not be achieved through the making of any other order and there is reasonable cause to believe that if the court's inherent jurisdiction is not exercised with respect to the child, the child is likely to suffer 'significant harm' (s 100(4)) (see *Devon County Council v B* [1997] 1 FLR 591). The courts have, however, emphasised that s 100 should not be restrictively interpreted and that it is perfectly in order for a local authority to seek leave to invite the court to exercise its inherent jurisdiction to protect children even where the exercise of such a power would represent an invasion of that person's parental responsibility, for example by ordering that there should be no attempt to contact or communicate with children (see Thorpe J in *Devon County Council v S* [1994] 1 FLR 355). The sorts of situations in which it is envisaged that the High Court's inherent jurisdiction may have to be invoked by the local authority include those situations: where an injunction is required to prevent an abusing parent or child from going near or having contact with the child in need of protection (see *Re S (Minors) (Inherent Jurisdiction: Ouster)* [1994] 1 FLR 623 and *C v K (Inherent Powers: Exclusion Order)* [1996] 2 FLR 506); or where some operative procedure is required in respect of the child, the child's parents are refusing to give consent or are not available to do so and the relevant doctors or hospitals are concerned about accepting the consent to operative treatment provided by the local authority holding a care order (see *Re W (A Minor) (Medical Treatment: Court's Jurisdiction)* [1993] Fam Law 64).

Appeals

4.59   A brief reference is made here to the appeals possible in respect of all the proceedings, which will be described in detail in Chapters **7** and **9**. Where criminal proceedings have been taken against an individual then, depending upon the court in which the proceedings are eventually determined, a decision can be made regarding an appeal. Where an offence has been tried in the magistrates' court, or in the youth court, there can be an appeal to the Crown Court either against conviction or sentence. Where a person is convicted in the Crown Court, there can be an appeal, under very strictly defined conditions, to the Court of Appeal Criminal Division against either conviction or sentence and this is considered in further detail in Chapter **9**.

4.60   In care and contact order proceedings, an appeal lies by the child usually through the guardian (since April 2001 an officer of CAFCASS) or by the parents or by any other persons who have been made parties to the proceedings from the magistrates' court to the Family Division of the High Court against the magistrates' decision to make or refuse to make any order (CA 1989, s 94(1)), except in the following situations, where there is no right of appeal, although since the implementation of the HRA 1998 it is possible that some of these restrictions on rights to appeal may be challenged using the provisions of Article 6 of the ECHR. There is thus currently no right of appeal:

(1) against the making or refusal to make an emergency protection order, the granting of an extension of or refusal to extend the effective period of the emergency protection order, the discharge or refusal to discharge the emergency protection order, or the giving or refusal to give any directions in connection with the order (see CA 1989, s 45(10) as substituted by the Courts and Legal Services Act 1990, s 116, Sch 16, para 19);

(2) where the magistrates' court has exercised its powers to decline jurisdiction because it considers that the case can be more conveniently dealt with by another court (s 94(2));

(3) against decisions taken by courts on questions arising in connection with the transfer or proposed transfer of proceedings except as provided for by orders made by the Lord Chancellor (under s 94(10) and (11)).

4.61 An appeal to the High Court against the making of any order or an order that no order should be made or against the refusal to make an order by any magistrates' court lies to a single judge of the Family Division unless the President otherwise directs (see *Handbook of Best Practice in Children Act Cases* (Children Act Advisory Committee, June 1997), at para 87). Leave to appeal is not required in relation to care and supervision order proceedings nor, generally, where provision is made for appeal in any part of Pt IV or Pt V of the CA 1989. Detailed rules of procedure are set out in the FPR 1991 (see further, Chapters 7 and 8) and generally all appeals should take place at the nearest convenient High Court centre (see *Practice Direction* [1992] 1 All ER 864). It is critical that an appeal is set down for hearing promptly so that if this is unlikely to be the case on Circuit, arrangements will be made for such an appeal to be heard in London (see *Handbook of Best Practice in Children Act Cases*, at para 90). On hearing the appeal the High Court Family Division judge can make such orders as may be necessary (s 94(4)), including such incidental or consequential provision as appears to be just (s 94(5)), in order to give effect to its determination of the appeal. Any order of the High Court made on appeal, other than one directing a rehearing by the magistrates shall for the purposes of the enforcement, variation, revival or discharge of the order, be treated as if it were an order of the magistrates' court from which the appeal was brought and not an order of the High Court (s 94(9)). The role and powers of the appellate courts in civil proceedings will be considered in more detail in Chapters 7 and **8**.

4.62 An appeal from the decision of a judge in a county court care centre or in the High Court is made direct to the Court of Appeal, but since 1 January 1999 leave is required for all appeals except those against:

– committal orders;
– refusal to grant habeas corpus;
– secure accommodation orders made under the CA 1989, s 25.

4.63   In addition, since 27 September 1999, where an appeal has already been made to the High Court (for example where there has been appeal from the magistrates' court to the High Court) no appeal against the decision of the High Court may be made to the Court of Appeal unless the Court of Appeal considers that:

(1)   the appeal would raise an important point of principle or practice; or
(2)   there is some other compelling reason for the Court of Appeal to hear it.

(See the Access to Justice Act 1999, s 65; RSC Order 59, r 1B, and see also Practice Direction (1999) at para 2.1.2.) These issues will be considered in more detail in Chapters **7** and **8**.

Exercise of parental responsibilities and children's rights where a child is in care

4.64   Where a care order is made with respect to a child, it is the duty of the local authority designated by the care order to receive the child into its care and to keep him in its care whilst the order remains in force (CA 1989, s 33(1)). As far as the exercise of parental responsibility in respect of the child is concerned, it is provided that whilst the care order is in force the local authority shall have parental responsibility for the child and shall have the power, subject to certain exceptions, to determine the extent to which a parent or guardian of the child may meet his responsibility for that child (s 33(3)). It should be noted that the parent does not cease to hold parental responsibility solely because some other person acquires it (see s 2(6)) but a person with parental responsibility is not entitled to act in any way which would be incompatible with any order made under the CA 1989 (see s 2(8)). It is further provided that the local authority may not exercise its powers to limit the exercise of parental responsibility unless it is satisfied that it is necessary to do so in order to safeguard or to promote the child's welfare (s 33(4)).

4.65   A parent or guardian may still do what is reasonable in all the circumstances of the case for the purpose of safeguarding or promoting the child's welfare (see s 33(5)) and retains any right, duty, power, responsibility or authority in relation to the child and his property under any other enactments (see s 33(9)). Such rights, powers and duties which the parent would still be entitled to exercise would include the right to consent to the child's marriage, to the child's adoption or emigration, rights in relation to the child's special educational needs (see Pt IV of the Education Act 1996), financial responsibility for the child and some responsibility for the child's acts where the child is placed by the local authority in the parent's charge and control. Where the local authority do make a decision to limit the exercise of parental responsibility by the parent as laid down in s 33(4) and the parents disagree with that decision, or, indeed, in relation to any of the other statutory duties which local authorities have in respect of the care and upbringing of children, then if the local authority fails to observe its duty or if the parent can show that the local authority has acted unreasonably in any decision reached with regard to the child, or to have acted in bad faith, an application may be made for judicial review. (See further, Chapter **11**.)

4.66 In addition to parents keeping such rights as the right to consent to the child's adoption or marriage, the provisions of the CA 1989 also make it clear that whilst the care order is in force the local authority cannot change the child's religion nor does it have the right to consent to, or refuse to consent to, the making of either a placement order or an adoption order in respect of the child, nor does it have the right to appoint a guardian for the child (s 33(6)). Furthermore, whilst a care order is in force with respect to the child, no person may cause the child to be known by a new surname or remove him from the UK without either the written consent of every person who has parental responsibility for the child or with the leave of the court (s 13). The court can give leave for a change of surname (see s 33(7)) and in an appropriate case where it is felt to be desirable that parents still considered to be dangerous should not be given notice of the application, then an order may be granted without the other parties being present (see *Re J (A Minor) (Child: Change of Name)* [1993] 1 FLR 699). It should also be noted that whilst the local authority does have certain powers to limit the parents' exercise of parental responsibility, this does not extend to preventing a mother from entering into a parental responsibility agreement under s 4 of the CA 1989 (see *Re X (Minors) (Care Proceedings: Parental Responsibility)* [2000] Fam 156.

4.67 Where an abused child is placed in care under the CA 1989, s 31, the local authority is then placed under a duty to safeguard and promote the child's welfare and to make use of such services available for children cared for by their own parents as appears to the local authority to be reasonable in the child's case (see s 22(3)). Before making any decision with respect to a child it is looking after, pursuant to a care order, the local authority must, so far as is practicable, ascertain the wishes and feelings of the child, his parents (including unmarried fathers), anyone else with parental responsibility and any other relevant person, which includes all the statutory agencies who might have been involved with the child, and the local authority may contact the child's school or GP (see *The Children Act 1989: Guidance and Regulations*, vol 3 'Family Placements' (HMSO, 1991), at para 2.51). Where the child has had the benefit of a guardian provided by CAFCASS, then the guardian should also be consulted, although there is no power in the court (even under the newly amended provision of s 31A of the CA 1989, as inserted by the Adoption and

Children Act 2002) to restrict the exercise of the local authority's powers by directing that any guardian should remain involved in order to oversee a planned rehabilitation of the child with a parent (see *Kent County Council v C* [1993] 1 FLR 308, and also *Re B (A Minor) (Care Order: Review)* [1993] 1 FLR 421). The power to re-engage the guardian's involvement in the case arises instead where, in any review under the newly amended provisions of s 26(2), the prescribed person thinks it would appropriate to refer the child's case to an officer of CAFCASS. Presumably, under these provisions for which Rules have yet to be provided, the prescribed person would seek to refer the child's case to the original guardian, who it appears from the amendments effected by the Adoption and Children Act 2002 will be able to commence proceedings to have the child's case reviewed by the courts (see s 26(2C) of the CA 1989, as amended; for further detail on this, see para **4.70**). In making any decision with regard to the child, a local authority is required to give due consideration to:

(1) such wishes and feelings of the child as it has been able to ascertain and having regard to his age and understanding;
(2) such wishes and feelings of any parent or person with parental responsibility or other relevant persons; and
(3) the child's religious persuasion, racial origin and cultural and linguistic background (s 22(5)).

4.68 Where it appears to the local authority that it is necessary, for the purpose of protecting members of the public from serious injury, to exercise its powers with respect to the child whom it is looking after in a manner which may not be consistent with its duties to the child, it may do so (see s 22(6)).

4.69 When a local authority is trying to determine where a child, who is being accommodated by it or who is in its care pursuant to a care order, is to live, then the local authority may provide accommodation and maintenance for any child by placing the child in one of a wide range of living situations (s 23(2)). Thus a local authority can provide accommodation and maintenance for any child whom it is looking after by:

(1) placing him with a family, a relative of his, ie any member of the extended family with whom it would be both safe and appropriate to place the child or any other suitable person on such terms as to payment by the authority and otherwise as the authority may determine;
(2) maintaining him in a community home, voluntary home or registered children's home;
(3) maintaining him in a home provided in accordance with arrangements made by the Secretary of State; and
(4) making such other arrangements as appear appropriate to the authority

and comply with any regulations made by the Secretary of State (s 23(2), as amended).

4.70 Where the child is accommodated with foster parents then the placement is now governed by the Standards and Regulations to be found in the document issued in April 2002 entitled *Fostering Services – National Minimum Standards – Fostering Services Regulations* (DOH, 2002), which replace the former guidance and the Foster Placement Regulations 1991. The regulations, as before, are mandatory and fostering providers must comply with them. The set of 32 National Minimum Standards provide, in a way similar to those provided for children in residential care (see below), a set of objectives against which to measure the perfomance of service providers as well as the care of the child in a particular foster home. This will be as a result of the DOH's systematic review of care standards in relation to children who are being looked after by local authorities. For children who are being looked after in residential care placements the imperative to attend first to the standards of care in such homes after the North Wales Children Inquiry was clearly urgent and so the new *National Minimum Standards for Children's Homes* was issued in March 2002, together with new *Children's Home Regulations* (see *Children's Homes – National Minimum Standards – Children's Homes Regulations* (DOH 2002, www.doh.gov.uk/ncs). These new national standards provide objectives against which to measure the performance of a particular children's home in terms of: planning for care; the quality of care which should be provided; the accessibility of complaints procedures; the quality of child protection procedures; the provision of care and control; the quality of the home's physical environment; the quality of staff; the monitoring of management and administration; and the setting of standards in relation to secure accommodation units and refuges. Critically, for children who feel in need of protection, Part 3 deals in a great deal of detail with arrangements to provide reassurance to the child who wishes to make a complaint (Standard 16) and to attempt to guarantee the protection of the child from abuse (Standard 17). As far as complaints are concerned, there is an emphasis on children being totally familiar with the procedures but also with precluding anyone who is the subject of a formal complaint from taking any responsibility for the consideration of or response to that complaint. The guidance stresses that children and, where appropriate, parents and others are provided with information on how to secure accesss to an advocate, who should be suitably skilled, for example in signing or in speaking the complainant's preferred language (para 16.2). Admittedly, these standards have only recently been introduced, but the Government promised as part of *Quality Protects*, after the North Wales Children's Homes scandal, that children would always have access to such advocates and yet, as noted above, the Joint Inspectorate report *Safeguarding Children* (DOH/SSI, 2002) (www.doh.gov/ssi/childrensafeguardsjoint/htm) noted that there were severe gaps in provision of advocacy services to children in such circumstances. This should be of major concern for it means that we are still failing properly to protect those children who are amongst the most vulnerable in the care system. In addition to being accommodated in local authority run children's homes, the child may, of course, be placed in a home run by a volunatary or private organisation. Alternatively, the child may be made the subject of a secure accommodation order under s 25 of the CA 1989 (see below) but the *National Minimum Standards* make it clear that their provisions apply equally to secure accommodation premises, and also to refuges. Thus Standard 36 emphasises that, apart from the measures necessary to the homes's status as a secure unit or refuge, children resident in secure units or refuges should receive the same measures to safeguard and promote their welfare as they should in other children's homes. There is, thus, an extremely wide range of provisions which can be made to cater for a child whilst the child is being looked after by the local authority. In addition, it should be pointed out that a child, while he is being looked after by the local authority, may, in certain circumstances, be placed in accommodation provided for the purpose of restricting his liberty (such proceedings when taken are known as secure accommodation order proceedings under the CA 1989, s 25(1)). Where the child or young person is being kept in secure accommodation for more than 72 hours in any 28-day period, an application must be made to a court for an order to keep the child in secure accommodation (see s 25(2)) and the Children (Secure Accommodation) Regulations 1991, SI 1991/1505, regs 20–22, as amended by the Children (Secure Accommodation) (Amendment) Regulations 1992, SI 1992/2117).

4.71 In order to cater for a large number of difficult situations with regard to the standard of care exercised in respect of children being looked after by a local authority, the CA 1989 provided for a system of reviews of cases to enable a child to be able to complain or to make their voice heard about any concerns the child might have in relation to his or her care whether such care was being provided by a foster family, within the child's own extended family or within a children's home (see s 26(1), (2)). Despite reassurances given by Virginia Bottomley, the then Minister of State at the DOH responsible for the CA 1989 that this system of reviews would ensure that children would in future be protected and feel able to voice their complaints, it has emerged that the current system is not viewed as one in which children can feel safe in raising their complaints within a review procedure controlled by the local authority providing for its care and accommodation (see *People Like Us: Report of the Review of the Safeguards of Children Living Away from Home* (DOH, Welsh Office, 1997), at chapters 10–18). The Adoption and Children Act 2002 at last seeks to address some of the concerns voiced in these reports. In particular, since local authorities will now be required to produce a s 31A care plan to the courts before a care order is made, the Act provides by an amendment to s 26(2)(e) that this plan must be kept under review in the reviews held on children in care. Where the child was made the subject of a care order before the implementation of the Act then the authority must prepare one and, again, then keep it under review in the s 26(2)(f), as amended, reviews. The teeth to the new system, as introduced under the Adoption and Children Act 2002, is that there is provision under the new s 26(2A) for the appointment of a prescribed person to participate in the review, to monitor the performance of the local authority in respect of that review, and most crucially to refer the child's case to an officer of CAFCASS, if that person thinks it appropriate to do so. Regulations will provide for the prescribed description of the person who will fulfil functions also as prescribed by the Regulations. It must be asssumed that such a prescribed person will be expected to be independent of the local authority and responsible for both the reviews and the child. The Lord Chancellor is then given power by the Act to extend any functions of CAFCASS officers to other proceedings, which will presumably be some form of children's care plan review proceedings. Thus, at last there is a response to the concern from the judiciary over the years and the concern, which followed the decision of the House of Lords in *Re S (Minors); Re W (Minors)* [2002] UKHL 10, [2002] 1 FLR 815, that children could be lost in the system with anyone having the right, not even the children themselves, to review the local authority's performance of its promises to the court when it obtained a care order on a child or to review serious complaints which the child might have had about his or her care. The provision of an independent person will hopefully mean that the child has more confidence in being able to raise such issues of concern which he may have, including the experience of abuse within the system in foster placements or in residential settings.

4.72 Where a child is complaining about abuse occurring in either a residential home provided by the local authority, a home provided by a voluntary organisation or a foster home, then *Working Together to Safeguard Children* (at para 6.22) advises that local child protection procedures should apply in every situation, including where children are living away from home. This is confirmed by Standard 17 of the *National Minimum Standards for Children's Homes* (DOH, 2002). *Working Together to Safeguard Children* directs (at para 6.5) that 'there are a number of essential safeguards which should be observed in all settings in which children live away from home, including foster care, residential care, private fostering, health setting, residential schools, prisons, young offenders institutions and secure units'. The guidance goes on to state that where such services are not directly provided by local authorities, then basic safeguards should be explicitly addressed in contracts with external providers. The safeguards set out are very detailed but include the fact that the child should have ready access to a trusted adult outside the institution which could be a family member, the child's social worker, an independent visitor or a children's advocate. The whole experience of the North Wales children enquiry is such that it is unlikely that a child's social worker could really be seen as an independent person to whom the child might feel safe in voicing complaints or concerns. (See *Lost in Care: Report of the*

Tribunal of Enquiry into the Abuse of Children in Care in the Former County Council Areas of Gwynedd and Clwyd Since 1974 (the Waterhouse Report) (The Stationery Office, 2000).) The provision of access to independent advocates as part of the *Quality Protects* framework was intended to address these issues but, as the Joint Inspectorates report *Safeguarding Children*, confirmed, this was found to be extremely patchy. Until improvements are made to this system, reliance may have to be placed instead on the new system being introduced as part of the review process under s 26 of the CA 1989, as amended by the Adoption and Children Act 2002.

4.73 *Working Together to Safeguard Children* and the *National Minimum Standards for Children's Homes* state that complaints procedures should be clear, effective, user friendly and readily accessible to children and young people, including those with disabilities and those for whom English is not a first language. *Working Together to Safeguard Children* states that procedures should address informal as well as formal complaints and it notes that systems that do not promote open communication about 'minor' complaints will not be responsive to major ones, and a pattern of 'minor' complaints may indicate more deeply seated problems in management and culture which need to be addressed. It goes on to advise that there should be a complaints register in every children's home which records all representations or complaints, the action taken to address them and the outcomes (at para 6.5). *Working Together to Safeguard Children* here again seems to be entirely missing the point that children who feel extremely vulnerable and who need to complain about the behaviour or action of the staff are scarcely likely to do so where the requirement is to make a complaint in the first instance to those against whom they may be making an allegation. The inadequacies of the current complaints procedures, their lack of independence and the lack of anyone independent to whom children could complain was voiced by Sir William Utting in his report (see *People Like Us*) but was also pointed up most markedly by Ernest Ryder QC, one of the counsel to the North Wales Children enquiry. He commented that:

> 'children should be given choices about their external contacts and these choices should include the right to speak to accredited lay advocates of their choice and be assisted by lay advocates in expressing their views and wishes. There should be total independence in the complaints process matched by effective rights of representation for the child, which will need to be mirrored by independent scrutiny of the effect upon the child, regardless of the result of the complaints determination' ('Lost and Found: Looking to the Future after North Wales' [2000] Fam Law 406, at p 408).

4.74 Whilst the introduction of the *National Minimum Standards for Children's Homes* and the Children's Homes Regulations 2002 and recent developments such as the *Quality Protects* initiative, including the wider provision of access to independent advocacy services for looked after children generally, the establishment of independent regional inspection units and the provision of a Commissioner for Wales (but not for England) may be seen as welcome steps, these are by no means sufficient to address the very real concern as to independence which many children who have been made the subject of care orders actually voice. If the Joint Inspectors are concerned that children cannot gain access to advocacy services then the system is still failing (see *Safeguarding Children* (DOH/SSI, 2002). Further concerns are raised by *Working Together to Safeguard Children* in relation to foster care. Thus, at para 6.9, it states that foster care is undertaken in the private domain of carers' own homes, which may make it more difficult to identify abusive situations and for children to find a voice outside the family. In order to try to ensure that the case social worker really does give the child adequate opportunity to be able to voice any concerns or complaints, *Working Together to Safeguard Children* now recommends that social workers are required to see the children in foster care on their own for a proportion of visits, and that evidence of this must now actually be recorded. The new *National Minimum Standards* expand upon these duties for the greater protection of the children (see *Fostering Services – National Minimum Standards – Fostering Services* (DOH, 2002)).

4.75 Whilst both the system of reviews under CA 1989, s 26(2) and representation procedures in s 26(3) (both as amended), the issuing of the new *National Minimum Standards* and the recent developments represented by the *Quality Protects* programme and the CSA 2000 are intended to improve the ability of children to make their voices heard, very considerable doubts remain. The new independent Regional Inspection Units should have as one of their priorities the duty to ensure that all children, wherever they are being looked after pursuant to a care order, can easily obtain access to a fully independent body to whom they can safely raise concerns or complaints. The CSA 2000 and the *National Minimum Standards* do not guarantee to advance the position of children who might wish to refer their position to an independent body, more especially when even access to independent advocacy services is proving problematical. For Wales, however, the situation is that s 72 of the CSA 2000 provides for the office of the Children's Commissioner for Wales. The appointment of an independent Children's Commissioner was first recommended by Sir Ronald Waterhouse in his report *Lost in Care*. Sir Ronald recommended that the Commissioner's duties should include ensuring that children's rights are respected through the monitoring and oversight of the operation of complaints and whistle-blowing procedures and the arrangements for children's advocacy; examining the handling of individual cases brought to the Commissioner's attention, including making recommendations on their merit when he considers it necessary or appropriate; and publishing reports, including an annual report to the Welsh Assembly. Provisions in Pt V of the CSA 2000 put these recommendations into effect for the full range of children's services, ie not just children looked after by local authorities but those being provided with domiciliary care, those in private hospitals or clinics, those being provided with care in day care or child-minding services and also to cover all children living away from home in boarding schools.

4.76 As far as England is concerned there is no exactly comparable provision to the Children's Commissioner for Wales established by Pt V of the CSA 2000 but the government did make provision for a Children's Rights Director to be established within the National Care Standards Commission (NCSC) contained in the CSA 2000, Sch 1, para 10. This was a follow up from *Learning the Lessons: the Government's Response to Lost in Care*, Cm 4776, chapter 4, at para 2. The appointment of a Children's Rights Director within the NCSC is not, however, further developed in the legislation and regulations therefore had to be issued to provide for further detail of the position (see CSA 2000, Sch 1, at para 10.2). The National Care Standards Commission (Children's Rights Director) Regulations 2001 were brought into force on 1 April 2002, and provide for the Children's Rights Director to have duties to monitor the work of the NCSC in relation to the provision of regulated children's services, which are defined to include the provision of all services to children whether provided by social services or any other agency. It is the clear intention from the way in which the regulations are framed that it will be no part of the director's role to hear complaints or concerns directly from individual children, but rather to generally safeguard and promote the rights and welfare of children who are provided with regulated children's services, to monitor and review the effectiveness of the NCSC in its regulation of children's services, and to monitor and review the effectiveness of the arrangements made by the providers of regulated children's services in relation to dealing with complaints and representations made by or on behalf of children about such services. Thus, rather than having any powers and responsibility in relation to individual children, the director is to be concerned with the overall operation of regulated children's services, and if individual concerns are raised in relation to the operation of a particular service the director must inform the police or social services for the area in which the service is provided or situated (National Care Standards Commission (Children's Rights Director) Regulations 2001, reg 3(a)–(p)).

4.77 Even in relation to Wales, the impact of the Commissioner and his or her powers and duties set out in the CSA 2000, ss 73–77 appear somewhat limited in that whilst s 73 provides for the Commissioner to be able to review and monitor certain arrangements made by providers of services in Wales or by the Welsh Assembly in respect of services for children regulated under the CSA 2000, the government has stated that it 'is not the Assembly's intention that the Commissioner should routinely take the place of existing complaints procedures but that he or she should investigate the situation in which a matter of principle is involved or in which there is evidence of a systematic breach of children's rights' (see Baroness Farrington, *Hansard*, HL, vol 615, col 960).

4.78   As well as such provision being made for Wales, as indicated, it remains to be seen whether the regulations governing the Office of the Children's Rights Director in England and the performance of the Director in office lead to parity as between the two jurisdictions. One is forced to ask why exactly the same office could not have been created for both Wales and England and there are therefore yet again serious questions which have to be asked in relation to the UK government's commitment to observing the principles of Art 3 of the UNCR, specifically Art 3(2) which provides that:

> 'States parties undertake to ensure the child such protection and care as is necessary for his or her well being, taking into account the rights and duties or his or her parents, legal guardians, or other individuals legally responsible for him or her and, to this end, shall take all appropriate legislative and administrative measures.'

It remains to be seen whether the appointment of the Children's Rights Director can be described as fulfilling the obligation to take *all* appropriate legal and administrative measures to ensure the child's care and protection as required by Art 3 of the Convention.

4.79   It also remains to be seen whether the provisions amending s 26 of the CA 1989 will have the desired effect of ensuring that children have clearly defined and accessible means of voicing concerns and complaints to people independent from those providing for their care away from their own parents and homes. The absence of such provision in the past has called into question the commitment of successive governments to safeguarding such children. Hopefully, the raft of new measures which have been introduced through the Adoption and Children Act 2002 amendments of the CA 1989 will render it less likely that the first decade of the new century will see many situations similar to those in the 1990s in which children were unable to feel that their safety and protection were being adequately safeguarded. It is clear that the government is beginning to acknowledge the force of the pressure now coming from children themselves for the appointment of a Children's Rights Commissioner for England, which was argued very persuasively by James Sweeney before the House of Commons Select Committee on Human Rights in June 2002 (see para **1.32**). Further pressure coming from the UNCRC Monitoring Committee following its examination of the UK's record on 19 September 2002 may yet see the introduction of a full Children's Rights Commissioner for all of the jurisdictions in the UK.

Children (Leaving Care) Act 2000

4.80 As well as the duties to children whom they are looking after imposed by s 22 of the CA 1989 (see para **4.66**), the Children (Leaving Care) Act 2000 has imposed a wide range of additional duties in relation to the care owed to those who are leaving care. This Act and the Children (Leaving Care) (England) Regulations 2001 implement the proposals set out in *Me Survive Out There – New Arrangements for Young People Living in and Leaving Care* (DOH, July 1999) and further honour commitments made in *Modernising Social Services* (Cm 4169) as well as in the government's response to the *Children's Safeguards Review* (Cm 4105) to strengthen the duties of local authorities towards care leavers.

4.81 Briefly, the new primary and subordinate legislation places a duty on local authorities to assess the needs of *eligible* and *relevant* children. An *eligible* child is defined as one aged 16 or 17 who has been continuously looked after for a period of 13 weeks continuously or in aggregate. A *relevant* child is a young person aged 16 or 17 who ceases to be looked after by the authority. The *responsible* authority which owes the various new duties imposed by the legislation is the one which last looked after the child. The Act imposes a new duty on the responsible authority to keep in touch with all qualifying care leavers and obliges the authority to formulate for all *eligible* and *relevant* children up to 21 years old regularly reviewed 'pathway plans' (which then replace the s 26(2A) or s 31A care plans) and these plans must cover education, training career plan and the financial support needed to enable the child or young person to realise these objectives. The Act introduces the concept of the personal adviser for all *eligible* and *relevant* children to help draw up and support pathway plans and keep in touch with the individual young person. The legislation requires the local authority to financially support care leavers and removes entitlement to specifically means-tested benefits, namely income-based job-seeker's allowance, income support and housing benefit from *eligible* and *relevant* young people. The Act also empowers the responsible authority to assist with the costs of education and training up to the age of 24, whenever the course may commence. The measures contained in the Children (Leaving Care) Act 2000 as now incorporated into the CA 1989, thus providing for the local authority to take on a far more supportive, safeguarding and protective role with regard to young people leaving care who would otherwise be cut off from all forms of support, very much as they were in the past (see *R v London Borough of Lambeth ex parte Cadell* [1998] 1 FLR 253).

Conclusion

4.82 It should be quite apparent from a reading of this chapter that the CA 1989 and the policies which informed both its development and that of the subsequent guidance and regulations have undergone a radical transformation, which is undobtedly due to the change in the political climate and a determination on the part of the Treasury to inject significant amounts of resource into preventive strategies. One of the major concerns when writing the second edition of this book was the failure already apparent by 1993 to make available sufficient resource to fulfil many of the preventive duties provided for in Part III of and Sch 2 to the CA 1989. The fact that the government of the time had not been prepared to ring-fence the money needed for implementation of the preventive work has shaped the interpretation and over-emphasis given to the importance of certain measures in the Act into the twenty-first century. The government is now desperate to direct all services down the preventive route as providing the panacea to all children's ills but is at the same time apparently committed to the concept of safeguarding where this is absolutely necessary. Only time and the next edition of this book will tell whether we have made the sort of significant steps towards the greater protection of children within our society now envisaged by the government, and whether the legal framework within which all services have to operate has contributed to rather than impeded the achievement of that goal.

CHAPTER 5

THE IDENTIFICATION, INVESTIGATION AND INITIATION OF PROCEEDINGS

'The prevention of child abuse is *everyone's* responsibility. If *anyone* has a concern about the wellbeing or safety of a child and they feel that it is not being dealt with they should take action. The appropriate action will depend on the particular circumstances but might include: asking the parent or carer if there is a problem; offering advice, help or support; and, if there are still concerns, contacting a professional or agency which can intervene, for example, a health visitor, doctor, police, social service or NSPCC. While some individuals and agencies have specific responsibilities, these should not be seen as detracting from the responsibilities which everyone should exercise.' (*Childhood Matters: Report of the National Commission of Enquiry into the Prevention of Child Abuse* (The Stationery Office, 1996), vol 1, at p 337.)

'Except in a few extreme cases where the decision is clear cut, as a society we have to decide which of the several million potentially harmful situations that occur each year require intervention? A threshold is drawn across behaviours which ordinarily happen and some, by virtue of their severity, context or duration, demand that professionals enquire into the situation to see what remedies are needed. Other thresholds are drawn at subsequent stages of the child protection process; at the first involvement of parents, when calling a protection meeting, convening a full conference or placing the child's name on the protection register. In deciding whether to act, professionals are influenced by legal/moral concerns which lay out the obligations of statutory authorities. But there are also practical considerations, not least the parents' willingness to cooperate and the child's reaction to the process. As well as stressing the value of outcome evidence, the researchers pointed out the importance of parental and child perspectives when deciding what action to take.' ('How can professionals best protect children?' in *Child Protection – Messages from Research* (HMSO, 1995), at pp 53–54.)

'Can the same child protection strategies serve for preventing and tackling maltreatment inside and outside the family? This question is most marked in the present study in relation to the differences between sexual abuse, primarily extra-familial, and other forms of ill treatment, which are primarily intra-familial. However, it also has broader implications. BATA (1999) in a review of the evidence on protecting children from racial abuse, discusses the limitations of a child protection structure which is family centred, when faced with a problem which is essentially community based. Similar limitations of present routine structures in dealing with "organised" abuse rings and large scale institutional abuse has become apparent in recent years, and it has become familiar practice to set up special multi-agency investigation and support structures, either on ad hoc or continuing basis. Studies of abused young people and young victims of crime commonly show that large proportions of victims tell no-one, or confide only in friends and relatives, rarely approaching official agencies. The present study, with its very low proportion of the sample seeking official help with sexual abuse, highlights again the importance of strategies and services which are known, available, accessible and acceptable to abused young people, and suggests that the traditional social services, police and health service framework may not be sufficient or appropriate for all needs.' (*Child Maltreatment in the United Kingdom – A Study of the Prevalence of Child Abuse and Neglect* (NSPCC, 2000), at pp 98–99).)

Introduction

5.1 These quotations, including the recent one from the study undertaken in 2000 by the NSPCC, reveal increasing levels of concern about past and current practices with regard to the process of notification leading to identification of potential child abuse, concerns about the nature and focus of child abuse investigations, and a continuing concern about the efficacy and appropriateness of the initiation of legal proceedings. As has been noted in Chapter 1, Article 19 of the UNCRC imposes an obligation to take such protective measures as are appropriate to protect children from abuse, including effective procedures for the establishment of social programmes to provide necessary support for the child and those who have the care of the child, as well as for other forms of prevention and for identification, reporting, referral, investigation, treatment, and follow up instances of child maltreatment, and, as appropriate, for judicial involvement. However, the messages from the various research studies would seem to indicate that there is a constant need, before the refocusing of efforts, to provide *effective procedures* for the establishment of social programmes to provide the relevant necessary support for the child and for those who have the care of the child in potential child abuse situations (see *Child Protection – Messages from Research* (HMSO, 1995), at pp 41–55 and see also *Children Act Now – Messages from Research* (DOH, 2001)). As has been seen in the previous chapter, there are provisions in s 17 of and Sch 2, Pt I to the CA 1989 which could be combined to respond to the problem but these provisions are largely discretionary, empowering of local authorities rather than duty imposing. As a result of the messages emerging from the various research studies, there has been increasing attention focused on the importance of providing continuing support to children in need and their families and the introduction of the *Quality Protects* programme has also sought to emphasise this within its first two objectives (see Chapters **3** and **4**). The combination of the CA 1989, the various volumes of DOH guidance (including, most importantly, *Working Together to Safeguard Children* (DOH, 1999, together with its two pieces of supplementary guidance, issued in 2000 and 2002 respectively) and the *Framework for the Assessment of Children in Need and their Families* (DOH, 1999)), have, nevertheless, provided the various professionals involved within the process with a more systematic and sensitive framework for the identification, reporting, referral, investigation, and follow up of child abuse cases. Even when such major and constructive steps have been taken, however, it is still the case that children slip through all of the safety nets which the system seeks to provide. Even whilst writing this book, the trial of the aunt of Victoria Climbie was taking place in the Old Bailey in London and the trial judge was referring to a catalogue of failure by all of the various agencies involved in the case to detect the extreme severity of the abuse in Victoria's case which ultimately led to her death. These failures became the subject of a hugely expensive two-part official inquiry, which reported on 28 January 2003 and indicated the same sorts of human and institutional failings and neglect of official guidance as such inquiries have revealed in the past (see the Report into the death of Victoria Climbie (DOH, 2003), cf *Child Abuse – A Study of Inquiry Reports 1980–1989* (DOH, 1991), *Out of Sight – Report on Child Deaths 1973–2000* (NSPCC, 2001) and *Learning from Past Experience – A Review of Serious Case Reviews* (DOH, 2002).

5.2 There are still arguments about whether the grounds for care proceedings introduced in the CA 1989 raised or lowered the threshold of State intervention in the lives of children and their families, but many believe that the CA 1989, taken together with the advisory guidance issued by the DOH and other involved departments, represents a potentially very responsive and effective framework when professional, and then judicial intervention may be necessary within a family. The further gloss put upon the provisions of the CA 1989 when dealing with child abuse by the HRA 1998 must also be considered. Thus, Article 8 of the ECHR as implemented by the HRA 1998 (see Chapters 1 and 4), requires that even greater consideration needs to be given to the issue of whether intervention in the private home and family life of the parents and children is really necessitated by the requirements to protect either the health or the rights and freedoms of the children. In addition, as was noted earlier, it must be possible to demonstrate that actual intervention is proportionate to the aim being sought to be achieved, namely the protection of the child or children (see paras **1.33** and **2.11**).

5.3 As *Working Together to Safeguard Children* indicates (in chapter 3), a very wide range of agencies or individual professionals may be called upon at different stages in situations where child abuse is suspected and individual professionals or members of the community may also be involved by reason of their initial voicing of concern about a child. Those often described as being 'in the front line' in cases of child abuse include social workers, those working in day care or child-minding situations, youth and community workers, leisure services staff, residential care staff, teachers and other education service staff including psychologists, all types of health workers, including especially health visitors, community nurses, general practitioners, psychiatrists, paediatricians, workers in child adolescent and adult mental health services, the police, the probation and prison service, housing authorities, the armed services, and of course all those in the voluntary and private sector who play an important role in children's services (see *Working Together to Safeguard Children*, at paras 3.4–3.89). In whichever way agencies or individuals are involved, all of the research studies seem to indicate that they are unlikely to view the law as any sort of universal panacea for dealing with problems of child abuse but rather as 'one *possible* resource for dealing with social troubles' (Dingwall, et al (1983)).

5.4   Since one of the most difficult tensions inherent in the CA 1989 is that of the balance to be struck between children's needs and families' rights, which is a tension at the heart of all child protection work, it is not surprising that both the official guidance issued by the DOH, and *Child Protection – Messages from Research* as well as *Children Act Now – Messages from Research*, recognise both the risk and the limits of law-based intervention in terms of successful outcomes for children. Thus, in *Care of Children – Principles and Practice in Regulations and Guidance* (DOH, 1989), it is stated that 'measures which antagonise, alienate, undermine or marginalise parents are *counter-productive*, for example, taking compulsory powers over children can *all too easily* have this effect though such action may be *necessary* in order to provide protection' (at para 2.7, emphasis added). Whilst pointing out that the Cleveland Report had emphasised the traumatic effects that an abuse investigation can have on families, *Child Protection – Messages from Research* emphasised that whilst the research studies had confirmed the sense of shock, fear and anger felt at the point of confrontation and the lingering bitter after-taste, on the brighter side there was evidence that although some trauma may remain, relations between social workers and parents often improved (at p 43). *Messages from Research* indicates that both the Dartington and Bristol research studies found that in 70 per cent of cases, parents became more sympathetic to professional concern and came to regard the enquiry as having been in some way beneficial (at p 43).

5.5   As far as *Child Protection: Messages from Research* is concerned, it is quite apparent that the quality and extent of partnership between professionals and families are major factors affecting the progress of cases and outcomes for children (with the exception of some extreme cases where the abuse is very serious or the family is antagonistic). Whilst it has to be admitted, and the document does this, that many of the research studies were being undertaken at a time when the then new *Working Together under the Children Act 1989* (DOH, 1991) was only in the course of being circulated, the research studies pointed up that the degree of partnership varied in quality and extent. *Child Protection – Messages from Research* emphasises that in one-quarter of cases such partnership is not achieved despite auspicious circumstances. Agency policy and procedures or social work practice, or both together, accounted, according to studies, for much of this failure (at p 47). It is important also to realise that the notion of partnership should not be seen as an end in itself, working together between professionals and families must always be done with the purpose of better protecting the child. This point is emphasised by *The Challenge of Partnership in Child Protection* (DOH, 1995), at pp 11–12 where it states that:

> 'The objective of any partnership ... must be the protection and welfare of the child; partnership should not be an end in itself. Workers should consider the possibility of a partnership with each family based on openness, mutual trust, joint decision making and willingness to listen to families and to capitalise on their strengths.'

5.6   *The Challenge of Partnership in Child Protection* does for the first time appear to recognise that understandings about partnership in child protection have evolved, and will continue to evolve. It distinguishes four levels of partnership operating within the arena of child protection and which may vary as between family members and over time. Thus the four levels of partnership are:

(a)   providing information;
(b)   involvement but predominantly passive, for example attending at conference;
(c)   participation on an active basis, contributing to information and decision-making;
(d)   partnership based on openness, mutual trust, joint decision-making and willingness to listen to and be influenced by families and to capitalise on their strengths.

5.7   The building of a partnership relationship between the child's family and the various concerned agencies may have been a continuing one, involving a prolonged period of contact with and service provision into the child's family. Regrettably, however, most cases of child abuse triggering intervention through the courts will come from those families with whom the relevant agencies have an existing contact (see Dale, et al (1986), at chapter 2 generally and see also *Child Protection – Messages from Research* (DOH, 1995) 'Factors associated with progress through the Child Protection process', at pp 33–34), rather than from families with whom there has been little or no pre-existing contact. As Morrison points out, 'whatever efforts and measures are directed towards voluntary partnership with parents, there will always be a significant proportion of abused children for whom a level of intervention involving court orders will be necessary' (see Morrison (1991)). What one might also add is that if intervention through court orders is not used then those children may continue to suffer seriously from continued further abuse and neglect. Farmer and Owen (*Child Protection Practice: Private Risks and Public Remedies – Decision Making, Intervention and Outcome in Child Protection Work* (DOH, 1995)) found that the most important element in the protection of children was the physical separation from the abusing parent. They report that:

> 'of the children who were effectively protected, this was achieved by total separation from the abusing parent in almost half the cases, while in over a quarter of the cases the children had been separated from the parent, who had abused them for a part of the follow up period. It is a sobering finding that only about a quarter of the children who had been effectively protected had achieved this safety whilst living continuously with the parent who was alleged to have abused them' (at p 69).

5.8   It is clear then that for a significant proportion of children the use of different legal procedures to protect them will be an absolute necessity. What is perhaps significant about the CA 1989 is that through the positive advantage principle contained in s 1(5), and the new requirements on the submission of care plans to the court (see s 31A of the CA 1989 as amended by the Adoption and Children Act 2002), local authority social services are required to demonstrate that the rights given them by the court orders will assist in the process of actually improving the child's situation and possibly changing the child's family conditions. This is even more the case where the demands of Article 8 of the ECHR also mean that the invoking of legal processes must be shown to be proportionate to the intended objective and that interference with both the parents' and child's rights to a private home and family life are thus justified by reference to the protection of the health of the children. The findings of such studies as Farmer and Owen must be of support to those who would make such arguments on behalf of local authority social services.

Prevention

5.9   The principle of prevention has been elevated by the CA 1989 to a provision of central importance in the work of all agencies concerned with the protection of children and the positive promotion of their health and welfare. It was no accident that Pt III of the CA 1989, coming immediately after, as it does, those parts dealing essentially with private law relating to children and their families, begins with the heading 'Local Authority Support for Children and Families'. What emerged in the CA 1989, therefore, was a recognition of the point made by the inter-departmental *Review of Child Care Law* (DHSS, 1985), that prevention 'was an inadequate term to describe the purpose of local authority provision for families with children'. That review indicated that there were two main aims for such a provision:

'To provide family support to help parents bring up their children; and to seek to prevent admission to care or court proceedings except where this was in the best interests of the child.'

The *Review* recommended that revised legislation should include:

'a broad power to provide services to promote the care and upbringing of children within their families as well as the specific preventive duties to seek to diminish the need for children to be received into care or brought before a juvenile court.'

5.10   This recommendation was enacted in s 17 of the CA 1989, which places a general duty on local authorities to safeguard and promote the welfare of the children in their area who are in need and, subject to that duty, to promote the upbringing of such children by their families. (This section has been subject to amendment by the Adoption and Children Act 2002, so that s 17(6) now provides that the services which may be provided by a local authority can, as well as providing assistance in kind or in exceptional circumstances in cash, now also extend to providing accommodation (Adoption and Children Act 2002).) This is further reinforced by the provisions in Sch 2, Pt I to the CA 1989, which imposes on local authorities the duties of identification of children in need and the provision of information to them about services provided by the local authority and voluntary organisations (Sch 2, Pt I, para 1); to take reasonable steps through the provision of such services to prevent children within their area suffering ill-treatment or neglect (Sch 2, Pt I, para 4); to take reasonable steps designed to reduce the need to bring care proceedings, criminal proceedings or any other sort of proceedings in respect of children (Sch 2, Pt I, para 7); and it provides local authorities with the power to provide services to help maintain the family home in which the child is living (Sch 2, Pt I, paras 8, 9 and 10). It can be seen that support for families with children in need is linked to the issue of whether the child is assessed to be a child in need. A child is taken to be in need if:

— the child is unlikely to achieve or maintain or to have the opportunity of achieving or maintaining a reasonable standard of health or development without the provision for him or her of services by a local authority;
— the child's health or development is likely to be significantly impaired or further impaired without the provision for him or her of such services; or
— the child is disabled (s 17 (10)).

5.11   The definition of a 'child in need' is further expanded by reference to the concept of health, development and disability in s 17(11). Thus, 'development' means physical, intellectual, emotional, social or behavioural development; 'health' means physical or mental health; and a child is described as 'disabled' where he is blind, deaf or dumb or suffers from a mental disorder of any kind or is substantially and permanently handicapped by illness, injury or congenital deformity or such other disability as may be prescribed.

5.12 As a result both of the requirement to produce children's services plans (inserted into the CA 1989, Sch 2, Pt I, para 1A) and as a result of the MAPs required pursuant to the *Quality Protects* programme, nearly all local authorities have expanded upon the definition of 'child in need' and have further produced information about types of services which are available for children in need within their areas. Professionals working within the area of child protection should, therefore, be aware of the contents of the children's services plans and the MAPs, together with the contents of any 'Children in Need' documents which have also been produced in a large number of authorities, in order to be able to identify which of the various services a family in need of protection not only requires but also actually has some reasonable chance of being given (see further, M Adcock in Adcock and White (1998), and Morrison (1991)). On 6 September 2002, the Minister for Young People, John Denham, announced that the government would be pressing local authorities in combination with all the other relevant agencies, to produce new local preventive strategies to improve services for all children at risk. He stated that the government expected that health bodies, the police, probation, youth offending teams and the voluntary sector all to be involved in the strategy, the development of which would be supported by government offices and the inspectorates, who where necessary would work with the local partners on ensuring that an effective strategy is in place. The Minister further indicated that 'essential parts of the strategy will be effective systems to identify children and families needing support, to exchange information between agencies and track the progress through agency referrals'. Such systems, he stated, were to be in place by 2003. He went on to emphasise that the government sees the establishment for every area in England of an effective preventive strategy as the next step in developing services for children at risk. He also repeated what had been announced in the Treasury White Paper on the Spending Review, published in July 2002, that the government also intends to pilot new organisational models for managing children's services to be known as Children's Trusts (see Statement of Youth Minister Announcing New Directions for Children's Services (DOH, 6 September 2002 on www.doh.gov). This is all very well but the major problem which needs to be addressed in all of this is not the creation of new tiers of managers in new Children's Trust structures, but recruitment of the people engaging in the actual work of the provision of services and the protection of children, namely social workers. The view of many social workers on the ground is that there has already been too great an increase in the number of management bureaucrats placing impossible demands on an ever diminishing number of workers on the ground as a result of ever increasing demands to meet central government performance indicators and management targets (see Chapter **12**).

5.13   The need for the sort of support services provided pursuant to Pt III of the CA 1989 may be identified by any of the professionals involved in working with the family or, indeed, if they can gain access to these plans and other documents laying out what local authorities are supposed to provide, by the family themselves. In addition to the more general duties described in Sch 2, Pt I to the CA 1989, Pt III goes on to identify a variety of other services to meet the needs of families for support and assistance in caring for children. Thus, a local authority is under a duty to provide such day care for children in need within their area who are aged 5 or under and not yet attending schools as is appropriate (s 18). This is, of course, a discretionary power and it would be virtually impossible to argue that any local authority is under an absolute duty to make wide-ranging provision for day care places. CA 1989 does go on to provide, in s 18(5), that local authorities must also provide the children in need within their area who are attending school, with care or supervised activities *as are appropriate* outside school hours or during school holidays. The key words, however, are those in italics since what might otherwise appear as a duty is now reduced by those words to a discretionary power within the local authority. As to the range of other services which could be provided by local authorities under the provisions of the CA 1989 to support the families of children in need, these include: advice, guidance and counselling (Sch 2, Pt I, para 8(a)); occupational, social, cultural or recreational activities (para 8(b)); home help, including laundry services (para 8(c)); facilities for, or assistance with, travelling to and from home for the purpose of taking advantage of any other service provided under the CA 1989 (para 8(d)); assistance to enable the child concerned and his family to have a holiday (para 8(e)); and family centres (para 9).

5.14   These then are the range and level of services which it might be appropriate to provide to meet children's needs and specific duties and powers to provide them are set out in the combination of s 17 of the CA 1989 and Sch 2, Pt I. Yet s 17 also contains within it (in 17(1)) a ranking order of priority which appears to have had a considerable effect on the work done for 'children in need' under the Act (see Tunstill (1997); Aldgate and Tunstill (1996) and Audit Commission (1994).)

5.15   Thus s 17(1) provides that it shall be the general duty of every local authority:

(a)   to safeguard and promote the welfare of children within their area who are in need;
(b)   so far as is consistent with that duty, to promote the upbringing of such children by their families;
(c)   by providing a range and level of services appropriate to those children's needs.

5.16 According to the various studies and according to other commentators, most of those working in local authorities are tending to prioritise and give greater priority to the requirement to comply with s 17(1)(a) rather than with s 17(1)(b). As a result of the very considerable economic forces bearing down and putting pressure upon the work of local authority social services, there has been a tendency to gatekeep resources and to target resource allocation in the direction of children at risk (see Tunstill (1997), at pp 54–56, and Parton, Thorpe and Wattan (1997), at pp 230–234). Tunstill points out the longstanding dominance of 'risk' as *the* factor in childcare decision-making and further that the root causes of the failure of s 17 so far to rebalance the relationship between child protection and family support are the adverse political and economic circumstances in which it has been introduced (at p 56). As she points out, the clause while masquerading as a 'pro-child in the family' measure is far from that. It is primarily designed to legitimate resource rationing. Social services, and therefore predominantly social workers, have now been given this task as part of their *professional* and *legal* (as opposed to merely administrative/bureaucratic) responsibility. That they and their managers have so far tended to frame such limited entitlement to services they are able to offer, in terms which reduce risk for themselves as well as the child, is not therefore surprising. Evidence from the research done by Tunstill, and by Tunstill and Aldgate, reveals that most local authorities determined priority access to family support services on the basis of those problems that conventionally attracted a definition of *high risk* under the aegis of earlier legislation, rather than basing their priorities on empirical data about the numbers of children *with needs*, such as living in poor households, in poor housing accommodation, or without gas, water and electricity supplies. What emerges from the figures is a hierarchy of access with children merely 'in need' given less attention (or at least less in the way of services) than those seen as being *at risk*.

5.17 The opportunity for social workers to act as a gateway to family support services in the early stages of a problem would seem to be curtailed, which is exactly the outcome the CA 1989 in theory was intended to avoid. Even whilst training was being done on the implications of the CA 1989, it was quite apparent that local authorities had simply not been given enough resources to even attempt to deal with the demands placed upon them by the new s 17. Two early reviews of personal social services funding (Harding (1992) and Schorr (1992)) found significant deficiencies in the funding of local authority social services which particularly affected children. Schorr's calculation of the necessary additional expenditure required by the CA 1989 was between £500m and £1bn per year. He also identified the fact that, given that the majority of social services clients are poor or live in adverse circumstances, their need for services was increasing because of growing poverty and unemployment. A report from Statham (Statham (1994)) highlighted the fact that most counties in Wales had insufficient resources at that stage to develop locally based family support services as clearly envisaged in Sch 2, Pt III to the CA 1989. Early on, even the *Children Act Report* which was required to be presented to Parliament in the early years of the operation of the Act, was forced to conclude that:

'a broadly consistent and somewhat worrying picture is emerging. In general, progress towards full implementation if Section 17 of the Children Act 1989 has been slow. Further work is still needed to provide across the country a range of family services aimed at preventing families reaching the point of breakdown. Some authorities are still finding it difficult to move from a reactive social policing role to a more proactive partnership role with families' (see *Children Act Report 1993* (DOH, 1994), at para 239).

5.18 As Tunstill points out, the root causes of the failure of s 17 so far as to rebalance the relationship between child protection and family support are the adverse political and economic circumstances in which it was introduced. She comments that:

'the process of replacing risk as the organising slogan for child care, with need, has to be understood in its political context, in idealogical as well as *resource* terms. It cannot be achieved by professional social work effort or reform alone. Once the clear commitment to meeting need on the basis of values such as equality and the normality of parenting problems has been proclaimed by governments, then the staff in statutory and voluntary agencies have an important part to play' (see Tunstill (1997)).

Parton et al also point out that 'simply shifting towards the child's welfare response in terms of s 17 of the CA 1989 will not overcome the problems. The choice of services is restricted and a whole range of possibilities are simply not on the menu' (see Parton et al (1997)). In recognition of the ever increasing number of problems being faced by families with children in need, and which could not be met by local authority provision, the government has now created a whole range of initiatives such as 'Sure Start', 'the Children's Fund' and 'Connexions', which aim to provide many of the services identified in the CA 1989 and are now seen by the government as a key part of local preventive strategies (see paras **1.12** and **5.12**).

5.19 Provisions of the CA 1989 and the DOH guidance (see *The Children Act 1989: Guidance and Regulations* (DOH, 1991), vol 6 'Disabled Children') further recognise the positive duties placed upon local authorities to provide services for children with disabilities within their area so as to minimise the effect of their disabilities and to give such children the opportunity to lead lives which are as normal as possible (see Sch 2, para 6 to the CA 1989). The range of services described earlier should also all be available for families with disabled children, and respite care, which formerly was always thought of as a particular service to meet the needs of families with disabled children, should also now be seen in a much wider context as being available to serve all families with children in need. The provision of temporary accommodation is governed by the provisions of s 20 of the CA 1989, and respite care is thus controlled by the protective provisions relating to the placement of children in accommodation provided by the local authority. (See *Fostering Services – National Minimum Standards* (DOH, 2002) accessible at *www.doh.gov.uk/ncsc*.) In many ways the same comments which have been made as to the limitation placed upon the provision of services to families of children in need with regard to economic resources can equally well be made in relation to the provision of services to families with disabled children. Disabled children also suffer directly as a result of the process of prioritisation – giving the highest priority to children at risk of abuse is unlikely to assist children with physical or other disabilities, and very often the families of such children feel themselves to be at the bottom of anyone's priority list (see *Don't Forget Us – A Report on Services Available to Children with Serious Learning Difficulties and Severely Challenging Behaviour* (Mental Health Foundation, 1997)).

5.20 In addition to those duties set out in s 17 of and Sch 2, paras 2 and 6 to the CA 1989, the Act has been further amended to allow either for direct payments to be made in order that parents may purchase particular services on behalf of their disabled child or, alternatively, for the provision of vouchers which are intended to assist in the purchasing of relevant respite care (CA 1989, ss 17A, 17B, as amended). Section 17A allows a local authority to make direct payments either to a person with parental responsibility for the disabled child or directly to a disabled child himself where he is aged 16 or 17 in order that services may be purchased which the local authority would otherwise have had to provide. The amount of money which will be paid over is provided by s 17A(6) as being the amount which would be equal to the local authority's estimate of the reasonable cost of securing the provision of the service concerned. The issuing of vouchers by local authorities under the provisions of s 17B are, as indicated above, intended to provide the person with parental responsibility with a break from caring by securing the temporary provision of services for the child, most particularly the service of respite care.

5.21 Regulations provide for the value of a voucher to be expressed in terms of money or of the delivery of a service for a period of time, or both; for the person who supplies the service against the voucher or for the arrangement under which it is supplied, to be approved by the local authority; and for a maximum period during which a service can be provided against a voucher (s 17B(3)(a), (b) and (c)). These amendments contained in ss 17A and 17B of the CA 1989 were made by the Carers and Disabled Children Act 2000. The *Policy Guidance* on the provisions of the Carers and Disabled Children Act 2000 emphasises that persons with parental responsibilities for a disabled child (usually the parents) now have the additional right to ask for an assessment.

The local council must take that assessment into account when deciding what services, if any, to provide under s 17 of the CA 1989 to support a disabled child and his or her family (see *Policy Guidance on the Carers and Disabled Children Act 2000* (DOH, 2001), at para 6). The guidance goes on to point out that the aim of direct payments to people with parental responsibility for a disabled child is to allow recipients to make more decisions for themselves, creating greater flexibility in the way their assessed needs are met and thus provide opportunities for families to have more control over their lives. It stresses that 'so long as the local council is satisfied that the assessed needs of the carer or disabled child and family will be met through the arrangements the carer or parent makes using the direct payment, then the local council is relieved of its responsibility to arrange those services' (at para 7).

5.22 The 'short term break voucher scheme' is further explained at the end of the *Policy Guidance*. The guidance states that short term break vouchers will enable parents to make arrangements for the additional support their disabled child will require whilst they take any breaks which they have been assessed as needing. The guidance emphasises that short-term break voucher schemes will thus offer flexibility in the timing of parents' breaks and choice in the way services are delivered to their children while they are taking a break (at para 79). The guidance points out that regulations have yet to be made and fuller guidance on development of local voucher schemes will be issued at the time when such regulations are introduced (at paras 80–81). Further practice guidance has been issued in relation to the assessment of carers' needs, the provision of the direct payment scheme and the voucher scheme in *Carers and People with Parental Responsibility for Disabled Children: Practice Guidance* (DOH, 2001).

Requests for help to other agencies

5.23 Whilst it might appear that an undue burden is placed upon local authorities, particularly on social services, to provide the various services under Pt III of the CA 1989, it should be noted that theoretically s 27 provides local authority social services departments with the ability to request help from a range of other authorities within the local area, such as local housing authorities, local education authorities, health authorities and health service trusts. Such a request of help made by social services or the particular local authority must be complied with by the other authorities, provided that it is compatible with its statutory functions and does not unduly prejudice the discharge of those functions. As the DOH guidance states, social services will, on occasion, turn to the education authority for assistance in meeting the duties placed on social services departments in respect of family support (see *The Children Act 1989: Guidance and Regulations* (DOH, 1991) vol 2 'Family Support, Day Care and Educational Provision for Young Children', at para 1.13). The type of service envisaged here might include the services of an educational psychologist or speech therapist where efforts are being made to mitigate the effects of possible child abuse or neglect. The guidance goes on to state that the local authority carries the principal responsibility for co-ordinating and providing services for children in need, although in some cases its services will be supported by other key agencies. Local authorities and other relevant agencies remain responsible for decisions about their own service provision or legal and administrative issues assigned to them. They should, however, seek out and have available the best relevant help from the other agencies. Similarly, they must 'be available and prepared to contribute to the work of other key agencies in meeting the legitimate needs of children and their families' (at para 1.14). The amendment of s 17(6) to provide that the giving of assistance to families of children in need can include the provision of accommodation serves to emphasise the duties which local housing authorities are under to respond to requests for accommodation made by social services (as confirmed in R *(on the application of W) v Lambeth LBC* [2002] 2 FLR 327 overruling in part *A v London Borough of Lambeth* [2001] 2 FLR 1201 and R *(on the application of J) v Enfield LBC* [2002] 2 FLR 1). (See Chapter **11** for a detailed discussion of cases on judicial review.)

The elevation of the prevention principle

5.24 Thus, it can be seen that the theoretical effect of the elevation of the prevention principle represented by the enactment of Pt III of the CA 1989 should have meant that the provision of day nursery places, playgroup places, child-minding facilities, family aid, family centres, respite care, short holidays and access to various educational and health facilities should be considered and some such provision used before resort is made to legal action such as the bringing of care proceedings. The various research studies would seem to indicate that if a family can be placed in the high risk category and the situation is brought within the definition of s 17(1)(a) then some such service provision should have been made (see *Children Act Now: Messages from Research* (DOH, 2000, at chapter 5). It is clear that the DOH has seen it as the task of all professionals working within the child protection arena to provide services to help to maintain the child within the family, provided always that to do so is consistent with the child's welfare (see *Working Together to Safeguard Children*, at para 7.5). The legislative support for the principles of prevention represented by the enactment of Pt III of the CA 1989 serves only to reinforce the good practice which had been carried out by a range of professionals prior to the enactment of the CA 1989. What does emerge from the research studies is that the ability to provide such support is only present at the point of quite serious risk to the child. The expectation that such support work could be carried out in order to prevent children falling into this category in the first place is as a result of the starving of local authorities of the necessary economic resources. What the various research studies which have been done so far on s 17 and Sch 2, Pt I show is that where children have been identified as being in need because of the need to safeguard their welfare (s 17(1)(a)), considerable efforts will be expended on keeping the family out of the framework of legal proceedings involving possible compulsory removal of the child from his family, but this does not necessarily mean that the child will be properly safeguarded (see Farmer and Owen (1995), Thoburn (1995) Gibbons (1995) and Gallagher et al (1995)).

5.25 The basic message in all the documents of guidance produced for social workers as the professionals in the front line of child abuse appears to be that, wherever it is possible to promote and protect the welfare of the child by leaving him in his family, then this approach is to be preferred to potentially damaging and possibly unnecessary removals (see *Child Protection: Messages from Research* (DOH, 1995); *Quality Protects* (DOH, September 1998) and *Children Act Now: Messages from Research* (DOH, 2001)). Even where social services or other professional agencies have had some continuing contact with the family, one particular incident may spark off a need for an investigation leading to a full child protection conference. Alternatively, in situations where families have previously been unknown to any agencies, a report of suspected abuse or concerns over a child may come through from another professional having contact with the child (eg a teacher), or from neighbours, relatives or friends of the family. In such circumstances the guidance as to how the various agencies and professionals should work together with the parents and other members of the family to safeguard the child and to ensure that the appropriate steps are taken are laid down in *Working Together to Safeguard Children* (DOH, 1999).

Working Together to Safeguard Children *and the new framework of assessment*

5.26 *Working Together to Safeguard Children* and the two additional pieces of supplementary guidance, *Safeguarding Children Involved in Prostitution* (DOH, 2000) and *Safeguarding Children in Whom Illness is Fabricated or Induced* (DOH, 2002), are further supported by the *Framework for the Assessment of Children in Need and their Families* (DOH, 2000) (now being referred to as the 'Lilac Book') and *Assessing Children in Need and their Families: Practice Guidance* (DOH, 2000) which builds on and supersedes earlier DOH guidance on assessing children (see *Protecting Children: A Guide for Social Workers Undertaking a Comprehensive Assessment* (1988) often referred to as the 'Orange Book'). That earlier publication was widely used by social work practitioners as a guide to comprehensive assessment for long-term planning in child protection cases. The purpose of the Orange Book was to assist social work practitioners, in consultation with other agencies, to understand the child's and family's situation more fully once concerns about significant harm had been established following initial enquiries and assessment. Much of the Orange Book's thinking about children's development and parents' capacity to respond to children's needs has been incorporated within the new assessment framework, generally referred to as the 'Lilac Book'. The DOH points out, however, that over the years concerns arose about the use made of the Orange Book. Both inspections by the Social Services Inspectorate and research studies (see *Child Protection: Messages from Research* (DOH, 1995) and *Children Act Now: Messages from Research* (DOH, 2000)) demonstrated that the guide was on occasions followed mechanistically and used as a checklist, without any differentiation according to the child's or family's circumstances. Assessment was regarded as an event rather than as a process and services were withheld awaiting the completion of an assessment. In some authorities, it was identified that an all or nothing approach had been adopted; either very detailed comprehensive assessments were carried out or there was no record of any analysis of the child and the family's situation.

5.27   The DOH thus emphasises that the *Framework for Assessing Children in Need and their Families* is now underpinned by a set of principles, which seek to remedy some of the misunderstanding about the task of working with children and families to find out what is happening, and how they might best be helped (see the Lilac Book, at p iv). The DOH has emphasised that arrangements have to be set in place to ensure successful implementation of the new framework for assessing children in need and their families. One of the most interesting directives to emerge from the new *Framework* is that an assessment plan should not only be agreed with the child and his family, but that:

> 'there is an expectation that within one working day of a referral being received or new information coming to an agency about an open case, there will be a decision about what response is required. A referral is defined as a request for services to be provided by the social services department' (at para 3.8).

5.28   The effectiveness of assessment processes will be measurable over time by evidence of improving outcomes for children and families known to social services departments. It declares, therefore, that the DOH will be working closely with those involved in providing services to children to develop appropriate implementation plans at national and local level, to learn from the experiences of children and families and to evaluate the contribution a new approach to assessment can make to improving outcomes for children in need.

Reporting

The absence of a reporting law

5.29   As identified in *Childhood Matters: Report of the Commission of Enquiry into the Prevention of Child Abuse and Neglect* (The Stationery Office, 1996), unlike many of the states in the USA or a number of countries within Europe, the law in England and Wales does not provide for the compulsory reporting of child abuse. The notion of a reporting law was discussed by the DHSS in the *Review of Child Care Law* (DHSS, 1985) but the working party decided against such a proposal (at para 12.4). There is, therefore, no provision in the CA 1989 providing for a legal duty to be placed upon members of the public to report suspicions or knowledge of incidents of child abuse.

5.30 Nevertheless, every encouragement is given to the public to ensure that where they do provide such information, their anonymity will be protected and it is likely that their anonymity will continue to be protected even given the provisions of Article 10 of the ECHR (see para **1.22**). This is suggested by the case of *D v NSPCC* [1997] 1 All ER 589, HL, which would almost certainly withstand any Article 10 challenge. Lord Diplock pointed out, in that case, that any private promise of confidentiality must yield to the general public interest that, in the administration of justice, truth will out, unless by reason of the character of the information or the relationship of the recipient to the informant, a more important public interest is served by protecting the information or the identity of the informant from disclosure in a court of law. Their Lordships concluded, in that case, that the public interest in ensuring the protection of children was greater than the public interest in ensuring that the whole truth be told. It thus refused to allow the disclosure of any details relating to the original informant, who had contacted the NSPCC to report her concern about the abuse of a particular child in the case. It is quite clear that organisations such as ChildLine and the NSPCC could not continue to perform the work which they do if there was any requirement that the identity of informants had to be disclosed before any action could be taken or that where action is taken, their right to anonymity could be breached.

Health professionals and the duty to report

5.31 Despite the absence of a mandatory reporting law, it is, nevertheless, the case that very many different professional groups working with children, whilst not subjected to any mandatory reporting law as such, may find that either their own professional association's guidance seeks very strongly to encourage them to do so, or else they are subjected to strong guidance being issued by their relevant supervising government department. For example, the BMA, GMSC, HEA, Brook Advisory Centres, FPA, and RCGP all combined together to produce guidelines for doctors which were published by all of the groups together in 1994. This remains the current Joint Guidance, even in 2002, and can be consulted on the different organisations' websites (see for example www.bma.org.uk/confidentiality+people+under+16), although further guidance on the subject has been issued by some of these different professional groups since (see, for example, BMA (2001) and www.bmjpg.com/consent, and see also paras **5.38–5.39**). The 1994 guidelines implicitly recognised that the notion of *Gillick*-competence of children may demand a different approach in cases of child abuse where the risk to a particular young person or other younger children demands that some disclosure must be made. The guidelines state that:

> 'The duty of confidentiality owed to a person under 16 is as great as the duty to any other person. The statutory body, the General Medical Council, states that: "patients are entitled to expect that the information about themselves or others which a doctor learns during the course of a medical consultation, investigation or treatment, will remain confidential. An explicit request by a patient that information should not be disclosed to particular people, or indeed to any third party, must be respected save in the most exceptional circumstances, for example where the health, safety or welfare of someone other than the patient would otherwise be at serious risk". The document goes on to emphasise that although respect for confidentiality is an essential element of doctor–patient relationship, "no patient, adult or minor, has an absolute right to complete confidentiality in all circumstances. Confidentiality must be balanced against society's interest in protecting vulnerable people from serious harm. Thus, in rare cases for example, a breach of confidentiality may be justified if the patient's silence puts others at risk and the doctor cannot persuade the patient to make a voluntary disclosure".
>
> In exceptional circumstances, a doctor may believe that the young person seeking medical advice on sexual matters is being exploited or abused. The doctor should provide counselling with a view to preparing the patient to agree, when ready, to confidentiality being relaxed. This task assumes greater urgency if the patient, siblings or other minors continue to be in a situation of risk so that in some cases, the doctor will have to tell the patient that confidentiality cannot be preserved. Disclosure should not be made without further discussing it with the patient whose cooperation is sought. To breach confidentiality without informing the patient and in contradiction of patient refusal may irreparably damage the trust between doctor and patient and may result in denial by the young person that abuse has taken place. In any situation where confidentiality is breached, the doctor must be prepared to justify his or her decision before the General Medical Council.'

5.32 Originally, it had been anticipated that when the various separate bodies came together to issue *Confidentiality and People under 16* (BMA, GMSC, HEA, BAC, FPA and RCGP, 1994) they would also go on to issue separate guidance documents, but as discussion continued it became quite clear that they should instead combine together to issue joint guidance. It thus emerged from the guidance that there is a clear *ethical imperative* upon the doctor to inform the relevant statutory agencies where the child has made disclosures or the doctor has observed any symptons or manifestations of any form of child abuse. In the case of older children, the guidance indicated that the doctor should, wherever possible, seek to encourage the child to agree to disclosure but that this might occur after a referral to expert counsellors very much following the model adopted in Holland in these sort of cases.

5.33 Following the publication of *Confidentiality and People under 16* in 1994, the DOH, the BMA and the Conference of Medical Royal Colleges got together to form a joint working party to produce further guidance for doctors working with child protection agencies. This resulting document *Child Protection: Medical Responsibilities* (DOH, BMA, Conference of Medical Royal Colleges, 1997) was intended to act as a supplement to the former *Working Together under the Children Act 1989* guidance issued in 1991. That guidance has again had to be revised to take account of the new guidance issued in *Working Together to Safeguard Children* (DOH, 1999) and was published in 2001 (see above at para **5.31**: *Consent, Rights and Choices in Health Care for Children and Young People* (BMA, 2001)). In Pt IV of *Child Protection: Medical Responsibilities,* the patient's entitlement to medical confidentiality is first emphasised and then circumstances are set out where the doctor's responsibility towards the child may appear to be in conflict with his or her ethical duties with regard to confidentiality. The guidance nevertheless stresses that the welfare of children must always be regarded as of first importance as their age and vulnerability renders them powerless to protect their own interests (at para 4.3). The guidance goes on to emphasise therefore that:

'there are overwhelming reasons why all doctors should be aware of factors relevant to the protection of children and the critical role they can play in safeguarding their interests. Doctors should be aware of the importance of safeguarding the interests of children and professional intervention should always have this in mind.'

5.34   The guidance further indicates that:

'in consultations where child abuse is alleged, promises of secrecy must not be given and it should be made clear to all parties in the consultation that information may be shared on a controlled "need to know" basis in the interests of the child. If an examination is carried out as part of the consultation the doctor should explain that information may have to be shared with other people, for example other doctors, social workers or the police on a similar basis. The doctor needs to be confident, however, that any information disclosed will not be further disclosed without his or her prior agreement' (at para 4.4).

5.35   The guidance does acknowledge that doctors may receive information suggesting concerns about child abuse from patients who are not the abused children. Such disclosures may come from the abusing or non-abusing parent and it is made clear that the same considerations will apply. Thus, where the doctor is in possession of information relating to a third party and which is of direct relevance to child protection issues, for example violent behaviour, sexual arousal to children or information about a known or alleged perpetrator who may pose a continuing risk to children, it is essential that doctors are aware of all these risk factors and weigh the information very carefully. The guidance advises that disclosure of such information will usually be justified in relation to child protection. As a result of the passage of the HRA 1998 and the Public Interest (Disclosure of Information) Act 1998, this advice now needs recasting to read that disclosure of such information is required in relation to child protection. Finally, in relation to the issue of confidential information and the circumstances which may lead to the sharing of that information, the guidance points out that doctors need to be fully aware of what factors are relevant to the protection of children and which therefore need to be shared with the statutory agencies (at para 4.7). Guidance issued by the General Medical Council and distributed to all GPs is much more prescriptive but this has the advantage of being written after the enactment of the HRA 1998, the Data Protection Act 1998 and the Public Interests (Disclosure of Information) Act 1998 (see *Confidentiality: Providing and Protecting Information* (GMC, 2000) at www.gmc-uk.org). Thus the guidance advises (at para 14), that 'disclosures of information without the patient's consent or where such consent cannot be obtained, cannot be made unless they can be justified in the public interest, usually where disclosure is essential to protect the patient, or someone else, from risk of death or serious harm'. The disclosure of information about the abuse of a child without the patient's consent and in some cases without the patient's knowledge, will usually therefore be covered if not required in certain circumstances, by this exception.

5.36 Virtually identical guidance to that issued in 1994 also exists for senior nurses, health visitors and midwives (see *Child Protection: Health Care Responsibilities – Guidance for Senior Nurses, Health Visitors and Midwives* (DOH, 1997)) and again the guidance makes it clear that in all such cases there is a similar ethical imperative imposed on these health care professionals to make the relevant disclosures in respect of any children suffering or at risk of suffering significant harm, in the same way as that laid out for the doctors in their guidance (see also *Designated Nurses – Child Protection* DOH, 2002). Given responsibilities imposed upon public authorities under the HRA 1998, this ethical imperative has now, of course, become a legal imperative.

Disclosures of information received by social workers

5.37 Guidance given to social workers and all those involved in the child protection arena is set out in *Working Together to Safeguard Children*. It is pointed out (at para 7.29) that professionals can only work together to safeguard children if there is an exchange of relevant information between them. It points out that this principle has been recognised by the courts and refers to the comments by Butler-Sloss LJ in *Re G (A Minor)* [1996] 2 All ER 65, at p 68. Thus, she stated that:

> 'the Working Together booklet does not have any legal status, but with the lesson of Cleveland in mind, the emphasis upon cooperation, joint investigation and full consultation at all stages of any investigation are crucial to the success of the government's guidelines ... The consequences of inter agency cooperation is that

there has to be free exchange of information between social workers and police officers together engaged in an investigation ... The information obtained by social workers in the course of their duties is however confidential and covered by the umbrella of public interest immunity ... It can however be disclosed to fellow members of the child protection team engaged in the investigation of possible abuse of the child concerned' (at p 68).

5.38 *Working Together to Safeguard Children* goes on to point out that any disclosure of personal information to others must always have regard to both common and statute law (at para 7.29). It states that, normally, personal information should only be disclosed to third parties (including other agencies) with the consent of the subject of that information. Wherever possible, consent should be obtained before sharing personal information with third parties. In some circumstances, consent may not be possible or desirable but the safety and welfare of a child dictate that the information should be shared (at para 7.30). The guidance states that the best way of ensuring that information sharing is properly handled is to work within carefully worked out information-sharing protocols between the agencies and the professionals involved, taking legal advice in individual cases where necessary. The guidance further points out that the Data Protection Registrar has produced a checklist for setting up information-sharing arrangements, which is reproduced in full at Appendix 4 of *Working Together to Safeguard Children*.

5.39 Whilst acknowledging that personal information about children and families held by professionals and agencies is usually subject to a legal duty of confidence, and should not normally be disclosed without the consent of the subject, the law does however permit the disclosure of confidential information necessary to safeguard a child or children in the public interest: that is, *the public interest in child protection may override the public interest in maintaining confidentiality*. The guidance states that disclosure should be justifiable in each case, according to the particular facts of the case, and legal advice should be sought in cases of doubt. The guidance emphasises that the children are entitled to the same duties of confidence as adults, providing, in the case of those aged under 16, they have the ability to understand the choices and their consequences relating to any treatment. Where it is believed that a child seeking advice is being exploited or abused then, in such cases, confidentiality may be breached, usually following discussion with the child.

5.40 It should be noted that, under the requirements of the Data Protection Act 1998, where personal information is obtained it must be processed fairly and lawfully; only disclosed in appropriate circumstances; must be accurate, relevant and not held longer than necessary; and must be kept securely. The Act provides for disclosure without the consent of the subject in certain conditions, including for the purposes of the prevention or detection of crime, or the apprehension or prosecution of offenders, and where failure to disclose would be likely to prejudice those objectives in a particular case.

5.41   *Working Together to Safeguard Children* points out the relevance of Article 8 of the ECHR in relation to the issue of disclosure of information and points out that disclosure of information without consent could give rise to an issue under Article 8. It does, however, point out that disclosure of information to safeguard children will usually come within the legitimate aims for interference with an Article 8 right. Thus such disclosure would usually be for the protection of the health or morals of the children, for the protection of the rights and freedoms of children and also for the prevention of disorder or crime as set out in Article 8(2). Disclosure should nevertheless be proportionate to the intended objective and thus should be appropriate for the purpose and only to the extent necessary to achieve that purpose (Article 8(2) and *Working Together to Safeguard Children*, at paras 7.35, 7.36).

Disclosure of information about sex offenders

5.42   The Home Office has also produced guidance (*Guidance on the Disclosure of Information about Sex Offenders Who May Present a Risk to Children and Vulnerable Adults* (Home Office, 2000)) on the exchange of information about all those who have been convicted of, cautioned for or otherwise dealt with by the courts for a sexual offence; and those who are considered by the relevant agencies to present a risk to children and others. The guidance further addresses issues in relation to people who have not been convicted or cautioned for offences, but who are suspected of involvement in criminal sexual activity. The guidance stresses that the disclosure of information should always take place within an established system and protocol between agencies, and should be integrated into a risk assessment and management system. Each case should be judged on its merits by the police and other relevant agencies, taking into account the degree of risk. The guidance further places on the police the responsibility of co-ordinating and leading the risk assessment and management process. It advises that agencies should work within carefully worked out information-sharing protocols, and refers to good practice material in existence. The Home Office guidance also advocates the establishment of multi-agency risk panels whose purpose is to share information about offenders and to devise strategies to manage their risk.

Disclosure of information by those in the prison service

5.43   *Working Together to Safeguard Children* also points out that the prison service works closely with other agencies to identify any prisoner who may represent a risk to the public on release. Regular risk assessments take account of progress made during the sentence, and informed decisions on sentence planning for individual prisoners, including sex offender treatment programmes. Governors of prisons are required to notify social services departments and the probation service of plans to release prisoners who have been convicted of offences against children and young people so that appropriate action can be taken by agencies in the community to minimise any risk.

Disclosure of information by those in the education service

5.44 Staff, particularly in the education service, may also be deemed to be in the front line as far as initial identification and referral processes in child protection cases are concerned. Local education authorities all over the country have, in compliance with local ACPC guidelines, issued education staff with explanations of the law and procedures which may flow from the referral of cases of suspected child abuse. Whilst local education authorities (LEAs) are responsible for staff in the education service, such as teachers, nursery staff including nursery nurses, educational welfare officers, educational psychologists and youth workers, they have no responsibility for the private sector. This, instead, falls on social services departments who are required to adopt the same principles with private schools in relation to child protection as they adopt in relation to any other school (see *Working Together to Safeguard Children*, at paras 3.15 and 6.5). *Working Together to Safeguard Children* emphasises that it is particularly important that independent schools (including independent special schools) establish channels of communication with local social services departments and ACPCs, building on existing links with the LEA, so that children requiring support receive prompt attention and any allegations of abuse can be properly investigated. It directs that independent schools which provide medical and/or nursing care should ensure that their medical and nursing staff have appropriate training and access to advice on child protection. It stresses that social services departments and ACPCs offer the same level of support and advice to independent schools in matters of child protection as they do to maintained schools (at para 3.15).

5.45 *Working Together to Safeguard Children* also emphasises the key contribution which education services can make to the process of safeguarding children, emphasising not only their pastoral responsibilities towards their pupils, but also the roles which schools can play in the prevention of abuse and neglect through their own policies and procedures for safeguarding children, and very importantly through the curriculum. *Working Together to Safeguard Children* emphasises that children can be helped to understand what is and is not acceptable behaviour towards them, and taught about staying safe from harm, and how to speak up if they have worries or concerns. It further states that the curriculum can also play a preventive role in developing awareness and resilience and in preparing children and young people for their future responsibilities as adults, parents and citizens. Despite this sentiment, increasingly research has identified that schools do not take on this role and, in particular, have not discussed with children the issue of appropriate behaviour within families. 'Stranger danger' is the type of advice which many children will receive but teaching about inappropriate behaviour within families is almost non-existent on the curriculum (see *Childhood Matters* (The Stationery Office, 1996), vol 2, at pp 127–131 and, see also *Child Maltreatment in the United Kingdom* (NSPCC, 2000), at p 61).

5.46 Education staff clearly have a critical role to play in noticing possible signs of abuse or neglect and in referring their concerns to the appropriate agency, normally the social services department. If a child has special educational needs, or is disabled, schools will have important information about the child's level of understanding and will generally be the most effective means of communicating with the child. They will also be well placed to give a view on the impact of treatment or intervention on the child's care or behaviour. Staff working in the education service will inevitably be asked questions where there are concerns about abuse or neglect in respect of a child attending their school. Whilst education staff do not have direct investigative responsibilities in child protection work they do nevertheless have a critical role to play in assisting the social services department by referring concerns and of course also in providing information relevant to s 47 of the CA 1989 'child protection enquiries'. In addition, where a child of school age is subject to an inter-agency child protection plan (see Chapter **4**) school staff should be involved in the preparation of the plan and the school's role and responsibilities in contributing to actions to safeguard the child, and promote his or her welfare, should be clearly identified.

5.47 Since the implementation of the CA 1989 in 1991, further steps have been taken to alert education staff to their role within the child protection system and also to provide advice relevant to those situations in which teachers and workers with children and young persons might be themselves accused of child abuse. The DfEE has issued two circulars. The first, Circular 10/95 entitled *Protecting Children from Abuse: the Role of the Education Service*, provides guidance to the education service on its role in helping to protect children from abuse. The main points emerging from this guidance are:

– all staff should be alert to signs of abuse and know to whom they should report any concerns or suspicions;
– all schools and colleges should have a designated member of staff responsible for coordinating action in the institution and liaising with other agencies, including the ACPC;
– all schools and colleges should be aware of the child protection procedures established by the ACPC and, where appropriate, by the local education authority;
– all schools and colleges should have procedures (of which all staff should be aware) for handling suspected cases of child abuse of pupils or

students, including procedures to be followed if a member of staff is accused of abuse;

– staff with designated responsibility for child protection should receive appropriate training;

– in every LEA, a senior officer should be responsible for coordinating action on child protection across the authority.

Circular 10/95 is also in the course of being revised as a result of the issuing of the new guidance from the DOH on *Working Together to Safeguard Children*, but according to the Child Protection Team Leader in the Schools Directorate of the DFES, this had not been done even by January 2003. Other documents being issued by the DFES are continuing to make reference to both Circulars 10/95 and 11/95 and so it would seem that they will remain current for some time yet. Partly as a result of the emerging findings from the Victoria Climbie inquiry, the government moved quickly to insert a new provision in the Education Act 2002 requiring LEAs to make arrangements for ensuring that the functions conferred upon them in their capacity as an LEA are exercised with a view to safeguarding and promoting the welfare of children (s 175 of the Education Act 2002). This provision mirrors the responsibilities imposed upon local authorities under s 17 of the CA 1989. The Act continues by providing that the governing body of each maintained school shall make arrangements for ensuring that their functions relating to the conduct of the school are exercised with a view to safeguarding and promoting the welfare of children who are pupils at the school. These provisions are potentially extremely onerous in terms of casting a legal duty upon schools to safeguard and promote the welfare of children who are in their schools and further duties are imposed in terms of requiring adherence to any guidance which is issued, which of course imposes a statutory duty to adhere to the guidelines laid down in *Working Together to Safeguard Children*. Failures to detect obvious signs of abuse on the part of education staff in the school which Lauren Wright attended were held to be in part responsible for the tragic events leading to her death. These new statutory duties inserted at a very late stage in the Bill's progress through Parliament are intended to emphasise the role of education staff in the area of child protection.

5.48 *Working Together to Safeguard Children* goes on to emphasise that there are other areas in which issues of child protection arise. Thus the guidance advises that all schools should have an effective whole school policy against bullying and head teachers should have measures in place to prevent all forms of bullying amongst pupils. In addition, where a State school is concerned that a child may have 'disappeared', or about any aspect of a pupil transfer which gives rise to concerns about a child's welfare, it should report its concerns to a person specified in the local ACPC guidance or to the LEA officer with designated responsibilities for child protection. *Working Together to Safeguard Children* goes on to emphasise that corporal punishment is outlawed for all pupils in all schools and colleges, including independent schools, although teachers at a school are allowed to use reasonable force to control or restrain pupils under certain circumstances. Further guidance is given on this in Circular 10/98 which provides that other staff employed at a school may also use restraint in the same way as teachers, provided they have been authorised by the head teacher to have control or charge of pupils. Again, Circular 10/98 emphasises that all schools must have a policy about the use of force to control or restrain pupils.

The role of the probation service

5.49   Probation officers may also have concerns about possible child abuse in cases in which they become involved, often as a result of their responsibility for the supervision of offenders, including those convicted of offences against children. In addition, probation services may be working with those who have children who may be in need and those whose convictions relate to domestic violence. Probation officers may also be supervising dangerous child sex offenders on licence after release from prison and, more generally, will also work with a range of offenders with convictions for less serious offences against children (for more detail on this, see Chapter **9**). They will therefore be alive to the risk posed by such offenders which may relate to children in the community in general or to specific children with whom offenders are, or are likely to be, living. Probation officers currently may also be working in the family court as court welfare officers and may be alerted to alleged or actual child abuse as a result of their investigations when providing reports in proceedings involving family relationship breakdown (see s 7 of the CA 1989). Through their work in preparing reports for courts, they may turn up concerns about whether a child is suffering or likely to suffer significant harm. In non-urgent cases they may refer their concerns back to court and the court is then able, under s 37 of the CA 1989, to direct a local authority to conduct an investigation into the child's circumstances to see whether or not it is necessary to take proceedings for a care or supervision order. In urgent cases, the probation service must notify social services of their concerns, and social services will then be under a duty to make enquiries and to take such action as may be necessary.

5.50   Of relevance also to the issue of reporting is the fact that arrangements exist to ensure that when offenders convicted of offences against children are discharged from prison, probation services inform the local authority in the area in which the discharged prisoner plans to reside. This allows the social services department to make enquiries and to take action where it is believed that there may be a danger to children residing at the same address. Inter-agency case conferences, focusing on the necessary action to manage the risk posed by offenders, have been introduced following the Sex Offenders Act 1997, with its requirement for sex offenders to register with the police (see further, Chapter **9**). Such conferences, often known as risk management meetings or panels, also agree action plans for potentially dangerous offenders who fall outside the scope of the Sex Offenders Act 1997. In many ways these processes mirror child protection conferences, but instead the focus is on managing the risk posed by the perpetrator and are central to the inter-agency approach supported by probation services. Such a meeting or panel should provide the forum in which appropriate arrangements can be agreed in order to safeguard and protect the relevant children. Where prisoners are being released from psychiatric units it may be appropriate to hold such a case conference at the psychiatric unit and to involve not only staff from the unit but those who may be involved in community psychiatric support. *Working Together to Safeguard Children* emphasises at para 3.67 that in any case where an imprisoned offender is considered to pose a risk to children, the social services department in the area where the offender lives (or intends to live in the case of prisoners) should be alerted and an inter-agency approach adopted. Probation services are required to work closely with social services and the prison services in such cases and have a central role in the resettlement of such prisoners.

The role of housing authorities

5.51   Housing authorities may also play a critical role in safeguarding children in terms of recognition, referral and the subsequent management of risk. Housing authority staff, through their day-to-day contact with members of the public, may become aware of concerns about the welfare of particular children and should refer these concerns to one of the statutory agencies in appropriate cases. *Working Together to Safeguard Children* points out that housing authorities may also have important information about families that could be helpful to local authorities carrying out assessments under s 17 or s 47 of the CA 1989. In accordance with their duty to assist under s 27, they should be prepared to share relevant information orally or in writing, including attending child protection conferences when requested to do so. The guidance points out that appropriate housing can make an important contribution to meeting health and developmental needs of children, including those who need safeguarding from significant harm. It states that housing authorities should be prepared to assist by the provision of accommodation either directly, through their links with other housing providers, or by the provision of advice and that examples of such situations could include those where women and children become homeless or at risk of homelessness as a result of domestic violence. The guidance further indicates that housing authorities will have an important part to play in the management of risk posed by dangerous offenders, including those who are assessed as presenting a risk, whether sexual or otherwise, to children. It emphasises that appropriate housing can contribute greatly to the ability of the police and others to manage the risk of such individuals' homes.

5.52 *Working Together to Safeguard Children* identifies a wide range of health care personnel who might potentially be involved in the identification of children at risk of abuse including GPs and other members of primary health care teams, midwives, health visitors and school nurses, those working in child adolescent and mental health services, those working with or for drug action teams and a whole range of other staff including accident and emergency staff, ambulance service staff, clinical psychologists, dental practitioners, staff in genito-urinary medicine services, obstetric and gynaecological staff, occupational therapists, physiotherapists, staff working in private health care, staff in sexual health services, pregnancy advisory services and speech and language therapists; and all other professions allied to medicine. The guidance states that all such staff should receive the training and supervision needed to recognise and act upon child welfare concerns, and to respond to the needs of children. It also points out that NHS Direct staff should also have access to clear procedures, training and advice on child protection. As a result of events in 1999, special guidance has been issued with regard to the visiting of psychiatric patients by children (see *Guidance on the Visiting of Psychiatric Patients by Children* (HSC 1999/222) and also see LAC(99)32 which has been issued to NHS Trusts, health authorities and social services departments). This states that:

> 'hospitals should have written policies on the arrangements about the visiting of patients by children, which should be drawn up in consultation with local social services authorities. A visit by a child should only take place following a decision that such a visit would be in the child's best interests. Decisions to allow such visits should be regularly reviewed.'

The role of the police

5.53 As far as police reporting of concerns about child abuse is concerned, this stems from their primary duty to protect members of the community and to bring offenders to justice. The police have special powers to take action in emergencies but, where they have concerns about the possibility of child abuse which is of a non-urgent nature, they would be expected to notify such concerns to social services. It should be noted that all police forces in England and Wales now have child protection units (CPUs) and although there may be differentiation in terms of their structures and staffing levels, they will normally take primary responsibility on behalf of the police for investigating child abuse cases. Despite the existence of such CPUs, safeguarding children is not solely their concern and all police officers need an understanding of child protection as part of their general responsibility. *Working Together to Safeguard Children* points out that patrol officers attending domestic violence incidents, for example, should be aware of the affect of such violence on any children within the household. It is further suggested that community beat officers should be made aware of any children in their area who are on the Child Protection Register, perhaps through links with police information systems. The guidance further emphasises that the police are committed to sharing information and intelligence with other agencies where this is necessary to protect children. This includes a responsibility to ensure that those officers representing the police at a child protection conference are fully informed about the case as well as being experienced in risk experience and the decision-making process. Clearly, it is anticipated that they would expect other agencies to share with them information and intelligence which they hold in order to enable the police to carry out their duties (at para 3.60). It is obviously the case that any evidence gathered during a criminal investigation by the police may also be of potential value to local authority solicitors who are preparing legal proceedings under the CA 1989 in order to protect the abused child. The police would normally consult first with the CPS but evidence will usually be shared where it is in the best interests of the child.

5.54 It should be noted that what has been said about the duties of the different agencies in respect of reporting concerns about particular children applies with equal force to later stages in the child protection process, such as investigation and assessment (see para **5.64** *et seq*).

Reporting by members of the public

5.55 Finally, whilst reporting of concerns about child abuse may come from any of the professionals in any of the agencies already discussed, and may come through to a social services department, the police or the NSPCC, referrals may also come from members of the public, or those working with children and families who are not accustomed to dealing with child protection matters. *Working Together to Safeguard Children* does not, unfortunately, reproduce the guidance set out in the 1991 version with regard to information which should be made available to members of the public. That document pointed out (at para 5.11.1) that:

> 'All referrals whatever their origin must be taken seriously and must be considered with an open mind which does not prejudice the situation. The statutory agencies must ensure that people know how to refer to them, and they must facilitate the making of referrals and the prompt and appropriate action in response to expressions of concern. It is important in all these cases that the public and professionals are free to refer to the child protection agencies without fear that this will lead to uncoordinated and/or premature action.'

5.56 As *Child Protection: Messages from Research* and *Children Act Now: Messages from Research* show, and, as a result of Article 8 of the ECHR, it is quite clear that a balance needs to be struck between taking action designed to protect a child from abuse and protecting that child and the family from the harm caused by unnecessary intervention. The best outcomes for children will only be achieved where there is a high level of commitment to the whole process of inter-agency working in child protection cases.

Stages of work in individual cases

5.57 Chapter 5 of *Working Together to Safeguard Children* (DOH, 1999) provides advice on what should happen if somebody has concerns about the welfare of a child (including those living away from home), together with concerns that a child may be suffering, or at risk of suffering, abuse or neglect. Whilst the guidance states that it is not intended as a detailed practice guide, it does set out clear expectations about the ways in which agencies and professionals should work together in the interests of children's safety and well-being. The latest version of *Working Together to Safeguard Children* is in fact the third version, the two previous ones having been issued in 1988 and 1991 respectively. Each version has undoubtedly been informed by the findings of different child abuse enquiries and also, and inevitably, by the course of legislation.

5.58 The moves to produce the first *Working Together* document occurred in 1987 even as the events of Cleveland were happening. The first draft appeared in April 1987 and had clearly been shaped by the findings of *A Child in Trust: Report of the Panel of Enquiry Investigating the Circumstances Surrounding the Death of Jasmine Beckford* (London Borough of Brent, 1985) but were given added impetus by the findings of the *Report of Enquiry into Child Abuse in Cleveland 1987* Cm 412 (HMSO, 1998), at p 248. The finalised version of the first *Working Together* guidance was published in 1988 in the wake of the Cleveland Report and followed very closely the Report's recommendations as to inter-agency working.

5.59 The second *Working Together* guidance (DOH, 1991) emphasised the importance of a shared clarity of purpose and stated that 'to be effective, co-operation between agencies providing protection to children must be underpinned by a shared agreement about the handling of individual cases' (para 5.10). That version of the guidance identified the various stages of work in individual cases of child abuse, but findings from *Child Protection: Messages from Research* (DOH, 1995) tended to suggest that on occasions social workers might apply the various steps identified in the guidance rather mechanistically.

5.60 Accordingly, *Working Together to Safeguard Children* (DOH, 1999) adopts a rather more fluid approach emphasising at every stage the importance of the assessments being conducted and the critical importance of a continuing evaluation as to whether more interventionist approaches are needed, especially where the child might otherwise be at risk of significant harm. Constant emphasis is laid on the importance of using the framework set out in the *Framework for the Assessment of Children in Need and their Families* (DOH, 2000) whilst at the same time it sets out clear expectations about the ways in which agencies and professionals should all work together in the interests of children's safety and well-being (see *Working Together to Safeguard Children*, at paras 5.1–5.104).

5.61 All the various agencies may thus be involved in different ways at different stages and what follows by way of the representation of these steps in a numbered sequence should not in any way be seen as describing steps which will take place independently or necessarily in the sequence indicated. The various stages do not necessarily stand alone nor are they clearly divided in time and, as can be seen, there is likely to be considerable overlap. Nevertheless, for the purposes of following the remainder of this chapter and also Chapter 7, which deals with the course of civil proceedings, it may be advantageous to set out the potentially relevant steps. Further detail on this guidance is given in Chapter 6, which engages in a more detailed analysis of *Working Together to Safeguard Children* from the perspective of inter-agency cooperation in child protection. Thus, the 14 steps which could be taken might include the following.

(1)   *Referral and initial consideration of the case.* According to *Working Together to Safeguard Children* (at para 5.10), social services should then decide on the next course of action within 24 hours, normally following discussion with any referring professional/service and looking at existing records and consulting other professionals and services as necessary (including the police where a criminal offence may have been committed against a child). Such initial consideration of the case should determine whether there are concerns about either the child's health and development, or actual and/or potential harm which justify further enquiries, assessment and/or intervention. If further action is needed, a decision will need to be taken on when the appropriate enquiries and/or investigation should take place. Sometimes it may be apparent even at this early stage that immediate emergency action should be taken to safeguard the child (at paras 5.12 and 5.23).

(2)   *Strategy discussions with police, social services and other agencies. Working Together to Safeguard Children* indicates that if emergency protection is necessary, this should normally, if possible, be preceded by an immediate strategy discussion between the police, social services and any other relevant agencies.

(3)   *Immediate protection.* This includes, for example, the taking of an emergency protection order (CA 1989, ss 44, 44A and 45) or in any case where immediate action is deemed to be absolutely critical then the exercise of police powers of protection (s 48) might be initiated. This is clearly only going to be case where there is a real fear that there is immediate risk to the life or limb of the child.

(4)   *Initial assessment, investigation and enquiries.* Where there is no such immediate risk to the child then, following on from the referral and initial consideration, there will be further investigation between various

agencies, which according to *Working Together to Safeguard Children* should be completed within a maximum of 7 working days from the date of referral. *Working Together to Safeguard Children* does, however, point out that the initial assessment period may be very brief where the criteria for initiating s 47 enquiries are met. The process of initial assessment should involve seeing and speaking to all family members, including the child, as appropriate and drawing together all relevant information from a range of sources including existing records and obtaining further relevant information from all professionals and others in contact with the child and the family.

(5)   *Core assessment and/or conducting s 47 enquiries and investigations.* The guidance deals with the situation where an initial assessment indicates the child may be in need, but where there are no substantiated concerns that the child may be suffering or at risk of significant harm. In such a case *Working Together to Safeguard Children* points out that the *Framework for the Assessment of Children in Need and their Families* provides a framework for a core assessment of a child's health and development, and the parents' capacity to respond to their child's needs. It states that such a core assessment can provide a sound evidence base for professional judgement on whether services would be helpful to the child and family and, if so, the types of service which would be most likely to bring about good outcomes for the child. In the case of *R (on the application of AB and SB) v Nottingham City Council* [2001] 3 FCR 350, it should be noted that the court found that where a local authority followed a path which did not involve the preparation of a core assessment as such, it had nevertheless to adopt a similarly systematic approach with a view to achievement of the same objectives. That involved an assessment of needs which took into account the three domains: the child's development needs, parenting capacity, family and environmental facts. It involved collaboration between all the relevant agencies so as to achieve a full understanding of the child in his family and community context. The authority then had to complete a three-stage process:

— to identify the child's needs;
— to produce a care plan; and
— to provide the identified services.

Failure to do so without good cause would constitute an impermissible departure from the *Framework for the Assessment of Children in Need and their Families*. In the instant case the court held that there was nothing in the documentation which approached an assessment capable of meeting those requirements. As to housing, it was common ground that accommodation could be provided under s 17 of the CA 1989 and that the assessment of the child's needs has to encompass the question of his housing needs. That assessment had to take into account the position of the child and the position of the carer with whom he lived. In the circumstances, there had been no proper assessment of housing need. Further, according to the court, even if there has been an assessment, there had been no proper provision of services to meet that need. The High Court judge found that it was the responsibility of the social services to meet the identified housing need. It could seek, he said, the assistance of the housing authority, but it could not simply wash its hands of the matter by referring those in need to the housing authority. The judge therefore found that the authority had been in breach of its duty under s 17 to assess the child's needs properly. The guidance goes on to indicate that Family Group Conferences may be an effective vehicle for taking forward work in this type of situation (at paras 5.20 and 7.13–7.18).

(6) *Conducting s 47 enquiries. Working Together to Safeguard Children* indicates that if the initial assessment reveals that a child is suspected to be suffering, or is likely to suffer, significant harm, then s 47 of the CA 1989 requires local authority social services to make enquiries so as to enable them to determine whether or not it should take any action to safeguard or promote the child's welfare. *Working Together to Safeguard Children* points out (at para 5.22) that the *Framework for the Assessment of Children in Need and their Families* is equally relevant in these circumstances as a structured framework for collecting, drawing together and analysing available information about a child and the family. The *Framework* will also assist in providing sound evidence on which to base often difficult professional judgements about whether to intervene to safeguard the child and promote his or her welfare and, if so, how best to do so and with what intended outcomes.

It should be noted that if emergency action has had to be taken to address immediate concerns about the family (as at (3)), then this should be followed quickly by any relevant s 47 enquiries as may be deemed necessary.

Running concurrently with the s 47 enquiries may well be police investigations concerning the commission of crimes arising out of the same facts. The guidance points out at para 5.32 that each ACPC should have in place a protocol for social services departments and the police to guide both agencies in deciding how s 47 enquiries and associated police investigations should be conducted and, in particular, in what circumstances s 47 enquiries linked to criminal investigation are necessary and/or appropriate.

(7) *Strategy discussion.* In very urgent situations as identified at (2) above, a strategy discussion will already have taken place. Where, however, an initial assessment has been begun, and this has identified that there is reasonable cause to suspect that a child is suffering, or is likely to suffer significant harm, then there should be a strategy discussion with all the relevant services including social services, police, education and health

and in particular any referring agency. The guidance provides that where a medical examination might be needed, a senior doctor from the providing service should be included in the strategy discussion. The strategy discussion is further analysed in Chapter **6**. *Working Together to Safeguard Children* points out (at para 5.30) that a strategy discussion may take place at a meeting or by other means but that any information shared, all decisions reached and the basis for those decisions, should be clearly recorded by all parties to the discussions.

(8)   *Child assessment orders.* The emphasis from *Working Together to Safeguard Children*, clearly influenced by *Child Protection: Messages from Research* (DOH, 1995), is that co-operation between social services, parents and all other potentially relevant agencies is not only desirable but will ensure the best outcomes for the child. However, where parents continue to refuse access to a child for the purposes of establishing basic facts about the child's condition, but concerns about the child's safety are not so urgent as to require an emergency protection order, then the local authority might apply to the courts for a child assessment order (CA 1989, s 43).

(9)   *Initial child protection conference.* The initial child protection conference should bring together family members, the child where appropriate, and those professionals most involved with the child and family, following s 47 enquiries.

(10)   *Registration and outline child protection plan.* In most circumstances, where it is determined that the child is at risk of suffering harm, has suffered or is likely to suffer significant harm, then the only decision-making power possessed by the child protection conference is to place the child's name on the child protection register and set to work on the outline child protection plan. It may be the case, however, that the circumstances are such that further legal intervention is necessary through the continuation of an emergency protection order, or an application being made for an interim care or supervision order. Where this is the case, the task of the initial child protection conference is to make such a recommendation to social services who will then instruct their lawyers accordingly. It must be noted that the action of registration itself will confer no protection on a child and must be accompanied by the child protection plan. The conference must take certain steps including the appointment of a key worker, usually to be drawn from social services, and the identification of the membership of a core group of professionals and family members who will develop and implement the child protection plan as a detailed working tool (see *Working Together to Safeguard Children*, para 5.68).

(11)   *Completion of core assessment.* Throughout the period of initial investigations, s 47 enquiries and other interviews and investigations, it is likely that the core assessment of the child and the family will be continuing. Since *Working Together to Safeguard Children* and the

Framework for the Assessment of Children in Need and their Families considers that this assessment will take some 42 days in total (when combined with the initial 7-day period) then it is apparent that information arising from the core assessment may well be informing the various stages of decision-making on an ongoing basis. Nevertheless, as much information as is possible to be derived from the core assessment should be provided in time for the conference (see para 5.61).

(12)   *Written agreement as to the child protection plan. Working Together* makes it clear that parents should understand the causes of concern which resulted in the child's name being placed on the Child Protection Register, what needs to change, and what is expected of them as part of the plan for safeguarding the child. To ensure that this is clear to all parties, it is stated that it is good practice to produce a written agreement as part of the plan to be negotiated between the child, the family members and professionals.

(13)   *Child protection review conference.* The first child protection review conference should be held within 3 months of the initial child protection conference, and further reviews should be held at intervals of not more than 6 months for as long as the child's name remains on the child protection register. *Working Together to Safeguard Children* emphasises that this is to ensure that the momentum is maintained in the process of safeguarding the registered child.

(14)   *Ongoing legal proceedings.* Where the recommendation of the initial child protection conference was that it was necessary to take further legal steps then an interim care or supervision order (CA 1989, s 38) will have been obtained and renewed at monthly intervals. When all the necessary investigations have been completed as well as the core assessment, then the matter should proceed to a full hearing of an application for a full care or supervision order (CA 1989, s 31).

5.62   The detail on all the various stages of work which involve the relevant concerned agencies, family members and, where appropriate, the child, will all be discussed in greater detail in Chapter 6 on inter-agency co-operation since the guidance and recommendations on the different roles of the parties are subject to detailed analysis in *Working Together to Safeguard Children*. What has been done here is merely to set out, in outline, the different stages incorporating, at the relevant points, those steps which are actually detailed in the law. It is proposed now to consider the various different legal provisions and the types of legal proceedings, which may issue as a result of a consideration that appropriate legal action must be taken.

Investigation

5.63   As *Working Together to Safeguard Children* emphasises, where a local authority receives information that there is a child in its area, who is subject to an emergency protection order, or is in police protection, or has contravened a ban imposed by a curfew notice under the Crime and Disorder Act 1998, or it has reasonable cause to *suspect* that a child in its area is suffering or is likely to suffer *significant harm*, the authority is under a duty to make or cause to be made such enquiries as it considers necessary (CA 1989, s 47(1)(a)(i)–(iii), (b)). The fact that it need only be reasonable cause to *suspect* rather than reasonable cause to *believe* was emphasised in the case of R *(on the application of S) v Swindon Borough Council and Another* [2001] 3 FCR 702. The purpose of such enquiries is to enable the local authority social services department to determine whether it should take any action to safeguard or promote the child's welfare, including the taking of any relevant further legal proceedings. It should also be remembered that a local authority may receive information about the possibility of a child suffering or being likely to suffer *significant harm*, via a court welfare officer engaged in providing a report to the court in family proceedings (as defined by s 8(4) of the CA 1989), or the local authority may receive a direction from the court itself to conduct an investigation into whether there is a need to institute care or supervision order proceedings under s 37 of the CA 1989.

The meaning of 'significant harm'

5.64 The meaning of *significant harm* is discussed in greater detail in Chapter 7, but it is worth examining briefly here since it is the trigger for much of what follows in the way of investigation. It is also the concept to which the concerned agencies and the courts must look when deciding whether to apply for orders, to exercise any special powers or, in the case of the court, to make any of the relevant orders. The relevant orders which the court may make include: emergency protection orders, child assessment orders, interim care or supervision orders, and full care supervision orders. Harm is defined by s 31(9) of the CA 1989 as meaning 'ill treatment or the impairment of health or development including impairment suffered from seeing or hearing the ill-treatment of another'; development is defined as meaning 'physical, intellectual, emotional, social or behavioural development'; health is defined to include 'physical or mental health' and, finally, ill-treatment is defined as including 'sexual abuse and forms of ill treatment which are not physical'.

5.65 When looking to satisfy the criterion of harm, it would appear that the court may be satisfied that the child is suffering from harm if any one of the three types of harm envisaged in s 31(9) is present. This is indeed the guidance offered by the DOH, which states in *Working Together to Safeguard Children* that each of these three different elements has been associated with the suffering of 'significant harm' by a child in different cases which have come before the courts. It also points out that the process of suffering such harm is a continual process but that 'sometimes, a single traumatic event may constitute significant harm, eg a violent assault, suffocation or poisoning' at para 2.17). The grounds for intervention can thus be seen to be very wide and, indeed, the Court of Appeal in *Newham London Borough Council v AG* [1993] 1 FLR 281, at p 289 has emphasised that the words of the CA 1989 must be considered, but are not meant to be unduly restrictive when the evidence clearly indicates that a certain course of action should be taken to protect a child. This point was reiterated by Thorpe J in *Re A* [1993] 1 FCR 824.

5.66 The condition as to *significant harm* is drawn with reference to the child concerned, and so those conducting the investigations and the courts which may be called upon to make orders, must look at the position, characteristics and needs of each particular child in respect of whom proceedings may have been taken, a point emphasised by the House of Lords in *Lancashire County Council v B* [2000] 1 FLR 583. The criteria which may trigger off an investigation and the subsequent making of orders are intended to cover situations where the child has suffered, is suffering or is *likely to suffer significant harm*. The use of the term 'is suffering' is intended to concentrate attention on present or continuing conditions where problems may have been temporarily ameliorated since the involvement of the investigating agency, but where the problem could, nevertheless, still give rise to legitimate concerns and justify considerable exploration and application for further orders.

5.67 Clearly, an investigation relating solely to past events is unlikely to proceed much further unless it is being linked in some way to the present evidence by some harm continuing, or being likely to continue (as emphasised in *Re M* [1994] 2 FLR 577, endorsing the earlier approach of *Northamptonshire County Council v S* [1992] 3 WLR 1010). It was stated very clearly in the case of *Re M* that a court could make a care order on the grounds that the child had been suffering significant harm at the point at which the local authority had intervened to initiate protective action in the courts in respect of the child. To do otherwise, of course, would have rendered it impossible for the local authority subsequently to succeed in gaining any further interim or full care or supervision orders where immediate intervention had been necessary to protect the child. The approach in *Re M* was adopted in later cases. Thus, in *Re K (Care Order or Residence Order)* [1995] 1 FLR 675, it was held that the court was able to make a care order even though, at the relevant time, the children were being properly looked after by their grandparents. Although in this case the local authority were no longer seeking a care order, it had initially applied for one and Stuart-White J ruled that there was no principle that a care order could only be made where the children were living with members of their family in exceptional circumstances. He felt that there would be cases in which either: (a) a care order would benefit the family providing care for the child, which was the situation in this case; or (b) cases in which a care order would be the only means of protecting children placed with members of the extended family from *significant harm* in the context of potential threats arising from the parents.

5.68 The cases of *Re SH (Care Order: Orphan)* [1995] 1 FLR 746 and *Re M (Care Order: Parental Responsibility)* [1996] 2 FLR 84 illustrate the problems which may face a local authority which provides accommodation to a child before a parent has died or where a baby has been abandoned. In the case of *Re SH* the child had been accommodated pursuant to the provisions of s 20 of the CA 1989 as a result of the illness of his mother and then later the death of his father. The local authority was pursuing a care order which was opposed by the child's guardian ad litem on the basis that the threshold criteria were not satisfied at the time of the making of the application and that, applying the principles set out in s 1(5), the local authority was able to look after the child pursuant to s 20 rather than obtaining a s 31 care order. The court held that the words 'is suffering' in s 31(2) meant 'was suffering' such harm at the time when the 'rescue operation' was instigated by the local authority, provided that such measures were continuing at the date of the final hearing. The importance of the decision in *Re SH* is that it affirms the principle that protective measures which commence with the provision of accommodation under s 20 can nevertheless qualify as the relevant local authority 'rescue operation'. The advantage which a care order offered over the continuing of s 20 accommodation was the very important one, specifically as it concerned the future welfare of the child, that it gave the local authority parental responsibility and the appropriate legal status to place the child for adoption, to be able to authorise medical operation and to be able to resist other applications made by relatives. No such similar protection was available using the status conferred by simply offering accommodation under s 20.

5.69 Similarly, in the case of *Re M*, a baby had been found abandoned on the steps of a health centre when only a few days old and was placed with foster parents using the provisions of s 20. The local authority subsequently sought a care order, arguing that there was a need for such an order to enable it to place the child for adoption. Cazalet J held that the fact of abandonment, with all the risks which it entailed, meant that the baby was suffering from 'significant harm' immediately before he was found on the steps of the health centre. The judge ruled that given his special needs, he was 'likely' to suffer 'significant harm' in the future as a result of having been abandoned and that under the principles of s 15 a care order should be made as it was necessary to preserve his future welfare that somebody should have parental responsibility for him. As to looking at the likelihood of the future possibility of harm as indicated by the words 'likely to suffer significant harm', the investigating agency in consultation with other professionals concerned with the child must seek to establish that there would be a greater risk to the child in leaving him in his current situation than by seeking to provide services to ameliorate the situation or, in the worst situation, by seeking the child's removal through an application for court orders.

5.70   Were an application to be based on the issue of the future possibility of harm by reference to past events, then the House of Lords has determined in *Re H and R* [1996] 1 FLR 80 that the standard of proof required of the likelihood of past events is proof on the balance of probabilities, except that where the allegation is an extremely serious one, the evidence required to satisfy the court that there was a real possibility of harm to a child must be even stronger. The basic message of this case somewhat controversially therefore was that the more serious the allegations made in respect of past events then the stronger the evidence will need to be to establish that it has actually occurred. In *Re H and R* itself, the risk to the complainant's younger sisters could only be established by accepting the evidence of the eldest 15-year-old that she had been abused by her step-father. Her evidence was the only evidence to suggest that she had been sexually abused by the step-father, and although the judge at first instance felt the girl was telling the truth, he had not felt that he was sure 'to the requisite high standard of proof' that her allegations were true. (See also *Re B* [2002] EWCA Civ 752, [2002] 2 FLR 1133 and *Re O and N* [2002] EWCA Civ 1271, [2002] 2 FLR 1167.)

5.71   The House of Lords in the case ruled that 'likely' in the context of s 31 of the CA 1989 was being used in the sense of a 'real possibility', a possibility that could not sensibly be ignored having regard to the nature and gravity of the feared harm in a particular case. The Lords went on the state that the standard of proof in cases involving the care of children was the ordinary civil standard of the 'balance of probability' but the more improbable the event, the stronger must be the evidence that it did occur before, on the balance of probability, its occurrence would be established. They further went on to emphasise that the rejection by the court of a disputed allegation as 'not proved on the balance of probability' might leave scope for the possibility that the non-proven allegation might be true after all. However, they stated that those unresolved doubts and suspicions could no more form the basis of a conclusion that the likelihood of suffering 'significant harm' had been established than they could form the basis of a conclusion that the criteria relating to the issue of 'is suffering' had been established. The House of Lords went on to emphasise that unproved allegations of maltreatment could not therefore form the basis for a finding by the court that either issue relating to the 'significant harm' had been established. They stated that it was, however, open to a court to conclude that there was a real possibility that the child would suffer harm in the future although harm in the past had not been established. They stressed that there would be cases where, although the alleged maltreatment had not been proved, the evidence before the court nevertheless established a combination of profoundly worrying features affecting the care of the child within the family, who was before the court.

They emphasised that in such cases, it would be open to a court in appropriate circumstances to find that, although not satisfied the child was yet suffering 'significant harm' on the basis of such facts as had been proved to the requisite standard of proof, there was a likelihood that the child would do so in the future.

5.72 It should be noted also that this approach has been taken by the courts when considering the appropriate standard of proof at the welfare stage of care proceedings. Thus, having established that 'significant harm' has occurred or there is a risk of 'significant harm' occurring to the child, the court then has to decide whether or not making a care or supervision order would be better for the child than making no order at all. In the case of *Re M and R (Child Abuse: Evidence)* [1996] 2 FLR 195 the Court of Appeal rejected this argument, emphasising that the court could only act on the basis of proven facts as opposed to suspicions. In this case the first instance judge had made interim care orders on the basis of emotional abuse and neglect of the children but he found that serious allegations of sexual abuse of the children by the mother and two men had not been proved to the requisite standard and refused to make a final care order, adjourning the case for 3 months. The local authority appealed but the Court of Appeal indicated that because the welfare of the child was paramount at the point of making the order, the standard of proof for establishing likely harm should again be on the basis of the test laid down in *Re H and R*. The Court of Appeal confirmed the judge's approach and did not agree with the local authority's arguments that, because the welfare of the child was paramount at the welfare stage, the standard of proof for establishing likely harm should be any less than the standard required by the case of *Re H and R*.

5.73 As to steps which may be taken to protect an unborn child on the basis that the child to be born may be at risk of suffering or being likely to suffer significant harm, the case of *A Metropolitan Borough Council v DB* [1997] 1 FLR 767 should be considered. In this case the mother was a 17-year-old crack cocaine addict who had a pathological fear of doctors, but whose medical condition raised considerable concern as she had suffered from eclamptic fits resulting from high blood pressure during the pregnancy. An application was made to the High Court for the 17-year-old to undergo such treatment as was necessary, including a Caesarean section, and an emergency protection order was obtained immediately the child was born. The local authority then sought to invoke the inherent jurisdiction of the High Court under s 100 of the CA 1989 in order to detain the mother in the hospital maternity ward which for these purposes would be deemed to be 'secure accommodation', since the mother had threatened to discharge herself in a situation which could be deemed to be life-threatening. Cazalet J allowed each of the orders which had been sought.

5.74 Some concern had been expressed with regard to the fact that emotional abuse was not specifically mentioned in the CA 1989 but, since ill-treatment can include forms of ill-treatment which are not physical, and the impairment of emotional development can constitute 'harm' under the CA 1989, such fears seem to have been unfounded. A number of cases including two which have already been mentioned, namely *Re H* and *Re M and R*, demonstrate that local authorities do not appear to be reluctant to base proceedings upon suggestions of 'emotional' or 'psychological' harm, and indeed Scott Baker J in *Re H* emphasised that 'the likelihood of harm is not confined to present or near future but applies to the ability of the parent or carer to meet the *emotional* needs of a child in years ahead'. (For a detailed analysis of the types of abuse which are now subsumed within the phrase 'significant harm' see Chapter 2).

5.75 The harm suffered or apprehended must be 'significant' and, where this turns on the child's health or development, his or her health or development is to be compared with that which could be expected of a similar child (s 31(10)). As far as the word 'significant' is concerned, the DHSS *Review of Child Care Law* (1985), stated that 'minor shortcomings in the health care provided, or minor deficits in physical, psychological or social development, should not give rise to compulsory intervention unless they are having, or are likely to have, serious and lasting effects upon the child' (at para 15.15). For an excellent multi-disciplinary discussion of the concept, see Adcock and White (1998). Lord Mackay, the Lord Chancellor at the time of the passing of the CA 1989, also indicated that 'unless there is evidence that a child is being, or is likely to be, positively harmed because of failure in the family, the State whether in the guise of a local authority or a court, should not interfere (see Lord Mackay, Joseph Jackson Memorial Lecture (1989) 139 NLJ 505, at p 508; and see *Working Together to Safeguard Children*, paras 2.16–2.18. In the case of *Humberside County Council v B* [1993] 1 FLR 257 at p 263, Booth J accepted that 'significant harm' should be interpreted in accordance with dictionary definitions of either 'considerable', or 'noteworthy', or 'important', and the Court of Appeal in the domestic violence case of *Chalmers v Johns* [1999] 1 FLR 392 also applied that interpretation to the same phrase used in s 33(7) of the Family Law Act 1996. Again, it has to be remembered that for action to be justified which breaches Article 8 of the ECHR 'right to private home and family life', it would have to be shown that the intervention was in response to 'significant' harm in order to claim the protection offered by the qualifications in Article 8(2).

5.76 The comparison to be made with a similar child is not without problems, however, since one is required to compare this subjective child with that hypothetically similar child. This issue came up for consideration by the court in the case of *Re O (A Minor) (Care Order: Education: Procedure)* [1992] 2 FLR 7, where Ewbank J took a very robust view of what constituted a similar child. In this particular case he was dealing with a young girl who had been truanting from school and the issue was whether she had suffered 'significant harm', what was significant turning on the comparison with a similar child. In Ewbank J's view a similar child in this case meant 'a child of equivalent, intellectual and social development who had gone to school and not merely an average child who may or may not be at school' (at p 12). Clearly, if a child is disabled in some way, and that has affected his health and development, the investigating agency must ask itself what the state of health or development could be expected of a similar child with a similar disability. As to whether 'similar' conotes any consideration being given to the child's background, this is doubtful since, according to Lord Mackay 'the care that a parent gives to his child must be related to the circumstances attributable to that child in the sense of his physical, mental and emotional characteristics' (*Hansard*, Deb Committee, vol 503, col 355). Other problems, however, arise from the use of this test; thus it has been pointed out that a deaf child of deaf parents may not be directly comparable to a deaf child of hearing parents (see Freeman (1992), at p 107). Whilst the child protection agencies when investigating issues of 'significant harm', will have to be sensitive to racial, cultural and religious issues (see Lau (1998)) nevertheless, what the Lord Chancellor was clearly indicating is that the agency must focus on the needs of a particular child.

Location of the abuse and identity of the perpetrator

5.77 The duty placed upon the local authority to investigate in cases of suspected child abuse is the same, no matter where that abuse has occurred or by whom it has been perpetrated. Thus, whilst *additional* special procedures may be invoked where children are abused in residential settings, outside the family home, in foster placements or in schools, the first duty upon the local authority is to engage in an investigation under s 47 of the CA 1989, which may well include taking steps to involve the police (see *Working Together to Safeguard Children*, at paras 6.1–6.13) or taking steps to minimise future risk (see *Re S* [2001] 2 FLR 776).

Processing the investigation

5.78 The provisions in s 47 of the CA 1989, which go into the processing of the investigation by social services, provide that enquiries must, in particular, be directed towards establishing whether they should make any application to the court or exercise any other of their powers under the CA 1989, which could include using any of the measures described at para **5.10** *et seq*. Where the local authority is carrying out an investigation in respect of a child on whom an emergency protection order has been made, and who is not in accommodation provided by or on behalf of a local authority, the local authority must further decide whether it would be in the child's best interests for him to be in such accommodation (s 47(3)). The local authority is not, apparently, in a position to be able to insist on taking over the child's accommodation but in most cases the other agencies concerned will deem it appropriate to transfer care of the child to the local authority, most particularly where the accommodation in which they might otherwise hold the child would be deemed to be wholly unsuitable (for example, police accommodation). The local authority is also under a duty to consider whether, in the case of a child in police protection, it would be in the child's best interests for the local authority to request that an application be made by the designated police officer (see para **5.87** *et seq*) for an emergency protection order on behalf of the local authority (ss 47(3)(c) and 46(7)).

Obtaining access to the child

5.79 In the course of pursuing its investigation under s 47 of the CA 1989, the local authority must take such steps as are reasonably practicable to obtain access to the child or to ensure that access is obtained on his behalf by a 'person authorised' by it for this purpose, unless it is satisfied that it already has sufficient information with respect to the child (s 47(4)). Such enquiries must be conducted with a view to enabling the authority to determine what action, if any, can be taken with respect of the child. Who might be authorised by the authority to assist it in the making of such enquiries is made clear by s 47(9)–(11), but it is the duty of any person employed by the local authority, any local education authority, any housing authority or any health authority, special health authority, primary care trust, or National Health Service trust to assist in the making of such enquiries unless it would be unreasonable in all the circumstances of the case. As was seen with the provisions on prevention contained in the CA 1989, Pt III (see para **5.10** *et seq*), s 27 contains a statutory enactment of the principles of *Working Together to Safeguard Children*.

5.80 The provisions of s 47(11) also indicate that the local authority could call upon any person authorised by the Secretary of State for the purpose of s 47 to assist it in making its enquiries. Thus far, no persons have been authorised under this provision, although presumably the local authority would be able to call in the services of the NSPCC, using the NSPCC powers of investigation provided under ss 31 and 44. It should be noted that the statutory list of those who can be called upon to assist the local authority does *not* include the police, but it was emphasised by the then Minister responsible for piloting the CA 1989 through the House of Commons, David Mellor, that 'police refusal to cooperate on any matter would be indefensible' (see *Hansard*, Deb Standing Committee B, col 317). It is also the case that *Working Together to Safeguard Children*, in chapter 3, which identifies all those with a role and responsibility in child protection investigations, includes the police. The probation service are not specifically included under these provisions but the Minister stated that 'probation officers are officers of the court and are already under a duty to assist in these matters'. Given the number of amendments which have now been made to the CA 1989, it would have made sense to have amended the list to have included probation officers and the police, most particularly when amendments were made following the amendment to s 47(1)(a)(iii) by the Crime and Disorder Act 1998 (CDA 1998). Considerable emphasis is given throughout chapter 3 of *Working Together to Safeguard Children* to the general responsibility of a whole range of agencies to co-operate with the performance by the local authority of its duties under s 47 to undertake child protection investigations. A considerable amount of joint training on the benefits to be derived from inter-agency co-operation across the board in any one area has also been provided under the auspices of local ACPCs and the critical role of all the various different agencies is emphasised throughout *Working Together to Safeguard Children.*

5.81 Where pursuant to s 47(4) the local authority social services do consider that they need the assistance of any of the agencies in trying to gain access to a child, it may well be that consideration is given to who might best seek such access. It is well known that in families where there are young children, in particular, health visitors may find it relatively easy to obtain access to the child. It is not, therefore, unreasonable for social services to make such a request of the health visiting service, although clearly, where there are concerns about the safety of any person seeking to gain such access, a refusal by the health visitor in certain circumstances would be deemed to be *reasonable* within the provisions of s 47(10).

5.82 In addition to engaging the assistance of any of the other relevant agencies in accordance with s 47(9) and (11), the local authority is required to consult the relevant LEA where, as a result of any such enquiries, it appears to the authority that there are matters concerned with the child's education which should be investigated. In those cases, therefore, where the concern is primarily focused on issues connected with the child's intellectual development, this should allow the local authority social services and the LEA to determine whether it would be more appropriate for the education service to deal with the child's case. This might then involve the services of an educational welfare officer, educational psychologist or counsellor and, in cases of non-attendance, might prompt the LEA to consider proceedings for an education supervision order under s 36 of the CA 1989.

5.83 Where the local authority's investigation under s 47 has been frustrated by an unreasonable refusal of access to the child, it should be noted that such refusal may constitute grounds for the local authority to seek an emergency protection order under s 44(1)(b) (see para **5.87**). In any event, under the provisions of s 47, where the local authority or person authorised by it has been refused access or denied information as to the child's whereabouts in the course of an investigation, the local authority is bound to apply for an emergency protection order, child assessment order, interim care or supervision order, 'unless they are satisfied that the child's welfare can be satisfactorily safeguarded without their doing so' (s 47(6)). These provisions, taken together, clarify the procedure to be followed by social workers when access to the child is being denied and addresses the problems raised specifically by *A Child in Mind: Protection of Children in a Responsible Society* (London Borough of Greenwich, 1987) ('the Kimberley Carlile Report'), which criticised the social workers for failing to be aware of, and to use, powers under the old law to gain access to Kimberley Carlile which, had they been invoked, might have prevented her death. (See the Children and Young Persons Act 1933 (CYPA 1933), s 40 which is further retained in the current law by virtue of s 48(9) of the CA 1989.)

5.84 In addition to the duties imposed on local authorities, the NSPCC is also empowered under s 44(1)(c) of the CA 1989 to take action to protect a child in situations where it has been unable to gain access or, more generally, to institute proceedings under s 31, and the police also have special powers under the provisions of s 46. The first and paramount concern of the social services, NSPCC or the police is to ensure that the child is protected. Where an allegation has been made or the suspicions of the police, social services or NSPCC officers have been aroused, then as previously identified in para **5.58** *et seq*, various investigations, together with an initial assessment, must be commenced and critically the Child Protection Register must be checked.

5.85 The various steps involving detailed inter-agency co-operation and the critically important work which must be undertaken with children and families in child protection investigations are dealt with in detail in Chapter **6** on inter-agency co-operation and reference to those various stages of working in this chapter will be very brief, simply to set the scene for those situations in which legal steps must be taken.

Application for an emergency protection order

Background

5.86 The detailed inter-agency work described in more detail in Chapter **6** should be pursued and in those cases where a child is already on the Child Protection Register, and is therefore the subject of an inter-agency protection plan, the key worker from social services ensures that such plans are formally reviewed in the child protection review conferences held in every period of 6 months. As well as checking the Child Protection Register, *Working Together to Safeguard Children* describes the various other checks which will be made with all the other agencies which might have connection with the child or the family (see *Working Together to Safeguard Children*, at chapter 3). All such checks provide essential information, as will the initial assessment of the child and the family, but it may be the case that speed is of the essence and, therefore, action is required without being able to make all the necessary enquiries. Discussions within a child protection conference setting or even within the strategy discussions may have to be postponed until after the taking of emergency action, involving the making of an emergency protection order (see s 44) and accompanying this with an exclusion order under s 44A. In a non-emergency situation where there is felt to be a risk of abuse which has not materialised, there may be on-going work with the family which has identified a looming, potential crisis. In such circumstances, it may be possible to hold the relevant strategy discussions, to carry on further investigations and enquiries, to begin the core assessment and to convene an initial child protection conference with all the relevant personnel, thus providing an opportunity for giving measured consideration to the taking of further legal steps, such as obtaining a child assessment order (CA 1989, s 43) or the institution of proceedings for a care or supervision order where there is no emergency (see CA 1989, s 31).

5.87 In an emergency situation, however, it may (as has been indicated) be impossible to hold the relevant strategy discussions or initial child protection conference, and the social workers, NSPCC officers or police officers may have to take action on their own initiative, perhaps without the time for consultation with other colleagues. As *Working Together to Safeguard Children* (at para 5.23) emphasises:

> 'Where there is a risk to the life of a child or likelihood of serious immediate harm, an agency with statutory child protection powers *should act quickly to secure the immediate safety of the child*. Emergency action might be necessary as soon as a referral is received or at any point in involvement with children and families … Neglect as well as abuse can pose such a risk of significant harm to a child that urgent protective action is needed. When considering whether emergency action is necessary, an agency should always consider whether action is also required to safeguard other children in the same household (eg siblings), the household of an alleged perpetrator, or elsewhere.'

5.88 It must be remembered, however, that even in an emergency it is essential to adhere to the principles underpinning the CA 1989 as emphasised by *Child Protection – Messages from Research* (DOH, 1995) and *Children Act Now – Messages from Research* (DOH, 2000), in particular, that of partnership with parents. The Cleveland Report had, as one of its major criticisms the failure to involve parents at an early stage when considering protective action, and this was highlighted subsequently in the *Report of the Inquiry into the Removal of Children from Orkney in 1991* (HMSO, 1992), at para 18.31, as well as in the DOH funded research studies including *Child Protection Practice: Private Risks and Public Remedies* (HMSO, 1995) and *Operating the Child Protection System: A Study of Child Protection Practices in English Local Authorities* (HMSO, 1995). *Working Together to Safeguard Children* constantly emphasises the importance of involving the parents wherever possible provided that this does not jeopardise the safety of the child (see eg paras 5.6, 5.11, 5.14, 5.17, 5.37, 5.43 and 5.44). As is pointed out in para 5.44, however, in the great majority of cases, children remain with their families following inquiries, even where concerns about abuse or neglect are substantiated. *Child Protection: Messages from Research* indicated that the work of Gibbons et al suggested that approximately 160,000 s 47 enquiries take place in England every year, including 25,000 where suspicions of maltreatment or neglect are in fact unsubstantiated (at p 25). It also reports, however, that in 96 out of every 100 cases, the children will remain at home with relatives and thus the importance of establishing a proper working partnership with parents is clearly absolutely critical.

5.89   It has already been noted that, where there is any possibility of a criminal offence having been committed against a child, the police will have been notified and will be involved at every stage of the process referred to in more detail in Chapter 6. It may be the case, of course, that the police have been involved in some way either in the initial referral or in the early stages of investigation following referral. Thus, an early strategy discussion between police and social services will often take place in order to plan the investigation properly and, in particular, the role of each agency and the extent of their joint investigations. (See Chapter 6; and see Parton, Thorpe and Wattham (1997), at pp 36–38.) It is the responsibility of the agency receiving the referral to initiate the whole process and, throughout the early stages of the investigation, both police and social services must keep in mind that it may be necessary to invoke civil child protection proceedings or criminal proceedings or both, against the perpetrator. Interviewing the child victim or the child or adult perpetrator must be conducted in accordance with established codes of practice and current case-law and this is considered in detail in Chapter 7 (in relation to civil proceedings) and Chapter 9 (in relation to criminal proceedings).

5.90   Against the background of on-going joint investigations, however, it must be remembered that if the case is an emergency then *Working Together to Safeguard Children* is absolutely clear that steps must be taken to apply for the relevant order to give the child the necessary protection in this emergency situation.

Making the application for an emergency protection order

5.91   Any person may apply to the court, usually a single justice in the magistrates' court, for an order authorising a child's removal to accommodation provided by or on behalf of the applicant or authorising the child to remain in the place in which he has been accommodated, provided that the court is satisfied (on the balance of probabilities) that there is reasonable cause to believe that to do otherwise would mean that the child would be likely to suffer significant harm (CA 1989, s 44(1)(a)). For a discussion of the meaning of 'significant harm', see para **5.65** and Chapter **7**. The order is referred to as 'an emergency protection order' (s 44(4)) and the fact that such orders are only to be made in real emergencies appears to have been understood by all the relevant agencies in England and Wales since the events of Cleveland, Rochdale and The Orkneys and the publishing of the various *Working Together* documents. Ever since the implementation of the CA 1989, on 14 October 1991, a very considerable decrease can be detected in relation to the use of emergency protection orders when compared with the number of place of safety orders taken out under the old law. Thus, a succession of *Children Act Reports*, including those published in 1993, 1994, 1995 and most recently *The Children Act Report 1995–1999* (DOH, 1999), and the supplements to *The Children Act Report 1995–1999* published on the internet by the DOH in December 1999, indicate that the making of emergency protection orders and emergency protection extension orders has remained at a remarkably consistent figure. Thus the *Children Act Report 1992* (DOH, 1993) reported that in 1992, 2,300 emergency protection orders had been made. There is then an upward turn through 1993 and 1994, a downturn and another upturn with the figures since 1998 showing a consistent decline to their lowest ever in 2001 (see *Children Act Report 2001* (DOH, 2002), at para 12.4). In tabular form the figures are as follows:

1993	1994	1995	1996	1997	1998	1999	2000	2001
2,546	3,144	3,054	2,565	2,393	2,473	2,454	2,232	2,127

5.92 These figures, as indicated, are very consistent and compare to approximately 5,000 children who were removed to a place of safety on the orders of a magistrate in the year ending 31 March 1991 before the implementation of the CA 1989 in October 1991 (*Children Act Report 1992*, at para 2.15).

5.93 An emergency protection order application can be made either without the other parties being present or on notice. Given the urgent nature of the grounds for making an order and the nature of the order itself, most applications are in fact made without notice being given and provision is made for this under the appropriate court rules (see FPC(CA 1989)R 1991, r 4(4)). It should be pointed out, however, that given the provisions of Article 6 of the ECHR an argument could be made that such orders made without notice being given to the other side, could be deemed to be in breach of parents' rights under that article to a fair trial, which includes the right to appear in person (see Swindells et al (2000), at para 6.78.) An application for an emergency protection order is made by filing the appropriate form (Forms C1 and C11) at the time the application is made or as directed by the justices' clerk (FPC(CA 1989)R 1991, r 4(1)(a)).

5.94 The fact that *any person* can apply for an emergency protection order under s 44(1)(a) of the CA 1989, means that the protective net could potentially be thrown very wide, but data from the first 10 years of the operation of the Act had tended to show that in child protection cases the applications come almost exclusively from child protection agencies. Those cases where emergency protection orders have been used by private individuals have tended to be in very rare cases which occurred very early on under the CA 1989, where attempts were made to use the orders to prevent a child abduction. It should be noted that the *The Children Act 1989: Guidance and Regulations* (vol 1 'Court Orders') (DOH, 1991) states that 'in dire circumstances a neighbour or a relative or school teacher may need to protect a child at risk by using the procedure for the application of an Emergency Protection Order' (at para 4.32). The police may also apply for an emergency protection order but they also have available to them the procedure under s 46 (see para **5.17**).

5.95 It should further be noted that rules of court necessitate the applicant notifying the local authority, as well as others, of the fact that an order has been made ((FPC(CA 1989)R 1991, r 21(8)(b)(iii)). Once the local authority has received such notification of an order having been made, it will be required to carry out an investigation under the provisions of s 47 (see para **5.61**(5) and (6)). Where an order has been made, the Emergency Protection Order (Transfer of Responsibilities) Regulations 1991, SI 1991/2003, commit the authority to take over the order itself and attendant powers and responsibilities, where it considers that it would be in the child's best interests to do so (reg 2(c)). In reaching a decision as to whether to take over an order, the local authority is required to consult the applicant and also to have regard to the ascertainable wishes and feelings of the child, the child's needs, the likely effect of any change in the child's circumstances, the child's age, sex and background, the circumstances which gave rise to the application, any directions of the court and any other orders, the relationship of any of the applicants to the child and any plans the applicant may have in respect of the child. This list mirrors, in broad terms, the CA 1989, s 1(3) checklist to which courts are required to have regard before they make any orders other than those relating to the protection of the child contained in Pt V of the CA 1989 (which includes emergency protection orders, child assessment orders and recovery orders). The NSPCC is also covered by these regulations.

5.96 A local authority, in addition to being able to rely on the more general grounds, can apply for an emergency protection order where enquiries are being made in the course of a local authority investigation under s 47 (see para **5.64**) and thus enquiries are being frustrated by access to the child being unreasonably refused and the applicant has reasonable cause to believe that access to the child is required as a matter of urgency (s 44(1)(b)). A similar power is vested in any authorised person under the CA 1989, which at the moment has only extended to the NSPCC (s 41(1)(c) and see s 31(9)).

Applying for directions to be included in emergency protection orders

5.97 The form which is used to make an application for an emergency protection order is eight pages long and requires the applicant to give as many details as he can about the child, the child's family, any other applications or orders which might affect the child and the grounds upon which the order is being sought. In response to criticisms made in the Cleveland Report, the emergency protection order gives the applicant the power to seek directions from the court with respect to the contact which is to be allowed between a named person and the child (s 44(6)(a)); or as to the medical or psychiatric examination or other assessment of the child (s 44(6)(b)). It should be noted that there is no reason why a direction on the latter provision may not be a direction for no or no further medical or psychiatric examination or other assessment. Where either direction is sought (or, indeed, further additional powers are sought, see para **5.107**) the applicant must be prepared to give reasons to the magistrates of seeking such directions from the court, although reasons as such are not required on the form itself. Where the court makes an order then the order will be as set out in Form C23.

The management of emergency protection order applications

5.98 Emergency duty teams in social services departments, or, where relevant, the NSPCC, will have available lists of magistrates' clerks providing cover at weekends and during the evening which are drawn up by the local magistrates' clerks themselves. This enables anyone to contact the relevant magistrates' clerk providing cover, who will then put the agency officers in touch with the relevant magistrate who has agreed to be available, and the clerk will generally also be with the magistrate when a protection order is granted. Because of the emphasis on the emergency nature of the provision in successive versions of *Working Together* and as a result of further guidance issued by the DOH, it would appear from the first 10 years working of the Act that applications are generally only sought where there is a real emergency. Even despite the presence of a clerk, it is difficult for justices to refuse to grant such orders, bearing in mind that they have to be satisfied on a balance of probabilities (the civil standard of proof) that there is reasonable cause to believe that a child is likely to suffer significant harm if an order were not made. Where a social worker or NSPCC officer states the circumstances giving rise to his or her belief, many magistrates would find it extremely hard to question the sincerity of that belief by denying the protection which would be afforded by an emergency protection order.

5.99 The only provision which might allow the magistrate some opportunity in an emergency situation of questioning the decisions of social services or the

NSPCC would be by the appointment of a children's guardian, an officer of CAFCASS. In theory this can be done at this much earlier stage of the emergency protection order by reason of s 41(6)(g). In order to cope with this provision, in the period up to April 2001, when CAFCASS was established, many guardian ad litem panel managers set up special arrangements to provide emergency guardians who could be summoned by the magistrate's clerk to meet at the magistrate's house in out-of-hours applications, and in some areas of the country special emergency duty teams of guardians ad litem were also available. Although there was much concern, early on, amongst those working as guardians ad litem that the service would not be able to cope with the demands of the CA 1989, this did not actually seem to have been borne out in practice, and where guardians were required to be present on emergency protection order applications, it was generally possible for one to be there. For a more detailed consideration of the work of the new officers of CAFCASS, see Chapters **7** and **8**. It should be noted here, however, that guardians drawn from CAFCASS are appointed to provide an *independent* social work perspective on what might be argued to be in the child's best interests. As a result of the establishment of the independent CAFCASS the guardian will be appointed from CAFCASS and thus there is no longer any risk of a link between the guardians and the social services department which is the applicant in the proceedings. This has beeen an important development since one aspect of the role in this early stage in the proceedings is to advise the court on the appropriateness of the social services department's or the NSPCC's application. Where the court, through the clerk, has ordered the appearance of a CAFCASS guardian in emergency protection order proceedings, then an order for the guardian's appointment should be made on Form C46. Once appointed at the emergency protection order stage, the guardian will generally stay involved in the case until the termination of proceedings involving the child, and may also go on to appoint a solicitor for the child, who will act as the child's representative and advocate for what the child wants (where the child is old enough) in the proceedings.

Effects of an emergency protection order

5.100 The emergency protection order requires any person who is in a position to produce the child to the applicant to do so and then provides that the child may either be removed to accommodation provided by or on behalf of the applicant or that the child may not be removed from premises in which he is then being accommodated (s 44(4)(a) and (b)). The order also operates to give the applicant parental responsibility for the child. The parental responsibility which the applicant acquires pursuant to these provisions is exercisable *only* so far as is necessary to safeguard the welfare of the child and *does not permit* (in response to the criticisms of the Cleveland Report) the denial of contact between the child, his parents and such other members of the family as it might be appropriate for him to see. Such contact between the child and these persons is presumed to be at a *reasonable* level and, where the local authority or NSPCC feel that the contact should not be allowed, it will have to seek a direction to this effect under s 44(6)(a). Again, in response to the Cleveland Report, such parental responsibility as is given *does not* extend to allowing the medical or psychiatric examination or other assessment of the child to take place without a specific direction to this effect from the court (s 44(6)(b)). Directions as to contact may impose conditions, and directions as to medical, psychiatric or other examinations or assessment may be to the effect that there are to be *no* medical, psychiatric or other examinations or assessments, or *no* such examination or assessment unless the court otherwise directs. It should also be noted that where, in the heat of the moment and under pressure, the applicant has forgotten to apply for such directions, s 44(9) makes it clear that such directions may be given at any time during the period of the emergency protection order, and that, similarly, where parents or children disagree with any such directions, they or the local authority may apply for such directions to be varied at any time.

Duration of emergency protection order

5.101 It is provided that an emergency protection order should have effect for such a period not exceeding 8 days as may be specified in the order (s 45(1)). The relatively short duration of emergency protection orders is a further response to concerns voiced at the height of the Cleveland crisis and represents the enactment of recommendations made originally in the government White Paper entitled *The Law on Child Care and Family Services* published in January 1987. However, where it appears to the applicant that since the granting of an order it has become safe for the child to be returned to a place from which the child had been removed, or it appears to the applicant that it is safe for the child to be removed from the place in which he was being detained, the applicant should either return him or (as the case may be) allow him to be removed (s 44(10)). The CA 1989 requires the return of the child to the care of the person from whose care he was removed or, if that is not reasonably practicable, to return the child to any parent, person with parental responsibility or such other person as the applicant (with the agreement of the court) considers appropriate (s 44(11)). The CA 1989 does, however, envisage situations in which the child has been returned pursuant to these provisions, but, within the duration of the emergency protection order, it becomes necessary once again to remove the child. This can be done within the terms of the original order for such period as remains unexpired of that order (s 44(12)).

Extending the duration of emergency protection orders

5.102 Whilst the initial duration of an emergency protection order is 8 days, except where the last of those 8 days is a public holiday, in which case the court may specify a period which ends at noon on the first later date which is not such a holiday, there is provision under the CA 1989 for application to be made to have the period of the emergency protection order extended for up to 7 days (s 45(4) and (5)). This appears generally in the *Children Act Report* to be referred to as an emergency protection order extension. Once such an application is made, the court may only make such an order if it has reasonable cause to believe that the child concerned is likely to suffer significant harm if the order is not extended (s 44(5)). Such an extension may only be granted on one occasion (s 44(6)). Interestingly, in the first 10 years of the operation of the CA 1989, the statistics show that emergency protection order extensions were made in approximately 220 cases per year and were only refused in an average of 10 cases per year. This would appear to suggest that an application for an extension is only made in approximately 10 per cent of cases but that they tend to be granted rather more easily than those who have to resort to such extensions may have expected (see *Children Act Report 1995–1999*, Supplement (November 2000), at chapter 10).

Applications to discharge emergency protection orders

5.103 If no such move to return the child to its family is made then, again, directly in response to the Cleveland Report, provision is made for the child, any parent, person with parental responsibility or any person with whom the child was living immediately before the making of the order, to apply to the court for the discharge of the order. Such an application for discharge, however, may only be made after the expiry of 72 hours, beginning with the making of the order. The statistics which have generally been made available (see *Children Act Report 1995–1999*, Supplement (November 2000) and the *Children Act Report 2001* (DOH, 2002)) do not reveal the numbers of applications for discharge of emergency protection orders under the CA 1989. It is felt, however, that a challenge could be mounted to the operation of this 72-hour barring period again using the provisions of Article 6 of the ECHR (see Swindells et al (2000)). Other than this provision for the making of an application for discharge of an emergency protection order, the CA 1989 makes it clear that no appeal may be made against the making of, or refusal to make, an emergency protection order, or against any direction given by the court in connection with such an order.

5.104 The possible concerns to which this provision might give rise where an application to social services is turned down by the magistrates were highlighted in *Essex County Council v F* [1993] 1 FLR 847. In this case, a 7-month-old baby had been in and out of hospital with problems relating to her immune system and feeding. The evidence of the social workers was that when the baby was with the mother she was not given proper medication nor proper feeding. In the 4-month period prior to the application for an emergency protection order, the baby had spent 14 days with her mother and had been returned to hospital on three occasions. The mother was living apart from the father and at the point when she proposed to resume care of the child she had no baby food or nappies. The mother appeared at the application but the magistrates declined to deal with the matter on the basis that the mother had not been given due notice under the rules. They refused to order short service and adjourned the application for 4 days and further refused to deal with the application on an ex parte basis. Counsel for the local authority and guardian ad litem argued that the refusal to make an order meant a refusal after hearing the application on its merits, which the magistrates had not done. On appeal, however, Douglas Brown J reluctantly reached the conclusion that the words of the CA 1989 compelled him to find that refusal meant any refusal and that the local authority had no right of appeal even though the case 'cried out for the intervention of the court'. In such a situation it would, of course, be possible to apply afresh to a different bench of magistrates although this would be subject to the co-operation of the clerk, or given Douglas Brown J's reaction it might have been appropriate instead to apply to the High Court to seek to ask it to exercise its inherent jurisdiction under s 100 of the CA 1989 to make an order for the child to stay in hospital or with relatives, since such an order would not be caught by the rules excluding orders in favour of local authorities provided by s 100 (see further, Chapter 7).

Evidential issues

5.105 Where an applicant for an emergency protection order seeks to rely not just upon their own evidence, but also upon evidence contained in reports made to the court, the rules of hearsay do not apply and the courts may take account of any material given in evidence or in writing which is relevant to the application (CA 1989, s 45(7)). (For further detail on this, see Chapter 8.)

Supplementary powers

5.106 Finally, a court making an emergency protection order may direct that the applicant may, whilst exercising any powers under that order, be accompanied by a registered medical practitioner, district nurse, or registered health visitor, if the applicant so chooses. This mirrors similar provisions made under the old law relating to place of safety orders and there appear to be no statistics available to indicate its level of use. It would appear to be rare that such powers are exercised therefore except where they relate to orders where additional powers have been sought under the provisions of s 48 (see para **5.112**).

Power to include exclusion requirements in emergency protection orders

5.107 As a result of amendments made to the CA 1989 by the Family Law Act 1996, a new s 44A was inserted into the CA 1989. This provides that the court may add an exclusion requirement to an emergency protection order granted under s 44(1) where the court is satisfied that the grounds for making an emergency protection order are made out, and where it has reasonable cause to believe that if a person is excluded from a dwelling house in which the child lives, then (i) in the case of an order made under s 44(1)(a) the child will not be likely to suffer significant harm even though the child is not removed or does not remain as provided in that section; or (ii) in the case of an order made under s 44(1)(b) or (c), the relevant enquiries will cease to be frustrated, and in addition where the court has reasonable cause to believe that another person living in the dwelling house (whether a parent of the child or some other person) is willing and able to give to the child the care which it would be reasonable to expect a parent to give to him, and consents to the inclusion of an exclusion requirement.

5.108 It is provided that an exclusion requirement is any one or more of the following:

(a) a provision requiring the relevant person to leave a dwelling house in which he is living with the child;
(b) a provision prohibiting the relevant person from entering a dwelling house in which the child lives; and
(c) a provision excluding the relevant person from a defined area in which a dwelling house in which the child lives is situated.

5.109 In addition, s 44A goes on to provide that the exclusion requirement may have effect for a shorter period than the other provisions of the order but critically the section also provides (s 44A(5)) that the court may attach a power of arrest to the exclusion requirement. These are critical new provisions intended to enable the local authority or other agencies involved to work closely with a parent who may be prepared to protect the child from the perpetrator of child abuse but who needs considerable support and assistance from the relevant agencies including the court in so doing.

5.110 Further amendments to the CA 1989, made by the Family Law Act 1996, include the addition of s 44B which provides that in any case where the court has power to include an exclusion requirement in an emergency protection order, the court may accept an undertaking from the relevant person in place of the making of such a requirement. It must be noted, however, that by s 44B(2) no power of arrest may be attached to any such undertaking. Nevertheless, such an undertaking given to a court is treated as enforceable as if it were an order of the court and shall further cease to have effect if, whilst it is in force, the applicant removes the child from the dwelling from which the relevant person is excluded to other accommodation for a continuous period of more than 24 hours. Thus, in those cases where it is felt that the risk to the child may be less serious than one in which it is felt that an exclusion requirement should be made, provision is made in the statute for the court to accept an undertaking, which should only be done where the court is satisfied that the child or children will receive the necessary protection from the court's acceptance of such an undertaking.

5.111   There are considerable differences with regard to the procedure which has to be followed if an exclusion requirement is made. The second condition which must be fulfilled before either an exclusion requirement is made or an undertaking is accepted, means that notice must be given to the proposed carer of the child, usually the mother, of the applicant's application for the inclusion of an exclusion requirement. Since their consent is necessary to the inclusion of an exclusion requirement, the rules of court have been amended to prescribe for consent to be given either orally in court or in writing to the court signed by the person giving consent (see FPC(CA 1989)R 1991, r 25(1)(b) as amended). Where written consent is given it must include a statement that the person giving consent is able and willing to give the child the required standard of care, and understands that the giving of consent could lead to the exclusion of the relevant person from the child's home (FPC(CA 1989)R 1991, r 25(2) as amended). It should be noted, however, that the application may be heard without notice being given to the party whose exclusion is sought, although again it must be remembered that the demands of Article 6 of the ECHR may well mean that the court will look very carefully at making such orders without the other party being present. Where a power of arrest is attached to an exclusion requirement then, save where the person who is to be excluded was given notice of the hearing and attended, the name of the person to be excluded must be announced publicly in open court at the earliest opportunity, as should the fact that an order has been made including an exclusion requirement to which a power of arrest has been attached. This may either be on the same day if the court proceeds to hear cases in open court, or at the next sitting of the court (see *Practice Direction* [1998] 2 All ER 928).

Further additional powers

5.112   Special provision is made under the CA 1989 to enable the court to require a person with information about a child's whereabouts to disclose that information when this is not available to the applicant (s 48(1)). The possibility of self-incrimination or the incrimination of a spouse does not excuse a person from compliance but, perhaps to the frustration of some police officers, any statement or admissions made in compliance are not admissible in evidence against that person in proceedings for any criminal offence other than perjury. It should be noted that this is an extension of the general principle contained in s 98, that statements or admissions made in actual proceedings are not admissible in evidence against the person making them or his spouse in proceedings of criminal offences. The interesting point to note about s 48(2) is that, of course, such statements will not generally be made in *the course of any proceedings*. The failure to comply with the court order to provide information is contempt of court and may amount to an offence under s 44(15).

5.113 The court is also able to authorise entry to premises to search for the child (s 48(3)) or any other child on the premises (s 48(4)). Interestingly, the section on the application form for an emergency protection order does not require that a separate application be made in respect of possible other children. If, however, on searching the premises a second or third child is found and the applicant believes that there are sufficient grounds for making an emergency protection order, the order authorising the search for the other child or children can be treated as an emergency protection order (s 48(5)). Where any person intentionally obstructs anyone exercising the powers for entry and search granted pursuant to s 48(3) and (4), that person will commit a criminal offence.

5.114 Where it is anticipated that the applicant will meet opposition to entry on the premises to execute an emergency protection order or to execute any additional powers under s 48, an application can be made for a warrant authorising a constable to assist the authorised person in entering and searching the named premises (s 48(9)). The *Children Act 1989: Guidance and Regulations* (vol 1 'Court Orders') recommends that whenever an application has been made for an emergency protection order the applicant should consider whether, at the same time, he needs to apply for a warrant for a police officer to accompany him when he is requesting authorisation to enter and search premises (para 4.57). The guidance goes on to state that:

'if any difficulties in gaining entry are foreseen, or if the applicant believes that he is likely to be threatened, intimidated or physically prevented from carrying out this part of the order, the possibility of simultaneously obtaining a warrant should always be considered.'

5.115 Where a warrant is issued it must be addressed to, and executed by, a police constable who can be accompanied by the applicant where that person desires and provided the court does not otherwise direct (s 48(10)). In addition to the issuing of a warrant, the court is further empowered to direct that a police constable may, in executing the warrant, be accompanied by a registered medical practitioner, registered nurse or registered health visitor where the constable so chooses. The guidance also states that it would always be good practice to request such a direction (at para 4.56).

5.116 Where a warrant is issued, it provides that the constable may use such reasonable force as is necessary in order to assist the applicant in the exercise of his or her powers to enter and search the premises for the child (s 48(9)).

Where the applicant has omitted to obtain a warrant at the same time as requesting authorisation to search and gain entry to premises, guidance issued to the police points out that where speed is essential to protect a child and a warrant would take too long to obtain, the police can act without a warrant to enter premises in order to save life and limb under s 17(1)(e) of the Police and Criminal Evidence Act 1984 (PACE). That Act goes on to provide, under s 25(3)(e), that police officers may arrest any person without warrant where this is necessary to achieve the protection of a child.

Police powers of protection

5.117 In some situations, it may be that the police are the first to discover that a child is suffering or is likely to suffer significant harm, and the CA 1989 provides the police with powers of protection to remove a child or to authorise the child remaining in a particular place such as a hospital (s 46(1) and (6)). This power can be exercised by the police for up to 72 hours, but where the police believe this period should be extended, they should either contact social services with a view to the local authority applying for an emergency protection order under s 44, or an interim care order (under s 38), or apply for and obtain an emergency protection order on behalf of the local authority (s 46(7)). While the police are exercising their powers of protection, they must notify parents and those with parental responsibility or with whom the child has been living of what is happening (s 46(4)), and afford such people reasonable contact with the child unless that would not be in the child's interests (s 46(10)). Police powers of protection have been described as 'occupying an anomalous position within the child protection framework in terms of decision making, accountability and control' (Masson (2002), at p 157). Unlike social services or the NSPCC, the police are not required to seek the court's permission for the exercise of their powers and there are no reported cases in the field of child protection where the police use of such powers has been challenged in the courts. The Home Office does not require forces to report on the use of the power and, in one study, three out of the 16 forces surveyed could not provide any statistics on its use at all and another two could only supply incomplete figures. Yet it has been estimated that the powers are used on 4,500 occasions per year on 6,000 children in England, excluding the area covered by the two London police forces (see Masson (2002), at p 159). Since estimates from the Metropolitan Police suggest that the power is used in London on at least as many occasions as in the rest of the country, this probably puts the annual figure at closer to 10,000. Masson's study found that in times of increasing pressure on understaffed social services, there is considerable reliance not only by social services but also by parents, children and the public on the police to respond to child protection crises and concerns arising outside office hours. She notes that the nature of these incidents and the organisation of police specialist child protection units meant that in the majority of cases uniform officers, with little experience in child protection, have to decide how to deal with them and whether to take children into police protection. Four factors are identified from the study which combined to encourage officers to use police protection: the breadth of possible interpretations, the lack of challenge, limited experience and concern about the consequences of failure to act. The study found that the social services surveyed were not able to provide support to families or the police, which could have reduced reliance on the police power or enabled more considered judgments particularly out of office hours. Although the social services managers in the study were critical of the 'overuse' of police protection, they also found it a convenient mechanism for emergency intervention (at p 172).

5.118 It should be noted that, where the police or the local authority apply for an emergency protection order, the period of police protection and the emergency protection order together cannot exceed 8 days (s 45(3)). Since the period to be spent in police protection is relatively short, as contrasted with the maximum period of an emergency protection order, the fact that the police do not acquire parental responsibility (s 46(9)(a)) but must nevertheless do what is reasonable in all the circumstances to safeguard or promote the child's welfare, may give rise to some confusion as to their powers in a case involving child protection. It is thought that whilst the police would be able to give consent to any required emergency medical treatment, it is unlikely that they can give consent to treatment which is not urgently required, but could give consent to any form of medical examination, psychiatric or other assessment. Where such an examination or assessment is required, this will necessitate an application for an emergency protection order and the request for directions from the court as to the conduct of such an examination or treatment.

Warrants under section 48(9)

5.119 It may sometimes be the case that those seeking to exercise an emergency protection order issued under s 44 may find difficulties in gaining entry to the premises and may therefore need the assistance to be found in s 48(9) of the CA 1989. Thus s 48(9) provides that where, on an application made by any person for a warrant to be issued, it appears to the court that a person attempting to exercise powers under an emergency protection order has been prevented from doing so by being refused entry to the premises concerned or access to the child concerned, or that any such person is likely to be so prevented from exercising any such powers, then the court may issue a warrant authorising any constable to assist the person mentioned in the exercise of those powers using reasonable force if necessary. It is further provided (s 48(10)) that every warrant issued shall be addressed to, and executed by, a police constable, who shall be accompanied by the person applying for the warrant where that person desires, and provided the court, by whom the warrant is issued, does not direct otherwise. In addition, the court granting an application for a warrant may direct that the constable concerned be accompanied by a registered medical practitioner, registered nurse or registered health visitor if he so chooses. Where, therefore, any social worker who has tried to exercise an order of the court issued under s 44 or s 44A has been frustrated in so doing then using these provisions the police are enabled to assist through the granting of the relevant warrant.

5.120 Police powers under the CA 1989 can, thus, be seen to be quite wide and attention should also be given to the provision in s 102 which allows an application to be made by any person (including a police constable) for a warrant to be issued by the court when that person has attempted to exercise powers under different parts of the CA 1989 and has been prevented from exercising such powers. The provision giving such persons the right to exercise the right of access to premises includes the CA 1989, ss 62, 64, 67, 76, 80, 86 and 87, Sch III, paras 8(1)(b), (2)(b) and the Adoption Act 1976, s 33. The primary power for the exercise of the right to enter premises falls chiefly upon social services, but the police can, where necessary, obtain a warrant under s 102 to enter the premises and search for children.

Court directions as to medical examination, psychiatric or other assessment of the child

5.121 Section 44(6) of the CA 1989 provides that where the court makes an emergency protection order it may give such directions, if any, as it considers appropriate with respect to the medical or psychiatric examination or other assessment of the child. Since the phrase *or other assessment* includes any form of social work assessment then, unless such a direction has been sought and obtained from the court, it will be virtually impossible for social services to determine whether to press forward with any further legal proceedings. Whether the child has been known to social services or any of the other agencies previously, or whether it is a completely new referral, considerable attention will have to be given to the process of engaging in the detailed assessment of the child as provided for in the *Framework for the Assessment of Children in Need and their Families* (DOH, 2000).

5.122 At the same time that the social workers may be undertaking their own assessment in accordance with the *Framework*, the court may also have imposed a direction that a psychiatrist should see the child for the purposes of a psychiatric assessment. It should be noted that where a request for such a direction has been made in the application for an emergency protection order, the request can be specific as to the person the applicant would like to carry out the psychiatric assessment.

5.123 A direction as to the medical examination of the child should be sought at the same time as seeking the granting of an emergency protection order and, again, specific requests can be made as to the sex of the doctor who is to carry out the medical examination and, even more specifically, a request can be made for a *particular* doctor to conduct the examination.

5.124 No matter what the nature of the assessment or examination is to be, it should be noted at this point that the child might *appear* to have the *right* to overrule the court's direction where he is deemed to be of sufficient understanding to make an informed decision (s 44(7)). This is one of the so-called *Gillick* provisions of the Act where not only are the child's wishes and feelings considered and taken into account but where it is apparent that the legislature had intended that they should be determinative of the issue. It would appear, however, that courts are not prepared to accept the child's autonomy interests in being able to make mistakes where acknowledgment of such an interest might lead to the child suffering harm. This was most starkly pointed up by the decision of Douglas Brown J in *South Glamorgan County Council v W and B* [1993] 1 FLR 574 dealing with the corresponding consent provisions contained in s 38(6) of the CA 1989 (see Chapter **12**). In that case, Douglas Brown J stated that the CA 1989 could not have been taken to have abrogated the power of the High Court in the exercise of its inherent jurisdiction to override, in a *proper* case, the wishes of a child and give consent for medical assessment, even where the child was of sufficient understanding and had refused such assessment. As Douglas Brown J put it, 'where other remedies within the CA 1989 have been used and exhausted and found not to bring about the desired results [the court] can resort to other remedies'. The question which must be asked is 'The result desired by whom?' and the clear answer is the result desired by the stautory child protection agencies and the courts.

Conclusion

5.125 The wealth of official guidance and statutory provisions governing the identification, investigation and initiation of child protection proceedings in those cases where concerns over child abuse have been raised is very considerable. This is why it seems so perplexing to realise that even with the benefit of all this material, tragedies such as those of Victoria Climbie and Lauren Wright can still occur in England in the new millennium. Critical shortages of front-line social work staff have been identified at a number of points in this chapter, but there are all sorts of reasons why such tragedies occur. Whilst it is easy to lay the blame at the door of various agencies, it must be remembered that it is those who abuse the children who are first and foremost at fault. Legislation and guidance can do much to asssist in improving our responses, but no system involving as it must human beings can ever probably be proof against the occurrence of the serious abuse or death of a child at the hands of a family member. We have spent so much money as a nation on very expensive child abuse and death inquiries and yet for the most part the results and recommendations of them all are very similar. Perhaps a better use of these very considerable sums would be on the provision of more and better-trained staff across all agencies, who are knowledgeable in the findings of previous inquiries and have been properly taught, with the relevant space and time to learn and reflect, as to how future tragedies might be avoided in their work.

5.126 In recognition of the need for increased training in child protection issues on an inter-agency basis, the Laming Report on the Inquiry into the Death of Victoria Climbie (28 January 2003 available at *www.victoria-climbie-inquiry.org/report*) made a number of recommendations about the provision of such training. Recommendation 7 of the report proposed the establishment of a Management Board for services to Children and Families, including senior officers from each of the key agencies, whose responsibilities would include ensuring that staff working in these agencies are appropriately trained and are able to demonstrate competence in their respective tasks. These Boards should be required under recommendation 15 to ensure that training on an inter-agency basis is provided, the effectiveness of which should be evaluated by the government inspectorates. Staff working in the relevant agencies should be required to demonstrate that their practice concerning inter-agency working is up to date by successfully completing appropriate training courses. In recommendation 14 it is proposed that the new national agency for Children and Families should require each of the training bodies covering services provided by doctors, nurses, teachers, police officers, housing department workers and social workers to demonstrate that effective joint working between each of these professional groups features in their national training programmes. Many of the other recommendations in the report, including those numbered 20, 31, 37, 43, 52, 59, also make detailed reference to the necessity of staff who are employed in the child protection arena being appropriately trained and being provided with training in relation to all the appropriate practice guidance, something which had patently not occurred in relation to the workers employed on Victoria's case. The Secretary of State, Alan Milburn, in his press conference on the same day indicated the government's unwillingness to implement a number of the recommendations but only time will tell as to whether both the monetary and the human resources are available (see further, Chapter **12**).

CHAPTER 6

INTER-AGENCY CO-OPERATION

'It is not widely accepted that child protection services need to be delivered through inter-agency and inter-disciplinary co-operation. Each succeeding child abuse enquiry, however, points out the difficulties for different disciplines and organisations in working effectively together ... One of the developments of the last 5 years has been an increasing devolvement of responsibility within the health service to independent trusts, within education departments to individual schools and within social services to individual localities. One of the results of these developments is a mushrooming of the number of separate operational units that will come into play in relation to child protection. Within this case, one of the features that comes into sharp focus is the number of operational units (at least 30) which attempted over 15 years to have an involvement with this family. Many of the operational units did so throughout the whole of that period, whilst others only had periodic involvement ... We have been able to identify the involvement of 28 social workers in Neighbourhood Services and 10 line managers. If the other organisations and the different groups of personnel who had a part to play are also included, the numbers involved are immense ... Within this complex organisational pattern there have been a range of professionals struggling day by day to make sense of *Working Together* .... . Any consideration of organisation and individual roles in relation to this family ... pinpoint very graphically the complexity of working on an inter-disciplinary and inter-agency basis' (*Paul: Death Through Neglect* (Bridge Child Care Consultancy Service, 1995), paras 131–140, at pp 159–161).

'The mandate is established for shared budgets, interdepartmental co-operation and collaboration which encourage the development of "joined up thinking" to address the multi-faceted needs of children. To implement such a strategy there must be a strong lead from elected members and chief officers as well as effective inter-agency working to plan, manage and deliver services. Social workers and other professional workers will need to work together to overcome barriers to effective joint working and consider the findings of research which show examples of effective practice and partnership in action. Professionals may be employed in different sectors, with different responsibilities but there are considerable overlaps in knowledge, understanding and overall aims, which can be pooled in the interests of children and their families. It follows that interdisciplinary research and training have a crucial role in developing attitudes and experiences of co-operation. Knowing who should be involved is only the first stage in working towards providing a seamless interdisciplinary service. An attitude of bridge building where commonalities are established by explicit linkages of budgets and planning infrastructure, as well as, professional understandings, training and common objectives, can best mobilise resources for the child' (*Studies Informing the Framework for the Asssessment of Children in Need and their Families* (DOH, 2001), at p 56).

'The *Working Together* booklet does not have any legal status, but with the lesson of *Cleveland County Council v F* in mind the emphasis upon co-operation, joint investigation and full consultation at all stages of any investigation are crucial to the success of the government guidelines ... The consequences of inter-agency co-operation is that there has to be free exchange of information between social workers and police officers together engaged in an investigation ... The information obtained by social workers in the course of their duties is, however, confidential and covered by the umbrella of public interest immunity ... It can however be disclosed to fellow members of the Child Protection Team engaged in the investigation of possible abuse of the child concerned' (Butler-Sloss LJ in *Re G (A Minor)* [1996] 2 All ER 65, at p 68).

Introduction

6.1   The above three quotations illustrate the primary importance of effective and properly co-ordinated inter-agency co-operation at every stage of a child's case coming to the notice of a particular agency. All agencies which have responsibility in the child protection field must now be familiar with the latest guidance on inter-agency co-operation issued by the government, namely *Working Together to Safeguard Children* (DOH et al, 1999, National Assembly for Wales, 2000)) and the two pieces of supplementary guidance, *Safeguarding Children Involved in Prostitution* (DOH, 2000) and *Safeguarding Children in Whom Illness is Fabricated or Induced* (DOH, 2002), and be aware of the inter-relationship between these documents and the *Framework for the Assessment of Children in Need and their Families* (DOH et al, 2000) together with its accompanying Practice Guidance (see *Assessing Children in Need and their Families – Practice Guidance* (DOH, 2000)).

Agencies and professionals responsible for child protection

6.2   Chapter 3 of *Working Together to Safeguard Children* opens with the words that 'An awareness and appreciation of the role of others is essential for effective collaboration' (at para 3.1). An even stronger emphasis on the critical understanding of a shared responsibility in this area is to be found in the latest supplement to *Working Together to Safeguard Children*, where it states that 'Promoting children's well-being and safeguarding them from significant harm depends crucially upon effective information sharing, collaboration and understanding between agencies and professionals' (see *Safeguarding Children in Whom Illness is Fabricated or Induced* (DOH, 2002), at para 1.23). Chapter 3 of *Working Together to Safeguard Children* then outlines the main roles and responsibilities of statutory agencies, professionals, the voluntary sector and the wider community, in relation to child protection. It emphasises that joint working should extend across the planning, management, provision and delivery of services, which is also emphasised in the quotations above. Thus, the roles of local authorities, social services, education services including independent schools, youth services, cultural and leisure services, health services, day care services, the police, probation, prisons, youth justice services, the voluntary and private sectors, housing authorities, CAFCASS, the armed services, and the wider community are clearly set out in chapter 3 with every opportunity being employed, as para 3.1 emphasises, to point out the vital importance not only of collaboration with all the other relevant agencies but of the awareness of each other's corresponding responsibilities and duties.

6.3 *Working Together to Safeguard Children* and its supplements apply to all services within England and Wales, and corresponding guidance exists for Scotland (see *Protecting Children: A Shared Responsibility* (The Scottish Office, 1998)) and for Northern Ireland (see *Co-operating to Protect Children: Children Northern Ireland Order 1995 Regulations and Guidance* (DHSS NI, 1995), vol 6). *Working Together to Safeguard Children* emphasises that voluntary organisations have a particularly important role to play in child protection. The guidance notes that national helplines are now operated on a free 24-hour basis by both ChildLine, whose service is available for children in trouble or in danger, and the NSPCC, whose services exist primarily for adults who have concerns about children. Parentline is also developing a national support helpline for parents under stress and all of these services, along with many smaller helplines, provide important routes into statutory and voluntary services for children in need and for those whose needs include safeguarding from significant harm. The guidance acknowledges that both voluntary and private sector organisations provide a range of services for children and families related to child protection issues. Such services include: advocacy projects for looked after children and for parents and children who are the subject of the CA 1989, s 47 inquiries and child protection conferences (see Chapter **5**); providing independent persons and visitors; home visiting and befriending/support programmes; support to disabled children and their families including the provision of short-term breaks; services for children who are victims or witnesses of crime; specialist services for disabled children and those with health problems; work in schools and other areas with peer support programmes; and therapeutic work with children and families particularly in relation to child sexual abuse.

6.4 The guidance states, however, that the NSPCC alone among voluntary organisations in England and Wales is authorised to initiate proceedings under the CA 1989 (at s 31) but it also acknowledges that other voluntary organisations undertake assessments of need and provide therapeutic and other services to children who have been abused. Many of these services are provided within the context of child protection plans for children whose

names are on the Child Protection Register (see Chapter **5**). The voluntary
sector also makes a significant contribution to the development and provision
of services for children abused through prostitution and for children who
abuse other children (see the work of the Children's Society and National
Children's Home, at Chapters **2** and **3**). *Working Together to Safeguard Children*
acknowledges that the range of roles fulfilled by organisations from the
voluntary and private sectors means that they need to have clear guidance and
procedures in place to ensure appropriate referrals and co-operation
procedures and that staff and volunteers must be trained to be aware of the
risks to and needs of children with whom they have contact.

The need for inter-disciplinary and inter-agency collaboration

6.5   No one reading the plethora of official government and local authority
child abuse and death inquiries (which now number at least 82 (see Corby,
Doig and Roberts (1998) and (2001) and see also *Learning from Past Experience –
A Review of Serious Case Reviews* (DOH, 2002) can doubt the vital importance of
the close co-operation between all professionals and agencies involved in child
protection. Nor, however, can one fail to be aware of the inevitable
breakdowns within the system of the levels of co-operation needed to ensure
that children do not slip through the safety net of all the processes and into
the abyss of undetected, unnoticed or misunderstood child abuse and neglect.
As has been seen from the quotations at the beginning of this chapter, the
CA 1989 was built on the philosophy that there should be much closer co-
operation between all professionals and agencies involved in child protection
and this is reflected in various sections of the Act such as s 27 which allows
different agencies to call upon the assistance of others in providing necessary
services to children and families and s 47 which provides direction as to the
assistance which must be rendered by different authorities when social
services require help in performing their duties. In addition, levels of co-
operation between local authorities, health authorities and the police are also
presumed in other sections, for example s 48 which provides that social
services may ask for the presence of police and health professionals when
trying to put into effect an emergency protection order.

6.6   A range of guidance issued by the government has, over the course of
the last 10 years, repeatedly pre-supposed close co-operation between
different agencies involved in child protection. Thus, the original *Memorandum
of Good Practice on Video Recorded Interviews with Child Witnesses for Criminal
Proceedings* (DOH, 1992) now replaced (since 24 May 2002) by Vol 1, Part 2
Planning and Conducting Interviews with Children of the three-volume *Achieving the
Best Evidence in Criminal Proceedings – Guidance for Vulnerable or Intimidated
Witnesses Including Children* (DOH, 2002) and the original guidance to police
officers and social workers in relation to children engaged in child prostitution

(DOH, 1999) since replaced by *Safeguarding Children Involved in Prostitution* (DOH, 2000), are based upon extremely close working relationships existing between police and social services in relation to the interviewing of children suspected of having been abused, and in relation to the type of work necessary with those children suspected of having been involved in child prostitution. The development of child witness packs (see *The Young Witness Pack* (1998) and (2000)) and the guidance issued on the *Provision of Therapy for Child Witnesses to a Criminal Trial* (DOH, 2001) testified to close working relationships between these agencies and the linking in with a child protection plan drawn up by social services. *Working Together to Safeguard Children* (at para 5.82) states that such plans should, along with other requirements, describe the identified needs of the child and what therapeutic services are required if a child is going to be a witness at a criminal trial (see further, Chapter **9**). In addition, the concurrent jurisdiction created by the CA 1989 (a lateral and vertical court transfer scheme) has also required co-operation between the judiciary and the court services agency working at different levels and in different courts, and special measures have been taken to try to progress both civil child protection proceedings and criminal proceedings against perpetrators of abuse more quickly through the system (see further, Chapter **9**). The production by the NSPCC of the video *A Case for Balance – Demonstrating Good Practice when Children are Witnesses – A Video Aimed at Judges and Lawyers* (NSPCC, 1997) indicates a recognition by the judiciary and lawyers that special levels of cooperation between judges and lawyers are also needed in child protection cases, where proceedings are taken in the criminal courts and rely crucially on the evidence of a child witness or witnesses. Guidance emphasising co-operation between all agencies and health service staff has been constantly revised and reissued throughout the 1990s and was discussed in detail in Chapter **5**. All of the various documents of guidance issued to the staff in the health services emphasise the importance of inter-agency collaboration and the necessity for early exchange of information between the various agencies which may be involved in child protection.

6.7   The need for a co-ordinated national approach to the problem of child abuse management was identified initially by two early guidance documents issued in 1970 and 1972 respectively which dealt with the need for inter-agency collaboration in relation to the problem of battered babies. The current system of child abuse management was, as Parton points out, effectively inaugurated with the issue of Circular LASSL 74/13 entitled *Non-Accidental Injury to Children* by the DHSS in 1974 (see Parton (1991), at pp 118–121). This Circular was issued in April 1974 in the wake of the Maria Colwell inquiry and whilst para 2 of the Circular engaged in an attempt to make the professionals aware of the first signs of the possible non-accidental injury, the remainder was taken up, as Parton comments, with how to manage individual cases and the local organisation of agencies, professionals and resources. The Circular emphasised the need for teamwork and 'strongly recommended' the establishment of case conferences, area review committees and child protection registers. Area review committees (now ACPCs) were to provide a forum for consultation between representatives of all local agencies and to be responsible for the formulation of local practice procedures, training, inquiries and general advice. Case conferences were to provide an arena for professionals who had knowledge of a particular child or family to share information and co-ordinate their efforts. The establishment of a register of cases was deemed to be essential as 'the outcome of any case will depend on the communicating skills of the professionals involved as much as upon their expertise' (see Circular 74/13). By the end of 1974, Area Review Committees had been established across England and Wales, together with Registers, while the convening of case conferences was 'recognised in all areas as a vital process in the handling of cases of children injured or at risk' (Circular 74/13, para 10). The system which currently operates is based very much on that originally established back in 1974 although much has now been adapted, improved and revised.

6.8   The current version of *Working Together*, now entitled *Working Together to Safeguard Children*, is the third version of a booklet originally published in 1988 which had itself been issued in response to various child abuse scandals and inquiries (see Chapter 5). Parton, Thorpe and Wattam have pointed out that a fundamental shift occurred between the issuing of the original 1986 draft guidance and that which ultimately appeared in 1988 in the aftermath of Cleveland (see Parton, Thorpe and Wattam (1997), at pp 32–33). Parton, Thorpe and Wattam identify the various stages of metamorphosis which the guidance has undergone between 1986 and 1997, detecting an emphasis on legalism and the construction of a new consensus as to the need to reconstruct the balance between the protection of children and the protection of the privacy of the family in order to maintain public confidence (at p 37).

6.9   That approach of getting the right balance between the protection of children and protection of the privacy of the family is further reflected in the 1999 version, *Working Together to Safeguard Children* (see further, para **6.21**). The 1999 document has, however, gone much further than this in that it demonstrates very clearly that it has been drawn up in response to the major research studies initiated by the DOH in the aftermath of the implementation of the CA 1989 (see *Child Protection: Messages from Research* (DOH, 1995)) and to the constructive criticisms made of the system introduced as a result of that Act (see eg Parton (1997)). In addition to the DOH's own study, the Audit Commission had produced in 1994 its report entitled *Seen But Not Heard: Co-ordinating Child Health and Social Services for Children in Need*, which identified in common with the results from the DOH's own research studies that one of the principal aims of the CA 1989, namely that of family support and the provision of services to children in need, was not actually being met but that far too much attention was focused on systems set up for responding to concerns about child abuse.

6.10 At the same time as the various research studies were being conducted into the workings of the new Act, further controversies surrounding child abuse and child deaths continued to surface, which emphasised yet again the problem of a lack of inter-agency co-operation and co-ordination. Such a lack was identified in the very influential report on *Paul: Death Through Neglect* (Bridge Child Care Consultancy, 1995) which was all the more important because this report emphasised the need for concerted working together to provide the relevant services into a family, where a child had died as a result of neglect. Paul's death was as much about neglect by the system as about neglect by his parents. The trial of Rosemary West in 1995 again emphasised failure by various agencies including social services, the NSPCC, the police, children's teachers, and the family GP, to take the necessary steps to safeguard the West's seven children, one of whom was murdered, and who had all been subjected to a terrifying regime of physical, emotional and sexual abuse. The response to the West case was undoubtedly to prompt demands for further tightening up of procedures related to interventionist approaches in families in the context of potential child abuse and a renewed emphasis on resort to legal proceedings where necessary.

6.11 Similar responses were again echoed in 2001 with the government's response to the death of Victoria Climbie, which again highlighted failures on the parts of different agencies to respond most appropriately to concerns which were being expressed. This case prompted the government to state that it would look again at systems of child protection. It is quite clear, however, that what is really necessary is to ensure that all professionals working together to safeguard children are thoroughly familiar with the guidelines which are laid down not only in *Working Together to Safeguard Children* and its supplements but also in the *Framework for the Assessment of Children in Need and their Families* (DOH, 2000) and the related *Practice Guidance* (DOH, 2000), as well as being aware that the messages from all the research which has been done has emphasised the importance of early support and the provision of services into families with children in need (see *The Children Act Now: Messages from Research* (DOH, 2001). The preventive approach, discussed in detail in Chapters **3** and **4**, is reinforced throughout the CA 1989 not only in Pt III but also and very critically in various paragraphs of Sch 2, Pt I which emphasise the obligation on local authorities to prevent children in their area suffering abuse and neglect (at Sch 2, Pt I, para 4) and also emphasise the need to reduce the bringing of care and supervision order proceedings in respect of all children (at Sch 2, Pt I, para 7).

6.12 The latest version of *Working Together to Safeguard Children* cannot be criticised for merely giving a nod in the direction of family support in the

Introduction, because it goes much further than this. The whole of the first chapter of this version emphasises the necessity for supporting children and families and then in chapter 2 draws out the lessons from research studies, professional practice and experience before then going on to consider the various roles and responsibilities of different agencies in responding to children in need. The whole look and feel of *Working Together to Safeguard Children* is very different from that of the 1991 version of *Working Together*, which even in its introductory chapter emphasised the role of ACPCs and the importance of the legal framework in responding to problems of child abuse. The 1991 document was extremely legalistic and focused upon the mechanics of procedures bound by different legal rules. *Working Together to Safeguard Children* puts, as has been stated, very much greater emphasis upon the roles and responsibilities of everyone in relation to children in need and the provision of relevant support and services and that all agencies involved are required to be aware of the *Framework for the Assessment of Children in Need and their Families* (DOH, 2000). This is critical for children and their families since, as the *Framework for Assessment* puts it, such awareness:

'when contributing to assessments of children in need will facilitate communication between agencies and with children and families. It will also assist the process of referral from one agency to another and increase the likelihood of acceptance of the contents of previous assessment thereby reducing unnecessary duplication of assessment and increasing local confidence in inter-agency work. Knowledge of the Assessment Framework can inform contributions by all agencies and disciplines when assessing children about whom there are safety concerns' (at pp ix, x).

6.13 The *Framework for Assessment* goes on to state that:

'effective collaborative work between staff of different disciplines and agencies assessing children in need and their families requires a common language to understand the needs of children, shared values about what is in children's best interests and a joint commitment to improving the outcomes for children. The *Framework for Assessment* provides that common language based on explicit values about children, knowledge about what children need to ensure their successful development, and the factors in their lives which may positively or negatively influence their upbringing. This increases the likelihood of parents and children experiencing consistency between professionals and themselves about what would be important for children's wellbeing and health development' (at p x).

6.14 What both *Working Together to Safeguard Children* and the *Framework for Assessment* emphasise is the need not only for a common language but also a common understanding about the various important factors in children's lives, and it has been encouraging to witness the national programmes of inter-agency training on *Working Together to Safeguard Children* and the *Framework for*

Assessment which have been conducted between social services and the other agencies all over the country.

6.15 Getting 'the right balance' is always difficult but, hopefully, the guidance provided in *Working Together to Safeguard Children* and the *Framework for Assessment* will help to achieve this, whilst not ignoring those factors which may point to negative outcomes for children. The importance of the enquiry into the death of Paul was that it emphasised what a number of the research studies and the DOH's own studies had shown, that there were continuing staff uncertainties in the assessment and identification of the serious consequences of neglect for children (see *The Children Act Report 1995–1999* (DOH, 1999), at para 3.13). One of the DOH's own studies, *Responding to Families in Need: The Inspection of Assessment, Planning and Decision Making in Family Support Services* (DOH, 1997) had found that some children were being left in neglectful situations for far too long while too many other children were the subject of unnecessary enquiries under s 47 of the CA 1989. (See also Beaumont (1999).)

6.16 The experiences of the children in the *Bedfordshire* case (see *Z v UK* [2001] 2 FLR 612, European Court) also pointed this up in that strenuous efforts had been made to keep the children in their family, whereas a focus on the actual extent of the impact of neglect on each of the children ought to have led to the inescapable conclusion that the parents were totally unable to cope, were totally failing to respond to the physical and emotional needs of their children, and that the children should have been removed long before the expiry of 5 years from the date of first coming to the attention of Bedfordshire Social Services. Reading the reports of the case, it is clear that social workers were indeed working towards what they saw as the demands of the CA 1989: that one should work together in partnership with the parents to achieve the best outcome for the children. Undoubtedly, they had taken this message on board whilst at the same time failing to recognise that the extent of the neglect suffered by the children was having such serious and long-term consequences for their physical, mental and emotional well-being.

6.17 The need for greater protection of children in residential care (see *Caring for Children Away from Home: Messages from Research* (DOH, 1998) has also been fully acknowledged by the DOH and has informed major new initiatives on the part of the government: in developing the *Quality Protects* programme; in the establishment of a Ministerial Task Force to develop a full programme of policy and management changes to deliver a safer environment for such children; and in the establishment of the Children and Young People's Unit, led by a Minister for Young People, to keep a focus on the needs of children and young people across all central government departmental boundaries. *Working Together to Safeguard Children* and its two supplements have as one of their key roles the task of ensuring effective child protection procedures for all children in whatever environment they are being looked after. As the *Children Act Report 1995–1999* stresses:

> 'the key message which the government wishes to promote is a new emphasis on looking more widely at the needs of the most vulnerable children and families in communities. Many of the families who find themselves caught up in the child protection system suffer from multiple disadvantages. They need help at an earlier stage to tackle their problems before parenting difficulties escalate into crisis or abuse. Assessment of the needs of children and their families will be key to providing better targeted support' (at para 3.10).

6.18   The criticisms levelled at earlier versions of *Working Together*, that they effectively ignored the effects of poverty and other inequities and inequalities within the system at large (see Parton (1997)) have also been responded to in great measure. *Working Together to Safeguard Children* and the *Framework for Assessment* continually seek to emphasise the problems which may be affecting children in need and their families. Thus, para 2.19 of *Working Together to Safeguard Children* identifies various sources of stress for children and their families, including poverty and social exclusion, as well as looking to such issues as domestic violence, the mental illness of a parent or carer and the problems of parents and carers being involved in drug and alcohol misuse. The *Framework for Assessment* now emphasises that safeguarding children should not be seen as a separate activity from promoting their welfare but rather that they are two sides of the same coin. 'Promoting welfare', it states, 'has a wider, more positive, action-centred approach embedded in a philosophy of creating opportunities to enable children to have optimum life chances in adulthood as well as ensuring they are growing up in circumstances consistent with the provision of safe and effective care' (see *Framework for Assessment*, at para 1.17). The *Framework for Assessment* points out that Hardiker et al have produced a very useful framework for looking at the policy context of children in need and the value of applying a twin approach of safeguarding and promoting welfare at different levels of intervention. The *Framework for Assessment* states that Hardiker et al's grid, which is reproduced in the *Framework for Assessment* at Appendix B, can be used to help the planning and appropriate provision of services to children in need and their families. The *Framework for Assessment* emphasises, however, that determining who is in need, what those needs are, and how services will have an effect on outcomes for children, requires professional judgement by social services staff *together with colleagues from other professional disciplines* who are working with children and families (at para 1.18.)

6.19   It is clear, therefore, that the DOH, together with the other government departments including the Home Office, the DfEE and the Assembly for Wales, have learned very substantially not only from their own research studies but also from the criticisms of others. Thus major changes have been made to the guidance on inter-agency co-operation in child protection to reflect the lessons which have been learned from successive child abuse enquiries including, most recently, the investigation into abuse of children in North Wales (see *Lost in Care: Report of the Tribunal of Enquiry into the Abuse of Children in Care in the Former County Council Areas of Gwynedd and Clwyd since 1974* (The Stationery Office, 2000)). There are now special sections within *Working Together to Safeguard Children,* which concentrate on issues of child protection arising in specific circumstances, including the difficulties faced by children living away from home and what action should be taken when investigating allegations of abuse made against professionals, foster carers or volunteers (see *Working Together to Safeguard Children,* at paras 6.1– 6.22). Further advice is given with regard to the investigation of organised or multiple abuse as well as to situations involving abuse of disabled children, and abuse of children by children and young people (at paras 6.24–6.37). Other key areas which have been said to be neglected in the past are further addressed within the new guidance. Thus, as well as establishing the key principle of working in partnership with children and families, there is also now considerable emphasis on the importance of addressing issues of race, ethnicity and culture in a sensitive and informed manner (at paras 7.2–7.26). Throughout the guidance, sensitivity to issues of race, ethnicity, religion, language and culture are evidenced including an awareness that bullying of children by other children and young people can very often have either implicit or explicit racial overtones (at paras 6.31–6.37).

6.20 The very marked change in emphasis in this latest version of *Working Together* has, of course, been influenced by other developments including the requirements since 1993 to produce children's services plans, which identify the range of services to be made available for children in need and their families but which have also required not only the identification of the role of other agencies but a real partnership to develop in terms of the delivery of services to children and families. That amendment to the CA 1989 arose, in part, as a result of the Audit Commission's findings which had not, at that stage, been made public, but it also has been accompanied by a much greater political willingness on the part of the Labour government to acknowledge the importance of having a clear steer from central government in terms of the direction in which all the various agencies working together to safeguard children should move. The importance of the *Quality Protects* programme, and the constant review of the performance of social services in their task constituted by the Performance Assessment Framework have undoubtedly focused attention on the importance of the delivery of services to children in need and their families. The new emphasis on assessing positive outcomes for children, including, in particular, the educational performance of children in care and the consideration given to their health needs, highlight the critical importance of all agencies working together to achieve the best possible outcomes for children.

Working Together to Safeguard Children in the new millennium

6.21 As successive enquiries and research studies have emphasised, inter-agency co-operation is by no means easy to achieve but the DOH indicates that the role of the guidance, which it has issued, is to provide a national framework within which agencies and professionals at local level – individually and jointly – draw up and agree upon their more detailed ways of working together (*Safeguarding Children Involved in Prostitution* (DOH, 2000), at para 1.3 and *Safeguarding Children in Whom Illness is Fabricated or Induced* (DOH, 2002), at para 1.2). All of the guidance documents which it has issued therefore are there to respond to the need for the best possible practice when concerns about a child's welfare surface. The guidance makes it clear that good practice calls for effective co-operation between different agencies and professionals; sensitive work with parents and carers in the best interests of the child; and the careful exercise of professional judgement based on thorough assessment and critical analysis of the available information. Many agencies have taken major steps forward in working together with other agencies, but the need for the advice and guidance provided by both *Working Together to Safeguard Children* and its supplements and the *Framework for Assessment* demonstrate that further improvements need to take place and must take place in order to bring about better outcomes for children. The key requirement of the CA 1989 for local authorities to adopt a more corporate approach in terms of its own constituent agencies has been pointed out earlier (see Chapter **5**). A number of agencies, however, do not come under the umbrella of the local authority and yet are key in providing support and services to children in need and their families, or in cases where there are grave concerns about the children, then in assisting in the assessment and investigative processes which may follow. The critical role of ACPCs is given considerable attention in the guidance as are the individual roles and responsibilities of all the potential constituent partners in the process of working together to provide support for children in need and their families as well as in the process of safeguarding children.

Key areas in Working Together to Safeguard Children *and the* Framework for Assessment

6.22 The identification of core principles informing the work of all the agencies is another key feature of the current guidance, as is the need for inter-agency training and development, which is the subject of a completely separate chapter of the 1999 document. It is therefore proposed to consider here in some detail those areas of both *Working Together to Safeguard Children* and the *Framework for Assessment* which have not already received attention in Chapters **2**, **4** and **5**. This examination will therefore include:

(1) an examination of the key principles which should inform all agencies' practice in working with children and families;

(2) an examination of the roles and responsibilities of all the different agencies who may provide support and assistance for children in need and their families, as well as participating in investigation and assessment in suspected cases of child abuse;

(3) the role of ACPCs;

(4) the issues posed by child protection arising in specific circumstances (the issues of handling individual cases having already been considered in Chapters **4** and **5**);

(5) the conduct of case reviews (considered briefly in Chapter **3**); and

(6) the issue of inter-agency training and development, which has not previously been touched on elsewhere.

Key principles and issues in inter-agency co-operation

6.23 Although the guidance on key principles for inter-agency co-operation appears in chapter 7 of *Working Together to Safeguard Children*, it is being considered here first because the guidance emphasises that these principles should underpin the practice of all agencies and professionals working together to safeguard children and promote their welfare. A number of these principles have already been considered elsewhere in other chapters (eg Chapters **3**, **4** and **5**) but others appear here for the first time. Thus, the key principles identified in chapter 7 of *Working Together to Safeguard Children* encompass: working in partnership with children and families and what, exactly, this means; issues associated with race, ethnicity and culture; the importance of sharing information and issues associated with the law of confidentiality and the practice of different professional groups such as doctors, nurses, health visitors and midwives; the importance of record-keeping; the critical role of supervision and support; and the importance of rigorous procedures associated with the recruitment and selection of staff.

Working in partnership with children and families

6.24 The importance of partnership has already been considered in a number of chapters and the emphasis which both *Working Together to Safeguard Children* and the *Framework for Assessment* place on the value of such partnership in terms of the best possible outcomes for children has also been repeatedly highlighted. *Working Together to Safeguard Children* not only emphasises the importance of working in partnership with parents, ensuring that parents will be helped and encouraged to play as full a part as possible in decisions about their child, but it also stresses that children of sufficient age and understanding should be kept fully informed of processes involving them, should be consulted sensitively, and decisions about their future should take account of their views. In illustrating what is meant by partnership in child protection, *Working Together to Safeguard Children* reproduces the 15 basic principles for working in partnership which were set out in *The Challenge of Partnership in Child Protection* (DOH, 1995)) (see *Working Together to Safeguard Children*, at p 76).

6.25 The guidance emphasises that the aim of child protection processes is to ensure the safety and welfare of a child, and that the child's interests should always be paramount. This, of course, reflects the principles set out in the CA 1989, s 1(1) that whenever the court makes a decision about the child's custody or upbringing, then the child's welfare is the court's paramount consideration. The agencies working together to safeguard children should agree a common understanding in each case, and at each stage of work, of how children and families will be involved in child protection processes, and what information is to be shared with them. The guidance states that there should be a presumption of openness, joint decision-making, and a willingness to listen to families and capitalise on their strengths, although some information known to professionals should be treated confidentially and should not be shared with some children or some adult members. Such information might include personal health information about particular family members unless consent has been given, or information which, if disclosed, could compromise criminal investigations or proceedings (at para 7.6). Whilst recognising that working relationships with families should develop according to individual circumstances, the guidance also recognises that family structures are increasingly complex and that there may be a wide number of family members playing a significant role in a child's life. It urges that professionals should make especially sure that they pay attention to the views of all those who have something significant to contribute to decisions about the child's future. This is more especially the case when considering the requirements of Article 8 of the ECHR in relation to the right of every family member to their private family life, which is being interpreted by the courts as entailing a positive duty on agencies to ensure the involvement and participation of all relevant family members in the consultative and decision-making processes in the child protection field unless to do so would endanger the child.

6.26 The guidance goes on to identify the importance of involving children not only so that they have a clear perception of what needs to be done to ensure their safety and well-being but also so that they are reassured that their safety is guaranteed. It indicates that children should be helped to understand how child protection processes work, how they can be involved, and what they can contribute to decisions about their future. In developing the theme of working in partnership with families, *Working Together to Safeguard Children* then describes the process of family group conferences, which has now been developed in a number of areas as a positive option for planning services for children and their families (at paras 7.13–7.18). The guidance notes that family group conferences do not replace or remove the need for child protection conferences but are a process through which family members, including those in the wider family, are enabled to meet together to find solutions to difficulties which they and the child and young person in their family are facing. According to *Working Together to Safeguard Children*, family group conferences may be appropriate in a number of contexts where there is a plan or decision to be made, for example: for children in need, in a range of circumstances where a plan is required for the child's future welfare; where s 47 enquiries do not substantiate referral concerns about significant harm but where there is a need for support and services; and where s 47 enquiries progress to a child protection conference, that conference may agree that a family group conference is an appropriate vehicle for the core group to use to develop the outline child protection plan into a fully worked up plan (see Chapters **4** and **5**). *Working Together to Safeguard Children* also states that where there are plans to use family group conferences, in situations where there are child protection concerns, they should be developed and implemented under the auspices of the ACPC. This will mean that all relevant agencies will be involved in their development and relate their use to other relevant child protection policies and procedures. It is emphasised that inter-agency training will be needed to build the relevant skills needed to work with children and families in this way, and to promote confidence in and develop a shared understanding of the process.

6.27 Still on the theme of partnership with families, the guidance goes on to deal with issues of support, advice and advocacy for children and families. Noting that children and families may be supported through their involvement in child protection processes by such services, the guidance states that families should always be informed as to those services which exist both locally and nationally. Where children and families are involved as witnesses in criminal proceedings, the police, witness support services and other services provided by Victim Support can do a great deal to explain the process, make it feel less daunting and ensure that children are prepared for and supported in the court process. In addition, the guidance indicates that information about the Criminal Injuries Compensation Scheme should also be provided in relevant cases (see further, Chapter **9**).

6.28 The guidance stresses that it is the responsibility of social services to make sure that children and adults have all the information they need to enable them to understand the child protection process and that information should be clear and accessible and available in a family's first language. It also goes on to note that if a child or family member has specific communication needs, because of language or disability, it may be necessary to use the services of an interpreter or specialist worker, or to make use of other aids to communication. The guidance advises that particular care should be taken in choosing an interpreter, having regard to their language skills, their understanding of the issues under discussion, their commitment to confidentiality, and their position in the wider community. The guidance warns that there can be difficulties in using family members or friends as interpreters and this should be avoided and that children also should not be used as interpreters.

Race, ethnicity and culture

6.29 As all the research studies in child protection have demonstrated, children from all cultures are subject to abuse and neglect but *Working Together to Safeguard Children* states that all children have a right to grow up safe from harm. It advises, however, that in order to make sensitive and informed professional judgements about a child's needs and parents' capacity to respond to their child's needs, it is important that professionals are sensitive to different family patterns and life-styles and to child-rearing patterns that vary across different racial, ethnic and cultural groups. Professionals should also be aware of the broader social factors that serve to discriminate against black and minority ethnic people. Working in a multi-racial and multi-cultural society requires professionals and organisations to be committed to equality in meeting the needs of all children and families and to understand the affect of racial harassment, racial discrimination and institutional racism, as well as cultural misunderstanding or misinterpretation (at para 7.24). Thus, the assessment process should always maintain a focus on the needs of the individual child, including a consideration of the way religious beliefs and cultural traditions in different racial, ethnic and cultural groups influence their values, attitudes and behaviour, and the way in which family and community life is structured and organised. Cultural factors neither explain nor condone acts of omission or commission which place the child at risk of significant harm. All professionals should be aware of and work with the strengths and support systems available within families, ethnic groups and communities, which can be built upon to help safeguard children and promote their welfare. Very importantly, *Working Together to Safeguard Children* advises that professionals should guard against stereotypes – both positive and negative – of black and minority ethnic families. But it also cautions that anxiety about being accused of racist practice should not prevent the necessary action being taken to safeguard the child. Careful assessment, based on evidence, of a child's needs, and a family's strengths and weaknesses, understood in the context of the wider social environment, will help to avoid any distorting effects of these influences on professional judgements.

Issues around the sharing of information

6.30 In this part of the Key Principles chapter, *Working Together to Safeguard Children* indicates that research and experience have shown repeatedly that keeping children safe from harm requires professionals and others to share information: about a child's health and development and exposure to possible harm; about a parent who may need help to or may not be able to care for a child adequately and safely; and about those who pose a risk of harm to a child. The guidance valuably points out that often, it is only when information from a number of sources has been shared and is then put together that it becomes clear that a child is at risk of or is suffering harm. In successive enquiry reports, it has been repeatedly emphasised that it is often this failure to share information which has ultimately led to the tragic circumstances of a child's death. The key piece of information which one particular agency may have may well be the piece which is required to complete the jigsaw puzzle to reveal that a child is or is not at risk of suffering significant harm.

6.31 Those providing services to adults and children may become concerned about the need to balance their duties to protect children from harm and their general duty towards their patient or service users and some professionals and staff face the added dimension of being involved in caring for, or supporting, more than one family member – the abused child, siblings and alleged abuser. Where there are concerns that a child is, or may be, at risk of significant harm, however, the needs of *that child* must come first. In these circumstances, the overriding objectives, according to *Working Together to Safeguard Children*, must be to safeguard the child. It also establishes that there is a need for all agencies to hold information securely. Thus, professionals can only work together to safeguard children if there is an exchange of information between them but that any disclosure of personal information to others must always have regard to both statute and common law. It advises that normally personal information should only be disclosed to third parties (including other agencies) with the consent of the subject of that information and that, wherever possible, consent should be obtained before sharing personal information with third parties. Very importantly, however, the guidance points out that in some circumstances, consent may not be possible or desirable but the safety and welfare of the child dictates that the information should be shared. The guidance advises that the best way of ensuring that information-sharing is properly handled is to work within carefully worked out information-sharing protocols between the agencies and professionals involved, and taking legal advice in individual cases where necessary. The guidance includes in Appendix 4 a very useful checklist produced by the Data Protection Registrar for setting up information-sharing arrangements.

6.32 The guidance restates the common law duty of confidence, which in general terms means that personal information about children and families held by professionals and agencies should be subject to a legal duty of confidence, and should not normally be disclosed without the consent of the subject. However, it points out that the common law permits the disclosure of confidential information necessary to safeguard a child or children in the public interests: that is, the public interest in child protection may override the public interest in maintaining confidentiality (see Chapter 5 and the case of *D v NSPCC* [1978] AC 171). The guidance correctly points out that children are entitled to the same duty of confidence as adults, provided that, in the case of those aged under 16, they have the ability to understand the choices and their consequences relating to any treatment (the so-called *Gillick*-competence test). The guidance does advise, however, that in exceptional circumstances where it is believed that a child seeking advice, for example on sexual matters, is being exploited or abused then confidentiality may be breached following discussions with the child.

6.33 Similar provisions apply pursuant to the Data Protection Act 1998 which requires that personal information is: obtained and processed fairly and lawfully; only disclosed in appropriate circumstances; accurate, relevant and not held longer than necessary; and kept securely. This Act again allows for disclosure without the consent of the subject in certain conditions, including very importantly for child protection purposes, for the purposes for the prevention or detection of crime or apprehension or prosecution of offenders, and where failure to disclose would be likely to prejudice those objectives in a particular case.

6.34 For those who might fear that Article 8 of the ECHR might be raised by parents or others to prevent disclosure of information without consent, the guidance indicates that disclosure of information to safeguard children will usually be within Article 8(2) and will be be done for the protection of health or morals, for the protection of the rights and freedoms of others or for the prevention of disorder or crime. The guidance advises, however, that disclosure should be appropriate for the purpose and only to the extent necessary to achieve that purpose.

6.35 *Working Together to Safeguard Children* goes on to indicate that the Home Office has produced guidance on the exchange of information about all those who have been convicted of, cautioned for, or otherwise dealt with by the courts for a sexual offence; and those who are considered by the relevant agency to present a risk to children and others. This guidance addresses issues arising in relation to people who have not been convicted or cautioned for offences but who are suspected of involvement in criminal sexual activity (see *Guidance on the Disclosure of Information about Sex Offenders Who May Present a Risk to Children and Vulnerable Adults* (Home Office, July 1999)). The Home Office guidance emphasises that the disclosure of information should always take place within an established system and protocol between agencies, and should be integrated into a risk assessment and management system. Each case should be judged on its merits by the police and other relevant agencies, taking account of the degree of risk. The Home Office guidance places on the police the responsibility to co-ordinate and lead the risk assessment and management process and advises that agencies should work within carefully worked out information-sharing protocols and refers to various good practice materials in existence. It also advocates the establishment of multi-agency risk panels whose purpose is to share information about offenders and to devise strategies to manage their risk (see further, Chapter **9**).

Guidance for doctors on confidentiality

6.36 As has been seen in Chapter **5**, the GMC has produced guidance which is more up to date than that which is referred to in *Working Together to Safeguard Children*. Practitioners should therefore be extremely cautious when referring to chapter 7 of *Working Together to Safeguard Children* (at paras 7.39–7.46) for information on the guidance issued by various branches of the medical profession. In particular, *Working Together to Safeguard Children* refers to the GMC document published in 1995 whereas the GMC has produced an updated version of this document entitled *Confidentiality: Providing and Protecting Information* (GMC, June 2000). Thus the guidance issued in 2000 states:

'Patients have a right to expect that information about them will be held in confidence by their doctors. Confidentiality is central to trust between doctors and patients. Without assurances about confidentiality, patients may be reluctant to give doctors the information they need in order to provide good care. If you are asked to provide information about patients you should:

(a) seek the patient's consent to disclosure of information wherever possible, whether or not you judge the patient can be identified from the disclosure,
(b) anonymise data where unidentifiable data will serve the purpose,
(c) keep disclosures to the minimum necessary.

Disclosure of personal information without consent *may be justified* where failure to do so may expose the patient or others to risk of death or serious harm. Where third parties are exposed to a risk so serious that it outweighs the patient's privacy interests, you should seek consent to disclosure where practicable. If it is not practicable, you should disclose information promptly to an appropriate person or authority. You should generally inform the patient before disclosing the information.

Problems may arise if you consider that a patient is incapable of giving consent to treatment or disclosure because of immaturity, illness or mental incapacity. If such patients ask you not to disclose information to a third party, you should try to persuade them to allow an appropriate person to be involved in the consultation. If they refuse and you are convinced that it is essential, in their medical interests, you may disclose relevant information to an appropriate person or authority. In such cases you must tell the patient before disclosing any information and, where appropriate, seek and carefully consider the views of an advocate or carer. You should document in the patient's record the steps you have taken to obtain consent and the reasons for deciding to disclose information.'

6.37 The United Kingdom Central Council for Nursing, Midwifery and Health Visiting has also produced *Guidelines for Professional Practice* (1996) which contain advice on providing information and are reproduced in *Working Together to Safeguard Children*. This advises (at para 55):

'Disclosure of information occurs:

- with the consent of the patient or client;
- without the consent of the patient or client;
- without the consent of the patient or client when the disclosure is required by law or by order of a court; and
- without the consent of the patient or client when the disclosure is considered to be necessary in the public interests.

The public interest means the interest of an individual, or groups of individuals or a society as a whole and would, for example, cover matters such as serious crime, child abuse, drug trafficking or other activities which place others at serious risk' (para 56).

'In all cases where you deliberately release information in what you believe to be the best interest of the public, your decision must be justified. In some circumstances, such as accident and emergency admissions where the police are involved, it may be appropriate to involve senior staff if you do not feel that you are able to deal with the situation alone' (para 57).

6.38 In the document *Confidentiality and Young People: A Toolkit for General Practice, Primary Care Groups and Trusts*, endorsed by the Royal College of General Practitioners, the General Practitioners Committee, the BMA, the Royal College of Nursing, and the Medical Defence Union, this guidance for nurses is reproduced with the additional advice that it is also 'considered good nursing practice that all patients, whenever possible, should be informed before confidentiality is broken unless to do so would be dangerous for the patient or others' (at p 11).

6.39 In addition to the two documents issued by the GMC for the guidance of doctors and by the United Kingdom Central Council for Nursing, Midwifery and Health Visiting, the BMA has also published a book entitled *Consent, Rights and Choices in Health Care for Children and Young People* (BMJ Books, 2001). This publication, which is intended for all health professionals, discusses the exceptional circumstances where it may be necessary to breach confidentiality or to disclose information relating to a patient. Such circumstances arise, according to the book, where 'disclosing information will protect the patient or others from a risk of serious harm' (at p 85). It points out that health professionals must weigh the advantages and disadvantages of disclosure versus non-disclosure and make a decision based on the individual circumstances. They must also be prepared to justify decisions, and be aware that they risk criticism for taking premature or inappropriate action as much as by delaying action, where there are serious grounds for concern. The book does canvas the possibility of discussing the need for disclosure with the patient if it is possible to do this safely and that the patient may then be persuaded to disclose information himself voluntarily. It goes on to advise, however, that the situations in which information might be disclosed without the patient's knowledge will be extremely rare. Where concerns about abuse are present and a child cannot be persuaded to agree to voluntary disclosure, and health professionals believe that there is immediate need to disclose information to an outside agency, then the child should be told what action is to be taken unless to do so would expose the child or others to increased risk of serious harm. The book does point out that children and young people sometimes try to elicit a promise of confidentiality from adults to whom they disclose information about abuse, but the book advises that doctors cannot promise to keep information confidential if a child's safety is threatened (at p 86).

6.40 Again, when considering the limits on confidentiality, the book acknowledges that the duty of confidentiality must always be balanced against the interests of others and the wider community and that there are exceptional circumstances where information about any patient may have to be disclosed without permission. This may include not only details about any child patient which the doctor or other health-care professional is dealing with but also an adult patient, where it may be necessary to disclose information in order to protect children and young people. As the book points out, this need to balance the fundamental aims of preserving trust and preventing harm is reflected in all the professional guidance which has been issued by the various bodies of health-care professionals. It notes that the exceptional cases where breach of confidentiality might be necessary can be described as disclosures 'in the public interest', and includes situations such as the prevention or detection of a serious crime, or the need to protect another person from a risk of serious harm. As this book notes, and it is a very good point, confidentiality is too valuable a principle to be sacrificed for vague goals or indefinable harm, but where information can be used to protect people from serious harm, the principle may have to give way (at p 81).

Record-keeping

6.41 *Working Together to Safeguard Children* emphasises that good record-keeping is an important part of the accountability of professionals to those who use their services but also that it helps to focus work and is essential to working effectively across agency and professional boundaries. Clear and accurate records therefore ensure that there is a documented account of an agency's or professional's involvement with a child and/or family and obviously help with continuity when individual workers are unavoidably replaced, and they also provide an essential tool for managers to monitor work or for peer review (see *Working Together to Safeguard Children*, at para 7.47). As has been pointed up by successive child abuse enquiries, records are also an essential source of evidence for investigations and enquiries, and may also be required to be disclosed in court proceedings (see especially, Owers, Brandon and Black (1999)). In those cases where a referral from any agency or member of the public does not result in any further action, then such records should still be retained to allow for prompt and efficient retrieval should circumstances arise when they need to be consulted again. In order that such records are clearly accessible, the guidance advises that records should use clear, straightforward language, be concise and be accurate not only in fact but also in differentiating between opinion, judgement and hypothesis.

6.42   *Working Together to Safeguard Children* emphasises that well-kept records provide an essential underpinning to good child protection practice and, again, successive enquiry reports have demonstrated that protecting children properly requires information to be brought together from a number of sources and careful professional judgements must then be made on the basis of such information. (see *Learning from Past Experience – A Review of Serious Case Reviews* (DOH, 2002), at chapters 6 and 7.) Where decisions to take further action have been taken jointly across agencies, or endorsed by a manager, this should also be made clear on the record.

6.43   Much attention has focused in recent times on the contents of social services departments' records. This is because relevant information about a child and family who are the subject of child protection concerns will normally be collated in one place by social services. Whether the case is going before a child protection conference or whether it finds its way into court, those asked to consider the case should be able to track the relevant history of the child and family which lead to the intervention; the nature of intervention, including intended outcome; the means by which change is to be achieved; and the progress which is being made (at para 7.50). Because of the problems there have been over the records kept by social services and the difficulties that can be engendered either as a result of poorly maintained files or a lack of familiarity with the detail on them, or as a result of a lack of clear management or a lack of respect for the concerns or views of other professionals, Bracewell J directed in *Re E (Care Proceedings Social Work Practice)* [2000] 2 FLR 254 that the following principles should be observed in child protection cases.

(1)   Every social work file should have as the top document a running chronology of significant events kept up to date as events unfold.
(2)   Lack of cooperation by parents or carers is never a reason to close a file or remove a child form a protection register.
(3)   Referrals by professionals such as health visitors and teachers should always be investigated and given great weight.
(4)   Those with the power of decision making should never make a judgement without having full knowledge of the files and consulting those professionals who know the family.
(5)   Children who were part of a sibling group should not be considered in isolation but in the context of the whole family history.

(6) Cases should be time-limited and an effective time-table laid down within which these changes need to be achieved.

In the Climbie case there was a failure to observe all of these guidelines except the fifth which did not apply as Victoria had no siblings in this country.

6.44 Failures in inter-agency co-operation which have been highlighted in recent child abuse enquiry reports have included failure to disclose changes of personnel at the various agencies or indeed the movement of a child into another local authority's boundaries. The guidance advises that the change of GP of a child who is on the Child Protection Register should be notified to all other agencies and professionals dealing with the child but the same holds true for any changes of other significant staff members of particular agencies involved in dealing with the child. The guidance recommends that each agency working with a child should ensure that when a child moves outside of their area, the child's records are transferred promptly to the relevant agency in the new area. Failure to make such notifications in the case of Kimberley Carlile was one of the factors contributing to Kimberley's death.

Supervision and support

6.45 For all those working in the field of child protection, the type of work which is entailed clearly involves making difficult and risky professional judgements and engaging in demanding work which can be both distressing and stressful and *Working Together to Safeguard Children* advises that all those involved should have access to advice and support, from peers, managers and named and designated professionals. It points out that for many practitioners involved in day-to-day work with children and families, effective supervision is important to promoting good standards of practice and to supporting individual staff members. Supervision should therefore help to ensure that: the practice is soundly based, consistent with ACPC and organisational procedures, practitioners fully understand their roles, responsibilities and scope of their professional discretion and authority; and identify the training and development needs of practitioners, so that each has the skills to provide an effective service. Failure to engage in such supervision has again repeatedly been pointed up in child abuse enquiry reports and was highlighted in the case of Victoria Climbie (2001).

The roles and responsibilities of other agencies

6.46 As *Working Together to Safeguard Children* emphasises: 'an awareness and appreciation of the role of others is essential for effective collaboration'. Chapter 3 of *Working Together to Safeguard Children* thus outlines the main roles and responsibilities of statutory agencies, professionals, the voluntary sector and the wider community in relation to child protection and emphasises that joint working should extend across the planning, management, provision and delivery of services (at para 3.1). This is further reflected in chapter 3 of the *Framework for Assessment* which states that a key principle of the assessment framework is 'that children's needs and their families' circumstances will require inter-agency collaboration to ensure full understanding of what is happening and to ensure an effective service response' (see *Framework for Assessment*, at para 5.1).

6.47 *Working Together to Safeguard Children* emphasises the key notion of working in partnership between the public agencies, the voluntary sector and service users and carers and identifies the fact that some authorities have put in place management structures which cut across traditional departmental and service boundaries. This again is reflected in the *Framework for Assessment* at para 5.2 where it identifies that 'increasingly, there are service developments designed on a multi-agency basis where teams operate with a pooled budget and shared objectives', an example of which is given as Youth Offending Teams (YOTs). The *Framework for Assessment* crucially identifies the fact that 'inter-agency, inter-disciplinary assessment practice requires an additional set of knowledge and skills to that required for working within a single agency or independently' (at para 5.4). Thus, the *Framework for Assessment* acknowledges that such practice requires all staff to understand the roles and responsibilities of staff working in contexts different to their own and that having an understanding of the perspective, language and culture of other professionals can inform how communication is conducted. This, the guidance points out, prevents professionals from misunderstanding one another because they use different language to describe similar concepts or because they are influenced by stereotypical perceptions of the other discipline. The guidance states that it is hoped that the use of the *Framework for Assessment* for assessing children in need provides a language which is common to children and their family members as well as to professionals and other staff (at para 5.4)

6.48 It is quite evident that the government believes that local authorities corporately have a responsibility to address the needs of children and young people and that there should be effective joint working by education, housing and leisure in partnership with social services and health. Whilst acknowledging the lead role which social services can play, the government has itself identified the fact that social services alone cannot promote the social inclusion and development of these children and families but that they can, in partnership with others, play a vital role (see *The Government's Objectives for Children's Social Services* (DOH, 1999), at p 4). *Working Together to Safeguard Children* states that 'a key objective for social services departments is to ensure that children are protected from significant harm' (at para 3.4) and it also emphasises the key role which social services play by placing the service first in terms of the identification of the roles and responsibilities of different agencies within the system in safeguarding children. It further notes that social services' responsibility towards children should be seen in the context of this broad range of care and support, so that children and families can be helped and supported in an integrated way which recognises the range and diversity of their needs and strengths (at para 3.5).

6.49 Both *Working Together to Safeguard Children* and the *Framework for Assessment*, however, acknowledge that local authorities, acting in order to fulfil their social services functions, have very specific legal duties in respect of children under the CA 1989. Thus, as well as the duty to safeguard and promote the welfare of children in their area who are in need, which the guidance documents emphasise should be done in partnership with parents in a way which is sensitive to the child's race, religion, culture and language, the guidance also points out that social services are rarely the only agency in contact with vulnerable children and their families, and partnerships with other agencies, especially health and education, are essential to help support such children and families.

6.50 The guidance acknowledges that where a child is at continuing risk of significant harm, social services are responsible for co-ordinating an inter-agency plan to safeguard the child which sets out and draws upon the contributions of family members, professionals and other agencies. It notes that, in a few cases, the social services department, in consultation with other involved agencies and professionals, may judge that a child's welfare cannot be sufficiently safeguarded if he or she remains at home and that in those circumstances application may be made to the courts for a care order which commits the child to the care of the local authority (see Chapter 7).

The role of social services

6.51 Both *Working Together to Safeguard Children* and the *Framework for Assessment* acknowledge that because of their responsibilities, duties and powers in relation to vulnerable children, social services departments will act as a principal point of contact for children about whom there are child welfare concerns and that they may be contacted directly by parents or family members seeking help, concerned friends and neighbours, or by professionals and others from statutory and voluntary agencies. Both documents thus emphasise the key role which social services play, as discussed in much greater detail in Chapters 4 and 5. All staff working in social services must therefore be fully aware of the imperative laid down both by *Working Together to Safeguard Children* and the *Framework for Assessment* for working in close co-operation and partnership with all the other agencies.

The education service

6.52 As with social services, the role of the education service in contributing to the welfare and safety of children has previously been discussed (see Chapter **5**). *Working Together to Safeguard Children* emphasises that all schools and colleges should create and maintain a safe environment for children and young people and should be able to manage situations where there are child welfare concerns. This is now reinforced by the statutory obligation to safeguard and promote the welfare of the children in their schools imposed upon school staffs and their governing bodies by s 175 of the Education Act 2002. *Working Together to Safeguard Children* points out that children can be helped to understand at school what is and is not acceptable behaviour towards them and taught about staying safe from harm, and how to speak up if they have worries or concerns. The guidance indicates that the curriculum can play a preventive role in developing awareness and resilience and in preparing children and young people for their future responsibilities as adults, parents and citizens. One of the problems, however, is that successive reports have identified the fact that schools have not developed this preventive educational role to any great degree and further attention now needs to be focused on how teachers can be assisted within the confines of the curriculum to discuss such critical issues as intra-family abuse and how to deal with it. Teachers and others within the education system, through their day-to-day contact with pupils and direct work with families, have a particularly critical role to play in noticing indicators of possible abuse or neglect and in referring concerns to the appropriate agencies, usually social services. Where the children have special educational needs or suffer from disabilities, schools will also be the possessors of key information about the child's level of understanding and the most effective means of communicating with the child.

6.53 Whilst acknowledging that the education service itself does not have a direct investigative responsibility in child protection work, both *Working Together to Safeguard Children* and the *Framework for Assessment* point out that staff working in the education service will on occasions be asked by social services departments for information on the child about whom there are concerns of abuse or neglect and staff may well be involved in child protection reviews. Where a child of school age is the subject of an inter-agency child protection plan, the school must be involved in the preparation of the plan and the school's roles and responsibilities in contributing to actions to safeguard the child and the promotion of his or her welfare should be clearly identified within the plan (see *Working Together to Safeguard Children*, at paras 3.12–3.13 and *Framework for Assessment*, at paras 5.41–5.50). Again, as has been seen earlier, staff in the education service have their own guidance issued by the DfEE for cases where there are concerns about a child's safety and welfare (see Circular 10/95 discussed in Chapter **5**). Children spend the greater part of their lives in schools, so it is particularly important that social services appreciate the critical contribution which education staff, including those operating playground and meal-time supervisions as well as those fulfilling care-taking roles, can contribute. The observations, for example, of the school care-taker, in the case of *Z v United Kingdom* [2001] 2 FLR 612, witnessing the children stealing waste food from dustbins around the school were missed until a number of years down the line.

Youth services

6.54 Both *Working Together to Safeguard Children* and the *Framework for Assessment* emphasise the close contact which many youth and community workers have with children and young people and advises that they should be fully familiar with local ACPC procedures and should provide written instructions on the circumstances in which youth and community workers should consult with colleagues, line managers and other statutory authorities when they have concerns about a child or young person (see *Working Together to Safeguard Children*, at para 3.16 and *Framework for Assessment*, at para 5.51).

Cultural and leisure services

6.55 *Working Together to Safeguard Children* acknowledges that cultural and leisure services provide and enable a wide range of facilities and services for children and that by the very nature of these activities personnel are in various degrees of contact with children. Again, the guidance emphasises that these departments should have in place procedures linked to local ACPC procedures detailing referral and other responses to information which may arise concerning child protection, and it also emphasises the requirements for staff training for all those working with children. Such staff may only rarely be involved in situations where they are the sole referring agency concerning a matter of child protection, but it can happen and in one or two situations their role may be critical. Their position is not in fact mentioned in the *Framework for Assessment* but the *Framework for Assessment* does refer specifically to chapter 3 of *Working Together to Safeguard Children* dealing with the role and responsibilities of all the various agencies who may have such concerns.

Health professionals

6.56 Again, both *Working Together to Safeguard Children* and the *Framework for Assessment* emphasise the critical role which will be played by a whole range of health professionals in terms of assessment and also in the provision of treatment services for children and families. Both point out that the health authority should take the overall strategic lead for health services in local inter-agency working on child protection matters and the *Framework for Assessment* further recognises that because of the universal nature of health provision, health professionals are often the first to become aware of the needs of children or that some families are experiencing difficulties looking after their children. This will more particularly be the case in the situation of children in whom illness is fabricated or induced (see *Safeguarding Children in Whom Illness is Fabricated or Induced* (DOH, 2000), at para 2.9). The *Framework for Assessment* points out that the health professionals should consider what help would benefit the families but at the same time acknowledges social services departments will have a crucial role to play in assisting health professionals by providing information about what help is available in the community and also through social services departments themselves.

6.57 There are a range of documents of guidance for different health professionals within the health-care system. A special explanatory booklet entitled *The Children Act 1989: An Introductory Guide for the NHS*, was first produced by the DOH for health professionals in 1991 and then, subsequently, further Addenda to *Working Together under the Children Act* (1991) were issued dealing with different parts of the NHS. These are all in the process of revision to take into account of the issuing of the new guidance, *Working Together to Safeguard Children* (1999).

6.58 The guidance for health professionals nevertheless extends from para 3.22 through to para 3.53 of chapter 3 of *Working Together to Safeguard Children* and is extremely comprehensive. The guidance identifies that each NHS Trust should, like the education service, identify a named doctor and a named nurse or midwife who will take a professional lead within the Trust on child protection matters. Such individuals are required to have expertise in children's health and development, the nature of child maltreatment, and local arrangements for safeguarding children and promoting their welfare. Whilst such individuals are an important source of advice and expertise for fellow professionals and other agencies, *Working Together to Safeguard Children* and the *Framework for Assessment* emphasise that all hospital and community health staff should be alert to the possibility of child abuse or neglect and be aware of local procedures as well as knowing the names and contact details of the relevant designated professionals. *Working Together to Safeguard Children* also points out that the staff working in Accident and Emergency departments and Minor Injury centres should also be familiar with local procedures for making enquiries of the Child Protection Register and they should particularly be alert to carers who seek medical care from a number of sources in order to conceal the repeated nature of a child's injuries. One of the features of the enquiry into the death of Sukina (at para **2.63**) was that the child was never taken to the same hospital for treatment although she was in fact taken to five different hospitals for treatment of quite severe minor injuries before she was ultimately killed. Primary Care Groups and Primary Care Trusts are also required to ensure that the services in their area make the relevant contribution to inter-agency working in child protection.

6.59 The critical role of the GP and other members of the Primary Health Care Team is also emphasised by both guidance documents, which point out that they are well placed to recognise when a child is potentially in need of extra help or services to promote health and development, or is at risk of harm. When those other then a GP become concerned about the welfare of a child, not only should action be taken in accordance with local ACPC procedures but, in addition, the GP should be informed immediately. *Working Together to Safeguard Children* emphasises that because of their knowledge of children and families GPs, together with other Primary Health Care Team members have an important role in all stages of child protection processes, from sharing information with social services when enquiries are being made about a child, to involvement in a child protection plan to safeguard a child. The guidance emphasises that GPs should make available to child protection conferences relevant information about a child and the family whether or not they, or a member of the Primary Health Care team, are able to attend (at para 3.30). Very usefully, it is stated that it is good practice to have a clear means of identifying in records those children, together with their parents and siblings, who are on the Child Protection Register. This, according to *Working Together to Safeguard Children*, will enable them to be recognised by the partners of the practice and any other doctor, practice nurse or health visitor who may become involved in the care of those children. The guidance also emphasises that each GP and member of Primary Health Care Team should have access to an up-to-date copy of local ACPC procedures.

6.60 Previous guidance issued as an addendum to *Working Together* (1991) in 1996 has been reissued to take account of the issuing of the new version of *Working Together to Safeguard Children* in 1999. In addition to the GP and members of the Primary Health Care Team, both of the guidance documents emphasise the very important role which midwives, health visitors and school nurses can play in identifying children in need and children at risk. They will then continue to work in partnership with social workers, GPs and others to contribute to integrated assessment, through sharing facts and professional opinion and by helping children and families identify and address their own needs (see *Framework for Assessment*, at para 5.24).

6.61 The *Framework for Assessment* further identifies the role of paediatric services in situations where in the course of the social services department's assessment of a child in need it is thought appropriate to obtain an opinion from a specialist paediatric service. The *Framework for Assessment* points out that many paediatric services have an identified lead community paediatrician for children in need who can advise social workers and parents on how to gain access to services. It acknowledges that within health services, community paediatricians can raise awareness of the difficulties faced by vulnerable and disadvantaged families and that one-stop shops where social services and health staff can work together to provide supportive and therapeutic services for children and their families have now been introduced within Health Action Zones.

6.62 Other health professionals who may become involved include a range of professionals across mental health services, including those in child and adolescent services as well as those in adult services. However they may become involved, the guidance points out that all have a duty to take steps where they identify or suspect instances of child abuse or neglect. The guidance emphasises that where there is concern this will require the sharing of information which is necessary to safeguard the child from the prospect of significant harm. *Working Together to Safeguard Children* points out that child and adolescent mental health services can help in facilitating communication between adult mental health services and children's welfare services, especially where there are concerns about responding appropriately both to the duty of confidentiality and the protection of children and that, again, the designated doctor or nurse can provide further advice in such situations.

6.63 *Working Together to Safeguard Children* points out the role of drug services where children may be suffering significant harm because of their own substance misuse, or where parental misuse may be causing such harm, and emphasises that referrals will need to be made by drug services in accordance with local ACPC procedures.

Day care services

6.64 Both documents recognise the increasing role which day care services are coming to play in children's lives and that many services will be offering help to children and families with problems and stresses, which makes them well placed to prevent problems from developing into abuse and neglect through the provision of support to families and also to recognise and act upon potential indicators of abuse and neglect (see *Working Together to Safeguard Children*, at para 3.54 and *Framework for Assessment*, at paras 5.59 and 5.60). Both documents stress that all those providing day care services should know how to recognise and respond to potential indicators of abuse or neglect and what to do when they have concerns about a child's welfare. The guidance states that day care providers in the private and voluntary sectors should have agreed procedures for when and how to contact the social services department about an individual child. In many areas local responsibility for the training of workers in 'Sure Start' provision and other day care providers across the voluntary and private sector in child protection issues has been taken on by the Early Years Development and Child Care Partnership Boards, which link in with training being provided by health social services and also by ACPCs.

The probation service

6.65 The role of probation in supervising offenders, both those coming out of prison on licence and those serving community sentences, means that they will come into contact with a great many children who may be in need, and will, in the case of sex offenders, be involved in inter-agency case conferences focusing on the necessary action to manage the risk posed by offenders which have been introduced following the Sex Offenders Act 1997 (see further, Chapter **9**). *Working Together to Safeguard Children* emphasises that in any case where an imprisoned offender is considered to pose a risk to children, the social services department in the area where the offender lives (or intends to live in the case of prisoners) should be alerted and that an inter-agency approach should be adopted entailing very close co-operation between probation, social services and the prison service.

The prison service

6.66 Both documents recognise that the prison service works closely with other agencies to identify prisoners who may present a risk to the public on release and note that governors are required to notify social service departments and the probation service of plans to release prisoners convicted of offences against children and young people so that appropriate action can be taken by agencies in the community to minimise any risk. The critical role which the prison service plays in helping prisoners to maintain contact with their children is noted and thus governors have the discretion to disallow any visits to prisoners if such visits would not be in the best interests of the visitor. In addition, governors have a discretion to stop correspondence from a prisoner to a child if a parent requests it. Prison governors are expected to seek and follow advice from social services departments where arrangements are being made for visits or other contact with convicted prisoners and social services receiving such a request for advice should assist the prison by assessing whether it is in the interests of a particular child to visit a named prisoner.

6.67 Further recognition has been given to the problems posed where prisoners are pregnant or have young babies and there is an emphasis on the paramount concern being the best interests of the child. Young children are allowed to remain with their mothers up to the age of 18 months, but as a child grows older prison becomes an increasingly unsuitable environment to enable normal child development and if the mother has not been released by then, attempts will be made to place the baby within the mother's own family or in a foster family.

6.68 Recognition of the duties which the prison service owes to young people under the age of 18 years whom it is accommodating can also be found within the guidance. Such prisons must appoint a child protection co-ordinator and establish, in consultation with local ACPCs, a policy governing arrangements for acting upon allegations or concerns that a young person may have suffered, or is at risk of suffering, significant harm. Such provisions are particularly important where secure units are to be found within the boundaries of a particular local authority since young people's experience of both prison and secure units is that they can be very brutal places where insufficient attention is given to the need to protect young prisoners from other prisoners (see *Banged Up, Beaten Up, Cutting Up – Report of the Howard League Commission of Inquiry into Violence in Penal Institutions for Teenagers Under 18* (The Howard League for Penal Reform, 1995); and *'Tell them so they Listen': Messages from Young People in Custody* (Home Office, 2000); and Goldson (2002) and see R *(on the application of the Howard League for Penal Reform) v Secretary of State for the Home Department* (unreported) 12 November 2002).

Youth justice services

6.69 *Working Together to Safeguard Children* and the *Framework for Assessment* recognise that a number of the children and young people who fall within the remit of YOTs will be children in need, including some whose needs will include safeguarding. The documents emphasise that there need to be clear links both at ACPC/YOT strategic level as well as at a child's specific operational level, between youth justice and child protection services. It states that these links should be incorporated in each local authority's children's services plan, the ACPC business plan and the youth justice plan itself. It is also noted that at the operational level, protocols are likely to be of assistance in establishing cross-referral arrangements.

Housing authorities

6.70 As has been identified earlier, housing authorities can play a critical role in safeguarding children in respect of recognition, referral and the subsequent management of risk (see Chapter **5**). Housing authority staff through their day-to-day contact with members of the public may become aware of concerns about the welfare of particular children and should refer to one of the statutory agencies in appropriate cases. The guidance notes that housing authorities may also have important information about families which may be helpful to local authorities carrying out assessment under s 17 or s 47 of the CA 1989, and that as part of their duty to assist under s 27 (see above), they should be prepared to share relevant information orally or in writing, including attending child protection conferences when requested to do so. The guidance recognises that appropriate housing can make an important contribution to meeting the health and developmental needs of children, including those who need safeguarding from significant harm, and that housing authorities should thus be prepared to assist by the provision of accommodation either directly, through their links with other housing providers or by the provision of advice. Such assistance would be of particular value in cases of domestic violence which result in the homelessness of women and children. Finally, the documents both recognise that housing authorities have an important part to play in the management of the risk posed by dangerous offenders, including those who are assessed as presenting a risk, whether sexual or otherwise, to children and that appropriate housing can contribute greatly to the ability of police and others to manage the risk which such individuals pose.

The police

6.71 *Working Together to Safeguard Children* proclaims that 'protecting life and preventing crime are primary tasks of the police' (at para 3.57). It also states that 'children are citizens who have the right to the protection offered by the criminal law'. This latter statement seems peculiarly at odds with the provision of the special defence of reasonable chastisement available to parents and carers of children under the age of 16 but this is a matter for the reform of the criminal law by the legislature (see Chapter **1**). Nevertheless, the police have a duty and responsibility to investigate criminal offences committed against children, and *Working Together to Safeguard Children* urges that such investigations should be carried out sensitively, thoroughly and professionally. *Working Together to Safeguard Children* states that the police recognise the fundamental importance of inter-agency working in combating child abuse, and that this is illustrated by well-established arrangements for joint training involving both police and social work colleagues. It points out that the police have invested a great deal in both training and resources to enhance their ability to offer the best possible service to child victims of crime. All forces now have CPUs, and despite variations in their structures and staffing levels, CPUs will normally take primary responsibility for investigating child abuse cases. *Working Together to Safeguard Children* emphasises that safeguarding children is not seen as solely the responsibility of CPU officers, and that all police officers should understand that it is a fundamental part of their duties. It notes that patrol officers attending domestic violence incidents should be aware of the effect of such violence on any children within the household and that community beat officers should be made aware of any children in their area who are on the Child Protection Register through links with police information systems (at para 3.59).

6.72 *Working Together to Safeguard Children* further emphasised that the police are committed to sharing information and intelligence with other agencies where this is necessary to protect children and that this includes a responsibility for ensuring that those officers representing the police at a child protection conference are fully informed about the case as well as being experienced in risk assessment and the decision-making process. It is also stated that the police can similarly expect other agencies to share with them information and intelligence they hold in order to enable the police to carry out their duties. It is noted that evidence gathered during a criminal investigation may be of use to local authority solicitors who are preparing for civil proceedings to protect the victim, and whilst the CPS should be consulted in such cases, normally evidence will be shared if it is in the best interests of the child.

6.73 *Working Together to Safeguard Children* states that the police should be notified as soon as possible where a criminal offence has been committed, or is suspected of having been committed against a child, although it does not mean in all such cases that a criminal investigation will follow or that there will necessarily be any further police involvement. However, the police must retain the opportunity to be informed and consulted, to ensure all relevant information can be taken into account before a final decision on whether to proceed with further investigation or with potential prosecution is made. Chapter 5 of *Working Together to Safeguard Children* states that ACPCs should have in place a protocol agreed between social services departments and the police, to guide both agencies in deciding how the child protection enquiry should be conducted and, in particular, the circumstances in which joint enquiries are appropriate (at para 5.38).

6.74 In determining whether or not criminal proceedings should be instituted, *Working Together to Safeguard Children* advises that three main factors will influence such a decision. Thus the police, together with the CPS in due course, will have to consider whether or not there is sufficient evidence to prosecute; whether it is in the public interests that proceedings be instigated against the particular offender; and whether or not criminal prosecution is in the best interests of the child. In most cases these days, advice from the CPS will be sought prior to proceedings being initiated (see further, Chapter **9**). *Working Together to Safeguard Children* emphasises that in dealing with offences involving a child victim, the police will normally work in partnership with social services and other caring agencies and whilst the responsibility to instigate criminal proceedings rests with the police, it states that they should always obtain and consider the views expressed by other partners about what is in a child's best interests. Differences in the standards of proof as between civil proceedings involving a child and criminal proceedings involving the prosecution of perpetrators often lead to misunderstandings between the different professions. Just because the police, together with the CPS, decide that it would not be appropriate to proceed with a criminal conviction this should in no way determine the decision with regard to the taking of child protection proceedings. The standard of proof required in criminal proceedings is much higher and also totally different from the issues which will be before the court and the relevant standards of proof required in civil proceedings (see further, Chapters **8** and **9**).

6.75 It should be remembered of course that in addition to their duties to investigate criminal offences, the CA 1989 confers special emergency powers on the police to enter premises and secure the immediate protection of children believed to be suffering from, or at risk of suffering, significant harm (see Chapters **4** and **5**) although evidence to the Climbie Inquiry suggested caution in the use of such powers.

Guardians in legal proceedings

6.76 Since the establishment of CAFCASS, the role of the former guardian ad litem is now taken on by the newly named children's guardian, but their role in proceedings is the same as before, that is to ensure that the child's best interests are always put before the court in any proceedings involving them and to carry out the task of selecting a lawyer to act on the child's behalf in the proceedings. Since guardians can be appointed at the stage at which an emergency protection order application is being heard, the critical role which guardians may play in such proceedings is also acknowledged in *Working Together to Safeguard Children* and it is suggested that guardians should always be invited along to all formal planning meetings convened by the local authority in respect of the child. It is also pointed out that this includes statutory reviews of children who are accommodated or looked after and child protection conferences and that the guardian may sometimes wish to attend such meetings in order to obtain information. *Working Together to Safeguard Children* emphasises, however, that the conference Chair should ensure that all those attending the meetings including, in particular, the child and any family members, understand that the guardian's presence does not imply any responsibility for decisions reached at such meetings.

Armed services

6.77 In England, social services departments have statutory responsibility for safeguarding and promoting the welfare of children of service families living within their area. If it becomes the case that social services are undertaking assessments of children in need then contact should be made with the welfare service appropriate to the particular service, details of which are given in Appendix 2 of *Working Together to Safeguard Children* (1999). The guidance states that the armed forces are fully committed to co-operating with statutory and other agencies in supporting families in this situation and have in place procedures to help in safeguarding children. In those areas where service families live, the armed forces seek to work alongside local social services departments and should also have representatives on the local ACPC and at child protection conferences when held.

6.78 When those serving with the armed forces are based overseas, the responsibility for their welfare is vested with the Ministry of Defence, although all three services provide professional welfare support through the Soldiers, Sailors, Airforce Association – Forces Help Network, who provide a fully qualified social worker and community health service in major overseas locations (eg in Germany and Cyprus). Instructions for the protection of children overseas, which reflect the principles of the CA 1989 and the philosophy of inter-agency co-operation, are issued by the Ministry of Defence as a Defence Council Instruction (Joint Service). *Working Together to Safeguard Children* also notes that larger overseas commands issue local child protection procedures, hold a Command Child Protection Register and have a Command Child Protection Committee which operates in a similar way to ACPCs in the UK in upholding standards and making sure that the best practice is reflected in procedures and observed in practice.

Comment

6.79 This part of the chapter has expanded upon the roles and responsibilities of all the different agencies who may be associated in any way with concerns about safeguarding children. As the *Framework for Assessment* comments, understanding these roles and responsibilities is a cornerstone of effective inter-agency, inter-disciplinary working and individual practitioners should use their professional relationships and networks to assist them in achieving good outcomes for children and their families. The *Framework for Assessment* also points out, however, that quality collaboration at an inter-personal level requires effective organisational arrangements to support these informal processes and that ensuring good inter-agency working is not solely dependent upon the commitment of dedicated individuals. This should be the critical role performed by ACPCs.

The role and responsibilities of Area Child Protection Committees

6.80 The ACPC is designated as the forum for inter-agency and inter-disciplinary work and is seen as bringing together representatives of each of the main agencies and professionals responsible for helping to protect children from abuse and neglect. *Working Together to Safeguard Children* emphasises that the ACPC should contribute to, and work within the framework established by, the children's services plan produced by each local authority. The clear function of ACPCs, therefore, is in identifying those children in need who are at risk of significant harm, or who have suffered significant harm, and in identifying resource gaps (in terms of funding and/or the contribution of different agencies) and better ways of working. The principal idea behind ACPCs is that there should be one umbrella group responsible for child protection across all services within an area, but *Working Together to Safeguard Children* notes that where boundaries between local authorities, the health service and the police are not co-terminous, there may be problems for some member agencies in having to work to different procedures and protocols according to the area involved or in having to participate in several ACPCs. *Working Together to Safeguard Children* recommends, therefore, that it may be helpful in these circumstances for an ACPC to cover an area which includes more than one local authority area, or for adjoining ACPCs to collaborate as far as possible on establishing common procedures and protocols and on inter-agency training. The failure of ACPCs to perform their functions as set out was the subject of much criticism in the Climbie Inquiry.

6.81 The pivotal role undertaken by ACPCs is underlined by the recommendation that all agencies should appoint to it officers from each of the main agencies responsible for working together to safeguard children, whose roles and seniority enable them to contribute to developing and maintaining strong and effective inter-agency child protection procedures and protocols, and ensure that local child protection services are adequately resourced (see *Working Together to Safeguard Children*, at para 4.10). Clearly, what is envisaged here is that such officers would have sufficient authority and autonomy to act on behalf of their member's service, but because of pressures on high-level managers within a number of different agencies, less senior representatives may be appointed and this can impede the critical work undertaken by ACPCs.

6.82 *Working Together to Safeguard Children* now requires that each ACPC should produce an annual business plan, setting out a work programme for the forthcoming year, including: measurable objectives; relevant management information on child protection activity in the course of the previous year; and progress against objectives set in the previous year. ACPC plans should both contribute to and derive from the framework of the local children's services plan and should be endorsed by senior managers in each of the main constituent agencies (para 4.19). ACPCs are encouraged to make the business plan, or an edited version of it, available to a wider audience, for example to explain to the wider community the work of local agencies in helping to keep children safe and thriving.

6.83 The specific responsibilities of an ACPC are set out at para 4.2 of *Working Together to Safeguard Children*. These are:

(1) to develop and agree local policies and procedures for inter-agency work to protect children within the national framework provided by the guidance;

(2) to audit and evaluate how well local services work together to protect children, for example through wider case audits;

(3) to put in place objectives and performance indicators for child protection, within the framework and objectives set out in children's services plans;

(4) to encourage and help develop effective working relationships between different services and professional groups, based on trust and mutual understanding;

(5) to ensure that there is a level of agreement and understanding across agencies about operational definitions and thresholds for intervention;

(6) to improve local ways of working in the light of knowledge gained

through national and local experience and research, and to make sure that any lessons learned are shared, understood and acted upon;

(7) to undertake case reviews where a child has died or – in certain circumstances – been seriously harmed, and abuse or neglect are confirmed or suspected; to make sure that any lessons from the case are understood and acted upon; to communicate clearly to individual services and professional groups their shared responsibility for protecting children, and to explain how each can contribute;

(8) to help improve the quality of child protection work and of inter-agency working through specifying needs for inter-agency training and development, and ensuring that training is delivered; and

(9) to raise awareness within the wider community of the need to safeguard children and promote their welfare and to explain how the wider community can contribute to these objectives.

6.84 *Working Together to Safeguard Children* goes on to emphasise that the scope of the responsibilities outlined in these nine objectives should, as a minimum, extend to the *relevant population*, ie:

– children abused and neglected within families, including those so harmed in the context of domestic violence;
– children abused outside families by adults known to them;
– children abused and neglected by professional carers, within an institutional setting, or anywhere else where children are cared for away from home;
– children abused by strangers;
– children abused by other people;
– young perpetrators who abuse;
– children involved in prostitution; and
– children who misuse drugs and alcohol.

6.85 They should extend also to *relevant activities*, ie:

– raising awareness within the wider community, including faith and minority ethnic communities, and amongst statutory, voluntary and independent agencies, about how everyone can contribute to safeguarding children and promoting their welfare;
– working together across agencies to identify and act upon concerns about a child's safety and welfare; and
– working together across agencies to help those children who have suffered or who are at continuing risk of suffering significant harm, in order to safeguard such children and promote their welfare (*Working Together to Safeguard Children*, at para 4.3).

6.86 The role performed by ACPCs is seen to be crucial for ensuring that all professionals working within the system recognise and appreciate the importance of a multi-agency approach. While *Working Together to Safeguard Children* indicates that ACPCs are accountable for their work to their main constituent agencies, it also lays particular responsibility on local authority social services for taking the lead responsibility in ensuring the establishment and effective working of ACPCs, although it also requires that all main constituent agencies should be responsible for contributing fully and effectively to the work of the ACPC. The ACPC has two other main roles, that of co-ordinating inter-agency training and development in the work of child protection, and in the conduct of Part 8 case reviews (at para **6.91**) and these will now be examined separately.

Co-ordination of inter-agency training

6.87 *Working Together to Safeguard Children* emphasises that it is the role of the ACPC to take a strategic overview of the planning, delivery and evaluation of the inter-agency training which is required in order to promote effective practice to safeguard the welfare of children. It points out that effective high-quality training is most likely to be achieved if the ACPC is strategically involved at all stages of the training cycle and it suggests that a training sub-committee should be established to be specifically responsible for all the tasks associated with the delivery of effective inter-agency training. It emphasises that all employers have a responsibility to resource and support inter-agency training by allocating sufficient resources to the task as well as by making available staff who can provide the training but also by ensuring the appropriate release of staff in order to attend training courses organised by the committee. It is also acknowledged that there are large numbers of people who are in contact with children away from their families, for example youth workers, child minders, those working with children in residential and day care settings and those working in sport and leisure settings in both a paid and unpaid capacity and it emphasises that they should as a minimum be provided with an introductory level of training on safeguarding children and that, given the range of personnel and the work patterns involved, creative methods should be adopted to provide them with the essential training.

6.88 The guidance also emphasises that managers at all levels within organisations employing staff to work with children and families, benefit from specific training on inter-agency practice to safeguard children and that some may need training on joint planning and commissioning; managing joint services and teams; chairing multi-disciplinary meetings; negotiating joint protocols and mediating where there is conflict and difference (at para 9.16). Considerable attention is given to the need for collaboration across agencies and disciplines in relation to the planning, design, delivery and administration of training and the guidance points out that in some areas the appointment of an inter-agency training co-ordinator funded by constituent members of the

ACPC and reporting to the ACPC, has proved an effective approach for managing the planning, administration and delivery of training. It recognises that this is only viable where an ACPC is sufficiently large to sustain such an appointment or where smaller ACPCs pool resources, but this has been done in a number of areas.

6.89 *Working Together to Safeguard Children* notes that training is most effective when those engaged in its planning, delivery and evaluation are aware of current policy and practice developments, and that such a position might be achieved by identifying and specifying training implications for all ACPC policy and practice developments, and by ensuring that subsequent training is informed by current research evidence, lessons from case reviews and local and national developments and initiatives.

6.90 The relevant section in *Working Together to Safeguard Children* (1999) is considerably longer than the previous section devoted to joint training in *Working Together under the Children Act 1989* (1991), at pp 53 and 54 of *Working Together* (1991)). This represents a recognition of the critical importance which inter-agency training and development fills in situations where so many different agencies may be involved with children and families. Such training and development is also crucial in terms of facilitating the shared understanding which is emphasised in the *Framework for Assessment* as being so critical to effective work in assessment of children and their families.

Part 8 case reviews

6.91 ACPCs are also crucial in terms of their role in conducting reviews when a child dies, or where abuse or neglect are known or suspected to be a factor in a child's death. *Working Together to Safeguard Children* advises that when a child dies in such circumstances, the ACPC should always conduct a review into the involvement with the child and family of agencies and professionals. It should further consider such a review where a child also sustains a potentially life threatening injury or serious and permanent impairment of health and development, or has been subjected to particularly serious sexual abuse; and the case gives rise to concerns about inter-agency working to protect children (see *Working Together to Safeguard Children*, at para 8.1). The purposes of such reviews (widely known as Part 8 reviews) are: to establish whether there are lessons to be learned from the case about the way in which local professionals and agencies worked together to safeguard children; to identify clearly what those lessons are, how they will be acted upon and what is expected to change as a result; and as a consequence to improve inter-agency working and better safeguard children. *Working Together to Safeguard Children* emphasises that case reviews are not enquiries into how a child died or who is culpable, since that is a matter for coroners and criminal courts respectively to determine as appropriate.

6.92 In many cases where a child dies or is subjected to serious abuse, not only will Part 8 reviews be held but there may also be some other sort of official enquiry into the child's death and into the arrangements made for managing the child's case between all the different agencies. When this occurs it may be the case that such further enquiry considers the circumstances surrounding the Part 8 case review. Such was the case in relation to *Paul: Death Through Neglect* (Bridge Child Care Consultancy Service, 1995). The previous Part 8 section in *Working Together to Safeguard Children* (1991) extended to only three pages and it is quite apparent that the newly drafted section now extending to some nine pages has taken on board a number of criticisms which have been made in successive official enquiry reports. Thus, for example, the report on *Paul* identified a lack of consistency in carrying out the Part 8 review by each agency, with some agencies simply reviewing their files, others interviewing their staff, and in one case, setting up alongside the review a serious incident investigation. The report indicated that it was inappropriate to produce a review report based solely on the file records. Since review reports may have to make criticisms of individual practice and the ACPC has to make a decision about publication about the report, it was felt to be inappropriate for those criticisms to be published without giving an opportunity to individual staff to provide information on the way in which they saw their involvement. In addition, the report felt that interviews were a useful way of checking the facts and the perceptions of the case, which again supported its conclusion that it was inappropriate to produce such a review based entirely on file records. The report indicated that what resulted in the case of *Paul* was a very inconsistent package of information and, in some instances, a failure to include significant information.

6.93 The ACPC was criticised for not having an agreed model for the conduct of such reviews and *Working Together to Safeguard Children* now itself sets out a model for the conduct of case reviews under Part 8. It lays down clear guidelines for consideration by the Review Panel and clear advice as to who should conduct such reviews, together with clear advice about the management review to be conducted by each service of its involvement with the child and the family as well as the commissioning of an overview report which can bring together and analyse the findings of the various reports from agencies and others, and which makes recommendations for future actions (at paras 8.17–8.18). The outline format guide for management reviews and that produced for the ACPC overview report are both extremely useful and set out in full on pp 92 and 93 of *Working Together to Safeguard Children*. (See also *Learning from Past Experience – A Review of Serious Case Reviews* (DOH, 2002).)

6.94 *Working Together to Safeguard Children* emphasises that there needs to be clarity over the interface between the different processes of investigation (including criminal investigations); case management, including help for abused children and immediate measures to ensure that other children are safe (a clear recommendation from the case of *Paul: Death Through Neglect*) and review, ie learning lessons from the case to lessen the likelihood of such events happening again. The different processes should inform each other and any proposals for review should be agreed with those leading criminal investigations to make sure that they do not prejudice the outcome of possible criminal proceedings.

6.95 Finally, *Working Together to Safeguard Children* notes that reviews are of little value unless lessons are learned from them and that at least as much effort should be spent on acting upon recommendations as on conducting the review and further sets out ways in which this may be achieved. The DOH also acknowledges its own role in using Part 8 case reviews as an important source of information to inform national policy and practice. It is responsible for identifying and disseminating common themes and trends across review reports and acting on lessons for policy and practice. The DOH states that it commissions overview reports at least every 2 years, drawing out key findings of case reviews and their indications for policy and practice. (For the latest of these see *Learning from Past Experience* (DOH, 2002). These lessons have clearly been learned in terms of the way in which the current Part 8 has been set out, so that it is as useful as it can be, not only to the various constituent agencies who may be involved, but also in assisting ACPCs to meet their responsibilities.

Child protection in specific circumstances

6.96 Another major change effected by *Working Together to Safeguard Children* and which represents a further improvement upon the 1991 document, is the collation in one chapter of specific issues which arise from dealing with child protection in specific circumstances. These are set out in chapter 6 of *Working Together to Safeguard Children* which states that the purpose of the chapter is to outline some special considerations that apply to safeguarding children in a range of specific circumstances. It is also stated to be seen as adding to chapter 5 of the guidance which deals with the handling of individual cases and should be seen as constituting further advice rather than substituting chapter 5.

6.97 Advice of this sort used to be included in the old *Working Together* (1988) within the chapter on individual cases, but clearly a number of separate issues arise for consideration when dealing with different types of situations involving allegations of abuse. The chapter deals with a range of issues including: children living away from home; allegations of abuse made against a professional, foster carer or volunteer; the impact of the Protection of Children Act 1999 (PCA 1999); investigating organised or multiple abuse; abuse of disabled children; abuse of children by children and young people; domestic violence; children involved in prostitution (now the subject of a separate guidance document namely *Safeguarding Children Involved in Prostitution* (DOH, 2002)); child pornography and the internet; children and families who go missing; and female genital mutilation. A number of these issues have already been tackled in earlier chapters (see Chapters **2**, **4** and **5**), but others have been left to be dealt with here more appropriately because they raise issues relating most particularly to inter-agency working.

Children living away from home

6.98   *Working Together to Safeguard Children* acknowledges that revelations of widespread abuse and neglect of children living away from home has done a great deal to raise awareness of the particular vulnerability of children in a residential setting. It notes that many of these focus on sexual abuse, but points out that physical and emotional abuse and neglect – including peer abuse, bullying and substance misuse – are equally a threat in institutional settings. (See *Caring For Children Away From Home* (DOH, 1998) and Goldson (2002).) The DOH emphasises that there should never be complacency that these are problems of the past and stresses that there is a need for continuing vigilance. In this it has clearly learned the lessons of the past since no sooner did it appear that the number of residential child abuse scandals was beginning to recede than the revelations about abuse of children in North Wales children's homes sprang to press attention in the late 1990s and the government was forced by media spotlight to announce a public enquiry into the allegations of abuse. As *Working Together to Safeguard Children* now emphasises, all agencies should ensure that children living away from home are protected by the same basic safeguards against abuse as all other children and that ACPC procedures should include a clear policy statement that local child protection procedures apply in every situation, including children living away from home in all environments including prison.

6.99   The guidelines lay down a number of basic safeguards which should be addressed in all residential settings and it is clear that where services are not directly provided, these basic safeguards should be explicitly addressed in contracts with external providers. Some of these basic safeguards have already been identified including: valuing and respecting children; ensuring openness on the part of the institution to the external world; training staff and foster carers in all aspects of safeguarding children and ensuring that they are knowledgeable about children's vulnerability, risk of harm and how to implement child protection procedures; that children should have ready access to a trusted adult outside the institution where he or she is being looked after; and that complaints procedures are clear, effective, user friendly and readily accessible to children and young people, including those with disabilities and those for whom English is not a first language (see Chapters **2** and **5**). Others which have previously not been discussed also include requirements that: recruitment and selection procedures are rigorous and create a high threshold of entry to deter abusers; clear procedures and support systems are in place for dealing with expressions of concern by staff and carers about other staff or carers, including a guarantee that procedures can be invoked in ways which do not prejudice the 'whistle blower's' own position and prospects; there is respect for diversity and sensitivity to race, culture, religion, gender, sexuality and disability; there is effective supervision and support which extends to temporary staff and volunteers; and staff and carers are alert to the risk of the children in the external environment from people prepared to exploit the additional vulnerability of children living away from home (see *Working Together to Safeguard Children*, at para 6.5).

6.100 The drafters of *Working Together to Safeguard Children* clearly demonstrate in these provisions a response to the findings of the various research studies as well as to the results of enquiry reports, particularly the *Children's Safeguards Review* and *Lost in Care*. In addition, chapter 6 of *Working Together* goes on to identify the extent to which children living away from home are also vulnerable to abuse by their peers including sexual abuse, racial harassment, discrimination and institutional racism and bullying. The findings of the National Commission Report (1996) and the NSPCC Report (2001) have clearly been responded to in terms of open acknowledgement of the problems, clear guidance on the need to identify such problems and a clear expression of the potential damage which such abuse may cause children and young people. There is also clear guidance on the difficulties which children and young people may face in trying to make complaints about foster carers as well as acknowledgement of the rights of foster carers who care for children who have been abused to be given full information both in the interests of the child being fostered and of the foster family itself. Again, the drafters appear to have been aware of developments in case-law recognising the legal right of foster parents in such circumstances to this information (see *W v Essex County Council* [2000] 1 FLR 657, HL).

6.101 The guidance goes on to discuss issues relating to the investigation of allegations particularly where, as in some circumstances, the nature of the allegations are historical. *Working Together to Safeguard Children* emphasises (at para 6.15) that where such allegations are made they should be responded to in the same way as contemporary concerns, in terms of prompt referral to the relevant social services department and discussion with the police if it appears that a criminal offence has been committed. The guidance goes on to identify that investigations may well have three related, but independent, strands: an investigation may consist of child protection enquiries; a police investigation into a possible offence; and disciplinary procedures where it appears that allegations may amount to misconduct on the part of a member of staff. The guidance also points out the fact that a prosecution may not always be possible but that this does not mean that action in relation to safeguarding children, or employing discipline, is not necessary or feasible. It advises that steps should be taken to evaluate the risk of harm to children posed by the person under investigation but that everyone who is being investigated is entitled to be treated fairly and honestly and to be provided with the relevant support throughout the investigation process. It points out (at para 6.19) that they should be helped to understand the concerns expressed and the processes being operated, and be clearly informed of the outcome of any investigation and the implications for disciplinary or related processes. It further advises that those undertaking investigation should be alert to any sign or pattern which suggests that the abuse is more widespread or organised than it appears at first sight or that it involves other perpetrators or institutions. As is the case with the most serious types of abuse occurring outside the institutional setting where allegations are substantiated, the guidance directs that the management or commissioners of services should think widely about the lessons of the case, how they should be acted upon and whether a full case review might be appropriate (at para 6.22).

Protection of Children Act 1999

6.102 *Working Together to Safeguard Children* emphasises that the PCA 1999 requires child care organisations (within the meaning of that Act) to refer the names of individuals considered unsuitable to work with children to a DOH list, along with List 99 maintained by the DFES. The Act requires child care organisations not to offer work to anyone so listed for any post involving regular contact with children in a childcare capacity but provides for rights of appeal to an independent tribunal against inclusion on either list (see further, Chapter **9**).

The investigation of organised or multiple abuse

6.103 As has been seen earlier, *Working Together to Safeguard Children* defines organised or multiple abuse as abuse involving one or more abuser and a number of related or non-related abused children and young people. It notes that the abusers concerned may be acting in concert to abuse children, sometimes acting in isolation, or may be using an institutional framework or position of authority to recruit children for abuse (see Chapter **2**). Organised and multiple abuse may occur as part of a network of abuse across a family or community, and within institutions such as residential homes or schools. Such abuse is profoundly traumatic for the children who become involved and its investigation is both time-consuming and demanding, requiring specialist skills from both police and social work staff. *Working Together to Safeguard Children* advises that some such investigations become extremely complex because of the number of places and people involved and the time-scale over which abuse is alleged to have occurred. The guidance also points out that the complexity is heightened where, as in historical cases, the alleged victims are no longer living in the situations where the incidents occurred or where the alleged perpetrators are no longer linked to the setting or employment role.

6.104 *Working Together to Safeguard Children* emphasises that each investigation of organised or multiple abuse will be different according to the characteristics of each situation and the scale and complexity of the investigation, but that each will require thorough planning, good inter-agency working, and attention to the welfare needs of the children involved. It also points out that the guidance given on investigating allegations of abuse against professionals is equally relevant to investigating organised or multiple abuse within an institution. In addition, however, it emphasises that there are some important issues which should be addressed in all major investigations, and which should be reflected in local procedures, set out at para 6.26. Thus, such major investigations should:

- bring together a trusted and vetted team from police and social work (either social services or the NSPCC or both) to manage and conduct major investigations where a criminal investigation runs alongside child protection enquiries and set out clearly the terms of engagement for the team, emphasising the need for confidentiality;
- involve the most senior managers from involved agencies at a strategic level in order that appropriate resources and staff can be deployed, who should agree upon the handling of political and media issues arising from the investigation;
- ensure that the police appoint a senior investigating officer of appropriate rank and experience, and consider the use of Major Incident Room Standard Administrative Procedures and the Home Office Large Major Enquiry System;
- ensure that records are safely and securely stored;
- recognise and anticipate that an investigation may become more expensive than suggested by initial allegations;
- where a social services department's own staff or foster carers are being accepted, ensure independence and objectivity on the part of the social work team, including ensuring sufficient distance in structural and geographical terms between such staff and those being investigated;
- begin every investigation with a strategy discussion to agree terms of reference and ways of working;
- secure access to expert legal advice, noting that the inter-relationship between criminal, civil and employment processes is complex;
- use regular strategic planning meetings and reviews to consider the conduct of the investigation, next steps and the effectiveness of joint working and ensure that minutes are kept of meetings;
- agree clear written protocols between police, social services and other agencies in relation to all key operational and policy matters, including information-sharing;
- consider first whether there are any children involved who need active safeguarding and/or therapeutic help, and how this should be achieved in a way which is consistent with the conduct of criminal investigations;

make a thorough assessment of the victim's needs, and provide services to meet those needs;

– provide a confidential and independent counselling service for victims and families, agreeing guidelines on disclosure of information to avoid the contamination of evidence;

– provide care and support for the investigation team, as much of the work may be difficult and distressing;

– put in place a means of identifying and acting upon lessons learned from the investigation; and

– at the close of the investigation, assess its handling and identify lessons for conducting similar investigations in the future.

6.105 The guidelines set out at para 6.26 of *Working Together to Safeguard Children* are extremely clear and careful attention has been given to the lessons learned from the various investigations into organised and multiple abuse conducted throughout the 1990s. What is set out above is not the full text of para 6.26 but the main headline points from each item and stage of the investigation.

Abuse of disabled children

6.106 *Working Together to Safeguard Children* includes for the first time detailed guidance in relation to the abuse of disabled children. In part, such inclusion is due to the increasing acceptance that disabled children are especially vulnerable to abuse and thus are at increased risk, and research has also shown that the presence of multiple disabilities appears to increase the risk of both abuse and neglect (see Hardiker (1994); and Russell (1996), at pp 42–66). One of the major problems in this area is, as the DOH notes in the *Children Act Report 1995–1999* (at para 7.2), a lack of statistical information. Whilst the most significant study in the United States demonstrated that disabled children were more than 1½ times as likely to be abused in any one year as other children (see Crosse, Kaye and Ratnofsky (1993)) and a 1989 study of deaf children found very high levels of suspected and confirmed physical, emotional and sexual abuse (see Kennedy, 'The Abuse of Deaf Children' in 3(1) *Child Abuse Review* 3–7), a proper research study into the incidence of abuse amongst disabled children has yet to be done. Other evidence made available to the National Commission of Enquiry into the Prevention of Child Abuse (*Childhood Matters* (The Stationery Office, 1996), at para 2.33) also indicated that children who are disabled in any way are also particularly vulnerable to bullying at school, especially verbal abuse, with consequent damaging effects on both education and social activities.

6.107 The DOH has acknowledged that further work needs to be done in this area since both *People Like Us: Report of the Review of the Safeguards for Children Living away from Home* (DOH, 1997) and *The Second Report of the Health Select*

Committee on Children Looked After by Local Authorities (DOH, 1998) has expressed concern about the inadequacy of the existing information base and recommended that reliable statistics should be obtained. The DOH has, however, acknowledged that there are problems in trying to collect relevant information since most disabled children known to social services have a multiplicity of disabilities and it is by no means straightforward to decide how best to capture their needs and circumstances statistically and none of the criteria currently used on Child Protection Registers separately records the numbers of children with disabilities who are on such registers.

6.108 Certainly, there is much greater emphasis on co-ordinating multi-agency services for disabled children, which should in turn reduce the incidence of abuse amongst this group of children. Joint planning of services across agency boundaries should help disabled children and their families who have persistently reported fragmentation and inconsistency between services. In November 1988, the DfEE published *Meeting Special Educational Needs*, a programme of action which set out what needed to be done to realise the government's vision for children with special needs, many of whom are disabled. Co-operation and multi-agency working have now become key themes of DfEE policy which are also replicated in current DOH priorities. The powers in the Health Services Act 1999 for pooled budgets and other organisational flexibilities should be particularly relevant to the development of services for disabled children and the message emphasising the importance of joint planning has been delivered to: the major agencies providing services for disabled children. Thus, this message has been provided to health services in the health improvement programmes and joint investment plans; to education services in the early years development plans and behaviour support plans; and to social services in the children's services plans and *Quality Protects* management action plans (see Chapter **1**).

6.109 Following the works of Gordon, Parker and Loughram (1992), (1996) and the Report of the Social Services Inspectorate, *Disabled Children: Directions for their Future Care* (1998), estimates have been derived for the potential numbers of children with disabilities who are being looked after in England and Wales. The estimates reveal that about a quarter of looked after children have disabilities compared with about 3.2 per cent of the under-18 age group as a whole. Disabled children, therefore, have a greater likelihood of being looked after, which is indicative of the huge amounts of stress under which the families of disabled children often labour and must be suggestive of failures in the system of the various agencies to work together to achieve the best outcome for such children and their families. This again was supported by the findings of Gordon et al who drew attention to the greater likelihood of disabled children coming from disadvantaged backgrounds, in that 55 per cent of households with children with disabilities were living in poverty or on its margins in 1985 and yet the families with the lowest 20 per cent of incomes received fewer services than all other families. The need for the government to give the sort of messages it has now given to the various departments, who have responsibilities for disabled children, is clearly pointed up by this work and must further be added to the list of factors which may render disabled children more vulnerable to abuse than others.

6.110 The guidance has already been considered in some detail in Chapter **2**, but it is worth emphasising that, once again, the drafters of *Working Together to Safeguard Children* have endeavoured to take into account criticisms made of the 1991 version in order to promote a higher level of awareness of the needs for safeguards for disabled children. Whilst acknowledging that safeguards should essentially be the same as those for non-disabled children, the guidance identifies measures which should be taken which will mean that children with disabilities are assisted in making their wishes and feelings known in respect of their care and treatment, that they receive appropriate personal, health and social education including sex education, ensuring that all disabled children know how to raise concerns if they are worried or angry about something, and crucially giving them access to a range of adults with whom they can communicate. There is also an explicit commitment to and understanding of all children's safety and welfare among providers of services used by disabled children, close contact with family, a culture of openness on the part of services, and guidelines and training for staff on good practice on intimate care, working with children of the opposite sex, handling difficult behaviour, issues of consent to treatment, anti-bullying strategies, and sexuality and sexual behaviour among young people living away from home.

6.111 *Working Together to Safeguard Children* states that where there are concerns about the welfare of a disabled child then they should be acted upon in exactly the same way as with any other child and that the same thresholds for action apply. It acknowledges that it would be unacceptable if poor standards of care were tolerated for disabled children which would not be tolerated for non-disabled children and points out that where a child has communication difficulties or learning difficulties, then special attention should be paid to communication needs in order to ascertain the child's perception of events, and his or her wishes and feelings. The guidance emphasises that in every area, social services as well as the police should be aware of non-verbal communication systems, when they might be useful and how to access them, and should know how to contact suitable interpreters or facilitators. It also stresses that agencies should not make assumptions about the inability of a disabled child to give credible evidence, or to withstand the rigor of the court process and that each child should be assessed carefully and helped and supported to participate in the criminal justice process when this is both in the child's best interests and the interests of justice.

6.112 The guidance also points out that ACPCs have a critical role in safeguarding disabled children through: raising awareness among children, families and services; identifying and meeting inter-agency training needs, which encourage the pooling of expertise between those with knowledge and skills in respect of disabilities, and those with knowledge and skills in respect of child protection; and in ensuring that local policies and procedures for safeguarding children meet the needs of disabled children. It is still the case, however, that many of those working with the voluntary sector in responding to the needs of disabled children and their families feel that ACPCs are in fact failing in each of these three critical areas.

6.113 As has already been indicated, the DOH acknowledges deficiencies throughout the system in relation to meeting the needs of disabled children and their families and particularly in relation to the protection of disabled children against abuse. In evaluating its findings from inspection reports and relating them to the objectives of *Quality Protects*, the DOH found that in relation to Objective 2, protecting children against abuse, the disabled child's welfare was not always central to the practice of workers and that specialist workers were often ill-informed about child protection issues (see *Removing Barriers for Disabled Children: The Inspection of Services to Disabled Children* (SSI/DOH, 1998) and *When Leaving Home is Leaving Care: The Inspection of Leaving Care Services* (SSI/DOH, 1997)). Clearly, it is of critical importance for those working with disabled children that they are fully aware of child protection issues and that they receive the relevant training in child protection. Where care of children with learning disabilities and challenging behaviour present particularly difficult problems, specialist disability workers must not turn their eyes away from potentially abusive situations just because they feel that parents are doing a wonderful job in extremely stressful circumstances. As *Working Together to Safeguard Children* emphasises, the thresholds must not be any higher for different children (see further, Lyon (1994)).

Abuse by children and young people

6.114 The need for close inter-agency co-operation in the provision of services for children and young people who have abused other children is particularly important and a number of paragraphs in *Working Together to Safeguard Children* emphasise the need for a properly co-ordinated approach (see, in particular, paras 6.33–6.36). *Working Together to Safeguard Children* draws fairly extensively on a number of studies which have been done in relation to this group of children. Farmer and Pollock found in their study *Sexually Abused and Abusing Children in Substitute Care* (1998) that half the sexually abused young people in their study had abused another child at some stage, generally another child in care. The evidence which they gathered suggested a likely connection in some cases between having experienced sexual abuse as a child and a later development of sexually abusing behaviour in the young person. They found that sexual abuse is part of a pattern of disadvantage which had serious emotional consequences for the majority of the young people in their sample.

6.115 Learning from such studies, *Working Together to Safeguard Children* emphasises that agencies should recognise that such children are likely to have considerable needs themselves, and also that they may pose a significant risk of harm to other children. Indeed, in Pollock and Farmer's study, almost one in five of the victimised young people sexually abused another child and a similar proportion of children who had already abused a child repeated this behaviour during the placements which constituted the focus of the study. Farmer and Pollock note that this was mainly abuse of other residents in children's homes, the children and grandchildren of foster carers, other foster children and siblings. *Working Together to Safeguard Children* emphasises that children and young people who abuse others should be held responsible for their abusive behaviour, whilst being identified and responded to in a way which meets their needs as well as protecting others. The importance of early intervention with children and young people who abuse others is stressed as this may play a critical part in protecting the public by preventing the continuation or escalation of abusive behaviour.

6.116 The guidance emphasises three key principles which should guide work with children and young people who abuse others. These are: first, that there should be a co-ordinated approach on the part of youth justice, child welfare, education, including educational psychology and health, including child and adolescent mental health agencies; secondly, the needs of children and young people who abuse others should be considered separately from the needs of their victims; thirdly, an assessment should be carried out in each case, appreciating that these children may have considerable unmet developmental needs as well as specific needs arising from their behaviour.

6.117 What appears to be lacking from these three principles is a need for continuing involvement, although the guidance points out that there may still be a need for a multi-agency approach if the young abuser's needs are complex (*Working Together to Safeguard Children*, at para 6.37). Pollock and Farmer's study found that although short-term outcomes for young abusers on placement were fairly good in that behaviour improved and major needs were then adequately met, because of the lack of therapeutic intervention, however, there was a danger that the young people's abusing behaviour would resurface after leaving care. In this area, as in so many others, *Working Together to Safeguard Children* appears to emphasise the need for immediate and medium-term action and for consideration to be given to appropriate placements for the children and young people, but appears to overlook the very serious need for further therapeutic assistance in order to ensure that the preventive aims of both the legislation and government policy are fully met. If young people who abuse are to be prevented from turning into adult abusers then a properly co-ordinated inter-agency assessment of needs beyond the immediate and medium term is absolutely crucial (see further, Farmer and Pollock (1998)).

6.118 *Working Together to Safeguard Children* emphasises that ACPCs and YOTs have a responsibility to ensure that there is a clear operational framework in place within which assessment, decision-making and case management can occur and that neither child welfare nor criminal justice agencies should embark upon a course of action that has implications for the other without appropriate consultation.

6.119 The guidance lays down that in assessing a child or young person who abuses another, relevant considerations include:

–   the nature and extent of the abusive behaviour, and in respect of sexual abuse it notes that there is sometimes perceived to be difficulties in distinguishing between normal childhood sexual development and experimentation and sexually inappropriate or aggressive behaviour, so that expert professional judgement may be needed within the context of knowledge about normal children's sexuality;
–   the context of the abusive behaviour;
–   the child's development and family and social circumstances;
–   the need for services, specifically focusing on the child's harmful behaviour as well as other significant needs; and
–   the risks to self and others, including other children in the household, extended family, school, peer group or wider social network.

6.120 *Working Together to Safeguard Children* points out that the risk of further abuse by the child or young person is likely to be present unless the opportunity for further abuse is ended, the young person has acknowledged the abusive behaviour and accepted responsibility and there is agreement by the young abuser and his/her family to work with relevant agencies to address the problem. Where a decision is made to place an abusing child with a foster family, social services must now be clear that there is a duty of care owed by them to the foster families to ensure that the foster families have all details regarding the child's history, particularly where the child is an abusing child. As the case of *W v Essex County Council* [2000] 1 FLR 657, HL emphasises, a failure to provide such information may lead to social services being found liable in negligence and the award of a considerable sum of damages. The situation in that case was clearly not an isolated example, since Farmer and Pollock point out that in a number of placements foster carers have not been provided with the relevant information in order to judge whether they were properly equipped to offer the child being placed with them, the appropriate support and family setting. Farmer and Pollock note that part of the problem in dealing with abusing children was that incidents of their abusing behaviour had been poorly recorded, partly because many of them had not been dealt with under child protection procedures, and since key information about children's histories was not held centrally on case files, new social workers sometimes did not know about past abuse by the child or else the facts were minimised in order to secure placements (see Farmer and Pollock (1998), at p 66).

6.121 *Working Together to Safeguard Children* recommends that the decisions to be made by local agencies, including the CPS where relevant, will include: the most appropriate course of action within the criminal justice system, if a child is above the age of criminal responsibility (see further, Chapter **9**); whether the young abuser should be the subject of a child protection conference; and what plan of action should be put in place to address the needs of the young abuser, detailing the involvement of all relevant agencies. The guidance further recommends that a young abuser should be the subject of a child protection conference if he or she is considered personally to be at risk of continuing significant harm but that where there is no reason to hold such a conference, there may still be a need for a multi-agency approach if the young abuser's needs are complex. As the guidance points out, issues regarding suitable educational and accommodation arrangements often require skilled and careful consideration (at paras 6.36–6.37). This is underlined both by recent case-law and by studies such as that conducted by Farmer and Pollock.

Conclusion

6.122 With so much guidance available on the processes of inter-agency co-operation, and with so many inquiry reports having focused on the calamitous effects for children if such co-operation breaks down, it may seem to many that it should be impossible that in 2001–2002 we are listening to yet another catalogue of failures in the inter-agency systems to protect children (see the *Hearings of Part 1 of the Inquiry into the Circumstances Surrounding the Death of Victoria Climbie*). We have to acknowledge that we still have a long way to go, not simply in the education and training of all the professionals who might be involved, but in a wider programme of education of the public into recognising their responsibility to the most vulnerable in our society, both as parents and as members of the community in which children live and move around. Children are not invisible, as was noted in *Z v UK* [2001] 2 FLR 612, it was not just a wide range of professionals who saw the children, but neighbours, shopkeepers and local residents. We all need to work together to protect the children in our society.

CHAPTER 7

CIVIL PROCEEDINGS: CARE AND SUPERVISION ORDER PROCEEDINGS IN THE FAMILY PROCEEDINGS COURT, THE COUNTY COURT AND THE HIGH COURT, AND THE MAKING OF SECURE ACCOMMODATION ORDERS

'The system in this country is terrible, we should be treated with respect. The courts make the child's life hell. You are told to tell the truth, which is pulled apart in court, so basically the child has to carry for the rest of its life that she was abused and also is a liar. Try and live with that' (*Childhood Matters* (The Stationery Office, 1996), at p 138).

'The whole system should be revised and geared more to helping the kids to deal with it all. I didn't cope very well and it makes me wonder how a younger child would have handled it' (ibid, at p 137).

'This legislation [the Children Act 1989] was influenced by the findings of major child abuse enquiries, especially that social workers failed to use their legal powers to protect children or abused families with those powers. It is unsurprising therefore that the Act took many decisions about children away from social workers and gave them to the courts, to be determined with the objectivity of the "due process of the law"' (Lane and Walsh (2002)).

Introduction

7.1   The latest figures available for the numbers of care and supervision orders made in the courts reveal that, in 2001, 5,984 care orders and 1,466 supervision orders were made (*Children Act Report 2001* (DOH, June 2002), at p 45, Figure 12.2.2). In the previous 2 years the breakdown shows that in 2000, 6,298 care orders and 1,326 supervision orders were made and in 1999, 5,081 care orders and 1,039 supervision orders were made. It is interesting to further note that in care and supervision order proceedings the courts, having regard to their powers under s 1(3)(g) of the CA 1989 to make any orders available to the court under the Act, made 1,093 residence orders in 1999, 1,365 in 2000, and 1,581 in 2001. In 1999 the courts made 236 prohibited steps orders, 227 in 2000, and 178 in 2001; and in 1999 they made 61 specific issue orders, 279 in 2000, and 178 in 2001 (see *Children Act Report 2001* (DOH, June 2002), at p 45, Figure 12.2.2). In a number of cases, therefore, the increasing number of supervision orders which were made may well have accompanied the making of residence orders and others of the s 8 orders as a way of safeguarding the child's position where the criteria for making a supervision order had been satisfied. The DOH has noted that the figures demonstrate a clear trend, during the period 1993–1999, of increasing numbers and proportion of children for whom care orders have been necessary to secure their health and development, and this trend has continued over the following 2 years. The DOH further notes that this implies that there has been a shift towards interventions sanctioned by the courts which is most apparent in the increased use of both interim and full care orders. Whilst noting that in general terms better outcomes are achieved through working, wherever possible, in partnership with parents and that the cost of taking cases to court is undoubtedly higher than action taken on the basis of the agreement with parents, the DOH would expect that for both these reasons hard-pressed social services departments would not be expected to take care proceedings without there being good reasons for doing so. The DOH states that the figures suggest that local authorities are seeking the authority of a court order in situations where parents will not voluntarily co-operate with a child protection plan, or do not have the capacity to respond appropriately to their children's needs, and the making of a care order is the best way of securing their safety and ensuring their health and development (*Children Act Report 1995–1999*, at paras 3.22–3.24). The upward trend towards the making of a greater number of care orders has continued through 2000 to 6,298 with a slight reduction in 2001 to 5,984 (*Children Act Report*, Figure 12.2). The latest figures available on the use of secure accommodation orders made under s 25 of the CA 1989 reveal that in 2000 some 784 orders were made, and that in the following year there was a substantial fall in the numbers of orders made to 583 (*Children Act Report 2001*). This reflects a continuing trend apparent from the *Children Act Reports* that there has been a very considerable reduction in the numbers of such orders made under s 25 from a high point in 1994 of 1,240 orders (see *Children Act Report 1995–1999*).

7.2   The making of secure accommodation orders under s 25 of the CA 1989 is a step which is usually taken only as a last resort in relation to children and young people who are already the subject of care orders or more unusually are being accommodated by a local authority, which is why they are being considered in this chapter after consideration of care and supervision order proceedings. It is proposed in this chapter, therefore, to consider all aspects of the law relating to the taking of civil proceedings for care and supervision orders, specifically including the critical roles of the children's guardian and the solicitor, who will be appointed to represent the child in all cases unless the court is satisfied that it is not necessary to do so in order to safeguard the child's interests in the court (CA 1989, s 41); and also the process in the civil courts leading to the making of a care or supervision order. The position with regard to the burden of proof and the type and quality of evidence which may be used in such proceedings, as well as various aspects of procedure, will be analysed in Chapter 8 together with the availability of supplementary procedures to protect children such as the invoking of the inherent jurisdiction of the High Court under the provisions of s 100 of the CA 1989 (see paras **8.166–8.176**), but the position on appeals generally will be considered at the relevant stages in this chapter. Finally, as already indicated, some consideration will also be given to the circumstances in which proceedings with regard to the making of secure accommodation orders may be instituted arising out of child protection concerns under the provisions of s 25 of the CA 1989. The use of orders remanding children to secure accommodation (under s 23(1) of the CYPA 1969, or para 7.5 of Sch 7 to the Powers of Criminal Courts Sentencing Act 2000 (PCC(S)A 2000), or detaining them in such accommodation whilst awaiting a court appearance (under s 38(6) of the Police and Criminal Evidence Act 1984), and the situation of those placed in secure units pursuant to sentences issued under s 73 of the CDA 1998, and ss 90–92 of the PCC(S)A 2000, will be considered in Chapter **9**.

7.3 All practitioners in any professional field who may be concerned with the taking of care or supervision order proceedings should be familiar with the *Handbook of Best Practice in Children Act Cases* (The Children Act Advisory Committee, LCD, June 1997). This guidance provides advice on such matters as preparation for court in such care proceedings, first appointment in public law cases in the county courts, appeals from the family proceedings court, disclosure of local authority held documents, and experts and the courts. The *Handbook* interestingly deals only with care and supervision order proceedings and makes no reference whatsoever to proceedings under s 25 for secure accommodation orders. Thus the title is somewhat misleading for those who might seek some assistance from it in secure accommodation proceedings. In addition, it should be noted that *A Handbook for Expert Witnesses in Children Act Cases* (Family Law, 2000) has been produced by Mr Justice Wall, the then Family Division Liaison Judge for the Northern Circuit, together with His Honour Judge Iain Hamilton. This provides extremely detailed guidance on the respective roles of the expert and the judge, the general duties of experts, the type of reports which should be prepared, giving of evidence in court, the ability of experts to ask for feedback at the end of the case after a decision has been made, and on the making of complaints about the way in which the expert has been treated (see Chapter **8**).

The persons who may initiate care and supervision order proceedings

7.4 The local authority or 'an authorised person' may initiate care proceedings under s 31 of the CA 1989. The only 'person' who has received specific authorisation so far have been officers of the NSPCC (s 31(8), (9)). The provisions in the CA 1989 marked a change from earlier law in that the police are no longer allowed to initiate care proceedings for any reason. In nearly all cases involving an application for a care or supervision order it has been local authorities who have been the applicants (see *Children Act Report 1995–1999* (DOH, 2000), chapter 10). Where an application is being made for a care or supervision order, such proceedings are generally referred to in orders directing the arrangements of court business issued by the LCD as public law applications.

Commencing proceedings

Which court?

7.5 Generally, all public law applications concerning children are commenced in the family proceedings courts (see CAPO 1991, art 3, as amended).

Criteria for transferring cases

7.6 Subject to a considerable number of restrictions, see CAPO 1991, art 7(2), (3) and (4) and arts 15–18 as amended, a family proceedings court may, upon application by a party or of its own motion, transfer to a county court proceedings of any of the kinds mentioned in art 3(1) of the CAPO 1991 where it considers it is in the interests of the child to do so having regard to a number of issues. Thus, the court must consider: whether any delay in determining the question raised in the proceedings is likely to prejudice the child's welfare; whether the proceedings are exceptionally grave, important or complex or that it would be appropriate for those proceedings to be held together with other family proceedings which are pending in another court; or where the transfer is likely significantly to accelerate the determination of the proceedings and there is no other method of doing so, including transfer to another magistrates' court, as appropriate, and delay would seriously prejudice the interests of the child who is the subject of the proceedings (see CAPO 1991, art 7(1)).

Restrictions on transfers

7.7 There are some restrictions on transfers. Thus, applications for emergency protection orders for child protection, a range of private law matters, and proceedings to give a police constable powers to assist in the removal of children under s 102 (see Chapter **5**) can only be transferred from a magistrates' court to a county court care centre in order to be heard together with other family proceedings which arise out of the same circumstances as gave rise to the proceedings to be transferred, and which are pending in another court (see CAPO 1991, arts 7(3) and 8).

Requirement to transfer

7.8   A magistrates' court *must* transfer proceedings to another magistrates' court where, having regard to the principle that any delay in determining the question is likely to prejudice the welfare of the child, the transferring court considers that the transfer is in the best interest of the child. The transferring court may consider this to be the case because it is likely to accelerate significantly the determination of the proceedings, or because it would be appropriate for those proceedings to be heard together with other family proceedings which are pending in the receiving court, or for some other reason (see Art 6 generally). The receiving court must, through its justices' clerk, also consent to the case being transferred (CAPO 1991, art 6(1)(b)).

Procedure on receipt of request for transfer

7.9   Where the justices' clerk or a family proceedings court receives a written request from one party to transfer proceedings, he or the court must issue a certificate (Form C49) granting, or refusing, the request in accordance with the relevant criteria. A copy of the certificate granting a request must be sent to the parties, any children's guardian and to the receiving court (see CAPO 1991, art 6(2)).

7.10   As to which county court a case may be transferred, if it is decided that a vertical rather than a horizontal transfer is in the best interest of the child, this is governed by special rules concerning the allocation of proceedings to particular levels of county court. In the case of public law proceedings (ie care and associated proceedings) these will have to be transferred to the relevant county court care centre (CAPO 1991, arts 14–20 as amended). Where the justices' clerk or family proceedings court has received a written request from a party for a transfer of proceedings to the county court, the procedure to be followed is exactly the same as that following the request to transfer proceedings for one magistrates' court to another (see above).

Judicial attitudes to transfer of cases

7.11   When magistrates are presented with complex or lengthy cases, there is now a considerable body of High Court opinion which suggests that they should immediately consider whether or not it is in the best interest of the child to transfer the case to the district judge in the county court care centre for his determination as to the appropriate level for the case to be heard. In

L v Berkshire County Council [1992] 1 FCR 481, the High Court stated that it was a matter of some concern that a lengthy hearing which was to go on before magistrates was going to be heard over a number of separate days because of the difficulty of reconvening the bench on consecutive days. Butler-Sloss LJ in *Re M* [1995] 1 FLR 546, did not merely express concern but gave strong advice to magistrates that they should 'in future' assess the difficulty and length of a case such as the present one and, especially when the bench cannot sit together continuously for several days, they should send these longer and more difficult cases to a higher court which has the ability to hear cases consecutively to their conclusion. As Thorpe J commented in *Re H (A Minor) (Care Proceedings: Child's Wishes)* [1993] 1 FLR 440, at p 445, 'It is vital for the success of the Family Justice System that has been introduced to accompany the Children Act 1989, that the allocation of cases to the appropriate level of court within the three tier system operates effectively'. Thorpe J, in that case, also stated that as a matter of course where the estimated length of the hearing was in excess of 2 or 3 days, magistrates should consider transferring the case to a district judge for consideration as to whether it should be heard by a circuit judge or a High Court judge. It was his view, clearly shared by Butler-Sloss LJ in *Re M*, that a complex case should always be transferred upwards. He went on to state that a case which seems to bristle with complexity at the outset and was transferred upward under the CAPO 1991 might, nevertheless, simplify as it progressed and might then justify a transfer back to the magistrates' court. A case might not manifest any of the criteria set out in Art 7 initially but if any of these factors subsequently developed the case should be swiftly transferred to a district judge. He stated that in a case with which he was dealing, 'it was manifest from the outset that it was an acutely difficult case where an able, intelligent adolescent was demonstrating a capacity to blight his prospect of achievement as a consequence of grossly disturbed behaviour'. It was, he said, a class of case more appropriately dealt with by a judge at the Family Division who would have the advantages of the services of the Official Solicitor. The view that care proceedings which are likely to run for 2 or, at most, 3 days constituted in itself a reason for transferring the case to a county court was reiterated by Thorpe J in *Re A (A Minor) (Care Proceedings)* [1993] 1 FCR 824. In that case, however, he went on to emphasise that it was important if an application for transfer on the grounds of duration was to succeed, it should be advanced at the earliest possible stage.

7.12   As to the types of issues which may be raised, it should be noted that it was stressed by Connell J is *S v Oxfordshire County Council* [1993] 1 FLR 452, that cases involving non-accidental injury and assessment of risk should, generally, always be transferred to a higher court. In *R v South East Hampshire Family Proceedings Court ex parte D* [1994] 2 FLR 190, Ewbank J gave detailed guidance on the effect of art 7 of the CAPO 1991. He stated that art 7 provides, as is well known, 'that the magistrates' court can transfer a case to the county court on an application by a party or of its own motion if it considers it to be in the interest of the child having regard first to the principle set out in s 1(2) of the CA 1989 which provides that the court shall have regard to the general principle that any delay in determining the question is likely to prejudice the welfare of the child. Secondly, it deals with a series of other questions relating to the gravity, importance or complexity of the case, (at p 192). Where it has been decided that a case should be transferred from the family proceedings court for consideration by the district judge then the *Handbook of Best Practice in Children Act Cases* (LCD, 1997) advises (at para 34) that the clerk of the family proceedings court should:

(a)   notify the care centre of the transfer by telephone and ask the date of the first appointment before the judge;

(b)   inform all parties of the directions appointment in the care centre;

(c)   ensure that the file of papers reaches the care centre not later than midday on the day before the hearing, using a courier service if necessary; and

(d)   alert the district judge, by telephone if necessary, to any unusual factor in the case.

Refusal of magistrates' court to transfer

7.13   Where a magistrates' court refuses to transfer proceedings to the county court care centre, any party may apply to the appropriate care centre for an order to transfer the proceedings to that centre (CAPO 1991, art 9). In determining whether or not to transfer the proceedings to itself, or whether those proceedings should be transferred to the High Court, the county court must consider the same criteria which the magistrates' court had to consider when deciding whether or not to grant the request for transfer (CAPO 1991, art 9(2)). In so doing, the county court may reach the decision that the proceedings are more appropriate for determination in the High Court and that such determination would be in the interests of the child (CAPO 1991, art 9(3)).

Right to apply for transfer after magistrates refusal

7.14   It is important that those representing children, parents or the local authority in care proceedings appreciate their rights to apply to the county court for a transfer of the case. This was illustrated by the case of *Essex County Council v L* [1993] Fam Law 458, where the local authority had sought to transfer care proceedings to a higher court but the justices had refused their application. By the commencement of the hearing, it was apparent that there was conflicting medical evidence and the hearing then took place on non-consecutive days over the course of several weeks. Bracewell J held that the practice of that magistrates' court was contrary to the best interests of children. She stated that 'where justices were told that a hearing was estimated for more than 2, or at the most, 3 days, or whether there was conflicting medical evidence, they should transfer the matter immediately to the nearest care centre.

Procedural steps on application to county court for transfer

7.15   The FPR 1991 provide for the steps to be taken and the time within which they should be taken where an application for transfer from a magistrates' court is made to a county court (r 4.6(1) as amended). The applicant is required to file the application for transfer together with the magistrates' Certificate of Refusal, and to serve a copy of the application and the certificate personally on all parties to the proceedings which it has sought to transfer within 2 days after receipt of the certificate by the applicant (r 4.6(2)). The court must deliver the application not before the fourth day after the filing of the application unless the parties consent to an earlier consideration, and either grant the application or direct that a day be fixed for the hearing of the application (r 4.6(3)). If the latter, the proper officer fixes the date and gives not less than one day's notice of the date to the parties (r (4.6)(3)(b)). Somewhat peculiarly, the rules do not provide for a copy of the original application to be lodged with the county court. It would clearly assist the district judge if this had already been done.

7.16   Where the county court is considering whether to transfer proceedings to the High Court it may, before deciding whether to make or refuse an order for transfer for the date of the hearing or whether such an order should be made, invite the party making the request for transfer to make written representations within the specified period as to whether such an order should be made (FPR 1991, r 4.6). After consideration of the written representation the court may make an order for transfer, determine that such an order should not be made or set a date for the hearing of the issue. However, as Thorpe J commented in *Re H (A Minor) (Care Proceedings: Child's Wishes)* [1993] 1 FLR 440, at p 445) where it becomes apparent in family proceedings that if a case was more complex than it had originally appeared, it was essential that action be taken swiftly to transfer it to the appropriate level of court within the three-tier system.

Horizontal transfer of case

7.17   There is provision for a county court care centre to transfer cases horizontally where, having regard to the avoidance of delay (see s 1(2) of the CA 1989), it considers the transfer to be in the child's interest, and the receiving court is of the same class or classes as the transferring court, or is to be presided over by a judge who is specified in the Family Proceedings (Allocation to Judiciary) Directions 1991 and 1993 for the same purposes as the judge presiding over the transferring court (see CAPO 1991, art 10, and see *The Children Act Advisory Committee Annual Report 1992* (LCD) (at chapter 4)).

Transfer of cases to the High Court

7.18 A county court may transfer proceedings to the High Court where, having regard to the principle of the avoidance of delay, it considers that the proceedings are appropriate for determination in the High Court and that such determination would be in the child's interest (CAPO 1991, art 12). It should also be pointed out that following the case of *Re AD (A Minor) (Child's Wishes)* [1993] Fam Law 405, the President of the Family Division has issued a Practice Direction that where children issue applications for s 8 orders (contact, prohibited steps, residence and specific issue orders), such applications raise issues which are more appropriate for determination in the High Court and should be transferred there for hearing (see *Practice Direction* [1993] 1 FLR 668). This may be relevant where a child, following concerns over significant harm, is offered accommodation by the local authority and then exercises his right to apply for a s 8 order under the CA 1989.

Transferring a case downwards

7.19 Reference was made earlier to the ability of the courts to transfer the cases downwards and it should be noted that the High Court can transfer a care case back for hearing in the county court where, having regard to the avoidance of delay principle, it considers that proceedings are appropriate for determination in such a court and that such determination would be in the best interests of the child (see CAPO 1991, art 13). It is further provided under the CAPO 1991 that the county court may transfer back to a magistrates' court before trial, proceedings transferred to it by a magistrates' court, having regard again to the 'avoidance of delay' principle in the interests of the child and where the criteria for transfer cited by the magistrates' court or the district judge as the reason for transfer either did not at the time apply or no longer applies (CAPO 1991, art 11).

Selecting the most appropriate court for a case

7.20 As has been seen from the various decided cases as well as from the orders and rules of court, there is the opportunity in public law for a certain amount of 'forum shopping'. Whilst the general rule, therefore, is that an application for a care or supervision order must initially be made to the family proceedings court, it should be noted that where such an application arises from a direction to conduct an investigation made by the High Court or county court under s 37 of the CA 1989, provided that court is a county court care centre, the application could be made there, or in such care centre as the court, which directed the investigation, may order (CAPO 1991, art 3(2)). Reference has also been made at paras **7.6** and **7.7** to the ability of anyone seeking to make an application for a care or supervision order to do so in a court where proceedings are already pending in respect of the child, provided this court is able to hear such an application.

Timetabling where there are simultaneous care and criminal proceedings

7.21 See Chapter 8 at paras **8.29–8.32** for a detailed explanation of these issues.

Making an application

7.22 An application for a care or supervision order may have been preceded by the granting of a child assessment order (CA 1989, s 43) or an emergency protection order (s 44), or by the exercise of police powers of protection (s 46) or as a result of a court directed investigation under s 37 (for a full discussion of these applications see Chapter **5**). Equally, the applicant may be applying to the court for an order where no previous action has been taken in respect of the child.

7.23 An applicant proposing to bring proceedings for a care or supervision order must file an application in Form C1 and supplemental Form C13, which combined are referred to as 'the application', along with sufficient copies for one to be served on each respondent and on anyone else to whom notice must be given (see (FPC(CA 1989)R 1991), r 4.4(1)(a), as amended and as substituted and r 4.7). Where an application is made in respect of more than one child, then all the children should be included on the one application form (r 4.4(1)(a)). The applicant must then serve a copy of the application, together with Form C6 and Form C7 where Form C7 has been given to him by the clerk in the court or the justices' clerk, on each respondent a minimum of 3 days prior to the hearing or directions appointment. Those persons who are respondents include the child, and anyone with parental responsibility for the child and the local authority, if it is not the applicant (see r 4.4(1)(b)). At the same time as the application is served, written notice of the proceedings must be given in Form C6A, which must be given to: any person caring for the child at the time proceedings were commenced; any local authority providing accommodation for the child; any refuge provider if the child is staying in a refuge; every person whom the applicant believes to be a party to pending relevant proceedings in respect of the child (see s 93(3) of the CA 1989); and every person whom the applicant believes to be a parent without parental responsibility for the child. It should be noted that, following implementation of the HRA 1998, the advice to most courts has been that copies of all notices in proceedings should be issued, as a matter of course, to unmarried fathers without parental responsibility otherwise they might be able to claim that their rights under Article 8 (right to private and family life) and Article 6 (right to a fair trial) had been jeopardised by the court's failure to keep them fully involved in such family proceedings as are contemplated here.

Directions appointments for first hearings

7.24 Upon receipt of the application, the justices' clerk in the family proceedings court or the clerk in the higher court will fix a date, time and place for the hearing or a directions appointment, allowing sufficient time for the applicant to comply with the rules as to service of a notice, and also the dates, time and place so fixed upon the copies of the application filed by the applicant and return the copy to the applicant for service (FPC(CA 1989)R 1991, r 4(2)). In most cases where there has been no preceding legal action, the justices' clerk or the court will usually find it appropriate to deal with a number of matters at a directions appointment prior to a first full hearing of an application. Further useful advice as to the conduct of first appointments in public law cases in the county court is also to be found in the *Handbook of Best Practice* (1997) at p 17, which also gives some more general advice applicable to all courts on the preparation for court in care proceedings (at p 7).

7.25 In the case of an application for a care or supervision order made in the family proceedings court, no provision is made in the rules for the filing of an answer by the respondents to the proceedings. Provision is, however, made in the county court and the High Court (see FPR 1991, r 4.9(3)) for the respondent to file a written answer, although no form is provided for this in the rules, and if the respondent does file a written answer then a copy must be served on the other parties (see r 4.9(4)).

7.26 Where a directions hearing is held, the justices' clerk or the magistrates in the family proceedings court or the relevant court in the county or the High Court, if a case has been transferred or consolidated, must consider giving, varying, or revoking directions for the conduct of the proceedings including: the timetable for the proceedings; the attendance of the child; the appointment of a CAFCASS officer (ie a children's guardian under s 41(1) of the CA 1989 or of a solicitor under s 41(3)); the submission of evidence including experts' reports; the possibility of transferring proceedings to another court and consolidation with other proceedings (FPC(CA 1989)R 1991, r 14(2).

7.27 At any stage in the proceedings any party may apply for, or the court may, of its own volition, hold directions appointments and issue the directions referred to earlier (FPC(CA 1989)R 1991, r 14(3)). Any party seeking directions must do so by written request specifying the direction sought, which must be filed and served on the other party, or to which the other parties have consented and they or their representatives have agreed in writing. Where the directions sought are not agreed, all parties having been served must be given the opportunity to attend or be heard or to make written representations. Experience of the first 10 years of the operation of the

CA 1989 has demonstrated that the presumptive 12-week timetable, felt to be desirable in care cases originally, has almost never worked out in practice (see *Avoiding Delay in Children Act Cases* (The Booth Report) (LCD, July 1996), at paras 3.8.29 and 3.8.31. See also *The Children Act 1989 – Timetabling of Interim Care Orders Study* (DOH, 1994), and also *Parental Perspectives on Care Proceedings* (The Stationery Office, 1998), at chapter 6)). *The Handbook of Best Practice in Children Act Cases* (LCD, 1997) advises (at para 4) that directions hearings should be used imaginatively to anticipate problems and address them in advance. It states that the directions hearing should be used to:

(a)   ensure strict compliance with timetables for filing evidence and documents;

(b)   inform the court, as a matter of urgency, if the timetable cannot be met for any reason;

(c)   be prepared in advance with dates and availability of witnesses and time needed to adduce evidence;

(d)   liaise with other agencies to ensure that all issues are addressed at an early stage, for example:
   –   where the transfer to the care centre would be appropriate;
   –   which other persons are seeking party status;
   –   issues of disclosure and confidentiality;
   –   any assessments or experts' reports sought by any other party;

(e)   fix the final hearing, even if only provisionally. Clearly, this guidance ties in not only with the 'delay principle' but also with a view that the presumption that delay could be prejudicial to the child's welfare may be rebutted by evidence on the basis of what is in the paramount interest of the child in each particular case. *The Handbook of Best Practice* also goes on to advise that all parties, and in particular the guardian have a duty to:
   –   advise the court on the timetable appropriate to the issues and timescales of the child concerned;
   –   keep the timetable under constant review throughout the preparation for the hearing;
   –   bring to the attention of the court promptly any significant development and seek further directions.

In addition, directions hearings should also be used to determine the necessity for a split hearing in care cases, that is the need for a factual hearing to determine the facts of the alleged abuse and a separate disposal hearing dealing with the future plans for the child. This is considered in detail in Chapter 8 at paras **8.25–8.28**, although it should be noted that a criminal conviction may well obviate the need for the fact-finding stage of the final hearing (see para **8.29**).

Party status

7.28 The applicant, which can be the NSPCC but will more usually be the local authority, is a party to proceedings for care or supervision orders, as is every person who has parental responsibility for the child and, in the case of care or supervision order proceedings, the child him or herself (FPC(CA 1989)R 1991, Sch 2, col (iii) and r 7(1)). The rules go on to provide, however, that any person may file a request in writing that he or someone else be joined as a party to the proceedings (r 7(2)). The court, on considering a request that the person be joined as a party, may: grant such a request without a hearing or representation, whereupon the justices' clerk or the court must inform the parties and the person making the request of that decision; order that a date be fixed for considering such a request and serve notice on the applicant and the parties; or invite the parties or any of them to make written representations as to whether a request should be granted and, after the expiry of a certain period, the court may then either grant such request or, again, order a hearing of such a request. In those circumstances where the court is determining whether to make a person a party to the proceedings or to discharge a party, the court does not have to apply the principle that the child's welfare is paramount since this is not a decision with regard to the upbringing of a child (see *North Yorkshire County Council v G* [1993] 2 FLR 732 and *Re W (Discharge of Party to Proceedings)* [1997] 1 FLR 128).

Unmarried fathers without parental responsibility as parties

7.29 In those circumstances where the person seeking to be joined as a party is an unmarried father without parental responsibility, the attitude of the court has been that such an unmarried father should be joined as a party unless there are extremely good reasons why he should not be so joined. It has been declared by the courts to be inappropriate to demand that the court should approach such an application by a parent with the provisions of s 10(9) of the CA 1989 in mind (see *Re B (Care Proceedings: Notification of Father Without Parental Responsibility)* [1999] 2 FLR 408).

7.30 Further, in *Re F (Care: Party Status Directions)* [1999] Fam Law 294, it was stated that a court should be especially reluctant to exclude a natural parent who wishes to be heard where serious allegations were being made against him which were likely to form the basis of meeting the threshold criteria laid down in s 31(2). Thus the basic principle must be that where the unmarried father without parental responsibility seeks to be joined, he should be allowed to do so and strenuous efforts should always be made on the part of social services to ensure that unmarried fathers without parental responsibility are given notice of the proceedings as is required by the Rules (FPR 1991, r 4.3 and Appendix 3, as amended). It is crucial that they are made aware of the circumstances and know what is going on if care or supervision orders are to be sought in respect of a particular child and this is more especially the case given the demands of Articles 6 and 8 of the ECHR.

7.31   In *Re B* [1999] 2 FLR 408, the unmarried father, who it was accepted had little contact with and had shown little active interest in the child up to this time, had not been given notice of the care proceedings because the local authority paperwork had another man's name down as the father. The local authority's care plan was that the child should be adopted by strangers whereas the father had understood that the child would return to the mother's care. As soon as he realised what was proposed, he applied to be joined to the care proceedings in order that he could be considered as a carer for the child. The justices refused the father's application, which they noted was very late, on the basis of the risk of disruption to the child as the result of delay to the care proceedings, and of the father's minimal involvement with the child. Holman J allowed the father's appeal holding that since both mother and father had been assserting that he was the father of the child, he should have been served with notice of the care proceedings, or at the very least the authority should have made an application to the court as to whether or not notice should be served. As the father had not been served with notice in breach of the Rules, the lateness of his application was not a powerful consideration. The court further held that the justices should not have approached the issue by asking whether the father had an arguable case since a father without parental responsibility was in a different position to others who required leave to be joined in care proceedings, as was demonstrated by the requirement that every father be served with notice of care proceedings. Holman J found that, broadly, a father ought ordinarily to be given the opportunity to be heard before major decisions were taken in relation to his child, and if he wished to participate as a party to care proceedings he should be permitted to do so unless there was some justifiable reason for not joining him as a party. In this case, said the judge, disruption to the child caused by delay was not sufficient reason for refusing to join the father, as there was no evidence that joining him as a party would delay proceedings, and any risk of delay could have been dealt with by the justices requiring as a condition of joining the father that the hearing go ahead as arranged. Holman J also criticised the guardian for failing to investigate the father's capabilities as a parent. Any father, said the judge, who was showing an interest in the child to the point of seeking to participate in the proceedings and to apply for orders himself, was entitled to be seen by, and have some investigation by, the guardian.

7.32   *Re B* must be seen as the correct approach, but in the case of *Re P (Care Proceedings: Father's Application to be Joined as Party)* [2001] 1 FLR 781, Connell J took a harder line in a situation where the father had been properly served with notice of the proceedings and had indeed attended court in person on a number of occasions when he was advised to get legal assistance. The guardian also wrote to the father offering to see him but received no reply, and when the child was about 13 months old the local authority produced their care plan proposing that the child be placed for adoption. During this period the father had spent some time in prison and maintained that the first he had heard of the adoption plan was upon his release. A directions hearing was then fixed at which a final date for hearing was set convenient to all parties. The father was again advised to seek legal assistance, and the guardian subsequently wrote to him asking him to contact her if he wished to particiapte in the proceedings and in the life of the child, but no response was received. In the following month the father contacted solicitors, who indicated to the local authority that he now wished to be joined as a party, and issued his application at the final directions hearing some 18 months after the proceedings had begun. That application was refused on the basis that the father's involvement would further delay the proceedings and that such delay would be damaging to the child's welfare. The father appealed, relying on *Re B*, arguing that his involvement would not necessarily result in delay, and that refusal to join him as party was a breach of his human rights. Connell dismissed his appeal finding there was no breach of the father's human rights in refusing to allow him to be joined as party as he had been given ample opportunity to be involved and had been advised early on to seek legal advice, which he had chosen to ignore. Connell J confirmed the principle set out in *Re B*, that as a general rule unless there was some justifiable reason for not joining him a natural father should be permitted to participate in care proceedings relating to his child, but distinguished this case from *Re B* emphasising that these proceedings had already beeen delayed for far too long, and that it was essential that the hearing date set should be adhered to. He noted that the father's involvement might not have required a postponement but it would certainly have prolonged the hearing beyond the 2 days listed because of the substantial disputes of fact betweeen mother and father, so that a resumption date would have had to be found. In all the circumstances of this case the denial of the father's rights of access to the court was justified by the legitimate aim of resolving the care issue without further delay and was proportionate to that aim. Connell J confirmed that the father still retained his right to be consulted and to apply for contact and parental responsibility orders.

7.33 For the sorts of extremely good reasons which might inhibit the local authority from seeking to give notice to an unmarried father without the authority of the court, and which would then justify the court in refusing to require that the unmarried father be given notice, the case of *Re X* [1996] 1 FLR 186 is of importance. In this case the mother of the child was an unmarried Bangladeshi girl aged 17 and the father of the child was the mother's brother in law. He did not know that the mother had given birth to a child by him, but the local authority was seeking a care order on the child with a view to an adoptive placement. The mother, supported by the guardian, sought a direction that notice of the proceedings should not be served on the father, since if the liaison between the mother and her sister's husband became known by the wider community the mother would be ostracised, the putative father's family would be put under great strain and the overall effect would be catastrophic. The local authority was contending that notice should be served on the putative father. The High Court held that r 4.8(8) of the FPR 1991 conferred upon the court a general discretion to direct that the rule requiring service upon the putative father should be disapplied. The court acknowledged that the welfare of the child was not the paramount consideration in such cirumstances but that the court was entitled to consider, quite independently of the welfare of the child, the effect on the child's family which would be likely if notice were served on the putative father. It also stated that there were factors in the case to which the local authority had pointed which indicated that the father should indeed be served with notice, but on balance the court determined that the well-being of the family and the long-term welfare of X were likely to be better served if the putative father was not served with notice of the proceedings and did not become a party to the care application. The overall discretion conferred on the courts by r 4.8(8) of the FPR 1991 is thus worth remembering, both generally in relation to all parties but especially when the provisions of the Adoption and Children Act 2002 amending the law relating to unmarried fathers and parental responsibility is implemented. Thus the newly amended provisions of s 4 of the CA 1989 will provide that all unmarried fathers who register the child's birth will obtain parental responsibility and will thus then automatically qualify as a party to be served with notice of the proceeedings. An early application would then have to be made by the mother and the child's guardian if in the circumstances there are good reasons arguing against automatic service.

Other additional parties

7.34   For others seeking to be made a party to the proceedings, the criteria which are laid down under s 10(9) which apply to applications for leave to apply for a s 8 order, have been held by the courts to apply to applications to be made by a party to care proceedings, namely: the nature of the application; the nature of the applicant's connection with the child; any risk that there might be to the child in an application being pursued; and, where the child is being looked after by a local authority, the local authority's plans for the child's future and the wishes and feelings of the child's parents (see s 10(9) of the CA 1989 and *Re M (Care: Contact: Grandmother's Application)* [1995] 2 FLR 86, see also *Re G (Child Care: Parental Involvement)* [1996] 1 FLR 857).

7.35 The Court of Appeal has also made it known, in the case of *Re M (Minors) (Sexual Abuse: Evidence)* [1993] 1 FLR 822 that additional parties should not be joined into proceedings as parties unless they have a separate view to put forward in the proceedings. In the particular circumstances of that case, the grandparents had been given leave to intervene and appeared, by counsel and solicitors, throughout the 20 days of the first instance hearing. The grandparents had offered an alternative home for the children in the event that the mother was not considered suitable by the court to have their care, but the court felt that their interests were identical to those of the mother. The Court of Appeal emphasised that there was no purpose in them being separately represented and they should have been called as witnesses for the mother and their offer could have been presented to the court both by the mother and the children's guardian ad litem. The court emphasised that grandparents, and others, should not intervene unless they could be seen to have a separate view to put forward (see also *Re G* [1993] 2 FLR 839, where the Court of Appeal stated that it would not normally be appropriate to join foster parents temporarily looking after the children as parties as they would be able to make their views known to the guardian. Also see *Re BJ (Care: Third Party Intervention)* [1999] Fam Law 613). Under the Court Rules the court does have a discretion to direct that a person who would not otherwise be a party may be joined or, alternatively, to direct that an existing party cease to be so (FPR 1991, r 4.7(5)). In exercising its discretion to join someone as an additional party, the court must, as was emphasised in the cases set out above, be of the view that they have a separate point of view to put forward.

7.36 It should be noted, however, that where allegations are made against a person in care proceedings and that person is not a party, he should be entitled to make an application to intervene and to take part in the proceedings to the limited extent that his case is being put before the court (see *Re S (Care: Residence: Intervener)* [1997] 1 FLR 497 where the Court of Appeal confirmed that the father, against whom allegations of sexual abuse had been made in the course of care proceedings on children now living with their mother, could be given leave to intervene to respond to such allegations but was not to be made a party. However, the restrictions put upon this principle of limited intervention by the Court of Appeal in *Re H (Care Proceedings: Intervener)* [2000] 1 FLR 775) should also be noted. Thus in *Re H*, where care proceedings had been taken in relation to a younger sister who alleged sexual abuse by the father and the parents accused the older sister of having lied and of seeking to pervert the course of justice. The older sister had made and retracted allegations of sexual abuse, the retraction was made because she wanted to end the criminal proceedings against her father because she was so lonely and wanted to go home. She did not, however, withdraw the truth of the allegations. She was given leave to intervene in the care proceedings on the basis of the case of *Re S*, but the Court of Appeal ruled, in allowing the parents' appeal against the daughter being given leave to intervene, that the judge had defined and applied the underlying principle in *Re S* too widely. The court confirmed that there is no right in satellite parties against whom allegations are made in care proceedings to intervene, and that each case had to be looked at on its own merits. The court might afford her such protection to intervene and be a party in the care proceedings, but it could not be extended to the criminal proceedings, and therefore it would not asssist the girl to have such protection in one set of proceedings and not in the other. To extend such protection in this case would also have unecessarily prolonged the care proceedings and increased the expenses.

Public funding (legal aid)

7.37 It is outside the scope of this book to enter into detailed discussion as to the provisions on public funding but it should be noted that under the provisions of the Access to Justice Act 1999, the Legal Services Commission has now been established to operate the Community Legal Service and to provide public funding for legal services, including legal advice and, where appropriate, legal representation in civil proceedings. Community legal service funding is available to all parties in care and supervision order proceedings, although different rules apply to cover the legal services position for children, parents and those with parental responsibility involved in care and supervision proceedings, secure accommodation proceedings and emergency protection order proceedings. For children, parents and those with parental responsibility, the standard legal services means and merits test is waived so that legal representation is available *as of right* to parents and children. There is no possibility of delaying the provision of legal services in these cases since solicitors are able to act immediately, provided they have the relevant Legal Services Commission franchise for this type of work, and they certify that a child or parent falls into the relevant category qualifying for legal services. The waiving of the means and merits test in respect of children, parents and those with parental responsibility continues until the proceedings are at an end and will cover all directly related issues, for example the making of interim care orders, or the making of s 8 orders in care proceedings. Where an appeal is lodged, however, although the waiver of the means test will continue to be applied, the Legal Services Commission will insist on an application of the merits test with regard to the appeal. As far as other parties are concerned, such as grandparents or other relatives who may seek to be joined as parties, provided they have a sufficiently separate view to be put forward (see *Re M* above), there will be no community legal services merits test but the usual rules concerning financial eligibility for legal services will have to be applied to such persons (Access to Justice Act 1999, s 21).

Representation of the child

Appointing a guardian

7.38 Reference has already been made (see Chapters **4** and **5**) to the relevant rules of court for providing for the early appointment of a guardian. Since April 2001, guardians have been drawn from the ranks of officers working for CAFCASS, referred to in the amended provisions of the statute (s 41(1) of the

CA 1989) and the Court Rules as 'The Service'. Where a guardian has been appointed at an early stage in proceedings, this may have been done by the clerk or by the court in proceedings for an emergency protection order or a child assessment order, and the name of the guardian will have been drawn from a list provided by CAFCASS. Court areas have been divided up into regions and there are regional offices providing officers from CAFCASS to service the courts' needs for guardians in care proceedings. The court rules relating to the work of guardians continue to apply with relevant amendments (see the Family Proceedings (Amendment) Rules 2001, SI 2001/821) and regulations providing for the operation of the CAFCASS service have been laid down and various Practice Statements have also been issued. It is anticipated that further volumes of guidance and regulations will be issued in due course in relation to the construction and management of the CAFCASS service and, as has been indicated, the duties laid down for guardians in the FPC(CA 1989)R 1991, (also as amended) apply as do those in the FPR 1991 which govern the work of the guardians in the county court and High Court (see FPR 1991, r 4.11 as amended by the Family Proceedings (Amendment) Rules 2001, see above).

Duties of the guardian

7.39 The children's guardian is appointed with a view to safeguarding the interests of the relevant child before the court and, thus, the rules direct him or her on a number of issues designed to achieve this end.

Promoting the welfare of the child

7.40 The first duty laid upon the children's guardian is provided for in the statute and is a duty to safeguard the interests of the child before the court in a manner described by the Rules. Indeed, the whole basis for the appointment of the guardian is that the court believes it is necessary for the purposes of safeguarding a child's interest before the court (see CA 1989, s 41(1)). The rules go on to provide (FPC(CA 1989)R 1991, r 11(1) and FPR 1991, r 4.11 as amended by the Family Proceedings Amendment Rules 2002) that in carrying out their duties, the guardian must have regard to the principle that delay should be avoided in children's cases and that whilst they are looking to safeguard the child's welfare before the court they must be bound by the principles laid down in the welfare checklist set out in s 1(3)(a)–(g) of the CA 1989. The welfare checklist should therefore be read as applying directly to the guardian and the guardian is, thus, required to ascertain the relevant wishes and feelings of the child and to consider these in the light of the child's age and understanding. This provision safeguards the idea that no matter what the guardian's views are of the child's wishes and feelings (and he must, of course, put these before the court in his report (r 11(7)) and separately in evidence on his own behalf (r 21(3)(d)), the guardian must ensure that the court is appraised of the child's own wishes and feelings. Where the guardian fails to communicate the child's wishes and feelings, then the solicitor for the child must recognise that it will be his or her duty to do so (see *Re P (Representation)* [1996] 1 FLR 486 considered at para **7.46**). Both the guardian and the court may need reminding that while a young or disabled child may be incapable of articulating or expressing wishes, even a very young or severely disabled child can give strong indications of his or her feelings on certain matters.

7.41   The guardian would be expected, in representing what is in the child's best interests to the court, to take into account the child's physical, emotional and educational needs as set out in s 1(3)(b) of the CA 1989. As was the case for ascertaining the child's wishes and feelings, the consideration of the child's physical, emotional and educational needs will require extensive consultation by the guardian where relevant, with the child, and with other agencies concerned for the protection of the child. It may also require detailed consultation between the guardian and other professionals requested by the court to provide reports. In the case of *Re B (Care or Supervision Order)* [1996] 2 FLR 693, the guardian liaised extremely closely and to good effect with the psychiatrists and psychologists appointed at various times to assesss the emotional needs of the children, who had been seriously sexually abused by their father, and was much influenced by them in her recommendation that the children could be cared for by their mother at home, but needed the greater protection offered by a care order rather than the lesser support which would be available on a supervision order. Nevertheless, whilst acknowledging the concerns of the guardian, Holman J in the High Court went ahead and made a supervision order. Linked with both of the previous items on the welfare checklist, the guardian is also expected to advise the court on the likely effects on the child, of any change in the child's circumstances (s 1(3)(c)) and this, again, involves the guardian checking evidence available from schools, foster parents, staff in children's homes, others who might have observed changes in the child since the commencement of proceedings, and other professionals, such as health professionals, who may be able to give advice on anticipated effects or changes in circumstances. The welfare checklist further requires the guardian to report to the court in respect of the child's age, sex, background and any characteristics of the child which the guardian may consider relevant and this must include the child's race, language, religion and culture (s 1(3)(d)). Considerable guidance on the importance of the guardian considering such factors was provided in the *Manual of Practice Guidance for Guardians ad Litem and Reporting Officers* (DOH, 1992), at pp 68–69, which it is presumed will be repeated in the form of some guidance issued in due course to officers of CAFCASS acting as guardians.

7.42   In care and associated proceedings the guardian has a special obligation to consider any harm which the child has suffered or is at risk of suffering and, clearly, in seeking to make recommendations to the court as to the best course of action to be followed in particular proceedings, the guardian will want to consider, very carefully, the evidence being put forward by the local authority with regard to the issue of significant harm and the issue of the experience of similar children (CA 1989, s 1(3)(e)).

7.43 The guardian must go on to consider how capable each of the child's parents are and any other person, in relation to whom they consider the question to be relevant, is, of meeting the child's needs (s 1(3)(f)). Clearly, when examining the proposed course of action to be taken by the local authority applicant, and the alternative proposals being put forward by parents or others, the guardian will have to look very closely at the capabilities of those persons who are seeking to have the child returned to them and should be satisfied that the child will not be placed at undue risk whilst in the care of any person seeking an order under the CA 1989 or any person in whose favour an order might be made. Failure by the guardian to consider and report on the capability of a natural father, who had previously shown little interest in his child but was putting himself forward as a potential carer in order to avoid the child being placed with strangers for adoption, was a matter for stinging censure by the High Court in the case of *Re B* [1999] 2 FLR 408 (see para **7.31**). Finally, the guardian, making recommendations to the court in the form of his report, is expected to consider the range of powers available to the court in the proceedings in question and to advise accordingly. It should be noted that where magistrates decide not to follow the recommendations of a guardian, the case of *S v Oxfordshire County Council* [1993] 1 FLR 452 makes it clear that the magistrates must give reasons for not doing so. In this particular case, the child had sustained a non-accidental injury and the magistrates had made a supervision order as requested by the local authority, although the guardian ad litem had contended that a care order was more appropriate. The guardian ad litem's appeal against the making of a supervision order was allowed and the care order was substituted. In *Re K* [1999] 2 FLR 303 (see para **7.129**)), on the other hand, where the mother and the local authority agreed on the making of a supervision order, the guardian had recommended that no order at all should be made as the child would receive all the necessary support under Part III of the CA 1989. In this case, Wall J stressed that the guardian's views had to be heard by the court, but where an agreement had been reached which was for the critical appropriate support to be given to the mother, then guardians should think long and hard before seeking to upset such agreements.

Instructing a solicitor

7.44 Unless a solicitor has already been appointed by the court under the provisions of s 41(3) of the CA 1989, the court rules provide that the guardian shall appoint a solicitor to represent the child and give such advice to the child as is appropriate, having regard to his age and understanding. Provided that the guardian and the child did not diverge in their views as to the conduct of the case, the guardian should instruct the solicitor representing the child on all matters relevant to the child's interest, including the possibilities of appeal, which might arise in the course of the proceedings (FPC(CA 1989)R 1991, r 11(2), as amended). Guardians may find that both they and the solicitors were appointed at a preliminary directions appointment and the guardian may be of the view that the court's choice would not have been their choice. Where the guardian feels that this is a problem, r 12(4) provides that the guardian may apply to the court for an order terminating the appointment of the solicitor, although the solicitor and, where he is of sufficient understanding, the child, must be given the opportunity to make representations. It should be noted as a matter of general principle that all solicitors appointed to represent children must be on The Law Society's National Childcare Panel of Solicitors, especially qualified to represent children in proceedings under the CA 1989. This Panel consists of local lists drawn up by The Law Society of especially qualified persons, and membership of the Panel is only open to those solicitors who can provide evidence of considerable experience in cases conducted on behalf of children, or those who have attended approved training courses. The Law Society has done a great deal to improve the standard of solicitors representing children by administration of this Panel, and it is a matter of some cause for concern that the Bar continues to feel a similar Panel should not be introduced for Barristers.

The solicitor and guardian partnership

7.45   Nevertheless, r 11(2) of the FPC(CA 1989)R 1991, as amended, does make it clear that it is the guardian who is to instruct the solicitor and, indeed, solicitors who are not trained to deal with children at all and who may have little or no experience of contact with disturbed or abused children, who often find the guardian's assistance invaluable. The rule therefore envisages a close working partnership between the guardian and the solicitor, both working together in what they consider to be the child's best interests. Wall J in the case of *Re CB and JB (Care Proceedings: Guidelines)* [1998] 2 FLR 211, at p 230 has emphasised that 'it is essential that solicitor and guardian work in partnership on every aspect of the case, including the definition of issues, the nature of the investigation to be undertaken, the need to instruct experts and the conclusions to be presented to the court in any interim or final report'. Wall J also stressed that it is very important that 'such a relationship should be intellectually rigorous, as well as professionally compatible. Each must be able to criticise the other; each must be able to curb any excesses or irrelevancies in which the other may be tempted to indulge' (at p 230). See also the work of Wall J on the *Report of the Children Act Sub-Committee of the Lord Chancellor's Advisory Board on Family Law on the Subject of the Separate Representation of Children in Public and Private Law Proceedings under the Children Act 1989* (LCD, 1989), at para 4.15 in particular.

7.46 The rules do, however, provide that if the solicitor considers, having taken into account the views of the guardian and any direction given to the guardian by the court at r 11(3), that the child wishes to give instructions which conflict with those of the guardian and that he is able, having regard to his understanding, to give instructions on his own behalf, then the solicitor must take instructions from the child and must see the child as his client. The Court of Appeal emphasised in *Re P (Representation)* [1996] 1 FLR 486 that once a conflict emerged, it was the duty of the solicitor to continue in the case acting upon the instructions of the child (see r 12(1)(a) and see further on this the comments of the Court of Appeal in *Re S (A Minor) (Independent Representation)* [1993] 2 FLR 437). Where it appears to the guardian that the child is either instructing the solicitor directly or where he finds there is likely to be a conflict between his recommendations and the child's views and the child is, or may be, capable of conducting the proceedings on his own behalf, Wall J suggested in *Re M (Minors) (Care Proceedings: Children's Wishes)* [1994] 1 FLR 749 that the guardian should: (a) take an early opportunity to discuss the likely difficulties with the solicitor instructed on behalf of the child; and (b) either take a summons out for directions for the point to be resolved or, where a summons for directions is already fixed or indeed a final hearing, bring the matter to the attention of the court and any other parties at that directions appointment or final hearing. In the case of *Re P* (above) the issue was raised at the final hearing. Where there is any concern about the issue of whether the child is able to give clear instructions or conduct the proceedings on his own behalf, that issue should be resolved by the court (see para **7.69**). This situation demonstrates the working of the unique system of dual representation operating within the structure of care proceedings in England and Wales. The child, when he is old enough to express his own views, thus has a representative to put these forward, ie the solicitor, and he also has a representative concerned with his best interests, ie the guardian. Where the guardian and the solicitor disagree and the solicitor determined that he must take instructions instead from the child (see the *Solicitors Family Law Association Guide to Representing Children* (7th edn, 2002), at p 8), the guardian has the right to give evidence on his own behalf when all other parties, except the child, have given their evidence, whether or not he has already been called as a witness by either side (FPC(CA 1989)R 1991, r 21(3)(d)). Nevertheless, where this occurs the guardian is acting completely on his own without legal advice unless arrangements are made through CAFCASS to provide legal advice for guardians who can no longer be said to be assisted by the solicitor for the child. The guardian is not, of course, entitled to community legal service funding because this will follow the child. The guardian must go on as an officer of the court to present his totally independent view of what he considers to be in the child's best interest. Also, in practice, whether in divergence situations or where still acting in conjunction with the solicitor for the child, some guardians have, in the past, experienced great difficulty in persuading the court to allow them to exercise their independent right to give evidence, and thus, both they and the solicitors must be aware of the rights under the rules.

7.47 Guardians in the new CAFCASS service acting for children in care proceedings are able to look to a range of guidance materials which were published for guardians ad litem under the old arrangments by the DOH and the Welsh Office. Thus the *Manual of Practice Guidance for Guardians ad Litem and Reporting Officers* (DOH, 1992) was followed in 1995 by *A Guide for Guardians ad Litem in Public Law Proceedings under the Children Act 1989* (DOH, 1995) and also the *National Standards for the Guardian ad Litem and Reporting Officer Services* (DOH/Welsh Office, 1995). New guidelines will no doubt be issued in due course once the first difficult period of 18 months following the establishment of CAFCASS is over and which, hopefully, will be influenced by the considerable amount of research which has now been done on the work of the guardian ad litem. See *The Guardian ad Litem, Complex Cases and the Use of Experts Following the Children Act 1989* (LCD, 1999). Guidance also exists for solicitors acting for children (see King and Young (1992)) and solicitors also have the benefit of the *Guide for Solicitors who Represent Children in Family Proceedings* produced by the Solicitors Family Law Association (7th edn, 2002). In addition, both guardians and solicitors should pay close regard to the guidance on best practice set out in the Child Act Advisory Committee's *Handbook of Best Practice in Children Act Cases* (LCD, 1997).

Attending directions appointments and other hearings

7.48 The children's guardian is under a duty, unless it is excused by the justices' clerk or the court, to attend all directions appointments in, and hearings of, the relevant proceedings. Ever since the implementation of the CA 1989, the courts have stressed the importance of guardians taking a more proactive role in processing cases through the court (see *Avoiding Delay in Children Act Cases* (The Booth Report) (LCD, 1996)). *The Handbook of Best Practice in Children Act Cases* (LCD, 1997) states that:

'all parties, and in particular the guardian, have a duty to:

(a)   advise the court on the timetable appropriate to the issues and timescale of the child concerned;

(b)   keep the timetable under constant review throughout the preparation of the hearing;

(c)   bring to the attention of the court promptly any significant developments and seek further directions. The guardian [ad litem] is further expected under the FPC(CA 1989)R 1991 to advise the court on the following matters (see r 11(4)):

- whether the child is of sufficient understanding for any purpose, including the child's refusal to submit to a medical or psychiatric examination or other assessment that the court has power to acquire, direct or order;
- the wishes of the child, in respect of any matter relevant to the proceedings, including his attendance at court;
- the appropriate forms for the proceedings;
- the appropriate timing of a proceeding or any part of them;
- the options available to it in respect of the child and the suitability of each such option, including what order should be made in determining the application;
- any other matter concerning which the justices' clerk or the court seeks the guardian's [ad litem's] advice or concerning which the guardian [ad litem] feels that the justices' clerk or the court should be informed. Any advice which is given may be given orally or in writing. The view that the guardian [ad litem] should take a proactive role relates particularly to the appropriate forum for proceedings and to the appropriate timing of such proceedings. These are both matters on which, given the guardian's [ad litem's] experience, you should be able to give much needed advice to magistrates' courts and their clerks and, more particularly, since the guardian [ad litem] is charged with the task, by virtue of r 11(1), of ensuring that the child's case is not subjected to delays.'

(Author's parenthesis added to reflect up-to-date position and nomenclature.)

Advice on parties

7.49 The guardian is required by the rules, as amended, to notify any person whom he believes should be a party to the proceedings and who would be likely, in the guardian's opinion, to safeguard the interests of the child, of that person's right to be joined as a party (see para **7.28** for the court's expectation with regard to the giving of such advice in particular cases). The guardian must then inform the justices' clerk or the court of any such notification given, of anyone of whom he intended to notify but was unable to contact, and anyone else whom he believes may wish to be joined to the proceedings (FPC(CA 1989)R 1991, r 11(6)).

Acceptance of service

7.50 It should be noted that when a solicitor has been appointed for the child and there is no one to accept or serve documents on his behalf, the guardian must do so and advise the child of the contents of such documents where the child is of sufficient understanding (FPC(CA 1989)R 1991, r 11(8)).

Investigation

7.51 The rules further provide (FPC(CA 1989)R 1991, r 11(9)) that a guardian is under a duty to carry out such investigations as may be necessary for him to perform his duties. A number of duties are then set out and these include contacting or seeking to interview such persons as the guardian thinks appropriate or as the court might direct. Obviously the guardian is expected to interview the child and any parent or persons with parental responsibility. It is critically important that the guardian is seen as independent from the other parties involved in the proceedings and the third Standard of the *National Standards for the Guardian ad Litem and Reporting Officer Services* (DOH/Welsh Office, 1995) states that 'the guardian is professionally independent from other parties and works impartially with parents, other family members, carers and professionals at all stages in the process, subject to the need to ensure the welfare of the child'. It would appear from research, however, that guardians do not always get across the message that they are independent of everyone else (see *Parental Perspectives on Care Proceedings* (The Stationery Office, 1998)).

7.52 Where the guardian is working with the child, the supporting criteria for Standard 4 direct that the guardian's work should be conducted in a manner and at a pace which is appropriate to the child's age and understanding, and the seriousness of the child's situation. The criteria goes on to advise that the guardian should develop a comprehensive understanding of the child's needs (physical, psychological, educational, health and development) given the child's age and maturity and should consider how these may be best met. Standard 7 goes on to advise that the guardian's intervention should be sensitive to the specific needs of family, carried out in a non-discriminatory manner. At all stages in the investigation process, the guardian should actively address issues of gender, race, culture, religion, language and disability and, where necessary, the guardian should seek advice or consultation to complement his knowledge and skills relating to such issues. The guardian or the court may feel it appropriate also to consider the possibility of making s 8 orders in favour of members of the extended family. Before the guardian will be able to put such a proposal to the court or before the court would feel happy in making an order in favour of such a relative or other person, the court would require evidence that such a person has been seen and would wish to consider the views of the guardian with regard to the capabilities of that particular person (see *C v Solihull Metropolitan Borough Council* [1993] 1 FLR 290). The guardian is further directed that where he inspects records belonging to the local authority he should bring to the attention of the court all such records and documents which may, in his opinion, assist in the proper determination of the proceedings. Under the provisions of s 42 of the CA 1989, local authorities are required to provide guardians with copies of any records of, or held by, the local authority which were compiled in connection with the making or the proposed making of an application under the CA 1989 with respect to the child concerned, or any other records of, or held by, the local authority which were compiled in connection with any functions referred to the social services committee so far as those records relate to that child.

These provisions give the guardian wide scope, particularly when local authorities often have materials on their files which are actually reports or letters from other agencies concerned for the protection of the child. There would appear to be nothing to prevent the guardian taking copies of such material held on the local authority's file.

7.53 One problem experienced by guardians in relation to records had been in those situations when they had felt it desirable to check police or other agencies' records, such as those of the health authority and the police or other agency are reluctant to reveal details to the guardians. In those situations, the guardian's ability to seek the assistance and directions of the court under rr 11(4) and 14 generally can be particularly useful, and the court, of course, may give an undertaking that any information disclosed will be treated in strict confidence and used solely for the purposes of the proceedings involving protection of the child, thus complying with the requirements of the Data Protection Act 1998.

7.54 The guardian is also able, in carrying out his duties under r 11(9), to obtain such professional assistance as is available to him, which he thinks is appropriate or which the court directs him to obtain. Given that it is understood that CAFCASS officers who serve as guardians have access to in-house legal advice, it would appear that the court would direct the officer to obtain such advice as is necessary in the particular case (see *Practice Statement (Officers of CAFCASS Legal Services and Special Caseworkers: Appointment in Family Proceedings)* [2001] 2 FLR 151, issued by the head of the CAFCASS Legal Service, Charles Prest).

Reports for the court

7.55 *The National Standards for the Guardian ad litem and Reporting Officer Services* states in Standard 10 that 'having brought together the relevant information, the guardian evaluates it and makes a judgement as to what future arrangements will be in the best interests of the child; whether any order is needed, because if it is whether the order sought is the one most likely to achieve the child's best interests'. Standard 11 goes on to provide that 'the guardian's report accords with both national and local guidelines on the report writing'. The guidance provides (at para 5.18) that for Standard 11 to be met satisfactorily, the guardian should ensure that the report format accords with any local guidelines which have been agreed, which now means that CAFCASS and the guardian should then ensure that the contents of the report follow professional guidance published nationally, unless the exceptional nature of the case requires otherwise. The rules require that a guardian file a written report advising on the interest of the child not less than 7 days before the date fixed for the final hearing of the proceedings, unless the justices' clerk or the court otherwise directs. The purpose of the report is to assist the court in reaching its decisions, once the case has been proved, as to whether any order at all should be made and, if so, which one (FPC(CA 1989)R 1991, r 11(7); see also s 1(4) and (5) of the CA 1989). Many guardians see the provision of a report for court as their primary task, not least because the courts are focusing such attention on the reports. The work surrounding the preparation of that report can take anything from 60 to 130 hours to prepare, which is now estimated to be the average time needed for the performance of the guardian's duties.

7.56   The courts jealously guarded the importance of the independence of the guardian ad litems under the old system. Thus in *R v Cornwall County Council ex parte G* [1992] 1 FLR 270, Sir Stephen Brown, then President of the Family Division, granted an order of *certiorari* quashing the decision of the director of social services for Cornwall who had attempted to set a limit on the number of hours spent by guardians on the cases, finding that this decision was arbitrary and unreasonable and amounted to an abuse of power and directly threatened the confidence which the courts, the public and guardian ad litems themselves should feel in a guardian ad litem independent status. It will be interesting to see how the new arrangements for CAFCASS will impact upon the number of hours which CAFCASS officers, appointed as guardians in care proceedings, are able to spend on such cases, and also the degree to which guardians will be perceived of as being independent by those involved in proceedings, most especially the children and young people. Early experiences of the workings of CAFCASS through 2001 and 2002 have not been happy ones with cases generally being subjected to even greater delays than was previously the case (see Chapter **12**) but evidence is yet to emerge as to whether the guardians are perceived by the chidren as being independent and whether in consequence there will be an increase in the number of cases in which children seek to instruct their solicitors to sever the relationship with the guardian.

7.57   The guardian's report should have been filed with the court at least 7 days in advance of the final hearing. In order to comply with r 21 of the FPC(CA 1989)R 1991, the justices who will be dealing with the case should have read, before the hearing, any documents filed under r 17, which will include the guardian's report. Inevitably, therefore, the guardian's report can now be seen as part of the overall evidence to be taken into account in care proceedings. It will certainly have a crucial bearing on the issue of whether making an order would be better for the child than not making an order at all, and, further, in assisting the court to exercise its discretion under s 1(4) of the CA 1989 which allows the court to choose from the range of orders available under that Act. In addition, however, there may be situations in which the guardian has seen some crucial piece of evidence which could be of importance in the adjudicative stage and which may have slipped the attention of the solicitors on all sides or, indeed, of the court. Where this is the case, the guardian should make his position known to the applicant or to the child's solicitor so that his evidence may be called. Where this is not done he still has the right to be given an opportunity to give evidence in the proceedings (FPC(CA 1989)R 1991, r 21(3)(d)).

7.58 Once the court has gone through the recommendations of the guardian in his report, the court does not have to follow the recommendations made by the guardian, but where it departs from them it must give reasons for doing so (see *S v Oxfordshire County Council* [1993] 1 FLR 452). In the case of *Re B (Care: Expert Witnesses)* [1996] 1 FLR 667 the Court of Appeal emphasised that in this case the judge had given proper reasons for departing both from the recommendations of the experts but also from that of the guardian.

7.59 The courts have constantly emphasised that guardians should limit their reports to factual observations and to assessments which are within the realms of their own professional expertise as a social worker (see *B v B (Child Abuse: Contact)* [1994] 2 FLR 713 and see also the comments of Wall J in *Re N (Child Abuse: Evidence)* [1996] 2 FLR 214). Wall J in *Re N* endorsed the passage in the *Manual of Practice Guidance for Guardians ad Litem and Reporting Officers* which recommends that:

> 'The guardian should not attempt to appear in court as an expert witness in matters on which he is not competent and credible in the Court guide as this can only undermine the child's case. The guardian is expected to be an expert in general childcare matters, not an expert in specialist areas.'

In *G v A Borough Council* [2000] Fam Law 11, it was acknowledged that this was a proper case for the guardian ad litem to offer his opinion on childcare and related matters since he had the necessary experience to be able to justify his opinions advanced in his report.

7.60 The court rules provide that no document can be disclosed without the leave of the court except to a party, their legal representative, a guardian, the Legal Services Commission or a Welfare Officer. It was held in *Oxfordshire County Council v P* [1995] 1 FLR 551 that these rules applied to a guardian ad litem's report as well as to the information collected by the guardian ad litem for the purpose of preparing the report. In the *Oxfordshire* case the court found that the police should not have attempted to make use of admissions made by the child's mother to the guardian ad litem that she had injured the child when distracted by the child's crying and that the guardian ad litem had been wrong in turn to have made a witness statement to the police, without the police having first obtained the leave of the court. The court found in that case that in order to encourage openness on the part of the parents, it was necessary for the court to terminate the appointment of the guardian ad litem.

7.61 In the case of *Re G (Social Worker: Disclosure)* [1996] 1 FLR 276, however, the Court of Appeal disapproved of both the decision of Ward J in the *Oxfordshire* case and Hale J in *Cleveland County Council v F* [1995] 1 FLR 797 in that both judges had appeared to extend the protection enjoyed by guardians ad litem in the preparation of their reports to a social worker's report or notes made in the case. In *Re G* the Court of Appeal emphasised that the rules only applied to documents held by the court in the court file and they did not apply to social workers' reports or notes in the social worker's file. In *Re W (Disclosure to Police)* [1998] 2 FLR 135 the Court of Appeal again adopted a much less restrictive interpretation of the rules and held that documents prepared and compiled by social workers when investigating a child's injuries, and which had not been filed with the court, could be disclosed to the police without obtaining leave either under the court rules or pursuant to s 12 of the Administration of Justice Act 1960. An assessment report, however, which had been filed with and was held by the court was found by the court to be covered by the rules and leave to disclose was required in that situation. Since it was feared that the rules against disclosure might mean that medical reports prepared for the court could not be released to the child's doctor in order to assist in the treatment of the child without the leave of the court, the Children Act Advisory Committee has advised that the following practice be observed by guardians and the newly named children's reporters in private law cases.

(a)   In every case in which a medical report on a child is made, consideration should be given to the desirability of releasing the report, or information from it, to the child's GP.

(b)   Where there are conflicting reports, or where the court's finding conflicts with the expert opinion (eg whether the child has been sexually abused), the question of whether the reports or extracts are to be released to the GP is to be raised as an issue.

(c)   Reports may contain information given by third parties in confidence, and the court's attention should be drawn to this when it is invited to make an order for release.

(d)   In any event, the court's leave should be sought to release relevant information to the child's GP, either to assist in current or proposed treatment, or as part of the confidential records of the child's medical history.

(e)   If the child has the capacity to make decisions with regard to treatment, his or her consent to the release of the information must also be obtained (see *Children Act Advisory Committee Annual Report 1994/1995* (LCD, 1995), at p 34).

7.62 The case of *Re C (Disclosure)* [1996] 1 FLR 797, emphasises that it is clear that it can never be proper for a guardian to promise to a child that any information given to the guardian would be withheld from the court.

Nevertheless, in an appropriate case, it was emphasised that confidential information could, if the welfare of the child demanded it, be withheld from a particular party and a guardian could properly tell a child that the judge would be told that the child did not want that information to be revealed to a particular party, and why. In such a case, Johnson J emphasised that the court was required to balance the right of a properly concerned party to disclosure of information significant to the court upon which the judge's conclusion might in some measure be based, upon the paramount interest of the child concerned. In that particular case, the court was satisfied that there was a high probability that disclosure of the information would cause harm to the child in that her trust in the guardian would be destroyed and, accordingly, leave was given to the guardian to withhold the information from the child's mother.

Other duties

7.63 The guardian, further, has general court duties, by reason of FPC(CA 1989)R 1991, r 11(10), as amended which provides that the guardian ad litem shall provide to the justices, clerk and the court such other assistance as may from time to time be required.

Appeals

7.64 When the court has finally disposed of the case, the guardian, acting together with the child's solicitor, is under a duty to consider whether it would be in the child's best interest to make an appeal against the making of, or refusal to make, any particular order (CA 1989, s 94). Where the case is heard in the family proceedings court, the appeal will lie to the High Court Family Division, and where the case is heard in the county court or in the High Court, the appeal lies to the Court of Appeal Civil Division (FPC(CA 1989)R 1991, r 11(2)). Where a guardian and a solicitor consider that it will be in the child's best interest to appeal, a notice of appeal can be lodged with the relevant court on behalf of the child. The guardian, however, may consider that an appeal is inappropriate and yet the solicitor, after consultation with his client, the child, may take the view that such an appeal should be lodged. In this case, the solicitor is able to take the instructions of the child if the solicitor deems the child old enough to give such instructions and an appeal can then be lodged on behalf of the child by the solicitor. The issue of whether the child is of sufficient understanding to instruct a solicitor and the duty of the solicitor to take instruction exclusively from the child, came up for consideration in *Re H (A Minor) (Care Proceedings: Child's Wishes)* [1993] 1 FLR 440. In this case, Thorpe J ruled (p 450) that:

'in cases involving intelligent, articulate but disturbed children it is necessary for the court to apply rr 11 and 12 of the rules realistically to ensure that not only is the professional voice of the guardian ad litem heard through an advocate's presentation but that also the wishes and feelings of the child, however limited the horizon, should be similarly presented.'

He pointed out that a child suffering from a mental disability or a pshychiatric disorder might not have sufficient understanding to instruct a solicitor but, in this particular case, by the time of the substantive hearing, the evidence was that the child was not suffering from such a disorder, although there was some doubt as to whether the child was actually able to give coherent and consistent instructions. Thorpe J pointed out that 'any question as to the child's ability in this respect, would be the subject of specific expert opinion'. He found, as a matter of fact, that 'the child did in fact in this give instructions to the solicitor but the solicitor fell into error in not giving proper weight to the terms of r 12 and in failing to take his instructions exclusively from the child'. Thorpe J, therefore, found that the child had not been properly represented at the hearing and this involved a fundamental forfeiture of a right of the child, which required the appellate court to exercise its discretion as to whether or not to order a rehearing. In fact, in the circumstances of this case, Thorpe J found, after examination, that it was inconceivable that the magistrates would have been dissuaded from the course they inevitably took, however ably and persuasively the child's disturbed and distorted views had been presented. In the circumstances of the case, therefore, he dismissed the appeal. As well as the child's right to appeal against the making of a care or supervision order, it should be noted that the persons who are, or who have been, made parties to the proceedings in addition to the child, such as parents and, perhaps, grandparents, will also have a right of appeal against the making of any order (see s 94 of the CA 1989).

Further action by the guardian

7.65 In certain circumstances where a court refuses to make a care or supervision order, and the applicant is determined that they are not going to pursue the matter by lodging an appeal, the question has to be asked as to whether the guardian has any locus standi to take the matter any further. As a result of the ability of any party to the proceedings to lodge an appeal, the guardian can, acting together with the solicitor, take the view that an appeal should be lodged on behalf of the child (see para **6.19**). Since implementation of the CA 1989, guardians ad litem have, together with the solicitor for the child, lodged a number of appeals both against the making of and the refusal to make orders. Where, however, the child is quite happy with the outcome of the proceedings and instructs the solicitor not to consider making an appeal, the guardian can, of his own volition, lodge an appeal against the refusal to make an order. The CA 1989 itself provides, in s 94(1) that 'an appeal shall lie to the High Court against the making, by a magistrates' court, of any order under this Act; or any refusal by a magistrates' court to make such an order'.

7.66   The issue of the extent to which guardians could apply for orders under s 8 was discussed in *Re M (Prohibited Steps Order: Application for Leave)* [1993] 1 FLR 275, where the guardian had been appointed to act as such in relation to a teenage girl who had run away from home and who had been made the subject of an emergency protection order. The local authority decided to take no further action in the case and, as a result, the guardian applied to a family proceedings court for leave to apply for a prohibited steps order so as to prevent the girl having contact with her father. Apparently, the local authority had reached its decision not to pursue care proceedings at a child protection conference, which the guardian had not attended. It had been decided, instead, that following the recommendation of the conference, the girl should be accommodated with foster parents in whose care she had been placed as a result of the emergency proctection order. The guardian, however, wished to challenge the local authority's decision, and to invite the court to prohibit contact between the girl and her father, to make an interim care order and to direct an investigation under s 37 of the 1989 Act. The case raised two important issues. First, how long is a guardian ad litem, once appointed, entitled to act in that capacity? Secondly, what should be the attitude of the court in dealing with applications by a person seeking leave under the CA 1989, s 10(9) to apply for a s 8 order? Johnson J, in ruling that the guardian had no capacity to have a continuing role in relation to the girl in the absence of continuing care or associated proceedings, followed a long line of pre-CA 1989 authority (*see Re T (Minors) (Care Proceedings: Wardship)* [1989] 1 FLR 313, CA; *A v Berkshire County Council* [1989] 1 FLR 273). Johnson J's ruling, that the guardian ad litem's role came to an end with the proceedings in respect of which he had been appointed, followed the policy line of the earlier decisions. In answer to the second question as to how the court should consider an application for leave to apply for s 8 orders, this was not a step which the guardian had to take since the court has power of its own motion in any family proceedings to make s 8 orders without an application having been made (see CA 1989, s 10(1)(b)). The issue of the continuing role of the guardian ad litem also came up for consideration in the case of *Kent County Council v C* [1993] 1 FLR 308. In that case, the local authority was seeking a care order with the intention of attempting a rehabilitation of the child with her mother and stepfather. In the light of evidence from an eminent psychiatrist, the guardian ad litem opposed the rehabilitation programme and invited the magistrates to make an order for no contact with the child by her mother or stepfather under s 34(2) of the CA 1989. The magistrates ruled that although they could have made such an order, they would not do so but instead, because of everyone's concern, they made a direction that the guardian ad litem continue to be involved in the case to assess the progress of rehabilitation. On appeal to the High Court it was confirmed that the justices could have made an order for no contact if it had been proved that such contact was not in the best interests of the child but they had *no* power to add a direction to a care order that the guardian ad litem be allowed to continue with his involvement with the child. The addition of such a direction, according to the High Court, was a fetter on the local authority's plans, authority and responsibility. For a different approach to whether the guardian ad litem should be involved, the court made what was, in effect, an interim contact order so that the guardian would continue to monitor the effects of contact on the child, see *Re B (A Minor) (Care Order: Review)* [1993] 1 FLR 421 (discussed in some detail in Chapter **10**).

The Role of CAFCASS in responding to the concerns of the presribed person arising out of a child's review

7.67 Under the new provisions inserted into s 26(2) of the CA 1989 by the Adoption and Children Act 2002, CAFCASS officers, presumably those who have been fulfilling the role of a children's guardian, can be approached by the prescribed person (see s 26(2A)(c) of the CA 1989), who is appointed to participate in reviews of the child's case (s 26(2A), where that person has concerns about the child's case, and court rules will provide for the CAFCASS officer to be able to initiate proceedings in the family courts under court rules yet to be made (s 26(2C) of the CA 1989). These provisions are a response to the disappointment and concerns of the judiciary and a great many others caused by the House of Lords' decision in *Re S (Minors); Re W (Minors)* [2002] UKHL 10, [2002] 1 FLR 815 overruling the Court of Appeal's approach to the starring of milestones in care plans. These new provisions will thus enable the courts to engage in the review of the operation of the s 31A care plans in relation to children in the care of the local authority and, interestingly, extend this supervisory power to all children in respect of whom plans must now be made (see s 26(2)(f)). The CAFCASS officers are thus envisaged as playing a key role in these provisions in consultation with the prescribed persons.

Other procedural issues

Attendance at directions appointment hearings

7.68 In the same way as the guardian is expected to attend directions appointments or hearings, other parties are required to attend such hearings, unless the clerk or the court otherwise direct (FPC(CA 1989) 1991, r 16(1)).

7.69 The FPC(CA 1989)R 1991 further provide that the proceedings may take place in the absence of any party, including the child (see para **7.71**) where the court considers it is in the interests of the child, having regard to the matters to be discussed or the likely evidence to be given, and the party concerned is represented by a guardian or a solicitor in the case of the child, or a solicitor in the case of other parties. The rules further provide that where the applicant appears for a direction appointment or for a hearing and one or more of the respondents does not, the clerk may proceed with the hearing or appointment in the absence of that respondent, provided it is proved, to the satisfaction of the court, that the respondent received reasonable notice of the hearing and the court is satisfied that the circumstances of the case justify proceeding with the hearing as happened in the case of *Re SW (A Minor) (Care Proceedings)* [1993] 2 FLR 609. The first 11 years of the operation of the CA 1989 has shown the courts using this power extensively due to a non-attendance by certain parties at directions hearings. Failure to proceed would necessarily lead to a delay in any particular child's case. Where one or more of the respondents appear at a hearing and the applicant has not, the court may refuse the application or, if sufficient evidence has previously been received, proceed in the absence of the applicant. Greater care must now be taken in the use of these provisions as a result of the demands of Article 6 of the ECHR. When neither the applicant nor the respondent appear, the court may refuse the application. The court is given the power, when hearing proceedings in relation to children, to determine that in relation to the child, the proceedings should go on in private when only the officers of the court, the parties, their legal representatives and such other persons as the court specifies may attend (FPC(CA 1989)R 1991, r 16(7)). In the High Court and county court, hearings or directions appointments take place in chambers unless the court otherwise directs (FPR 1991, r 4.16(7)).

Evidence

7.70 The provisions dealing with evidence across all three tiers of courts concerning the child protection proceedings are dealt with in detail in Chapter **8**. That discussion also includes discussion as to the duties and roles of experts in relation to which detailed judicial guidance has been given by Mr Justice Wall, Family Division, Liaison Judge for the Northern Circuit, in *A Handbook for Expert Witnesses in Children Act Cases* (Family Law, 2000).

Attendance of the child at hearings

7.71 The CA 1989 provides that the court has a discretion as to whether to order that the child be present in court at any stage of the proceedings (s 95(1)). The relevant rules of court provide that proceedings may take place in the absence of the child where the court considers this in the interest of the child having regard to matters to be discussed or the evidence likely to be given, and the child is represented by a guardian or solicitor (FPC(CA 1989)R 1991, r 1 and FPR 1991, r 4.16(2)). Before making any such direction, the rules require that the court should give the guardian, the solicitor for the child and, if he is of sufficient understanding, the child an opportunity to make representations. Most courts believe that where a child is represented by both a solicitor and guardian, it constitutes an unnecessary trial for the child to be present in court during the hearing for care or supervision orders. In some cases, however, the child may wish to be present and it is clear that many judges are not happy with the presence of children in court. This was evidently so in the case of *Re C (A Minor) (Care: Child's Wishes)* [1993] 1 FLR 832 where a 13-year-old girl had been present throughout the proceedings and was further present on a subsequent appeal to the High Court. The guardian ad litem had followed the provisions in the FPC(CA 1989)R 1991 in that the girl had indicated a clear desire to be present and the magistrates had exercised their discretion under s 95(1) of the CA 1989 to allow the child to be present in court at their hearing. The child was present in court throughout the hearing before the justices, save for brief intervals when evidence was being given which the child's guardian thought it better for her not to hear. None of the other parties had raised any objections at this stage nor in the appeal. Notwithstanding this, Waite J ruled that the presence of children should not be encouraged to develop into a settled practice. He further directed that guardians ad litem who arranged for children to be present at hearings should consider their reasons for doing so carefully and be prepared to state those reasons in court if asked. Given that the philosophy which underpinned the CA 1989 was that of according increased recognition and respect for the wishes and feelings of children, this seems quite an extraordinary direction and one which suggests that it is the judges rather than the child who find the child's presence in court proceedings uncomfortable. No one would suggest that a child should ever be forced to be present in court but where a young person has indicated to the guardian a very clear desire to be in court during the proceedings or a wish to see the judge privately, such a request should be very carefully considered by the court, especially in the light of Article 6 of the ECHR which provides for the right to a fair trial. Where the child asks to see the judge it should, however, be made clear to the child that even though he may see the judge in private, confidentiality of such discussions cannot be guaranteed.

7.72 In the case of *J v Lancashire County Council* (reported at p 72 of the *Children Act Advisory Committee Annual Report 1992/1993* (LCD, 1993)) the guidance issued by the court was to the effect that the courts should be informed in advance of any application for the child to be present, which would be ruled upon by the court before any substantive hearing commenced. The court in the *Lancashire* case advised that such a procedure would prevent the child from being exposed to any distressful harm and would enable the court to consider representations, with the welfare of the child as the court's paramount consideration. In *J v Lancashire County Council*, the 15-year-old girl was ordered to leave the court during the hearing of her appeal against a care order made in the family proceedings court, which she had attended all the way through, because the judge concluded that she was emotionally disturbed and that the concerns about her would inhibit submissions to the court. The court further ruled that the matters under discussion could represent a source of potential emotional damage and that there would have to be exceptional circumstances for a girl of 15 to be present in court whilst her situation was being discussed, having regard to the principle of the paramountcy of the child's welfare. Nevertheless it is left to the judge in each individual case to determine whether the child should be allowed to be present or not. Thus in *Re A (Care: Discharge Application by a Child)* [1995] 1 FLR 599, Thorpe J stated that:

> 'The balance to be maintained between recognising and upholding the rights of children who are parties to Children Act litigation to participate and be heard, and the need to protect children from exposure to material that might be damaging is a delicate one and one essentially to be performed by the trial judge with a full perspective of the issues and the statements and reports, and at a relatively early stage in the proceedings' (at p 601 and see also the *Children Act Advisory Committee Annual Report 1994/1995*, at p 52).

7.73 As we have now implemented the ECHR and have moved towards an increasing understanding of the rights accorded by Article 12 of the UNCRC (see Chapter **1**), more and more of the judges have become dissatisfied with the old stance adopted by a significant proportion of the judiciary towards the child's presence in court. Holman J has written very persuasively in favour of allowing children to attend part or, in appropriate cases, all of the proceedings where it can be shown that this will not damage the child. (See Holman J, 'Allowing Children into Court' in *Representing Children*, vol 12, at p 336, and see also Lyon (2000b)), at pp 67–81.)

Withdrawal of an application for a care or supervision order

7.74 The leave of the court is required before any application for a care or supervision order may be withdrawn (FPR 1991, r 4.5(1) and FPC(CA 1989)R 1991, r 5(1)). The person seeking leave to withdraw an application must file and serve on the parties a written request for leave setting out the reasons for the request unless the request is being made orally in court and the parties and the guardian are present. Where this is the case, if the party is concerned as to whether the guardian (where he has been involved in the case) has had an opportunity to make written representation, the court can grant the request if it thinks fit. It is clear from the case of *Re F (Care Order: Withdrawal of Application)* [1993] 2 FLR 9 that under this rule the guardian must be present personally and cannot be deemed to be present solely because the child's legal representative was present.

7.75 It is clear from the case of *Re F (Care Order: Withdrawal of Application)* [1993] 2 FLR 9 that under this rule the guardian must be present per se and cannot be deemed to be present solely because the child's legal representative was present. In *Re F*, the family proceedings court had failed to give proper notice to the guardian ad litem of the local authority's application to withdraw the proceedings. The High Court found that the magistrates were in error and should not have given leave for the application to be withdrawn on the material before them. Hollings J further gave guidance on how courts should consider an application to withdraw. He emphasised that an application for withdrawal of care or supervision order proceedings had to be considered as carefully by the court as any other application for an order in respect of a child under the CA 1989. He emphasised that there was a statutory duty upon the court to have regard to the welfare of the child, and this included the duty to hear expert evidence from the guardian ad litem prepared in accordance with the guardian ad litem's statutory duty, before the courts could allow proceedings to be withdrawn. This point was further emphasised in the case of *Re N (Leave to Withdraw Care Proceedings)* [2000] 1 FLR 134. In this case the parents had been married in December 1995 and the child, the subject of the proceedings, was born in November 1998. The mother also had four older children by three other fathers, and concerns about the second and third child, which arose after the family had moved to Scotland, led to these two children being made the subject of a child protection order by the Sheriff in Scotland. Following this, both children had been placed with foster parents where they flourished and wished to stay and were doing extremely well. When the mother became pregnant in 1998 the parents moved back to England and when the child was born the local authority obtained an emergency protection order and applied for a care order. At this point, a full psychiatric assessment of both parents was carried out which demonstrated that their care of the baby was exemplary and that the baby should remain with them. Accordingly, on 23 August 1999 the local authority had sought leave to withdraw its application for a care order under the provisions of r 4.5(1) of the FPR 1991. The parents had also supported their application to withdraw relying upon Art 8(1) of the ECHR that the continuation of the proceedings constituted a breach of their right to private and family life and was disproportionate to the needs of the child in the case. The main plank of the local authority's application was the independent psychiatric assessment which had commented very favourably on the care given by the parents to the baby since her birth, whereas the guardian ad litem was opposed to the application to withdraw on the main ground that the local authority had failed properly to investigate or consider the wealth of evidence in Scotland regarding the difficulties of all four older children and the failure of the parents to accept or co-operate with the advice given to them by the social services, the education authority and medical experts with regard to these four other children. Bracewell J, refusing the local authority's application for withdrawal, held that there was nothing in the ECHR which required the court to act otherwise than in the interest of the child. Bracewell J conceded that whilst it was true that the parents were caring well for the baby, nevertheless under the provisions of s 31(2)(b)(i) of the CA 1989 the court also had to be concerned about the care likely to be given to the child if the order was not made. Bracewell J emphasised that this encompassed the capacity of the parents to provide appropriate care throughout childhood, and in this case there was evidence to be tested which if found established would give rise to a real possibility of future harm to the child. The assessment relied upon by the local authority in seeking to withdraw the case had failed to investigate properly the significance of the two children in foster homes in Scotland or the history of the two oldest children. There had been no consultation with anyone in Scotland nor any check of the records against contentions of the parents. Whether the local authority assessment was valid could only be ascertained by testing of the evidence in court and there was therefore a clear need to proceed for the benefit of the child. To do otherwise, argued Bracewell J, would leave the child unprotected. She therefore refused the local authority's application to withdraw and ordered that the case had to proceed as timetabled.

7.76 It should also be noted that where a case has been taken on appeal, and the Appeal Court refuses to allow a party to withdraw an application, this may be done because the court is of the view that the guardian's opposition to the withdrawal of the case should be heard by evidence being presented by the guardian to the court (see *Oldham Metropolitan Borough Council v E* [1994] 1 FLR 568).

7.77 It is nevertheless possible for an application to be made where not all the other parties have to be present. Where this is the case the application must be made in writing, setting out the reasons for the request and the person seeking leave to withdraw must file his request, and serve it on the parties (see FPC(CA 1989)R 1991, r 5(2) and FPR 1991, r 4.5(2)). Provided all the other parties consent and the guardian has had an opportunity to make written representations, the court may grant the request if it thinks it appropriate (FPC(CA 1989)R 1991, r 5(4)(a)). In deciding whether or not to do so, the court must consider the matter as carefully as it would any other application for an order (see above) and it must further treat the child's welfare as paramount (see *Re N (Leave to Withdraw Care Proceedings)* [2000] 1 FLR 134 and also *London Borough of Southwark v B* [1993] 2 FLR 559). Where the court does allow the application to be withdrawn then the justices' clerk or the proper officer, as appropriate, must inform the parties and the guardian of the granting of the withdrawal. Where the court does not think it appropriate to grant a withdrawal, then the justices' clerk or the proper officer in the High Court or in the county court can fix a date for hearing of the request to withdraw. In such circumstances, the parties and the guardian must be given at least 7 days' notice of the hearing (see FPC(CA 1989)R 1991, r 5(4)(b) and FPR 1991, r.4.5(4)(b)).

The various stages in proceedings for a care or supervision order

7.78 The *Handbook of Best Practice in Children Act Cases* (Children Act Advisory Committee, LCD, 1997) advises that by the first directions hearing, all parties and their legal advisers should have considered whether the issues of fact are stark enough to justify a split hearing, with an early resolution of factual disputes in order to enable a definitive care plan to be formulated and also to enable the guardian to make recommended actions as to outcome. The *Handbook* suggests, for example, that this is likely to arise in cases of alleged non-accidental injury where different persons are in the frame as possible perpetrators and/or accomplices, and in cases of sexual abuse. The advice in the *Handbook* follows on from the advice first given by the Children Act Advisory Committee in its report for 1994–1995 where the Committee recommended that consideration should be given to the benefits of a preliminary stage hearing on questions of fact in just such cases. This advice had in fact been followed by Bracewell J in *Re S (Care Proceedings: Split Hearing)* [1996] 2 FLR 773 where she stated that such a procedure could and should have been adopted at a much earlier stage in the case so as to avoid the appalling 14-month delay. Even then, as Bracewell J pointed out, after such a lengthy period it was still not possible for the local authority to present a definitive care plan for the child, nor was it possible for the guardian ad litem to recommend any particular outcome by reason of the stark factual issues which had required determination before any future placement could be considered. In the case of *Re S*, Bracewell J made a care order on the child and then opened the court in order to issue the following guidelines to prevent delay in contested abuse cases.

(1)   Judges and practitioners should be alert to identify those contested care proceedings cases which would be suited to a split hearing.

(2)   To identify those cases where there would be a clear issue of sexual and/or physical abuse.

(3)   The identified cases should then have an early hearing to decide factual issues. The substantive hearing would then be able to focus on the welfare of the child with greater clarity.

(4)   Experts in the same field of expertise should meet in advance of the preliminary hearing to identify areas of agreement and dispute which should then be incorporated into a schedule for the court.

7.79   Given the clear message sent out by this case, then repeated in the *Handbook of Best Practice in Children Act Cases* (LCD, 1997), Wall J was all the more critical of both the legal advisers and the guardian ad litem for failing to ensure that there was an early preliminary hearing at which the factual issues could have been detailed in the case of *Re CB and JB (Care Proceedings: Guidelines)* [1998] 2 FLR 211. As a result of the failure to concentrate on the principal issue of determining who was responsible for the severe shaking of CB, there had been obfuscation of that issue, delay, waste of social work resources and unnecessary escalation of legal costs. In addition, 13 expert witnesses had made reports. Again, in order to assist practitioners, Wall J adjourned the case into open court and issued a number of additional guidelines which generally related to the issue of the evidence being presented in this particular case but which stressed the critical importance of the benefits of a split hearing in clearly identifying the factual issues relevant to the establishment of the threshold criteria under s 31 of the CA 1989.

7.80 In the preliminary stage of the split hearing to determine factual issues (see para **8.28**), or in those circumstances where there is no split hearing and the final hearing is under way, the applicant must first prove on the balance of probabilities that:

(1) the child concerned is suffering or is likely to suffer significant harm (often referred to as the first limb of the care grounds);

(2) that the harm or likelihood of harm is attributable to:

    (a) the care given to the child, or likely to be given to him if the order were not made, not being what it would be reasonable to expect a parent to give to him; or

    (b) the child being beyond parental control (these alternatives are often referred to as the second limb of the care grounds).

After the preliminary stage is completed or at the conclusion of the part of the hearing dealing with the threshold criteria, and provided the court is satisfied that both limbs in s 31(2) of the CA 1989 are satisfied, then the court must further be satisfied that:

(3) making an order in respect of the child will be better for the child than making no order at all (s 1(5) of the CA 1989 the so called 'positive advantage' principle). The court must satisfy itself that such is the case by applying the welfare principle (CA 1989, s 1(1) as informed by the welfare checklist (s 1(3)(a)–(g)).

Problems can, however, arise where more than one child is the subject of applications in the same proceedings and the court is then faced with the difficulty of determining whether it is possible to achieve an outcome which is in the best interest of each child (see *Re T and E (Proceedings: Conflicting Interests)* [1995] 1 FLR 581).

7.81 Where the court is satisfied that making an order would be better for the child than making no order at all, it must then consider the range of options open to it under s 1(4) of the CA 1989 (see also *Humberside County Council v B* [1993] 1 FLR 257; *F v Leeds City Council* [1994] 2 FLR 60; *Leicestershire County Council v G* [1994] 2 FLR 329; *Re V (Care or Supervision Order)* [1996] 1 FLR 776; *Re O (Care or Supervision Order)* [1996] 2 FLR 755).

7.82 The court will no doubt have been considering throughout the course of the presentation of evidence on both sides, whether the making of a care or supervision order would be appropriate or whether the making of orders under s 8 would be more likely to achieve what is in the best interest of the child as, for example, in *C v Solihull Metropolitan Borough Council* [1993] 1 FLR 290. The court will have a range of evidence before it including, possibly, experts' reports, the views of the parents or other carers of the child, the views of the child as represented by the child's solicitor, and the views of the guardian as expressed in his report, which may have been amplified in the course of cross-examination. In many cases the courts may find the guardian's report to be persuasive, but in others it may be prepared to overrule the guardian's recommendations, more particularly where the guardian has stepped outside his particular realm of expertise (see para **7.59**).

7.83 It should be noted that the courts may find both the limbs of s 31 of the CA 1989 to be proved but may then decide that to make an order is not in the child's best interest. This may be because, in child protection cases, the process of negotiation and working in partnership by the local authority with the parents together should be ongoing, even whilst proceedings are under way and, by the time proceedings get to a final hearing, it may be that that process has resulted in an entirely satisfactory voluntary arrangement between the child's family and social services, such that it is not necessary for the court to make an order. The applicant and the court will have to be convinced that the child will be better protected under this sort of arrangement and to argue this position before the court, since the court may have legitimate concerns for the safety of the child under voluntary arrangements and it is the court which has to be satisfied that it is not right to make an order (see Bracewell J in *Re S (Care Proceedings: Split Hearing)* [1996] 2 FLR 773). The view of the Children Act Advisory Committee in their annual report for 1992/1993 indicated that in their view the issue before the court in such circumstances was not whether future working in partnership with the parents was possible but whether, in all of the circumstances of the case, the paramountcy of the child's welfare would be better safeguarded by the local authority having parental responsibility for the child by virtue of the making of a care order under s 31 and the provisions giving effect to this under s 33.

The threshold criteria

Parental concessions and the threshold criteria

7.84 Even where the parents of a child or children who are the subject of care proceedings concede that the threshold conditions are met, this cannot absolve the court from its duty to investigate and to satisfy itself that the evidence clearly discloses that the threshold criteria in any child's case are substantiated. These principles were first established in the case of *Re G (A Minor) (Care Order: Threshold Conditions)* [1994] 2 FLR 69 and have since been further expanded upon in *Re B (Agreed Finding of Facts)* [1998] 2 FLR 968, *Re M (Threshold Criteria: Parental Concessions)* [1999] 2 FLR 728, and *Re D (Child:*

Threshold Criteria) [2001] 1 FLR 274. All of these cases are discussed in detail in Chapter **8** which deals with all matters of evidence in care or supervision order proceedings, but it is important to state the general principles which are to be derived from the cases here. Thus the court in *Re G* emphasised that whilst it had to satisfy itself of the evidence, the nature of the investigation required would depend on the facts of the particular case. In *Re B* the court acknowledged that whilst it might go ahead on the basis of a parent's concessions and dispense with a long complex civil hearing, if the parent was later convicted or acquitted in criminal proceedings, then a new order or a new hearing might be necessary to take account of the conviction or acquittal.

7.85 In *Re M* (above), the Court of Appeal held that it is an appropriate exercise of the court's powers to determine whether or not on the individual facts the parents' concessions fulfilled the justice of the case and met the children's best interests. In that case, the court determined that the concessions needed further investigation where three children of adoptive parents made allegations of sexual abuse against the adoptive father who was acquitted in two of the cases. The parents did not wish for the children to return to live with them or to have contact with them, and conceded that the threshold criteria were met on the grounds that they had caused the children significant harm by rejecting them following the allegations of sexual abuse; by their use of inappropriate methods of punishment; and by their failure adequately to attend to the children's emotional needs. The further investigation was however necessary because: there was potential for further contact between the children and the adoptive parents and the court's attitude would be very different if there had been sexual abuse by the father; the care plan for the children including any therapy would have to take account of the actual harm the children had suffered; and the court's examination of the children's evidence would give the children the sense that the court was listening to them.

7.86 In *Re D* (above), the Court of Appeal again stressed that it is up to the individual judge in the particular circumstances of each case to determine in the exercise of his discretion whether or not he needed to allow a full hearing involving evidence from forensic experts to proceed in order to determine whether the threshold criteria were met. In this case the experts had indicated very clearly that they were unable to advise on issues of child protection without a preliminary judicial determination of the core factual issue, which was whether the mother was a deliberate abuser or a thoroughly careless parent.

Satisfying the threshold criteria

The child concerned is suffering or likely to suffer 'significant harm' (s 31(2)(a))

7.87 The condition as to 'significant harm' laid down in the first limb of s 31(2) of the CA 1989 has already been considered in some detail in Chapters **4** and **5** since it is the basis for the making of any orders for the initial protection of the child, including in emergencies, and also for the making of any interim care or supervision orders. The condition as to 'significant harm' is drawn with reference to the child concerned in a particular case so that the court in care or supervision order proceedings must look at the position, characteristics and needs of each particular child. Thus, before any order can be made the court must be satisfied that in relation to each child the threshold criteria are met and must then go on to consider, in relation each child, the welfare stage.

7.88 The first limb of s 31(2) of the CA 1989 covers situations both where the child is suffering or is likely to suffer significant harm. The use of the term 'is suffering' is intended to concentrate attention on present or continuing conditions. The problems that have temporarily been ameliorated since the commencement of proceedings or even since the involvement of the local authority with the family, can still found an application (see *Re M (Care Order: Threshold Conditions)* [1994] 2 FLR 577). In *Re M*, the baby boy's mother had been murdered by his father in the presence of all four children when the baby was only 8 months old. The children were removed on an emergency protection order with the three eldest children going to live with a cousin of the mother and the baby being placed in short-term foster care. The father was convicted of the murder of the mother and sentenced to life imprisonment with a recommendation for deportation. Bracewell J made residence orders in favour of the mother's cousin in respect of the three elder children although, in respect of M, a care order was made with a view to adoption outside the natural family. The Court of Appeal held that the relevant date for the purposes of determining whether the threshold criteria were met was the date upon which the case came before the court for disposal; and therefore at the relevant date the s 31(2) criteria was not met and there was therefore no jurisdiction to make a care order. The Court of Appeal substituted a residence order in favour of the mother's cousin and the baby went to stay with her, in whose care he thrived. On appeal to the House of Lords, their Lordships unanimously reversed the Court of Appeal ruling and restored the care order made on M by Bracewell J. In doing so, it quoted with approval the approach which had been adopted by Ewbank J in *Northamptonshire County Council v S* [1993] 1 FLR 554. The House of Lords emphasised the critical importance of looking at the purpose behind the legislation and stated that if the court could only look at the situation as it was at the date of the hearing, then it would mean that the local authority would always be prevented from obtaining a care order because of its own intervention to protect a child. The critical date, therefore, which the court could look back at was the date at which the local authority had initiated any protective action in order to safeguard the child. In this case that point was the date at which the emergency protection order had been taken out and the children were removed from their home.

7.89 When looking at the evidence necessary to cross the threshold for the making of the care or supervision order the local authority was nevertheless entitled to rely on information acquired after the date of intervention, and even on later events if those later events were capable of proving the state of affairs at the date of intervention. This was emphasised in the case of *Re G* (above), where the first instance judge held that he could not make an order on the elder of two boys because the local authority had not established that he was suffering actual harm at the date of the intervention. He had made an order, however, on the second boy because an assesssment on the mother had shown that at the date of that intervention she was incapable of providing the necessary care or stimulation of young children and that she was vulnerable to the attentions of men who posed a real risk to children. The Court of Appeal held that the judge had been entitled to make an order on the elder of the two boys because of the information which by then was available in relation to the mother's abilities and susceptibilities which had all posed a risk to both children at the date of both interventions, even though the evidence only came to light after the interventions.

7.90 The court in *Re M* (above) quoted with approval the approach of Ewbank J in *Northamptonshire County Council v S and Others* [1993] 1 FLR 554, where he had similarly found that the court had to consider the position immediately before a protection order, if there was one; or an interim care order, if that was the initiation of the protection. Ewbank J went on to refer to the possibility of when a child went into 'voluntary' care. It should be noted that in such a situation the children would now be described as being 'accommodated' by the local authority under s 20 and, thus, when giving effect to the phrase 'is suffering significant harm' this could apply, inter alia, to the position immediately before the child was accommodated under s 20. Applications relating solely to past events could, therefore, not found an application unless linked in some way to the present evidence by some harm continuing or being likely to continue (as was the case in *Re B (Care Order: Criteria)* [1993] 1 FLR 815).

7.91 As to relying on the future possibility of harm as is indicated by the phrase 'likely to suffer' significant harm, the court in *Newham London Borough Council v AG* [1993] 1 FLR 281 indicated that it would be wrong to equate the phrase 'likely to suffer' with 'on the balance of probabilities'. The Court of Appeal emphasised in this case that the court, in such circumstances, was not applying a test to events which had happened in the past, and deciding on the evidence, on the balance of probabilities, whether an event had in fact happened. Rather, in considering the phrase 'likely to suffer' the court was looking to the future and had to assess the risk. When looking to the future, all the court could do was to evaluate the risk. The Court of Appeal found that in the present case the judge had to make an assessment of the future risk to the child in the light of the evidence before him. He had found that there was a real significant risk of the child suffering significant harm if he did not make a care order. His conclusion was amply supported by the evidence given by the mother's psychiatrist as to the mother's unstable and unpredictably violent psychiatric condition. Thus, in compliance with the correct procedure, when relying on the future possibility of harm as indicated by the phrase 'likely to suffer significant harm', the applicant must seek to show there would be a greater risk to the child in leaving him with his family than by seeking his removal. As was the case in *Newham*, when balancing these risks the court will have to decide, on all the evidence including experts' reports and guardian's reports, which constitutes the greater risk.

7.92 Where the applicant does seek to rely on the fact that the child 'is likely to suffer significant harm' the House of Lords has determined in *Re H and R* [1996] 1 FLR 80 that 'likely' in the context of s 31(2)(a) is being used in the sense of a real possibility, a possibility that could not sensibly be ignored, having regard to the nature and gravity of the feared harm in the particular case. Whilst holding that the standard of proof in cases involving the care of children with the ordinary civil standard of balance of probability, the House of Lords went on to stress that the more improbable the event, the stronger must be the evidence that it did occur before, on the balance of probability, its occurrence will be established. Their Lordships emphasised (at p 96) that when assessing the probabilities the court will have in mind as a factor, to whatever extent is appropriate in the particular case, that the more serious the allegation the less likely it is that the event occurred and, hence, the stronger should be the evidence before the court concludes that the allegation is established on the balance of probabilities. They went on to state that this does not mean that where a serious allegation is in issue the standard of proof required is higher, but rather that it 'means only that the inherent probability or improbability of an event is itself a matter to be taken into account when weighing the probabilities and deciding whether, on balance, the event occurred'. In *Re H and R*, the eldest of four children who was not a child of the mother's cohabitant, alleged that she had been sexually abused by him and he had been charged with rape. Interim care, followed by interim supervision orders were made in respect of the three other girls and the local authority proceeded with care applications in respect of each of them, the authority's case being based solely on the alleged abuse of the 15-year-old by the step-father. The judge at first instance was asked to find that the step-father had sexually abused the eldest child or at least that there was a substantial risk that he had done so, thereby satisfying the conditions of s 31(2) of the CA 1989 for the making of a care order. The judge at first instance, however, could not be satisfied, he said, 'to the requisite high standard of proof' that the 15-year-old's allegations were true and dismissed the applications for care orders by the local authority. The Court of Appeal confirmed this approach and again dismissed the applications. On appeal to the House of Lords their Lordships found that, since sexual abuse had not been proved to the requisite standard of proof, there were no facts upon which the judge could properly conclude that there was a likelihood of harm to the three younger girls. The House of Lords emphasised that whilst unproven allegations of maltreatment could not form the basis for a finding by the court that either limb of s 31(2)(a) was established, it was, however, open to a court to conclude that there was a real possibility that the child would suffer harm in the future although harm in the past had not been established. There would be cases said the court where, although the alleged maltreatment was not proved, the evidence did establish a combination of profoundly worrying features affecting the care of the child within the family. In such cases, it would be open to a court in appropriate circumstances to find that, although not satisfied the child was yet suffering significant harm, on the basis of such facts as were proved there was a likelihood that he would do so in the future. (See for further detailed analysis of this case from the evidential perspective Chapter **8** and see also the case of *Re C and B (Care Order: Future Harm)* [2001] 1 FLR 611 discussed at para **7.94** and the cases of *Re B* [2002] EWCA Civ 752, [2002] 2 FLR 1133 and *Re O and N* [2002] EWCA Civ 1271, [2002] 2 FLR 1167.)

7.93 Whilst the view had been expressed by the review of child care law (DHSS, 1985) that in cases of emotional or psychological harm, the approach which would be taken would be that which would prevent an unwarranted intervention (at para 15.18), the courts seem to have taken a much more robust view regardless of the species of the apprehended harm. Thus, Scott Baker J in *Re H (A Minor) (Section 37 Direction)* [1993] 2 FLR 541, stated that 'the likelihood of the harm is not confined to present or near future but applies to the ability of a parent or carer to meet the emotional needs of a child for years ahead'. This applicability of the phrase 'likely to suffer' means that it is possible to look to satisfaction of the grounds solely on the basis of the fear of future harm and in assessing the likelihood of future significant harm, past and present behaviour may, but does not have to, be relevant. The case of *Re H* emphasises that the court is thus not able only to look at the immediate or even medium-term position, but also to the long-term future needs of the child. In that particular case, the judge expressed doubts concerning the ability of either of the women looking after the child to fully appreciate the difficulties which the child would face growing up in an area where her parents and brother also lived and in adjusting to the circumstances giving rise to her placement with the applicants for the residence order.

7.94   When considering the action to be taken in relation to a case based on the real risk of future harm, which could not sensibly be ignored, the Court of Appeal in *Re C and B* [2001] 1 FLR 611, CA has emphasised the fact that action taken by a local authority in response had to be proportionate to the nature and gravity of the feared harm. This approach by the courts takes into account the need for proportionality in actions taken by public authorities as required by the ECHR (see para **1.32**). In that case, care orders were made in 1997 under s 31(2)(a) of the CA 1989 in respect of the eldest girl of the family, and her half sister. The care orders were made on the basis that the elder girl had suffered actual harm to her intellectual and emotional development, and the likelihood of such harm occurring to the younger girl in the future, and the care plan was for both children to remain in long-term foster care. A year later the mother gave birth to a baby boy and 6 months later, at the instigation of the girls' guardian in the proceedings concerning the girls, a report under s 37(b) of the CA 1989 was ordered into the boy's welfare. The social worker's report indicated that although there was no evidence that the boy was currently suffering any harm, 'it was highly likely that he would suffer similar significant harm as his sisters in the future', and that drastic intervention was required. The local authority applied for and were granted an interim care order on him and he was removed from his parents when he was 10 months old. Four months later the mother gave birth to another boy, C, and the local authority obtained an emergency protection order in respect of him the same day. Three months later the county court made an interim care order in relation to C and both the boys were placed with the same foster carers. A month later the judge found there was a likelihood of each child suffering significant emotional harm in the future and she made care orders under s 31 and approved the care plan which was for adoption. The parents appealed and the court held that where there was a real possibility of future harm to a child which could not sensibly be ignored, the action to be taken by the local authority in response had to be proportionate to the nature of the gravity of that feared harm. The principle had to be that the local authority worked to support and essentially to reunite the family unless the risks were so high that the child's welfare required alternative family care. Cases where intervention would be appropriate to protect the child from future harm were likely to involve long-standing problems interfering with the capacity to provide even 'good enough' parenting in a serious way such as serious mental illness or a serious personality disorder, or intractable substance mis-use, or evidence of past chronic neglect or abuse, or evidence of serious ill-treament and physical harm. Since none of these situations had arisen in this case, the court allowed the parent's appeals, ordered the care orders set aside and remitted the case to a High Court judge for consideration.

7.95   As has already been noted (see Chapters **4** and **5**), the CA 1989 defines the concept of harm very widely indeed and reference should be made back to Chapter 5 for a detailed discussion of the concept of 'harm'. The meaning of the phrase 'significant' was also discussed at length in that section (see para **5.131**).

Comparison with a similar child

7.96 When looking at whether harm suffered by a child is significant, comparisons have to be made with a similar child (CA 1989, s 31(10)). The comparison to be made with a similar child is not a problem-free one, since it is required that a comparison is made between this subjective child with that hypothetically similar child. This issue came up for consideration by the courts in the case of *Re O (A Minor) (Care Order: Education: Procedure)* [1992] 2 FLR 7, which concerned a girl aged 15 years and 4 months who had persistently truanted from school for over 3 years. Ewbank J had supported magistrates who had made a care order on the basis that the girl's intellectual and social development was suffering and was likely to suffer and that the harm that she was suffering from or was likely to suffer from, was significant. It was further urged on behalf of the girl that, in determining whether the harm was significant, the comparison that had to be made was with a 'similar child', and there was no evidence that she had suffered harm compared with a similar child. Ewbank J took a rather more robust view of what constituted a similar child in such circumstances. He stated that, in his view, 'similar child' meant a 'child of equivalent intellectual and social development, who had gone to school, and not merely an average child, who may or may not be at school' (at p 12). Clearly, if the child is disabled in some way, and that has affected his health and development, the court must ask itself what state of health and development could be expected of a child with a similar disability. As to whether 'similar' connotes any consideration being given to the child's background, this is doubtful since, according to the Lord Chancellor, 'the care that a parent gives to his child must relate to the circumstances attributable to that child in the sense of physical, mental and emotional characteristics' (*Hansard* (HL) Deb Committee, vol 503, col 355). The child's background, however, may be considered relevant once the care conditions are satisfied when the court is considering the welfare stage and thus whether or not to make an order (see s 1(3)(d)).

Proof that the harm, or likelihood of harm, is attributable to the care given to the child, or likely to be given to him if the order were not made, not being what it would be reasonable to expect a parent to give to him (s 31(2)(b))

7.97 In addition to proving that the child is suffering or is likely to suffer significant harm, the applicant for a care or supervision order must go on to prove to the court's satisfaction that the harm or likelihood of harm is attributable to, even if not directly the result of, a failure by the parents to provide an appropriate level of care. Thus, there is no requirement by the words of the section to prove that a particular individual caused the harm but rather that the harm suffered by the child was attributable to 'the care given to the child' (see *Lancashire County Council v B* [2000] 1 FLR 583). In the *Lancashire* case, a child's care was shared between the parents and a child-minder. After the child had sustained serious non-accidental head injuries as a result of at least two episodes of violent shaking, the local authority applied for a care order in respect of the child, and also in respect of another child, who was the child-minder's own child. The judge at first instance dismissed both care order applications on the basis that it was not possible to tell which of the child's carers as between the parents and the child-minder was responsible for the injuries. The Court of Appeal had held (in *Re B and W (Threshold Criteria)* [1999] 2 FLR 833) that in the first child's case, the threshold conditions had been met, as the child had clearly suffered harm and apportionment of responsibility was irrelevant, as a child should not be left at risk simply because it was not possible for the court to be sure which part of the care network had failed. The parents appealed, arguing that the child should not be placed in local authority care if the court had not been able to satisfy itself that the harm suffered by the child was attributable to the care provided by the parents themselves. They also raised the argument that continuation of the care proceedings infringed their right to family life, guaranteed under Article 8 of the ECHR. The House of Lords dismissed the parents' appeal stating that the threshold conditions could be satisfied when there was no more than a possibility that the parents, rather than one of the other carers, were responsible for inflicting the injuries which the child had suffered. The House of Lords held that the court had to be satisfied that harm suffered by the child was 'attributable to the care given to the child'. That phrase, according to the House of Lords, referred primarily to the care given by a parent or parents or other primary carers, but where care was shared the phrase was apt to embrace the care given by any of the carers. This interpretation, according to the Lords, was necessary to allow the court to intervene to protect a child who was clearly at risk, even though it was not possible to identify the source of the risk. It by no means followed that because the threshold conditions had been satisfied, the court would go on to make a care order, and when considering cases of this type, judges should keep firmly in mind, in the exercise of their discretionary powers, that the parents have not been shown to be responsible for the child's injuries. The steps taken in this case had been those reasonably necessary to pursue the legitimate aim of protecting the child from further injury, which was an exception under Article 8(2) to the guarantee for respect for private and family life contained within Article 8(1).

7.98 When looking at the care given to the child, or likely to be given to the child if an order were not made, it is not what it would be 'reasonable' to expect the parent to give, the type of care is not further defined in the CA 1989. Clearly, if harm can encompass, as it does, the impairment of mental, physical, emotional, intellectual and social development (CA 1989, s 31(9)), 'care' can then be defined in the same way and may include the lack of emotional care demonstrated by a complete disregard to the child's feelings.

This was indeed a point made by Douglas Brown J in *Re B (Care Order: Criteria)* [1993] 1 FLR 815, where he stated that 'care' for these purposes goes 'beyond physical care and included emotional care which a reasonable parent would give a child'. He went on to state that 'in the case of a child who has been sexually abused, that reasonable emotional care includes listening to the child and being able to monitor the child's words and actions so that a professional assessment can be carried out'. In *Re B* the child had been placed with foster parents who had been specially trained to deal with children who had been victims of sexual abuse and the judge felt it important that she remained with those foster parents who were giving her the right degree of emotional care and support as one would reasonably expect from a parent.

7.99 Again, in *Re C (A Minor) (Care: Balancing Exercise)* [1992] 2 FCR 65, Thorpe J found that while there were doubts as to whether the father had sexually abused the first five children in the family, there was undoubtedly evidence that they had been sexually abused and whilst it would be wrong to make a specific finding that the father had abused the children, it would have been equally wrong to ignore the risk that the father might pose to the sixth child. The judge also found that the catalogue of inadequate parenting of the elder children meant that there was evidence of physical abuse and of emotional abuse and that the totality of the evidence established the local authority's case on both the first and second limb in relation to the first five children. The issue which he then had to consider was whether the parents' performance in respect of the five eldest children was so inadequate that it would be inappropriate to expose the sixth child to the risk of repetition, ie that the likelihood of harm would be attributable to the absence of reasonable care likely to be offered to the child. As Thorpe J pointed out, this involved a balancing exercise and the balance was a fine one. Thorpe J indicated that the expert evidence of experienced child psychiatrists and developmental paediatricians would have been particularly valuable. He felt that in this case the decision was not so plain that the past record outweighed the mitigating circumstances that could be urged for the parents in that they had been very young when they embarked on family life, and the accepted failures were almost inevitable given the size of the family with which they had burdened themselves. In the circumstances, the chances for natural parenting, although slender, would be served by further investigation by an independent expert and the case was adjourned for this to take place.

7.100 As was pointed out earlier, this condition also has a prospective element so that even where the child is being provided with accommodation at the time any proceedings are instituted, the court can look to a previous lack of care and of the likelihood of this being repeated if the child is returned to the parents' care (see *Northamptonshire County Council v S and Others* [1993] 1 FLR 554). Furthermore, if other children have remained in the family setting and there are now concerns about them, the care of the child dealt with in earlier proceedings may become relevant when considering the likelihood of harm to them and the standard of care which they may have received. It is, however, important to remember that each child's case must be considered individually.

7.101 Whilst the test is subjective in looking at the child, it is clearly objective in looking at the standard of care offered by the parents. Thus, it must be an objectively reasonable standard of care offered by the hypothetical reasonable parent. A parent cannot rely on his or her personal inadequacies to argue that he or she could not provide a better standard of care because parents are expected to seek assistance from the local authority in order to enable them to provide the requisite degree of care (see Chapter 4 and Part III of the CA 1989). Where the parent has failed to avail himself or herself of the packages of services made available by the local authority and the child goes on to suffer significant harm, the local authority would then be expected to intervene through the taking of care or supervision order proceedings in such circumstances.

The child being beyond parental control

7.102 The second limb in s 31(2)(b) of the CA 1989 refers to the child being beyond parental control, which is a matter of fact on which evidence can be presented. Simply because a parent argues that a child is beyond their parental control does not mean that the local authority will wish to take action on this ground unless the breakdown is really so serious that court intervention is justifiable, and thus parents are not able to avoid taking responsibility for their troublesome teenagers or even younger children. Where a parent has done all in his or her power to offer good quality care and advice to a child, but the child has rejected this by opting at an early age for a life of crime, or a life on drugs or on the streets, the child will be deemed to be beyond parental control and the quality of care limb will not be an issue.

7.103 This is illustrated again by the case of *Re O (A Minor) (Care Order: Education: Procedure)* [1992] 2 FLR 7, where Ewbank J illustrated the alternative nature of the two parts of the second limb. Thus he held in his judgment that 'where a child is suffering harm in not going to school and is living at home, it will follow that either the child is beyond her parents' control or that they are not giving the child the care that it would be reasonable to expect a parent to give'.

7.104 In the case of *Re M v Birmingham City Council* [1994] 2 FLR 141, it was emphasised that the fact that the 'child's being beyond parental control' was capable of describing a state of affairs in the past, in the present or in the future according to the context in which it fell to be applied. On the facts of the case as presented, not withstanding the fact that the child had been in the care of the local authority since November 1993, all of the evidence pointed to the conclusion that the child was, at all times material to the magistrate's consideration, beyond parental control. Two other matters in relation to the interpretation of s 31(2)(b)(ii) of the CA 1989 were canvassed before the court. Stuart-White J stated that he was prepared to assume for the purposes of the appeal in the *M* case without deciding the point, that 'parental control' refers to the parent of the child in question and not to parents, or reasonable parents, in general. In construing the word 'parental' in relation to this subsection, however, he was prepared to hold that the 'control' in question is that exercised, or to be exercised, not simply by the mother but by the mother in conjunction with her cohabitant. Stuart-White J drew support in determining this by making reference to s 2(9) of the CA 1989 and from the fact that many parents share de facto although not legal parental responsibility with cohabitants who are not related to the children and in respect of whom there is no parental responsibility order or formal parental responsibility agreement.

The welfare checklist

7.105 Once the court is satisfied that the threshold care conditions are met, it must go on to satisfy itself that making an order is better for the child than making no order at all. In considering this, the court will regard the child's welfare as its paramount consideration and must be bound by the welfare checklist. An important item on the checklist for these purposes is the range of orders available in the proceedings (CA 1989, s 1(3)(g)). For this reason, this stage of the proceedings is often referred to as the 'welfare stage'. Four separate issues come up for consideration as part of the welfare stage, all of which are contained in s 1 of the CA 1989. Thus, s 1(1) requires that the court should treat the child's welfare as its paramount consideration when deciding whether or not to make an order and, in determining whether or not to make any of the orders in Part IV of the CA 1989 the court must pay particular regard to the welfare checklist contained within s 1(3) (as provided for by s 1(4) of the CA 1989). The welfare checklist itself provides another very important part of the welfare stage in that the court must consider the powers which it has available to it in the proceedings in question, which directs the court to the possibility of making not just a care or supervision order but also any of the range of s 8 or s 16 orders available under the provisions of Part II of the CA 1989 (s 1(3)(g)). The avoidance of delay principle contained within s 1(2) should already have been attended to by the time of the final hearing and the court bears a considerable degree of responsibility for ensuring that the requirements of s 32 are adhered to and the timetable is drawn up with a view to ensuring that any application is heard without delay. It must be pointed out, however, that just because parties and their legal advisers agree and co-operate over the production and presentation of relevant evidence in time for a particular hearing date, this does not affect the court's duty to be vigilant under the provisions of s 32 in ensuring that unnecessary and wasteful proliferation of expert evidence does not occur (see Wall J in *Re CB and JB (Care Proceedings: Guidelines)* [1998] 2 FLR 211, at p 231 endorsing the view of the court's proactive duty described in *Re G (Minors) (Expert Witnesses)* [1994] 2 FLR 291).

7.106 Where pursuant to s 1(3)(g) of the CA 1989 the court is considering making any private law orders in proceedings, the court must consider the evidence of the local authority, any experts and the recommendations suggested by the guardian to the court. If, having taken all this evidence into account, the court decides to make a residence order in favour of a member of the family, subject to certain conditions in favour of the parents, the residence order may be combined with, for example, a supervision order. This was the solution adopted in *C v Solihull Metropolitan Borough Council* [1993] 1 FLR 290 by Ward J. In this case, there had been an application for a care order but the magistrates had made a supervision order. Neither order was appropriate in Ward J's view, since, in the absence of a final assessment, it would be better to make a residence order in favour of the parents subject to conditions, and an interim supervision order also subject to conditions. The conditions to be attached to the residence order were that the parents would undertake a programme of assessment and access to the child and the condition attaching to the interim supervision order was that the child be subject to various medical assessments (see also *Humberside County Council v B* [1993] 1 FLR 257 considered in detail in Chapter **4**).

Making an order is better for the child than making no order at all – A consideration of the impact of Re S and Re W – the new s 31A care plans, the new provisions on review of such plans and the potential for referring cases back to court

7.107 The last element in the welfare stage is that part which I have preferred to call the 'positive advantage principle' which is contained within s 1(5) of the CA 1989. Thus, where a court is considering whether or not to make one or more orders under the Act with respect to a child, it shall not make the order or any of the orders unless it considers that doing so would be better for the child than making no order at all. In deciding whether or not the making of an order will produce a positive advantage for the child, the court will need as much information as possible placed before it with regard to the local authority's s 31A plans for the child. The provisions of the CA 1989 have now been amended as a result of the case of *Re S (Minors); Re W (Minors)* [2002] UKHL 10, [2002] 1 FLR 815 HL, to provide that much greater attention should be focused on the care plan and not only by the courts. In *Re S*, the local authority had undertaken on the making of the care orders to attempt rehabilitation of the children with the family supported by a package of resources. Being short of money, it failed to deliver. The appeal process, however, resulted in the authority concentrating its mind and its resources so that by the time the case ultimately reached the House of Lords, the care plan was operating as originally promised. In *Re W*, there was some hope of rehabilitating the children with their family but not for some 12–18 months beyond the final hearing. The trial judge wanted to make interim care orders but felt constrained by previous case-law from so doing and thus made final care orders. That decision was reversed by the Court of Appeal and the grandparents who had planned to come from the USA to the UK to care for the children did not do so. In consequence, before the case reached the House of Lords, final care orders were reinstated by consent of all the parties. In these two cases, the Court of Appeal determined after the hearing of the two appeals, that it was necessary to introduce two 'major innovations in the construction and application of the Children Act 1989', namely the starred care plan, the starring being used to identify key elements in the plans which if not met would prompt a court-based review of the case, and 'a wider discretion' to use interim care orders as a means to supervise the actions of the local authority where the court was disatisfied as to the authority's proposals for the care of the child. The Court of Appeal adopted this approach, it said, because of the impact of the implementation of the HRA 1998, incorporating the Articles of the ECHR, on the CA 1989. The House of Lords unanimously rejected the reasoning adopted by the Court of Appeal in relation to the starring of care plans, stating that this was a 'judicial innovation passing well beyond the boundary of statutory interpretation' which would have constituted an amendment of the CA 1989. The effect of this is that the starring of any orders in existence, and there were a number after the CA 1989 ruling, are treated as set aside, although the original care orders remain in effect. With regard to the use of interim orders the House of Lords did not overrule the Court of Appeal but Lord Nicholls (at paras 89–102), whilst acknowledging that trial judges were afforded the degree of flexibility in the use of such orders as indicated by the Court of Appeal, did not see this as the major innovation, which the Court of Appeal thought it was. Lord Nicholls concluded his analysis of this power thus: 'what is more important is that … the court must always maintain a proper balance between the need to satisfy itself about the appropriateness of the care plan and the avoidance of over-zealous investigation into matters which are properly within the administrative discretion of the local authority'. This balance is a matter for the good sense of the tribunal, assisted by the advocates appearing before it. (For an exceptionally well argued and detailed analysis of all the implications of these decisions, see Tolson (2002.))

7.108 The reversal of the Court of Appeal's decisions was greeted with dismay by many guardians and children's lawyers, who had seen the decision as very necessary for children cared for by local authorities, and the comments of the House of Lords that this sort of amendment could only come about through legislation prompted the DOH to announce that amendments would be made to the CA 1989 in an effort to achieve some measure of the greater scrutiny of local authority proposals for the care of children both on the making of care orders, and of the execution of these plans. Thus s 26(2) of the CA 1989 has been extensively amended and a new s 31A has been added by the Adoption and Children Act 2002. The new s 31A provides that where proceedings are underway in which a care order might be made, then the local authority must, within such time as the court may direct, prepare a care plan (s 31A(1)). While the application is pending, the authority must keep any care plan prepared by them under review and, if it is of the opinion that some change is required, revise the plan or make a new plan accordingly (s 31A(2)). These new provisions give the courts much greater power not only as to the timing of the preparation of the plan but also, and inevitably, control over the sorts of issues the court might want the plan to specifically address. The provisions of s 26(2A) go even further, in that they provide for the reviews held on children to keep the s 31A care plan under review, and where there is no plan they provide that one should be made (s 26(2)(e) and (f)). They also provide for the appointment of a prescribed person to participate in the review, monitor the local authority's performance and, where the person considers it appropriate to do so, refer the child's case to a CAFCASS officer (s 26(2A)), who can then take the child's case back to court under court rules yet to be made (s 26(2C)). Thus the amendments to the CA 1989 potentially provide for the prescribed person to refer the case to a CAFCASS officer, who will presumably be able to return to court for review of the child's position if critical goals are not achieved, the very result the Court of Appeal had hoped to reach in the two cases. The new s 31A goes on to provide that the care plan must give any prescribed information and do so in a prescribed manner (s 31A(3)). Thus it is likely that there will be a new set of Regulations issued with regard to this prescribed information, but these were not available at the time of writing. According to the Local Authority Circular LAC 1999 (29) *Care Plans and Care Proceedings under the Children Act 1989* (which was of course released before the amendments to the Act and will be replaced in all likelihood by a new circular once the new provision is implemented), the care plan is 'one of the most important documents considered by the courts in care proceedings'. In putting its plan before the court the local authority is also expected to clarify why a package of support methods provided under Part III of the CA 1989 would be ineffective in safeguarding the child's welfare as this sort of provision would always be considered preferable to the making of compulsory orders. There is no *pro forma* for a care plan prior to implementation of s 31A, but the advice given by the DOH at the present time through the Local Authority Circular LAC 1999 (29) does provide some guidance on the structure and content of the care plan. Thus it advised that a separate care plan is required for each child who is the subject of care proceedings and the court's attention should be drawn to any important differences between the plans reflecting the individual needs of brothers and sisters (at paras 11–19). The Circular also states that one or more relevant senior officers within the local authority should have endorsed the care plan before it is presented to the court in the final hearing. The Children Act Advisory Committee has also given guidance in the past recommending in 1994 that the authority's care plan should be as full as the facts of the case would allow (at p 32). In its *Handbook of Best Practice in Children Act Cases*, the Committee gives the following advice as to the care plan (at paras 7–12).

– Ensure that the issues raised by the local authority are clearly set out with a fully researched care plan, to enable the parties to know what case they have to meet.

– If permanent placement in an alternative family is the care plan, prepare the ground as far as possible without pre-empting the court's decision.

– If the plan is for an adoptive placement, the court will be handicapped in assessing the plan and time scale, unless the child concerned has already been considered and approved by the adoption and fostering panel, and potential suitable adoptive families have been identified. It is not good practice to await the making of a care order before obtaining such information because the court is deprived of important background information and significant delay can occur in placing the child in the event of the court approving the plan.

– If the plan involves a specialist placement with therapy and/or further assessment, identify the placement of any professionals involved, together with the time scale and availability of the appropriate funding.

– If the plan depends upon the finding of facts or determination of particular issues by the court, state why and set out clear alternative proposals.

– If no firm proposal can be made, then that should be made clear by the authority and explained.

7.109 The *Handbook of Best Practice* clearly anticipated that local authorities should appreciate that their care plans will be subjected to very careful judicial scrutiny. That approach was endorsed by Wall J in *Re J (Minors) (Care: Care Plan)* [1994] 1 FLR 253 where he emphasised that if the court was not satisfied that the care plan was in the best interest of the child, or all of the facts were not known to the court, it could refuse to make a care order. He further stated that where evidence was available in relation to material parts of the care plan, such evidence and details of the placement should be made available and form part of the care plan. Wall J also emphasised, as is now regularly the case pursuant to the Directions in the Circular, that the care plan should be made before the final hearing and in consultation with the parents and the other parties, or should, at least, take their views and wishes into account. In the case of *Re T (A Minor) (Care Order: Conditions)* [1994] 2 FLR 423, the Court of Appeal stressed that it was the duty of any court hearing an application for a care order to scrutinise the local authority's care plan, and, if the court did not agree with the care plan, then it was stressed by Nourse LJ that it might refuse to make a care order although he went on to state that the cases in which it is appropriate to take such a course would no doubt be rare. The emphasis on this being a rare course of action, as referred to by Nourse LJ, was approved by Butler-Sloss LJ in the case of *Re L (Sexual Abuse: Standard of Proof)* [1996] 1 FLR 116, at p 126.

7.110 The case of *Re D and K (Care Plan: Twin Track Planning)* [1999] 2 FLR 872 has already been referred to in Chapter **5**. But the effect of the case is to underline the importance of those issues identified at para 9 of the *Handbook of Best Practice in Children Act Cases* (Children Act Advisory Committee, LCD, 1997) set out above with regard to the possibility of adoptive placements. As can be seen from the law report description of the case, ie twin track planning, the situation envisaged is where a local authority realises that there is one of two possibilities open to it with regard to the best outcome for the children: namely rehabilitation within the natural family, or adoption placement outside the family. Bracewell J considered herself handicapped in the instant case by the lack of information as to the availability of suitable adoptive parents and so repeated the guidance given by the *Handbook of Best Practice* to the effect that adoption should be considered by the panel and suitable adopters identified before the final hearing (referred to as 'twin track planning'). The judge went on to state that the court should be proactive at the early stages of a case to ensure that permanency options were investigated and described the benefits of 'concurrent planning'. The judge emphasised that concurrent planning is 'the process of working towards family reunification, while at the same time establishing an alternative permanent plan'. Local Authority Circular LAC 1999 (29) also gave specific guidance where adoption is, or may be, the plan and states that it will depend on the need for a fact finding hearing prior to planning the possibilities for the child. However, where fact finding is not crucial, and rehabilitation with the family has been ruled out, then the case of a child should go to the adoption and fostering panel and steps towards placement (and timetable) should be identified.

7.111 Once it is possessed of all the relevant information contained within the s 31A care plan, and it is fully appraised of all the options before it both in terms of which orders can be made and in favour of whom (generally this may be included within the guardian's report), then the court must go on to decide whether in all the circumstances making an order would be better for the child than making no order at all and that, indeed, making an order is in the paramount interests of the child. Again, depending on all the evidence which has been offered to it, the court will then have to decide whether it should make a care order or a supervision order.

Conduct of proceedings for a care or supervision order

7.112 The relevant court rules provide that the court may give directions as to the order of speeches and evidence at a hearing but, in the absence of such directions, the rules provide that the parties and guardian should adduce their evidence in the following order (FPC(CA 1989)R 1991, r 21 and FPR 1999, r 4.21(1) and (2)):

(1)   the applicant;
(2)   any parent or person with parental responsibility for the child;
(3)   other respondents;
(4)   (the guardian);
(5)   (the child, if he is a party to the proceedings and there is no guardian or solicitor representing the child).

The justices' clerk or a proper officer of the court or the court itself must keep a note of the substance of the oral evidence given during the course of the proceedings in relation to a care or supervision order.

7.113 Generally, the applicant local authority would seek in its opening speech to lay the evidence before the court upon which it has based an application for a care or supervision order. The local authority will then call witnesses in any order which facilitates the presentation of the case to the court as clearly as possible. Witnesses are usually called in a chronological order in which signs of significant harm to the child might have been noted. This may be followed by calling for a social workers' testimony regarding family circumstances which may indicate that the child was not receiving the requisite degree of care or that the child was beyond parental control. There will first be the 'examination-in-chief' of these witnesses, wherein the applicant will endeavour to elicit testimony from the witnesses he has called, in support of the particular interpretation of the facts which he seeks to establish. Any of the other parties may, at the completion of the evidence of any particular witness, request the right to question the witness concerned and this process is called 'cross-examination' (see further on this, Chapter **8**).

7.114 At the completion of the applicant's case any party with parental responsibility for the child or any other respondent may seek to present their side of the case and cross-examination may be undertaken by the applicant and the child's solicitor. Once the other respondents have completed their evidence the guardian can be called upon to give evidence on behalf of the child, in particular where the guardian has a contribution to make with regard to the main substantive issues in the hearing. Much of the work which guardians now do is intended to elicit whether the child has suffered or is likely to suffer significant harm and the degree to which this is attributable to the absence of reasonable parental care or control. Where there is no guardian the child, through his solicitor, can make any points which he wishes to make. Given the fact that the child would be rarely in court, there is, however, no opportunity to cross-examine him in respect of any evidence given on his behalf. This is felt by some to be unduly prejudicial to parents and those with parental responsibility where evidence is sought to be produced to the court by means of video-recorded interviews with the child. The courts will be extremely cautious in attaching weight to such video evidence (see further, Chapter **8**).

7.115 It should be stressed that the whole point of the CA 1989 was to try to steer the courts into adopting a far more inquisitorial approach in care proceedings than the traditional adversarial approach previously adopted. Extensive training is now given to judges to try to ensure that the judges, as far as possible, try to encourage this more inquisitorial approach.

7.116 It has already been noted that the reports of experts and the guardian will have had to have been circulated to all parties and will have to have been lodged with the court in advance of the hearing. Indeed, the court dealing with the case must have read in advance any documents which have been filed under r 17 of the court rules in respect of the hearing. This should enable courts better to follow the evidence of expert witnesses when they are called by any party to the proceedings. The *Handbook of Best Practice in Children Act Cases* (LCD, 1997) at para 21 actually advises that it is both desirable and saves court time if the judge who is to be listed for the full hearing in the care case is also the judge who has the determination of the final directions appointment.

7.117 Finally, after hearing all the evidence, the court must make its decision as soon as is practicable (FPC(CA 1989)1991, r 20(4)). When making any order or refusing any application the court must state any findings of fact, complete Form FC22 and give the reasons for its decision (see r 21(6) as substituted). The justices' clerk must record any reasons given by the magistrates in writing (see r 21(5)) since the parties are entitled to know the reasons and findings. Any failure to put the reasons and the findings down in writing renders the decision void (see *W v Hertfordshire County Council* [1993] 1 FLR 118 and *Devon County Council v S* [1993] 1 FLR 842). It is also important in giving the reasons for their decision that the court mentions any factors, even if these appear obvious, which they brought into the balancing exercise (see *Re B* (1992) *The Times*, July 16). Where the magistrates have decided to take a different course from that recommended by a guardian ad litem, then it was very important for them to state their reasons for adopting a different course (*S v Oxfordshire County Council* [1993] 1 FLR 452). It was also made clear in that case that when justices are giving their findings of fact and their reasons they should first set out the relevant facts in chronological order or under such headings as might be convenient, making it clear what was in dispute and what was not, and that they made findings on any matter in dispute.

7.118 Where a care order is made, it must be recorded in writing on Form C32 and where a supervision order is made it must be recorded in writing on Form C35. A copy of the relevant order must then be served as soon as is practicable by the justices' clerk or the proper officer on the parties and any person with whom the child may be living (see FPC(CA 1989)R 1991, r 21(7)).

7.119 Although the court rules do not now require the court to engage in an oral explanation to the various parties involved of the effect of the making of a care order, it is suggested that good practice would dictate that the court should engage in such an oral explanation.

7.120 An example for the format of this explanation was given first in *A Child in Trust: Jasmine Beckford* (the Jasmine Beckford Report) (DHSS, 1985), at pp 169–170. It was suggested that the explanation should contain the following information.

(1)   A statement that upon the court's decision to make a care order, the particular local authority, through its appropriate committee and officers in the social services department, will be responsible for the child until he is aged 18. (Where a supervision order is being made instead, the court should explain that the child is being placed under the supervision of the local authority social services and that this supervision will continue for at least one year.)

(2)   A statement that it will be for the local authority to decide, under a care order, where the child will live; and that the local authority has the right to decide whether the child would be allowed to go home. (Similarly, for supervision orders, a statement should be made that it will be for the supervising officer to give directions as to where the child should live, what activities the child might engage in and whether the court has decided to make any directions for psychiatric or medical treatment of the child.)

(3)   An explanation that where a care order has been made and the local authority decides to allow the child home, it will be for social workers to visit him at home in pursuance of the exercise of their parental responsibilities under s 33, in order to ensure that the child is being properly looked after.

(4)   A statement that if at any time it is thought that the child is not likely to be treated properly he may be removed from home by the local authority, as the local authority is still holding a care order which gives it parental responsibility under s 33 of the CA 1989.

(5)   A statement to the parents and the child (where the child is in court) that each has a separate independent right at any time to apply to the court to put to an end to the care order; and that if they decided to take this step they could apply for public funding (legal aid) in their application. No promises would be given by the court that the order

would be discharged. The local authority itself may also ask the court at any time to discharge the order. In that event, it was more likely that the court would agree to do so, because the social services generally know when it is no longer necessary for the child to be away from his parents' home. (In addition, under the Review of Children's Cases Regulations 1991, SI 1991/894 local authorities, when conducting reviews of the children subject to care orders, must actively consider in the review, together with the child, whether it is appropriate either for the authority or the child to apply for the discharge of any orders in respect of the child.)

(6)   A question directed to the parties asking if they understood and whether they wished to say anything more.

It was further stressed in the Jasmine Beckford Report that in making a care order the court had no power then to make any recommendations or to endorse the expectations of the local authority.

Consideration of contact

7.121   It should be noted that before making a care order with respect to any child, the court has to consider the arrangements which the authority has made or proposes to make for affording any personal contact with a child to be made a subject of an order; and invites the parties to the proceedings to comment on those arrangements (see s 34(11) of the CA 1989; see also Chapter **10** where the whole issue of contact is considered in detail).

Orders which may be made when the case is proved

7.122   In addition to the range of private law orders under ss 8 and 16 of the CA 1989, which may now be made in proceedings brought under s 31 of the CA 1989 (see para **7.140**), the court also has the power to choose to make either a care order (s 31(1)(a)) or a supervision order (s 31(1)(b)). Just because the local authority is requesting that the court makes a supervision order linked to a residence order under s 8, rather than a care order, does not mean that the court must accede to its request (see *Re K (Supervision Orders)* [1995] 1 FLR 675.

The effects of making a care order

Who is the designated authority?

7.123   Where the court decides to make a care order, the local authority designated in a care order must be the authority within whose area the child is ordinarily resident or, where the child does not reside in a local authority area, the local authority within whose area any circumstances arose in consequence of which the order has been made (CA 1989, s 31(8)(a) and (b)). In the case of *Northampton County Council v Islington LBC* [1999] 2 FLR 881, a question arose on the point of interpretation of s 31(8) as between two local authorities. In this case, following the parents separation, the care of N (aged 12) varied between London and Northampton. Care proceedings were begun by Islington LBC at a time when N was living in that borough but he was then removed and placed in a children's home in Croydon. Quite separately, proceedings were commenced in Northampton with respect to his two sisters who lived there with their mother. The s 31 criteria were not contested and there was no opposition to the making of a care order to Northampton with regard to the sisters. The issue in the case was which authority should be the designated authority for N. The judge at first instance favoured the designation of Northampton so that N could ultimately be placed in a foster home near to his maternal family. He held that this could be achieved because, on the facts, he held that N was not 'ordinarily' resident in any authority and therefore the court had discretion under s 31(8)(b) to determine which of the two authorities should be designated. Northampton appealed against this decision and the Court of Appeal found instead that Islington should be the designated authority and the appeal should be allowed. In the course of giving judgment, Thorpe LJ reviewed the main first instance reported decisions on the issue, starting with that of Grace LJ in *Re BC (A Minor) (Care Order: Appropriate Local Authority)* [1995] 3 FCR 598 in which it was held that ordinary residence if it is to be determined by reference to where the child is living before being placed in interim care (the 'stop the clock' approach), that approach had been criticised in subsequent decisions, see for example, *Gateshead Metropolitan Council v L and Another* [1996] 2 FLR 179 and Holman J in *North Yorkshire County Council v Wiltshire County Council* [1999] 2 FLR 560. In all the circumstances, Thorpe LJ concluded that:

(a) the word 'ordinary' should be read into s 31(8)(b) so that it should then read 'where the child does not ordinarily reside';

(b) the disregard provision in s 105(6) of the CA 1989 is to be construed as Bracewell J had done in *Re BC* (ie adopt the 'stop the clock' approach);

(c) developments affecting the family during the disregard period should only be considered as an exceptional case;

(d) where a child is not ordinarily resident in any authority, and therefore s 31(8)(b) applies, the liberal approach of the reported decisions in drawing in so many considerations is not correct. The relevant parts of s 31(8) were intended to achieve a simple mechanism to determine the question of designation of the appropriate authority and on the facts of this case Islington would be designated and the appeal allowed.

7.124 Where during the period between the making of an application for a care order and the making of the order the child becomes ordinarily resident in the area of a new local authority, the order must be in favour of that new authority, even although the previous authority has had the conduct of the application and has been providing social work support to the family. In this sort of situation, it was held in *L v London Borough of Bexley* [1996] 2 FLR 595 (and approved in *Re C (Care Order: Appropriate Local Authority)* [1997] 1 FLR 544) that the new authority should be involved in and send a representative to attend the proceedings. This is in order that the court can be satisfied that the new authority is committed to and has the financial and practical resources to implement the proposed care plan. It should also be determined whether or not it is appropriate for the new local authority to become a party to or take over the conduct of the proceedings. Whichever of the two actually conducts the proceedings, there must be close, early and full co-operation between the two authorities and the s 31A care plan must be prepared with close liaison between the two of them. It should be submitted as a joint plan and if there are any problems with any aspect of it which requires clarification before the final order the court must be made clear as to who bears the responsibility for a particular feature.

Duties and responsibilities of the designated authority

7.125 The care order places the designated authority under a duty to receive the child into its care and to continue to keep him in its care while the order remains in force (CA 1989, s 33(1) and (2)), and it further gives the authority parental responsibility for the child (s 33(3)–(7), and see earlier in this chapter for a detailed discussion of these provisions). Given that the effect of the care order is to give local authorities the power to determine the extent to which parents can exercise their parental responsibilities then, where parents wish to challenge the exercise of the local authority's discretion, they will have to do so by means of judicial review unless they can bring themselves within the operation of the representations procedure provided by the local authorities pursuant to s 26(3) of the CA 1989 (see Chapter **11** for an analysis of both approaches).

The extinguishing or cessation of other orders

7.126 The making of a care order will operate to extinguish a residence order or any s 8 order, and any wardship order can also cease to be of effect. The making of a care order will also bring to an end a supervision order under s 35 and a school attendance order. The care order will continue in force until the child reaches the age of 18, unless brought to an end earlier. It should be noted that no care or supervision order can be made in respect of a child who has reached the age of 17 (or 16 in the case of a child who is married) (s 31(3)). Where the court makes a care order, it has no power to add any direction as the responsibility for the child who is then placed firmly with the local authority and it cannot seek to control any of the local authority's actions. It was emphasised, in *Kent County Council v C* [1993] 1 FLR 308, that the court cannot, as happened in that case, direct that a guardian be allowed to have continued involvement in order to investigate the rehabilitation process and apply to have contact terminated if the guardian thought this appropriate. Thus, once the care order has been made, it gives the local authority the right to follow through on its s 31A care plans for the child, and to place the child in accordance with those plans. Under the newly amended provisions of s 26 of the CA 1989 (see para **7.108**) the prescribed person has the duty to be present at the reviews, which must consider the plans, monitor the local authority's performance, and refer the child's case to a CAFCASS officer, who then has the right to take the child's case back to court (s 26(2C) of the CA 1989).

The effects of making a supervision order

7.127 It may be thought appropriate in some cases involving issues of child protection to continue to involve the local authority in some way without using the measure of a care order. This can be done by the making of a supervision order under s 35 of the CA 1989; the effect of the supervision order is governed both by the provisions of s 35 and Sch 3, Parts I and II which also provide for the powers and duties of the supervising officer.

7.128 There are a very considerable number of cases which consider in detail the criteria for choosing between making a care or a supervision order. In the important case of *Re O (Care or Supervision Order)* [1996] 2 FLR 755, Hale J reviewed the authorities stating that the wide range of local authority powers under Part III of the CA 1989 and Sch 2, coupled with s 1(5) meant that the court should begin with the preference for the less interventionist approach unless there are cogent reasons to the contrary and also stated that care orders do not allow the court to assist in the ongoing care of the child, whereas a supervision order does permit the court to do so. Hale J held that the magistrate in this particular case should have been prepared at least to consider the effect of supervision orders and the benefits which could have been derived from them before going straight to the most Draconian order, namely a care order, provided for by the CA 1989. Following on this decision Hale J returned to give further guidance upon the choice between the two orders in the case of *Oxfordshire County Council v L (Care or Supervision Order)* [1998] 1 FLR 70. In this case, Hale emphasised that where a local authority does not seek a full care order, then whilst the court has the power to force the more Draconian order upon it, the court should only make a care order where there are strong and cogent reasons for doing so. It was wrong to impose a care order simply in order to encourage the local authority by placing statutory duties upon it. She also emphasised that where a child is to be placed at home, it should be remembered that Parliament intended the very serious step of removing a child from home only to occur where the circumstances warranted it and normally via independent judicial authority, rather than as a result of a purely administrative decision. Hale J is here recognising the ability of local authorities, who do obtain a care order but where the child is then placed at home, to be able to remove the child at will given the powers of parental responsibility which they are able to exercise pursuant to a care order. As to the role of an appellate court in circumstances where it could not be said that the magistrate had been plainly wrong to hold that a child's continuing protection requires a care order, Sir Stephen Brown, then President of the Family Division, ruled that it was therefore not the place of the appellate court to intervene (see *Re C (Care or Supervision Order)* [1999] 2 FLR 621).

7.129 Since the implementation of the HRA 1998, the courts must also be mindful that the making of any order on their part must be a proportionate response to the feared risk to the child. Thus, the Court of Appeal emphasised in *Re O (Supervision Order: Future Harm)* [2001] 1 FCR 289 that where the risk to the child is at the lower end of the spectrum, the making of a supervision order instead of a care order accords more with the demands of Article 8(1) of the ECHR (right to respect for one's private and family life). A rather more unusual problem arises if the choice is as between a supervision order and either no order or a s 16 family assistance order, although the demands of Article 8(1) are just as relevant. This situation was before the court in *Re K (Supervision Orders)* [1999] 2 FLR 303 where a child had died in suspicious circumstances only a few days after birth, and the local authority had commenced care proceedings in respect of the mother's three elder children, who were initially placed with foster carers. The children were returned to the mother under the care plan, and the family moved into a different local authority area. Both authorities argued for a supervision order in favour of the second authority, on the basis that there was insufficient evidence to establish that the mother was responsible for the death of the baby but that the threshold criteria were met in other ways. The mother denied any involvement in the baby's death and considered that the children had not suffered significant harm, but she accepted that because of her personal circumstances there was a risk that the children could suffer significant harm in the future, and that therefore a supervision order for one year was appropriate. The guardian opposed the agreement between mother and the authorities arguing either that unless some finding of fact was made in relation to the baby's death, the threshold criteria were not met, or if they were met, the so-called 'no order principle' prohibited the making of a supervision order. He submitted that the supervision order would not improve the children's situation as in any event they would remain with their mother, and, because they were already on the child protection register, with or without an order the local authority had a duty to monitor their situation. Wall J made the supervision order observing that a guardian's opinions about the threshold criteria could not be ruled inadmissible, even if they were at odds with the views of all the other parties. The guardian had a duty to represent the child and to place all matters relevant to the child's welfare before the court.

However, where, as here, the local authority and the parents had reached a sensible agreement which clearly protected the child and was in no sense collusive, then the guardian should think long and hard before seeking to upset that agreement or putting forward alternative contentious proposals. The judge held that the threshold criteria were met in this case because of the mother's isolation and vulnerability, particularly her history of relationships involving domestic violence. The court held that a supervision order should only be imposed if it made things better for the children. It observed that it would be wrong to make a supervision order which was not in the interests of the children simply to encourage the local authority to perform its statutory duties, and where performance of the duties under Part III of the CA 1989 would meet the children's needs, a supervision order ought not to be made. In this case, however, the court held that it was appropriate to make a supervision order rather than no order because, although the children would in any event remain in the mother's care with local authority supervision, under a supervision order the mother was more likely to co-operate with the authority, the authority would allocate greater resources to monitoring the family, the authority would be fully involved in the family's progress, and the mother would have obligations placed upon her. Wall J here was correctly observing the principles of s 1(5) of the CA 1989 and of Article 8(1) of the ECHR in that the supervision order should only be made if the child needs more protection than that afforded by provision under Part III, or by voluntary arrangements and that was clearly the case here.

7.130 Where a supervision order is in force, it is the duty of the supervisor to advise, assist and befriend the supervised child, to take such steps as are reasonably necessary to give effect to the order and, where the order has not been fully complied with, or the supervisor considers that the order may no longer be necessary, to consider whether or not to apply for the discharge of the order. While the order is in force, the supervisor can direct that the child participate in certain activities, undergo medical or psychiatric assessment, or can ask the court to direct that the child undergo medical or psychiatric treatment (CA 1989, Sch 3, paras 2–5). It should be noted that whereas directions for treatment are wholly the responsibility of the court and must be laid down by the court, the court can, however, delegate to the supervisor the specification of directions regarding examination (see *Re H (Supervision Order)* [1994] 2 FLR 979, and see also *Re B (Supervision Order: Parental Undertaking)* [1996] 1 FLR 676). The supervisor can direct with the consent of any responsible person, that that person takes all reasonable steps to ensure that the supervised child complies with any directions or activities, medical and psychiatric examinations or with any directions as to medical and psychiatric treatment, and that the responsible person participate in certain activities. This particular provision may be extremely useful in dealing with cases where there are real concerns as to the continuing possibility of significant harm, because the supervisor can require the parent to participate in such activities as attending a family centre for assessment. This option was considered but ultimately rejected by the court in favour of a care order in *Re D (Care or Supervision Order)* [1993] 2 FLR 423.

7.131 A supervision order has a limited life, ending one year from the date upon which it was made and the prescribed number of days in respect of which, for example, a residence condition might now be included without limitation, following amendments effected by the Courts and Legal Services Act 1990, Sch 3, para 7(1). The supervision order can be extended or further extended for such periods as the court thinks fit, except that it cannot be extended to run beyond the end of 3 years beginning with the date on which it was made (Sch 3, para 6(4)).

7.132 One of the factors which might influence either a guardian in making a report to the court, or the court itself in considering a supervision order, is the availability to the court of the range of private law orders in ss 8 and 16 of the CA 1989 to complement the supervision order. Thus, the court might wish to make a residence order to a grandparent whilst recognising the risk to the child, and may decide to make a supervision order alongside the residence order. It should, perhaps, be made clear at this stage that a residence order will settle the arrangements as to whom the child should live with and will further give that person parental responsibility (see ss 8(1) and 12 of the CA 1989). Contact with the child's parents might be controlled, if necessary, so that an order might be made allowing contact with the mother in the grandparents' home but a prohibited steps order also made forbidding the father from having contact with the child.

Variation, discharge and termination of care and supervision orders

7.133 Under the CA 1989, the court does not possess any power to vary a care order, but can, on the application of any person entitled to apply for the discharge of the care order, substitute a supervision order for a care order (see s 39(4) of the CA 1989 and *Re O (Care: Discharge of Care Order)* [1999] 2 FLR 119). Before the court can order such a substitution it must be able to satisfy itself that the welfare principle has been adhered to, and that, by making a substitution, it does not have to be satisfied again that the threshold conditions are met (s 39(5)). The rationale for this must be that the conditions were obviously met at the time the original order was made and, rather than redirecting the court to go over conditions which have already been satisfied, it is better to focus on whether the substituted order will be in the child's paramount interest (s 1(1) and (3)) and will be better for the child than not ordering such a substitution (s 1(5)).

7.134 A care order, including an interim care order can be discharged by the court on the application of the child himself, the local authority designated in the care order or any person with parental responsibility for the child (s 39(1)). It should be noted that this will include parents, since the making of a care order does not operate to terminate their responsibility, but it would exclude grandparents or former foster parents with whom the child had lived under a residence order and who had previously held parental responsibility in consequence of that order, because the making of a care order will have discharged the residence order (s 91(2)). This will mean, therefore, that such persons will be unable to apply for the discharge of the care order.

7.135 The conditions which must be satisfied before the court can grant an order discharging the care order are contained within s 1 of the CA 1989. The court must determine that the discharge will be in the paramount interest of the child and, since the order is an order under Part IV of the CA 1989, the welfare checklist comes into operation and the court must, therefore, consider the likelihood of harm occurring to the child. The fact that there is no likelihood of harm occurring is not in itself justification for discharging the order. Instead, the question is whether the child's welfare will best be served by being discharged from care. In all these circumstances the onus of proving this lies with the person seeking discharge of the order (see *Re S (Discharge of Care Order)* [1995] 2 FLR 639, and *Re O (Care: Discharge of Care Order)* [1999] 2 FLR 119).

7.136 A phased return home may be achieved by substituting a supervision order together with a residence order containing specific conditions. In such situations, an application would have to be made by the local authority for such a variation, so that the court may be dealing with an application by a parent for discharge of a care order which is then being countered by the local authority applying for a substituted supervision order together with a residence order to achieve a phased return of the child to his home.

7.137 In those circumstances where the court refuses an application for the discharge of a care order or the substitution of a supervision order for a care order, the CA 1989 provides that no further application can be made within 6 months of the determination of such application, unless the court grants leave (s 91(15)(a)).

7.138 A care order will terminate when the child reaches the age of 18, unless it is brought to an end earlier (CA 1989, s 91(12)). It will also be terminated by the making of a residence order (s 91(1)), since an application can be made for such an order even though the child is the subject of a care order (s 91(1)). The child can also make an application for a residence order to be made in favour of a particular person if, for some reason, that person is unable or unwilling to make an application himself and provided that the child is of sufficient understanding. This may certainly be the case where such person would be ineligible for public funding (legal aid), whereas the child would generally be eligible for public funding subject to the means and merits test in respect of an application for a s 8 order.

7.139 It is further provided in the CA 1989 that a care order will also terminate where the child is taken to live in Northern Ireland, the Isle of Man or any of the Channel Islands, provided the court's prior permission for such removal has been obtained and the relevant authorities in those jurisdictions have indicated their willingness to take over the care of any such child, and the court has since been notified of their willingness (see s 101(4) and for the conditions, and the Children (Prescribed Orders (Northern Ireland, Guernsey and Isle of Man)) Regulations 1991, SI 1991/2032).

7.140 As far as supervision orders are concerned, these can be varied or discharged on an application being made by the child, the supervisor or any person who has parental responsibility for the child. The conditions which must be satisfied before the court can order variation or discharge of the terms of the supervision order are, once more, those provided by s 1 of the CA 1989. Where the variation sought is actually the substitution of the supervision order by a care order this cannot in fact be done under these provisions, and so the requirements of s 31(2) would again have to be met, since s 39(5) only applies to the substitution of a care order by a supervision order and not vice versa. Where such an application is made the court must consider whether it is necessary to appoint a guardian (s 41(6)(d)). This will more especially be the case where concerns have previously been focused around issues of the risks to the child and the child is now felt to be at great risk whilst on a supervision order. The supervisor may seek variation of the terms of the supervision order where the earlier order is not being complied with, which may include a requirement that the child live in a specified place for a period or periods so specified, participate in certain activities and undergo a medical examination or psychiatric examination or psychiatric or medical treatment (Sch 3, Part 1, paras 2–5). No court should include the requirement that the child undergo such assessment or treatment unless it is satisfied that where the child has sufficient understanding to make an informed decision, he has consented to its inclusion (Sch 3, Part I, para 5(5)(a)). Where a supervision order has imposed a requirement on a 'responsible person', not being a person with parental responsibility, that person can also apply for variation of the order as it relates to him (s 39(3)). No further application can be made for the discharge of a supervision order within 6 months of the previous application except with the leave of the court (s 91(15)(b)). It should be noted that a supervision order will terminate when the child reaches the age of 18 (s 91(13)), or when a care order is made (s 91(3)), or when an adoption order is made, or when the court takes action in respect of the child by making orders under the Child Abduction and Custody Act 1985 (Sch 3, Part II, para 6(2)).

7.141 Where the application being made is an application to extend the period of the supervision order there is no power to make a care order in the absence of a specific application under s 31 (see *Re A (A Minor) (Supervision Order: Extension)* [1995] 1 FLR 335). In the case of *Re A*, it was however held that s 31 criteria do not need to be satisfied where there is an application for extension of a supervision order, since otherwise Sch 3, para 6 enabling an extension application being made by the supervisor would have no purpose.

Appeals

7.142 The CA 1989 provides that any party to proceedings for a care or supervision order (including interim orders) has a right of appeal (s 94(1)). The appeal lies to the High Court Family Division against the making of or refusal to make any such order by a magistrates' court. An appeal against the making of or refusal to make any such orders by a judge in the county court or in the High Court lies to the Court of Appeal, Civil Division. In contrast with the old law, this meant that children, parents, local authorities and anyone else who attained party status in the proceedings, have equal rights to appeal against decisions made by the courts with which they are dissatisfied. This right of appeal has been exercised extensively in the first 11 years of the operation of the CA 1989, and since 1999, as a result of the number of appeals which were being made, appeals to the Court of Appeal now require leave so that hopeless cases can be filtered out of the system and prevent wastage of time and resources. (See RSC Ord 59, r 1A and 1 B and see *Practice Note* [1999] 1 All ER 186 which sets out the practice and procedure for dealing with applications for leave to appeal to the Court of Appeal. See also *Re N (Residence: Hopeless Appeals)* [1995] 2 FLR 210.) Whereas local authorities used to have to seek to use wardship as a means of remedying their lack of a right of appeal under the old law where a court had refused to make an order, there has been no shortage of cases brought by local authorities under the 1989 Act exercising the local authority's right to appeal against the courts' refusal to make orders (see, eg, *Croydon London Borough Council v A (No 1)* [1992] 2 FLR 341; *W v Hertfordshire County Council* [1993] 1 FLR 118; *Gateshead Meropolitan Borough Council v N* [1993] 1 FLR 811; and *Suffolk County Council v C* [1999] 1 FLR 259).

Procedure

7.143 Specific guidance on appeals from family proceedings courts under s 94 of the CA 1989 are provided in section 6 of the *Handbook on Best Practice in Children Act Cases* (Children Act Advisory Committeee, LCD, 1997). The guidance is very clear (at p 31) that careful attention needs to be paid to the requirements of r 4 of the FPR 1991, as amended. An appeal against the making, varying or discharging of or the refusal to make, vary or discharge any care or supervision orders (including interim orders) is lodged by filing in the court in which the appeal is to be heard, and serving on the parties to the proceedings and any guardian a notice of appeal in writing setting out the grounds upon which the appellant relies (FPR 1991, r 4.22(2)(a), as amended). Accompanying this, there must be filed a certified copy of the summons or application and of the order appealed against and of any order staying its execution, a copy of the notes of evidence, including any reports and witness statements which form part of the evidence in the court below (see *Re U (T)* [1993] 2 FCR 565, at p 572), and a copy of any reasons given for the decision. It has been emphasised by the former President of the Family Division, Sir Stephen Brown, in a direction issued by him, that these documents must be filed in the registry (which is also a care centre) nearest to the court in which the order appealed from was made (see *President's Direction* [1992] 1 FLR 463). The notice of appeal must be filed and served within 14 days after the determination against which an appeal is brought (FPR 1991, r 4.22(3)(a)), unless it is an appeal against an interim care or supervision order, in which case it must be within 7 days or with the leave of the court to which, or judge to whom, the appeal is to be brought, within such other time as that court or judge may direct (r 4.22(3)(c)).

7.144 Where the appeal is brought in the Family Division of the High Court by a party other than the child, but the child was a party to the proceedings in a lower court and is affected by the appeal, the procedure to be followed is laid down in *Practice Direction* [1985] 1 All ER 896. The notice of motion should be served on the children's guardian appointed in the court below, and no order is required appointing him guardian in the High Court proceedings providing his consent to act and his solitictor's certificate, referred to in the Rules of Court, are filed in the Principal Registry by that solicitor as soon as practicable after the service of motion (FPR 1991, r 9.2(7)). Where any parties who were respondents in the earlier proceedings wish to contend, on appeal, that the decision of the lower court should be varied, either in any event or in the event of the appeal being allowed in whole or in part, or by way of cross-appeal that the decision of the lower court was wrong in whole or in part, then they must, within 14 days of receipt of the notice of appeal, file and serve on all other parties to the appeal, notice in writing, setting out the grounds upon which they rely (r 4.22(5)). No such right exists, however, in respect of an appeal against an interim care or supervision order made under s 38.

7.145 An appeal to the High Court will be heard and determined by a single judge who will normally sit in open court (*President's Practice Direction (Children Act 1989) Appeals* [1992] 1 FLR 463 and see also *Re PB (Hearings in Open Court)* [1996] 2 FLR 765) and an application to that court to withdraw the appeal and have it dismissed with the consent of all the parties to amend the grounds of appeal may be heard by a district judge of that court (FPR 1991, r 4.22(7)).

7.146 Where it is sought to bring fresh evidence before the appeal court, the case of *Croydon London Borough Council v A (No 3)* [1992] 2 FLR 350 provides guidance as to how such fresh evidence should be dealt with. In that case the court ruled that the proper approach for the appellate court to take was to consider, first, what view to take of the judge's decision below on the material that was before him, ignoring, at that stage, any fresh evidence which might have been adduced before the appellate court. If the judge below was plainly wrong, or had misdirected himself by taking into account some matter he should not have done or by failing to take into account some matter he should have done, the appeal should be allowed, unless the fresh evidence led to a different conclusion. Where the appellate court was minded to dismiss the appeal, it would be necessary to look at the fresh evidence, having regard to the disadvantages of having to decide on statement evidence only. It has been emphasised in *Croydon London Borough Council v A (No 1)* [1992] 2 FLR 341, that on an appeal from the magistrates' court under the CA 1989, the appeal court has wide-ranging powers to consider and deal with the case in the same way in which the court below would have done, but it is not empowered to hear evidence save in *exceptional* circumstances.

Powers of the appellate court

7.147 It should be noted that the power of the appellate courts in children's cases may be exercised in any one of three ways.

(1)　*Remit the case with directions.* Where the appellate court is satisfied that the order was wrong but is uncertain, on the basis of evidence before it, as to what order should be made, it may remit the case with such directions for the care of the child in the interim period as are consistent with the paramountcy of the child's welfare. This was done, for example, in *Humberside County Council v B* [1993] 1 FLR 257, where Booth J discharged an interim care order on appeal and remitted the matter back to the magistrates to consider what order to make.

(2)　*Substitution of orders.* Where the appellate court is satisfied that the lower court's order was plainly wrong in law and it has before it all the relevant evidence, the court may substitute its own order where it reaches a different conclusion. See, for example, the care orders made by the Court of Appeal in *Lancashire County Council v B* [1999] 2 FLR 833, where the first instance judge had found that the threshold criteria could not be established because he could not determine who had been responsible for the injuries but made an interim care order pending the appeal; and the orders again made by the Court of Appeal in *Re G (Children) (Care Order: Threshold Criteria)* [2001] 2 FLR 1111, where the first instance judge had declined to make a care order in relation to the elder brother but the Court of Appeal found that the threshold criteria were satisfied and made the care order requested by the local authority.

(3)　*Hearing evidence.* In very exceptional circumstances, as has already been noted, the appellate court may hear evidence, although where it is the case that either or both of the parties are seeking to put fresh evidence before the court, then, again, as has been noted, great care will be exercised by the court in such circumstances in accordance with guidance issued by the Court of Appeal in both the pre-CA 1989 case of *M v M (Transfer of Custody: Appeal)* [1987] 2 FLR 146 and in the post-CA 1989 cases of *Hounslow London Borough Council v A* [1993] 1 FLR 702, where there was fresh evidence that the father's cohabitation had broken down, and in *Croydon London Borough Council v A (No 3)* [1992] 2 FLR 350, where there was fresh evidence that rehabilitation of the child with the parents was not working well. The appellate court may then either allow the appeal and substitute its own orders or dismiss the appeal. In cases where new evidence suggests the lower court reached its decision without being aware of some crucial factors, the appellate court may remit the case for reconsideration in the wake of such evidence.

When drafting a notice of appeal in all these situations, it is vital that the document reports fully the reasons upon which the lower courts' decision was based and, where the sequence of events in the case is very complex, it is further helpful to the appellate court to have before it a chronology of events (see *Re B* (1992) *The Times*, July 16). The court rules require magistrates, as well as judges, to provide written reasons for their decisions which must be announced at the time of the decision (see *Hillingdon London Borough v H* [1992] 2 FLR 372, *W v Hertfordshire County Council* [1993] 1 FLR 118 and *London Borough of Croydon v R* [1997] 2 FLR 675) and these reasons must be sufficiently detailed for an appellate court to be able to scrutinise them and must be set down in the manner prescribed by the Court of Appeal (see *Re M (s 94 Appeals)* [1995] 1 FLR 546).

Orders pending appeals

7.148 It was provided for the first time by the CA 1989 that the court has power to make orders pending appeals in care or supervision order proceedings (s 40). It was clearly the intention of Parliament to provide some continuity in the child's life by reason of the powers which had been given and, since such orders come within Part IV of the CA 1989, they are again subject to the application of the three limbs of the welfare principle (s 1(4)(b)). The criteria which must be met are that there must have been some intervention already in the child's life in the proceedings represented by the making of a care or supervision order or an interim order (s 40). There is, however, a lacuna if the intention is to appeal against a refusal to make a first interim order since an earlier emergency protection order would not seem to qualify as an order being made pending such an appeal in order to provide for the child to remain in the care of the local authority (s 40(1)(b) and (2)(b)).

Where the court dismisses an application for a care order and the child is, at that time, subject to an interim care order, the court may make a further interim care order pending appeal (s 40(1)) as, for example, in *Lancashire County Council v B* [2000] 1 FLR 583. Where a court dismisses an application for a care order or supervision order, the court may make a supervision order pending the appeal (s 40(2)). The court, further, has the power in each case to include directions in the order on any matter to do with the child's welfare as it sees fit. Where the court grants an application to discharge a care or supervision order, it can order that, pending the appeal, the decision is not to have effect (s 40(3)(a)), or that the order should remain in force subject to any directions it gives (s 40(3)(b)). Where an appeal is lodged against a decision of another court with respect to an order pending appeal, the appellate court may extend these orders (s 40(5)). Those orders which are made pursuant to this provision can only have effect until the date upon which the appeal is determined (s 40(6)(a)) or, where no appeal is made, the period during which an appeal could have been made (s 40(6)(b)). Where the court has made a residence order, together with any other s 8 orders in care or supervision order proceedings as it has the power to do under s 1(3)(g), it further has the power to postpone the coming into effect of the order or to impose temporary requirements pending an appeal (s 11(7)). It should be stressed that under no circumstances should the power to make these orders pending the outcome of the appeals lead to unnecessary delay or contribute to adverse effects on the child's welfare as a result of lingering uncertainty. Appeals should generally be heard by the High Court Family Division within 28 days, and the Court of Appeal is equally bound in children's cases by the 'no delay' principle to be found in s 1 (2) of the CA 1989. Other issues relating to evidence on appeals is considered in detail in Chapter **8**.

Secure accommodation proceedings under s 25 of the CA 1989

7.149 The introduction of regulation by the courts on the use of secure accommodation by local authorities took place for the first time in 1983, with the Secure Accommodation Regulations 1983, SI 1983/99. The workings of the Regulations were, however, extensively criticised (see Bullock (1988)) and the government conducted its own review of secure accommodation in 1988. Another study identified severe problems in the court process revealing that: court proceedings were frequently cursory, an average hearing lasting 13 minutes, the shortest 3 minutes; legal representation of children was extremely variable but predominantly passive, with solicitors observed taking instructions from child clients at the very last moment, seen as siding with the social worker, not contesting orders but proceeding in what the solicitors perceived to be in the client's best interests; and magistrates were seen as simply rubber-stamping appplications especially renewals. The report concluded that it was 'clear that the idea that judicial hearings protect the liberty of individuals against excessive State intervention is, so far as secure accommodation is concerned, little more than libertarian rhetoric'. The report also specifically recommended the extension of the guardian ad litem system to cover children in secure accommodation since:

> 'no independent assessment of the children's needs, rights and interests was provided to the courts and it was assumed that the care authority's social worker would without conflict be dispassionate expert and prosecution witness. This seemed to us a point where ambiguity was both unnecessary and unhelpful and it is to be hoped that the extension of the guardian system will go some way towards resolving the problem' (see Harris and Timms (1993), at p 211).

As a result of all these trenchant criticisms, the provisions in s 25 were included in the CA 1989 and new Regulations, the Children (Secure Accommodation) Regulations 1991, were issued subject to very detailed guidance contained in *The Children Act 1989: Guidance and Regulations* vol 4 'Residential Care' (DOH, 1991). In addition, the list of specified proceedings in which guardians were to be appointed included secure accommodation proceedings (s 41(6)(i) of the CA 1989). As was pointed out in para **7.2**, it is only proposed in this chapter to examine the making of secure accommodation orders under s 25 of the CA 1989, the so called 'civil route' into secure accommodation (see J Timms, *Representing Children* (Sweet & Maxwell, 1995) at p 219). The use of such orders in criminal proceedings is examined in Chapter **9**.

The role of secure accommodation in the child care system

7.150 The guidance as well as successive government reports states that secure accommodation has an important role to play amongst the range of residential services and facilities provided by local authorities. Both in terms of the safety and security of the premises, the skills and enhanced levels of staff available and the specialist programmes which can be provided these days, a secure placement may be the most appropriate and *only* way of responding to some of the most serious cases of children who may be at risk of suffering significant harm, who may engage in serious episodes of self-harm (as in the case of *Re D*, see para **7.133**) or who pose a risk to others (as in *Re K* [2001] 1 FLR 527, also at para **7.133**). However, as the guidance emphasises, restricting the liberty of children is a serious step which must only be taken where there is no appropriate alternative. It must be a last resort in the sense that all else must first have been comprehensively considered and rejected, never because no other placement was available at the relevant time because of inadequacies in staffing, because the child is simply being a nuisance or runs away from his accommodation and is not likely to suffer harm in doing so, and never as a form of punishment. It is important, in considering the possibility of a secure placement that there is a clear view of the aims and objectives of such a placement and that those providing the accommodation can fully meet those aims and objectives, and this is more particularly the case if it is being considered as part of a programme to provide protection for the child. The guidance stresses that secure placements, once made, should only be for so long as is necesssary and unavoidable, and that care should be taken to ensure that children are not retained in security simply to complete a predetermined assessment of the treatment programme. It is obviously critical that plans should be made for continuity of care, education and, where appropriate, access to professional (eg psychiatric) support when the child leaves secure accommodation. Disappointingly, as is noted in Chapter **10**, the guidance does not focus on the importance of continuity in terms of the support which may be provided crucially by friends or other members of the child's own support networks. Paragraph 7(c) of Sch 2, Part I imposes a duty on local authorities to avoid the necessity for children in need within their area to be placed in secure accommodation, and the guidance states that careful consideration should be given to the existing range of alternative facilities and services available locally, identifying any gaps or inadequacies in such provision and how these might best be met, either by the authority itself or in co-operation with other agencies. In addition, steps should be taken to ensure that all decisions to seek a placement for a child in secure accommmodation are taken at a senior level within the authority. This should be at not less than Assistant Director level and such a person should be accountable to the Director of Social Services for that decision. Local authorities managing secure units have a particular responsibility to ensure that children accommodated in the non-secure part of the home are not unnecessarily placed in the associated secure facility and that the criteria for restricting liberty are applied equally rigorously to such children as to those being considered for admission from outside the home.

General principles

7.151 The guidance states that any placement by a local authority of a child whom it is looking after should, wherever practicable, arise as part of the local authority's overall plan for the child's welfare. In planning such a placement, and in considering any decision with respect to a child looked after in such accommodation, a local authority is still of course bound by the duties under s 22 of the CA 1989, including the duty to safeguard and promote the child's welfare (s 22(3)(a)), and as far as is reasonably practicable must ascertain the wishes and feelings regarding the use of such accommodation of the child, his parents and any other person who has parental responsibility, and anyone else whose wishes and feelings it considers relevant (s 22(4)). It remains to be seen whether the prescribed person (appointed under s 26(2A) of the CA 1989, as amended) will be deemed to be a relevant person, but there seems no reason why they should not be so considered. For children who are provided with accommodation on a voluntary basis under s 20, it should be noted that any person with parental responsibility for a child may remove him at any time from accommodation which has been provided (s 20(8)). This, the guidance advises, includes removal from placements in secure accommodation, whether or not the authority of the court to restrict the liberty of the child under s 25 has been obtained, although the guidance further notes that this should be in line with any agreements made with the local authority by the parents.

Grounds for the making of orders under s 25

7.152 As was pointed out in para **7.2**, a local authority looking after a child can, in certain circumstances, seek an order under s 25 of the CA 1989 to provide that the child should be kept in secure accommodation. Where, therefore, it is proposed to keep a child in secure accommodation for a period exceeding 72 hours, the local authority can only do so where it has obtained an order from the court. The court may only grant such an order where it is satisfied that the child has a history of absconding and is likely to abscond from any other description of accommodation; that if he absconds he is likely to suffer significant harm; or that if he is kept in any other description of accommodation he is likely to injure himself *or others*. It can be seen that these provisions are not only directed at child protection concerns with regard to the individual child (as seen in *Re D* (above), where there were concerns as a result of past episodes of self-harm including overdoses and cutting herself with a razor; and in *A Metropolitan Borough Council v DB* [1997] 1 FLR 767, where the girl was a crack cocaine addict living in squalor who had been admitted to hospital 2 days before the birth of her child suffering from pre-eclamptic fits brought on by high blood pressure and was still dangerously hypertensive), but can also focus on the risk the child may pose to members of the public, including children. (See, for example, the risk posed to female children by the boy in *Re K* (above.) Pursuant to s 25(2), the Children (Secure Accommodation) Regulations 1991 were made and provide that the maximum period for which a child may be held in secure accommodation without the authority of the court is 72 hours in any period of 28 days. The regulations also provide that applications under s 25 may only be made by the local authority looking after the child. The criteria for the making of such orders under s 25(1)(a) also look to the issue of the child suffering 'significant harm' and this is interpreted in exactly the same way as it is when establishing grounds for the making of care and supervision orders (see para **7.78**). The criteria for the making of orders under s 25(1)(b), on the other hand, focus on the factual issue of whether there is evidence to suggest that if the child is kept other than in secure accommodation he is likely to injure himself or others, as was seen in the case of *Re K*.

7.153 Again, as was noted in para **7.1**, the number of applications made to the courts to exercise their powers under s 5 has been diminishing dramatically over recent years, and has now fallen to 583 in 2001 from 1,240 in 1994. The over 50 per cent reduction in the number of applications being made demonstrates a recognition by local authorities that this is really a measure of last resort, but is also likely to be reflective of the fact that increasing numbers of children who might previously have been looked after by local authorities and placed in secure acccommodation after the making of such orders have been finding their way instead into the criminal justice system.

Meaning of secure accommodation

7.154 Section 25(1) of the CA 1989 defines secure accommodation as that which is 'provided for the purpose of restricting liberty' and this is further expanded upon, not in the Act or the regulations, but in *The Children Act 1989: Guidance and Regulations* – vol 4 – 'Residential Care' (DOH, 1991) (referred to in the following paragraphs of this chapter as the *Guidance* (at chapter 8, para 8.10). Whilst the *Guidance* recognises that the interpretation of this term is ultimately a matter to be determined by the court, it stresses that it is important to understand that any practice or measure which prevents a child from leaving a room or building of his own free will, may be deemed by the court to constitute 'restriction of liberty'. The *Guidance* suggests that while, for example, it is clear that the locking of a child in a room or a part of a building to prevent him leaving voluntarily is caught by the statutory definition, other practices which place restrictions on freedom of mobility, for example by creating a human barrier, are not so clear cut. Thus the *Guidance* suggests in these circumstances seeking the advice of the local authority's legal department in the first instance and then the Social Services Inspectorate as to the legality of the practice or measure. In *A Metropolitan Borough Council v DB* [1997] 1 FLR 767, the High Court confirmed that secure accommodation is not limited to that which is approved by the Secretary of State, as it is restriction of liberty which is the essential factor in determining what was secure accommodation. Thus, in that case the maternity ward from which the nurses had to prevent the 17-year-old girl from leaving was secure accommodation and the girl herself came within the criteria in s 25(1)(b) as if she was to leave the ward and the medical care provided there she would be likely to injure herself. By contrast, in *Re C (Detention: Medical Treatment)* [1997] 2 FLR 180 the girl was the subject of wardship proceedings and the ward in the eating disorder clinic where she was being treated had no restrictions on entry or exit, and thus Wall J had no hesitation in finding that the accommodation did not fall within s 25, even were the court to have exercised its wardship powers to make an order that the girl be detained against her wishes using reasonable force if necessary because this would have been an exercise of the wardship's courts powers.

Minimum age

7.155 The regulations provide that no child under the age of 13 may be placed in secure accommodation in a community home without the prior approval of the Secretary of State of the placement. This replaces the previous minimum age of 10 years, thus the *Guidance* advises that a local authority wishing to restrict the liberty of a child under 13 should first of all discuss the case with the Social Services Inspectorate, and subject to their advice a formal written submission should then be submitted to the Secretary of State for his consideration providing details of why the restriction of liberty is considered to be the only appropriate way of dealing with the child.

Use of secure accommodation without the authority of the court

7.156 Regulation 10(1) of the Children (Secure Accommodation) Regulations 1991 places a limit on the maximum period a child, to whom s 25 of the CA 1989 applies, may have his liberty restricted without the authority of the court. The maximum period is 72 hours either consecutively or in aggregate in any period of 28 consecutive days. Some relaxation of this provision is contained in reg 10(3) to meet difficulties which may be faced by authorities in arranging applications to be heard at short notice where the 72-hour period expires over a weeked or other public holiday. Where the authority uses its powers to detain for a period of up to 72 hours under reg 10(1) without having to go to court this will enable it to determine whether secure accommodation is needed as a longer-term measure and thus as to whether it needs to make an application to the court for a longer period in secure accommodation.

Applications to the court

7.157 An application must be made to the family proceeedings court by the local authority looking after the child, except that an application may be made to the county court or High Court where there are other proceedings in respect of the same child (CAPO 1991, art 3(1)(a)). Proceedings are begun in the family proceedings court for the area in which the child normally has his home as otherwise courts and guardians in the areas of secure units would become overburdened. Staff working in accommodation which restricts liberty, and field social workers working with children in respect of whom an order is sought, will be aware of the need to prepare children adequately for the court hearing and in this respect particular regard should be paid to the age and understanding of the child, although the child should have the benefit of a children's guardian in respect of the application (see para **7.159**). Where the decision is made by the family proceedings court then the case of *R v Oxfordshire County Council (Secure Accommodation Order)* [1992] Fam 150 established that the magistrates must give full reasons for their decision in s 25 applications.

Legal representation

7.158 Section 25(6) provides that a court is unable to exercise its powers to authorise a period of restriction of liberty if the child is not legally represented in court, the only exception being where the child, having been informed of his rights to apply for public funding of legal representation and having had an opportunity to do so, has refused or failed to apply.

The role of the children's guardian

7.159 Applications to the court for authority to restrict the liberty of children are 'specified proceedings' within the meaning of s 41 and thus the court is required to appoint a guardian unless it is of the opinion that it is unnecessary to do so in order to safeguard the children's interests. It is the usual practice for the guardian therefore to be involved in the appointment and the giving of initial instructions to the child's solicitor. The solicitor will represent the child in accordance with FPC(CA 1989)R 1991, r 12 as in other specified proceedings. If, as may well be the case given that secure orders involve children usually over the age of 13, the guardian and the child have a divergence of opinion about the recommendation to be put to the court, then, as is the case with care and supervision order proceedings, the legal representation stays with the child and the guardian where he needs legal support will have to seek assistance from CAFCASS legal services. The powers and duties of the guardian are similar to those in care and supervision order proceedings, but other key considerations might include: the need to ascertain the child's wishes and feelings as a matter of urgency; the need to identify a divergence situation at an early stage; the need to know exactly where it is proposed the child should be placed, thus orders should not be made for any available bed; and particular consideration should have been paid by the local authority, which should be checked by the guardian, to the suitability of the placement in terms of the child's race, language, religion and culture (s 22(5)(c)); and to the location in terms of proximity to the child's family (s 23(7)(a)); and guardians should also be especially aware of the impact of delay.

Evidence

7.160 Save where the matter proceeds by agreement between the parties, the court is obliged to make findings of fact based on sworn evidence which it has heard. Douglas Brown J in *R v Oxfordshire County Council (Secure Accommodation Order)* [1992] Fam 150 emphasised that evidence of attempted self-injury and threats to others could be evidence on which the likelihood of self-harm or threats, when in the community, could be assessed by the court, but that psychiatric evidence would be of assistance in such a case.

Consideration of the welfare of the child

7.161 The issue of the precise weight to be accorded to the welfare of the child in s 25 proceedings has caused problems. In the case of *Hereford and Worcester County Council v S* [1993] 2 FLR 360 it was held, in accordance with para 8.9 of the *Guidance*, that s 1 applied to s 25 applications and that the court must therefore make the welfare of the child its paramount consideration. Subsequent case-law, particularly *Re M (Secure Accommodation Order)* [1995] 1 FLR 418, has now established, however, that although the welfare of the child is of great importance, where the court has found any of the criteria under the Act or regulations is satisfied, it is bound to make a secure accommodation order. In the case of *Re M* the child had a history of absconding, violent and disruptive behaviour and drug abuse. He had criminal convictions and had been expelled from various schools. The local authority's application for a secure accommodation order was made on one day's notice. The guardian's application to the court for an adjournment to enable enquiries to be made was refused by the magistrates who applied the s 1 welfare principle to the local authority's application and made a final order. Both the guardian and M appealed to the High Court where Ward J dismissed both appeals. The guardian appealed to the Court of Appeal. The Court of Appeal held that the criteria laid down in s 1 did not apply to Part III of the Act. If the relevant criteria under s 25(4) were met, it was mandatory for the secure accommodation order to be made. It followed that, whilst the child's welfare was of great importance, it was not paramount for the purposes of s 25. The appeal was dismissed because although the magistrates had been in error in applying the welfare criteria, that error had been in favour of M and the secure accommodation order had been properly made.

Interim orders

7.162 If the court is not ready to make a final decision because of some uncertainty as to whether the criteira will be met, it has power to make an interim order for the child to be kept in secure accommodation. It is not possible to continue such an order simply to ensure the ongoing involvement of the guardian. This was emphasised by the Court of Appeal in *Re B (A Minor) (Secure Accommodation Order)* [1994] 2 FLR 707. The guardian and the court must be aware of the very real risk that a child may remain in secure accommodation as a consequence of a series of interim orders for longer than would have been possible following the making of a full order, which is manifestly unsatisfactory.

Duration and effects of orders

7.163 Regulation 11 of the Children (Secure Accommodation) Regulations 1991 provides that, subject to reg 12 (which deals with later applications) the maximum period that a court may authorise a child to be kept in secure accommodation on a first application is 3 months. It was established in *Re B (A Minor) (Secure Accommodation Order)* [1994] 2 FLR 707 that detention in secure accommodation dates from the date of the court order, and not from the date when the child is placed in secure accommodation. Where the local authority looking after the child believes that the placement should continue beyond the period specified in the order, then further applications must be made to the court, as happened in the case of *LM v Essex County Council* [1999] 1 FLR 988. Orders may be renewed under reg 12 on further applications being made for periods of up to 6 months at a time. The order is permissive, ie the authority is not required to use the secure accommodation, and must also ensure that the statutory criteria under which the court made the order continue to apply (reg 16). After an order has been made the local authority must appoint at least three persons, one of whom must be independent of the authority, to review the keeping of the child in secure accommodation, once within the first month and thereafter at intervals not exceeding 3 months (reg 17). This was also emphasied in *LM v Essex County Council* where the panel reviewing the secure accommodation order of a 16-year-old girl concluded on 6 January 1999 that the criteria no longer applied to her. They directed that the local authority should make immediate arrangements to remove her from secure accommodation. The local authority, for practical reasons, informed the solicitor for the girl that they would continue her placement until 8 February. He sought *habeas corpus* to allow the immediate release of his client. At the hearing the local authority agreed to relocate her immediately. The court making the consent order held that the local authority could not continue to detain a child under s 25 when the local authority itself did not consider that the criteria continued to apply. The court noted that it was no longer asked to decide whether the powerful practical arguments about the difficulty of relocating a child immediately should prevail over the obvious arguments relating to the liberty of a subject. It left open whether, where there was disagreement as to whether the criteria were still satisfied, the appropriate remedy would be *habeas corpus* or judicial review of the local authority's decision.

Appeals

7.164 Under s 94, appeals against the making of, or refusal to make, an order for the restriction of liberty in the family proceedings court lie to the Family Division of the High Court, in the same way as for care proceedings (see para **7.142**). Such an appeal against the making of an order should be listed as a matter of urgency affecting as it does the liberty of the child, and the child's placement will continue during the time it takes for the appeal to be heard. Where, however, the court has refused to authorise the restriction of liberty, and the authority is appealing against that decision, the child must not be retained or placed in secure accommodation pending consideration of the appeal.

Use of secure accommodation as constituting a breach of Article 5 of the ECHR

7.165 In the case of *Re K (Secure Accommodation Order: Right to Liberty)* [2001] 1 FLR 526, an attempt was made to challenge secure accommodation orders

on the basis that such orders were incompatible with the right to liberty under
Article 5 of the ECHR. In this case the child, now aged 15, had been
permanently excluded from nursery when aged 2 as a result of his destructive
behaviour, and had been referred to an educational psychologist at the age of
4 because of generally aggressive behaviour. He had then been placed in a
special school, but it became increasingly difficult for his parents to manage
his behaviour, which included serious sexual behaviour and the destruction of
property, including fire setting, and the local authority became involved.
Eventually the child was placed in a residential home. Following an assault on
a female member of staff, an assessment of the child, then aged 11, diagnosed
him as having hyperkinetic conduct disorder, and described him as presenting
a serious risk to himself and others. Although another residential placement
was successful for a time, after the child's thirteenth birthday there was a
further deterioration in his behaviour and, following indecent assaults,
incidents of fire setting and assaults on staff, he was eventually placed at a
secure unit under a secure accommodation order within s 25 of the CA 1989.
The child appealed the most recent of a series of such orders, on the basis that
secure accommodation orders were incompatible with Article 5 of the ECHR
and also damages in respect of the alleged breach of his right to liberty. The
Court of Appeal refused a declaration that s 25 was incompatible with the
provisions in Article 5 and made a secure accommodation order until
February 2001, a period of 3 months, with a review at the end of the period.
The court held that s 25 did constitute a deprivation of liberty, but was not
incompatible with the Convention where it was justified within Article 5(1)(d)
as being the detention of a minor for the purpose of educational supervision.
Educational supervision, ruled the court, was not to be equated rigidly with
notions of classroom teaching, but particularly in the care context should
embrace many aspects of the exercise by the local authority of parental rights
for the benefit and protection of the child concerned. The court stated that if
a young person were to be detained under a secure accommodation order,
without any educational provision being made for that young person, there
would be a breach of the Convention right to liberty, but on the basis that the
duty of the court was to find a compatible interpretation of legislation, s 25
was not incompatible with the Convention notwithstanding the fact that it did
not itself mention educational provision.

Conclusion

7.166   The case of *Re K* (above) illustrates the best of the working of the
system of child protection proceedings from care and supervision order
proceedings through to secure accommodation proceedings, where the aim is
to prevent the child from suffering further significant harm, or the likelihood
of such harm, and to provide an alternative means of care. In the case of *Re K*,
a failure to use the provisions of s 25 would almost certainly have meant
resort to criminal proceedings in respect of the criminal offences he was

prone to commit, and orders being made which would not have attracted the welfare regime of measures attached to orders made under s 25, in particular the provisions relating to the maintenance and support of contact (see Chapter **10**). All aspects of care and supervision order proceedings and the circumstances in which a local authority looking after a child may seek a secure accommodation order have been considered. The legislature has been prepared to respond to the continuing judicial concern over plans for children in care, culminating in the decision of the House of Lords in *Re S (Minors); Re W (Minors)* [2002] UKHL 10, [2002] 1 FLR 815 and it appears to have laid down a means, through the prescribed person's right to refer matters to a CAFCASS officer who can then take the case to court, of providing the court with the opportunity to assess whether the local authority's plans for the child are being properly pursued (ss 26(A) and 26(C) of the CA 1989, as amended). It will be interesting to see by the time of the next edition of this book just how well these provisions are working out in practice to protect the lives of children in the care of local authorities.

CHAPTER 8

EVIDENCE AND PROCEDURE IN CIVIL CHILD ABUSE CASES

'Too often lawyers limit their role to simply preparing for the hearing of a case and there is little attempt to relate what is happening within the court process to the practicalities of family life. Our concerns are that the system itself, rather than protecting and helping children, may increase their difficulties' (*Association of Lawyers for Children Evidence to Childhood Matters* (1996) Volume 1, at para 5.10).

'It was accepted that unconscious processes were at work in every courtroom setting. As a simple illustration, it was accepted that most judges would react differently to witnesses of different appearance. Most judges would be influenced by parents acting "impeccably" in the witness box as contrasted with those who went "berserk". However, at a deeper level it had to be accepted that there were built in prejudices, factors of background, and the unconscious process at work, all of which would affect a judge's evaluation of the evidence. Naturally judges ... by the very nature of their work, had acquired skills and developed an insight born of experience and collected professional expertise. But all judges needed to be cautious and should be made aware of their own fallabilities – many of which are unconscious' (*Rooted Sorrows* (Family Law, 1997) First Plenary Session, at p 17).

'Like most things which are worthwhile, developing skills and confidence as a witness in court takes practice and experience. A respect for, and acceptance of, the unique rules and procedures of the judicial process are a good beginning. Whilst social workers and health professionals have different training and often different values from lawyers, there is no reason teamwork cannot be achieved, with roles and skills being complementary, ensuring that the right decisions are made for children who need the protection of the courts' (Lane and Walsh (2002), at p 354).

Introduction: civil and criminal proceedings

8.1 In circumstances where child abuse becomes a matter for the courts, practitioners in the field will become involved in the separate jurisdictions of the criminal and civil courts. Each jurisdiction represents the intervention by the state into the arena of child abuse. There are important differences between how each jurisdiction works, how information is processed and how decisions are made within each jurisdiction. Despite these differences, the operation of each jurisdiction may be triggered by the same set of facts.

The criminal justice system

Example 1

8.2   Sally Edwards aged 13 lives at home with her mother Amy Edwards and her mother's cohabitee Bill Brown. Sally has an elder brother Graham Edwards aged 15. Amy and Bill have twins, a daughter Mary Brown and a son George Brown aged 5. The father of Sally and Graham is David Edwards. David and Amy were divorced 5 years ago. Amy goes out several evenings a week, leaving Bill at home with the children. Sally tells her school friend that she has had sexual intercourse with Bill when her mother is out. Their class teacher overhears the conversation and tells the head teacher, who calls in the police. Sally is medically examined and is found to be 12 weeks' pregnant. She is interviewed by the police and discloses that she has had intercourse with Bill. Bill is interviewed by the police and makes no admissions.

8.3   The child protection team refer the case to the CPS. There is a prima facie case against Bill, who the police discover has a previous conviction for sexual intercourse with a minor. Bill is charged on an indictment with a number of counts alleging that on specific days he had unlawful sexual intercourse with Sally. The case proceeds to trial before a judge and jury at the Crown Court. The purpose of the Crown Court trial is to establish as a question of fact whether Bill has committed the offences with which he is charged: whether he had sexual intercourse with Sally.

8.4   The burden is on the prosecution to prove the case. The Crown attempts to prove the facts of the case by calling live evidence as to what happened. Sally is deemed a competent child witness and gives her evidence. The police surgeon who examined her gives evidence as to her medical condition. Amy gives evidence that on the dates particularised on the indictment Bill looked after Sally, Mary and George in her absence. The police officer gives evidence as to Bill's interview. The prosecution evidence is principally given orally or 'live' so that it can be tested by defence cross-examination. After legal argument, Bill's previous conviction is not introduced in evidence. Bill is at liberty to give evidence denying the allegation, and to call defence evidence from a neighbour stating that he was in Bill's company on the stated dates.

8.5   The principal features of the criminal sytem may therefore be summarised as follows:

–   the burden of proof lies with the prosecution, who present their case and call their evidence first;

– the jury decides the factual basis of the allegation and whether the defendant is guilty or not guilty, upon the evidence which they have heard in court;

– the judge rules on the law, specifically upon what is admissible in evidence to be placed before the jury, and what must be excluded as inadmissible and withheld from the jury, because it is unfair and prejudicial, or irrelevant;

– the emphasis is upon live oral testimony as to the facts of the allegation; other uncontroversial evidence may be given in written form, but only subject to the agreement of the defence;

– the child victim will give evidence orally, although the provision of a video-link may shield her from the intimidation of the courtroom; her role in the proceedings ends with the giving of her evidence;

– evidence is limited to what is strictly relevant to the charges: there may be legal argument about what the jury may be told: the judge in his discretion may exclude or rule inadmissible material which is prejudicial to the defendant rather than probative of the prosecution case;

– the presentation of the court is both formal and public: the judge, the advocates for the prosecution and the defence will normally wear robes. Members of the public and the press will be present, and, subject to any direction by the judge, the proceedings of the court may be published in the media;

– the function of the court is to provide the proper forum for the verdict: following a 'guilty' verdict, the judge must sentence the defendant in a way which marks the proper disapproval of society for the crime which has been committed, and is consistent with established sentencing practice. The workings of the criminal justice system in relation to child protection matters are dealt with fully in Chapter **9**.

The civil system

8.6 The allegations made by Sally against Bill will also be the focus of parallel proceedings in the Family Court. The public policy foundation for this is the desire of society to protect children from abuse. The legal process is that provided for by the CA 1989, which imposes a statutory duty upon local authorities to protect children living in their area who may be at risk of significant harm. The overriding focus of the CA 1989 is the welfare principle. Thus, as was detailed in Chapter **7**, s 1(1) of the CA 1989 provides that:

'When a court determines any question with respect to –

(a) the upbringing of a child; or
(b) the administration of a child's property or the application of any income arising from it,

the child's welfare shall be the court's paramount consideration.'

8.7   The paramountcy of the welfare principle is thus the driving force behind the operation of the civil courts dealing with children's cases. The effect of this is that the way in which the courts work in child abuse cases and, in particular, the handling of evidential material is entirely different from the practice in the criminal courts. In particular, the factual nexus for the family court is likely to be much more complex and discrete.

Example 2

8.8   Amy, Sally's mother, has had difficulties in parenting her four children. Amy has had a long-standing problem with alcohol. This was a factor in the breakdown of her marriage to David, the father of Robert and Sally. David, a long-distance lorry driver, was regularly away from home. Amy's drinking came to the attention of the children's school, which notified social services. Following a case conference, Robert and Sally were placed upon the Child Protection Register on the grounds of neglect. Following the breakdown of David and Amy's marriage, David issued applications under s 8 of the CA 1989 for residence and contact, raising concerns about Amy's drinking and her new boyfriend Bill. The local authority provided a report for the court under s 37 of the CA 1989, addressing the risk presented by Amy's parenting. Amy was able to curb her drinking and was felt to be otherwise a 'good enough' mother. Residence orders for Robert and Sally were therefore granted to Amy. Amy subsequently gave birth to twins Rose and George. Amy suffered from post-natal depression and her drinking continued. Sally and Robert were often involved in the care of the twins, and all four children were registered on the Child Protection Register under the category of emotional abuse. The children were allocated a social worker. Regular case conferences reviewed the situation in relation to the children but a decision to issue care proceedings was never taken because Amy was able to moderate her drinking for lengthy periods. Bill, her cohabitee, was unemployed and shared the care of the children with whom he appeared to have a good relationship. Social services were unaware of Bill's conviction for unlawful sexual intercourse with a minor which occurred when he was 19 and living in another city.

8.9   Following Sally's disclosure at school, the allocated social worker was contacted and a child protection investigation was begun. Sally told the social worker and the police officer that she and the other children had watched pornographic videos at home, which were kept in an open cupboard by Bill and Amy's bed. The school reported that Rose and George were often absent, and that their mother smelt of drink when collecting them. Amy, when told of Sally's pregnancy, denied that Bill was responsible and accused her daughter of acting provocatively to men. The maternal grandmother Barbara Smith had played an active role in helping to care for the children and social services placed all the children with her pending further investigation.

8.10   Care proceedings in relation to all four children were necessary in order to safeguard the children from further harm and to plan for their future. In many cases, the allegation of sexual abuse will become the trigger for the issue of proceedings, against a long-standing background of emotional abuse and neglect. Procedurally, the application will be for a care or supervision order under s 31 of the CA 1989. A care or supervision order may only be made if a court is satisfied:

(a)   that the child concerned is suffering, or is likely to suffer, significant harm; and
(b)   that the harm, or likelihood of harm, is attributable to:
    (i)   the care given to the child, or likely to be given to him if the order were not made, not being what it would be reasonable to expect a parent to give to him; or
    (ii)   the child's being beyond parental control.

8.11   This application will be made in the first instance to magistrates or a district judge in the family proceedings court. Cases involving the abuse of children are properly dealt with at county court or High Court level and will be transferred upwards subject to the CAPO 1991. It is usual for the local authority to seek interim care orders pursuant to s 38(2) of the CA 1989, on the basis that there are reasonable grounds to suppose that the s 31 conditions are made out; in the absence of concessions by the parents and clear written agreements about the children's placements and contact, interim care orders are likely to be necessary.

Nature of evidence in children's proceedings

8.12   The function of children's proceedings is to make decisions about the upbringing of children with regard to what is in their best interests, in line with the paramountcy of the welfare principle. Criminal proceedings arising from the same basis of fact are concerned with the identification of the perpetrator of the crime and the determination of the punishment appropriate to the crime.

Children's proceedings are inquisitorial

8.13   Prior to the CA 1989, many children's cases between the State and parents, or between parents as private individuals, were decided under the wardship juridsiction of the High Court. Historically, this was founded on the concept of *parens patriae*, where the court, by delegation of the sovereign's duties, had a parental relationship with the ward of court, and assumed protective responsibility towards the ward, effectively displacing the parental responsibility of the parents. (For what remains of this jurisdiction, see paras **8.166–8.176**.) Practice since the CA 1989 derives from the inquisitorial system, the power to control the evidence which it receives and the conduct of the proceedings, and to make decisions about the welfare of children independently of those urged by the parties. This is at its most fully developed at the higher level of children's cases, in the hands of High Court judges, although the power of the judges in the English children's courts does not go as far as the fact-finding undertaken by, for example, French examining magistrates. The way in which the court in children's proceedings exerts its control upon the parties will be developed below. The adversarial element remains in children's proceedings in determining issues of fact. It is the duty of each party to subject the case of an opponent to testing by rigorous forensic cross-examination (see further for interesting observations on the nature of the influence of these adversarial elements, Lane and Walsh (2002)).

The judge as a finder of fact

8.14   In common with most other civil proceedings, findings and decisions in children's cases have been exclusively the province of the judge or the lay magistrates: there has never been any role for a jury in children's cases. Children cases are heard by High Court, county court or district judges who are trained lawyers, or by lay magistrates who sit in the family proceedings court assisted by qualified court clerks and have received special training since the CA 1989.

8.15   The function of the family judge is on consideration of the evidence to make the best decision for the child, subject to the paramountcy of the welfare principle. In essence, this decision can be reduced to two elements: first, where a child should live, whether with a parent, or a relative, or in an alternative permanent family secured by the State; secondly, with whom the child should have contact, in terms of his parents, extended family or others. In the determination of these questions, the family court will assess the allegations of abuse. Where an allegation of sexual or physical abuse is central to the proceedings, a 'finding' of the court as to whether acts of abuse occurred and who was the perpetrator has to be made, in order to decide on where and with whom a child should live in the future. In cases where the thrust of the allegations concern chronic neglect and parental incapacity, an allegation of abuse may appear to be peripheral, and a 'finding' therefore may not be necessary to determine a child's future. It follows from this that the function of the Family Court in child abuse cases is not the detection and punishment of a crime: the child, not the perpetrator, is the focus of the proceedings, and the language of guilt or innocence and retribution is not used.

Representation

8.16   Criminal proceedings arising out of child abuse are an adversarial contest between the State and the defendant or defendants. The criminal case triggered by Sally Edward's disclosure has two parties and would simply be described as *R v Bill Brown.* In the parallel children's case, the family court may be hearing a number of applications: alongside the application of the local authority for care orders there may be competing residence applications from the children's maternal grandmother, Barbara Smith, and from Bill Edwards, the father of Robert and Sally. Who should become a party is governed by the FPR 1991: Amy Edwards and David Edwards as parties with parental responsibility will automatically be parties. Other potential parties seeking to make an application will be required to satisfy the criteria set out in the CA 1989, s 10(9). Barbara Smith as maternal grandmother has played an active role in the children's lives over the years and would be likely to be given leave to make an application for residence. Bill Brown, as the non-marital father of Rose and George, would be given notice of the proceedings and could apply for party status, in order to be heard as to his role in the abuse allegations and in relation to the future of Rose and George who are his children. (For more detail in relation to who may be parties to proceedings see Chapter 7.)

The child as a party

8.17 The point has been made that the role of the child victim in a criminal abuse case ends upon the giving of her evidence: she remains a witness, not a party. In contrast, s 41 of the CA 1989 stipulates that children who are subject to specified (public law) proceedings shall be represented through an officer of CAFCASS, normally a children's guardian (see Family Proceedings (Amendment) Rules 2001). The guardian, through detailed enquiries and commissioning the appropriate assessments, assists the court as to the best future arrangements for the children and informs the court of the ascertainable wishes and feelings of the child (considered in the light of his age and understanding) under the CA 1989, s 1(3)(a) (see Chapter 7). The importance given to the wishes of the child increases in relation to his or her age. Where a teenage child disagrees with the recommendations or approach of the guardian, he or she may be permitted his or her own lawyer to represent them, separately from the guardian, subject to the discretion of the court and the representations particularly of the children's guardian and solicitor. Therefore, in our example, the family case triggered by Sally Edwards' allegations may have no less than seven parties and their legal representatives and be dealt with by the Family Court as *Barsetshire County Council v (1) Amy Edwards (mother), (2) David Edwards (father), (3) Bill Brown (father), (4) Barbara Smith (grandmother and applicant for residence) and (5)–(8) Edwards Brown (children through their guardian).* (For further detail on this see Chapter 7.)

Documentary material: accumulating the evidence

8.18 It follows that the distinctive function of children's cases gives rise to a greater volume and range of evidence than a parallel criminal case. Subject only to relevance, there is no limit to the type of material which may be received as evidence in child abuse cases in the Family Court. Various distinctions may be made in the types of evidence likely to be part of a family case concerning child abuse.

Statements

8.19   Chronologically, first will come the setting out of the local authority's case, alleged in brief particulars in the application Form C1 and its supplement Form C2, and enlarged upon in social workers' statements of evidence. The local authority will also provide interim and final care plans, setting out the proposals for the children (for current detailed guidance as to the appropriate contents of care plans, see Circular LAC (99) 29, *Care Plans and Care Proceedings under the Children Act*, which will be replaced when the Adoption and Children Act 2002 is implemented, see further Chapter 7). Parents will also file statements, replying to the allegations made against them, or to support applications for residence or contact. Relevant secondary material such as case conference minutes, reports from school teachers, health visitors or correspondence is commonly exhibited to parties' statements.

Primary raw material

8.20   Abuse cases alleging sexual abuse or physical injury to children will generate extensive material which, whilst not created for the purpose of court, becomes highly relevant to the proceedings. Specific to abuse cases are the medical notes of the duty doctor, registrar or GP on first presentation, including x-ray material and skeletal surveys, the nursing log and discharge summary if the child is hospitalised, and the GP's records for the child and possibly the parent. Where issues of fact are disputed, extracts of the running log kept by social services may be relevant evidence.

Aural and video material

8.21   Video-recording of any formal memorandum interview of a child alleging abuse, together with an agreed transcription, will be available. Other video- or tape-recorded material may be also before the court, subject to its probative effect: for example, a neighbour's video of a 3-year-old child balancing semi-naked on a first floor window sill may be highly probative of neglect and is likely to be admissible evidence.

Experts' reports

8.22   These are an essential component of abuse cases. A case of sexual abuse will depend on the intimate examination of the child by a consultant paediatrician. Paediatric radiologists and neurologists will review and report on x-rays and scans where there is suspected non-accidental injury. Such reports are directly relevant to the fact-finding exercise as to the nature of the harm. It is usual for a consultant child and family psychiatrist to report on attachment and relationships within the family. Where a parent is directly suspected of abuse, an assessment from an adult psychiatrist will address propensity and risk. The intellectual functioning and capacity of parent or child may be reported on by a psychologist.

Material from other civil and criminal cases

8.23 It is usual practice for the parties and the court in children's cases to receive relevant material from a parallel criminal case, including videos and transcripts of interviews, medical evidence and witness statements. Where there are previous children's proceedings in relation to children currently under consideration, documents from those proceedings will also be admitted.

Lawyer's documents

8.24 These are documents prepared by advocates to assist the court in dealing with cases in which the filed evidence may be voluminous. Care cases are usually factually complicated: it has become customary for the applicant to provide a chronology listing the relevant factual events in a non-contentious way. It is now mandatory for applicants to provide a succinct summary of the background, a statement of the issues to be determined, a summary of the orders and directions sought by each party, a chronology for a final hearing or if the background summary is insufficient, and skeleton arguments (where appropriate) outlining each party's legal arguments (see *Practice Direction (Family Proceedings: Court Bundles)* [2000] 1 FLR 536). There has been express sanction of other types of document: the local authority should provide a threshold document setting out how the s 31 criteria are said to be satisfied, a clear statement of the facts which they wish the court to find, and the basis upon which it is alleged that the threshold is crossed (see *Re G (Care Proceedings: Threshold Conditions)* [2001] 2 FLR 1111, CA). Where experts of similar disciplines disagree, a schedule setting out areas of agreement and disagreement normally compiled by the guardian is good practice (see *Re C (Expert Evidence: Disclosure: Practice)* [1995] 1 FLR 204). In the family proceedings court, where lay magistrates are obliged to provide full written reasons for their decisions, it is customary for the parties to provide a consensual document or documents dealing with the threshold criteria and also the agreed facts which form the basis for the court's decision.

Hearings: split hearings

8.25 Both the criminal and the family jurisdictions have fully developed procedures for the marshalling of evidence in preparation for the main hearing. The pleas and directions of the criminal court are mirrored by the directions hearings in the Family Court; the pre-trial review or final directions perform the same task in each jurisdiction. A criminal trial dispenses justice as a single exercise, although a conviction may lead to an adjournment for considerations of sentencing. Family cases involving abuse lend themselves to several separate substantive hearings, often several months apart, but which are conducted on oral evidence as formal hearings. Parents may wish to challenge the successive renewals of interim care orders, and request the return of their children; however, holding numerous contested hearings at the interim stage has been disapproved (see *Re B (Interim Care Orders: Renewal)* [2001] 2 FLR 1217). Other common areas of dispute which give rise to contested hearings are applications by parents for contact to children in care under s 34 of the CA 1989, and for residential assessments of parent and child under s 38(6) of the CA 1989.

8.26 The children's courts have a discretion to determine how they conduct their hearings. Even where applications are contested, hearings may vary through what has been described as a 'spectrum of procedure' (see *Re B (Minors) (Contact)* [1994] 2 FLR 1, CA). Hearings may involve short legal submissions, oral evidence on behalf of a social worker or perhaps a parent, or a full-blown hearing, with witnesses giving evidence and being cross-examined over a lengthy period. Subject to the agreement of the parties and the court, there may also be flexibility about the order in which the witnesses give their evidence, although in practice the applicant local authority or parent will call their evidence first. In private law proceedings between parents, the CAFCASS reporting officer will customarily give evidence first, while in care cases as befits a party with an inquisitorial role the guardian will always go last. It is a clearly understood principle that a party who contests evidence should have the opportunity to hear that evidence from the witness and to have it cross-examined.

8.27 The intrinsic importance of determining allegations of child abuse before proceedings to make final decisions about where a child should live has given rise to the developing practice of split hearings in children's cases, where a 'factual hearing' determining the facts of the alleged abuse is followed by a 'disposal hearing' dealing with the future plans for the child. A preliminary hearing on the factual basis of allegations of sexual abuse or non-accidental injury can clarify issues and prevent delay. The practice has no statutory basis within CA 1989, but developed as a judicial response to recommendations in the *Children Act Advisory Committee Annual Report 1994–1995* (at p 19). In *Re S (Care Proceedings: Split Hearing)* [1996] 2 FLR 773, the need for the early factual determination of issues was clearly demonstrated in a case where a baby of 10 months sustained serious non-accidental injuries. The full hearing of the local authority's application for a care order began 14 months later. No definitive care plan was even then possible, as the perpetrator of the injuries had not been proved, and the various assessments by highly qualified experts of the parenting capacity of the mother, father and stepfather could make no firm recommendation because of the fundamental dispute of facts.

8.28   Current Court of Appeal guidance in relation to split hearings is contained in *Re G (Care Proceedings: Split Trials)* [2001] 1 FLR 872, CA, in which a local authority had made a care application for a little boy whose baby half-brother had died following serious physical injuries in the care of his parents. From the judgment of Hale J, the following points may be drawn:

- split hearings may be useful where there needs to be early decisions about the causation of injury;
- split hearings need to be early in the case and clearly focused;
- expert assessments can be made after the hearing, in the light of judicial findings;
- the making of findings 'may often promote acceptance, understanding and movement on the part of those who will be involved in the child's future' (at p 882);
- best practice is to timetable at the same time the 'fact finding' and the 'disposal' parts of the split hearing, to be heard by the same judge, even if the disposal hearing has to be rearranged for this purpose.

Timing of criminal and children's hearings

8.29   The example of Sally Edwards shows how the same set of facts may trigger two separate sets of proceedings. Where there are reasonable grounds for believing that significant harm has occurred to a child, or that there is a likelihood of significant harm, a local authority may respond quickly with an application for an emergency protection order or a care application, in order to set in motion risk assessments and proper planning for the future of the children. A formal criminal charge may only follow formal interviewing, the collection of evidence and consideration of the merits of the case by the CPS. A criminal conviction may obviate the need for the 'fact-finding' stage of a split hearing. However, it is not the practice of the Family Court to wait for a criminal determination where the future of the children needs to be determined without undue delay: s 1(2) of the CA 1989 expressly provides that:

> 'In any proceedings in which any question with respect to the upbringing of a child arises, the court shall have regard to the general principle that any delay in determining the question is likely to prejudice the welfare of the child.'

8.30   In *Re TB (Care Proceedings: Criminal Trial)* [1995] 2 FLR 801, the Court of Appeal held that the fact that there were criminal proceedings for neglect of two elder children pending against a mother and stepfather was not in itself reason to adjourn the care proceedings which concerned all four children of the family. The issue of delay was all important. The court must consider what is in the child's best interests: the Court of Appeal has stated that even in a case of murder, it should not be assumed that the criminal trial should precede the care proceedings, unless there were exceptional circumstances: each case has to be determined on its own facts.

8.31 Parents giving evidence in care proceedings who also face criminal charges are afforded protection in several ways. The inquisitorial nature of the children's jurisdiction means that the evidence of parents may be essential. Section 98 of the CA 1989 provides that no person may be excused from giving evidence in care proceedings on the grounds that he may incriminate himself or a spouse, but:

> 'A statement or admission made in such proceedings shall not be admissible in evidence against the person making it or his spouse in proceedings for an offence other than perjury' (CA 1989, s 98(2)).

8.32 Although the police may seek disclosure of what a parent has said, a confession in care proceedings may not be admitted in criminal proceedings (see *Re EC (Disclosure of Material)* [1996] 2 FLR 725). Parents facing criminal charges will not be prejudiced by a prior finding of fact by a care court, as this would not be admissible in criminal proceedings.

Burden and standard of proof

8.33 The burden of proof in civil proceedings concerning children, in common with other areas of civil law, lies with the party making the application or assertion of fact. However, the CA 1989 has introduced a complexity to this process: there are several criteria which must be sequentially proved, or on which the court must be satisfied, before an order is made.

8.34 A local authority applying for a care or supervision order in care proceedings will first have to satisfy the threshold criteria (see para **8.10**) as set out in s 31(2) of the CA 1989. Where a child has been found to have been sexually abused or suffered non-accidental injury, the making of an order is not automatic: CA 1989, s 1(5) imposes a second burden in that the court is prohibited from making orders under the Act 'unless it considers that doing so would be better for the child than making no orders at all'. In public law proceedings, it is usually possible to demonstrate a case for the making of an order, because of the need for the local authority to share parental responsibility under a care order, or to 'advise, assist and befriend the child' under a supervision order (s 35(1)(a)). In private law proceedings between parents, it may be possible to have no order where there is full agreement. However, before orders can be made in care and contested residence cases, the third burden to be satisfied is the 'welfare checklist' as set out in s 1(3).

8.35 The standard of proof which is applied by the family court in all cases involving the welfare of children is the ordinary civil standard. This is proof on the balance of probabilities, defined by Denning J in *Miller v Ministry of Pensions* [1947] 2 All ER 372: 'if the evidence is such that the tribunal can say "We think it more probable than not", the burden is discharged'. However, if the probabilities are equal in weight, then the burden is not discharged, and the applicant fails. For practitioners dealing with parallel criminal and children's proceedings it is essential to be aware that the standard of proof for the prosecution in a criminal trial is a higher standard: a jury will be directed that in order to convict a defendant, it must be satisfied so that it is sure, or beyond reasonable doubt. A decision by a jury that guilt is probable but not certain should result in the acquittal of the defendant.

Proof in child abuse cases

8.36 In cases of sexual abuse or non-accidental injury, the current state of the law is expressed by a majority of the House of Lords in *Re H and R (Child Sexual Abuse: Standard of Proof)* [1996] 1 FLR 80, which remains the current law. The court must be satisfied on the balance of probabilities that the occurrence of abuse as particularised in the evidence was more likely than not. Their Lordships' view was that the more serious the allegation in any particular case, the less likely it was that the event occurred, and therefore the stronger or more cogent the evidence needed to establish the allegation on the balance of probabilities. This does not mean that the more serious the allegation, the higher the standard of proof which is required: rather, 'the more improbable the event, the stronger must be the evidence that it did occur before, on the balance of probability, its occurrence will be established' (at p 96E).

8.37 This means that, in practical terms, the Family Court may, on the evidence before it and having assessed the credibility of the witnesses, make a finding that a teenage girl has been sexually abused by her mother's boyfriend on the basis of her pregnancy and a clear disclosure by her, taking into account evidence of opportunity and giving some weight to his previous conviction. On the other hand, on the same evidence, a jury in a criminal court may not necessarily convict.

8.38 However, the Family Court is occasionally presented with scenarios that appear to be inherently improbable: for example, ritualised sexual abuse in the context of satanic practices, the use by parents of animals in the sexual abuse of their children, or the administration of poison by a mother to her baby. The standard of proof remains the balance of probabilities, but the court is required to look for stronger or more cogent evidence: this may take the form of admissions, medical evidence, evidence from third party witnesses or other forms of corroboration. Evidence of abuse which may appear ostensibly to be compelling in isolation will be weighed and tested against other evidence by the adversarial process of cross-examination, and may well be mitigated in its effect by this.

8.39 Certain evidence may need especially meticulous testing by the court. Children's disclosures of sexual abuse give rise to particular difficulty, being potentially probative, but also highly prejudicial to the parent or party implicated (see *Report of the Inquiry into Child Abuse in Cleveland 1977* (HMSO, 1988) especially paras 12.1–12.69). *Re E (A Minor) (Child Abuse: Evidence)* [1991] 1 FLR 420, CA, arose out of allegations to parents, police and social workers by three children aged between 3 and 4 years of age of sexual abuse by neighbours. The parents and social workers accepted uncritically what the children said. However, there were inconsistencies in the children's accounts and in their behaviour. There were serious deficiencies in the interviewing of the children and no other reliable supporting evidence. The High Court judge therefore found that the evidential value of what the children said was very limited, and that none of the children had been abused.

8.40 In *Re E*, Scott Baker J (at p 425) set out his analysis of the proper judicial approach to disclosures by children:

'very great caution is necessary in evaluating what weight is attached to each child's evidence. I bear in mind the following:

(1)   Where a child has been interviewed more than once, second and subsequent interviews are likely to be of diminishing, if not negligible, value.
(2)   These children are all of very tender years.
(3)   Great care must be taken in assessing the reliability of the adults who report what the children said.
(4)   I have to look at the climate in which the children made their disclosures, and decide whether the children may have been influenced in what they have said by the adults' words or behaviour.
(5)   I have to consider what the children are reported as having said is likely to be fact or fiction or a mixture of the two.
(6)   I have to consider the consistency of each child's accounts.
(7)   I have to consider whether each child's behaviour, before and after the disclosures, is consistent with the truth of them.
(8)   I have to look for reliable independent evidence to corroborate what the children have said.'

8.41 In cases alleging child abuse, there is need for meticulous care in the collection of evidence. Where more extreme allegations are made, such as ritual or satanic abuse, it has been held that for the allegations to be proved, it is necessary to establish that what the children have said has been recorded in a reliable form, and that such evidence has been correctly and accurately analysed. In *Rochdale Borough Council v A and Others* [1991] 2 FLR 192, 20 children from six families were the subject of care applications following the children's descriptions of ghosts, drinks that made them fly and the killing of babies. The court found that interview techniques had been adopted with little regard to the recommendations of the Cleveland Report, and were therefore unreliable. The local authority had uncritically believed the children and had removed them from their homes without the benefit of any independent evidence to corroborate the children's allegations.

Admissibility and judicial discretion: the inclusionary rule

8.42 In contrast with criminal proceedings, the rules of evidence in children's proceedings are inclusionary rather than exclusionary. In criminal proceedings, strict rules of evidence apply which exclude or limit the evidence which may be heard by the jury. The prosecution may apply to admit evidence necessary for proving the prosecution case which may be prejudicial to the defence, and therefore fiercely opposed. The merits of such applications are determined by the judge in the absence of the jury, and the battle over admissibility is a characteristic feature of criminal cases.

8.43 In children's cases there is a duty to enquire how best to secure the welfare of the child: because the welfare of the child is the paramount consideration, it is proper that all relevant issues are brought to the attention of the court. Accordingly, evidence which is second- or third-hand hearsay, and evidence which may in other proceedings claim the protection of privilege, confidentiality or public interest immunity, is likely to be admissible in children's cases.

8.44 The court in children's cases, whether a professional judge or lay magistrates assisted by the court clerk, has ultimate discretion over the admissibility of evidence. Evidence deriving from covert video surveillance showing a mother harming her child, even where it has been improperly or illegally obtained, has been held to be admissible in children's cases (see *Re DH (A Minor) (Child Abuse)* [1994] 1 FLR 679). The receiving of prejudical evidence into children's proceedings is broadly capable of challenge, because it may be irrelevant. Where evidence is deemed to be prejudicial to a party, reliance may now be made upon Article 6 of the ECHR which provides the right to a fair trial. Some categories of evidence are deemed to be too unreliable to be admitted into children's proceedings: in *Re D (Evidence: Facilitated Communication)* [2001] 1 FLR 148, the President of the Family Division ruled that evidence obtained from a technique whereby a victim of sexual abuse, who suffered cognitive disability and was unable to speak, was assisted in pointing towards a communication board, should be not used to confirm or deny allegations of sexual abuse.

8.45 In any event, evidence admitted into the Family Court is subject to the normal judicial process of evaluation. Evidence which is corroborated by other witnesses or other evidence, or where it is given by a credible, reputable or authoritative witness is likely to be given the appropriate weight. Evidence which is unsupported by other evidence or is unconvincing may be rejected or ignored by the court.

Hearsay evidence: in general

8.46   Hearsay arises in judicial proceedings where evidence of something that has been said or an event which has happened comes before the court, other than as a result of the direct oral evidence in court of a witness to the event who is sworn or has affirmed to tell the truth. A witness may give oral evidence of something she has seen or has heard said in her presence. Evidence of anything said or done other than in her presence, reported to a witness by a third party, is therefore hearsay. Historically, the rules of evidence have not permitted such evidence to be before the court to prove the truth of matters contained within it: hearsay evidence is intrinsically less reliable and inferior and is therefore excluded.

8.47   In civil proceedings, generally, there has been a move towards the admissibility of hearsay. Section 1(1) of the Civil Evidence Act 1995 provides that in all civil proceedings evidence shall not be excluded on the ground that it is hearsay. Because children's proceedings are inquisitorial, courts dealing with children's cases need to be able to receive evidence which may in other courts be excluded as hearsay. Section 96(3) of the CA 1989 entitled the Lord Chancellor to make provision for the admissibility of hearsay in respect of children's cases. The children's courts were therefore permitted to accept hearsay evidence ahead of the general civil courts.

8.48   The current order governing the admissibility of hearsay in children's proceedings is the Children (Admissibility of Hearsay Evidence) Order 1993, SI 1993/621 (superseding the 1990 and 1991 Orders). The present state of the law is that in civil proceedings before the High Court or a county court, in family proceedings, and in civil proceedings under the Child Support Act 1991 in a magistrates' court, evidence given in connection with the upbringing, maintenance or welfare of a child will be admissible notwithstanding any rule of law relating to hearsay.

Forms of hearsay admissible

8.49   The use of the word 'evidence' in the order does not limit the type or origin of admissible hearsay in any way. Thus, medical or scientific records such as charts showing paediatric measurements, are admissible The expert responsible for the compiling of those measurements or tests may be needed to give oral evidence as to their interpretation, but will not be required to prove their provenance. Reports from consultant psychiatrists or doctors which are the foundation of the average care case are therefore admissible as documents without the need for the maker to attend court, although any party who disagrees with their content will in practice require the witness for cross-examination.

8.50   The evidence admitted need not be confined to first-hand hearsay, but may be second- or third-hand or even more remote. The consecutive running records compiled by social workers, general practitioners and social workers will be admissible as evidence, even in circumstances where the individual makers of each part of the document may no longer be traceable.

8.51 The evidence of children also becomes admissible, without their having to attend court to give evidence, or be cross-examined (see *C v C (Contempt: Evidence)* [1993] 1 FLR 220, CA). This may take the form of a written letter or picture sent to the judge, a note by the guardian of what a child has said directly to him or her, and the video and written evidence of what a child has said when asked questions by police or social worker in the form of the memorandum interview. Attempts by parties to care proceedings to secure the live attendance of children for the purpose of cross-examination have been expressly disapproved by the High Court in *Re P (Witness Summons)* [1997] 2 FLR 447. A mother and stepfather sought a witness summons against a 12-year-old child who had alleged that the stepfather had abused her. Wilson J referred to the damage that can be caused by questioning a child complainant, and indicated that generally in cases involving children of 12 or younger, the absence of the child's oral evidence was desirable.

Weight given to hearsay evidence

8.52 The admissibility of hearsay within children's proceedings does not absolve the court of its duty to consider and assess the appropriate weight to be placed upon evidence received by it. The difficulty with admitting hearsay evidence is that it is not possible to cross-examine the person who originally observed or reported the incident being recounted at second hand by the witness. The question of relevance arises at every stage and in relation to every piece of evidence. Whilst it is axiomatic that the court should always receive the best evidence available to it, there are circumstances in which written evidence which is technically hearsay may be preferred to oral evidence which is inaccurate, self-serving or deliberately untruthful.

8.53 The children's courts are aware that in the interests of justice to all the parties concerned, including considerations of the right to a fair trial under Article 6 of the ECHR, as well as the need to make the best decision for the child concerned, hearsay evidence has to be carefully handled. There must be proper judicial recognition of the fact of hearsay, and consideration of the extent to which it may be relied upon. By direction of the President of the Family Division, where hearsay evidence is adduced, 'the source of the information must be declared, or good reason given for not doing so' (see *Practice Direction of 31 January 1995 (Case Management)* [1995] 1 FLR 456, at para 3).

8.54 The proper approach to hearsay evidence is thus to address the extent to which surrounding circumstances indicate the accuracy or otherwise of the statement received in evidence: whether the maker of the statement was a credible witness, or had any motive to conceal or to misrepresent, and whether the statement was made contemporaneously with or as close as possible to the events alleged to have occurred. The further the evidence is from the original source of the statement, the less weight the court is likely to attach to it.

Hearsay evidence in applications for emergency protection orders

8.55   An emergency protection order entitles the applicant immediately to remove a child from his carer where there is reasonable cause to believe that the child is likely to suffer significant harm (CA 1989, s 44(1)). The paramount need to protect the welfare of the child in an emergency provides an example of how strict rules of evidence may be subordinated to welfare considerations in children's cases. Section 45(7) of the CA 1989 provides as follows:

> 'Regardless of any enactment or rule of law which would otherwise prevent it from doing so, a court hearing an application for, or with respect to, an emergency protection order may take account of –
>
> (a)   any statement contained in any report made to the court in the course of, or in connection with, the hearing; or
> (b)   any evidence given during the hearing,
>
> which is, in the opinion of the court, relevant to the application.'

8.56   It is consistent with the aims of the CA 1989 that where abuse may be alleged, emergency protection orders can be made quickly. Section 45(7) ensures that this can be done without the need for first-hand oral evidence as to the facts relied upon. The rights of parents are, however, recognised by the prohibition against the renewal of the emergency protection order on more than one occasion, and the right to apply for the discharge of the order after 72 hours (s 44(6) and (9)).

Hearsay evidence in reports of the guardian

8.57   The CA 1989 makes further statutory provision for the admissibility of hearsay. Guardians in public law proceedings for care and supervision orders have a special status, in that they are intended to be seen as independent of the conflicting interests of parent and local authority. Their primary duty is to safeguard the welfare of the child. Their power is quasi-inquisitorial, in that there is a requirement upon the guardian to make such investigations as are necessary, and to bring to the attention of the court 'all such records and documents which may in his opinion assist in the proper determination of the proceedings' (see FPR 1991, r 4.11(9)(b); FPC(CA 1989)R 1991, r 11(9)(b)).

8.58   The special position of the children's guardian is undefined by statutory exceptions relating to the admissibility of his evidence. Thus the CA 1989, s 41(11) provides:

'Regardless of any enactment or rule of law which would otherwise prevent it from doing so, the court may take account of –

(a) any statement contained in a report by a guardian ad litem who is appointed under this section for the purpose of the proceedings in question; and

(b) any evidence given in respect of the matters referred to in the report,

in so far as the statement or evidence is, in the opinion of the court, relevant to the question which the court is considering.'

8.59 This section covers 'any statement', not just one made personally by the guardian: as such, anything told to a guardian by, for example, a health visitor or school teacher, who may not have provided their own statements within proceedings, immediately becomes admissible.

8.60 The children's guardian may also be the conduit for the admissibility of material contained within local authority records which relate to the child. The guardian has the right 'to examine and take copies of' local authority records (CA 1989, s 42(1)). A copy of such a record taken by a guardian is 'admissible as evidence of any matter referred to in any report which the guardian makes to the court, or evidence which he gives in the proceedings' (s 42(2)). Even where a local authority claims public interest immunity to protect its records from inspection or disclosure, it cannot prevail over the express provisions of s 42 (see *Re T (A Minor) (Guardian ad Litem: Case Record)* [1994] 1 FLR 632).

Evidence in interviews with children

8.61 The purpose of an interview of a child victim, which has been done in accordance with the *Achieving the Best Evidence in Criminal Proceedings: Guidance for Vulnerable or Intimidated Witnesses, Including Children* (DOH, 2002) is to provide the best possible device for placing the evidence of a child before the family court, without the need for a live appearance by the child: the interview is available to the court through the medium of video-tape, and thus is obviously hearsay in form. Difficulties in dealing with the evidence of children in child abuse cases were raised in cases dealing with satanic abuse in the early 1990s (see *Re A and Others (Minors) (Child Abuse: Guidelines)* [1992] 1 FLR 439; *Rochdale Borough Council v A and Others* [1991] 2 FLR 192). The *Memorandum of Good Practice* was issued by the Home Office and the DOH in 1992. For research on memorandum interviews see *Interviewing Child Witnesses under the Memorandum of Good Practice* (Home Office, 1999). See also *Re N (Child Abuse: Evidence)* [1996] 2 FLR 214, CA. Although the *Memorandum* was intended solely for dealing with child witnesses in criminal proceedings, it led to great improvements in the practice of interviewing children, and its principles were therefore adhered to in children's cases in the civil courts also. The *Memorandum* has been replaced since 2001 by Volume 1 Part 2 of *Achieving Best Evidence in Criminal Proceedings* (Home Office, 2001) and this should now be the baseline guidance for all those interviewing children in whatever format for the purpose of court proceedings, including those taking place in the civil courts. The detail of the new guidance with regard to best practice on the process of interviewing children and the recording of such interviews can be found at paras **9.81–9.93**.

8.62 In practice, all video interviews of children by police and social workers will be admissible in the children's courts, where their content is relevant. It is for the judge alone to decide what weight and credibility attach to video material. There is inherent in the guidance interview a tension between the police officer trying to secure clear and cogent evidence for use in a prosecution, and the social worker attempting to place the child at ease and provide reassurance and support. It has not been uncommon for interviews to fall short of the earlier *Memorandum* guidelines, for example by using leading questions, failing to approach the interview with an open mind or pressure on the child to make disclosures. Under the terms of the *Achieving the Best Evidence* guidance, such inadequacies do not render the interview inadmissible but may seriously devalue the evidential weight of what a child may say. This was indeed found to be so in cases when the *Memorandum* was still the operative guidance. Thus, in *Re D (Child Abuse: Interviews)* [1998] 2 FLR 10, CA, the Court of Appeal allowed the appeal of a father from findings made against him of sexual abuse. A 4-year-old child had made no disclosure in a *Memorandum* interview, but had been repeatedly interviewed by social workers before producing drawings and making further allegations against the father. The Court of Appeal concluded 'where these general guidelines were not followed, although evidence was unlikely to be excluded entirely, it would usually be of such little weight that the court would not be able to rely upon it'.

Disclosure

8.63 The inquisitorial nature of children's proceedings means that a wide range of evidence may be placed by the parties before the court through the process known as 'disclosure'. Because of the inquisitorial process, in children's proceedings a *duty of disclosure* has developed, which has been described as being 'almost unknown in other jurisdictions, save in the arena of the interlocutory injunction' (see Burrows (1999), at p 101). The term 'discovery' is sometimes used in association with disclosure, to describe the process by which documents or material are asked for, in order to be disclosed into legal proceedings.

8.64 In children's cases, in particular those in which child abuse is alleged, and where there may be criminal or other proceedings in train, there may be parties who wish to resist the normal process of disclosure. In theory, a party to care proceedings who seeks to prevent prejudicial evidence being received by the family court may rely on three arguments: that material is subject to privilege, is covered by public interest immunity or is confidential. The importance of the welfare principle since the CA 1989, and the extent to which the court is willing to adopt an inquisitorial role, has seen the erosion of these principles in the direction of blanket disclosure *into* children's proceedings. Evidence may also be disclosed *out of* children's proceedings, for use by parties to those proceedings in other arenas, or to third parties not involved in the children's proceedings.

8.65 However, there are important restrictions in the disclosure of material filed in children's cases to individuals who are not parties to the proceedings, and to the outside world in general. Since the adoption of the ECHR by the HRA 1998 which came into force in October 2000, disclosure in child abuse cases in England and Wales now has to be considered in the light of the ECHR, principally but not exclusively those Articles establishing the right to a fair trial and the right to family life.

Disclosure of social work records

8.66 A local authority which takes public law proceedings against parents has to cross the 'threshold' in order to secure an interim care order under the CA 1989, s 38(2) or a final order under s 31. Cases of child abuse will often have had the involvement of social workers where neglect or emotional abuse is also a factor. There may be forensic issues about factual material or allegations held by the local authority in their social work records. A local authority thus has a high duty in the interests of the welfare of the child to disclose 'all relevant material' save that protected by public interest immunity, to parties in care proceedings (see *R v Hampshire County Council ex parte K and Another* [1990] 1 FLR 330). The incorporation of the ECHR into English domestic law also entitles parties to rely on Article 6 which provides for the right to a fair trial. Previous decisions in European law have held that this includes the right of a parent to consult the relevant evidence which is available to the authorities (see *Feldbrugge v The Netherlands* (1986) 8 EHRR 425). It is therefore good practice for local authorities to disclose the social work records which form the foundation for their court statements of social workers.

8.67 Judicial guidance has been given on what categories of social work documents ought normally to be disclosed within children's proceedings. In *Re A and Others (Minors) (Child Abuse: Guidelines)* [1992] 1 FLR 439, a case involving allegations of ritual and sexual abuse to a number of children by members of an extended family, the local authority freely disclosed a variety of evidence, including notes made by the social workers and foster parents, the running log of the social workers, and the minutes of case conferences and reviews. This was approved by the court, who held that a local authority should provide discovery of original material recording matters of fact in relation to children, parents or other relevant persons, especially transcripts and records of matters in issue. The court recognised that notes or records of case conferences or meetings where opinions were given were in a different category: professionals attending who may be from other disciplines and not in the employment of the local authority should be able to express opinions freely, without having to look over their shoulder. It is thus open to a local authority to assert public interest immunity for this category of material, although any privilege attaching to those documents may be voluntarily waived by the local authority.

Present practice in disclosure

8.68 The present practice in disclosure is that local authorities generally recognise that parents who are parties to children's proceedings and who have to deal with allegations of child abuse need to have access to social work records to address the allegations against them. In care proceedings, it has been held that a local authority has a duty to disclose all relevant information which may assist parents in rebutting allegations against them, or may modify or cast doubt upon the case advanced against them (see *Re C (Expert Evidence: Disclosure: Practice)* [1995] 1 FLR 204).

8.69 The local authority may therefore volunteer disclosure, despite the cost in time and money in providing multiple copies of records which may be numerous, difficult to read and of varying degrees of relevance. Where there are likely to be factual issues arising out of social work records, parties should apply their minds to pre-trial discovery, to avoid unnecessary delay during the trial while material is obtained and distributed (see *Re JC (Care Proceedings: Procedure)* [1995] 2 FLR 77, at p 82C). However, there is little point in disclosure of material which may be irrelevant. The guardian, who is permitted access to local authority files under s 42 of the CA 1989, may determine which documents should be disclosed to the parents. It is not the position that there be 'carte blanche disclosure of social work notes and records' (at p 83C), as in each case a proper case for discovery must be made out.

Disclosure of medical records and reports

8.70 Medical records may be relevant material in child abuse cases. The medical recording of a child's injuries are fundamental to the proceedings and therefore will be admissible. In certain circumstances, the records of a GP or hospital notes may also be relevant: for example, where a child is admitted to hospital after an injury, nursing notes may contain highly relevant material about the attendance of the parents and their demeanour to the child.

8.71 Medical notes are privileged documents. They may also be subject to public interest immunity. The preservation of the confidence which exists between a patient and the doctors, nurses and other medical staff who have dealings with him is a matter of fundamental principle, and is enshrined within the codes of conduct which govern the medical profession (see eg *R v Mid Glamorgan Family Health Services and Another ex parte Martin* [1995] 1 FLR 283, CA). It is axiomatic that a doctor must refrain from disclosing information about a patient to a third party. There is nevertheless a recognition that, exceptionally, the professional obligation of confidence may be overridden where disclosure is in the public interest. A doctor owes a duty to his patient to preserve confidentiality, but he owes a duty to the public which may be greater than his duty to the patient. In particular, where a doctor has reason to believe that a child is being physically or sexually abused, it is permissible for a doctor to disclose information to a third party; it is the view of the GMC that there is a positive duty upon a doctor to do so (see *General Medical Council Annual Report 1987*, cited in *Working Together under the Children Act 1989: A Guide to Inter-Agency Cooperation for the Protection of Children from Abuse* (DOH, 1991), at p 12).

8.72 The trend towards disclosure is reflected in *Re C (A Minor) (Evidence: Confidential Information)* [1991] 2 FLR 478, CA, in which proposed adopters sought to rely upon a sworn statement from a mother's GP which was adverse to her. It was held by the President of the Family Division that the statement of the GP was admissible: the public interest in the restricted disclosure to the court of relevant confidential material concerning the mother's medical condition in the special circumstances of the case prevailed over the public interest in the need to maintain confidentiality between doctor and patient. Any reluctance by a doctor to produce medical records may be overcome by a witness summons to give evidence, since it has always been accepted that doctors are obliged to answer questions put to them in court about their own patients (see Kingham (1991)).

Disclosure of video evidence

8.73 Doctors may also be obliged to disclose material including video-recordings to parties in children proceedings. Such disclosure may in the children's interests be limited to the lawyers but withheld from the parents. In *B v B (Child Abuse: Evidence)* [1991] 2 FLR 487, Johnson J considered a submission by the Hospital for Sick Children, Great Ormond Street, that video-recordings of a child in which allegations of sexual abuse against a father were made were confidential to the child, and should only be disclosed to the doctors and lawyers involved, not to the parents. The judge held that the video material was not privileged, but should not be shown to the parents because of the potential damage to the child that might flow from the parents seeing the disclosure.

8.74   It now seems likely that parents should have video material disclosed to them. In *TP and KM v United Kingdom* [2001] 2 FLR 549, a case decided in the European Court, a mother and daughter were awarded damages for breach of both applicants' right to respect for family life under Article 8 of the ECHR and breach of their right to an effective remedy under Article 13. A local authority had removed the daughter temporarily from the mother's care on the basis of an ambivalent disclosure about the mother's boyfriend in a video interview, and on the advice of a social worker and psychiatrist who conducted the interview, failed to disclose the video to the mother or the court.

8.75   The decision in *TP and KM v United Kingdom* flowed from a decision to withhold video evidence in care proceedings as long ago as 1987. It is now accepted practice that legal advisers and medical experts instructed by them, should have access to videos made in hospitals. The practice of hospitals of declining to permit video-tapes or copies of video-tapes to leave their premises has been disapproved by the High Court: see *Re R (Child Abuse: Video Evidence)* [1995] 1 FLR 451 and *Re M (Child Abuse: Video Evidence)* [1995] 2 FLR 571. Solicitors should be permitted custody of video-tapes, on the receipt of specific undertakings as to their use, as travel costs to view videos can add disproportionately to legal costs, and may inhibit experts from having free access to such material. Such procedures apply equally to videos compiled in the course of child protection or criminal investigations and held in police stations.

Legal privilege

8.76   There is a fundamental principle that certain documents are regarded as privileged. This means that they are absolutely private and immune from discovery by any third party. Included in the category of legal privilege are communications between an individual and his lawyers, and documents produced to assist the lawyers in the preparation for and the conduct of legal action. Legal professional privilege has been described as:

> 'much more than an ordinary rule of evidence, limited in its application to the facts of a particular case. It is a fundamental condition on which the administration of justice as a whole rests' (*R v Derby Magistrates ex parte B* [1996] 1 FLR 513, HL).

Lawyers are therefore bound absolutely by the concept of privilege from disclosing documents. Privilege may be waived only with the express permission of the party concerned.

The limitations of privilege in children's cases

8.77   Occasionally, an issue may arise as to the discovery of expert or other evidence which is adverse to the interests of a parent, although highly relevant to the question of the welfare of the child. The welfare principle thus comes directly into conflict with the principle that information given by a party in confidence to his legal adviser, or evidence collected on his behalf for the advancement of his case, is privileged.

8.78 Prior to the CA 1989, in *Re A (Minors) (Disclosure of Material)* [1991] 2 FLR 473, a mother was suspected of causing the death of one of her children by deliberate suffocation. She failed to file a report from a paediatric pathologist instructed on her behalf, which was adverse to her. Johnson J referred to the parental, administrative and non-adversarial character of the wardship jurisdiction, and held that the High Court did have the power to override the legal professional privilege which attached to such a report. That power, however, was to be exercised 'only rarely, and only when the court is satisfied that it is necessary for it to be exercised in order to achieve the best interests of the child involved'.

Privilege in CA 1989 cases

8.79 The current position is that the legal professional privilege which attaches to communications between a party and his lawyer remains intact and such documents are not subject to disclosure. Where there were parallel criminal and care proceedings following injuries to a child, the High Court has upheld the father's right to claim the protection of legal professional privilege in respect of the non-disclosure of the identity of medical experts he had instructed in the criminal proceedings, their notes and reports. The court upheld legal privilege, despite the welfare of the child being the court's paramount consideration, and the high duty of disclosure in such proceedings (see *S County Council v B* [2000] 2 FLR 161).

8.80 Within care proceedings, the position is different in relation to documents obtained by a party once proceedings have been issued. It is now clear that a parent or party in children's proceedings must disclose to the court any expert report commissioned on the instruction of the party which then turns out to be adverse to his interests.

8.81 In *Re L (Police Investigation: Privilege)* [1996] 1 FLR 731, HL, a child had been admitted to hospital having consumed methadone. It was suspected that the mother had deliberately administered the drug to the child. The mother obtained leave of the court subject to r 4.23 of the FPR 1991 to instruct a chemical pathologist as to the drug taken by the child, and filed the report with the court. The police, supported by the guardian, sought the disclosure of the report to themselves, as they were considering criminal proceedings against the mother. The mother's appeal to the House of Lords against disclosure of the document to the police was dismissed by a 3:2 majority. The mother's subsequent appeal to the European Court also failed: it was held that she had not been deprived of the right to a fair trial, as she was legally represented and able to cross-examine and adduce other evidence to counteract that part of the report which was adverse to her. There was no unfairness in the requirement to disclose the expert's report, as this applied equally to all parties in the care proceedings (see *L v UK* [2000] 2 FLR 322, ECHR).

8.82 It is therefore clear that where a party to children's proceedings has been given leave to disclose confidential material to a third party in order to obtain a report, it is a condition of leave that the report must be filed at court and served upon all parties, and may be vulnerable to further disclosure to third parties outside the proceedings, such as the police.

8.83 The existence of adverse material may come about in the course of day-to-day dealings between solicitor and client. It is established that such communication may not attract the shield of privilege, and therefore may be disclosable, where it is not strictly concerned with legal advice (see *R v Manchester Crown Court ex parte Rogers* [1999] 1 WLR 832). In *C v C (Evidence: Privilege)* [2001] 2 FLR 184, the Court of Appeal permitted the use by the mother of an affidavit sworn by the father's solicitor in an application to the court to come off the record, detailing the content of telephone calls which were abusive and threatening. The father's behaviour as revealed in the affidavit was evidence of the very type of conduct at issue in CA 1989 proceedings between the parties which had been denied by the father, and its discovery into those proceedings was therefore permitted.

8.84 The question of whether there is a duty placed upon legal representatives who may handle or receive material damaging to their clients to make voluntary disclosure of all matters relevant to a child's welfare remains unresolved. The existence of a positive duty placed upon an advocate to disclose matters pertaining to the welfare of a child where against the interests of the client was raised speculatively in *Essex County Council v R* [1993] 2 FLR 826 (per Thorpe J), but has not been approved by case-law. In principle, solicitor–client communications therefore remain privileged and confidential. However, in wardship proceedings a solicitor may be ordered to disclose information as to the location of a parent who has abducted a child in order to assist in tracing their whereabouts (see *Re H (Abduction: Whereabouts Order to Solicitors)* [2000] 1 FLR 766).

Public interest immunity

8.85 Public interest immunity is a doctrine developed to enable the courts to protect information from disclosure, on the grounds that public interest requires it. Therefore, documents or information coming into existence at the highest level of government and policy-making will not be disclosed where the public interest requires non-disclosure, irrespective of the hardship occasioned to a litigant who may wish to rely upon them.

8.86 Public interest immunity therefore attaches primarily to documents held by public bodies, such as local authorities in pursuance of their social services function, or, for example, by the NSPCC. It may be in the public interest that such documents are not disclosed. The justification for this principle has been explained in *Re D (Infants)* [1970] 1 WLR 599. Harman LJ held (at p 610E) that disclosure of such documents was contrary to public policy:

> 'Because these records must not be kept by people looking over their shoulders in case they should be attacked for some opinion they may feel it their duty to express.'

8.87 A public authority with a statutory duty to keep records would find it difficult to perform that public duty if it were under the apprehension that such material might come under public scrutiny in a court of law. It is therefore open to social workers to contend that material within their files relating to children is subject to an absolute assurance of confidentiality, and should not be disclosed. This may particularly be the case where there are allegations of child abuse from named third party sources who may otherwise fear reprisal. Other bodies such as the probation service may also claim the shield of public interest immunity in relation to documents held by them (see *Re M (Minors) (Confidential Documents)* [1987] 1 FLR 46).

Public interest immunity and waiver

8.88 Historically, one of the defining features of the doctrine of public interest immunity, and one that precisely distinguishes it from privilege, is that it cannot be waived by the organisation protecting its documents from disclosure. In *Campbell v Tameside MBC* [1982] QB 1065, CA, the Court of Appeal held that public interest immunity is capable of being waived in respect of documents dealing with matters of day-to-day administration and record-keeping, as opposed to matters of central government policy. In practice, therefore, organisations holding documents required for disclosure into children's cases prefer that the courts should make the decision over disclosure.

Public interest immunity in children's cases

8.89 Circumstances may arise within children's proceedings where a party seeks to advance his case by the disclosure of documents covered by public interest immunity. In *Re M (A Minor) (Disclosure of Material)* [1990] 2 FLR 36, CA, a father applied for general discovery of social work records relating to his elder daughter, which contained allegations of rape and incest against him, in wardship proceedings relating to a younger half-sister. Refusing the father's appeal, the Court of Appeal held that social work documents were covered by public interest immunity, although there was no absolute rule against disclosure. An application for specific documents was possible, but the party applying for discovery must establish the need for the production of a specific document. It was for the court to perform the balancing exercise between the competing interests of public interest immunity and disclosure, but the court itself should inspect the documents only where there were definite grounds for expecting to find material of real importance to the applicant (at p 44C). A current view expressed in *Re R (Care: Disclosure: Nature of Proceedings)* [2002] 1 FLR 755 is that as a class of documents, social work records are not subject to public interest immunity, so that any claim to resist disclosure based on public interest immunity must set out the particular harm that it is alleged will be caused to the public interest if the matter is disclosed.

8.90	In *Re C (Expert Evidence: Disclosure: Practice)* [1995] 1 FLR 204, Cazalet J considered the role of public interest immunity and set out the following guidelines to be considered when deciding whether immunity applied to a particular document or class of document in care proceedings:

– A local authority has a duty to disclose all relevant information which might assist parents to rebut allegations made against them, save for documents which might be protected by public interest immunity.
– It was then for the party seeking disclosure to show the reasons why the documents should be produced, but it was for the court to decide whether documents covered by public interest immunity should be disclosed.
– The local authority is under a duty to disclose relevant documents, not protected by public interest immunity, which modify or cast doubt upon its case.
– If a relevant document appears protected by public interest immunity, the local authority should draw the existence of the document to the notice of the other parties. The local authority should prepare a précis of the information, which would be disclosed if ordered.
– The local authority should draw the guardian ad litem's attention to any matters of concern within the documents. Moreover, if in the course of inspecting social services files, the guardian ad litem finds relevant records which have not been disclosed, he should invite disclosure by the local authority. The guardian ad litem, however, is not entitled to disclose documents covered by public interest immunity.

8.91	The main feature which emerges from these guidelines is the general duty of the local authority to give discovery of documents. The local authority may claim public interest immunity, in which case the onus then shifts to the party seeking the documents to persuade the court that they should be discovered. It is then for the court to decide whether public interest immunity should apply.

Public interest immunity in criminal cases

8.92   Where criminal charges are laid alleging the abuse, neglect or physical assault of children, parallel material may be held in social services files, in addition to the documentary evidence filed in care proceedings. Defence lawyers in criminal prosecutions involving children may apply within children's proceedings for the disclosure of documents held by social services. Of particular interest to the defendant would be records showing that a child alleging abuse had been recorded as having a history of similar allegations against others, was believed to be a liar or had an unstable lifestyle (see *Re D (Minors) (Wardship: Disclosure)* [1994] 1 FLR 346).

8.93   In such cases, it has been recommended that the question of disclosure be left to the trial judge in the criminal proceedings: 'he alone will be in a position to assess the relevance and likely effect of the disclosure of any material which might be contained in the documents' (see *Re H (Criminal Proceedings: Disclosure of Adoption Records)* [1995] 1 FLR 964). The family court should not therefore make an order or ruling binding the judge conducting a criminal trial. Application is made to the criminal court by subpoena to the local authority social services department for public interest immunity to be set aside and for material held by social services to be disclosed (see also *Handbook of Best Practice in Children Act Cases*, reprinted in *The Family Court Practice* (Family Law, 2002), at section 7 which deals with the recommended procedure for prosecution and defence to obtain disclosure of local authority records).

Principles to be applied in determining disclosure of social services files

8.94   Applications in criminal proceedings for the disclosure of social services documents relating to children are now governed by the decision in *R v Reading Justices ex parte Berkshire County Council* [1996] 1 FLR 149. This case involved an application for documents to the magistrates' court under the Magistrates' Courts Act 1980, s 97, but the principles deriving from the judgment were expressly approved by the Lord Chief Justice in *R v Derby Magistrates' Court ex parte B* [1996] AC 487, HL, and are therefore relevant to applications made directly to the Crown Court.

8.95   The *Reading Justices* case establishes that only 'material evidence' should be disclosed. The principles are as follows:

'(i)   to be material evidence, documents must not only be relevant to the issues arising in the criminal proceedings, but also documents admissible as such in evidence;

(ii)   documents which are desired merely for the purpose of possible cross-examination are not admissible in evidence, and thus not material for the purpose of s.97;

(iii) whoever seeks the production of documents must satisfy the justices with some material that the documents are "likely to be material" in the sense indicated, likelihood for this purpose involving a real possibility, although not necessarily a probability;

(iv)   it is not sufficient that the applicant merely wants to find out whether or not the third party has such material documents. This procedure must not be used as a disguised attempt to obtain discovery.'

8.96 Bodies such as social services resisting an application to set aside public interest immunity therefore may succeed where the application is to gain sight of material to use solely in cross-examination of a prosecution witness, because documents are not admissible in their own right in criminal proceedings. Similarly, hearsay and the written opinions of social workers and third parties are not admissible in criminal proceedings, save under limited statutory exceptions. (Section 23 of the Criminal Evidence Act 1988 provides for the admissibility of hearsay evidence where hearsay is made in a document, and the author of the statement could have given direct oral evidence of the facts contained within it, but is prevented from doing so by specified circumstances.) It is also open for the local authority to argue the immateriality of the documents or information sought, because their contents are irrelevant to the defence case.

8.97 Once a judge decides that documents are material, by virtue of their relevance and admissibility, the question of public interest immunity falls to be considered. The local authority must then argue that disclosure should not be ordered, by asserting public interest immunity. In reality, once the court is satisfied that the documents are material, disclosure is likely to be ordered, subject to performing the 'balancing exercise' of weighing the need of the defendant to defend himself against the public interest in maintaining confidentiality.

8.98 The Court of Criminal Appeal has held that it is not necessary for the trial judge to read social services files in order to determine an application for disclosure: the judge may properly accept the assurances of 'an independent competent member of the Bar that the documents requested were irrelevant' (see *R v W(G); R v W(E)* [1996] Crim LR 904). The Court of Appeal envisaged that counsel for the local authority would determine which documents were relevant by reading them through in the light of the particulars in the summons. The judge could accept that submission and order disclosure, or go on to read the files himself. The obligation upon a local authority engaged in a search through its files is only to indicate the relevance of documents it holds to the questions asked in the summons, not to help the defence by providing documents which have not been asked for. Public interest immunity must then be asserted and cannot be waived by the local authority: the formal setting aside of public interest immunity remains a matter for the judge.

Confidential documents

8.99 The welfare of children demands that there should be a full exchange of information between professionals prior to and after the inception of proceedings. Conversely, circumstances may also arise where material is held to be confidential and therefore withheld from or not shared with other parties in children proceedings.

Disclosure of confidential information among professionals

8.100 It is in the interests of child protection that there should be a proper exchange of information between the multiple agencies jointly concerned in child protection work.

8.101 The final conclusions of the Cleveland Report made a strong recommendation for the development of inter-agency co-operation between health and social services professionals, police and voluntary organisations, and for proper channels of communication to be set up between these bodies (*Report of the Inquiry into Child Abuse in Cleveland* (1987), at pp 248–250).

8.102 On the other hand, the FPR 1991 established the statutory requirement of confidentiality in children's cases. In the family courts, the rules provide as follows:

> 'Notwithstanding any rule of court to the contrary, no document, other than a record of an order, held by the court and relating to proceedings to which this Part applies shall be disclosed, other than to –
>
> (a) a party
> (b) the legal representative of a party
> (c) the children's guardian
> (d) the Legal Aid Board, or
> (e) a welfare officer or children and family reporter
> (f) an expert whose instruction has been authorised by the court
>
> without leave of the judge or district judge' (FPR 1991, r 4.23(1); FPC(CA 1989)R 1991, r 23, as amended by SI 2001/821).

8.103 This means that any document other than a court order relating to children's proceedings and filed at court may not be disclosed to third parties without the express leave of the court. This rule sits uncomfortably with the inter-disciplinary co-operation envisaged by the Cleveland Report. In *Re G (A Minor) (Social Worker: Disclosure)* [1996] 1 WLR 1407, CA, a local authority appealed against a ruling that a social worker was not entitled to disclose documents to the police. The Court of Appeal restated the Cleveland principles that multi-disciplinary agencies engaged in child protection must not be fettered in the free exchange of information through formal channels such as a case conference, or informal communications. It was held by a majority of the court that the leave requirement applied only to documents actually filed with the court (at p 282G; *Oxfordshire County Council v P (A Minor)* [1995] 1 FLR 552 disapproved on this point; see also Chapter **7**; for more detailed discussion of this issue). A social worker does not need leave to disclose information recorded in case files, or a report which for whatever reason has never reached the court. Where the document is created in contemplation of proceedings, leave is not needed in the interests of promoting co-operation between professionals such as police and social workers in dealing with allegations of child abuse. This principle has been confirmed by the Court of Appeal in *Re W (Disclosure to Police)* [1998] 2 FLR 135, CA, in respect of documents and information in existence where proceedings are pending.

8.104 Since 1998, the Data Protection Act 1998 has further developed the access allowed in limited circumstances by individuals to documents in social services files, from that previously allowed under the terms of the Access to Personal Files Act 1987. Access may be refused where serious harm may result to the person requesting the data, or to some other person (Data Protection (Subject Access Modification) (Social Work) Order 2000, SI 2000/415). However, s 35 of the Act provides that personal data may be disclosed where required by an order of the court, or where it is necessary for the purpose of any legal proceedings. Confidential files may be disclosed with third party identities concealed. (For further discussion on this see Chapters **5** and **6**.)

Duty of statutory bodies to provide information

8.105 Statutory bodies have a duty to disclose information to a local authority where its staff believe that a child may be suffering significant harm (CA 1989, s 47). This duty extends to the education and housing authorities, to health authorities and anyone else authorised by the Secretary of State. To this extent, therefore, confidentiality between professionals has been reduced by statute. Such information may relate to a child, or to an adult, such as an alleged perpetrator. Material obtained in this way could then be disclosed in subsequent children's proceedings. Further, their discovery could be compelled, subject to issues of public interest immunity, and the guardian would have access to such information under s 42. Application by a guardian to see a wide range of material is likely to be successful. In *Re R (Care*

Proceedings: Disclosure) [2000] 2 FLR 751, the Court of Appeal held that a report compiled by an area child protection committee into the death of a child's half-brother should be disclosed to the guardian in order to assist in assessing the mother's future capacity to care for the surviving child. In *Nottinghamshire County Council v H* [1995] 1 FLR 115, a local authority successfully sought disclosure from the police of documents relating to forthcoming criminal prosecution, in order to enable it to make a more informed decision about the future of children who were the subject of care proceedings.

Oral admissions

8.106 It follows from the above that a social worker is free to pass on spoken admissions which may have implications for child protection: admissions made to social workers and recorded in writing in the social work files are not governed by the FPR 1991, r 4.23. However, an oral admission by a parent to a guardian may be treated differently to those received by social workers. This is because the role of the guardian is essentially created by the court proceedings; thus a guardian should seek the leave of the court before disclosing information to the police (see *Oxfordshire County Council v P* [1995] 1 FLR 552).

Confidentiality between parties

8.107 It is a fundamental principle that a court should not make findings or draw conclusions upon evidence or information which a party to legal proceedings has not seen, and is not therefore in a position to deal with. Occasionally, in children's proceedings, a party may wish to rely upon material in court which he wishes to keep confidential. Another party may then not know of its existence or content. In *Official Solicitor v K* [1965] AC 201, HL, a case heard prior to the CA 1989, the House of Lords held that within the wardship jurisdiction, confidential reports might exceptionally be submitted to the court but withheld from the parties; the test is whether the material is reliable, and whether 'real harm' to the child might ensue if the material is fully disclosed.

8.108 In *Re B (A Minor) (Disclosure of Evidence)* [1993] 1 FLR 191, CA, the Court of Appeal ruled that the court had jurisdiction to direct that material, disclosure of which might be damaging to the child, should not be disclosed to a party. The disclosure had to be so detrimental to the child's welfare as to outweigh the normal requirements of a fair trial, and was only to be ordered in exceptional circumstances and for the shortest period possible. The procedure to be adopted in cases where leave to withhold material is sought was addressed in *Re C (Disclosure)* [1996] 1 FLR 797, where the court suggested that contentious material could be disclosed only to a party's legal adviser; in practice, it is open to a legal representative to decline to receive information in this way, since in legal proceedings the lawyer does not have an existence independent from his client, and should in principle communicate such information as he receives to his client. It was accepted in *Re C* that where a legal representative declines to take part in that procedure, it was open to the court to grant leave to withhold disclosure. In doing so, the principles to be followed were:

–   first, whether disclosure carried with it 'a real risk of significant harm to the child';
–   if yes, whether the overall interests of the child would benefit from non-disclosure;
–   these interests then had to be weighed against the interests of the other party in being allowed access to the material upon which the court's conclusion might be based;
–   non-disclosure was the exception not the rule and would only be ordered where the risk and gravity of the feared harm to the child was compelling (at pp 797–798).

8.109 Where the application to withhold material is motivated by the desire to conceal information potentially prejudicial to a party's case, and there is no real possibility of significant harm to the children through disclosure, such an application is likely to fail (see *Re M and A (Disclosure of Information)* [1999] 1 FLR 443).

8.110 Withholding information from a party within children's proceedings has been made more difficult since the adoption in October 2000 of the ECHR through the coming into force of the HRA 1998. Article 6(1) of the ECHR states that 'everyone is entitled to a fair and public hearing within a reasonable time by an independent and impartial tribunal established by law'. In 1995, in the case of *McMichael v United Kingdom* [1995] Fam Law 478, the European Court of Human Rights ruled unanimously that the withholding of documents in care proceedings relating to a child from the mother of the child was a violation of Article 6(1). A fair adversarial trial demanded that parties should have knowledge of and an opportunity to comment on the other side's case, and the failure to disclose documents meant that parents were hindered in their ability to influence the outcome of the case. A High Court Practice Direction in the same year further stressed the duty of full and relevant disclosure in all family proceedings (*Practice Direction of 31 January 1995 (Case Management)* [1995] 1 FLR 456, at para 3; see also Brasse (1996); Burrows (1996); and also see Chapter 7).

8.111 Now that the HRA 1998 is in force, applications which seek the withholding of documents from a party in a manner which breaches Article 6(1) of the ECHR may also attract argument in relation to Article 8 which establishes the right to respect for private and family life, and limits the ways in which these may be interfered with by a public authority. In *Re B (Disclosure* *to Other Parties)* [2001] 2 FLR 1017 (followed in *Re R (Care: Disclosure: Nature of Proceedings)* [2002] 1 FLR 755; see Philimore (2001)), a case involving four children with three different fathers, the father of one of the children, against whom there were allegations of serious domestic violence, claimed the right under Article 6 to see all the papers. The mother successfully resisted the application for disclosure on the grounds that full disclosure to him would violate her own and the children's privacy. The court held that since the HRA 1998 had come into force, it was not just the rights of children which could deny a litigant access to documents, but the competing interests of others involved as a victim, party or witness who could rely on their Article 8 rights. The father had an absolute right to a fair trial, and in principle was therefore entitled to see the papers. However, this right was balanced against the Article 8 rights of the other parties. The court ruled that the restriction on disclosure did not violate the overriding requirements of a fair trial and was proportionate. Nevertheless, non-disclosure was justified only where the case was 'compelling or strictly necessary', and the court must be rigorous in examining the feared harm (see *Z v Finland* (1997) 25 EHRR 371 for the statement of this principle).

Disclosing documents out of care proceedings

8.112 Rule 4.23 of the FPR 1991 has the effect of making documents filed in children's proceedings confidential to the parties, their legal advisers, the CAFCASS reporting officer (or guardian ad litem) and the court-appointed expert. Circumstances may arise in which disclosure of documents out of children's proceedings is sought by parties to those proceedings who wish to use documents for their own purposes in another arena, or by third parties who seek information contained within them. It has been held by the Court of Appeal that the leave of the court is required for the disclosure of information contained within the confidential documents, as well as for sight of the documents themselves (see *Re A (Criminal Proceedings: Disclosure)* [1996] 1 FLR 221, CA), where the accused in a pending murder trial successfully won the right to information already known to his solicitor. The leave of the court is therefore necessary for the disclosure of the confidential information filed within children's cases in the following contexts.

Disclosure of reports relating to children to family centres

8.113 Leave is required for such disclosure to family centres or other therapeutic bodies, even where they are part of the local authority social services department (see *Re C (Guardian ad Litem: Disclosure of Report)* [1996] 1 FLR 61). In *Re X (Disclosure of Information)* [2001] 2 FLR 440, leave was given to: a local authority to disclose the judgment in care proceedings which reflected the unchallenged evidence that a party had sexually abused a number of children; a number of the victims who were not parties to the proceedings, to social workers and health professionals who worked with them; and the Criminal Injuries Compensation Authority (CICA) in pursuance of a claim for compensation. Disclosure was justified as it would be of positive benefit to the children involved, and would be largely confined to persons who had a close and confidential relationship with the children.

Disclosure to the police to assist investigations

8.114 In the pursuit of their investigations, the police may request the disclosure of documentary material filed within children's proceedings, or records of evidence given at trial during application for orders under the CA 1989. Police will be refused sight of medical records or other documentary material only rarely.

8.115 Recent applications by the police within the CA 1989 cases have raised issues as to confidentiality, as well as solicitor–client privilege and privilege against self-incrimination. The current state of the law is represented by the majority judgment of the House of Lords in *Re L (Police Investigation: Privilege)* [1996] 1 FLR 731, where a drug addict mother whose child had become seriously ill after ingesting methadone had filed an expert report in children's proceedings which cast serious doubts on the mother's explanation of accidental ingestion. The police applied for copies of the report for the purpose of investigating criminal offences. The House of Lords approved the disclosure to the police, which had been ordered by the High Court on the grounds that a potential prosecution was important for planning the children's future and the nature of their contact to their mother, in the context of the suspicion that she had administered life-threatening drugs to them. The European Court, addressing potential breaches of the ECHR, in *L v UK* [2000] 2 FLR 322, found there had been no breach of the mother's right to a fair trial on the basis that the disclosure provisions applied equally to all the parties to the care proceedings, and the mother was legally represented and not prevented from dealing with adverse evidence in cross-examination.

8.116 It is now clear that the courts have jurisdiction to hear applications for disclosure of documents by a body such as the police who are not parties to care proceedings. The court has an unfettered discretion when dealing with such applications. The judge must consider a number of potentially competing interests: the interests of the child concerned; the public interest in encouraging frankness by preserving confidentiality; and the public interest in upholding the legal process by providing evidence for use in other proceedings. The welfare of the child is a major factor, but not necessarily paramount (see *Oxfordshire County Council v L and F* [1997] 1 FLR 235).

Privilege against self-incrimination

8.117 In order that the children's court be assisted in receiving full and frank information, the CA 1989 introduced a statutory protection from self-incrimination. Under s 98 of the CA 1989, in proceedings for care or supervision orders, emergency protection orders or child assessment orders, no person shall be excused from giving evidence on any matter, or answering any question put to him in the course of his evidence, on the ground that it would incriminate him or his spouse of an offence. However:

> 'A statement or admission made in such proceedings shall not be admissible in evidence against the person making it or his spouse in proceedings for an offence other than perjury' (CA 1989, s 98(2)).

8.118 This means that statements or admissions made in such proceedings may not be used in prosecutions for other criminal proceedings, other than perjury. This is to encourage witnesses in children cases to be frank with the local authority and the courts, and to facilitate further investigations and assessments. The protection offered by s 98(2) protects against statements such as confessions within care proceedings being used in criminal proceedings.

8.119 However, there is no promise of confidentiality generally. The fact of an admission otherwise covered by s 98(2) may nevertheless be disclosed to the police to assist them with their investigations. Although statements and admissions made in care proceedings are not admissible in themselves in a criminal trial, s 98(2) does not protect a party from being cross-examined about having made such statements or admissions (see *Re L (Care: Confidentiality)* [1999] 1 FLR 165).

8.120 Guidelines about dealing with confessions and admissions were set out by the Court of Appeal in *Re EC (Disclosure of Material)* [1996] 2 FLR 725, CA, in care proceedings relating to a 3-year-old child, following the death of her baby sister from alleged non-accidental injuries. The father was advised that he had the protection of s 98(2), and in evidence then admitted throwing the baby onto a settee. The police then sought disclosure of a wide range of material, including transcripts of the evidence directly relating to the baby's injuries. It was held on appeal that the police should have had disclosure of all the material requested by them. The factors which the court should consider on an application for disclosure were:

– the welfare and interests of the child or children concerned in care proceedings and other children generally;
– the maintenance of confidentiality in children cases and the importance of encouraging frankness;
– the public interest in the administration of justice and the prosecution of serious crime;
– the gravity of the alleged offence and the relevance of the evidence to it;

– the desirability of co-operation between the various agencies concerned
   with the welfare of children;
– in cases where s 98(2) applies, fairness to the person who had
   incriminated himself and any others affected by the incriminating
   statement;
– any other material disclosure which had already taken place.

8.121 The Court of Appeal recognised that disclosure may not be ordered if
the welfare of the affected child is likely to be adversely affected in a serious
way, or if the evidence has little or no bearing upon a police investigation. It is
open to the court to decide on the facts of each application, whether a balance
was tipped towards the importance of maintaining frankness and
confidentiality, notwithstanding the serious nature of the offence. In *Re M
(Care Proceedings: Disclosure: Human Rights)* [2001] 2 FLR 1316, the court refused
to order the disclosure to the police of the mother's letter of admission made
during care proceedings as to her responsibility for causing serious injuries to
her baby by shaking: the parents were under intensive psychiatric and social
work assessment, with a view to deciding whether the child could be returned
to their care, and the disclosure sought by the police raised the real possibility
of a criminal conviction which would jeopardise the prospect of the child
being reunited with its parents.

8.122 However, the strong public interest in making available to the police
material relevant to the prosecution of persons involved in violent or sexual
offences against children is likely to be a very important factor in whether or
not to order the release of information to the police. Where there is an
admission of culpability for the death of a child (as in *Re EC*), the case for
disclosure is likely to be strong. In *Re W (Disclosure to the Police)* [1998] 2 FLR
135, a mother admitted to a social worker in an assessment interview that she
had shaken her 8-month-old baby: the Court of Appeal held that where police
and social workers were working together, a family judge should hesitate
before refusing to provide relevant and significant information to the police.

8.123 Where disclosure is ordered, admissions or confessions made in the
care proceedings are still inadmissible in any criminal case, but could form the
basis of a formal police interview with a suspect and, if repeated in such a
context, would be likely to be admitted in a criminal trial.

Disclosure to other public bodies

8.124 Disclosure of information as to an individual's risk to children given in
children's proceedings may be sought by regulatory bodies or by public bodies
such as local authorities (see Smith(1999) and (2000)). In *A County Council v W
and Others (Disclosure)* [1997] 1 FLR 574 (see also *Re A (Disclosure of Medical
Records to the GMC)* [1998] 2 FLR 641), the GMC successfully secured the

disclosure of documents in care proceedings where a finding had been made that a medical practitioner had sexually abused his daughter, on the basis that there was an overwhelming and overriding public interest that the GMC should be in a position to review the professional status of the father as a registered medical practitioner. In *Re L (Care Proceedings: Disclosure to Third Party)* [2000] 1 FLR 913, the UK Central Council for Nursing has made a similar successful application for disclosure where a mother in care proceedings was found to have caused significant harm to her child, and there was concern about her continued employment as a paediatric nurse. In *Re R (Disclosure)* [1998] 1 FLR 433, the court gave leave for the disclosure of information to an employer about a father employed in the field of social welfare who was found to be a threat to children, at the request of the father's chief probation officer.

8.125 In *A Health Authority v X (Discovery: Medical Conduct)* [2002] 1 FLR 383, a health authority wished to see documents held by a local authority and produced in care proceedings, as well as those generated by those proceedings, in order to investigate allegations of misconduct in an NHS practice. The court balanced the interests of the children in the care proceedings against the public interest in health and safety. Disclosure was permitted, but subject to conditions to protect patient confidentiality in the light of Article 8 of the ECHR, as well as the common law right of confidentiality between a patient and his doctors (see *R v Mid Glamorgan Family Health Services and Another ex parte Martin* [1995] 1 FLR 283, CA).

8.126 The position in relation to disclosure to other local authorities is more complex. There is clearly a tension between the duties of all local authorities to safeguard and promote the welfare of children in their area under ss 17 and 47 of the CA 1989, the principle of confidentiality in children's proceedings, and the right to privacy under the ECHR.

8.127 Recent case-law has expressed caution over the disclosure of information. The duty of the local authority to disclose the identity of convicted child abusers to the owner of a caravan site where the men were living on release from prison was considered in *R v Chief Constable of North Wales ex parte Thorpe* [1998] 2 FLR 571, CA. The Court of Appeal ruled that disclosure should only be made where there was a 'pressing need' for it; the fact that there were criminal convictions which were in the public domain did not entitle the police or the local authority to publicise them in the absence of proof of 'pressing need'. In *Re V (Sexual Abuse: Disclosure); Re L (Sexual Abuse: Disclosure)* [1999] 1 FLR 267, men against whom findings of sexual abuse had been made in care proceedings successfully appealed against the disclosure of this information to the local authorities in whose areas they currently lived. The Court of Appeal considered the guidelines previously given in relation to disclosure to the police in *Re EC (Disclosure of Material)* [1996] 2 FLR 725, CA, and declined to order disclosure on the grounds that there was no pressing need. Neither man had been convicted in a criminal court, and the balance was firmly against disclosure (see further, Chapter **11**).

8.128   R *v Local Authority and Police Authority in the Midlands ex parte LM* [2000] 1 FLR 612 (see further, Chapter **11**) concerned the power of the police and the local authority to disclose old and unproven allegations against an individual who sought to take up a voluntary teaching post with the youth service. The principles governing the exercise of the power to disclose in *ex parte Thorpe* were followed. Disclosure should only be made if there were real and cogent evidence of a 'pressing need'. Disclosure should be the exception rather than the rule, and a blanket policy of disclosure was specifically disapproved. The impact of the ECHR was influential in *ex parte LM*, and the ECHR is likely to tip the balance further away from disclosure without evidence of immediate risk to children. Caution is also reflected in the current Home Office guidelines in relation to sex offenders (*Guidance on the Disclosure of Information about Sex Offenders who may Present a Risk to Children and Vulnerable Adults* (Home Office, 1999)), which states:

> 'A decision to disclose to third parties will always need to be justified carefully in both legal and moral grounds, and should be taken only as part of a carefully managed process ... the general presumption is that information should not be disclosed, not least because of the potentially serious effect on the ability of an offender to live a normal life, the risk of violence to offenders, and the risk that disclosure might drive them underground.'

8.129   The difficulty for those concerned with child protection is that without disclosure to the relevant local authority, evidence of 'pressing need' may be difficult to gather. The current state of the case-law suggests conflicting views over whether local authorities should not be pro-active in informing other local authorities that individuals convicted of offences against children or against whom findings have been made in the family court have moved into their area. (See further on this Chapters **5**, **6** and **11**.) Nevertheless, local authorities may answer enquiries from other local authorities and social services may pass on information from their files in the form of closing summaries when families with children move on to another area.

Disclosure to parties for use in other legal proceedings

8.130   The courts have the power to grant applications by a party to family proceedings for the disclosure of material filed with them for use in other proceedings to which they are parties. Such proceedings may be civil, such as actions in negligence against individuals or public bodies, or criminal, where there is an obvious nexus with the circumstances that give rise to CA 1989 proceedings. Historically, applications by parties in parallel proceedings for disclosure out of children's proceedings into other litigation have been looked at with sympathy by the courts, in contrast to the sometimes restrictive approach taken in third party applications for disclosure.

8.131 The groundwork for disclosure was laid in *Re D (Minors) (Wardship)* [1994] 1 FLR 346, CA, a wardship case decided in 1991. It was held that a judge in the exercise of his discretion must balance the importance of confidentiality in wardship proceedings and the need for frankness by persons giving evidence in the wardship court, against the public interest in seeing that justice is done in a wide context:

> 'In relation to criminal proceedings, it is clear that the wardship court should not, as it were, seek to erect a barrier which will prejudice the operation of another bench of the judicature' (at p 351).

A similar approach was taken by the Court of Appeal in *Re Manda (Wardship: Disclosure of Evidence)* [1993] 1 FLR 205, CA, where the parents of an elective mute won the right to disclose the wardship papers to an expert for the purpose of a proposed claim in negligence against a local authority, health authority and a consultant paediatrician. It was held in *Manda* that where disclosure is sought to assist a party in other areas of litigation, 'the public interest in the administration of justice required that all relevant information should be available for use in those proceedings'.

8.132 This decision contrasts with the restrictive approach of the High Court in *Re X, Y and Z (Wardship: Disclosure of Material)* [1992] Fam 124, where the court declined to order the disclosure of wardship material relating children in the Cleveland child abuse cases to a newspaper which wished to use unspecified material to defend a libel action brought by two paediatricians. The applicant newspaper was not of course party to the wardship action and was unable to particularise the documents sought or to demonstrate the real risk of injustice in the libel action if the documents were not disclosed; therefore the court concluded that the damage which disclosure would do to the family jurisdiction outweighed 'the unproved and uncertain advantage which it might secure in advancing the prospect of a fair trial'. Following the adoption of the ECHR into English law, the right to a fair trial set out in Article 6 may lend extra weight to the claim for disclosure.

Disclosure in criminal proceedings

8.133 Parties to children's proceedings also seek disclosure of relevant but confidential material, where they are not only parties to children's proceedings but defendants in criminal proceedings, with obvious implications for the liberty of the individual. The approach of the Court of Appeal in relation to disclosure out of wardship proceedings has been extended to apply to CA 1989 cases. In *Re K and Others (Minors) (Care Proceedings: Disclosure)* [1994] 1 FLR 377, a father charged with the rape of his two children applied for the disclosure of statements made by the mother, transcripts of video interviews with the children filed within the care proceedings and for leave for his defence counsel to see all documents filed within the care proceedings. It was held that the disclosure would not be to the detriment of the children as 'it is in fact greatly in their interests that their father should have a fair trial and greatly in the interests of justice that there should be no impediment to this'. Leave of the court is required even for the disclosure of factual information filed within children's cases, where this may be relevant to assist a defendant in cross-examination of witnesses in a criminal trial (see *Re A (Criminal Proceedings: Disclosure)* [1996] 1 FLR 221, CA).

8.134 This may be contrasted with the type of application dealt with in *R v Reading Justices ex parte Berkshire County Council* [1996] 1 FLR 149 (discussed at para **8.94**) where a party to care proceedings faced with criminal charges sought disclosure of the social services files that stood behind the papers filed in the care proceedings. The current approach of the courts to such applications is likely to be restrictive.

Restrictions on publicity

8.135 In addition to the restrictions on the disclosure of documents provided for by r 4.23 of the FPR 1991, there are important restrictions against publicity in children's cases. These have been created in a piecemeal fashion by statute, and by decisions of the courts in case-law (see Dixon (2001)).

Statutory restrictions

8.136 There are four principal statutes providing for protection against identification for children involved in court proceedings. Under s 97(2) of the CA 1989, no person shall publish any material which is intended or likely to identify:

'(a) any child as being involved in any proceedings before the High Court, a county court or a magistrates' court in which any power under this Act may be exercised by the court with respect to that or any other child; or

(b) an address or school as being that of a child involved in any such proceedings.'

8.137 Breach of this section is a criminal offence. Furthermore, under the Administration of Justice Act 1960, s 12(1), as amended by the CA 1989, the publication of information relating to proceedings under the High Court's inherent jurisdiction over minors under the CA 1989 or otherwise relating to the maintenance or upbringing of a minor is a contempt of court and therefore punishable by the court. Protection for child defendants and witnesses in criminal proceedings is provided by s 39(1) of the CYPA 1933, which permits the court to direct that no newspaper shall identify the child or publish photographs without leave of the court. Under the Magistrates' Courts Act 1980, s 71(1), it is a criminal offence to publicise other than limited details in relation to family proceedings and proceedings under the Adoption Act 1976.

Case-law

8.138 The effect of statute is therefore to prevent and to punish publicity which identifies the names and addresses of children, or information relating to proceedings before the courts. However, in the area of case-law, there are a number of tensions in play which the courts have attempted to reconcile. These are the concern of the courts to protect children from potentially harmful public attention, the desire of the media in a democratic society to promote public discussion where there is a legitimate public interest, and the desire of parties to children's proceedings to seek publicity for their own reasons. The adoption into English law of the ECHR has increased these tensions: Article 6 which provides that a judgment shall in principle be pronounced publicly and Article 10 which provides for freedom of expression are potentially in collision with Article 8 which provides for the right of respect for private and family life.

8.139 Where the court determines that publicity will have a direct effect on the child's upbringing, under s 1(1) of the CA 1989 the child's welfare becomes the court's paramount consideration. The paramountcy principle means that other factors are unlikely to be determinative, and publicity is likely to be refused: see *Re Z (A Minor) (Freedom of Publication)* [1996] 1 FLR 191, CA, where the mother of a child with special educational needs whose existence was already in the public domain was refused permission to have the child appear in a television film about the unit attended by the child. The Court of Appeal held that the question they were asked to determine related to the upbringing of the child, and were clear in deciding that her welfare would be harmed and not advanced by involvement with the projected film.

8.140 *Re Z* represents the high watermark of the restrictive approach to publicity. The imperative of confidentiality has been found to be an overriding consideration in relatively few cases in recent years: in *A v M (Family Proceedings: Publicity)* [2000] 1 FLR 562, injunctions were granted to prevent a mother who had failed in court to obtain the residence of her children from repeating her allegations against the father to the press because of further damage to the children.

8.141 The discretion of the court is very wide: where a teenage boy developed a relationship of which the court disapproved but was unable to prevent, the court determined that publication would 'introduce reality and force him to confront his behaviour' and gave leave for publicity (see *Re H (Publication of Judgment)* [1995] 2 FLR 542).

8.142 Where the welfare of the child is not paramount, because the application does not relate to the child's upbringing, the court must conduct a balancing exercise. The competing interests are whether the child would suffer clear and identifiable harm, together with the interests of free speech and the benefits of an open court, considered against the importance of confidentiality. For example, it has been held that it is not a contempt of court to publish an interview with a boy who was a ward of court who had gone to live with a religious sect as no harm would follow (*Kelly v BBC* [2001] 1 FLR 197). It has been held that where a television programme proposed to identify a father imprisoned following a conviction for indecency, there was no evidence that publicity would affect the care or upbringing of the child. Therefore, there was no balancing exercise to conduct, and publication should be permitted (see *R v Central Independent Television plc* [1994] 2 FLR 151, CA).

8.143 The importance of free speech and the need for openness in legal proceedings has lead to a greater inclination to permit publicity in recent cases. In *Clibbery v Allen and Another* [2001] 2 FLR 819, a case concerning cross-applications for non-molestation and occupation orders between former lovers, issues arose over the legality of injunctions restraining the woman from disclosing material used in proceedings to the press. It was held that where proceedings relating to property or money (as opposed to children) were held in chambers, disclosure of any material not expressly determined to be confidential by the court was permissible. It was held that:

> 'the right of parties to privacy conflicted with the right of freedom of expression, and a rule restraining participants in hearings held in private from ever disclosing anything connected with those hearings could not be justified as necessary in a democratic society, or as proportionate to the legitimate aim pursued' (at p 820).

8.144 Residence disputes between celebrities which have attracted the attention of the press have seen a greater willingness to permit publication of information. In *Re G (Celebrities: Publicity)* [1999] 1 FLR 409, CA (see Pears, (1999)), the Court of Appeal deprecated orders made in the High Court prohibiting the publication in the news media even of a summary of the orders which had been made in cross-applications for residence between parents in the public eye, stating 'the extent to which family proceedings were conducted in private hearings has been much criticised recently, and there are powerful arguments for more openness'. However, in *X v Dempster* [1999] 1 FLR 894, a case arising from the same litigation, a newspaper columnist who publicly disclosed the tenor of forthcoming testimony from witnesses to be called on behalf of the father was fined for contempt of court, because it placed in the public domain matters which the court had yet to consider in private. The court stated that it was permissible in the absence of a specific injunction to publish the name, address and photograph of the parties and children involved, and to identify the witnesses.

8.145 Cases involving the publicising of social services material filed in care proceedings are still likely to attract the protection of the courts. In *Oxfordshire County Council v L and F* [1997] 1 FLR 235, parents suspected of non-accidental injury who had been vindicated by the court were refused permission to publish information deriving from the case. In conducting the balancing exercise, the public interest in the confidentiality of proceedings relating to children and the importance of social workers and others concerned with the protection of children performing their duties with candour and frankness were the determinative factor.

Expert evidence in child abuse cases

Function and scope

8.146 Many children cases inevitably involve allegations of physical, emotional or sexual abuse of children. There may be factual disputes about what has happened to a child, or argument about the capacity of a mother or a father to provide adequate parenting (see *Re B* [2002] 2 FLR 1133 and *Re O and N* [2002] 2 FLR 1167). Parties may wish to adduce evidence from a variety of medical, psychiatric or other expert witnesses. Frequently, courts will be assisted by an appropriate expert, and it is the function of that expert to assist in the proving of the factual substratum as well as providing an opinion as to the question before the court. Judicial concern about the proper and effective use of experts in children cases has resulted in best practice guidance from the Children Act Advisory Committee, *Handbook of Best Practice in Children Act Cases* (see section 5, 'Experts and the Courts', set out as 'Best Practice Guidance June 1997' in Part IV of *The Family Court Practice 2002* (Family Law, 2002); see also Wall and Hamilton (2000)), which should be consulted for detailed procedural guidance in relation to the instruction of experts. Case-law since the CA 1989 also reflects the way in which the children's courts have increasingly assumed control over the appointment and management of expert evidence (see *Re G (Minors) (Expert Witnesses)* [1994] 2 FLR 291; *Re C (Expert Evidence: Disclosure: Practice)* [1995] 1 FLR 204; *Re R (Child Abuse: Video Evidence)* [1995] 1 FLR 451; *Re A and B (Minors) (No 2)* [1995] 1 FLR 351; *Re T and E (Proceedings: Conflicting Interests)* [1995] 1 FLR 581; and *Re CS (Expert Witnesses)* [1996] 2 FLR 115).

8.147 Expert evidence in children's proceedings may be summarised as follows:

- admissible evidence of facts observed by an expert;
- explanation and interpretation of evidence of fact adduced by another witness or by the expert himself;
- opinion evidence as to the significance of facts before the court.

It is important to be clear that the expert may be both a witness of fact (eg a child) and of opinion (eg giving an explanation to the court as to whether bruises were accidental, and if not, how they might have occurred).

The expert and the judge

8.148 The function of the expert in children proceedings is wholly different from that of the judge. It is for the expert to conduct an assessment and express an opinion within the particular area of his expertise. *The Handbook of Best Practice in Children Act Cases* states that:

'the role of the expert is to provide independent assistance to the court by way of objective, unbiased opinion, in relation to matters within his expertise. Expert evidence presented to the court must be, and be seen to be, the independent product of the expert, uninfluenced by the instructing party' (at section 5, para 74).

8.149 The admissibility of expert evidence is provided for by the Civil Evidence Act 1972: 'where a person is called as a witness in any civil proceedings, his opinion on any relevant matters on which he is qualified to give expert evidence shall be admissible in evidence' (s 3). The question of the weight to be given to the opinion of the expert is a matter for the judge: while the court is likely to be heavily dependent upon the skill, knowledge and intellectual integrity of the expert, he cannot usurp the function of the judge, who must decide the particular issue in each case.

Judicial assessment of expert evidence

8.150 The court is entitled to reject even the unanimous opinions of experts: there is 'no rule that the judge suspends judicial belief simply because the evidence is given by an expert' (see *Re B (Care: Expert Witnesses)* [1996] 1 FLR 667, at p 670E, CA). The task of the judge has been expressed as follows: 'I have to remind myself that the question is whether I believe the child, not whether I believe those who believe her' (see *Re FS (Child Abuse: Evidence)* [1996] 2 FLR 158, at p 169A, CA). Expert opinion as to the truth or otherwise of a witness's evidence has been held to be inadmissible because it usurps the function of the judge (see *Re S and B (Minors) (Child Abuse: Evidence)* [1990] 2 FLR 489, CA; *Re N (Child Abuse: Evidence)* [1996] 2 FLR 214, CA). Because it is for the judge alone to decide whether a child should be believed, evidence from the expert should be couched in terms of consistency or inconsistency of a fact, in relation to the event which is alleged to have occurred (see *Re N (Child Abuse: Evidence)* [1996] 2 FLR 214, at pp 221F–222F).

8.151 The judge by definition is not an expert in the field about which an expert may be giving evidence: 'the court has no expertise of its own other then legal expertise … the expert advises but the judge decides' (see *Re B (Care: Expert Witnesses)* [1996] 1 FLR 667, at p 670, CA. It is permissible for a judge to decline to follow the recommendations of experts, as long as the judicial finding is not against the weight of evidence as a whole. The court should always give reasons for departing from the recommendations of the instructed expert. The judge should not become involved in controversy between the experts, except where such controversy is an issue in the case, and the judge has to decide which expert is preferred or a proper resolution of the proceedings.

Procedure in relation to expert evidence: the principles

8.152 The convention within the wardship jurisdiction that the court should take control of the involvement of the expert with the child has been retained and extended following the CA 1989. This is now governed by the FPR 1991. As in wardship, a child should not be examined without leave of the court. Rule 4.18 provides that:

'(1)   No person may, without the leave of the court, cause the child to be medically or psychiatrically examined, or otherwise assessed, for the purpose of the preparation of expert evidence for use in the proceedings.
(2)   An application for leave under paragraph (1) shall, unless the court otherwise directs, be served on all parties to the proceedings and the children's guardian.
(3)   Where the leave of the court has not been given under paragraph (1), no evidence arising out of an examination or assessment to which that paragraph applies may be adduced without leave of the court.'

8.153 Thus no one without leave of the court may have a child medically or psychiatrically examined for the purpose of obtaining a report for use in the proceedings. This would also prevent examination without leave by a broad range of experts, including psychologists. It applies to children in all family proceedings whether in care proceedings or private law cases.

8.154 Previously, the FPR 1991 made no provision for the release of the case papers to an expert except by specific leave of the court. Rule 4.23 governing the confidentiality of material filed in children's cases has now been amended by the Family Proceedings (Amendment) Rules 2001 to provide that documents may be disclosed to 'an expert whose instruction by a party has been authorised by the court'. Therefore, so long as the court approves the expert, a further direction for disclosure of documents to the expert is otiose.

Leave to instruct an expert

8.155 Leave to instruct an expert may be sought by application on Form C2 for directions (see FPR 1991, r 4.14), or by agreement between the parties. Advocates who seek the leave of the court to disclose papers to an expert must apply their minds at an early stage of the proceedings to issues which are likely to need expert evidence to resolve. Applications for leave to instruct experts should be made as early in the proceedings as possible, commensurate with the state of the evidence. This is because an assessment or report to the necessary standard is likely to take several months to complete, and experts may be unable to commence work straight away through professional commitments. Wherever possible, enquiry should be made to ensure that the expert can meet the likely timetable of the case.

8.156 The grant of leave will depend on the circumstances of the case. As the involvement of an expert is not a question directly relating to the upbringing of the child, the welfare principle is not paramount. The interests of the child will be considered alongside the interests of the parties, the need for a fair hearing at which the issues can be properly determined, and the delay principle. In considering whether to grant leave, the court should seek to identify the issues which need to be determined, and consider whether the proposed expert would assist: leave to obtain expert evidence has been refused on the grounds that his expertise would not bear sufficiently upon the issue the court has to decide (see *H v Cambridgeshire County Council* [1996] 2 FLR 566).

8.157 No expert should be involved in a case without the approval of the court and a specific direction as to his involvement. It is contrary to good practice to produce evidence from an expert instructed separately by a party on the basis of anonymous information. Experts should be told explicitly that the court had given permission for their instruction, and what the terms of the court order were in relation to their instruction: in *Re A (Family Proceedings: Expert Witnesses)* [2001] 1 FLR 723, a father who without the leave of the court obtained a report from a clinical psychologist commenting on a video of his contact with the child based upon anonymous background information was specifically disapproved of by the court.

Choosing the expert

8.158 In order to be effective in assisting the court, the expert needs to have appropriate qualifications and experience and to be recognised within his or her profession. It is normal for the curriculum vitae of an expert to be available to the court and the parties. Where a medical expert is required, it is usual to prefer an expert who holds a position at consultant level (for assistance in the identification of experts in the appropriate disciplines for non-accidental injuries, see Temple-Bone (2002)).

8.159 Care should be taken over the identification of the expert. There is a fundamental duty upon the expert to be independent. This principle is expressd in the CPR 1998, Part 35 of which emphasises that the expert's duty is to assist the court in matters which are within his or her own expertise. This duty overrides 'the obligation to the person from whom he has received his instructions or by whom he is paid' (CPR 1998, r 35(3)). The duty of absolute independence has been emphasised by Thorpe LJ in *Vernon v Boseley (Expert Evidence) (Note)* [1998] 1 FLR 297, at p 302:

> 'The area of expertise in any case may be likened to a broad street, with the plaintiff walking on one pavement and the defendant walking on the opposite side. Somehow the expert must be ever mindful of the need to walk straight down the middle of the road and to resist the temptation to join the party from whom his instructions come on the pavement.'

8.160 The choice of experts has, in certain circumstances, been disapproved. Experts who do not represent mainstream opinion, or whose evidence has been shown to be unreliable, unproven or unscientific should not be instructed. The instruction of a named expert who has identified a bone condition described by him as 'Temporary Brittle Bone Disease' has been roundly criticised on a number of occasions by the High Court (see *Re R (A Minor) (Experts' Evidence) (Note)* [1991] 1 FLR 291; *Re AB (Child Abuse: Expert Witnesses)* [1995] 1 FLR 181; *Re X (Non-accidental Injury: Expert Evidence)* [2001] 2 FLR 90; see also Williams (2000)).

8.161 Evidence from an expert already involved in a therapeutic capacity with a party or child is disapproved. In *Re B (Sexual Abuse: Experts' Report)* [2000] 1 FLR 871, CA, a mother sought to prove that a father was sexually abusing their child by adducing evidence from the child psychiatrist already treating the child. The Court of Appeal held that the role of the expert who treats an individual and the role of the expert who provides a forensic report must not be confused.

8.162 Where leave for an examination is given, the court will usually try to limit the number of examinations to which a child is subjected. The dangers of the court giving general leave, rather then specific leave for the instruction of a particular expert or experts, can be seen in *Re B (Child Sexual Abuse: Standard of Proof) (Note)* [1995] 1 FLR 904, in which following the grant of general leave without limitation, 11 psychologists and psychiatrists became involved in the proceedings. The recent trend towards the court being active in managing the expert evidence has been reflected in *Re CB and JB (Care Proceedings: Guidelines)* [1998] 2 FLR 211, where Wall J excluded the evidence of four of the six psychiatrists and psychologists as being of no relevance to the issues before the court.

8.163 The involvement of multiple experts inevitably extends the length and costs of the litigation. It may also be potentially abusive for the children concerned to be subject to repeated examinations by several experts. Where possible, the courts will consider the instruction of a single joint expert, usually a new forensic instruction, to overcome the partiality of existing experts who may have been previously involved with one side only, and the perception of unfairness to the other side (*Re B (Sexual Abuse: Expert's Report)* [2000] 1 FLR 871; see also Mitchell (2000)). Their expertise and identity should be agreed by all parties prior to approval by the court. In default of agreement, the Official Solicitor holds lists of experts and could nominate an appropriate person. Alternatively, the court may grant leave to the guardian to arrange an examination or assessment by a sole expert.

8.164 Where there are serious or difficult allegations in respect of non-accidental injury, the court is likely to need all the help that it can get, and the instruction of a second expert is not unusual. For example, more than one consultant paediatric radiologist may be required to give their opinion on the timing and causation of bone injuries. This is usually done by reviewing the medical material, not by examining the child. Where a 'paper opinion' is sought, the court is far more likely to be amenable for a second expert to be instructed, because it can be done relatively speedily and without exposing the child to further examination.

Disclosing material to experts

8.165 It is of the utmost importance that experts see all the relevant material. This will be the case for papers filed in the proceedings, as well as medical records or background material. These should be particularised in the letter of instruction to the expert. Experts who are likely to be called to give evidence at trial should be kept up to date with recent developments and read any recent statements from the parties and the children's guardian before going into court. Lawyers may well be penalised by costs orders where adjournments are necessary to enable experts to catch up with necessary reading (see *Re G, S, and M (Wasted Costs)* [2000] 1 FLR 52). It is good practice for experts in the same discipline to confer before the trial and to produce a schedule of issues which are agreed or remain in dispute between them, to assist the court. Current best practice is for the guardian or the solicitor for the child to chair a meeting of experts, although difficulties may arise from a lack of medical or scientific expertise (see Meadows (1999)). For guidance on chairing expert meetings, see Winter (2001)).

Supplementary legal routes to protect children

High Court applications: wardship

8.166 Some children's applications are heard in the High Court under the wardship jurisdiction. This is an entirely separate jurisdiction from the High

Court hearing CA 1989 cases. If especially difficult or complex, CA 1989 cases may be deemed appropriate for determination by the High Court and are therefore transferred upwards from the county court (see the CAPO 1991, art 12). In practice, the judges who deal with wardship will be drawn from the Family Division, and are the same as the judges who determine CA 1989 applications.

8.167 Historically, the wardship jurisdiction in relation to children was exercised by the High Court, where private disputes over children led to the child becoming a ward of court. By the 1980s, the wardship procedure was being increasingly harnessed by the local authorities as a way of taking children into care in complex or difficult cases, or where rapid protective action was necessary. It was possible to come before the High Court on an ex parte basis without notice to parents, on an undertaking to issue an originating summons, the issue of which would result in the child becoming immediately a ward of court. Full parental rights were thus vested in the court alone, but the local authority would seek care and control to exercise day-to-day responsibilities for the child (see the Family Law Reform Act 1969, s 7, abolished by the CA 1989, s 100).

8.168 Wardship meant that parental rights remained vested in the court until the child reached the age of 18 or the wardship was discharged. The effect of this was that the leave of the court was necessary for significant steps in a child's life, such as hospital treatment, a change of residence or school, interview by the police or removal from the jurisdiction of England and Wales for a holiday. Failure to obtain the consent of the court to such steps was a contempt of court and made the offender liable for punishment. The care given to a child by a local authority was also subject to the scrutiny of the court which could exercise its power to review until the end of the wardship. The high-water mark for wardship was reached in 1991, the year the CA 1989 came into force, when there were 4,961 cases of wardship in the High Court; in the 3 previous years, the number of wardship cases had risen by 34 per cent (cited in Mitchell (2001a). The current annual figure is said to be about 430 per year (see Mitchell (2001b)).

8.169 The CA 1989 effectively brought to an end the role of the wardship court in care cases. Section 100 of the Act expressly prohibits the court from exercising the inherent jurisdiction of the High Court in order to place a child in care. The local authority may not apply under the inherent jurisdiction without leave of the Court, save in very limited circumstances (CA 1989, s 100(3), (4) and (5)). A local authority therefore has to apply under the CA 1989 in order to take a child into care. Upon the making of an interim or full care order, the parental responsibility vested in the mother and father (subject to their marriage or agreement) is shared with the local authority, which has power to determine how it is exercised by the parents. Parental responsibility is at no time held by the court.

8.170 The courts have expressed concern in recent years about the lack of jurisdiction to review or control local authorities who may fail to implement care plans or allow children to drift in the care system. The impact of the adoption of the ECHR means that the right to family life of a child and its parents is perforce breached by a local authority which is unwilling or unable to progress its care plan for the child. Such dissatisfaction had led the Court of Appeal to recommend 'starred milestones', which if not achieved would trigger the reinvolvement of the court (see *Re W and B; Re W (Care Plan)* [2001] EWCA Civ 757, [2001] 2 FLR 582, CA). However, the principles of the CA 1989 were roundly reaffirmed on appeal to the House of Lords, which asserted that 'it was a cardinal principle of the 1989 Act that courts were not empowered to intervene in the way local authorities discharged their parental responsibilities under final care orders' (*Re S (Minors); Re W (Minors)* [2002] UKHL 10, [2002] 1 FLR 815). The local authority therefore remains in the driving seat after the making of a care order, and under the CA 1989 the courts currently have no power to review their actions or to intervene.

8.171 The rights of private individuals such as parents or relatives to apply under the wardship jurisdiction have not been curtailed by statute. However, the Court of Appeal has held that the wardship jurisdiction should be invoked only in exceptional circumstances 'where a question concerning the child's upbringing or property could not be resolved under the CA 1989 so as to secure his best interests' (see *Re CT (A Minor) (Wardship: Representation)* [1993] 2 FLR 278). An example would be an application by local authority foster parents to ward a child to prevent the removal of the child from their care by a local authority who wished to place the child elsewhere for welfare reasons; under s 9(3) of the CA 1989, a foster parent in such circumstances is debarred even from making an application for leave to make a s 8 application, where the local authority does not consent, and the child has been placed with him for less than 3 years. Only an application under wardship would enable the court to make an immediate injunction preventing the child being moved, and provide a forum for the proper judicial evaluation of the foster parents' application.

8.172 One benefit of wardship is the ongoing protective jurisdiction which it provides over a child. Historically, wardship was used on the application of a parent or relative trying to prevent a child meeting or forming an association with an undesirable adult. This has had application in *Re R (A Minor) (Contempt)* [1994] 2 FLR 185, CA, where wardship and its injunctive powers were used to try to prohibit contact between a 14-year-old girl and a married man in his 30s. This was ultimately ineffective, as despite repeated breaches of the orders, culminating in the imprisonment of the man for contempt of court for the maximum of 2 years, the liaison continued and resulted in pregnancy.

8.173 Boys who run away from home have also been warded, as in *Re H (A Minor) (Role of the Official Solicitor)* [1993] 2 FLR 552 where a boy developed an obsessive enthusiasm for a dance academy and its male proprietor, and *Kelly v British Broadcasting Corporation* [2001] Fam 59 where a boy who had run away to join a religious cult was warded to permit a 'seek and find' order.

8.174 Wardship is also used where children have been removed from the jurisdiction of England and Wales by a parent, or there is the threat of such a removal. Although the 'seek and find' orders available under wardship are similar to those already available under s 34 of the Family Law Act 1986, it has been suggested that wardship has advantages (see Mitchell (2001b), at pp 214–215): this is because it vests parental rights in the court, making any removal automatically wrongful, and may secure compliance abroad as in *Re KR (Abduction: Forcible Removal by Parents)* [1999] 2 FLR 542, where the return of a Sikh girl taken to the Punjab for an arranged marriage was secured on the wardship application of her sister.

8.175 Because of the exceptional nature of such applications, the first consideration should be to consider the range of remedies under the CA 1989. Individuals who have child protection concerns should contact the relevant local authority to investigate. Alternatively, an individual has powers under s 44 of the CA 1989 to seek an emergency protection order where there is reason to believe that a child is likely to suffer significant harm. An application by an individual in such circumstances is rare, and the court is likely to involve the social services department of the local authority forthwith, which has under s 47 of the CA 1989 a statutory duty to make 'such enquiries as they consider necessary to enable them to decide whether they should take any action to safeguard or promote the child's welfare'.

High Court applications: the inherent jurisdiction

8.176 The High Court retains its inherent jurisdiction to make decisions about children. This has survived the implementation of the CA 1989. This is a power specific only to the High Court, and is exercisable whether or not a child is a ward of court. It has been stated that 'for practical purposes, the jurisdiction in wardship and the inherent jurisdiction over children is one and the same' (*Re Z (A Minor) (Freedom of Publication)* [1996] 1 FLR 191, at p 197, CA). With the decline in the use of the wardship jurisdiction, most applications made directly to the High Court in relation to children are therefore now likely to be under the inherent jurisdiction. The jurisdiction of the High Court has survived because it offers a flexible, immediate and available remedy for problems which lie outside the scope of the CA 1989.

Most applications under the inherent jurisdiction in the High Court are made by local authorities.

Local authority applications

8.177 Section 100(3) of the CA 1989 provides that a local authority must seek the leave of the High Court in making an application under the inherent jurisdiction. In essence, the court may only grant leave if there is no other remedy available to the local authority, and there is reasonable cause to believe that otherwise the child is likely to suffer significant harm.

8.178 The inherent jurisdiction will have to be invoked where there is an issue about the urgent medical treatment for a child in care. In *Re W (A Minor) (Consent to Medical Treatment)* [1993] 1 FLR 1, CA, the Court of Appeal authorised the treatment of a 16-year-old girl with anorexia who was refusing treatment. An order under the inherent jurisdiction was necessary, because the girl was already in the care of the local authority, and therefore could not be made a ward of court. Where a child is already in care, s 9(1) of the CA 1989 prohibits the court from making any order under s 8 save a residence order. The jurisdiction of the High Court was exercisable without the child being a ward and it is therefore not necessary to make the child a ward of court to invoke the inherent jurisdiction.

8.179 Where the issue of medical treatment arises and a child is not already in care, the local authority may take alternative routes available under the CA 1989. Cases have arisen where a blood transfusion is medically necessary, but parents have refused their consent. In *Re R (A Minor) (Blood Transfusion)* [1993] 2 FLR 757, the High Court held that the local authority could apply for permission to use blood products by way of a specific issue order under s 8 of the CA 1989. In earlier cases the local authority was permitted to take the route of invoking the inherent jurisdiction to achieve the same result (see *Re S (A Minor) (Medical Treatment)* [1993] 1 FLR 376; *Re O (A Minor) (Medical Treatment)* [1993] 2 FLR 149). Where a child is at immediate risk of significant harm, a local authority may use the CA 1989 remedies such as applying for an emergency protection order (s 44(1)) or a child assessment order (s 43(1)).

8.180 Where a child is in care, and s 9(1) provides that no specific issue or prohibited steps order can be made, it has been suggested that the local authority may invoke the inherent jurisdiction to declare the lawfulness of a mentally handicapped child being sterilised or having an abortion, or a life-saving operation (see Hershman and McFarlane *Children Law and Practice* (Family Law) looseleaf, at para C1171).

8.181 Under the Supreme Court Act 1981 s 37, the High Court has the power to make injunctions ancillary to a care order. An injunction may be necessary to support the power bestowed upon a local authority by s 33(3) of the CA 1989 to exercise parental responsibility for a child, and determine the extent to which a parent may exercise such parental responsibility. Injunctions may be necessary to protect a child under a care order from the actions of a parent, for example in exercising unauthorised contact to disrupt a placement. Such orders are not permitted by the CA 1989 but are necessary in the interests of a child.

8.182 In *Re S (Minors) (Inherent Jurisdiction: Ouster)* [1994] 1 FLR 623, an order compelling a father to leave his own home was made by the High Court under the inherent jurisdiction. The Court of Appeal has ruled that the county court has no power to grant an injunction in care proceedings (*Devon County Council v B* [1997] 1 FLR 591, CA), so such an application has to be heard in the High Court under the inherent jurisdiction. In practice, High Court judges hearing CA 1989 applications will be ready to make such orders if they are necessary, and it may be good practice to secure the transfer of such applications vertically to the High Court in anticipation of the need for such an order. No leave is necessary for a local authority to apply for such an injunction.

Applications by individuals

8.183 In contrast to local authorities, individuals who wish to invoke the inherent jurisdiction in relation to children do not need to seek the leave of the court to make an application. However, a better remedy is by way of an application for judicial review, discussed in detail at Chapter **11**, which permits the High Court to exercise supervisory control over statutory bodies where a local authority is believed to have acted unreasonably or beyond its powers, and has disregarded the right to family life under the ECHR.

CHAPTER 9

CRIMINAL PROCEEDINGS

'The research consistently indicates that criminal court involvement is stressful for many children and their families. Furthermore, children's recovery may be delayed by lengthy and multiple legal proceedings. Adverse emotional effects are not manifested by all children, even in the short term, and some children may regret not having their day in court' (*Childhood Matters, A Report of the National Commission of Inquiry into the Prevention of Child Abuse and Neglect* (1996), at p 250).

'Child abuse victims involved in the criminal justice system require co-ordination among prosecutors, police, child protection service workers, and, when available, victim/assistance programme staff to ensure that cases are dealt with in an integrated and child-focussed manner from the moment of disclosure though sentencing and beyond' (Sas, Wolfe and Gowdey (1996), at pp 355–356).

GROUNDS OF CRIMINAL LIABILITY

Basic principles of criminal liability

9.1   The vast majority of criminal offences relating to child abuse are now defined by statutes, some of which date back to the nineteenth century. The one important exception is the law relating to homicide, where murder and manslaughter remain common law offences, derived from the decisions of the courts.

9.2   The majority of criminal offences, whether common law or statutory, consist of two essential elements, technically described as the *actus reus* (the actual deed) and *mens rea* (the mental element required). The former consists of the external elements of an offence, which will usually consist of acts or, exceptionally, omissions in specified circumstances and may sometimes also include prohibited consequences (such as harm or death). The latter consists of the fault element required for the offence, which may be satisfied by states of mind such as knowledge, intention, wilfulness, recklessness or negligence. As a general rule, both elements must exist contemporaneously before criminal liability will arise. For example, the *actus reus* of a murder would be satisfied if a child dies as a result of physical abuse. However, the perpetrator of the abuse would only be liable for murder if, at the time of inflicting the abuse, he had the necessary *mens rea*, ie he either intended to kill the child or intended to cause the child grievous bodily harm. Although there is a strong common law presumption that all offences require *mens rea*, the presumption can be rebutted if Parliament has indicated a contrary intention, either expressly or by necessary implication (*Sweet v Parsley* [1969] 1 All ER 347). Offences where no *mens rea* is required as to one or more elements of *actus reus* are called offences of strict liability. In the past, where the age of the victim is an essential component of the *actus reus* of a sexual offence, the courts have tended to interpret the offence as imposing strict liability in relation to the victim's age. Thus an offender who honestly (and perhaps reasonably) believed that a girl was over the age of 16 would have no defence to a charge of taking an unmarried girl under the age of 16 out of the possession of her father against his will (*R v Prince* (1875) LR 2 CCR 154). However, the approach has been subject to sustained criticism and the House of Lords has made it clear that there is no special principle applicable to age-based sexual offences, and that the presumption of *mens rea* applies (see paras **9.41** and **9.44**).

Young offenders and the age of criminal responsibility

9.3   A child under the age of 10 is said to be *doli incapax*, ie incapable of crime, and therefore a child under the age of 10 cannot be convicted of a criminal offence. Children below this age whose behaviour causes concern may be made the subject of a care order if they are suffering or likely to suffer significant harm and the harm, or likelihood of harm, is attributable to, inter alia, the child's being beyond parental control (see para **8.92** *et seq*). The Crime and Disorder Act 1998 also provides further powers to deal with children under 10 who have committed acts which, in the case of those over 10, would have constituted criminal offences. The local authority may apply to the magistrates' family proceedings court for a child safety order, which places the child under the supervision of a responsible officer for a period of up to 3 months and subjects the child to certain restrictions or conditions (s 11).

9.4   In the past, where a child was 10 years of age or over but under the age of 14 at the time of the alleged offence, there was a rebuttable presumption at common law that the child was *doli incapax*. The prosecution could rebut this presumption by calling evidence to show that a child had 'mischievous discretion', ie that the child knew that what he was doing was seriously wrong. In *C v DPP* [1994] 3 All ER 190, the Divisional Court expressed the view that the presumption did a serious disservice to the law and ruled that it was no longer part of the law of England and Wales. However, the House of Lords took the view that any change in the law was a matter for Parliament, not the courts (*C (A Minor) v DPP* [1995] 2 All ER 43). The issue has now been resolved by s 34 of the Crime and Disorder Act 1998, which abolished the rebuttable presumption of *doli incapax* for children aged between 10 and 14 years. As a result, all children over the age of 10 years are now assumed to have reached the same level of moral culpability as adults and may be convicted of any offence. The only exception to this general principle is where the age of the offender is specified as an essential ingredient of a statutory offence. For example, the offence of wilfully ill-treating or neglecting a child under the CYPA 1933 can only be committed by a person who is at least 16 years old.

Boys and sexual offences

9.5   Prior to 1993, there was an irrebuttable presumption that boys under the age of 14 were incapable of sexual intercourse. This meant that they could not be convicted as perpetrators of rape or any offence involving sexual intercourse, or of buggery, whether as agent or patient. In recent years the presumption had increasingly come under attack as being outdated and the presumption was therefore abolished by the Sexual Offences Act 1993. Thus there is no longer any restriction on convicting boys over the age of 10 of offences involving sexual intercourse.

Children as parties to crimes created for their own protection

9.6   When an indictable offence is committed, criminal liability will generally be imposed not only on the principal offender, but also on accomplices who aid, abet, counsel or procure the commission of the offence (Accessories and Abettors Act 1861, s 8). However, where a statute is designed for protection of a certain class of persons, it may be construed as excluding by implication the liability of any member of that class who is the victim of the offence, even though that person does in fact aid, abet, counsel or procure the offence. There is clear authority for the application of this principle to sexual offences. In the case of *R v Tyrrell* [1894] 1 QB 710, it was held that a girl between the age of 13 and 16 who encouraged a boy to have sexual intercourse with her could not be liable as an accomplice to the offence of having unlawful sexual intercourse with a girl under the age of 16 because the offence had been created for her own protection. Thus, if a sexual offence has been specifically created for the protection of a certain class of individuals, a member of that class will not incur criminal liability by aiding, abetting, counselling or procuring the offence when they are themselves the victim of the offence.

Physical abuse and neglect

Cruelty to persons aged under 16

9.7   Statutory offences of cruelty to children have existed since the nineteenth century. The relevant law is now contained in s 1 of the CYPA 1933, as amended by the CA 1989, which provides that it is an offence for any person who is at least 16 years old and has responsibility for a child or young person under that age, to wilfully assault, ill-treat, neglect, abandon or expose the child in a manner likely to cause him unnecessary suffering or injury to health, or to cause or procure the child to be so treated. The offence is subject to a maximum penalty of 10 years' imprisonment.

Persons who may be liable

9.8   By virtue of s 17 of the CYPA 1933, liability may be imposed on any person who has parental responsibility for the child or young person (within the meaning of the CA 1989) or who is otherwise legally liable to maintain him; and any person who has care of him. Therefore liability may be imposed not only on parents and primary carers, but also on people such as schoolteachers and anyone over the age of 16 who acts as a babysitter for the child.

9.9   Parents or carers may be charged jointly. Even if only one of them is proved to have abused or neglected the child, the other will be liable for neglect if they realised that the abuse was taking place, but failed to take steps to protect the child. For example, in R *v Creed* [2000] 1 Cr App R (S) 304, a mother had failed to protect a child from sustained violence over a period of 7 months from the man with whom she was living, and had delayed calling for medical attention following the infliction of grave injuries by him which had caused the child's death. She was convicted of an offence under s 1 and was sentenced to a total of 5 years' imprisonment.

The offending behaviour

9.10   The offence is not divided into watertight compartments. It creates a single offence which may be committed by a wide range of behaviour – assault, ill-treatment, neglect and abandonment or exposure – each of which must be carried out in a manner likely to cause the child unnecessary suffering or injury to health (which includes injury to or loss of sight, or hearing, or limb, or organ of the body, and any mental derangement). It is clear that the child need not actually suffer or be injured, as s 1(3) of CYPA 1933 provides that the offence is committed notwithstanding that actual suffering or injury to health, or the likelihood of actual suffering or injury to health, is obviated by the action of another person.

Assaults and ill-treatment

9.11   It will usually take the form of a battery, that is the actual infliction of unlawful personal violence. This is subject to the right of the parent or any other person having the lawful control or charge of the child or young person (subject to s 548 of the Education Act 1996) to administer punishment to him (see para **2.62** *et seq*). However, a simple common assault will not suffice unless it is committed in a manner likely to cause unnecessary suffering to the child or injury to his health (R *v Hatton* [1925] 2 KB 322). Ill-treatment is not defined by the CYPA 1933, but obviously includes a wide range of behaviour, including bullying or frightening the child.

Neglect

9.12   Cases of neglect have received frequent attention in the courts. By virtue of s 1(2) of the CYPA 1933 the parent or guardian of a child or young person will be deemed to have neglected him in a manner likely to cause injury to his health if he fails to provide adequate food, clothing, medical aid or lodging, or, if unable to provide them, he fails to procure them, for example, by requesting assistance from the authorities. However, even where neglect is deemed, it must still be established that the neglect was 'wilful' (*R v Wills* [1990] Crim LR 714). Many of the cases arise from the defendant's culpable failure to summon medical assistance for a child. In *R v Taggart* [1999] 2 Cr App R (S) 68, the defendant's 3½-year-old child had suffered severe scalding while in the bath. Although it was accepted that the scalding had been accidental, the defendant pleaded guilty on the basis of his failure to summon medical attention for the child until more than 24 hours later.

Abandonment and exposure

9.13   Abandonment means leaving a child to its fate. For example, in *R v Boulden* (1957) 41 Cr App R 105, a father of five children was held to have abandoned them in a manner likely to cause unnecessary suffering when he left them to travel to Scotland. The court held that the father should have taken all reasonable steps to ensure that the children had been received into care. The offence of exposing a child in a manner likely to cause unnecessary suffering or injury has had little consideration in case-law. It is clear that exposure need not necessarily consist of physically placing the child somewhere with intent to injure him (*R v Williams (John)* (1910) 4 Cr App R 89). If a child under the age of 2 is abandoned or exposed so that the child's life is endangered, or his health is or is likely to be permanently injured, a separate offence under s 27 of the OAPA 1861 will be committed.

'Wilful' behaviour

9.14   In order to constitute the offence, the behaviour must be 'wilful'. In the case of *R v Shepherd* [1981] AC 394, it was held that 'wilfully' is not limited to requiring an intention to do one of the physical acts described in the section, but also extends to the consequences. In this case a child of 16 months died of hypothermia following severe gastro-enteritis. The parents were poor and of low intelligence, and had not appreciated the seriousness of the child's condition. The parents were initially convicted under s 1 on the basis of an objective test, ie that a reasonable parent would have realised the risk. Their appeal was allowed, the House of Lords deciding that the jury must be satisfied: (1) that the child did in fact need medical aid at the time at which his parents were charged with failing to provide it; and (2) either the parents were aware at the time that the child's health might be at risk if it were not provided with medical aid, or that the parents' unawareness of this fact was due to their not caring whether the child's health was at risk or not. Following *Shepherd*, a person will only be liable for the offence if he either knows that his conduct might cause suffering or injury to health or if he does not care whether this results or not. Therefore, a carer who genuinely does not know that a child in their care requires medical attention, either through stupidity or ignorance, will not commit the offence under s 1 by failing to call for medical assistance.

Other offences involving physical abuse

Assault and battery

9.15　In lay terms, the word assault is commonly used to describe unwanted physical contact. The strict legal definition of assault is much narrower and is restricted to causing another to apprehend the infliction of immediate unlawful personal violence, sometimes referred to as 'psychiatric assault'. If unlawful personal contact with the victim actually occurs, this amounts to a battery, sometimes referred to as 'physical assault'. In either case the defendant must have intended the outcome, or have been aware of the risk that his behaviour would result in the prohibited consequence (*R v Savage and Parmenter* [1991] 4 All ER 698). However, the term assault has generally come to be used to include both assault and battery, although the two remain distinct offences. In the majority of cases, assault and battery will be committed together and both will involve a positive act by the defendant. For example, an abuser approaches a child, shouting and raising his hand (assault) and then strikes the child (battery). In exceptional cases, liability for assault or battery may arise from an omission if the defendant is under a duty to act. For example, if the defendant's behaviour has created a dangerous situation, he will be under a duty to take steps to alleviate the danger (*R v Miller* [1983] 1 All ER 978). In practice, it is unlikely that an abuser would face charges of these summary offences of assault or battery, as the relevant conduct will inevitably fall within s 1 of the CYPA 1933, which will be the preferred charge. However, if the child suffered any significant injury as a result of the abuse, the abuser may be charged with one of the statutory offences under the OAPA 1861 involving actual or grievous bodily harm.

Actual bodily harm

9.16　Section 47 of the OAPA 1861 provides that it is an offence, subject to a maximum penalty of 5 years' imprisonment, to assault a person occasioning them actual bodily harm. The assault may take the form of a technical assault or battery and must cause the victim to suffer actual bodily harm. The level of harm required is relatively low, a typical example being bruising. The harm need not be permanent, but must be more than merely transient or trifling

(R *v Donovan* [1934] 2 KB 498) and can include psychiatric harm in the form of an identifiable clinical condition (R *v Ireland and Burstow* [1997] 4 All ER 225). Although the defendant must have the *mens rea* required for the assault or battery, there is no need for the defendant either to intend the actual bodily harm or be aware of the risk of such harm (R *v Savage and Parmenter*, above). For example, a defendant who admits causing bruising to a baby by rough handling, but claims that he did not foresee the risk of the bruising occurring, perhaps because he had no experience of handling babies, would be liable for an offence under s 47 of the OAPA 1861.

Grievous bodily harm

9.17 Section 20 of the OAPA 1861 provides that it is an offence, subject to a maximum penalty of 5 years' imprisonment, unlawfully and maliciously to wound or inflict grievous bodily harm on any other person. Section 18 of the same Act provides that it is an offence unlawfully and maliciously to wound or cause grievous bodily harm to any person with intent to do some grievous bodily harm (or with intent to resist arrest). The requirement of ulterior intent makes the offence under s 18 a very serious one, which is reflected in the maximum penalty of life imprisonment. A wound is a break in the continuity of the whole skin (*JJC v Eisenhower* [1983] 3 All ER 230). Grievous bodily harm has simply been defined as 'really serious harm' (*DPP v Smith* [1960] 3 All ER 161), which may include psychiatric harm (R *v Ireland and Burstow*, above). Typical examples of grievous bodily harm include broken bones and serious internal injuries. Although in the majority of cases the harm will be inflicted or caused by an assault or battery, this is not an essential element of the offence.

9.18 For the offence under s 20 of the OAPA 1861, the defendant must intend or foresee that his actions may cause *some* harm to the victim (R *v Savage and Parmenter*, above). Thus a defendant who punches a child, causing serious internal injuries, will be liable for the offence under s 20 if he foresaw that he may cause the child some harm, even if he did not foresee the extent of the harm he actually caused. If, however, when he punched the child it was the defendant's intention to cause serious injury, he would be liable for the offence under s 18.

Criminal liability when the child dies

9.19 If a child dies as a result of abuse or neglect, criminal liability will be dependent on the abuser's state of mind, or culpability, at the time of the abuse.

Murder

9.20 Murder is the most culpable criminal offence and carries a mandatory sentence of life imprisonment. A defendant will be liable for murder if he causes the death of another with 'malice aforethought', which is defined as either intending to kill or intending to cause grievous bodily harm (R *v Moloney* [1985] 1 All ER 1025). For these purposes, a person intends a consequence when it is his aim or objective. Alternatively, if death or grievous bodily harm is not the defendant's aim or objective, but he foresees either consequence as virtually certain to occur, that is evidence from which the jury may find he had the necessary intention (R *v Woollin* [1998] 3 WLR 382). Therefore, if a child dies as a result of physical abuse or a deliberate omission (such as starving the child) the abuser will be liable for murder if the child's death or the infliction of grievous bodily harm on the child was either his aim or objective, or he foresaw that death or grievous bodily harm was a virtually certain consequence, which would be evidence from which the jury may find he had the necessary intention. In exceptional circumstances, where a defendant has killed with malice aforethought, the resulting conviction may be reduced to either infanticide or manslaughter, both of which carry a maximum penalty of life imprisonment.

Infanticide

9.21 Section 1 of the Infanticide Act 1938 provides that, where a mother kills her child by any wilful act or omission when the child is under 12 months old, she will not be liable for murder if the balance of her mind was disturbed by reason of her not having fully recovered from the effect of giving birth to the child or by reason of the effect of lactation consequent upon the birth of her child. Although there are comparatively few convictions for infanticide each year (in 2000/01 there were only five convictions for infanticide in England and Wales), the statutory provision has been the subject of considerable criticism, not least because it is based on the belief that the ordinary conditions of childbirth and lactation have a potentially disruptive effect on the mental state and behaviour of women. However, it does appear to be a useful tool to ensure lenient sentences for women who kill their young children, most of whom are viewed overwhelmingly as tragic cases (see further, Mackay (1993)).

Partial defences to murder – voluntary manslaughter

Diminished responsibility

9.22 Section 2 of the Homicide Act 1957 provides that where a person kills or is party to the killing of another, he shall not be convicted of murder if he was suffering from such abnormality of the mind as substantially impaired his mental responsibility for his acts and omissions in doing or being party to the killing. Although the provision applies to both men and women, research has shown that, in relation to parents who kill their children, women are far more likely to be dealt with on the basis of diminished responsibility (see further, Wilczynski and Morris (1993)).

Provocation

9.23 Provocation was originally a common law concept. Section 3 of the Homicide Act 1957 now provides that, where there is evidence on which the jury can find that a person charged was provoked (whether by things done or by things said or by both together) to lose his self control, the question whether the provocation was enough to make a reasonable man do as he did shall be left to be determined by the jury; and in determining the question the jury shall take into account everything both done and said according to the effect which, in their opinion, it would have on the reasonable man. The potential scope of provocation is wide. In the case of *R v Doughty* (1986) 83 Cr App R 319, the Court of Appeal held that the persistent crying of a young baby fell within the scope of 'things said or done', and that, if there was evidence on which the jury might find that the crying had caused the defendant to lose self-control, then the issue of provocation should be left to the jury. In deciding whether the provocation was enough to make a reasonable person do as the defendant did, it is now clear that the reasonable person will be attributed with any relevant characteristics of the defendant, including any mental characteristics which reduce the defendant's power of self-control (*R v Smith (Morgan James)* [2000] 4 All ER 289). So a mother suffering from post-natal depression, who 'snaps' under the stress of caring for a baby who cries persistently, may be able to rely on provocation to reduce a murder charge to one of manslaughter.

Involuntary manslaughter

9.24 If the defendant does not have any intention to kill or cause grievous bodily harm, but is nevertheless still held to be culpably responsible for the death of a child, the appropriate charge will be one of manslaughter. Liability may arise in two ways – constructive manslaughter or gross negligence manslaughter.

Constructive manslaughter

9.25 Liability for this form of manslaughter is constructed out of the performance of an unlawful dangerous act. The unlawful act must be a crime requiring a degree of fault greater than negligence (*Andrews v DPP* [1937] 2 All ER 552). It is clear that a negligent omission such as might constitute wilful neglect of a child will not be sufficient to form the basis of constructive manslaughter (*R v Lowe* [1973] 1 All ER 805), although there is some doubt as to whether the same would apply to a deliberate omission. Given the existence of gross negligence manslaughter, where an omission may clearly form the basis of liability, this issue is unlikely to be problematic. In the vast majority of cases the unlawful act will be an assault on the victim. The unlawful act must be dangerous, which means it must be such as all sober and reasonable people would inevitably recognise must subject the other person to, at least, the risk of some harm resulting therefrom, albeit not serious harm (*R v Church* [1966] 1 QB 59). Thus, whenever an abuser commits an assault on a child that results in the child's death, this will inevitably constitute manslaughter, whether or not the abuser actually foresaw the possibility of death or even harm resulting.

Gross negligence manslaughter

9.26 This form of manslaughter will be relied on where the victim's death was caused by an omission, or where the defendant's act was not otherwise unlawful. For liability to arise three factors must be established. First, the defendant must owe a duty of care to the victim. Secondly, there must be a breach of that duty which causes death. Finally, the required degree of negligence must be established. This was described by Lord Mackay in *R v Adomako* [1994] 3 All ER 79 as follows:

> 'The essence of the matter, which is supremely a jury question, is whether, having regard to the risk of death involved, the conduct of the defendant was so bad in all the circumstances as to amount in their judgment to a criminal act or omission.'

9.27 This last requirement has been the subject of much criticism as it is circular in its reasoning, leaving the jury to decide whether they think the acts or omissions of the defendant amount to criminal behaviour. It is clear that negligent parents and carers may face the prospect of being charged with gross negligence manslaughter if a child in their care dies. In July 2000 two young girls, aged 7 and 8, were killed by a train in west Wales while playing on an unfenced railway line (*Daily Telegraph*, 31 July 2000). At the time of the incident, they were in the care of the mother and step-father of one of the girls, who were subsequently charged with the manslaughter of the girls through gross negligence (*Daily Telegraph*, 14 December 2000). The prosecution alleged that the defendants had left the children unsupervised for half-an-hour while they played on the railway line. A jury convicted the defendants of gross negligence and manslaughter (*Daily Telegraph*, 28 July 2001) and they were sentenced to 12 months' imprisonment on each count, suspended for one year. Imposing liability for manslaughter on the basis of a negligent omission, as opposed to a positive act, will invariably be controversial. Presumably no jury will convict on the basis of a momentary lapse of attention by a carer. In the case of the children killed by the train, the judge commented that the defendants had been 'appallingly negligent' (*Daily Telegraph*, 19 October 2001), but in many circumstances the line between 'mere' negligence and the gross negligence required for a criminal conviction will potentially be a difficult one to draw.

Sexual abuse

9.28 The law has regulated sexual activity with children from early times but the criminal law relating to child sexual abuse is diverse and complex. There is no single offence of sexually abusing a child. The vast majority of sexual offences are not age-specific and therefore sexual activity with a child when the child does not, in fact, consent can be prosecuted as rape or indecent assault. However, the protection afforded by the general law of sexual offences has been found to be insufficient to protect children from sexual abuse and exploitation and so further provisions have been enacted for the specific purpose of protecting children from what is deemed to be inappropriate sexual behaviour.

The age of consent

9.29 One of the methods used to protect children has been to impose a statutory age of consent. Although there is no universally agreed age of consent and views on the appropriate age inevitably vary, the law in England and Wales is based on the assumption that children under the age of 16 years should not be indulging in any form of sexual activity and thus since 1885, 16 has been the age of consent for heterosexual activity. The age of consent for homosexual activity has been more controversial. Originally set at 21 years by the Sexual Offences Act 1967 (SOA 1967), it was reduced to 18 years by the CJPOA 1994. Spurred on by the ruling of the European Commission on Human Rights in *Sutherland v United Kingdom* (1997) 24 EHRR CD 22, the government expressed its commitment to equalising the age of consent for heterosexual and homosexual activity at 16 years. Following unsuccessful attempts in July 1998 and April 1999, when the government was defeated on this issue by the House of Lords, the government resorted to the use of the Parliament Acts, which allow a Bill which has been passed by the House of Commons in two successive sessions but rejected by the House of Lords in each of those sessions to be presented for Royal Assent, to secure the change. Section 1 of the Sexual Offences (Amendment) Act 2000, which was implemented on 8 January 2001, reduces the age of consent for homosexual activity to 16 years. Thus children under the age of 16 cannot, in law, consent to any sexual activity.

9.30 However, a distinction must be made between consent in law and consent in fact. Whereas a 15-year-old girl cannot, in law, consent to sexual intercourse, it is clear that she can, and frequently will, consent in fact. Therefore, a man who has consensual sexual intercourse with a 15-year-old girl may commit the offence of having unlawful sexual intercourse with a girl under the age of 16, but he will not commit the offence of rape.

Rape

9.31 Rape is defined by s 1 of the Sexual Offences Act 1956 (SOA 1956) (as amended) as sexual intercourse (defined as penile penetration of the vagina or anus) with a person who at the time of the intercourse does not consent to it and at the time the man either knows that the person does not consent or he is reckless as to whether there is consent. The maximum penalty which may be imposed on conviction for rape is life imprisonment.

Age and the absence of consent

9.32 The essential ingredient of the offence of rape is the absence of consent. There is no statutory definition of consent and the word is given its ordinary meaning. For example, there will be no consent if any apparent agreement is achieved by the use of force or fear of force. Nor will there be consent if the victim is incapable of consenting because she is unconscious or asleep, or if she is deceived as to the nature of the act (R *v Williams* [1923] 1 KB 340). The law recognises a distinction between 'real consent' and 'a lack of consent or mere submission', although it is not always easy to draw a line between the two. It is also clear that there will be no consent if the victim did not have the understanding and knowledge to decide whether to consent or resist (whether by age, disability or illness) (R *v Lang* (1975) 62 Cr App R 50). Clearly, few problems arise if the victim is very young. In the case of R *v Howard* [1965] 3 All ER 684, the alleged victim of rape was a girl of 6 years of age. Lord Parker CJ commented 'it would be idle for anyone to suggest that a girl of that age had sufficient understanding and knowledge to decide whether to consent or resist'. In the case of older child victims, it will be a matter for the jury to decide whether the individual child had sufficient understanding and knowledge to decide whether to consent. If the prosecution does not think it can prove absence of consent by virtue of the child's level of understanding and knowledge alone, if the child is under 13 years, an alternative charge may be brought under s 5 of the SOA 1956, which carries the same maximum penalty as a charge of rape – ie life imprisonment. Where the victim is between 13 and 16, in many cases it will be difficult to prove the absence of consent by virtue of the child's understanding and knowledge alone and so the prosecution will need to rely on other evidence, such as the use of force or threats, to establish the absence of consent. If it fails to do so, alternative charges may be brought under ss 6, 14 or 15 of the SOA 1956, all of which carry lesser maximum penalties.

Knowledge or recklessness as to the absence of consent

9.33 In addition to proving the absence of consent, the prosecution must also prove that the defendant either knew that the victim was not consenting, or that he was reckless as to whether the victim consented or not. This fault element is subjective and depends on the belief in the defendant's mind at the time of the offence. If he honestly believed the victim was consenting (even if he had no reasonable grounds for that belief) then he will not be liable for rape (*DPP v Morgan* [1976] AC 182). However, a jury is unlikely to believe a defendant who claims to have held a totally unreasonable belief in consent. The jury will be instructed that the presence or absence of reasonable grounds for an alleged belief in consent is a matter to which it is to have regard, in conjunction with other relevant matters, in considering whether the belief was actually held (Sexual Offences (Amendment) Act 1976, s 1(2)). In the case of a very young victim, a defence of mistaken belief in consent will inevitably fail as no jury would believe a defendant who claims he honestly believed that a 6-year-old child was consenting to the intercourse. However, with older child victims, once again the prosecution will need to rely on other evidence, such as the use of force or threats, to rebut a claim of honest belief in consent.

Unlawful sexual intercourse

9.34 Whereas an absence of consent is an essential ingredient to a charge of rape, consent is irrelevant to the offences in ss 5 and 6 of the SOA 1956. By virtue of s 5 of the Act, it is an offence for a man to have unlawful sexual intercourse with a girl under the age of 13. The offence is punishable with life imprisonment. Section 6 of the SOA 1956 provides that it is an offence (subject to the exceptions provided for in the section) for a man to have unlawful sexual intercourse with a girl under the age of 16. The offence is punishable with a maximum of 2 years' imprisonment. The requirement that the intercourse be 'unlawful' means that it must be outside the bonds of marriage (R v Chapman [1959] 1 QB 100). As the age of marriage is now 16, intercourse with a girl under that age is necessarily unlawful, except in the case of a marriage valid under foreign law. Offences under both sections are committed irrespective of any consent the girl may, in fact, give.

Mistaken belief as to age

9.35 A man has a defence under s 6(3) if he is under the age of 24, has not previously been charged with a like offence, and he believes the girl to be of the age of 16 or over and has reasonable cause for the belief. This so-called 'young man's defence' allows for a limited defence of a reasonable mistaken belief as to age, but only as to the offence under s 6, the defence is not applicable to the offence under s 5 of the SOA 1956. Subject to the 'young man's defence' liability in respect of the age of the victim is strict in both sections, a view which has recently been affirmed by the House of Lords (B v DPP [2000] 1 All ER 833; R v K [2001] 3 All ER 897). As a result, a man (of whatever age) who has consensual sexual intercourse with girl of 12, believing on reasonable grounds that she is 16, will be liable for the offence under s 5 and subject to a maximum penalty of life imprisonment. Yet if the girl is 13 and the man meets the criteria of the 'young man's defence' he will be entitled to an acquittal. In creating the offences in ss 5 and 6, Parliament was understandably anxious to afford greater protection to younger girls, but the imposition of strict liability for the more serious offence is questionable, particularly in view of the recent approach of the House of Lords to other age-based sexual offences.

Buggery

9.36   Section 12 of the SOA 1956 provides that it is an offence for a person to commit buggery with another person or an animal. Buggery is not defined by the statute and so the common law definition of intercourse per anum by a man with a man or woman, or intercourse per vaginum by man or a woman with an animal is applicable. However, the scope of the offence has been modified over the years. As non-consensual anal intercourse now constitutes rape, buggery is restricted to consensual anal intercourse. Buggery between males over the age of 21 years in private was initially decriminalised by the SOA 1967. As a result of the extended definition of rape enacted in 1994 and the equalisation of the age of consent for heterosexual and homosexual activity, anal intercourse with a boy or girl under the age of 16 is now an offence subject to a maximum penalty of life imprisonment.

Indecent assault

9.37   Section 14 of the SOA 1956 provides that it is an offence for a person to make an indecent assault on a woman. Section 15 of the Act provides for a similar offence of making an indecent assault on a man. Both offences are punishable with a maximum of 10 years' imprisonment. The prosecution must prove an assault, which may be a technical assault or a battery (see para **9.15**). Therefore, a defendant who merely invites another person to touch him will not commit an assault. In *Fairclough v Whip* [1951] 2 All ER 834 a defendant had exposed himself in the presence of a 9-year-old girl and invited her to touch his exposed person, which she did. It was held that this did not amount to an indecent assault.

9.38   The assault must be accompanied by circumstances of indecency. The appropriate test is whether right-minded persons would consider the conduct as being 'offensive to contemporary standards of modesty and privacy' (*R v Court* [1989] AC 28). If the circumstances of the assault are inherently indecent when viewed objectively, the defendant's purpose or motive will be irrelevant. However, if the circumstances of the assault are not inherently indecent, but are merely capable of being considered indecent, the defendant's motive will be a crucial factor. For example, in the case of *Court* (above), the defendant spanked a 12-year-old girl several times across her shorts. In the House of Lords Lord Ackner commented:

> 'The conduct of the appellant in assaulting the girl by spanking her was only *capable* of being an indecent assault. To decide whether or not right-minded persons might think that assault was indecent, the following factors were clearly relevant: the relationship of the defendant to this victim (were they relatives, friends or virtually complete strangers?), how had the defendant come to embark on this conduct and *why* was he behaving in this way?'

9.39 If, however, right-minded persons could not consider the circumstances of the assault indecent, any secret motive of the defendant will be irrelevant. For example, in the case of *R v George* [1956] Crim LR 52, there was held to be no indecent assault where the defendant, who had a 'shoe-fetish', tried to remove the victim's shoes, even though his motive for acting was sexual gratification.

Children and the legal fiction of non-consent

9.40 Sections 14(2) and 15(2) of the SOA 1956 provide that a girl or boy under the age of 16 cannot in law give any consent that would prevent an act being an assault for the purposes of the sections. This legal fiction of non-consent means that virtually all sexual activity with children under the age of 16 amounts to an indecent assault. This results in an uneasy relationship between the offences of unlawful sexual intercourse and indecent assault. The slightest indecent touching of a girl under the age of 16 renders the defendant liable for indecent assault (regardless of any consent the girl has given), subject to a maximum penalty of 10 years' imprisonment. Yet if the couple proceed to have consensual sexual intercourse (and the girl is 13 or over), the defendant would be liable under s 6 of the SOA 1956 and subject to a maximum penalty of 2 years' imprisonment. As a matter of logic, any sexual intercourse involves an indecent assault, so the legal fiction of non-consent arguably obviated the need for the offence under s 6 of the SOA 1956.

Mistaken belief as to the age of the victim

9.41 For many years, liability in respect of the victim's age was strict, so that an honest (and maybe reasonable) belief that the victim was aged 16 or over would not amount to a defence to a charge of indecent assault. This view was supported by the Court of Appeal in *R v K* [2001] Crim LR 134 when it was decided that, in s 14(2) of the SOA 1956, Parliament had excluded any defence based on mistaken belief, although such a defence is available under s 14(3) (reasonable cause to believe that the victim is the defendant's wife), and s 14(4) (indecent assault on a defective). However, following their own previous decision in *B v DPP* [2001] 1 All ER 833 in relation to the offence of indecency with children (see para **9.44**), the House of Lords in *R v K* [2001] 2 All ER 897 reserved the decision of the Court of Appeal and held that the presumption of mens rea applies to s 14(2). As a result of the House of Lords' decision in *R v K*, if a defendant honestly believes that the victim was 16 or over, he is entitled to an acquittal.

Indecency with children

9.42 Whereas the offences of indecent assault criminalise a wide range of sexual behaviour with children, the coverage is not fully comprehensive. Cases such as *Fairclough v Whip* (see para **9.37**), revealed a lacuna in the law and in

1959 the Criminal Law Review Committee was established to review the law. Following the Committee's first report, the Indecency with Children Act 1960 (ICA 1960) was passed. Section 1 of the Act provided that an offence is committed by any person who commits an act of gross indecency with or towards a child under the age of 14, or who incites a child under that age to such an act with him or another. This clearly created an anomaly as the section afforded no protection to 14- and 15-year-olds, yet the anomaly remained untouched for 40 years. The Criminal Justice and Court Services Act 2000 (CJCSA 2000) has now amended the ICA 1960 with effect from January 2001 so that the offence protects all children under the age of 16. The maximum penalty for the offence is 10 years' imprisonment.

9.43   The offence obviously includes an indecent assault, but is much wider than that. This is illustrated by the facts of the case of *R v Speck* [1977] 2 All ER 859, in which an 8-year-old girl, uninvited, placed her hand on a man's penis, outside his trousers and continued to keep her hand there for 5 minutes. In consequence, the man had an erection, but stayed passive and did nothing to encourage her. He was convicted under s 1 of the ICA 1960, the Court of Appeal holding that his conduct amounted to 'an invitation to the child to do the act'. The decision has been criticised as being an abuse of language because there was no invitation in the ordinary sense of the word. Yet the Court of Appeal clearly felt that liability should arise in such circumstances and was prepared to stretch the wording of the Act in order to obtain a conviction. Had the draftsman extended the offence to include 'permitting an act of gross indecency to be performed', no such problems would have arisen.

Mistaken belief as to age of the victim

9.44   The ICA 1960 does not expressly provide a defence based on mistaken belief in the victim's age. For many years, in line with the offences of indecent assault and unlawful sexual intercourse, the Act was thought to impose strict liability as to age. However, a recent decision of the House of Lords has made it clear that an honest belief that the victim is 14 or over (now raised to 16 or over) will result in the acquittal of the defendant. In the case of *B v DPP* [2000] 1 All ER 833, the defendant, a 15-year-old boy, sat next to a 13-year-old girl on a bus. He asked her to perform oral sex on him but she refused. He repeated his request several times and she repeatedly refused. He was charged with an offence under s 1 of the ICA 1960 Act. At his trial in the youth court it was accepted that he honestly believed that the girl was over 13 (the relevant age at the time of the offence), but, in line with previous authority (*R v Prince*, see para **9.2**), the court ruled that this was not a defence. The Divisional Court upheld this ruling and a further appeal was taken to the House of Lords. The House of Lords could not find, either on grounds of general principle or case-law authority, any indication of sufficient cogency to displace the application of the common law presumption of *mens rea*. It was decided that an honest belief that the victim was over 13 would result in an acquittal, regardless of whether or not the defendant had reasonable grounds for that belief. There is, therefore, no consistency in the law regarding a mistaken belief in the victim's age in relation to sexual offences.

Incest

9.45 Incest became a criminal offence in England and Wales for the first time in 1908 and is now contained in ss 10 and 11 of the SOA 1956. Sexual intercourse between parent and child, grandfather and granddaughter, and brother and sister is prohibited. The offence may be committed by a man (s 10) or a woman over the age of 16 (s 11), provided in each case the man or woman knows that the person with whom they are having intercourse is one of the prohibited relations. The offence is punishable with a maximum of 7 years' imprisonment, or life imprisonment if committed with a girl under 13 years. The relationships within ss 10 and 11 are restricted to blood relationships. Therefore, if a father has consensual sexual intercourse with his 14-year-old daughter, he commits incest and is liable to a maximum of 7 years' imprisonment. But if a step-father commits the same act with his step-daughter, he is only liable under the SOA 1956, s 6 and may face a maximum of 2 years' imprisonment. It is irrelevant that the step-father may have played a far more active role in the girl's upbringing. For example, the father may have deserted the mother before the daughter was born, yet if he has intercourse with the daughter, presuming he knows she is his daughter, he will be guilty of incest. In today's society, with a high divorce rate and step-families becoming more common, it is difficult to see that such a distinction is logical.

Abuse of a position of trust

9.46 Section 3 of the Sexual Offences (Amendment) Act 2000 (SO(A)A 2000) creates a new offence of abuse of a position of trust. A person aged 18 or over commits the offence if they have sexual intercourse (whether vaginal or anal) or engage in any other sexual activity with a person under that age where they are in a 'position of trust' in relation to the younger person. The offence carries a maximum penalty of 5 years' imprisonment.

9.47 The enactment of the offence is closely linked with the move to equalise the age of consent for homosexual and heterosexual activity. Whereas the previously existing criminal law generally protected children under the age of 16 from inappropriate sexual activity, concern had been expressed that the lowering of the age of consent for homosexual activity could lead to the exploitation of vulnerable young people over the age of 16 by older men, particularly by those in a position of trust or authority over the young person. Many jurisdictions have recognised the danger of exploitation and have adopted measures to protect vulnerable young people. For example, in

Austria, it is illegal for a male over the age of 19 to commit homosexual acts with a male between 14 and 18, and in Portugal it is illegal for a person aged 18 or over to commit sexual acts with a person under 18. In Canada, a specific offence has been created of sexual exploitation of a young person by one who is in a position of trust (Article 153 of the Canadian Criminal Code).

9.48 When amendments were introduced to the Crime and Disorder Bill which would have had the effect of lowering the age of consent for homosexual activity to 16, amendments were also tabled which aimed to introduce protections similar to those which exist in other jurisdictions. However, these amendments were rejected by the House of Commons before the Bill went to the House of Lords and in June 1998 the government announced the establishment of an inter-departmental working group of officials to consider how to prevent those who were unsuitable from working with children and to look at further possible measures to protect 16- and 17-year-olds who may be vulnerable to abuse by those in a position of trust such as carers, teachers and leaders of organised residential activities (HC Deb, vol 31, col 304, 4 June 1998).

9.49 The working group was asked to prioritise work on the issue of abuse of trust because of the government's commitment to give Parliament a second opportunity during the 1998–99 session to consider the equalisation of the age of consent and so the group published an interim report in November 1998 dealing solely with this issue (*Working Group on Preventing Unsuitable People from Working with Children and Abuse of Trust. Interim Report: Abuse of Trust* (25 November 1998)). Although the large majority of organisations that responded to the consultation exercise carried out by the group in August and September 1998 believed that conduct amounting to abuse of a position of trust in relation to those over the age of consent was better regulated by professional codes than by a criminal offence, the group concluded that a new criminal offence would be justified in certain limited circumstances. The group also recommended a major initiative to strengthen codes of conduct generally to protect young people from those in a position of authority over them (see now *Caring for Young and Vulnerable People?: Guidance on Preventing Abuse of Trust* (Home Office, 1999)). The recommendations of the group in relation to a new criminal offence of abuse of trust were enacted in s 3 of the SO(A)A 2000 which was brought into force in January 2001.

9.50 The SO(A)A 2000 does not specify a lower age-limit for the younger person below which only pre-existing criminal offences apply and so there are a number of circumstances in which several alternative charges are possible. The offence under s 3 of SO(A)A 2000 is included in Sch 1 to the SOA 1997, so that anyone cautioned or convicted of the offence is subject to the notification requirements of the 1997 Act (see para **9.245** *et seq*). The government has suggested that the offence of abuse of trust will act more as a deterrent than result in a large number of actual prosecutions and has estimated that prosecutions will amount to around 10–15 per year (*Explanatory Notes on the Sexual Offences (Amendment) Bill*). The accuracy of this prediction remains to be seen. In 2001/02, 408 offences of abuse of trust were recorded by the police (Home Office Statistical Bulletin 7/02).

'Sexual intercourse' and 'sexual activity'

9.51 Sexual intercourse includes both vaginal and anal intercourse and thus covers homosexual activity. Sexual activity is defined objectively, as activity which a reasonable person would regard as sexual in the circumstances, but behaviour which a reasonable person would only regard as sexual activity if he was aware of the parties' intentions, motives or feelings is specifically excluded (SO(A)A 2000, s 3(5)).

'Position of trust' (s 4)

9.52 A person aged 18 or over is said to be in a position of trust in relation to a younger person if he is regularly involved in caring for, training, supervising or being in sole charge of persons under 18 at the relevant institution and:

- the younger person is detained in an institution under a court order and any other enactment;
- the younger person is resident in a home or other place in which accommodation (or accommodation and maintenance) are provided by a local authority or a voluntary organisation;
- the younger person is accommodated and cared for in any of the following institutions:
  - a hospital;
  - a residential care home, nursing home, mental nursing home or private hospital;
  - a community home, voluntary home, children's home or residential establishment;
  - a home provided under s 82(5) of CA 1989; or
- the younger person is receiving full time education at an educational institution (s 4(8)).

Defences

9.53 It is a defence for a person charged with the abuse of a position of trust if at the time of the intercourse or sexual activity he did not know or could not reasonably have been expected to know that the younger person was aged under 18 or that he was in a position of trust in relation to the younger person. It is also a defence if the older person was married to the younger person (s 3(2)). This latter defence was thought necessary in order to ensure compliance with the ECHR, although the working group was concerned that such a defence would provide a means to 'marry your way' out of an offence. Transitional provisions apply to ensure that the offence does not apply where the older person was in a sexual relationship with the younger person at the time when he was in a position of trust in relation to the younger person immediately before the enactment of the legislation (s 3(3)).

Indecent photographs

9.54 The problems of paedophile sex rings and the distribution of indecent photographs and images involving children have received an increasing amount of attention in recent years. The general criminal law relating to pornography is contained in the Obscene Publications Acts 1959 and 1964. However, specific offences have been created with a view to protecting children who may become victims of pornography. The initial impetus came from the case of *R v Sutton* [1977] 1 WLR 1086, which revealed a lacuna in the law. The defendant in this case photographed small boys (aged 11 to 13 years) in the nude for the purposes of selling the photographs to magazines. He did not touch the boys except to arrange their poses. He was charged with indecently assaulting the boys but was acquitted. The touching was held not to be an indecent assault as it was not indecent. (There was also held to be no common assault as the boys had consented.) Parliament stepped in to remedy the defect in the form of the Protection of Children Act 1978 which provides that it is an offence to take indecent photographs of persons under 16 years, or to distribute or show or advertise such photographs. In 1988, this offence was extended by s 160 of the CJA 1988 which created a summary offence of possession of an indecent photograph of a person under 16 years.

Child sexual abuse and the internet

Child pornography

9.55 In the 1990s, further reform to the criminal law relating to indecent photographs of children was found to be necessary because advances in computer technology had led to a considerable increase in both the creation and distribution of digital images resembling photographs and concerns were mounting over the use and transmission of such material via the internet, especially by organised paedophile rings and networks. The CJPOA 1994 amended the Protection of Children Act 1978 and the CJA 1988 to include references to making pseudo photographs (images made or manipulated by computer which are not photographs in the technical sense) and also extended liability to data stored on a computer disk or by other electronic means which is capable of conversion into a photograph. The use of the internet for the distribution of child pornography has now become a matter of national concern. In February 2001 seven paedophiles, who were members of the world's biggest child pornography ring known as 'Wonderland', were convicted of conspiring to distribute indecent images of children. The men traded over 120,000 pornographic images with one another and more than 100 Wonderland members throughout Britain, the United States, Europe and Australia. At the time the offences were committed the maximum penalty for offences under the Protection of Children Act 1978 was 3 years' imprisonment and the summary offence under the CJA 1988 was restricted to 6 months' imprisonment. Section 41 of the CJCSA 2000 has now increased the maximum sentence under the 1978 Act to 10 years' imprisonment with effect from January 2001. The offence under the 1988 Act is made triable either way and the maximum penalty is raised to 5 years' imprisonment.

Paedophiles and internet chatrooms

9.56 The amendments contained in the CJCSA 2000 have gone some way towards addressing concerns which have been raised about the coverage of the criminal law in respect of paedophile abuse on the internet. However, the internet can also be used by paedophiles as a point of contact with children with a view to developing a sexual relationship with them in the 'real world'. Internet 'chatrooms' enable individuals to hold typed conversations with people of all ages and backgrounds from across the world. Risk assessment studies have identified the most likely targets of 'online enticement' as being teenagers, mainly girls, between the ages of 13 and 17.

9.57 In March 2001, the Internet Crime Forum published a detailed report (*Chat Wise Street Wise*) which made a number of recommendations for Internet Service Providers (ISPs), the police, government and children's charities with a view to protecting children using internet chatrooms. The recommendations include the following:

- education programmes should be aimed at parents and other carers to advise them of the potential risks to children using chat services and appropriate steps they can take to protect them;
- ISPs should provide clear advice to their subscribers about child-friendly chat, and actively promote chat services specifically targeted at their age range;
- children's chatrooms should be supervised and a user-friendly reporting mechanism should be available for users to report incidents in chatrooms for investigation;
- ISPs, user groups and children's organisations should develop a kitemarking scheme which would offer a simple way for parents to identify chat services which are safe for children;

- the IT industry should continue to research better, cheaper and more user-friendly technical solutions to the potential dangers of chatrooms, including measures to ensure an appropriate level of traceability of online abusers;
- police officers should have specialised training and increased resources to ensure a prompt and effective response to reports of incidents in chatrooms;
- relevant UK legislation should be kept under review to ensure that it can meet changing circumstances, on- and offline, to protect children from abuse.

9.58 The Report recommended a number of safety messages that parents and carers should pass onto their children:

- do not give out personal details, photographs or any other information that could be used to identify you;
- do not take other people at face value – they may not be what they seem;
- never arrange to meet someone you have only ever met on the internet without first telling your parents, getting their permission and taking a responsible adult with you;
- always stay in the public areas of chat where there are other people around;
- do not open an attachment or downloaded file unless you know and trust the person who has sent it;
- if you find something you do not like, save it, print it, log off and tell an adult.

Reform of sexual offences – 'setting the boundaries'

9.59 In recent years the issues of child sexual abuse and the activities of paedophiles have become a matter of increasing public and professional concern. As a result, the final decade of the twentieth century saw numerous procedural changes taking place in the policy, law and practice relating to the protection of children from sex offenders. However, with the exception of a small number of piecemeal changes and amendments, the substantive criminal law has remained virtually unchanged for many years. The SOA 1956 was a consolidating measure passed under the fast-track provisions of the Consolidation of Enactments (Procedure) Act 1949 and, as a result, it was debated in Parliament for only 3 minutes. The SOA 1956 simply re-enacted in virtually identical language provisions of the OAPA 1861, the Criminal Law Amendment Act 1885 and the Vagrancy Act 1898, which was itself amended by the Criminal Law Amendment Act 1912, all of which had been enacted without detailed debates in either the House of Commons or the House of Lords (Martin Bowley QC 'A Sexual Scandal' *The Times*, 23 June 1998).

9.60 In 1998 the government announced its intention to reform the law relating to sexual offences and the terms of reference of a review of the law were announced in January 1999 (Home Office Press Release 028/99). An initial canvassing of views took place between January and March 1999, with contributions passed to a Steering Group of officials, lawyers and advisers for consideration of the whole framework of sexual offences. The Steering Group was advised by an external reference group, which included individuals and organisations concerned with women's issues, children's charities, gay and lesbian groups, and medical, ethical and religious interests. Following wide-ranging consultation, the Steering Group published a consultation document, *Setting the Boundaries: Reforming the Law on Sex Offences*, in July 2000.

The age of consent

9.61 In considering whether or not there is a need to retain the age of consent, the Review recognises that there are strong arguments on both sides, but concludes that the overriding argument for its retention is one of child protection, both from predatory adults, and from other children (at para 3.5.6). As a matter of public policy, it is recommended that the age of legal consent should remain at 16. This recommendation is unlikely to meet with fierce opposition. Although the age of consent varies between 12 and 18 in other countries, there is a trend towards standardisation between 15 and 17. In 1998 it was suggested in the media that ministers were to examine the possibility of reducing the age of consent to 14 (*Daily Mail*, 25 August 1998). This brought an immediate response from the Home Secretary, referring to the suggestion as 'absolute nonsense' and having no basis in fact whatsoever.

9.62 Having agreed that 16 should remain the age of legal consent, the Review then considered the issues of consenting sexual behaviour, or 'mutual agreement'. The Review was persuaded by the argument that, whilst teenagers have developing capacities to consent, and may actually agree to sex upon occasions, the situation of younger children was different as very young children will not know or understand sufficiently to give free and informed agreement to sex. In order to provide absolute protection for younger children, it is recommended that, in relation to consensual offences, the law should state that below the age of 13 a child cannot effectively consent to sexual activity.

The proposed offences

9.63 The consultation document contains proposals for reform of the entire law relating to sexual offences. Children will, of course, continue to be potential victims of the non-consensual sexual offences which are not age specific. The most significant proposals in this respect include the redefinition of rape to include penetration of the mouth, anus or female genitalia by a penis and the creation of a new offence of sexual assault by penetration to deal with all other forms of sexual penetration of the anus and genitalia. It is proposed that both offences, which could be committed with intent or recklessly, should be seen as equally serious and should carry a maximum penalty of life imprisonment. A new offence of sexual assault would replace other non-penetrative sexual touching currently covered by the offence of indecent assault, with sexual touching being defined objectively as behaviour that a reasonable bystander would consider to be sexual.

9.64   The issue of consent in relation to sexual offences has long been problematic for both legal practitioners and juries. The Review does not seek to change the meaning of consent, but rather to clarify the law so that it is clearly understood. It is proposed that consent should be defined in law as 'free agreement' and that the law should set out a non-exhaustive list of circumstances where consent was not present.

9.65   In relation to the protection of children, the general policy underlying the proposals is to have clear, gender neutral offences to enable the law to deal appropriately with all those who abuse children, whether the abusers are male or female and the victims are boys or girls. It is therefore recommended that the age of legal consent should be retained at 16 years and it is proposed that the offences of sexual intercourse with girls under the age of 16 and 13, buggery with a child under the age of consent, and indecency with a child under 16 be replaced by two new offences – adult sexual abuse of a child and sexual activity between minors.

Adult sexual abuse of a child (Recommendation 19)

9.66   The offence would be committed by any person of 18 or over who was involved in sexual penetration with a child under 16; or who undertook any sexual act towards or with a child under the age of 16; or who incited, induced or compelled a child to carry out a sexual act, whether on the accused, another person or the child himself; or who made a child witness a sexual act (whether live or recorded). The offence is essentially about the adult's responsibility towards the child and so there would be no criminal liability on the child, however much the child may appear to have consented or encouraged the offence.

9.67   The Review recommends that a mistaken belief that the child was aged 16 or over would only be a defence where the child was in fact 13 or over. The mistaken belief must be an honest and reasonable belief and the defendant must have taken all reasonable steps to ascertain the age of the child. However, the use of the defence of mistaken belief in age should be limited to raising the defence in court on one occasion only.

Sexual activity between minors (Recommendation 27)

9.68 The offence would apply to those under the age of 18 who indulged in sexual activity with children under the age of 16. It is recommended that, where the younger child is aged between 13 and 16, the same statutory defence of mistake of age as applies to the offence of adult sexual abuse of a child would apply. Where one of the partners is over the age of consent, or one of the partners is below the age of 13, then the older partner would be criminally liable. In all other cases, the Review points out that criminal justice action is not the best or most effective way to tackle the problem of mutually agreed under-age sex between peers and recommends that further consideration should be given to appropriate non-criminal interventions for young people under 16 engaging in under-age sex who are not now, and should not in future, normally be subject to prosecution.

Persistent sexual abuse (Recommendation 25)

9.69 In addition to these two offences, it is proposed that a new offence of persistent sexual abuse of a child be introduced, in order to ensure that effective sentencing measures are available to deal with offenders who abuse a child over a long period of time. Views are sought as to whether there should also be a similar offence relating to the abuse or sexual exploitation of a number of different children.

Familial sexual abuse (Recommendation 35)

9.70 The proposed offences of adult sexual abuse of a child and sexual activity between minors would, of course, impose criminal liability for all forms of intra-familial sexual abuse involving a child under the age of 16. Despite this, the Review concluded that it was important that the law should make special provision for such abuse within the family in order to increase protection and provide appropriate remedies. It is therefore proposed that there should be an offence of familial sexual abuse, which would replace the existing offences of incest by a man and incest by a woman and which would reflect the looser structure of modern families. For the purposes of the new offence, the prohibition on sexual relations with a child should apply until the child is 18. The offence would apply to sexual penetration with or of a child by all of those relations included in the existing offence of incest with the addition of uncles and aunts who are related by blood, adoptive parents and adoptive siblings, step-parents and foster parents and any other person who is living in the household and in a position of trust or authority over the child. It is also proposed that sexual penetration by adult close family members (defined as certain blood and adoptive relationships) should continue to be forbidden by law, and views are sought as to whether the prohibition should extend to adult sexual relationships between step-parents and step-children.

9.70A The concept of 'grooming' involves a potential offender making contact with potential victims (who will usually be children), either directly or through internet chat rooms, with a view to building a relationship of trust which can subsequently be exploited by engaging in sexual activity with the victim. Under the existing law, whereas the actual exploitation of the position of trust will amount to a criminal offence, behaviour prior to that will not generally be caught by the criminal law. In November 2002, the government announced its intention to introduce a new offence of sexual grooming (*Protecting the Public* (2002) Cm 5668). The offence will be designed to catch those aged 18 or over who undertake a course of conduct with a child under 16 leading to a meeting where the adult intends to engage in sexual activity with the child. To complement the new offence of grooming, a new civil order is imposed, which will contain such prohibitions as are necessary to protect a child or children in general. For example, the order could prohibit explicit communication with children via email, or hanging around schools or playgrounds. It is anticipated that a maximum penalty of 5 years' imprisonment will be available for both the offence of grooming and breach of the civil order.

THE PRE-TRIAL PROCESS

Gathering the evidence

9.71 Child abuse typically takes place in private and independent witnesses are rare. In cases of abuse on babies and very young children, in the absence of a confession from the abuser, any investigation must rely primarily on medical evidence of the injuries sustained and circumstantial evidence as to who was caring for the victim at the time the injuries were inflicted. Whilst this may be sufficient to satisfy the court in child protection proceedings, where the burden of proof is the civil standard of the balance of probabilities, at a criminal trial, the jury must be satisfied of the defendant's guilt beyond all reasonable doubt, making a conviction very difficult to obtain. The difficulties are exacerbated in cases of sexual abuse, where there may be little or no medical evidence. When a child is old enough to communicate, and relate details of abuse to third parties, the child's evidence will often be central to a successful prosecution.

Competence of child witnesses

9.72 When investigating a case of suspected child abuse with a view to prosecuting the abuser, one the first factors which must be considered is whether the child victim will be competent to give evidence at any subsequent trial. Traditionally, children were not thought to be competent, trustworthy witnesses, therefore, it was argued, why waste the court's valuable time listening to a child's evidence? (see Cobley (1991)). However, in recent years, traditionally held beliefs about the competence of children have been challenged, causing society's attitude towards children as witnesses to change dramatically. There is no doubt that one of the major factors instrumental in bringing about such a change has been the increase in societal awareness of the existence of child abuse, both physical and sexual. In many cases of child abuse, the victim will be the only witness. If the child is not to be believed or not permitted to give evidence in court, the abuser cannot be punished. The younger the child, the more acute the problem. This unsatisfactory state of affairs, combined with psychological research on the credibility of children, has led in recent years to a review of the competence of child witnesses.

9.73 Section 38(1) of the CYPA 1933 allowed a child of tender years to give unsworn evidence provided that, in the opinion of the court, the child was possessed of sufficient intelligence to justify the reception of the evidence and understand the duty of speaking the truth. It was the responsibility of the trial judge to examine a potential witness in court to ascertain whether they had the necessary understanding of the oath or of the concepts of truth and duty, and the burden of proving this rested with the party who had chosen to call the witness. Although in theory the CYPA 1933 allowed more children to be heard in court, it proved to be a bar in many cases because, while young children may be perfectly reliable witnesses, they were not always able to explain abstract concepts like 'duty' and 'truth'. Furthermore, the judiciary were themselves reluctant to admit the evidence of young children. In 1958 the Lord Chief Justice commented that it was 'ridiculous' to suppose that any value could be attached to the evidence of a 5-year-old child (R v *Wallwork* (1958) 42 Cr App R 153).

9.74 In 1989, the *Report of the Advisory Group on Video Evidence* (Home Office, 1989) criticised this approach, which was said to lead to the abandonment of prosecutions for a large number of serious violent and sexual offences against children. As the Advisory Group commented, it seemed logical to suppose that a child who was not able to explain what the oath signified, or what concepts like truth and duty meant, was rather less likely to be sophisticated enough to invent and consistently and successfully sustain falsehoods than other witnesses (para 5.11). The Advisory Group recommended that the competence requirement for child witnesses should be dispensed with and not be replaced. Instead, it was proposed that if, once any witness had begun to testify, it became apparent that they could not communicate in a way which made sense, the judge should rely on his existing power to rule the witness incompetent (para 5.13).

9.75 As a result of the growing pressure for change, the Criminal Justice Act 1991 (CJA 1991) provided that all children under the age of 14 years must give unsworn evidence, those over 14 being required to give sworn evidence (CJA 1988, s 33A). The CJA 1991 was clearly intended to implement the proposals of the Advisory Group and create a presumption that all children were competent witnesses. However, the wording of the Act was open to the interpretation that, contrary to Parliament's intention, it in fact created a new competence requirement for children under 14 years. To clarify the situation, the CJPOA 1994 made the presumption of competence explicit by providing that the evidence of a child under the age of 14 years shall be received unless it appears to the court that the child is incapable of giving intelligible testimony (CJA 1988, s 33A(2A)). These provisions have been replaced by the YJCEA 1999. Section 53 of the YJCEA 1999 provides that at every stage in criminal proceedings all persons are (whatever their age) competent to give evidence. This is subject to two qualifications:

(1) a person is not competent to give evidence in criminal proceedings if it appears to the court that he is not able to:

  (a) understand questions put to him as a witness, and
  (b) give answers to them which can be understood;

(2) a person charged in criminal proceedings is not competent to give evidence in the proceedings for the prosecution (whether he is the only person, or is one of two or more persons, charged in the proceedings).

9.76 The YJCEA 1999 also permits witnesses over 14 years of age to give unsworn evidence if they are not capable of taking the oath. These provisions were brought into force on 24 July 2002.

Corroboration and child witnesses

9.77 Corroboration is evidence which tends to support or confirm other evidence. The belief that children do not make reliable witnesses has been traditionally reinforced by a mandatory requirement of corroboration. Prior to 1988, a defendant could not be convicted on the uncorroborated evidence of a young child who gave unsworn evidence (CYPA 1933, s 38). If a child gave sworn evidence, a conviction without corroboration was possible, but only after the judge had warned the jury that it would be 'dangerous' to convict on the child's evidence without corroboration (R v Buck [1981] Crim LR 108). Once the warning had been given, the jury were free to convict without corroboration. In 1987 Home Office research concluded that a general legal requirement that children's evidence be corroborated did not appear to be necessary (*Children's Evidence: The Need for Corroboration* (Home Office, 1987)). As a result, s 34 of the CJA 1988 removed the corroboration requirement for both the sworn and the unsworn evidence of children. Thus there is no longer any legal requirement to corroborate the evidence of a child witness.

Corroboration and sexual abuse

9.78 In cases of child sexual abuse, there existed a further hurdle in relation to corroboration. Traditionally, the judge had to warn the jury of the danger of convicting on the uncorroborated evidence of the victim of a sexual offence. The rationale for requiring a corroboration warning was that sexual offences were said to be capable of being feigned more plausibly than other crimes and that the jury could not be expected to know about the psychological motives for so doing without special instruction. For many years the general consensus of opinion was that the requirement should be retained, although research with mock juries in the early 1970s suggested that the jury was more likely to convict if a corroboration warning was given, arguably because the warning served to emphasise the evidence required to be corroborated by repeating it and reminding the jury of it ([1973] Crim LR 208). In recent times attitudes towards victims of sexual offences have changed dramatically. Although the warning was required regardless of whether the victim or defendant was male or female and whether or not consent was an ingredient of the offence, in practice defendants are more likely to be male and victims female and thus the requirement was perceived to be an insult to women as it was based on a fundamental mistrust of the credibility of their evidence. This, combined with the growing awareness of the impact of the requirement on the prosecution of child sex abusers, led to calls for its abolition. By virtue of s 32 of the CJPOA 1994, any requirement to give a warning about convicting on the uncorroborated evidence of the victim of a sexual offence has been abrogated.

9.79 Although there are no longer any legal requirements relating to the corroboration in cases of child abuse, corroboration inevitably strengthens the prosecution case and, in practice, those responsible for gathering the evidence would be well advised to look for corroborating evidence of a child's evidence wherever possible.

Interviewing child witnesses: general issues

9.80 As previously noted, the evidence of the child victim of abuse will often be central to a successful prosecution. However, the way in which this evidence is gathered is crucial if it is to be admitted in criminal proceedings.

The Memorandum of Good Practice

9.81 Following the crisis in Cleveland in 1987, concerns were expressed that evidence gathered from children could be tainted by poor interviewing by non-lawyers, unfamiliar with the rules of evidence. When the CJA 1991 permitted a video-recording of an interview with a child witness to be admitted in place of the child's evidence-in-chief at a criminal trial (see para **9.162**), the DOH and Home Office published a Memorandum of Good Practice on interviewing child witnesses (*Memorandum of Good Practice on Video Recorded Interviews with Child Witnesses for Criminal Proceedings* (DOH, 1992). The

Memorandum contained a recommended protocol for interviewing based on a phased approach which was designed to ensure that the child is encouraged to recall events freely, followed by closed questions or prompts where necessary.

Revising the Memorandum of Good Practice

9.82 In 1999 a research review of interviewing child witnesses under the *Memorandum* was undertaken on behalf of the Home Office (*Interviewing Child Witnesses under the Memorandum of Good Practice: A Research Review* (Police Research Series Paper 115, Home Office, 1999). The report summarised the findings of recent research on children as witnesses and drew out the implications for the conduct of interviews under the *Memorandum*. The report urged that any revision of the *Memorandum* should be informed by recent research, and located within a strategic, comprehensive and nationally agreed framework for reform. More specifically, it suggested that any revision of the *Memorandum* should:

–   stress the importance of establishing and addressing children's needs and concerns prior to interview and highlighting the role of appropriate rapport and closure in that process;
–   outline the need for flexibility in styles of interviewing, particularly for children with communication or learning impairments;
–   include a specific section(s) devoted to the interviewing of very young and particularly vulnerable witnesses;
–   stress the evidential value of responses to open-ended questions, the importance of following closed questions with further open questions and the importance of giving the initiative for responding to the child;
–   provide examples of productive and counter-productive questioning techniques;
–   acknowledge that there will be exceptions to the 'one-hour rule' on interviewing; and,
–   provide further guidance on tests of truth and lies, the duration, pace and number of interviews, the use of drawings, props, toys and anatomically-detailed dolls and specialised questioning techniques.

Achieving the best evidence in criminal proceedings

9.83 Further impetus to revise the *Memorandum* was provided by Part II of the YJCEA 1999 which extends the special measures introduced for child witnesses to other vulnerable or intimidated witnesses (see para **9.166** *et seq*). The decision was therefore taken to revise and extend the *Memorandum* to incorporate guidance on interviewing vulnerable and intimidated adults as well as children and to include guidance on the pre-trial treatment of witnesses and their appearance in court, so as to reflect the commitment of all parties within the criminal justice system to ensuring that all witnesses may give their best evidence. Drawing on the research findings and practical experience, a team of psychologists and lawyers with expert knowledge of the field produced an initial draft of guidance to revise and update the *Memorandum*. Further revisions were made to the guidance after piloting with focus groups and in the light of feedback from a Home Office consultative conference. In 2001, revised guidance was published. The following summarises the most recent guidance on interviewing child witnesses for criminal proceedings, contained in *Achieving the Best Evidence in Criminal Proceedings* (DOH, 2001), Vol 1, Part 2, at paras 2.0–2.154.

The different purposes of the interview *(*Achieving the Best Evidence, *at paras 2.1–2.32)*

9.84 Any video-recorded interview serves two different purposes – evidence gathering for use in criminal proceedings and the examination-in-chief of the child witness. However, although the guidance concentrates on the evidential implications for criminal proceedings, any information gained during the interview can also be used to inform enquiries under s 47 of the CA 1989 and any subsequent actions to safeguard and promote the child's welfare. The interview may additionally serve a useful purpose in other proceedings, such as civil childcare proceedings or disciplinary proceedings against adult carers, for example in residential institutions, which should not be overlooked. However, in practice, research has shown that the tension between different objectives can result in testimony which is incomplete, inadmissible or difficult for the jury to understand and evaluate (*An Assessment of the Admissibility and Sufficiency of Evidence in Child Abuse Prosecutions* (Home Office, 1999)).

Planning the interview *(*Achieving the Best Evidence, *at paras 2.0–2.72)*

9.85 If the child is giving evidence in a sexual offence case or a case involving an offence of violence, abduction or neglect, a video-recorded interview will normally take place, unless the child objects, and/or there are insurmountable difficulties which prevent the recording taking place (this may include that the child has been involved in abuse involving video-recording or photography). Interviewers must take steps to prepare the child before the interview itself. At a minimum, this means explaining to the child what an interview is, who will be present and when/where it will happen, in a manner appropriate to the child's age and understanding. The child should also be told of the purpose of the interview. Written consent to be video-recorded is not necessary from the child, but it is unlikely to be practicable or desirable to video-record an interview with a reluctant or hostile child. Wherever possible, older children should be consulted about matters appropriate to their age and understanding, and contribute to the planning and preparation of the interview, for example when and where the interview takes place, who is present and who conducts the interview. The interviewing team (which at a minimum should include representatives of both police and local authority social services) should plan in advance the expected duration of the interview. It will help both the interviewer and the child to have a clear idea how long the interview is likely to last, although the pace and duration of the interview will depend upon the individual child, his or her attention span and any specific needs. The *Memorandum* initially suggested that the interview should usually last less than an hour. The most recent guidance states that it is not possible or desirable to posit an ideal duration for an interview, although it notes that most interviews in practice last around one hour (*Achieving the Best Evidence*, para 2.98).

Who should lead the interview? (**Achieving the Best Evidence,** at paras 2.72–2.76)

9.86   The investigating team should consider who is best qualified to conduct the interview, and whether there should be a second interviewer/supporter present to support the interviewer (para 2.72). A special blend of skills is required to interview children and the lead interviewer should be a person who has, or is likely to be able to establish, rapport with the child, who understands how to communicate effectively with children, including in sometimes disturbed periods, and who has a proper grasp of the rules of evidence and knowledge of the points needed to prove particular offences. He or she must also be prepared to testify about the interview in court if required to do so. This is described in the guidance as a 'formidable job specification' and some compromise will probably be necessary (para 2.73). A rigid definition of the roles of police and social services professionals is not likely to be possible or desirable and a high degree of flexibility and responsiveness within the joint investigating team is required in the interests of an effective interview. The presence of a second interviewer is desirable as he or she can help to ensure that the interview is conducted in a professional manner and that the child's needs are kept paramount. The second interviewer should be alert to identifying gaps in the child's account, interviewer errors and apparent confusions in the communication between the lead interviewer and the child, and can communicate with the lead interviewer as necessary (para 2.76). A support person may also be present at the interview, although the supporter must be clearly instructed not to participate in any way in the interview itself (para 2.75). Parents or carers should not be automatically excluded from this role, although anyone involved as a witness in the case (including a parent to whom the child first disclosed abuse) cannot take on the role of supporter.

The interview

Phase 1: establishing rapport (**Achieving the Best Evidence,** at paras 2.100–2.105)

9.87   The main aim of the first phase of the interview is to build up a rapport between the interviewer and the child in which the child is helped to relax and feel as comfortable as possible in the interview situation. The rapport stage should normally encompass the following:

– discussing neutral topics and, where appropriate, playing with toys;
– establishing the purpose of the interview. The reason for the interview needs to be explained in a way which makes the focus of the interview clear but does not specify the nature of the offence as to do so would be regarded as unnecessarily leading;
– reassuring the child they have done nothing wrong;
– drawing attention to the video equipment;
– explaining the ground rules; it should be made clear to the child that it is acceptable to say 'I don't know' or 'I don't understand' in response to any question (para 2.101);
– exploring the child's understanding of truth and lies (para 2.105); although there is no legal requirement to administer the oath, since the video may be used as evidence in court, it is helpful to the court to know that the child was made aware of the importance of telling the truth; it is inadvisable to ask children to provide general definitions of what is a truth and a lie, rather they should be asked to judge from examples;
– supplementing the interviewer's knowledge of the child's social, emotional and cognitive development; the interviewer will learn more about the child's communication skills and degree of understanding of vocabulary and so can adjust their language use and complexity of their questions in the light of the child's responses (para 2.105).

Phase 2: free narrative account (Achieving the Best Evidence, at paras 2.106–2.111)

9.88 The aim of this phase of the interview is to secure a full and comprehensive account from the child of the alleged incident, in the child's own words. The child should be asked to provide in his or her own words an account of the relevant event(s). This is the core of the interview and the most reliable source of accurate information. The interviewer's role is that of facilitator, not an interrogator, and every effort should be made to obtain information which is spontaneous and free from the interviewer's influence. The interviewer can offer prompts and encouragement if the child's account falters, but this must be neutral ('and then what happened?') and must not imply positive evaluation ('right', 'good'). Reassurance can be offered if the child is reluctant to talk freely ('I know this must be difficult for you. Is there anything I can do to make it easier?'), but the use of terms of endearment ('dear', 'sweetheart'), verbal reinforcement (telling the child he or she is 'doing really well') and physical contact between the interviewer and the child (hugging, holding a hand) are inappropriate in the context of a formal interview.

9.89 If nothing of significance emerges during the free narrative phase, or if a satisfactory, verifiable explanation has emerged for the original cause of concern, it may be necessary and proper to proceed directly to the closure phase of the interview.

Phase 3: questioning (Achieving the Best Evidence, at paras 2.112–2.130)

9.90 In nearly all cases it will be necessary to expand on the child's initial account through questions. These should be kept as short and simple in construction as possible and should not involve vocabulary with which the child is not familiar. The four most important types of questions which may be used are as follows:

– *Open-ended questions*: questions which are worded in such a way as to enable the child to provide more information about any event in a way that is not leading, suggestive or putting the witness under pressure. They can provide the child with the opportunity to expand on relevant issues raised in their free narrative account (eg 'You told me he climbed into bed with you, can you tell me a little bit more about what happened then?'). Research and practice shows that the most reliable and detailed answers from children of all ages are secured from open-ended questions and the questioning phase should always begin with this type of question (paras 2.118–2.120).

– *Specific questions:* questions which serve to ask in a non-suggestive way for extension or clarification of information previously supplied by a witness (paras 2.121–2.125). Examples of specific questions are the so-called 'wh …' questions – questions which begin who, what, where or why (although care should be taken with 'why?' questions as they may be interpreted by children as implying guilt or blame to them). For example, a child in a sexual abuse investigation may have responded to an open-ended prompt by mentioning that a named man had climbed into bed with her. A specific but non-leading follow up question might be, 'What clothes was he wearing at the time?' If this yielded no clear answer, a further, more-explicit question might be, 'Was he wearing any clothes?'

– *Closed questions:* questions which pose fixed alternatives and the child is invited to choose between them. They can be useful if a specific question proves unproductive. For example, 'Were you in your bedroom or the living room when this happened or can't you remember?' (para 2.126).

– *Leading questions:* questions which imply the answer or assume facts which are likely to be in dispute. For example, 'Daddy hurt you, didn't he?' or, 'When did you first tell anyone what Daddy did?', put to a child who has not alleged that Daddy did anything. Psychological research indicates that interviewee's responses to leading questions tend to be determined more by the manner of questioning than by valid remembering. Leading questions will not normally be allowed if a witness is giving evidence in open court. If used in an interview, it is likely that portions may be edited out or, in the worst case, the whole recording ruled inadmissible. Good interviewing practice should discourage leading questions with all but youngest and most reticent witnesses (paras 2.127–2.130).

*Phase 4: closing (*Achieving the Best Evidence, *at paras 2.131–2.135)*

9.91 Every interview should have a closure stage which should normally involve the following features:

— check with the second interviewer, if present, as to whether there are any additional questions which need to be raised or ambiguities or apparent inconsistencies which could be usefully resolved;
— summarise what the child has said; where the child has provided significant evidence, the lead interviewer should check with the witness that the interviewer has correctly understood the important parts of the witness' account;
— answer any questions from the child; children frequently ask what will happen next; answers and explanations should be appropriate to the age of the child and promises which cannot be kept should not be made;
— thank the child for their time and effort;
— provide advice on seeking help and a contact number should the child wish to discuss any matters of concern with the interviewer;
— return to rapport or neutral topics; the aim of closure should be that, as far as possible, the child should leave the interview in a positive frame of mind and it may be useful to revert to neutral topics discussed in the rapport stage to assist this;
— report the end-time of the interview.

Provision of therapy for child witnesses prior to criminal trial

9.92 Child victims may be severely traumatised by abuse and in many cases may benefit from therapy to assist their recovery. However, when it is anticipated that a child will be required to give evidence at a subsequent criminal trial, concerns have been expressed that, if the child receives therapy before the trial, the child's evidence may be tainted and the prosecution lost. Any discussion with witnesses prior to a criminal trial is generally discouraged as it may be argued by the opposing side at the trial that the discussion has resulted in fabrication, for example if the witness becomes aware of gaps or inconsistencies in his or her evidence, or becomes more convinced (or convincing) in his or evidence, but no less mistaken. Such claims may be raised in relation to various types of discussions, including therapy. However, to delay therapy until after the trial may not be in the child's best interests (see *Achieving the Best Evidence*, at paras 2.90–2.91). The decision as to whether or not a child witness should receive therapy prior to a criminal trial therefore requires a balancing of interests. Following widespread consultation within the criminal justice system, and with those professionals who provide therapeutic help to abused children, guidance on this issue has now been issued (*Provision of Therapy for Child Witnesses Prior to Criminal Trial: Practice Guidance* (DOH, 2001)). The guidance is primarily aimed at therapists and lawyers involved in making decisions in cases where the provision of therapy for child witnesses prior to a criminal trial is a consideration, but it is hoped that it will be helpful to everyone who comes into contact with child victims of abuse, particularly teachers, health visitors, social workers and police who are often the first to hear an allegation.

Who decides?

9.93 The guidance makes it clear that the decision as to whether a child should receive therapy before a criminal trial is not one to be taken by the police or the CPS. Such decisions can only be taken by all of the professionals from the agencies responsible for the welfare of the child, in consultation with the carers of the child and the child himself or herself, if the child is of sufficient age and understanding. In making the decision, the best interests of the child are the paramount consideration. If there is a demonstrable need for the provision of therapy and it is possible that therapy will prejudice the criminal proceedings, consideration may need to be given to abandoning those proceedings in the interests of the child's well-being. Alternatively, there may be some children for whom it will be preferable to delay therapy until after the criminal trial, to avoid the benefits of the therapy being undone. While some forms of therapy may undermine the evidence given by the witness, this will not automatically be the case. The CPS will offer advice, as requested in individual cases, on the likely impact on the evidence of the child receiving therapy. Clear lines of communication are required to ensure that everyone involved in the process is fully and reliably informed.

Confidentiality and disclosure

9.94 The administration of justice and the need to ensure a fair trial demand that any information and evidence which could have an impact on the decision to prosecute, the conduct of the case, or the outcome of proceedings is made available to the police and prosecution. At some stage during the trial process the prosecution must provide the defence with such information and evidence as may undermine the prosecution case or assist the defence case (see para **9.130**) and it is important that careful records of therapy are maintained. Where a therapist receives a request for information or documents, legal advice should be sought before complying with the request. In addition to informal requests for information, if there are real grounds to believe that material which could affect the outcome of the prosecution is being withheld, an application may be made to the court for a witness summons to obtain the material. If, as will usually be the case, a therapist, having taken appropriate legal advice, believes that the material should not be disclosed, he or she may oppose the witness summons application. In that case the court may hold a hearing at which the therapist's employer may be legally represented. The court, having heard representations from the advocate for the therapist's employer, will decide whether or not to issue a summons requiring the disclosure of the material. Because of the recognition that maintaining a child's trust is central to the provision of therapy, it will usually only be appropriate to breach confidentiality in compliance with these procedures. Because confidentiality cannot be guaranteed in advance, it is important that an understanding is reached with the child and carers at the outset of therapy of the circumstances under which material obtained under treatment may be required to be disclosed.

Guidelines on the use of therapy

9.95 The following guidelines should be followed.

(1) The term 'therapy' covers a range of treatment approaches, including counselling, but in this context it does not include any physical treatments. There should be a clear distinction between preparing a child for the experience of giving evidence in court (see para **9.183** *et seq*) and the provision of therapy or counselling to address trauma. Some types of therapeutic work are more likely to be seen as prejudicial and thereby undermine the perception of a child's credibility and reliability or as influencing a child's memory of events or the account they give. Interpretative psychotherapy may present evidential problems even if carefully conducted. Hypnotherapy, psychodrama, regression techniques and unstructured groups would very definitely present problems as far as evidential reliability is concerned. Hence, there is a spectrum of evidential risk to the criminal trial which should be considered.

(2) Professionals offering therapy may be working within the NHS, social services, the voluntary sector or privately. Providers and purchasers of therapy must ensure that any therapist or counsellor has appropriate training according to the level of work to be undertaken, as well as a thorough understanding of the effects of abuse. Membership of an appropriate professional body or other recognised competence would be expected in these circumstances. They must also have a good understanding of how the rules of evidence for witnesses in criminal proceedings may require modification of techniques.

(3) Assessment of the need for therapy of any child during the pre-trial period should only be undertaken following consultation with the relevant other professionals involved, when the needs and best interests of the particular child should be discussed. The discussion should include the logistics of setting up a specialist assessment of the child. It is vital

that a trained professional person with a recognised competence in such assessments should see the child and any relevant family members. One or more careful assessment interviews should be conducted in order to determine whether and in what way the child is emotionally disturbed and also whether further treatment is needed. In particular, the assessment should address the child's development in both emotional and cognitive terms, any specific needs the child may have and the issue of possible suggestibility of the child. The assessor should use a limited range of selected assessment tools, such as drawing materials and appropriate toys, to supplement questioning within a session. If deemed clinically appropriate, children should also have a separate psychological and/or developmental assessment to obtain baseline data on their cognitive and emotional functioning. Such a psychological assessment will indicate whether the child has specific needs which may require assistance in court, for example an intermediary or interpreter (see para **9.179**), as well as contributing to an understanding of the child's emotional needs. Not all children who are assessed will need therapy. Final recommendations from the assessment will indicate the type of therapy or intervention, if any, required for the particular child.

(4) In newly arising allegations, therapy should not usually take place before a witness has provided a statement or, if appropriate, before a video-recorded interview has taken place. If therapeutic work is already in progress when new allegations come to light, disruption of therapy should be avoided even if new investigations must be conducted. If the prosecutor advises that the proposed therapy may prejudice the criminal case, those responsible for the child's welfare should take this into account when deciding whether to agree to the therapy. It may still be in the best interests of the child to proceed with the therapy. Therapists or counsellors should avoid using leading questions or discussing the evidence which the individual or any other witness will give, including exploring in detail the substance of specific allegations made. As a general principle, group therapy should not be offered to the child witness prior to the trial.

(5) Prosecutors must be informed that the witness has received therapy. Prosecutors must then obtain an assurance that the witness did not, in the therapy session(s), say anything inconsistent with the statements made by the witness to the police.

Police powers and the criminal law as a method of child protection

'Arrestable offences'

9.96 Police powers of arrest are contained within the Police and Criminal Evidence Act 1984 (PACE). The most important factor in determining an officer's power of arrest is the offence under consideration. Section 24 of PACE provides a power of summary arrest in respect of arrestable offences defined in that section. (Summary in this context means done with despatch and without formalities.) Arrestable offences include offences for which a person, 21 years of age or over, may be sentenced to imprisonment for a term of 5 years and also offences specifically listed. The listed offences include offences under s 1 of the Protection of Children Act 1978. Thus the more serious offences will be arrestable offences within the meaning of PACE. Where a constable has reasonable grounds for suspecting that an arrestable offence has been committed, he may arrest without warrant anyone who he has reasonable grounds for suspecting to be guilty of the offence. Thus two tests of reasonable suspicion must be employed – there must be reasonable grounds to suspect an arrestable offence has been committed and reasonable grounds to suspect the person arrested is guilty of the offence. The fact that an arrestable offence has not actually been committed, or that the person arrested is not actually guilty of the offence, does not render the arrest unlawful.

General arrest conditions

9.97 However, even if an offence is not classified as an 'arrestable offence', a power of arrest may arise under s 25 of PACE if it appears to a police officer that service of a summons is impracticable or inappropriate because any of the 'general arrest conditions' are satisfied. These conditions include the condition that the officer has reasonable grounds for believing that arrest is necessary to protect a child or other vulnerable person from the relevant person.

'Reasonable grounds to suspect'

9.98 A definition of what constitutes reasonable grounds to suspect has proved elusive. Although PACE contains no definition, the Code of Practice issued under the Act does attempt to give some guidelines as to what constitutes reasonable grounds for suspicion (Code A, Annex B). These relate specifically to the powers of stop and search, but the annex makes it clear that the level of suspicion required is the same as the level that would justify arrest. Paragraph 1 states:

> 'Reasonable suspicion, in contrast to mere suspicion, must be founded on fact. There must be some concrete basis for the officer's suspicion, related to the individual concerned, which can be considered and evaluated by a third person. Mere suspicion, in contrast, is a hunch or instinct which cannot be explained or justified to an objective observer.'

9.99 The Divisional Court has suggested that the words 'has reasonable cause to suspect' import the requirement that the constable in fact suspects (*Siddiqui v Swann* [1979] Crim LR 318). But the officer's personal suspicion is not sufficient. The test as to whether or not reasonable grounds exist is an objective one, and if the exercise of the power is challenged on the basis that there were no reasonable grounds to suspect, the onus of establishing them lies on the officer. However, in practice there has been a notable absence of reported cases where such challenges have been made. It would seem that as long as the police officer can show some grounds for suspicion, then that will suffice.

Arrest as a means of child protection

9.100 The criterion of 'reasonable grounds to suspect' is the legal threshold for the exercise of coercive police powers under PACE. In contrast, the legal threshold for the exercise of emergency child protection measures under the CA 1989 is the criteria of 'reasonable cause to believe'. Generally, 'suspicion' requires a lower level of proof than 'belief'. It has been said, 'If ... there are 10 steps from mere suspicion to a state of certainty ... then reasonable suspicion may be as low as step two or three, whilst reasonable belief may be as high as step 9 or 10' (Bevan and Lidstone (1985), at p 5). Therefore, whenever it is believed that a child has been abused and there are grounds for a court to make an emergency protection order or for the police to take the child into police protection, then, provided there is reasonable suspicion as to the identity of the abuser, a power of arrest will usually arise. This may obviate the need to remove the child from home if there is a non-abusing carer willing and able to look after the child.

Child protection following arrest

9.101 As a general rule, an arrested person may only be detained without charge for up to 24 hours (PACE, s 41). The period following arrest will often be a vital one as far as the gathering of evidence from the abuser is concerned. If at any time during the investigation the police have sufficient evidence for a prosecution to succeed, the arrested person should be asked no further questions. In the majority of cases the arrested person will then be charged with an appropriate criminal offence. The main advantage of proceeding by way of charge is that the police can continue to have a measure of control over the movements of the abuser, and thereby continue protecting the child victim, either by detaining the abuser in custody for a further period after charge before making an application for a remand in custody to the court, or by imposing conditions of bail.

Releasing the abuser on police bail

9.102 Once the abuser has been charged, in most cases there is a presumption in favour of bail and the abuser must be released, either on bail or without bail (PACE, s 38). The presumption in favour of bail does not apply to those charged with murder, attempted murder, manslaughter, rape or attempted rape, when the onus falls on the person charged to show that there are exceptional reasons why he should not be kept in custody (Crime and Disorder Act 1998, s 56).

Conditions of bail

9.103 Although the courts have long had the power to impose conditions on a grant of bail, before 1994, if there were no grounds to justify the continued detention of a defendant after charge, although the police could bail the defendant, thereby imposing the standard duty to surrender to custody, and could require the defendant to provide a surety or sureties, there was no power to attach any further conditions to the bail. However, following the implementation of CJPOA 1994 (which amends s 3 of the Bail Act 1976) the police may now require a defendant to comply with such requirements as appear to be necessary for the purpose of preventing the defendant from:

- failing to surrender to custody;
- committing an offence whilst on bail; or
- interfering with witnesses or otherwise obstructing the course of justice, whether in relation to himself or any other person.

Taking the defendant before the court

9.104 If there is evidence to rebut the presumption in favour of bail, the police may detain the defendant after charge. This may be done if, inter alia, there are reasonable grounds for believing that detention is necessary to prevent the commission of a further offence or to prevent the defendant causing physical injury to any other person (PACE, s 38, as amended). Thus, if there are reasonable grounds to believe (note: believe not suspect) that the abuse would continue if the abuser were to be released, he may be detained and brought before the local magistrates' court as soon as is practicable, and in any case not later than the first sitting after he is charged with the offence (PACE, s 46(2)).

Remands in custody

9.105 When a defendant first appears before the magistrates' court, the Bail Act 1976 provides what is commonly referred to as a 'right to bail'. However, where the offence charged is punishable with imprisonment (as the vast majority of child abuse offences are), the statutory right to bail can be denied if the court is satisfied that certain conditions are met (Bail Act 1976, Sch 1). These conditions include there being substantial grounds for believing that, if released on bail, the defendant would commit an offence whilst on bail, or interfere with witnesses. The court will take various factors into account, including the seriousness of the offence and the probable method of dealing with the defendant for it, the character, antecedents associations and community ties of the defendant, his record in respect of the fulfilment of his obligations under previous grants of bail (if relevant) and the strength of evidence against him, as well as any other factors which appear to be relevant.

9.106 In cases of intra-familial abuse, the likelihood of the abuser committing further offences or interfering with witnesses may well depend on whether the child is still at home. In cases where the abuse is sufficiently serious to justify the police detaining the abuser after charge and taking him before the court, the court may take the child's presence at home into consideration in deciding whether to remand the abuser in custody. However, in view of the presumption in favour of bail and the fact that alternative methods of protecting the child will be available, including the imposition of conditions of bail, it is unlikely that the presence or absence of the child at home would be the sole determining factor.

Custody time-limits

9.107 If a defendant is remanded in custody, regulations prescribe the maximum period for which he may be held in custody pending trial:

–   70 days between first appearance in the magistrates' court and committal proceedings;
–   70 days between first appearance and summary trial for an offence which is triable either way (reduced to 56 days if the decision for summary trial is taken within 56 days); and
–   112 days between committal for trial and arraignment.

9.108 The prosecution may make an application for an extension before the custody time-limit expires, but such extension will only be granted if the court is satisfied that:

–   there is good and sufficient cause for an extension; and
–   the Crown has acted with all due expedition.

Should the time-limit expire, the exceptions to the right to bail contained in Sch 1 to the Bail Act 1976 no longer apply and the defendant is effectively given a right to bail. However, the court can attach conditions to the bail as long as they are conditions that must be complied with after the grant of bail, thereby allowing the court to restrict the movements of a defendant who is released pending trial.

Remands on bail by the court

9.109 The balance of the decision of the court to remand a defendant in custody or on bail may well rest on the ability of the court to impose meaningful conditions of bail. The court has the same power as the police to require a surety or sureties, and to require the defendant to comply with such other conditions as appear necessary to ensure that he does not abscond, commit further offences whilst on bail or interfere with witnesses or otherwise obstruct the course of justice whether in relation to himself or any other person.

Conditions of bail

9.110 The conditions imposed can restrict the movements of the defendant to a considerable degree. Conditions frequently imposed include the following:

- a condition of residence, frequently expressed as a condition that the person is to live and sleep at a specified address;
- a condition that the person is to notify any changes of address to the police;
- a condition of reporting (whether daily, weekly or at other intervals) to a local police station;
- a curfew (ie that the person must be indoors between certain hours);
- a condition that a person is not to enter a certain area or building, or to go within a specified distance of a certain address;
- a condition that the person is not to contact (whether directly or indirectly) the victim of the alleged offence and/or any other probable witnesses; and
- a condition that the person's passport should be surrendered to the police.

9.111 Thus, in cases of intra-familial abuse, as long as there is a non-abusing parent or carer available to look after the child victim at home, the arrest of an abuser may well act as a form of protection for the child, obviating the need to remove the child from home. If there is insufficient evidence to charge, the protection will be short-lived, but if an abuser is charged, the protection may continue right up until the trial – and beyond if the trial results in a conviction.

Alternatives to prosecution

Cautions

9.112 If the police have gathered sufficient evidence to justify a prosecution, a decision may be taken to caution the abuser, rather than to proceed to a full trial. The practice of cautioning a defendant as an alternative to prosecution was initially developed as a means of diverting young offenders from the criminal justice system, but cautions are now only administered to adults, whereas the new system of reprimands and final warnings has replaced the issuing of cautions for young offeneders (see para **9.117**). Cautioning practice is dealt with by a Home Office Circular (18/1994), which incorporates

National Standards for Cautioning. The main aim of the Circular is to discourage the use of cautions in appropriate cases (particularly indictable only offences), to increase consistency between forces and to promote better monitoring and recording of cautions. Following the publication of the Circular, the Association of Chief Police Officers (ACPO) issued more detailed and prescriptive guidance on cautioning which recommended the use of 'gravity factors' to improve objectivity and thereby improve consistency. The system suggested involved the allocation of a score according to the seriousness of the offence and a range of aggravating or mitigating factors. The final score would be a guide when deciding on a suitable disposal. Subsequent research undertaken on behalf of the Home Office found that 25 out of 42 police forces in England and Wales accepted gravity factors as a guide for cautioning decisions (*Police Cautioning in the 1990s* (Home Office Research Findings No 52, 1997)).

Criteria for administering a caution

9.113 In order to administer a caution:

– there must be sufficient evidence to justify a prosecution, ie there must be sufficient evidence of the defendant's guilt to offer a realistic prospect of conviction;
– the defendant must admit the offence;
– the defendant must understand the significance of the offence and give informed consent to the caution.

9.114 In deciding whether or not to administer a caution, the police must consider if it is in the public interest. The following factors should be considered.

– The police should take into account the public interest principles contained in the Code for Crown Prosecutors.
– Commission of an indictable-only offence should lead to prosecution, regardless of the age or previous record of the defendant, other than in the most exceptional circumstances. Home Office research found that the cautioning rate for indictable-only offences was 12 per cent in 1994 and 11 per cent in 1995 and that only six forces said that they would not, under any circumstances, caution for a serious indictable offence.
– Triable either way offences may also be too serious for a caution. Consideration should be given to, inter alia, the harm resulting from the offence, whether the offence was racially motivated, whether the offence involved a breach of trust, and whether the offence was carried out in an organised way.

- The defendant's attitude should be considered – in particular the wilfulness with which the offence was committed and the defendant's subsequent attitude.
- The victim's view of the offence, and whether a caution is appropriate, should be sought and considered, although this is not conclusive.
- There should be a presumption in favour of cautioning rather than prosecuting certain categories of defendant, such as the elderly and those who suffer from mental illness or impairment or a severe physical illness.
- A defendant should only be cautioned for a second time if the subsequent offence is trivial or where there has been a sufficient lapse of time since the first caution to suggest that it had some effect.

The status of a police caution

9.115 There is no statutory basis for administering a caution; however, the Home Office guidance on cautioning makes it clear that a caution is to be recorded by the police and should be cited in court proceedings if they are relevant to the offence under consideration. However, it is noted in the guidance that, in presenting antecedents, care should be taken to distinguish between cautions and convictions, which should usually be listed on a separate sheet of paper. Cautions also form part of the criminal statistics collated by the Home Office. Following the enactment of the Police Act 1997, the creation of a Criminal Records Bureau within the Home Office and answerable to the Home Secretary will bring all criminal record information under central control. Those who are cautioned for specified sexual offences are subject to the notification requirements imposed by the SOA 1997 (see para **9.245** *et seq*).

Young offenders

9.116 The procedures for arrest and detention of those suspected of committing criminal offences are generally applicable to all persons, regardless of age. However, special provision is made for young persons. For these purposes, a young person is defined as someone under the age of 17 years. Those aged 17 or over are treated while in police detention as if they were adults, although, if a prosecution is commenced, those under the age of 18 will fall within the jurisdiction of the Youth Court (see para **9.140** *et seq*). When a young person is arrested, all reasonable steps must be taken to inform his parents of what has occurred (CYPA 1933, s 34) and the young person should not normally be interviewed or asked to provide a statement unless an 'appropriate adult' is present (Code C, paras 11.14–11.16). An appropriate adult is defined as either his parent or guardian, a social worker, or some other responsible adult unconnected with the police. The appropriate adult's role is not merely to act as an observer, but also to advise the young person and, if necessary, to facilitate communication with him. Following police investigations, if the young person is charged but not released, arrangements will usually be made for him to be taken into the care of the local authority and detained by them until he can be brought before the Youth Court (PACE, s 38(6)). In practice, the young person will often be released without charge to allow consultations with other agencies as to whether a prosecution should proceed, whether a reprimand or warning should be given, or whether it would be more appropriate to pursue an alternative, non-criminal form of intervention.

Young offenders and the final warning scheme

9.117 Section 37 of the CDA 1998 provides that the principal aim of the youth justice system is to prevent offending by children and young people. Although cautions were initially developed as a means of diverting young offenders from the criminal justice system, ss 65 and 66 of the CDA 1998 now provide for a new scheme of police reprimands and warnings, known as the final warning scheme, which replaces cautioning for young offenders. The main objectives of the scheme are to end repeat cautioning and provide a speedy and progressive response to offending behaviour, to ensure appropriate and effective action when a young person starts to offend so as to help prevent re-offending, and to ensure that those who do re-offend after a final warning are dealt with quickly and effectively by the court system. Under the scheme, instead of receiving a caution, young offenders may receive a reprimand, or in more serious cases, a warning. Those who have not previously been reprimanded, warned or charged, may be reprimanded provided that the offence is not so serious as to require a warning. Those who have not previously been warned, or those whose previous warning was received more than 2 years previously, may receive a warning as long as the police officer considers the offence to be not so serious as to require a charge to be brought. The warning is a serious matter and any further offending behaviour will result in charges being brought in all but the most exceptional circumstances. In no circumstances can a young person receive more than two warnings.

Youth offending teams

9.118 Section 39 of the CDA 1998 places a duty on local authorities with social services and education responsibilities to establish one or more YOTs for their area. YOTs are responsible for co-ordinating the provision of youth justice services for those in the area who need them, and for carrying out the functions assigned to the teams in the Youth Justice Plan, which the local authority are required to formulate and implement annually. The YOTs are multi-agency and include probation officers, social workers, police officers and members nominated by the health authority and chief education officer for the area. When a warning is given to a young person, he will be referred immediately to the local YOT. The YOT is then under an obligation to assess the young person and arrange for him to participate in a rehabilitation programme, unless it is considered inappropriate to do so. Each rehabilitation programme is individual to the young person, but will always be targeted at achieving the overall aims of addressing offending behaviour and preventing re-offending.

Young abusers: protection or prosecution?

9.119 The decision to prosecute any young offender is given careful consideration. Under the final warning scheme, depending on the severity of the offence, the young offender can be 'fast-tracked' to court without a reprimand or final warning having been given. Specific reference is made in the Code of Practice for Crown Prosecutors to young offenders. Crown prosecutors are required to consider the interests of a young offender when deciding whether it is in the public interest to prosecute, but it is also pointed out that Crown prosecutors should not avoid prosecuting simply because of the offender's age and that the seriousness of the offence or the offender's past behaviour is very important. Thus, for example, when James Bulger was killed by two boys aged 10 years, a prosecution was deemed to be in the public interest, despite the very young age of the boys. The decision to proceed with a prosecution in this case has been subjected to sustained criticism, particularly from those who believe that the killers were, in reality, victims of their upbringing who were in need of care and protection, rather than prosecution and punishment.

Sexual experimentation or sexual abuse?

9.120 The question of whether young abusers are offenders or victims is probably most acute in cases involving sexual activity. There is evidence to suggest that around one-third of sexual offences committed against children are committed by other children (*Sex Offending Against Children: Understanding the Risk* (Home Office, 1999)). The review of sex offences undertaken by the Home Office felt it was important to draw a distinction between sexual experimentation and sexual abuse. In cases of mutually agreed under-age sexual activity, where it was clear that the children were not involved in abusive or exploitive sexual activity, the review recommended that the children should not be prosecuted, and should not automatically fall under the reprimands and final warning scheme, but should have a non-criminal alternative. Consideration was given to the possibility of making a referral to the YOTs. However, it was pointed out that many of those working in the field of child protection felt that referral of a child to any panel concerned with youth offending would provide a negative effect by tainting the whole process – that children would automatically equate such panels with criminalisation, and would be reluctant to seek their help. The review concluded that what was really needed was a process to run in parallel with investigation procedures, which could give individual assessment and possible referral to a range of services from sex education to other forms of intervention, ensuring that these reflected the aims of a national sexual health strategy (*Setting the Boundaries*, at paras 3.9.18–3.9.19).

9.121 In cases where the sexual activity was regarded as abusive or exploitive, a variety of suggestions were made as to the best way to treat young abusers, including that they should be treated separately from adult sex abusers. It was also suggested that, wherever possible, they should be removed from the criminal justice system, and civil remedies, together with welfare support, should be used to tackle abusive behaviour. The review considered that whatever approach was adopted needed to reflect the basic principles of protecting the community and the individual and preventing re-offending. Although the review did not give specific consideration to the issue, the final warning scheme does have the potential to ensure that young abusers receive treatment without the need for a criminal conviction via a rehabilitation programme (something that the system of cautioning offenders does not provide). The Home Office guidance on the establishment and operation of the rehabilitation programmes refers to the possibility of short-term counselling or group work to bring about behavioural change, although no specific mention is made of addressing the issue of treatment for sex offenders (*The Establishment and Operation of the Rehabilitation (Change) Programmes under the Final Warning Scheme* (Home Office, 1999)). If a prosecution does take place, it is important that young abusers are given appropriate sentences and disposals to ensure that they do not continue to pose a risk to others, and that they receive appropriate treatment.

Handing over to the CPS

9.122 The CPS was created by the Prosecution of Offences Act 1985. The overall head of the service is the Director of Public Prosecutions, who is assisted by Chief Crown Prosecutors, each of whom is responsible to the Director for supervising the operation of the service in a particular area. In many cases the police may seek advice from the CPS at an early stage of an investigation, but once a suspect has been charged or informed he may be reported for summons, the entire conduct of the case is passed to the CPS and the evidence compiled by the police during their investigations is passed to the local office of the CPS. The case is then reviewed by a CPS lawyer. One of the major reasons for the creation of the service was to provide an independent check on whether police prosecutions were justified and, if not, to halt them at an early stage. For this reason, the CPS has a right to discontinue proceedings (s 23), and thus the final decision as to whether a prosecution proceeds rests with the CPS, not the police. Guidance for the CPS in making this decision is contained in the Code for Crown Prosecutors issued by the DPP. The police will already have considered many of the criteria laid down in the Code when making the initial decision to charge the defendant or report him for summons (Home Office Circular 18/1994). The

Code lays down two tests that must be satisfied before a prosecution can proceed – the evidential test and the public interest test.

The evidential test

9.123 Crown prosecutors must be satisfied that there is enough evidence to provide a 'realistic prospect of conviction' against each defendant on each charge. This is an objective test, meaning that a jury or bench of magistrates, properly directed in accordance with the law, is more likely than not to convict the defendant on the charge alleged. In deciding this, Crown prosecutors must consider both the admissibility and reliability of the evidence in court. This will be particularly relevant in cases involving children as witnesses. Although attitudes towards the veracity and reliability of child witnesses have changed dramatically over the past two decades and the growing concern over the physical and sexual abuse of children has resulted in changes to the way in which children's evidence can be received by a court, the decision to proceed with a prosecution in such cases will require careful consideration of the willingness and ability of the prosecution witnesses to give evidence in court.

The public interest test

9.124 Once the evidential test has been satisfied, the Crown prosecutor must then decide whether a prosecution is in the public interest. The Code states that, in cases of any seriousness, a prosecution will usually take place unless there are public interest factors tending against prosecution which clearly outweigh those tending in favour. A list of common public interest factors, both for and against prosecution, are provided, followed by a caveat that deciding on the public interest is not simply a matter of adding up the number of factors on each side and that Crown prosecutors must always think very carefully about how important each factor is in the circumstances of each case and go on to make an overall assessment.

Some common public interest factors in favour of prosecution

9.125 The more serious the offence, the more likely it is that a prosecution will be needed in the public interest. A prosecution is likely to be needed if:

- a conviction is likely to result in a significant sentence;
- a weapon was used or violence was threatened during the commission of the offence;
- the offence was committed against a person serving the public (eg a police or prison officer, or a nurse);
- the defendant was in a position of authority or trust;
- the evidence shows that the defendant was a ringleader or an organiser of the offence;
- there is evidence that the offence was premeditated;

- there is evidence that the offence was carried out by a group;
- the victim of the offence was vulnerable, has been in considerable fear, or suffered personal attack, damage or disturbance;
- the offence was motivated by any form of discrimination against the victim's ethnic or national origin, sex, religious beliefs, political views or sexual preference;
- there is a marked difference between the actual or mental ages of the defendant and the victim, or if there is an element of corruption;
- the defendant's previous convictions or cautions are relevant to the present offence;
- the defendant is alleged to have committed the offence whilst under an order of the court;
- there are grounds for believing that the offence is likely to be continued or repeated, for example by a history of recurring conduct; or
- the offence, although not serious in itself, is widespread in the area where it was committed.

Some common public interest factors against prosecution

9.126 A prosecution is less likely to be needed if:

- the court is likely to impose a small or nominal penalty;
- the offence was committed as a result of a genuine mistake or misunderstanding (these factors must be balanced against the seriousness of the offence);
- the loss or harm can be described as minor and was the result of a single incident, particularly if it was caused by a misjudgement;
- there has been a long delay between the offence taking place and the date of the trial, unless:
  - the offence is serious;
  - the delay was caused in part by the defendant;
  - the offence has only recently come to light; or
  - the complexity of the offence has meant that there has been a long investigation;
- a prosecution is likely to have a very bad effect on the victim's physical or mental health, always bearing in mind the seriousness of the offence;
- the defendant is elderly or is, or was at the time of the offence, suffering from significant mental or physical ill-health, unless the offence is serious or there is a real possibility that it may be repeated; the CPS, where necessary, applies Home Office guidelines about how to deal with mentally disordered offenders; Crown prosecutors must balance the desirability of diverting a defendant who is suffering from significant mental or physical ill-health with the need to safeguard the general public;

– the defendant has put right the loss or harm that was caused (but defendants must not avoid prosecution simply because they can pay compensation); or

– details may be made public that could harm sources of information, international relations or national security.

Child victims and CPS decision-making

9.127 The decision to proceed with a prosecution in a case involving a child victim will inevitably focus initially on the credibility of the child. However, this will not be the only influential factor. A study conducted for the Home Office on the admissibility and sufficiency of evidence in child abuse prosecutions studied 94 cases of child abuse, involving 124 complainants (*An Assessment of the Admissibility and Sufficiency of Evidence in Child Abuse Prosecutions* (Home Office, August 1999)). The cases were secured in September and October 1996 and were obtained from three CPUs and from the CPS in those areas: 61 of the cases (65 per cent) involved sexual abuse; 19 cases (20 per cent) involved physical abuse; 6 cases (7 per cent) involved physical abuse and neglect; 5 cases (5 per cent) involved physical and sexual abuse; 2 cases (2 per cent) involved neglect and 1 case (1 per cent) involved physical and sexual abuse and neglect. As the cases originated from CPUs, they were almost exclusively cases of intra-familial abuse or cases where the complainant knew the alleged abuser.

9.128 The study found that the cases reviewed were often multi-faceted and that it was the interaction between several features that determined the prosecution decision. In particular:

– The most crucial piece of evidence in sexual abuse cases was the child's account. In judging the evidential strength of this account the police and CPS looked for clarity, detail and consistency.

– An assessment of the child's demeanour in giving the account included a consideration of whether the child's manner of describing the abuse was in keeping with the researcher's image of how an abused child 'should' behave in an interview.

– CPS lawyers found the introduction of video-taped testimony enormously helpful in their evaluation of the strength of a child witness, albeit very time-consuming to review.

– Some evidence supporting the child's account was felt to be necessary before a case of sexual abuse could be prosecuted. However, the strength of the additional evidence required was dependent on the clarity and consistency of the child's account. Where a child's testimony was considered to be exceptionally clear and detailed, evidence of opportunity might be considered sufficient. When the child's account was vague or inconsistent, a case would only be prosecuted where there was other strong evidence supporting the child's account, such as clear medical signs or testimony from other children who were making similar allegations.

- Cases of alleged sexual abuse were examined to see whether there was anything in the child's past which could be used to suggest that she was an untruthful or otherwise unreliable witness.

- In contrast, the child's account had little weight in a decision to prosecute physical abuse. Cases were most likely to be prosecuted which had medical evidence of a serious assault on a young child and where the suspect had previously been suspected of assault on a child.

- Conversely, cases of physical assault were less likely to be prosecuted when the complainant was older and had behaved badly in the prelude to the assault. In these cases it was considered that the suspect could raise the defence of 'reasonable parental chastisement'. Cases were also less likely to be prosecuted when social services were working with the suspect to modify his behaviour.

- The police and CPS viewed a court appearance as an arduous, painful experience for the child and this could lead to the conclusion that it was not in the public interest to prosecute.

Disclosure of unused material

9.129 In order to ensure a fair trial for the defendant, for many years the prosecution has been under a common law duty to disclose to the defence not only the evidence on which it proposes to rely at trial, but also any evidence pertaining to the case which will not be relied upon at trial. The duty to disclose unused material is now subject to the statutory scheme set out in the Criminal Procedure and Investigations Act 1996 (CPIA 1996), as supplemented by a Code of Practice issued under Part II of the Act.

9.130 The scheme of the legislation can be divided into four stages as follows.

(1) The investigator's duty

The Code of Practice issued under s 23 of the CPIA 1996 makes investigators (which includes police officers and others such as trading standards officers) responsible for ensuring that any information relevant to the investigation is recorded and retained, whether it is gathered in the course of the investigation (eg documents or indecent photographs seized) or generated by the investigation (eg interview records). Where the investigator believes that the defendant is likely to plead not guilty at a summary trial in the magistrates' court, or that the offence will be tried on indictment at the Crown Court, he is required to prepare a schedule listing material which has been retained and which does not form part of the case against the defendant. If the investigator has retained any sensitive material which he believes it is not in the public interest to disclose, this should be listed in a separate schedule (see para **9.131**).

(2) Primary prosecution disclosure

Section 3 of the CPIA 1996 requires the prosecutor to disclose previously undisclosed material to the defence if, in the prosecutor's opinion, it might undermine the case for the prosecution. The material may be disclosed either by giving it to the defence, or allowing them to inspect it at a reasonable time and place. This step is called 'primary prosecution disclosure' and must be carried out as soon as reasonably practicable (CPIA 1996, s 13).

(3) Defence disclosure

Once primary disclosure has taken place and the case is committed to the Crown Court, the defendant must give a written statement to the prosecutor setting out in general terms the nature of the defence and matters on which the defendant takes issues with the prosecution, with reasons (CPIA 1996, s 5). This statement must be served within 14 days of the prosecution's compliance with the duty of primary disclosure.

(4) Secondary prosecution disclosure

Once the defence statement has been served, the prosecution must disclose to the defendant any previously undisclosed prosecution material 'which might reasonably be expected to assist the accused's defence as disclosed by the defence statement' (CPIA 1996, s 7).

Local authority records, disclosure and public interest immunity in criminal proceedings

9.131 The prosecution duty to disclose is subject to immunity when the public interest so dictates. Although the CPIA 1996 generally disapplies the rules of common law in relation to the prosecution duty of disclosure, it expressly preserves the rules of common law as to whether disclosure is in the public interest (s 21). As noted above, the investigator may list 'sensitive' material on a separate schedule if he thinks it should not be disclosed in the public interest. Public interest immunity applies to both primary and secondary disclosure. The Code of Practice issued under Part II of the CPIA 1996 gives examples of sensitive material. The examples include material supplied to an investigator during a criminal investigation which relates to a child or young person and which has been generated by a local authority social services department, an ACPC or other party contacted by an investigator during the investigation (para 6.12). However, the categorisation of material as sensitive is in no way conclusive of whether its disclosure is in the public interest. The court is the final arbitrator of whether the material should be withheld. If the prosecution wish to rely on public interest immunity or sensitivity to justify non-disclosure, then, whenever possible, they should notify the defence that they are applying for a ruling by the court, and indicate to the defence at least the category of the material which they hold. The defence must then have the opportunity of making representations to the court. In exceptional circumstances, the application may be made ex parte, without the defence being notified. The court will then perform a balancing exercise, balancing the weight of the public interest in non-disclosure against the importance of the material for which the immunity is claimed to the issues of interest to the defence.

9.132 It has been made clear by the courts that social work and analogous records are in a special category of immunity, justified by the particular circumstances of the welfare of children. Although the immunity is not absolute, in many cases disclosure will be refused. In *Re M (A Minor) (Disclosure of Material)* [1990] 2 FLR 36 the Court of Appeal set out the criteria to be applied in wardship proceedings and the same approach has been adopted by judges trying criminal cases involving child abuse. Access to such records may be of crucial importance to defendants accused of abusing children who are already in the care of a local authority, particularly when the accusations are only made several years after the alleged abuse. In *R v B (Derek Anthony)* (2001) *The Times*, January 17 the defendant was convicted in 1999 of various offences of child cruelty, assault occasioning actual bodily harm, indecent assault and buggery. All of the offences were committed whilst he was headmaster of a Community School between 1974 and 1980. The victims were pupils at the school aged between 10 and 15 years who had either been voluntarily placed in care by their parents or a care order had been made by the court. The reasons for them being in care varied but in the main it was either because their parents could not cope with them, or because they were beyond the control of their parents, or because they had committed crimes. The defendant appealed against his convictions on the ground that he was denied access to documents in social services files which would have assisted him in undermining the prosecution case. These files had been provided to the prosecution by social services, but the defendant had been denied access on the grounds of public interest immunity. The Court of Appeal held that the correct approach had been taken to disclosure. The judge had balanced the need to protect the victims against the public interest in ensuring that there was a fair trial. Certain documents had been disclosed to the defence and the judge was entitled to take account of the fact that the purpose of disclosure is to ensure a fair trial, and not to enable endless cross-examination as to credit on very peripheral matters affecting young men then aged between 10 and 15 years. The Court of Appeal also rejected the defendant's contention that he had been deprived of his right to a fair trial under the HRA 1998 (ECHR, Article 6), stating that the human rights jurisprudence recognises that legitimate restrictions must be placed upon the defendant's right to disclosure in the public interest.

Third party disclosure

9.133 Sometimes material relevant to the prosecution or defence case will be in the hands of someone other than the prosecution, for example, confidential records of any therapy received by a child victim of abuse (see para **9.94**). The *Attorney-General's Guidelines on Disclosure of Information in Criminal Proceedings* suggest that, where the prosecution suspects that a third party (eg a local authority, a social services department, a hospital, a doctor, a school, providers of forensic services) has material or information which might be disclosable if it were in the possession of the prosecution, consideration should be given as to whether it is appropriate to seek access to the material or information. If so, steps should be taken by the prosecution to obtain such material or information, and it will be particularly important to do so if the material or information is likely to undermine the prosecution case, or assist a known defence (para 30).

9.134 If the material remains in the hands of the third party, then the defendant is entitled to request it. If the third party is not prepared to hand it over, the defendant may seek a witness summons under the Criminal Procedure (Attendance of Witnesses) Act 1965 for trials in the Crown Court, or under Magistrates' Court Act 1980, s 97 for summary trials. At the resultant hearing, the third party would then be able to argue that any sensitive material should not be disclosed on grounds of public interest immunity.

The effect of delay on prosecution

9.135 In recent years, a number of cases of child abuse, particularly abuse which has taken place in institutions, have come to light some considerable time after the abuse actually occurred. Although the Code for Crown Prosecutors mentions delay as a factor which could militate against a prosecution in certain circumstances, in the vast majority of cases where the offence is to be tried on indictment, there exists no specific time-limit within which a criminal prosecution must be brought. The Crown Court has inherent power to prevent its process from abuse (*Connelly v DPP* [1964] AC 1254), and if a long delay has made it impossible for the defendant to have a fair trial, the proceedings will be stayed. When considering an application to stay proceedings, the court will consider the reasons for the delay and whether there is a risk of serious prejudice to the defendant in meeting the stale allegations (*R v Jenkins* [1998] Crim LR 411). However, delay, even a very long delay, will not automatically result in serious prejudice to the defendant sufficient to justify staying the proceedings. In *R v Wilkinson* [1996] Cr App R 81, the defendant faced trial for indecent assault and incest against his two daughters and step-granddaughter some 28 years after the first incidence of abuse and the Court of Appeal held that the trial judge had correctly decided that the prosecution was not an abuse of process. If such cases do proceed to trial, the judge has a duty to confront the jury with the fact of delay and its potential impact on the formulation and conduct of the defence and on the prosecution's fulfilment of the burden of proof (R *v Percival* (1998) *The Times*, July 20 and R *v GY* [1999] Crim LR 825).

THE CRIMINAL TRIAL

Classification of offences and mode of trial

9.136 Criminal offences are categorised for the purpose of determining the court in which they will be tried. An offence may be classified as: a summary offence, which means that it may only be tried at a summary trial in the magistrates' court; an indictable offence, which means that it may only be tried on indictment at the Crown Court; or as a 'triable either way' offence, which means that it may be tried either at the magistrates' court or at the Crown Court. The vast majority of criminal cases begin in the magistrates' court, where summary offences will be tried and indictable offences will be committed for trial at the Crown Court.

Determination of the mode of trial

9.137 Determination of the mode of trial of either way offences takes place in the magistrates' court. A defendant charged with such an offence has a right to elect trial by jury at the Crown Court, regardless of the view of the magistrates' court. Similarly, if the court considers the offence is more suitable for trial on indictment, it may send the case to the Crown Court for trial, regardless of the views of the defendant. In deciding this, s 19 of the Magistrates' Courts Act 1980 requires the court to have regard to the following matters in deciding whether an offence is more suitable for summary trial or trial on indictment:

(1) the nature of the case;
(2) whether the circumstances make the offence one of a serious character;
(3) whether the punishment which a magistrates' court would have power to inflict for it would be adequate;
(4) any other circumstances which appear to the court to make it more suitable for the offence to be tried in one way rather than the other;
(5) any representations made by the prosecution or the defence.

National Mode of Trial Guidelines

9.138 The most important factor that the magistrates will consider in determining mode of trial will be whether they could impose adequate punishment if the defendant is convicted. The maximum penalties they can impose are 6 months' imprisonment and/or a fine of £5,000 for any one offence and, for two or more offences, an aggregate of 12 months' imprisonment and/or fines of £5,000 for each offence. Further guidance is given in the *National Mode of Trial Guidelines* issued in 1995 by the Criminal Justice Consultative Council. The guidelines set out general considerations and then suggest features that are relevant in forming a judgement on the seriousness of particular types of offences as follows:

Violence to and neglect of children
(1)   substantial injury;
(2)   repeated violence or serious neglect, even if the physical harm is slight;
(3)   sadistic violence (eg deliberate burning or scalding).

Indecent assault
(1)   substantial disparity in age between victim and defendant, and the assault is more than trivial;
(2)   violence or threats of violence;
(3)   relationship of trust or responsibility between defendant and victim;
(4)   several similar offences, and the assaults are more than trivial;
(5)   the victim is particularly vulnerable;
(6)   serious nature of the assault.

Unlawful sexual intercourse
(1)   wide disparity of age;
(2)   breach of a position of trust;
(3)   the victim is particularly vulnerable.

Restricting the defendant's right to trial on indictment

9.139 Under the present system, a defendant has the right to elect trial on indictment for a large number of offences, many of which, it is argued, are more suitable for trial in the magistrates' court. In recent years concern has been expressed about defendants 'working the system' and demanding trial on indictment for no good reason other than to delay proceedings. Efforts have been made to abolish the defendant's right to choose trial on indictment for offences triable either way, and allow magistrates to make the final decision. The government has estimated that removing the right of the defendant to elect trial on indictment would reduce the number of trials in the Crown Court by around 14,000 per annum, representing a net resource saving of about £128 million. However, the government's efforts have met with fierce opposition. Two Criminal Justice (Mode of Trial) Bills were introduced in the 1999–2000 session of Parliament, but neither Bill received Royal Assent. More far-reaching proposals for reform of the criminal courts were published in October 2001 (Sir Robin Auld, *Review of the Criminal Courts in England and Wales*). The review proposed that committal proceedings should be abolished (see para **9.147**) and that a defendant should no longer have an elective right to trial by jury. The government has expressed support for these proposals (*The Criminal Courts Review Report: A Government Statement* (LCD, 2001)).

Young offenders

9.140 Whereas adult defendants will have their case heard in the magistrates' court or the Crown Court, the desirability of making special arrangements to cater for criminal cases involving young offenders has been recognised since the Children Act 1908 established the first juvenile court. Subsequent legislation firmly established the procedures whereby young offenders were separated from their older counterparts and dealt with in a way thought to be more appropriate to their age, needs and understanding. More recently, the CJA 1991 established the Youth Court that exists today. The Youth Court is a magistrates' court specially constituted for the purpose of hearing charges against young offenders under the age of 18 years. As a general rule, when a defendant below this age is charged with any offence (other than homicide), he must be tried summarily by a Youth Court, and not by the magistrates court or the Crown Court. There are, however, a number of exceptions to this general rule. By virtue of s 46 of the CYPA 1933 and s 18 of the CYPA 1963, a young offender can be dealt with by the magistrates' court in the following circumstances:

- he is charged jointly with an adult; or
- he appears before the magistrates together with an adult and although he is not charged jointly with the adult if the prosecution have chosen to charge them separately, the charge against him is that he aided and abetted the commission of the offence alleged against the adult or vice versa; or
- he appears before the magistrates together with an adult, and the charge against him arises out of circumstances the same as or connected with the circumstances giving rise to the charge against the adult; or
- the adult magistrates' court began to hear the proceedings against him in the erroneous belief that he was an adult.

9.141 If a young offender is dealt with by the magistrates' court and he pleads guilty or is found guilty, his case will be remitted to the Youth Court for sentence, unless the magistrates are satisfied that such a remittal would be undesirable and that the case can be dealt with by a discharge, a fine or binding over the parent or guardian.

Young offenders and the Crown Court

9.142 Unlike adult defendants, young offenders have no right to elect to be tried on indictment at the Crown Court. By virtue of s 24(1) of the

Magistrates' Courts Act 1980, a young offender must be tried summarily (either in the Youth Court or the adult magistrates' court) unless:

— he is charged with an offence of homicide; or
— he is charged jointly with an adult who is going to be tried on indictment, and the magistrates consider that it is in the interests of justice to commit them both for trial; or
— the magistrates consider that he could properly be sentenced under s 91 of the PCC(S)A 2000 (under which young persons convicted on indictment of certain grave crimes may be sentenced to be detained for long periods), and either:

- he is charged with an offence carrying a maximum sentence of 14 years' imprisonment or more, or with indecent assault on a woman or a man; or
- he is a young person (ie has attained the age of 14 or more) and is charged with causing death by dangerous driving or causing death by careless driving while under the influence of drink or drugs.

Young abusers

9.143 A young offender who abuses another child, either physically or sexually, will usually be tried in the Youth Court. However, if the offence with which he is charged is a serious one, a decision will be made by the Youth Court before the case starts as to whether the matters should be committed to the Crown Court so that that Court can consider the long-term detention provisions of the PCC(S)A 2000 if the young offender is found guilty. In making the decision, a balance must be struck between the objectives of keeping young offenders out of long-term custody on the one hand and, on the other, the need to impose sufficiently substantial sentences on people who have committed serious crimes so as to provide both appropriate punishment and a deterrent to protect the public. Thus, for example, a young offender charged with rape should always be tried in the Crown Court. Most other 'grave crimes' that may be tried in the Crown Court carry a sentence of 14 years or more. Section 64 of the CJA 1991 provided that the offence of indecent assault on a woman under s 14 of the SOA 1956 was also regarded as a qualifying offence, despite the fact that it carries a maximum sentence of 10 years' imprisonment. The rationale behind this amendment is not clear and the fact that it did not originally include an offence of indecent assault on a man under s 15 of the SOA 1956 was clearly anomalous. This anomaly was rectified by s 44 of the Crime (Sentences) Act 1997, which extended the provision to include the offence of indecent assault on a man.

Young offenders, trial procedures and human rights

9.144 Following a ruling of the European Court of Human Rights in

December 1999 in the case of *T v UK; V v UK* [1999] TLR 871, trial procedures for young offenders charged with serious offences are to be changed. In 1993 Jon Venables and Robert Thompson were charged with the murder of 2-year-old James Bulger. Both offenders were aged 10 at the time of the offence. Their trial took place over 3 weeks at Preston Crown Court, where modifications, such as raising the floor level of the dock and shortening sitting hours were made to the courtroom and trial, to take account of their youth. The boys were convicted and sentenced to be detained under s 53(2) of the CYPA 1933 (now s 90 of the PCC(S)A 2000). The boys took their case to the European Court of Human Rights, complaining, inter alia, that, in view of their young age, their trial in public in an adult Crown Court and the punitive nature of their sentence constituted violations of their rights not to be subjected to inhuman or degrading treatment or punishment as guaranteed by Article 3 of the ECHR. They further complained that they were denied a fair trial in breach of Article 6 of the ECHR. The European Court of Human Rights acknowledged that, while the public nature of the proceedings might have exacerbated the feelings of guilt, distress, anguish and fear experienced by the applicants, it was not convinced that the particular features of the trial process caused, to a significant degree, suffering going beyond that which would inevitably have been engendered by any attempt by the authorities to deal with the applicants and therefore it did not find that the boy's trial gave rise to a violation of Article 3. However, the Court found that, despite the special measures which were taken in view of the boys' age, the formality and ritual of the Crown Court must at times have seemed incomprehensible and intimidating for a child aged 11. In the circumstances, the Court did not consider that it was sufficient for the purposes of Article 6 that the boys were represented by skilled and experienced lawyers and therefore found that the boys had been denied a fair hearing in breach of Article 6.

9.145 As a result of the ruling, reforms to the way in which young offenders are tried for serious crimes are inevitable. The most likely model to be adopted is expected to be a criminal court in which judges and lawyers remove wigs and gowns and an informal environment is created. To a certain extent, this would mirror reforms made in recent years to ease the stress experienced by young victims and witnesses and which are currently being extended to other vulnerable or intimidated witnesses. The Home Secretary is said to be against trying young offenders charged with serious offences in a Youth Court and will not countenance a lowering of the age of criminal responsibility, which at 10 years is one of the lowest in Europe (*T v UK; V v UK* (above)). Any reforms to trial procedures would apply not only to young offenders charged with murder, as in the James Bulger case, but also, at the discretion of the magistrates, to those charged with other serious offences which may currently be tried in the Crown Court.

Practice Direction: trial of children and young persons in the Crown Court

9.146 In February 2000, the Lord Chief Justice issued a Practice Direction (*Practice Direction (Crown Court: Young Defendants)* [2000] 1 WLR 659) containing the following guidance:

'*The overriding principle*
3. Some young offenders accused of committing serious crimes may be very young and very immature when standing trial in the Crown Court. The purpose of such trial is to determine guilt (if that is in issue) and decide the appropriate sentence if the young offender pleads guilty or is convicted. The trial process should not itself expose the young offender to avoidable intimidation, humiliation or distress. All possible steps should be taken to assist the young offender to understand and participate in the proceedings. The ordinary trial process should so far as necessary be adapted to meet those ends. Regard should be had to the welfare of the young offender as required by section 44 of the Children and Young Persons Act 1933.

. . .

The trial
9. The trial should, if practicable, be held in a courtroom in which all the participants are on the same or almost the same level.
10. A young offender should normally, if he wishes, be free to sit with members of his family or others in a like relationship and in a place which permits easy, informal communication with his legal representatives and others with whom he wants or needs to communicate.
11. The court should explain the course of proceedings to a young offender in terms he can understand, should remind those representing a young offender of their continuing duty to explain each step of the trial to him and should ensure, so far as is practicable, that the trial is conducted in language which the young offender can understand.
12. The trial should be conducted according to a timetable that takes full account of a young offender's inability to concentrate for long periods. Frequent and regular breaks will often be appropriate.
13. Robes and wigs should not be worn unless the young offender asks that they should be or the court for good reason orders that they should be. Any person responsible for the security of a young offender who is in custody should not be in uniform. There should be no recognisable police presence in the courtroom save for good reason.
14. The court should be prepared to restrict attendance at the trial to a small number, perhaps limited to some of those with immediate and direct interest in the outcome of the trial. The court should rule on any challenged claim to attend.
15. Facilities for reporting the trial (subject to any direction restricting reporting of the proceedings given under section 39 of the Children and Young Persons Act 1933 or section 45 of the Youth Justice and Criminal Evidence Act 1999) must be provided. But the court may restrict the number of those attending in the courtroom to report the trial to such number as is judged practicable and desirable. In ruling on any challenged claim to attend the courtroom for the purpose of reporting the trial the court should be mindful of the public's general

right to be informed about the administration of justice in the Crown Court. Where access to the courtroom by reporters is restricted, arrangements should be made for the proceedings to be relayed, audibly and if possible visually, to another room in the same court complex to which the media have free access if it appears that there will be a need for such additional facilities.

16. Where the court is called upon to exercise its discretion in relation to any procedural matter falling within the scope of this Practice Direction but not the subject of specific reference, such discretion should be exercised having regard to the overriding principle.'

Committal proceedings

9.147 Before a criminal case can be tried on indictment at the Crown Court, it must be committed for trial by the magistrates' court. Historically, committal proceedings were designed to act as a filter to prevent weak cases reaching the Crown Court. Prior to 1967 the magistrates would review the evidence presented by the prosecution in order to decide if there was sufficient evidence on which a reasonable jury could convict the defendant. However, this was time-consuming for both the court and witnesses and was deemed to be unnecessary in cases where the defence conceded that there was a prima facie case. The Criminal Justice Act 1967 (CJA 1967) therefore introduced an alternative procedure whereby the magistrates could commit the case for trial without consideration of the evidence, if the defence agreed. Despite this, pressure for reform of the system continued. It was argued that committal proceedings, whether with or without consideration of the evidence, were not an effective filter and that they were expensive, cumbersome and time-consuming. Furthermore, concern was expressed that the right of the defence to insist on consideration of the evidence, and thereby ensure that prosecution witnesses were required to give evidence at the committal proceedings as well as at the trial, could be abused.

Child witnesses and notices of transfer

9.148 Concern about the potential abuse of committal proceedings by the defence was particularly acute when one of the prosecution witnesses was a child. In 1989 the *Advisory Group on Video Evidence* (see para **9.162**) concluded that, in cases which involve children, the existing committal proceedings were irredeemably flawed. The Group made recommendations aimed at protecting children from being required to give evidence at committal proceedings and which would also reduce the time taken for the case to come to trial at the Crown Court, thereby ensuring the events were fresher in the child's mind and enabling any therapy the child needed to be commenced at an earlier stage. The recommendations were enacted by s 53 of the CJA 1991. In certain circumstances, the Director of Public Prosecutions may now issue a notice of transfer, which effectively allows the case to proceed directly to the Crown

Court. In order to issue such a notice, the proceedings must relate to one of the following offences:

(1) an offence which involves an assault on, or injury or a threat of injury to, a person;

(2) an offence under s 1 of the CYPA 1933 (cruelty to persons under 16);

(3) an offence under the SOA 1956, the ICA 1960, the SOA 1967, s 54 of the Criminal Law Act 1977 or the Protection of Children Act 1978; and

(4) attempting or conspiring to commit, or aiding, abetting, counselling, procuring or inciting the commission of any of the above.

9.149 The Director of Public Prosecutions must be satisfied that:

(1) the evidence of the offence would be sufficient for the accused to be committed for trial;

(2) a child (defined to mean a person aged under 14 if the offence is one of violence or cruelty and a person under 17 for sexual offences) who is alleged to be the victim or to have witnessed the commission of the offence, will be called as a witness at trial; and

(3) for the purpose of avoiding any prejudice to the welfare of the child, the case should be taken over and proceeded with without delay by the Crown Court.

9.150 References to the welfare of the child have traditionally been associated with civil proceedings. Whereas previous statutory provisions allowed concessions for child witnesses in criminal proceedings, these generally required a 'serious danger to the juvenile's life or health' (ss 42 and 43 of the CYPA 1933). The express requirement that the *welfare* of the child should be taken into account in the conduct of criminal proceedings relating to an abuser reflects the growing concern with children's needs and rights.

9.151 Provision exists for the defence to apply to the Crown Court for dismissal of the charges. The judge must dismiss any of the charges specified in the notice of transfer in respect of which it appears to him that the evidence against the applicant would not be sufficient for a jury properly to convict him. Although the judge can give leave for oral evidence to be given at the application, oral evidence cannot be adduced from the child witness.

Further changes to committal proceedings

9.152 Following the reforms relating to child witnesses, there was continued pressure to reform committal proceedings for all witnesses. The CJPOA 1994 contained provisions to abolish committal proceedings and replace them with a system of transfer for trial. The proposed system, which was purely administrative rather than judicial, was perceived by practitioners as a 'bureaucratic nightmare' and was never brought into force. Instead a revised committal procedure was introduced by the CPIA 1996 (see Card and Ward (1996)). The magistrates' court continues to act as a filter, deciding whether there is sufficient evidence to commit a case to the Crown Court. The committal may take place without consideration of the prosecution evidence if the defence agree. The crucial change is that, if the defence contend there is not sufficient evidence to justify committal or the offender is not legally represented, the prosecution evidence which the magistrates consider is restricted to written evidence. Thus no witness can now be required to give evidence on two occasions, thereby removing a potential source of additional stress.

The course of the trial – the principle of open justice

9.153 Article 6 of the ECHR provides that 'in the determination ... of any criminal charge against him, everyone is entitled to a fair and public hearing within a reasonable time by an independent and impartial tribunal established by law' and that 'everyone charged with a criminal offence has the following minimum rights: ... to examine or have examined witnesses against him and to obtain the attendance and examination of witnesses on his behalf under the same conditions as witnesses against him'. An important assumption underlying the trial procedure in England and Wales is that the oral testimony of witnesses in open court is superior to any other type of evidence and thus the adversarial system of trial accords precedence to the oral testimony of witnesses. This, together with the rule against hearsay evidence, which generally prevents the repetition of an out-of-court statement in order to prove its truth, ensures compliance with Article 6 because witnesses are generally required to appear in court in person at the trial of a defendant, give their evidence orally in open court and face cross-examination by the opposing party.

The admission of written statements

9.154 Although witnesses are generally required to give oral evidence in open court, in certain limited circumstances a written statement of their evidence may be admitted at the trial. If the opposing party does not object to the admission of a witness's written statement in place of the oral testimony of the witness, then, provided the statement it signed by the witness and contains a declaration that it is true to the best of his or her knowledge and belief, the statement can be admitted as an exception to the hearsay rule (CJA 1967, s 9). However, if the defendant pleads not guilty to the charges he is facing, this provision is unlikely to assist the victim, who will usually be a crucial prosecution witness. The exceptions to the hearsay rule contained in ss 23–26 of the CJA 1988 may be of more assistance. The Act provides that a statement made by a person in a document shall be admissible in criminal proceedings as evidence of any fact of which direct oral evidence by him would be admissible if, inter alia:

—   the person who made the statement is dead or by reason of his bodily or mental condition unfit to attend as a witness; or
—   if the statement was made to a police officer or some other person charged with the duty of investigating offences or charging offenders, the person who made it does not give oral evidence through fear or because he is kept out of the way.

9.155 Thus victims who have been so severely traumatised by events that they are unfit to attend as witnesses may have a written statement admitted in place of oral testimony. In these circumstances, although the statement will usually have been made to the police during the initial investigation, this is not a prerequisite to its admission. However, the court may refuse to admit the statement if it is of the opinion that in the interests of justice the statement ought not to be admitted (CJA 1988, s 25(1)). In so deciding the court must have regard, inter alia, to any risk, having regard in particular to whether it is likely to be possible to controvert the statement if the person making it does not attend to give oral evidence in the proceedings, that its admission or exclusion will result in unfairness to the accused, or, if there is more than one, to any of them. The inability of the defence to cross-examine a witness who is central to the prosecution case would undoubtedly result in unfairness and it is therefore unlikely that a prosecution could proceed without the oral evidence of the victim.

9.156 If the witness is not unfit, but merely in fear of giving oral evidence, then a statement made to the police may be admitted. 'Fear' has been widely interpreted. It is sufficient to prove that a witness is in fear as a consequence of the offence or of something said or done subsequently in relation to the offence and the possibility of giving evidence in relation to it (*R v Acton Justices ex parte McMullen* (1990) 92 Cr App R 98). Thus a traumatised victim may come within this provision. However, further restrictions apply in these circumstances in that the statement cannot be admitted without the leave of the court and the court can only give leave if it is of the opinion that the statement ought to be admitted in the interests of justice (CJA 1988, s 26). Once again, it is highly unlikely that the statement of a key prosecution witness will be admitted in place of oral testimony.

Written statements and Article 6 of the ECHR

9.157 A further consideration would, of course, be a potential breach of Article 6 of the ECHR. The admission of hearsay evidence by the prosecution does not automatically constitute a breach of Article 6. The European Court of Human Rights has expressed the view that, in determining whether there has been a breach of Article 6, its task is to ascertain whether the proceedings considered as a whole, including the way in which the evidence was taken, were unfair (*Asch v Austria*, Series A, No 203 (1991), para 26). It would appear to be crucial that a defendant should not be convicted solely on the basis of hearsay evidence (*Kostovski v Netherlands*, Series A, No 166 (1989) 12 EHRR 434 and *Doorson v Netherlands* (1996) 22 EHRR 330). The right of a defendant to cross-examine prosecution witnesses, or to have them cross-examined on his behalf, will continue to be of fundamental importance, despite recent changes to the way in which child witnesses may give evidence.

Children as witnesses: in general

9.158 It is generally acknowledged that giving evidence in open court and facing cross-examination can be a traumatic experience for any witness. The stress is inevitably exacerbated when the witness is a child, particularly when the child is a victim of the offence. To be expected to stand in open court and repeat allegations of abuse in front of the alleged abuser was often more than many children were capable of, and frequently resulted in the child breaking down and being unable to give evidence. As a result of these concerns, various procedural reforms to the way in which children give evidence have been made in recent years.

Use of screens

9.159 At common law, a defendant was said to have a right to confront his accuser, although precisely how far this right extends has not always been clear. At the beginning of the twentieth century, it was generally thought that this included a right of face-to-face confrontation with a witness. However, in 1919 the Court of Appeal held that if there was a fear that the witness may be intimidated, the witness could give evidence out of sight of the defendant. In the case of R *v Smellie* (1919) 14 Cr App R 128, the defendant was required to sit on the stairs leading to the dock, where he could not be seen by the witness, but could nevertheless hear the evidence being given. A somewhat more sophisticated method of achieving the same objective is to erect screens in the courtroom which shield the witness from the defendant, but allow the jury to see both the defendant and the witness. The Court of Appeal first gave formal approval for the use of screens for child witnesses in 1989 in R *v X, Y, Z* (1989) 91 Cr App R 36, when the Lord Chief Justice pointed out that a trial judge has a duty to see that justice is done, which means that he has to see that the system operated fairly, not only to defendants, but also to the prosecution and witnesses.

Video links

9.160 Advances in video technology in recent years have led to further reform. Section 32 of the CJA 1988 for the first time permitted certain witnesses, with the leave of the court, to give evidence by live television link. The provision only extended to two categories of persons – those who are outside the UK and children under 14 years where the charge involved a violent offence or children under 17 years where the charge involved a sexual offence. Violent and sexual offences are defined by s 32(2) as offences involving assault on, or injury or a threat of injury to, a person; offences under s 1 of the CYPA 1933 (cruelty to persons under 16); offences under the SOA 1956, ICA 1960, SOA 1967, s 54 of the Criminal Law Act 1977 or the Protection of Children Act 1978; and attempting or conspiring to commit, or aiding, abetting, counselling procuring or inciting the commission of any of these offences. The provisions are available to trials on indictment in the Crown Court, proceedings in Youth Court and appeals to the Court of Appeal. Video link systems have been set up in Crown Courts throughout the country so that child witnesses can sit in a separate room in the court building that is linked by closed circuit television to the courtroom. Although the child can be seen on screens in the courtroom, the child can only see the judge, prosecution and defence counsel on a monitor in the room as questions are being asked. An evaluation of the video link for child witnesses was conducted 2 years after its introduction and concluded that the link enjoyed widespread acceptance amongst all those with experience of its use (*An Evaluation of the Live Link for Child Witnesses* (Home Office, 1991)). The research found that the majority of child witnesses (76 per cent) were able to give evidence without being reduced to tears at any point and only one child was visibly distressed at all stages of examination. Unfortunately, very little research had been carried out on children testifying under traditional procedures, so comparison is difficult, but it was generally accepted that video links reduced the stress experienced by the child witness and hence improved the quality of the evidence they were able to give.

9.161 Whilst such a move is to be welcomed in that it undoubtedly alleviates the stress associated with giving evidence in open court and thus hopefully improves the quality of the evidence given, concerns have been expressed about removing the witness from the courtroom. One objection is that by avoiding a direct confrontation with the offender, whether by the use of screens or video links, this could indicate to the jury that the witness has good cause to fear the offender, thereby indicating his guilt. Furthermore, it has been argued that allowing a witness to give evidence via a live link enhances the credibility of the witness (Haugaard and Reppucci (1988)). It is argued that the media bestows prestige and enhances the authority of an individual by legitimising his status, and that such considerations are of particular importance in a trial when the demeanour and credibility of the witness are crucial. Conversely it can be argued that the screen image of a witness lacks the power of the witness's own presence, the offender being more real to the jury as they see him throughout the trial (McKewan (1988)). On occasions it seems that prosecution counsel, when faced with a particularly impressive and resilient witness, have quite deliberately opted for an in-court appearance on the grounds of its greater impact (*An Evauluation of the Child Witnesses*, op cit).

Video-recorded evidence

The Advisory Group on Video Evidence

9.162 During the passage of the CJA 1988 through Parliament an Advisory Group on Video Evidence was set up, chaired by His Honour Judge Thomas Pigot QC. The Group reported in December 1989 (*Report of the Advisory Group on Video Evidence* (Home Office, 1989)) and proposed that the law should be changed so that at trials on indictment for violent and sexual offences, video-recorded interviews with children should be admissible in criminal trials. A scheme was suggested whereby the child would not be involved in the actual trial of the offender. The Advisory Group envisaged that an interview with the child would be video-recorded and the trial judge would subsequently rule on the admissibility of the video in place of the child's evidence-in-chief at a pre-trial application. The defendant's right to cross-examine the child would then be retained by holding a preliminary hearing which would be held in less formal, more comfortable surroundings than the courtroom, with only the judge, counsel for each side, the child and either a parent or supporter present. The defendant would be able to hear and view the proceedings through closed circuit television or a one-way mirror and would be able to communicate with his counsel in order to direct him or her to put any required questions to the child. At the preliminary hearing, any video recordings which had been allowed in evidence would be shown to the child witness, who may be asked to expand on certain aspects of it. The child would then usually be cross-examined by defence counsel. The Advisory Group emphasised that these proceedings should be as informal as possible, and that the judge should control cross-examination with special care. The preliminary hearing would itself be video-recorded. At the eventual trial, the initial video-recorded interview would be shown at the point in which the child would tradition-ally give evidence-in-chief and the video-recording of the preliminary hearing would be shown at the time when cross-examination would usually follow. The Advisory Group also expressed the opinion that, once the recommendations in relation to child witnesses had been implemented, a high priority should then attach to extending the new measures to vulnerable adult witnesses, such as the elderly, handicapped or badly traumatised. If this proved not to be possible within a reasonable time, the Group thought that priority should be given to victims of serious sexual offences, who were said to face special and generally recognised difficulties.

Evidence-in-chief and the CJA 1991

9.163 The recommendations of the Advisory Group were generally greeted with hope and enthusiasm, but when the CJA 1991 was introduced, those who had anticipated full implementation of the proposals were disappointed. The Act amended the CJA 1988 to allow a video-recording of an interview conducted with a child witness and which related to any matter in the proceedings, to be given in evidence with the leave of the court, as an exception to the hearsay rule. The same restrictions apply regarding the court, the age of the child and the offence charged as apply to the use of giving evidence via a video link. But the video-recording can only be admitted at the actual trial, no provision was made in the CJA 1991 for a preliminary hearing to be held. Furthermore, the video will only be admitted if the child is available for cross-examination at the trial. The cross-examination can, of course, be conducted via a live video link, but nevertheless the child is still required to be in court on the day of the trial – something which many reformers had hoped to avoid.

9.164 Research indicates that the main benefit of allowing video-recorded evidence in court is the reduced stress on child witnesses (*Video Taping Children's Evidence: An Evaluation* (Home Office, 1995)), although concerns have been expressed that its use means that the child is precipitated straight into court for cross-examination – 'the nastiest bit of the court appearance' (J Spencer, the *Guardian*, 17 August 1994). The CJA 1991 prevented the child being examined in chief on any matter which in the opinion of the court had been dealt with in the recorded testimony (s 32A(5)), which was initially interpreted by some judges to mean that the child could not be asked any friendly questions by prosecuting counsel as a 'warm-up' to cross-examination. This problem was alleviated by s 51 of the CJPOA 1994 which amended the legislation so that a child could be questioned on any matter not *adequately* dealt with in the recorded testimony. Following the CJA 1991, it seems that the practice of admitting video-recordings is by no means universal. Between October 1992 and June 1994, 1,199 trials took place in England and Wales involving child witnesses. From these, there were 640 applications to admit video-recorded interviews, 470 applications were granted, but in only 202 cases was the video known to have been shown in court (*Video Taping Children's Evidence*). In January 1998 the Crown Prosecution Service Inspectorate published a report on its thematic review of cases involving child witnesses, concluding that the quality of video evidence had steadily improved, both technically and in terms of interviewing skills (*The Inspectorate's Report in Cases Involving Child Witnesses – Thematic Report* (Crown Prosecution Service Inspectorate, 1998)).

'*Speaking up for justice*': other vulnerable witnesses in the criminal justice system

9.165 The initial impetus for making it easier for witnesses to give evidence in court came from the growing acknowledgement of the existence of child abuse as a serious problem in society and the realisation that children, even at a very young age, could make reliable, competent witnesses. Whereas the last decade of the twentieth century saw various measures put in place to alleviate the stress experienced by child witnesses, it was also acknowledged that many adult victims and witnesses find the criminal justice process daunting and stressful, particularly those who are vulnerable because of their personal circumstances, including their relationship with the defendant or because of the nature of certain serious crimes, such as rape. Concerns were also expressed about witnesses with learning difficulties and the intimidation of witnesses. In 1997, the government established an inter-departmental working party to undertake a wide-ranging review on the treatment of vulnerable or intimidated witnesses in the criminal justice system. The group reported in June 1998 (*Speaking Up for Justice* (Home Office, 1998)) and recommended a coherent and integrated scheme to provide appropriate support and assistance for vulnerable or intimidated witnesses, with proposals covering the investigation stage, pre-trial support, the trial and beyond.

Youth Justice and Criminal Evidence Act 1999

9.166 Part II of the YJCEA 1999 contains those recommendations of *Speaking up for Justice* which require legislation. Many of these provisions replace the provisions of the CJA 1988 and the CJA 1991 which made special provision for child witnesses. The YJCEA 1999 makes provision for a magistrates' court, Youth Court, the Crown Court or the Criminal Division of the Court of Appeal to make a special measures direction in relation to certain witnesses in order to improve the quality of their evidence. Such measures were implemented in relation to all courts except the magistrates' courts on 24 July 2002 (see Home Office Circulars 6, 35 and 38 of 2002).

Eligible witnesses

9.167 Sections 16 and 17 of the YJCEA 1999 provide that witnesses other than the accused will be eligible for special measures if:

- they are aged under 17;
- they suffer from a mental disorder, mental impairment or significant learning disability which the court considers likely to affect the quality of their evidence;
- they suffer from a physical disorder or disability which the court considers likely to affect the quality of their evidence; or
- the court is satisfied that the witnesses are likely, because of their own circumstances and the circumstances relating to the case, to suffer fear or distress in giving evidence to an extent that is expected to affect its quality.

9.168 Thus witnesses under the age of 17 will always be considered eligible. In other cases, in deciding eligibility, the court must consider any views expressed by the witness. In determining whether the fear and stress of a witness is likely to affect the quality of the evidence given, the court must take into account in particular:

– the nature and alleged circumstances of the offence to which the proceedings relate;
– the age of the witness;
– where relevant the social and cultural background and ethnic origins of the witness, the domestic and employment circumstances of the witness, and any religious beliefs or political opinions of the witness;
– any behaviour towards the witness on the part of the accused, members of the family or associates of the accused, or any other person who is likely to be an accused or witness in the proceedings.

Victims of sexual offences

9.169 Where the witness is a complainant in respect of a sexual offence, the witness is eligible for assistance unless the court is informed that the witness does not wish to be so eligible (YJCEA 1999, s 17(4)). A sexual offence is defined as:

– rape or burglary with intent to rape;
– an offence under any of ss 2–12 and 14–17 of the SOA 1956;
– an offence under s 128 of the Mental Health Act 1959;
– an offence under s 1 of the ICA 1960; and
– an offence under s 54 of the Criminal Law Act 1977.

Special measures directions

Evidence given in private

9.170 Section 25 of the YJCEA 1999 provides that, if the proceedings relate to a sexual offence or it appears to the court that there are reasonable grounds for believing that any person other than the accused has sought, or will seek, to intimidate the witness in connection with testifying in the proceedings, a special measures direction may include a provision that certain people be excluded from the courtroom while the witness gives evidence. The direction will describe individuals or groups of people who are to be excluded although, for obvious reasons, the accused, legal representatives and any interpreters may not be excluded. The court must also allow at least one member of the press to remain if one has been nominated by the press. The freedom of any member of the press who is excluded from the courtroom to report the case will be unaffected, unless a reporting restriction is imposed separately.

Removal of wigs and gowns

9.171 If the trial takes place on indictment, the judge and counsel will usually be attired in wigs and gowns. Whilst many witnesses expect this, and indeed it may even make the court appearance more 'exciting' in that it reminds them of courtroom dramas portrayed on the television, the wigs and gowns can be intimidating for some witnesses. The court has always had a discretion to order the removal of wigs and gowns, and indeed has often done so in the case of child witnesses. The discretion is now placed on a statutory basis in that a special measures direction may provide for the wearing of wigs or gowns to be dispensed with during the giving of an eligible witness's evidence (YJCEA 1999, s 26).

Screening witness from accused

9.172 Although the Court of Appeal has given formal approval for the use of screens to shield a child witness, it has also made clear that, whereas it was permissible to use screens in the case of adult witnesses if it was otherwise impossible to do justice, such a course should be adopted only in the most exceptional cases (R v *Schaub and Cooper (Joey)* [1994] Crim LR 531). The discretion of the court to give leave for the use of screens has now been placed on a statutory basis by s 23 of the YJCEA 1999. A special measures direction may provide for the witness, while giving testimony or being sworn in court, to be prevented by means of a screen or other arrangement from seeing the defendant. However, the witness must be able to see, and be seen by, the persons judging the case (the judge, magistrates or jury) and by at least one legal representative of the prosecution and defence.

Evidence by live link

9.173 The apparent success of video links resulted in pressure for the provision to be extended to other witnesses who may benefit. As a result, a special measures direction may now provide for an eligible witness to give evidence by means of a live link (s 24). As such special measures may now also be used in the magistrates' court, this greatly extends the potential use of video links. In order to address some of the concerns raised in relation to the use of video links by child witnesses, s 32 of the YJCEA 1999 provides that where, at a trial on indictment, evidence has been given in accordance with a special measures direction, the judge must give the jury such warning (if any) as he considers necessary to ensure that the fact that the direction was given in relation to the witness does not prejudice the offender.

Video-recorded evidence-in-chief

9.174 Section 27 of the YJCEA 1999 provides that a special measures direction may provide for a video-recording of an interview of the witness to be admitted as evidence-in-chief of the witness, both at the trial and for the purposes of committal proceedings. The recording can be edited or excluded if the interests of justice so require. If a direction is made for a recording to be shown to the court, the court can later exclude the recording if there is not enough information about how and where the recording was made or if the witness who made the recording is not available for further questioning (whether by video, in court or by live link) and the parties have not agreed that this is unnecessary. The video-recording forms the whole of a witness's evidence-in-chief unless the witness is asked to give evidence about matters not covered in the recorded interview or the court gives permission for the witness to be asked further questions about matters not covered adequately in the recorded interview.

9.175 Thus, following the enactment of the YJCEA 1999, all eligible witnesses may have their evidence-in-chief replaced by a video-recorded interview, thereby enhancing the quality of their evidence and also reducing the stress traditionally associated with giving evidence in court. In order to address the problem of sworn evidence, when a video-recording is made of an interview with a witness aged 14 or over then, in anticipation of the recording being admitted as evidence-in-chief, the witness should swear an oath at the beginning of the interview, if someone is available to administer the oath and they are capable of being sworn. If an oath is not taken, the evidence admitted will be evidence given unsworn.

Video-recorded cross-examination or re-examination

9.176 Section 28 of the YJCEA 1999 provides that, where the court has already allowed a video-recording to be admitted as the witness's evidence-in-chief, the witness may be cross-examined before trial and the cross-examination, and any subsequent re-examination, recorded on video for use at trial.

9.177 The cross-examination will not be recorded in the physical presence of the defendant, although he will have to be able to see and hear the cross-examination and be able to communicate with his legal representative. The recording may, but need not, take place in the physical presence of the judge or magistrates and the defence and prosecution legal representatives, although all these individuals must be able to see and hear the witness being cross-examined and communicate with anyone who is in the room with the witness, such as an intermediary. Witnesses who have been cross-examined on video may not be cross-examined again unless the court makes a direction permitting another video-recorded cross-examination. The court will only do so if the subject of the proposed cross-examination is relevant to the trial and something which the party seeking to cross-examine did not know about at the time of the original cross-examination and could not have reasonably found out about by then, or if it is otherwise in the interests of justice to do so.

9.178 The video-recording of cross-examination as permitted by the YJCEA 1999 attracted strong opposition during the passage of the legislation through Parliament. Although the provisions were welcomed by the NSPCC, who had been calling for the implementation of the remaining recommendations from the Advisory Group on Video Evidence for some years, The Law Society, the law reform pressure group, Justice, and the civil liberties pressure group, Liberty, all expressed concern (Research Paper 99/40 (Home Affairs Section, House of Commons Library, 1999)). Whilst the principle of cross-examining vulnerable witnesses outside the courtroom was generally accepted, it was argued that this would only be feasible during the course of the trial itself. Liberty argued that effective cross-examination of a witness was dependent on the evidence of other witnesses, which would only be put to proof and therefore fully available at the trial. To allow for cross-examination of a witness prior to trial would arguably place that witness's evidence in a different position to that of other witnesses and would be in breach of Article 6. Furthermore, both Liberty and Justice pointed out that provision for re-opening cross-examination of the witness at a later date if necessary illustrated the practical difficulties which may occur if, as anticipated, there were many applications to do so. The government's response to such arguments was pragmatic. Acknowledging that there would inevitably be cases where the defence would only be ready or willing to cross-examine witnesses shortly before a trial begins, Lord Williams of Mostyn pointed out that 'unless we start, we shall get nowhere' (HL Deb, vol 596, col 376, 1 February 1999). Clearly, the provisions have the potential to benefit some cases. If there are genuine reasons why cross-examination cannot take place before the trial without prejudicing the defence case, then little more can be done – vulnerable witnesses can at least have the benefit of other special measures available at the trial. The real concern is that the defence will be tempted to use delaying tactics to defeat the objective of the legislation. The courts will need to be alive to this possibility and take active steps to ensure that such abuse of the system does not occur to the detriment of vulnerable witnesses.

Use of intermediaries and aids to communication

9.179 The provision of special measures, such as the use of screens or video-recorded testimony, will undoubtedly enhance the quality of the evidence given by many witnesses, whilst at the same time making the whole experience less traumatic for them. Yet it is acknowledged that there will continue to be a small number of witnesses who, although competent to give evidence, nevertheless have difficulty communicating in the usual way. This may be because the witness is very young or suffers from a disability which affects his ability to communicate. In 1989 the Advisory Group on Video Evidence recommended that a trial judge should be able to make special arrangements for the examination of very young or very disturbed children, extending where necessary to allowing the relaying of questions from counsel through a paediatrician, child psychiatrist, social worker or person who enjoys the child's confidence. The Advisory Group recognised that this would be a substantial change and that there would be unease at the prospect of interposing a third party between advocate and witness. The dissenting member of the Group believed that the intervention of a specialist interlocutor would hinder rather than assist counsel in conducting the case – inevitably some of counsel's forensic skills, timing and intonation would be lost. The recommendation of the majority was not enacted in CJA 1991, but the issue was returned to by the Working Group in 1998 when it was pointed out that, in addition to the potential use of intermediaries in communicating with children, there may be adult vulnerable witnesses with language and comprehension difficulties who could also benefit from the assistance of an intermediary in relaying questions. However, the Group expressed reservations about the use of an intermediary in interpreting the witness's reply to the court.

9.180 Sections 29 and 30 of the YJCEA 1999 provide that a special measures direction may provide for any examination of the witness (however and wherever conducted) to be conducted through an interpreter or intermediary, and may provide for the witness to be provided with any aid to communication that the court considers appropriate. An intermediary is someone whom the court approves to communicate to the witness the questions the court, the defence and the prosecution ask, and then communicate the answers the witness gives in reply. The intermediary will be allowed to explain questions and answers if that is necessary to enable the witness and the court to communicate. The aids to communication are intended to be aids to overcoming physical disabilities with understanding or answering questions, such as sign-boards and communication aids; the provision is not intended to cover devices for disguising speech.

9.181 However, intermediaries and aids to communication are only available to witnesses eligible for special measures due to their age, or because they suffer from a mental disorder, mental impairment, significant learning disability or physical disorder or disability which the court considers likely to affect the quality of their evidence (s 18(1)). Thus the measures may prove valuable for child witnesses, but adult witnesses are excluded unless they suffer from a relevant disability.

Implementation of the YJCEA 1999

9.182 Special measures directions were introduced in the Crown Court in July 2002 allowing:

- the use of screens (YJCEA 1999, s 23);
- the exclusion of certain people from the courtroom (YJCEA 1999, s 25);
- the removal of wigs and gowns (YJCEA 1999, s 26);

–   evidence by live link for all eligible witnesses (YJCEA 1999, s 32);
–   video-recorded evidence-in-chief for witnesses eligible by virtue of age or
     disability (YJCEA 1999, s 27).

It is anticipated that pilot studies on the use of intermediaries will begin by
December 2002 and a study on the best way to introduce video-recorded pre-
trial cross-examination is planned (*Home Office Press Release* 211/2002). In
magistrates' courts, TV links and video-recorded evidence for child witnesses
in certain cases were introduced in July 2002 and it is anticipated that most of
the other measures will be extended to magistrates' courts in 2003/04,
following evaluation of how the measures are working in the Crown Court.

Preparing young witnesses for court

9.183   National Standards on preparing young witnesses for court have been
agreed by the Home Office, LCD, CPS, DOH, Childline and the NSPCC,
The Law Society and the Criminal Bar Association. These are published in
Volume 3 Appendices of *Achieving the Best Evidence in Criminal Proceedings*
(Home Office, 2001), at Appendix J. Volume 2 of *Achieving the Best Evidence*
contains guidance on witness support and preparation for children and
includes the following suggestions.

Memory refreshing (paras 4.33–4.38)

9.184   Witnesses generally are entitled to be shown a copy of their statement
before being called to give evidence. The videotape is commonly used to
refresh a young witness's memory before the trial – the equivalent of reading
the statement beforehand. Viewing the video ahead of time in more informal
surroundings helps young witnesses 'get over' seeing themselves on the screen
and makes it more likely that they will concentrate on the contents. It is not
satisfactory to show the video for the purpose of refreshing on the day of the
trial, and before the young witness watches it again with the jury, as most
young witnesses find it difficult to concentrate through two viewings on the
same day.

The young witness's preparation for court

9.185   As well as Volume 2 of *Achieving the Best Evidence* giving similar advice at
para 4.51, the Bar Code of Conduct states that 'it is a responsibility of a
barrister, especially when the witness is nervous, vulnerable or apparently the
victim of criminal or similar conduct, to ensure that those facing unfamiliar
court proceedings are put as much at ease as possible'. The Code supports the
view that it is of benefit to young witnesses to meet both prosecuting and
defence advocates before trial, providing there is no discussion of the
evidence. Meetings with advocates go some way to demystifying the court
process for the young witness. Experience suggests that meeting the judge

before the case starts can also have this effect. Putting young witnesses more at ease assists them to give best evidence.

Breaks for young witnesses (para 4.54)

9.186 Although judges and lawyers should invite young witnesses to tell the court when they need a break, or should tell them how to use a touch card where one is available in court, young witnesses' ability to identify when this is necessary should not be relied on. The prosecution should provide information, from home or school, bearing in mind that it is likely to be shorter in the stressful atmosphere of the court. This will enable the judges and advocates to plan breaks in the young witness's testimony. Planned breaks are less likely to occur at a time that would favour one side over another.

Case management

9.187 Cases need to be managed robustly to ensure that the case is ready for trial. The commitment to give high priority to child abuse cases is contained in many documents, including the Victim's Charter.

Defence witnesses

9.188 Although most witnesses give evidence on behalf of the prosecution, arrangements for preparation and pre-trial court visits should also be made available on request to young witnesses called by the defence.

SENTENCING

9.189 With the exception of the offence of murder, which carries a mandatory sentence of life imprisonment, each offence has a prescribed maximum penalty, but no minimum penalty. Thus the court exercises an element of discretion in determining the appropriate sentence to be passed when a defendant is convicted. However, the court's discretion must be exercised within the legislative framework which is now set out in the PCC(S)A 2000. The basic principle underlying the sentencing framework is that of proportionality – that those convicted of criminal offences are punished justly and suitably according to the seriousness of their offences. However, those convicted of violent or sexual offences may be sentenced to longer custodial sentences if it is thought to be necessary to protect the public from serious harm.

Custodial sentences

Criteria for custody

9.190 Section 79 of the PCC(S)A 2000 provides that, where a person is convicted of an offence punishable with a custodial sentence other than one fixed by law or under the provisions of the Act which require an automatic life penalty for a second 'serious' offence (s 109) or minimum custodial sentences for third convictions for drug trafficking (s 110) or domestic burglary (s 111), the court cannot pass a custodial sentence on the offender unless one of two conditions is satisfied:

–   the court is of the opinion that the offence, or combination of the offence and one or more offences associated with it, was so serious that only such a sentence can be justified for the offence (s 79(2)(a)); or
–   where the offence is a violent or sexual offence, the court is of the opinion that only such a sentence would be adequate to protect the public from serious harm from him (s 79(2)(b)).

Length of custodial sentence

9.191 The PCC(S)A 2000 also lays down specific criteria for the proper determination of the length of any custodial sentence imposed. The Act provides that the custodial sentence shall be:

–   for such term (not exceeding the permitted maximum) as in the opinion of the court is commensurate with the seriousness of the offence, or the combination of the offence and one or more offences associated with it (s 80(2)(a)); or
–   where the offence is a violent or sexual offence, for such longer term (not exceeding that maximum) as in the opinion of the court is necessary to protect the public from serious harm from the offender (s 80(2)(b)).

Abusers and custodial sentences

9.192 The majority of abusers who receive a custodial sentence will receive a commensurate sentence, based on the seriousness of their offence or offences. The PCC(S)A 2000 does not define the word 'serious', although several of its provisions govern the way in which the seriousness of the offence is considered:

–   the sentencer is required to have regard to mitigating and aggravating factors which impinge upon offence seriousness (s 81(4)(a));
–   the sentencer is permitted to take account of any other mitigating factor (s 158(1));
–   the sentencer may take into account any previous convictions of the offender or any failure of his to respond to previous sentences (s 151(1));
–   the sentencer is required to treat offending while on bail as an aggravating feature (s 151(2)); and
–   when an offender has pleaded guilty, the sentencer is required to take into account the stage in the proceedings for the offence at which the

offender indicated his intention to plead guilty and the circumstances in which this indication was given (s 152).

9.193 In cases of intra-familial abuse, the abuse of a position of trust which is inevitably involved, combined with the vulnerability of the child victim is likely to be an aggravating factor. If the defendant pleads guilty at an early stage in the proceedings, thus obviating the need for the child to give evidence in court, this will be a mitigating factor.

'Dangerous' offenders: violent and sexual offences

9.194 However, child abusers will invariably be convicted of violent or sexual offences, and may therefore be 'dangerous' offenders to whom the usual restrictions on custodial sentences do not apply. A violent offence is defined to mean an offence which leads, or is intended or likely to lead, to a person's death or to physical injury to a person (s 161(3)). A sexual offence includes offences under the SOA 1956 (other than an offence under ss 30, 31 or 33–36 of that Act), s 128 of the Mental Health Act 1959, the ICA 1960, s 54 of the Criminal Law Act 1977, or the Protection of Children Act 1978; an offence of burglary with intent to rape under s 9 of the Theft Act 1968; and conspiracy, attempts and incitements to commit any of these offences (PCC(S)A 2000, s 161(2)).

Serious harm

9.195 References to protecting the public from serious harm from an offender are to be construed as references to protecting members of the public from death or serious personal injury, whether physical or psychological, occasioned by further such offences committed by him (s 161(4)). However, PCC(S)A 2000 makes no mention of the likelihood of risk which must be perceived by the sentencer before the provisions of s 79(2)(b) can be relied upon and does not require a court to consider psychiatric or psychological reports. It will be sufficient if an individual or a small group of people are at risk of serious harm (*R v Hashi* (1994) 16 Cr App R (S) 121) and, in determining whether the harm to the public will be serious, the sentencer can have regard to the vulnerability of particular potential victims, for example children who may be in need of protection from a paedophile (*R v Bowler* (1994) 15 Cr App R (S) 78).

9.196 The only statutory restriction placed on the length of a sentence imposed under s 80(2)(b) is that it must be within the statutory maximum for the offence. The court is required to explain in open court that it is of the opinion that s 80(2)(b) applies and why it is of that opinion, and it must explain to the offender in open court and in ordinary language why the sentence is for such a term (s 80(3)). The decisions of the Court of Appeal provide some guidance on the correct approach to take to the calculation of the appropriate length of sentence, but this guidance has remained at a fairly general level. The usual approach is first to calculate what the proportionate sentence would be based on the seriousness of the offence and then to add the period of detention deemed to be necessary for public protection. This latter calculation will inevitably be greatly influenced by the sentencer's prediction of the risk posed by the offender. The Court of Appeal has made it clear that some element of proportionality should be retained (R *v Mansell* (1994) 15 Cr App R (S) 844, R *v Crowe and Pennington* [1994] Crim LR 958), and thus a sentence under s 80(2)(b) should not be out of all proportion to the sentence which would be imposed under s 80(2)(a), ie one commensurate with the seriousness of the offence. The Court of Appeal has indicated that factors which would normally mitigate the sentence should be given less weight when considering a sentence under s 80(2)(b) than when considering a sentence under s 80(2)(a) (R *v Walsh* (1995) 16 Cr App R (S) 204). However, in many cases factors which mitigate the seriousness of the offence will also affect the risk posed by the individual offender and will thus have been taken into account, both in deciding whether a custodial sentence was justified in the first place and in determining whether a longer sentence is necessary for public protection.

Abusers and extended sentences

9.197 All prisoners given a custodial sentence of 12 months or more will be subject to a period on licence following their release, during which time they will be supervised by the Probation Service in order to help them adjust to life in the community and address their offending behaviour. Those who commit violent or sexual offences on or after 30 September 1998 and are subsequently convicted of the offence may be given an extended sentence if the court is satisfied that the normal period of supervision to which they would be subject would not be adequate to prevent the commission of further offences or to secure their rehabilitation (PCC(S)A 2000, s 85). The extended sentence consists of two distinct components: the custodial term and the extension period. The custodial term may be either a commensurate sentence imposed under s 80(2)(a) or a longer than commensurate sentence passed under s 80(2)(b). The defendant will be released at the end of the custodial term in the same way as other defendants, but he will be subject to licence, and thus supervision, for the whole of the extension period and will be liable to be recalled to custody at any time up to the end of that period. The length of the combined custodial term and extension period must not exceed the maximum term permitted for the offence. Subject to this, the extension period itself may not exceed 10 years in the case of a sexual offence and 5 years in the case of a violent offence. Extended sentences may not be passed on violent offenders if the custodial term imposed is less than 4 years.

Community sentences

9.198 The PCC(S)A 2000 creates a threshold provision for community sentences, similar to that created for the imposition of custodial sentences. A community sentence may only be imposed if the sentencer is of the opinion that the offence, or the combination of the offence and one or more offences associated with it, was serious enough to warrant such a sentence (s 35). Once the threshold criterion has been satisfied, the sentencer must choose the community order or orders which are thought to be most suitable for the defendant, and must ensure that the restrictions on the liberty of the defendant are commensurate with the seriousness of the offence or offences. In deciding whether a community sentence is justified and whether the restrictions on the liberty of the defendant are commensurate with the seriousness of the offence, the sentencer *must* take into account all such information about the circumstances of the offence or offences as is available and, in deciding which order or orders are most suitable for the defendant, the sentencer *may* take into account any information about the defendant which is before the court (s 36). A community sentence consists of one or more of the following community orders.

9.199 *Community rehabilitation orders* (formerly probation orders): a court may make a community rehabilitation order on defendants aged 16 or over if it is of the opinion that the supervision of the defendant is desirable in the interests of securing his rehabilitation or protecting the public from harm from him or preventing the commission by him of further offences (PCC(S)A 2000, s 41). The order must last for not less than 6 months and not more than 3 years. It may include various requirements with which the defendant must comply, such as requirements as to residence, attendance at a probation centre and treatment for mental conditions and for drug and alcohol dependency, as listed in Sch 2 to the PCC(S)A 2000.

9.200 *Drug treatment and testing orders*: if the court is satisfied that a defendant aged 16 or over is dependent on or has a propensity to misuse drugs and that his dependency or propensity is such as requires or may be susceptible to treatment, a drug treatment and testing order can be made (PCC(S)A 2000, s 52). There need be no causal link between the dependency or misuse and the offence committed. The order has effect for a period specified in the order, of not less than 6 months or more than 3 years, and the offender must consent to the making of the order. The order includes a requirement that the defendant must submit to treatment, which may include residential treatment by or under the direction of a specified person with a view to the reduction or elimination of the offender's dependency on or propensity to misuse drugs. The order also includes a testing requirement which requires the defendant to provide a specified minimum number of samples during the period of the order. Throughout the period of the order, the defendant will be placed under the supervision of a probation officer whose role is to supervise the offender to the extent necessary to enable him to report on the offender's progress to the court, and to report to the court any failure by the defendant to comply with the requirements of the order and matters relating to revocation or amendment of the order. The order cannot be made at the same time as a custodial sentence, but can be combined with other community orders, such as community rehabilitation orders and curfew orders. Section 47 of the CJCSA 2000 gave the courts a further power to make a *drug abstinence order* in relation to defendants aged 18 or over. The order requires the defendant to abstain from using class A drugs and to provide, when instructed to do so, a sample for the purpose of ascertaining whether he has any specified class A drug in his body.

9.201 *Community punishment orders* (formerly community service orders): a community punishment order is an order which requires the defendant to perform unpaid work in the community for not less than 40 and not more than 240 hours (PCC(S)A 2000, s 46). The court may only make the order where it is satisfied that the defendant, who must be 16 or over, is a suitable person to perform work under such an order. A community punishment order may, on occasion, be appropriate in a case involving violence, as long as the violence is not serious (*R v Hefron* (1980) 2 Cr App R (S) 230). However, if the defendant has been convicted of an offence against a child, careful consideration must be given to the kind of work he is required to do in the community. In particular, concern has been expressed about the suitability of a community punishment order for sex offenders as it contains no provision to address the sexual offending, but yet leaves sex offenders in the community (*Exercising Constant Vigilance: The Role of the Probation Service in Protecting the Public from Sex Offenders* (Home Office, 1998), para 1.11).

9.202 *Community punishment and rehabilitation orders* (formerly combination orders): as the name suggests, this order combines the requirements of a community rehabilitation order and a community punishment order. The supervision period must last for not less than 12 months and not more than 3 years and the number of hours' work must be not less than 40 nor more than 100 (PCC(S)A 2000, s 51).

9.203 *Curfew orders:* a curfew order requires the defendant to remain at a specified place for between 2 and 12 hours on any days over a period which must not exceed 6 months from the date when the order was made (or 3 months if the defendant is under 16 years) (PCC(S)A 2000, s 37). The order may also include requirements for electronic monitoring in order to keep a check upon the defendant's whereabouts.

9.204 *Supervision orders:* the Youth Court or the Crown Court can make an order placing a defendant under the age of 18 years under the supervision of a local authority, a probation officer or a member of a YOT for a period of up to 3 years (PCC(S)A 2000, s 63).

9.205 *Attendance centre orders:* a court may make an attendance centre order in relation to a defendant under the age of 21 who has been convicted of an imprisonable offence provided that the court has been notified that there is a suitable centre for him to attend (PCC(S)A 2000, s 62).

9.206 *Action plan orders:* the Crown Court and the Youth Court may make an action plan order in relation to a defendant under the age of 18 (PCC(S)A 2000, ss 69–71). The order requires the defendant to comply for a period of 3 months with an action plan which lays down certain requirements about his actions and whereabouts. The defendant will be under the supervision of a probation officer for the period of the order.

Absolute and conditional discharges

9.207 If any court feels that it is inexpedient to inflict punishment on a defendant, of whatever age, the court may make an order either discharging him absolutely or, if the court thinks fit, discharging him subject to the condition that he commits no offence within a specified period, which must not exceed 3 years (PCC(S)A 2000, s 12).

Sentencing young offenders

9.208 For the purposes of sentencing, the age of the young offender and the sentence imposed will determine whether or not he is treated as an adult. The underlying principles of sentencing of young offenders are the same as for adult offenders, although a wider range of orders is available in the Youth Court, which will generally hear cases involving offenders under the age of 18 years, and there are restrictions and limitations on the use of some orders by the Youth Court. Thus a sentence passed on a defendant of any age must generally be commensurate with the seriousness of the offence, or offences associated with it, or, in the case of a custodial sentence imposed for a violent or sexual offence, only such a sentence would be adequate to protect the public from serious harm from the defendant. However, a court is also required to have regard to the welfare of any child or young person brought before it, either as an offender or otherwise, and must in a proper case take steps for removing him from undesirable surroundings, and for securing that proper provision is made for his education and training (CYPA 1933, s 44). There is no statutory guidance on the interaction of the often competing welfare and just deserts considerations and so, when a court is dealing with an offender under the age of 18, it must itself decide what weight to give to each in a given case and deal with any resulting tensions (see Gordon et al (1999)).

Young offenders and custodial sentences

9.209 The basic criteria for custody for both young offenders and adults are the same, but there is a different scheme of custodial provision. The age of the young offender is crucial. An offender under the age of 21 years may not currently be sentenced to imprisonment, but there are alternative custodial sentences available, depending on the age of the offender.

Offenders aged 18–20 years

9.210 When s 61 of the CJCSA 2000 is brought into force, imprisonment will become the standard custodial sentence for offenders aged 18–20 inclusive as well as for offenders aged 21 and over. At present, offenders aged 18 or over but under 21 when they commit the offence of murder must be sentenced to custody for life (PCC(S)A 2000, s 93). Those convicted of an offence punishable with a maximum of life imprisonment for those over the age of 21 years, may be sentenced to custody for life if the court thinks that such a sentence would be appropriate (PCC(S)A 2000, s 94). In other cases, if a custodial sentence is justified the young offender will be sentenced to detention in a young offender institute (PCC(S)A 2000, s 96). The minimum term is 21 days' detention but the only maximum term is that which can be imposed for the offence itself.

Young offenders under 18 years

9.211 Young offenders convicted of murder who were under the age of 18 at the time of the offence are sentenced to detention during Her Majesty's pleasure (PCC(S)A 2000, s 90, which replaces the previous provisions under s 53 of the CYPA 1933). Those convicted following trial on indictment at the Crown Court of an offence punishable in the case of a person aged 21 or over with imprisonment for 14 years or more, or an offence of indecent assault on a man or woman (see para **9.142**) may be sentenced to detention for a fixed term, not exceeding the maximum for the offence.

Detention and training orders

9.212 In all other cases where a custodial sentence is justified, following the implementation of ss 100–107 of the PCC(S)A 2000 on 1 April 2000, the sentence that the court is to pass is a detention and training order. The order replaces the sentences of detention in a young offender institution and secure training orders for offenders under the age of 18 years. The order can be made in respect of:

- 15–17-year-olds for any imprisonable offence which is so serious as to justify a custodial sentence;
- 12–14-year-olds who, in the opinion of the court, are persistent offenders;

–   10- and 11-year-olds where, in the opinion of the court, only a custodial
     sentence would be adequate to protect the public from further offending
     by him and the offence was committed on or after such date as the
     Secretary of State may by order appoint.

The term of the order can be 4, 6, 8, 10, 12, 18 or 24 months, although the
total length of the order must not exceed the maximum term of imprisonment
that a Crown Court could impose on an adult offender (s 101). The order will
usually be divided equally between time spent in detention and training, on the
one hand, and supervision on the other (s 102).

Young offenders and community sentences

9.213 Community rehabilitation orders, drug testing and treatment orders,
community punishment orders, community punishment and rehabilitation
orders and curfew orders are available for 16- and 17-year-old offenders in the
same way as they are for adult offenders. Attendance centre orders are
available for offenders under the age of 21. Supervision orders and action plan
orders are only available for offenders under the age of 18.

9.214 The Crown Court and Youth Court also have power to impose a
reparation order on defendants under the age of 18 who have been convicted of
any offence except murder (PCC(S)A 2000, ss 73 and 74). The order requires
the defendant to make reparation to the victim or a person otherwise affected
by the offence, or to the community at large. A reparation order is not a
community order, and so can be used where the defendant has committed an
offence which is not serious enough to justify the use of a community
sentence.

9.215 Under Part III of the PCC(S)A 2000, a Youth Court or, exceptionally,
an adult magistrates' court, dealing with a defendant under the age of 18 for
his first conviction is in certain circumstances required to sentence the young
offender by ordering him to be *referred to a youth offender panel*. In other
circumstances, the court has a discretion to deal with the defendant in this
way. The youth panel will agree a 'contract' with the defendant and his family
which is aimed at tackling the offending behaviour and its causes (PCC(S)A
2000, ss 16 and 17). Powers to make referral orders have initially been made
available only to certain courts on a pilot basis.

Information available to the sentencer

9.216 Before passing sentence, the court must ensure that it has before it all
relevant information in order to determine the appropriate sentence. If the
defendant pleads not guilty and a full trial takes place, the sentencer (who will
be the magistrates following a summary trial in the magistrates' court or the

judge following a trial on indictment in the Crown Court) will usually be fully aware of the facts of the offence. If the defendant pleads guilty, the prosecuting counsel will summarise the facts of the case. The sentencer will be provided with details of the defendant's antecedent history, which will include a complete record of his criminal history, in some cases dating back many years. Although the provisions of the Rehabilitation of Offenders Act 1975 do not apply to criminal proceedings, the Court of Appeal has recommended that effect should be given to the rationale underlying that Act and reference should not be made to convictions which are 'spent' when that can reasonably be avoided.

Pre-sentence reports

9.217 In many cases, before deciding on the appropriate sentence, the court will obtain a pre-sentence report on the defendant. There is a mandatory requirement to obtain and consider such a report when the offender is under the age of 18 years, unless the offence is triable only on indictment or there is a pre-existing report and the court relies on that report, and, in either case, the court thinks that a report would be unnecessary. Where the defendant is over the age of 18, the court is under a duty to obtain and consider a pre-sentence report before forming an opinion that only a custodial sentence can be justified or before making a community order, unless it is of the opinion that such a report is unnecessary (PCC(S)A 2000, s 81).

Contents of pre-sentence reports

9.218 Pre-sentence reports are prepared by probation officers if the defendant is an adult and by local authority social workers if he is aged under 13. For intermediate ages the work is shared between the probation service and social workers, with social workers generally taking responsibility for the report if a teenage offender or his family are already known to the local authority. The preparation of pre-sentence reports is governed by national standards. A pre-sentence report is made with a view to assisting the court in determining the most suitable method of dealing with a defendant and should address:

- the current offence(s) in the proceedings, summarising the facts and assessing the seriousness of the offender's attitude to the offence(s);
- relevant information about the defendant setting the current offence in context, including his or her previous offending, and strengths and problems; and
- a conclusion and, where relevant, a proposal for the most suitable community sentence.

9.219 In the case of a violent or sexual offence, the information about the defendant should include evidence of the risk to the public of serious harm from the offender. This information may then be used by the sentencer in the process of determining whether a longer than normal sentence can be justified on the grounds of protecting the public from serious harm.

The victim and the sentencing process

9.220 Although traditionally the role of the victim in a criminal trial has been confined to appearing as a witness for the prosecution, in recent years increasing attention has been focused on the needs and rights of victims and their role in the criminal justice process. However, there has been particular controversy over the involvement of victims in the sentencing process, especially in cases of intra-familial child abuse where the offence and resulting sentence may have a considerable effect on the child's welfare. It has been argued that there are three areas which could conceivably permit victims to influence the sentencing decision – victim impact statements, victim forgiveness and the effect of the sentence on the victim (Gillespie (1998)).

9.221 Victim impact statements may be used to provide the sentencer with information about the impact of the offence on the victim, without the need for a further court appearance. Many jurisdictions have made statutory provision for the admission of such statements, some of which require the court to consider such statements before passing sentence. Although no similar statutory provision exists in England and Wales, the Victim's Charter of 1996 formally set out the rights of victims to make a statement explaining how the crime has affected them. The underlying rationale is that the impact of the crime helps to illustrate the totality of the offence. Whether or not the relative resilience of the victim should be a factor affecting the punishment imposed is a matter of some debate, but the 'egg-shell skull' principle, whereby the offender must take his victim as he finds him, has been accepted in our jurisdiction for many years (R v Blaue [1975] 3 All ER 466). The issue is likely to be of specific relevance to sexual and violent offences, where the psychological impact on the victim may be particularly severe. When a defendant has been convicted of rape, the Court of Appeal has made it clear that the offence should be treated as aggravated where the effect upon the victim, whether physical or mental, is of special seriousness (R v Billam (1986) 82 Cr App R 347). More radical versions of victim impact statements admitted in other jurisdictions allow the victim to make 'penal demands' and to express an opinion as to the appropriate sentence to be passed. Whilst the Court of Appeal has made it clear that it is acceptable for a sentencer to consider a victim impact statement before passing sentence, this is to be done for the purpose of ascertaining factual evidence relevant to sentencing and does not extend to allowing the victim to make penal demands.

9.222 In *Attorney General's Reference (No 2 of 1995)* [1996] 1 Cr App R (S) 274, the offender had been convicted of offences of indecency relating to his daughter. In imposing a probation order on the defendant, the trial judge declined to look at a statement made by the daughter as to the impact of the offences on her, taking the view that it was inappropriate to receive evidence which sought to aggravate the impact which the offending had on the victim. On appeal by the Attorney-General, the Court of Appeal varied the sentence to 2 years' imprisonment and expressed the view that it was wholly appropriate that a judge should receive factual information as to the impact of the offending on a victim. Furthermore, the judge was said to be well equipped to know whether the statement put before him contained evidence of fact relevant to sentencing or whether an attempt had been made to try to 'hot up' the case against a defendant. In practice, it appears that victim impact statements seldom influence sentencing decisions. When they do, it is always to increase their severity. Research has shown that most impact information which influences sentences is of a type which is, or should be, already available or is of a type which Crown Court judges often seek at the sentencing stage anyway, leading to the conclusion that support for victim impact statements is largely at the level of rhetoric as distinct from practice (*The Uses of Victim Statements* (Home Office Research Development and Statistics Directorate, December 1999)).

9.223 In cases where there has been a close relationship between the defendant and victim prior to the offence, the victim may well be prepared to forgive the defendant. However, just as the views of the victim, as opposed to the impact of the offence on the victim, will not be allowed to increase the sentence passed, so too the views of the victim should not be allowed to mitigate the sentence. It has been suggested by the Court of Appeal that victim forgiveness can have an effect, albeit an indirect effect, upon the sentencer as the forgiveness may reduce the possibility of re-offending and it may reduce the public outrage which sometimes arises where a defendant has been released into the community early (*R v Darvill* (1987) 9 Cr App R (S) 225). Yet, unless victim forgiveness is taken to reduce the seriousness of the offence, in the case of custodial sentences, these considerations could not effect a sentence imposed under the PCC(S)A 2000, s 80(2)(a), which requires the sentence to be commensurate with the seriousness of the offence. The reduced risk of offending could only affect the imposition of a longer than normal sentence under s 80(2)(b) of the Act.

9.224 The final factor that may influence a sentencer is the effect of the proposed sentence on the victim. In contrast to victim impact statements and taking account of victim forgiveness, whereby the sentencer may be influenced by the harm caused by the offender and by the subjective feelings of the victim, in considering the effect of the sentence on the victim the sentencer is influenced by the potential harm caused to the victim by the criminal justice system rather than the offender. Once again, this will be of particular relevance to cases of intra-familial child abuse, where a custodial sentence imposed on an abusing parent or carer may have an adverse effect on the child. One of the main principles enshrined in the CA 1989 is that children are best cared for by both parents wherever possible. Whilst no one would suggest leaving a child with an abusing parent, in some cases of intra-familial abuse where the offence would ordinarily be sufficiently serious to justify a custodial sentence, a non-custodial sentence with the long-term aim of re-integrating the offender back into the family when he no longer poses a risk to the child, would be the preferred outcome from the child's point of view. In such cases it has been asked whether society is really willing to see a child harmed just so that they can see a parent placed in prison (Gillespie (1998), see para **9.220**). In many cases the answer will inevitably be 'yes'.

Sentencing guidelines

9.225 The appropriate sentence in each case must be determined by reference to the statutory framework, the maximum penalty specified for the offence and the sentencing powers of the court. If a defendant is convicted following summary trial in the magistrates' court, the maximum penalty the court can impose is 6 months' imprisonment and/or a fine. However, no such restrictions are placed on the Crown Court. The following paragraphs contain illustrative examples from the cases of the range of sentences imposed in cases of child abuse.

Physical abuse and neglect

Cruelty to persons aged under 16

9.226 The maximum penalty on conviction on indictment for an offence under s 1 of the CYPA 1933 is 10 years' imprisonment.

Assaults and ill-treatment

9.227 The longest custodial sentences are passed in cases where there has been a sustained period of ill-treatment including deliberate assaults or intentional ill-treatment. If two carers are prosecuted, the court will take account of their respective roles in the abuse. In R v A *(Lavinia)* [1999] 1 Cr App R (S) 240, A pleaded guilty to three counts of cruelty to her child. She had moved in with S, bringing her two young children with her. The older child, aged about 15 months, was subjected to sustained violent treatment. S admitted squeezing the child's head between his legs and A admitted biting her. When the child was taken to hospital she was found to have a fractured skull and irreversible brain damage. She died a few days later and a post-mortem examination disclosed numerous injuries, including bruising consistent with her face having been gripped between fingers and thumbs, and bite marks. S was sentenced to 7 years' imprisonment and A was sentenced to 5 years' imprisonment. S's appeal was dismissed as the Court of Appeal held he had been the dominant partner and his sentence of 7 years was fully justified. However, A's sentence was reduced to 4 years' imprisonment as she was of low mentality and the court felt that insufficient distinction had been drawn between them.

Failure to protect a child from violence

9.228 If a child has been subjected to a sustained period of severe abuse from one carer, and another carer has failed to take steps to protect the child, a substantial custodial sentence is likely. In *R v Creed* [2000] 1 Cr App R (S) 304, C lived with a man who was not her child's father. Over a period of several months the man assaulted the child on a number of occasions. On one occasion C was called home from work and called an ambulance for the child some 30 minutes after she had returned home. The child was taken to hospital but was found to be dead. A post-mortem revealed extensive injuries, including a split liver, which would have caused death within 15 to 20 minutes of its infliction, during which time it would have been obvious that the child was in urgent need of medical attention. The man was convicted of murder and sentenced to life imprisonment. C pleaded guilty to two counts of child cruelty, the prosecution case being that over a period of 7 months she had failed to protect the child from violence and that, on the occasion of the child's death, she had caused unnecessary suffering by the delay in calling for an ambulance. Her sentence of 5 years' imprisonment was upheld by the Court of Appeal, which held that C had acted with utter selfishness, relegating the interests of the child below her own interests in pursuing a relationship with the man.

Neglect

9.229 In many cases, if the defendant does not admit causing physical injury to a child, they may be liable for neglect on the basis of failure to summon medical assistance for the child and sentenced accordingly. In *R v Taggert* [1999] 2 Cr App R (S) 68, the defendant was initially sentenced to 4½ years' imprisonment having pleaded guilty on the basis that he had neglected a child by leaving her unattended in a bath while very hot water was running and that he had then failed to ensure that medical assistance was summoned within an appropriate time. However, the Court of Appeal reduced the sentence to 2½ years' imprisonment, pointing out that this was a case of failure to obtain medical assistance, not a prolonged series of cruel and injurious acts.

Abandonment and exposure

9.230 A custodial sentence will also usually be considered appropriate in cases of abandonment or exposure. In *R v C (Paul John)* [2000] 2 Cr App R (S) 329, S was a mother of three children, aged 13, 9 and 7. She lived with C, who was a drug addict. S and C left the children alone for a period of about 7 hours, during which time the eldest child gained access to C's methadone and subsequently died from pneumonia caused by methadone poisoning. S and C were sentenced to 12 months' imprisonment. In each case the Court of Appeal held that the sentences were not manifestly excessive.

Offences under the Offences Against the Person Act 1861

9.231 The maximum sentence under the OAPA 1861, ss 47 (assault occasioning actual bodily harm) and 20 (inflicting grievous bodily harm) is 5 years' imprisonment, whereas the maximum sentence under s 18 (causing grievous bodily harm with intent) is life imprisonment. These charges may be brought as alternatives to the offence under s 1 of the CYPA 1933 in cases involving the physical ill-treatment of a child, the appropriate charge depending on the severity of the injuries inflicted and the culpability of the defendant.

9.232 In *R v O (David)* [1999] 2 Cr App R (S) 280, O pleaded guilty to assault occasioning actual bodily harm and child cruelty. He lived with a woman who had an 8-year-old son. O returned home after drinking and found the child's room untidy. He assaulted the child over a period of 2 hours, striking him and throwing him about the room. He also put the child's head in a toilet bowl and flushed the toilet. The child was later found to have swellings and bruises consistent with a history of repeated forceful blows. O was sentenced to 2½ years' imprisonment. The Court of Appeal held that this was not a case of a person cracking under domestic or economic pressure. Anyone who used violence of this nature to a child could expect to lose his liberty, and when the violence was prolonged, a substantial period of imprisonment could be expected. However, the sentence was reduced to 21 months' imprisonment as it was held that the sentencer's starting point had been too high and insufficient credit had been given for O's guilty plea.

9.233 Longer custodial sentences will be imposed when the injury is more severe and deliberately caused. The Court of Appeal has made it clear that a sentence of between 4 and 5 years' imprisonment will be appropriate for an isolated incident of causing grievous bodily harm with intent on a baby, by a person of previous good character, which gave rise to an offence under the OAPA 1861, s 18 (*Attorney General's Reference (No 34 of 2000)* (2000) *The Times*, August 23).

Murder and voluntary manslaughter

9.234 A defendant convicted of murder is subject to a mandatory sentence of life imprisonment. Although voluntary manslaughter is committed with the same fault element as murder and the maximum penalty is life imprisonment, the cases in these categories tend to involve strong mitigating factors which are usually reflected in the sentence. In *R v Leggett* [1996] 2 Cr App R (S) 77, the defendant had pleaded guilty to the manslaughter of her 14-month-old baby. Psychiatric reports indicated that she had an immature personality disorder and that at the time of the killing she was in a state of emotional turmoil. A sentence of 4 years' imprisonment was upheld by the Court of Appeal. In R v Yeomans (1988) 10 Cr App R (S) 63 the defendant drowned his 18-month-old daughter in the sea while suffering from acute reactive depression. A sentence of 8 years' imprisonment was reduced to 5 years by the Court of Appeal.

Involuntary manslaughter

9.235 Manslaughter of a young child arising out of the performance of an unlawful dangerous act normally attracts a custodial sentence of between 2 and 8 years, depending upon the degree of culpability. In R v Bashford (1988) 10 Cr App R (S) 359, the child died from violent shaking after persistent crying, but there was no evidence of violence having been used on any other occasion. A sentence of 2 years' imprisonment was upheld by the Court of Appeal. In R v Ali (1988) 10 Cr App R (S) 59, a 4-year-old child had been abused over a lengthy period and died of a fractured skull. The child was found to have a number of other fractures caused on various other occasions. The Court of Appeal upheld a sentence of 8 years' imprisonment. Sentences will rarely be imposed in excess of 8 years. In R v Piggot [1999] 1 Cr App R (S) 392, the defendant had been drinking and admitted striking a 9-month-old baby with the back of his hand or fist when the child kept crying. The child was found to have a head injury consistent with the head having impacted against a hard surface with some force. A sentence of 10 years' imprisonment was found by the Court of Appeal to be excessive and outside the normal sentencing bracket. The sentence was accordingly reduced to 6 years. To date, there have been no appellate cases where liability for a child's death has arisen through gross negligence (see para **9.27**).

Infanticide

9.236 Although the maximum penalty for infanticide is life imprisonment, few defendants receive a custodial sentence as the mitigating factors are frequently overwhelming (see R v Sainsbury (1989) 11 Cr App R(S) 533).

Sexual abuse

Rape

9.237 The maximum penalty for rape is life imprisonment. It has always been regarded as a serious offence and the Court of Appeal has commented on several occasions that, other than in wholly exceptional circumstances, rape calls for an immediate custodial sentence. In 1986 Lord Lane CJ delivered the judgment in R v Billam [1986] 1 WLR 349, giving guidance to trial judges on sentencing offenders convicted of rape. For rape committed by an adult without any aggravating or mitigating factors, a figure of 5 years should be taken as the starting point in a contested case. If aggravating factors are present, such as the man being in a position of responsibility towards the victim, the starting point should be 8 years.

9.238 If further aggravating factors are present, such as the victim being very young, the sentence should be substantially higher than the figure suggested as the starting point. In *Attorney General's Reference (No 8 of 1999)* [2000] 1 Cr App R (S) 56, a defendant was convicted of five counts of rape of his 8-year-old daughter and one rape of the 13-year-old daughter of a friend. The Court of Appeal said that the lowest sentence which could properly have been imposed at trial was 12 years.

9.239 The Court of Appeal has made it clear that, whilst immediate custodial sentences will be appropriate in the vast majority of cases of rape, a non-custodial sentence may be appropriate if there are exceptional circumstances. The case of *R v D* [1996] 1 Cr App R (S) 196, provides a useful illustration of what the court deems to be 'exceptional circumstances'. The defendant had pleaded guilty to rape, indecent assault and incest. He had committed a number of indecent assaults on his sister, who was 2 years younger than him. The assaults included sexual intercourse without consent and were committed over a period of 7 years, beginning when he was 12 years old. The assaults ended in 1992 and the victim confided in her parents the following year. The defendant was initially sentenced to 4 years' imprisonment. On appeal, new evidence was produced in the Court of Appeal which consisted of a letter from the victim, expressing her concern at the sentence and the fact that the defendant was not receiving the treatment he was deemed to be in need of whilst he was in prison, which was having a detrimental effect on the victim's own mental state. The court took the view that this was a case where it was unlikely that the prison sentence would be of assistance to the victim, or to the general public or to the defendant himself. Noting in particular the fact that the prison sentence had a positively adverse effect on the victim, the court felt able to take a 'more merciful' approach and quashed the original sentence, substituting it with a probation order for 2 years, with a condition that the defendant joined an extended group work programme for sex offenders.

Unlawful sexual intercourse

9.240 The maximum sentence for unlawful sexual intercourse is life imprisonment if the girl is aged under 13 and 2 years' imprisonment if the girl is aged under 16. If the girl is aged between 13 and 16 and the defendant is not in a position of trust or authority, in cases where there is a substantial difference in age between the defendant and victim and a custodial sentence is appropriate, on a guilty plea the sentence will be in the region of 6–9 months' imprisonment (*R v Carter* [1997] 1 Cr App R (S) 434). If the offence involved a breach of a position of trust or authority, the appropriate sentence will range between 9 months (*R v Wood* (1990) 12 Cr App R (S) 129) and 18 months (*R v Forsyth* (1987) 9 Cr App R (S) 126). If the girl is aged under 13, the Court of Appeal has emphasised that unlawful sexual intercourse is an extremely serious offence and must remain so, even in the relaxed time in which we live (*R v Bulmer* (1989) 11 Cr App R (S) 586). The age of the girl and her relationship with the defendant will often be the decisive factors in determining the appropriate sentence. In *R v Robertson* (1988) 10 Cr App R (S) 183, the defendant, who had pleaded not guilty, was convicted of four counts of indecent assault and one of unlawful sexual intercourse arising out of conduct with his two stepdaughters on various occasions over a period of years. The Court of Appeal stated that the sentence of 10 years' imprisonment was not wrong in principle, neither was it excessive in the circumstances. At the opposite end of the spectrum, in *R v Brough* [1997] 1 Cr App R (S) 55, the 22-year-old defendant was intellectually impaired and was initially sentenced to 2 years' imprisonment for having sexual intercourse with a girl under the age of 13 on three occasions. The Court of Appeal substituted a sentence of 15 months' imprisonment.

Indecent assault and indecency with children

9.241 The maximum sentence for indecent assault on a man or a woman is now 10 years' imprisonment. Prior to 16 September 1985, indecent assaults on a women attracted a maximum penalty of only 2 years' imprisonment. If the offence charged is one of indecency with a child, for offences committed on or after 1 October 1997 the maximum sentence is also 10 years' imprisonment, but for offences committed before this date, the maximum sentence is 2 years' imprisonment. The Court of Appeal has noted that the public rightly and strongly condemn offences of indecent assault committed on children. In *Attorney General's Reference (No 34 of 1997)* [1998] 1 FLR 515, the defendant had pleaded guilty to six counts of indecent assault on three boys aged between 6 and 11 by touching their genitalia under their clothing, in incidents spanning a period of 2½ years. The Court of Appeal held that, in a contested case, the appropriate sentence would range between 30 months and 3 years' imprisonment, and, after a guilty plea, between 18 months and 2 years. More substantial custodial sentences may be justified by the nature of the indecency and the period over which the assaults take place. In *R v Cook* (1988) 10 Cr App R (S) 42, the Court of Appeal upheld sentences totalling 11 years' imprisonment. The defendant had pleaded guilty to eight counts of indecent assault and one of buggery, committed against his four stepchildren, as part of a pattern of offending which took place over a 9-year period.

Incest

9.242 The maximum sentence for incest is life imprisonment if committed with a girl under the age of 13, and 7 years' imprisonment in all other cases. In *Attorney General's Reference (No 1 of 1989)* (1989) 11 Cr App R (S) 409, the Court of Appeal gave guidance as to the appropriate sentence to be imposed. Where the girl is over 16, generally speaking a range from 3 years' imprisonment down to a nominal penalty will be appropriate depending, in particular, on the one hand whether force was used, and upon the degree of harm, if any to the girl, and on the other the desirability where it exists of keeping family disruption to a minimum. The older the girl, the greater the possibility that she may have been willing or even the instigating party to the liaison, a factor which will be reflected in the sentence. In other words, the lower the degree of corruption, the lower the penalty. Where the girl is aged from 13 to 16, a sentence between about 5 years and 3 years seems on the authorities to be appropriate. Much the same principles will apply as in the case of a girl aged over 16, although the likelihood of corruption increases in inverse proportion to the age of the girl. Nearly all cases in this and in other categories have involved pleas of guilty and the sentences in this category seem to range from about 2 years and 4 years, credit having been given for the plea. Where the girl is aged under 13 the widest range of sentence is to be found. If one can properly describe any case of incest as the 'ordinary' type of case, it will be one where the sexual relationship between husband and wife has broken down; the father has probably resorted to excessive drinking, and the eldest daughter is gradually, by way of familiarities, indecent acts and suggestions, made the object of the father's frustrated sexual inclinations. If the girl is not far short of her thirteenth birthday and there are no particularly adverse or favourable features on a not guilty plea, a term of about 6 years on the authorities would seem to be appropriate. It scarcely needs to be stated that the younger the girl when the sexual approach is started, the more likely it will be that the girl's will was overborne and accordingly the more serious would be the crime.

Abuse of a position of trust

9.243 The maximum penalty following conviction on indictment is 5 years' imprisonment. No opportunity for the Court of Appeal to give guidance on sentencing for this offence has yet arisen, although the age of the victim, the age difference between the victim and the defendant and the position of trust involved will undoubtedly be influential factors.

Indecent photographs and child pornography

9.244 The maximum penalty following conviction on indictment for an offence under the Protection of Children Act 1978 is 3 years' imprisonment for offences committed before 11 January 2001, and 10 years for offences committed after that date. For the offence of possession under the CJA 1988, the maximum penalty is 6 months' imprisonment for offences committed before 11 January 2001 and 5 years' imprisonment following trial on indictment for offences committed after that date. General guidance was given for sentencing in cases where child pornography is downloaded from the internet in *R v Toomer and Others* [2001] 2 Cr App R(S) 30, although this must now be viewed in the light of the increased sentences available since January 2001. The factors to be considered in determining the appropriate sentence include: the quantity, nature and quality of the material and whether it was for personal use or was prepared for distribution; the character of the defendant; the effect that the offence had on the victim; the co-operation offered by the defendant during the investigation; the amount of material found in the defendant's possession; and whether the defendant pleaded guilty. Non-custodial disposals should be reserved for isolated offences committed by first offenders on a guilty plea, where the amount was very small and there was no commercial element. In *Wild (No 1)* [2002] 1 Cr App R (S) 37, the Court of Appeal asked the Sentencing Advisory Panel for advice on the sentencing of offences involving indecent photographs or pseudo-photographs of children. The Panel issued a consultation paper in January 2002 (*Sentencing of Offences Involving Child Pornography*) and new sentencing guidelines are awaited.

Child sexual abuse and the sex offender register

9.245 In recent years there has been increasing concern about the activities of sex offenders, particularly paedophiles who abuse children. One of the responses to this concern has been the creation of the sex offender 'register'. Although the Police National Computer has for many years held details of convicted sex offenders, prior to 1997 there was no provision for keeping the information up to date and so keeping track of the movements of such offenders in society was difficult. The SOA 1997 now requires certain categories of sex offenders to notify the police of any change of name and address during a specified period. Schedule 5 to the CJCSA 2000 makes further amendments to the SOA 1997 with a view to improving protection of the public. These amendments were implemented in 2001. The notification requirements apply to all those convicted or cautioned in respect of an offence listed in Sch 1 to the SOA 1997, and to those who are found not guilty of such an offence by reason of insanity, or found to be under a disability and to have done the act charged in respect of the offence, after the commencement of the SOA 1997. The requirements also apply to those who were convicted before the commencement of the Act but had not been dealt with at the time of commencement of the Act, and to those who had been convicted and, at the time of commencement of the Act, were serving sentences of imprisonment or detention, were subject to a community order or supervision following imprisonment, or were detained in hospital or subject to a guardianship order.

The Schedule 1 offences

9.246 During the passage of the Bill through Parliament, there was concern that the list of those subject to the notification requirements should not include 'unnecessary' names where, for example, there were adult consensual acts or sexual offences of a comparatively minor nature. As a result, the notification requirements do not attach to offences under the SOA 1956, ss 10, 12, 13 and 16 (incest by a man, buggery, indecency with men, and assault with intent to commit buggery) if the victim or other party was aged 18 or over. In the case of indecent assault (SOA 1956, ss 14 and 15), if the victim is aged 18 or over, the notification requirements will only apply if the offender is or has been sentenced to imprisonment for a term of 30 months or more, or is or has been admitted to hospital subject to a restriction order.

9.247 The question of whether the notification requirements should be imposed on young offenders was also the subject of considerable debate. It was argued that, as the criminal justice system treats children differently from adults and the provisions were primarily concerned with the protection of children, young offenders should be treated separately from adult defendants. Attempts were made to remove children aged under 16 from the ambit of the provisions completely, or alternatively to give the court a discretion to direct that the notification requirements should apply to those aged under 16 (HC Deb, vol 291, col 235, 25 February 1997). Whilst there was clear agreement that young offenders could be distinguished, particularly in cases where the 'victim' was close in age to the offender, the government was not prepared to accept the automatic exclusion of a young offender simply by virtue of age. The resulting compromise excludes from the notification requirements those under the age of 20 who commit offences under ss 6, 12 and 13 of SOA 1956 (intercourse with a girl between 13 and 16, buggery and indecency between men). This still, however, means that the notification requirements may be imposed on very young offenders. In August 1999 a 10-year-old boy was found guilty of indecently assaulting an 8-year-old girl and was made the subject of a 3-year supervision order. He would also be subject to the notification requirements for 5 years from the date of his conviction (*The Times*, 24 August 1999). Referring to the outcome as a 'legal quirk', the boy's solicitor pointed out that the boy would not have been subject to the notification requirements if he had assaulted an 18-year-old woman.

9.248 In summary, the notification provisions attach to the following offences:

- SOA 1956, s 1 (rape);
- SOA 1956, s 5 (intercourse with a girl under 13);
- SOA 1956, s 6 (intercourse with a girl between 13 and 16) (except where the offender is under 20);

- SOA 1956, s 10 (incest by a man) (except where the victim of or, as the case may be, the other party to the offence was 18 or over and the offender has not been sentenced to imprisonment for a term of 30 months or more and is not admitted to a hospital subject to a restriction order);
- SOA 1956, ss 12 and 13 (buggery and indecency between men) (except where the offender is under 20, or where the victim of or, as the case may be, the other party to the offence was 18 or over and the offender is not sentenced to imprisonment for a term of 30 months or more and is not admitted to a hospital subject to a restriction order);
- SOA 1956, ss 14, 15 and 16 (indecent assault on a woman, indecent assault on a man and assault with intent to commit buggery) (except where the victim of or, as the case may be, the other party to the offence was 18 or over and the offender has not been sentenced to imprisonment for a term of 30 months or more and is not admitted to a hospital subject to a restriction order);
- SOA 1956, s 28 (causing or encouraging prostitution of, intercourse with, or indecent assault on, a girl under 16);
- ICA 1960, s 1(1) (indecent conduct towards young child);
- Criminal Law Act 1977, s 54 (inciting girl under 16 to have incestuous sexual intercourse);
- Protection of Children Act 1978, s 1 (indecent photographs of children);
- Customs and Excise Management Act 1979, s 170 (penalty for fraudulent evasion of duty etc) in relation to goods prohibited to be imported under s 42 of the Customs Consolidation Act 1876 (prohibitions and restrictions) (except where the prohibited goods did not include indecent photographs of persons who were, or appear to have been, under the age of 16);
- CJA 1988, s 160 (possession of indecent photographs of children).

The notification requirements

9.249 The SOA 1997 initially required those subject to the provisions of the legislation to notify to the police their name and home address within 14 days of the conviction or the commencement of the Act (s 2(1)). Under the CJCSA 2000 this period is reduced to 3 days. Any subsequent changes of name or address must be notified within 14 days, together with any address in the UK where the offender has stayed for a period or periods amounting to 14 days in any 12-month period, which would, of course, cover any holiday in the UK in excess of 2 weeks. The requirements of the SOA 1997 are restricted to providing information about addresses in the UK. The CJCSA 2000 will give the Secretary of State power to make regulations requiring those subject to the notification requirements to give notice of their intention to leave the UK, together with details of the country to which they are travelling, and to give notice about their return to the UK.

9.250 The SOA 1997 allowed the notification to be given orally or in writing. The CJCSA 2000 specifies that the notification must be in person and that the individual may be required to allow his fingerprints and photograph to be taken. During the passage of the SOA 1997 through Parliament, the NSPCC suggested that the inclusion of a 'domestic profile' in the notification requirements would be of benefit (HC Deb, vol 291, col 220, 25 February 1997). It was argued that this would help combat registration of mere postal addresses and would obviously act as a useful trigger to warn the relevant authorities if there were vulnerable children in the household, but the suggestion has not been acted upon.

The registration period

9.251 The length of time the individual will be subject to the notification requirements is dependent upon the sentence imposed (SOA 1997, s 1(4)):

– an indefinite period is imposed on those sentenced to a term of imprisonment of 30 months or more and those admitted to a hospital subject to a restriction order;
– sentences of more than 6 months' but less than 30 months' imprisonment attract a period of 10 years;
– sentences of 6 months' imprisonment or less and admissions to hospital without a restriction order attract a period of 7 years;
– any other offenders are subjected to the requirements for a period of 5 years.

9.252 In practice, research suggests that about 20 per cent of individuals subject to the notification requirements will remain subject to them for an indefinite period (*The Prevalence of Convictions for Sex Offending* (Home Office Research Findings No 55, 1997)). It had been argued that, given the deep-seated nature of paedophilia, an indefinite period should be imposed on all offenders or, alternatively, that the court be given a discretion to extend the period in the interests of justice. In a similar vein, it was argued that the courts should have a discretion to vary the period so as to lift the notification requirements where there was evidence that an individual no longer presented a risk to the public. The government resisted all attempts to introduce an element of flexibility, arguing that the set periods were proportionate to the seriousness of the offence as it was established at the time of sentencing and that it would be inappropriate to expect a court, perhaps years after the original trial, to reassess the risk posed by an individual (Standing Committee D, 4 February 1997, cols 24–25). The refusal to build any form of discretion into the provisions is one which could lead to unacceptable bureaucratic requirements being imposed in certain circumstances.

Enforcement

9.253 The effective enforcement of the notification requirements obviously requires a sanction to be imposed on those who fail to comply. One option would have been to rely on the usual sanctions for breaching an order of the court, but it was decided to create a new criminal offence of failing, without reasonable excuse, to comply with the notification requirements and of providing information which the individual knows to be false. Under s 3 of the SOA 1997, the offence is a summary one, subject to a maximum penalty of 6 months' imprisonment. The CJCSA 2000 makes the offence triable either way and increases the maximum penalty to 5 years' imprisonment following conviction on indictment.

Restraining orders under the Sex Offenders Act 1997

9.254 Despite the implementation of the SOA 1997, concern continued to be expressed that communities were not being adequately protected against the activities of paedophiles. Section 2 of the CDA 1998 introduced the sex offender order, which is a civil order, breach of which constitutes a criminal offence. On an application by the chief officer of police, the magistrates' court, acting in its civil capacity, can make an order in relation to a convicted sex offender (and those who fall within s 3 of the CDA 1998) who has acted in such a way as to give reasonable cause to believe that an order is necessary to protect the public from serious harm from him. The order prohibits the offender from doing any act specified in the order. However, sex offender orders require an application to be made to the court some time after the original conviction for the offence and the power has not been widely used. The CJCSA 2000 inserts a new s 5A into the SOA 1997 giving the court a power to impose a restraining order when sentencing a sex offender if it is satisfied that it is necessary to do so in order to protect the public in general, or any particular members of the public, from serious harm from him. As with a sex offender order, a restraining order may prohibit the individual from doing anything described in the order. Thus specific restrictions may be imposed on an abuser when he returns to the community, without the need for his behaviour to be monitored and a further application made to the court.

Use of the information

9.255 If the notification requirements are complied with, the police are now able to keep track of all sex offenders convicted of the offences specified in the SOA 1997. Although popularly described as a 'register', the SOA 1997 made no provision for the creation of a separate register and attempts during the passage of the Bill through Parliament to impose a duty on the Secretary of State to maintain such a register failed. In practice, this is unlikely to be of any real significance as the information is stored on the Phoenix database of the Police National Computer and is accessible by all police forces in England

and Wales and by the National Criminal Intelligence Service. The government claims to have made it clear that the information must not just sit on the computer or gather dust on a file (HC Deb, vol 313, cols 304–305, 4 June 1998). The police undoubtedly make use of the information for the investigation of crime, but far more controversial issues arise in the dissemination of the information to other agencies and, in some cases, to the community at large (see further, Cobley (2000)).

Child protection and disqualification orders

The background

9.256 It has long been acknowledged that individuals who are thought to present a risk to children should not be allowed unrestricted access to them through employment, whether paid or voluntary. In the past, employers had three potential sources of information which could be consulted in order to check the background of a potential employee: a criminal record check, 'List 99' and the DOH's Consultancy Index.

9.257 Under administrative arrangements between the Home Office and the ACPO, criminal record checks could be made against those applying for work in the public sector which would give them substantial unsupervised access, on a sustained or regular basis, to children under the age of 16, or children under the age of 18 who have special needs. For residential staff the checks could be carried out when such access will be to children under the age of 18 who are looked after by the local authority. Checks were not available to private organisations or to the majority of voluntary bodies, although certain national voluntary childcare organisations (including Barnardo's and the NSPCC) had access to criminal record checks through their membership of the Voluntary Organisations Consultancy Service.

9.258 'List 99' was the list maintained by the DfEE containing details of those barred from employment as a teacher or related position on medical grounds or grounds of misconduct under the Education Reform Act 1988. Access to the List is strictly limited to individuals responsible for checking the suitability of those applying for relevant positions.

9.259 The DOH's Consultancy Index had no statutory basis but operated on an advisory basis whereby local authorities, private and voluntary organisations could check the suitability of those they proposed to employ in a childcare post.

Increasing awareness of the problem

9.260 Whilst the availability of criminal record checks, List 99 and the DOH's Consultancy Index provided certain safeguards, in recent years concerns were expressed that these safeguards were not fully integrated and that there was a need for a more streamlined approach to ensure that there were no loopholes. In 1997 *People Like Us: Report of the Review of Safeguards for Children Living Away from Home* (DOH/Welsh Office) made a number of recommendations for improving recruitment and selection procedures in the childcare field (at chapter 13). In 1998, in an effort to address these concerns, the government set up an inter-departmental working group of officials to consider additional safeguards to prevent those who are unsuitable from working with children, including the possibility of a central register backed up by a new criminal offence to prevent those on the register applying for work with children.

Legislative reform

9.261 The main report by the group was published in January 1999 (*Report of the Interdepartmental Working Group on Preventing Unsuitable Persons from Working with Children and Abuse of Trust* (Home Office, 1999)). Several of the Report's recommendations were enacted in the PCA 1999 which made four principal changes:

–   placing the DOH's Consultancy Index on a statutory basis and providing for the referral of names and creating a right of appeal to a new tribunal;
–   amending the Education Reform Act 1988 to provide a power permitting inclusion on List 99 on grounds that individuals are not considered fit and proper persons to work as teachers or work involving regular contact with children, thus enabling a distinction to be drawn between those who are included on List 99 because they are unsuitable to work with children and those who are included on the List for other reasons, such as offences of dishonesty, and creates a right of appeal to the new tribunal;
–   amending Pt V of the Police Act 1997 to enable the Criminal Records Bureau to disclose information about people who are included on either list along with their criminal records;
–   requiring childcare organisations proposing to employ someone in a childcare setting to ensure that individuals are checked through the bureau against the DOH Consultancy Index and the relevant category of List 99 and not to employ anyone identified on either list.

Further legislative reform

9.262 Whereas for several years the Secretary of State has had statutory powers to ban unsuitable people from working in the field of education and the PCA 1999 also provides the Secretary of State with powers to ban unsuitable people from working with children in the health and social care fields, in July 1999 the inter-departmental working group published further proposals for reform (*Report of the Interdepartmental Working Group on Preventing Unsuitable Persons from Working with Children and Abuse of Trust: Update* (Home

Office, 1999)). These proposals were enacted in the CJCSA 2000 which makes a further four principle changes:

—   creating a new way for the courts to disqualify unsuitable people from working with children, in addition to the existing schemes in education and childcare areas;
—   providing a review process for the disqualified person;
—   providing criminal sanctions against those who breach the disqualification, whether by the new order imposed by the courts or as a result of being listed, barred or disqualified by the previously existing schemes;
—   providing a new comprehensive definition of working with children.

Guidance was published by the Home Office in December 2000 (*Criminal Justice and Court Services Act 2000: Protection of Children Guidance* (Home Office, 2000)) and the relevant provisions of the CJCSA 2000 came into force on 11 January 2001.

Disqualification orders

9.263 When sentencing a defendant, in certain circumstances the court may now make an order which disqualifies the defendant from working with children (CJCSA 2000, ss 26–30). In order for a disqualification order to be made, the defendant must have committed 'an offence against a child', as defined by Sch 4 to the Act. The offences are mainly offences of a sexual or violent nature. Some offences will automatically be offences against a child as the age of the victim is an essential element of the offence, such as child cruelty or unlawful sexual intercourse. Other offences are more general, such as rape and murder, which will only be offences against a child if the victim is someone under 18 years of age.

9.264 If a defendant has committed a qualifying offence, one of two further conditions must apply before a disqualification order can be made. The first condition is the imposition of a qualifying sentence by a senior court (defined as the Crown Court, the Court of Appeal, a court-martial or the Courts-Martial Appeal Court). A qualifying sentence can be very broadly defined as a sentence of imprisonment for a term of 12 months or more (including suspended sentences) or a hospital or guardianship order within the meaning of the Mental Health Act 1983. The second alternative condition is the making of a relevant order by a senior court, which is an order that the defendant be admitted to hospital or a guardianship order (within the meaning of the Army Act 1955, the Air Force Act 1955, the Naval Discipline Act 1957 or the Mental Health Act 1983).

9.265 If the defendant was aged 18 or over when the offence was committed, the court must impose a disqualification order upon him to prevent his working with children, unless the court believes that it is unlikely that the defendant will commit a further offence against a child, in which case the reasons for not imposing the disqualification order must be stated and recorded. If the defendant was aged under 18 at the time he committed the offence, the court should only impose a disqualification order on him if it believes that there is a likelihood of the defendant committing a further offence against a child, in which case the reasons for imposing the order must be stated and recorded.

9.266 When a disqualification order is imposed, court officers should ensure that before the defendant leaves court he is provided with written notification that he is subject to an order disqualifying him from working with children. The notification should spell out in simple language the effect and implications of the disqualification order, and the review process.

The review process

9.267 The CJCSA 2000 establishes a review process for those disqualified from working with children. The review process is not part of the criminal proceedings, which are complete at the sentencing stage, it is a review of the disqualification order only. The tribunal responsible for the review is that established by the PCA 1999. Disqualified individuals are entitled to make an application for leave to have their case reviewed only once 10 years (or 5 years in the case of individuals who were aged under 18 at the time of the offence) has passed from the date on which the order was imposed, or on release from custody, whichever is the later (CJCSA 2000, s 33). In deciding whether or not to grant leave, the tribunal must consider whether or not the individual's circumstances have changed since the order was made, and whether or not those changes are sufficient to warrant leave to apply for review of the disqualification order. If leave is granted the disqualified individual must demonstrate to the satisfaction of the tribunal that he is now suitable to work with children. It is not sufficient for the individual to prove that he is no longer a risk to children, rather the individual must prove that they are now positively suitable for such work (s 32). If the tribunal is not so satisfied, it must dismiss the application and the individual must wait another 10 years (or 5 years in the case of those aged under 18 at the time of the offence) before applying for a further review. When the tribunal is satisfied that the individual is suitable to work with children, it must direct that the disqualification order is to cease to have effect, although provision exists for the order to be restored if it is proved necessary (s 34).

Criminal offences

9.268 Section 35 of the CJCSA 2000 creates two new offences, which may be committed by individuals who are disqualified from working with children and those who offer or procure work in a regulated position to a disqualified person. For these purposes, it is immaterial whether the disqualification arises as a result of a disqualification order or by inclusion on the lists maintained by the DOH of people considered unsuitable to work with children, or on the list maintained by the DfEE on the grounds of not being a fit and proper person to be employed as a teacher or worker with children or young persons.

9.269 The first offence is committed if an individual who is disqualified from working with children knowingly applies for, offers to do, accepts, or does any work with children. The individual must therefore be aware that the work involved in their application, offer, acceptance, or activity, was indeed work with children for this to be an offence and so organisations recruiting staff or volunteers to work with children should ensure that the status of such work is clear. The individual will have a defence if they did not know, or could not reasonably be expected to know, that they were disqualified from working with children.

9.270 The second offence is committed by a person who knowingly offers work with children to, or procures work with children for, an individual who is disqualified from working with children, or allows such an individual to continue in such work. No statutory defence is provided, but the offence will only be committed if the person concerned acts knowingly. Both offences are triable either way and are subject to a maximum punishment of 5 years' imprisonment following conviction on indictment.

'Working with children'

9.271 Section 36 of the CJCSA 2000 provides a comprehensive definition of working with children. The definition of work is itself very broad and includes any kind of work, whether paid or unpaid, whether under a contract of service or apprenticeship, under a contract for services, or otherwise than under a contract. It therefore covers the public, private, voluntary and volunteering sectors. A child is defined as a person aged under 18 years, except that, where children in employment are concerned, a child is someone aged under 16 years. The basic building block of the definition is called a 'regulated position'. There are eight basic sets of regulated positions, some of which are broad and comprehensive, covering particular roles in all organisations, others are aimed at particular functions or specific places of work or areas of concern. With one exception (s 36(1)(g)), all definitions of a regulated position are limited to 'normal duties'. The intention is to exclude the one-off work. Thus if a parent rings a mini-cab firm and arranges for a driver to take their child to some activity on a one-off basis, the driver's position would not be regulated. But if a mini-cab firm offers a service to parents for driving unaccompanied children, such work would form a normal part of the duties of such drivers and would therefore be regulated.

9.272 The following categories provide a broad outline of the regulated positions:

- *employment in certain establishments (CJCSA 2000, s 36(1)(a)):* primary or secondary carers, or ancillary staff, whose normal duties involve carrying out work of any sort in establishments exclusively or mainly for children;
- *day care premises (s 36(1)(b)):* a position whose normal duties include work on day care premises;
- *caring for, training, supervising or being in sole charge of children (s 36(1)(c)):* a position whose normal duties include caring for, training, supervising or being in sole charge of children;
- *unsupervised contact (s 36(1)(d)):* a position whose normal duties involve unsupervised contact with children under arrangements made by a responsible person;
- *child employment (s 36(1)(e), (f)):* a position whose normal duties include caring for children under the age of 16 in the course of the children's employment or a position a substantial part of whose normal duties include supervising or training children under the age of 16 in the course of the children's employment;
- *other positions (s 36(1)(g)):* 'The great and the good' – individuals who, by virtue of the authority and responsibility inherent in the posts they hold, might be expected to be positively suitable to work with children; these include charity trustees of a children's charity, relevant local bodies, members of the Youth Justice Board and the Children's Commissioner for Wales;
- *supervising or managing someone in a regulated position (s 36(1)(h)):* a position whose normal duties include supervising or managing an individual in his work in a regulated position; as well as immediate managers and supervisors, it covers those with authority to dismiss an individual in a regulated position.

THE RIGHTS OF VICTIMS AND COMPENSATION

9.273 In recent years there has been a growing movement towards according rights to victims of crime. The first Victim's Charter was published in 1990 and a substantially revised charter was issued in 1996 which set out the standards of service which victims could expect to receive. In February 2001, the government announced a review of the Victim's Charter and commenced a consultation process, seeking views on whether the 'service standard' approach should be replaced by a 'rights' approach, possibly placing victims' rights on a statutory basis. Views are also sought as to whether a new post of Victim's Ombudsman should be established (*Review of the Victim's Charter* (Home Office Communication Directorate, February 2001)).

Victim personal statements

9.274 From October 2001, victim personal statements are being introduced. Any victim who makes a witness statement (which will include a video-recorded interview) will have the opportunity to make a personal statement enabling them to tell the criminal justice agencies how the crime has affected them, and identify and protect their interests in general. The agencies will take the statement into account when they make decisions, including those made when a defendant has been convicted. The views of victims are already taken into account at various stages in the criminal justice process, and in cases of child abuse the child's best interests must often be balanced against competing interests. It is now envisaged that the carers of child victims will also be invited to make a personal statement, which will allow account to be taken of the impact of the abuse on the immediate family. In cases of child abuse, the extent to which victim personal statements will enhance what can already be a difficult balancing exercise remains to be seen.

Compensation for victims of abuse

9.275 One of the guiding principles underlying the review of the Victim's Charter is the need to provide compensation or reparation to the victims of crime. There are two sources of compensation currently available to victims without the need to resort to taking personal civil action against the defendant: the courts may order a convicted defendant to pay compensation to the victim or the victim may be eligible for compensation from the government through the Criminal Injuries Compensation Scheme.

Criminal compensation orders

9.276 Since 1973, the courts have had a general power to order compensation to be paid to the victim of an offence for personal injury, loss or damage caused by the offence. In an effort to encourage the use of such orders, the CJA 1988 introduced a requirement that if a court, having power to make a compensation order, chooses not to do so, it must give reasons. A compensation order may be made instead of or in addition to dealing with the defendant in any other way for the offence and so an order can be combined with any other sentence the court may impose. The compensation is to be of such an amount as the court considers appropriate, having regard to any evidence and to any representations that are made by or on behalf of the defendant and the prosecutor (PCC(S)A 2000, s 130). The court collects the compensation, pays it to the victim and enforces the order if the defendant defaults. The government is now said to be looking carefully at whether to establish a 'Victim's Fund' to ensure that victims receive the financial compensation they deserve from defendants more quickly.

Criminal Injuries Compensation Scheme

9.277 The Criminal Injuries Compensation Scheme was introduced in August 1964 as a non-statutory scheme to provide payment from public funds to the innocent victims of crimes of violence and those injured in attempting to apprehend criminals or prevent crime. Awards were initially made on an ex gratia basis and were assessed on the basis of common law damages. The Criminal Injuries Compensation Act 1995 placed the scheme on a statutory basis and changed the way awards were assessed. Awards are now based on a tariff of awards that groups together injuries of comparable severity and allocates a financial value to them (see further, Cobley (1998)).

Crimes of violence

9.278 To qualify for an award, an applicant must have sustained 'personal injury directly attributable to, inter alia, a crime of violence'. The scheme does not define a 'crime of violence'. In R *v Criminal Injuries Compensation Board ex parte Clowes* (1977) 120 Sol Jo 856, it was held that a crime of violence is one which contains an element of potential danger to personal safety. Guidance issued in relation to child abuse by the CICA responsible for administering the scheme states:

> 'Physical assault is the most obvious example [of a crime of violence], but the term may also include sexual abuse or interference which is not always thought of as a crime of violence. Rape, incest and buggery are further clear examples, but we can consider indecent assault too' (CICA, 1996).

'Personal injury' includes physical injury and mental injury (ie a medically recognised psychiatric or psychological illness). However, compensation will not normally be payable for mental injury alone unless the applicant was, inter alia, the non-consenting victim of a sexual offence. Trivial injuries are excluded from the scheme as the injury must be serious enough to qualify for at least the minimum award available under the scheme, currently £1,000.

Time-limits

9.279 Applications initially had to be made within 3 years of the incident giving rise to the injury, although this requirement could be waived in exceptional cases, especially if the application was made within a reasonable time of the child reaching majority. Under the tariff scheme, the time-limit for making the application has been reduced from 3 years to 2 years and guidance issued by the CICA explains that the 2-year limit is necessary because of the difficulties involved in investigating and substantiating late claims, as it is often not possible to obtain reliable evidence of police involvement and medical treatment given at the time because records are no longer available. Ideally, the claim should be made as soon as possible after the abuse comes to light even if the victim is still a child. Although the scheme itself makes no specific mention of applications on behalf of a person under the age of 18, guidance issued by the CICA indicates that such a claim must be made by an adult with parental responsibility for the child. Usually, this will be one of the child's parents, but, obviously, if the child has been subjected to abuse within the immediate family this may not be possible. If the child is in care, it is expected that the claim will be lodged by or on behalf of the authority to whom care has been granted.

Restrictions on eligibility

9.280 The abuser need not necessarily be convicted of a criminal offence, although the CICA must be satisfied on the balance of probabilities that the events alleged actually occurred and may withhold or reduce compensation if an applicant has not taken, without delay, all reasonable steps to inform the police or other appropriate authority of the circumstances of the injury with a view to bringing the abuser to justice. On the face of it, this may preclude many claims by abused children, but the guidance issued by the CICA makes it clear that every case is to be treated on its merits and a more sympathetic view will be taken in the case of children who may be too young or too frightened to appreciate the right course of action. However, victims of intra-familial abuse face further hurdles. Prior to 1979, no compensation was payable if the victim and offender were living together at the time as members of the same family. The scheme was extended to include victims of violence within the family in October 1979, but claims based on abuse within the family before that date will necessarily fail (*R v CICB ex parte P* [1993] 2 FLR 600). During 1998–99, the CICA disallowed 150 claims because the injury had been sustained in a family setting before October 1979 (*Criminal Injuries Compensation Authority Annual Report 1998/99*).

9.281 Even under the extended scheme, where the victim and the person responsible for causing the injury were living in the same household at the time of the injury as members of the same family, compensation will only be paid if the person responsible has been prosecuted in connection with the offence, unless the CICA considers that there are good reasons why a prosecution has not been brought (para 16). In such cases, a full explanation on the child's behalf will be required, but, as there are a number of reasons why a prosecution may not have been brought – including the strict eviden-tial requirements and the high standard of proof in criminal proceedings – in many cases a satisfactory explanation will be available. However, compensation will only be awarded if the CICA is satisfied that the abuser will not benefit, as may happen if the child and the abuser are still living under the same roof, and, if the applicant is under 18 years of age, it would not be against his or her interests for an award to be made (para 15). Guidance issued by the CICA suggests that, in the case of a child who was very young at the time of a very minor assault and could reasonably be expected to make a full recovery and forget that it had happened, an award may not be in the child's best interests because, when released to him or her at the age of 18, it might well re-open the incident and cause considerable distress. However, in 1998–99 the CICA disallowed only five claims as being against a minor's interest.

Amounts payable

9.282 The amount payable will depend upon the severity of the abuse. The tariff was revised in April 2001 (see Miers (2001)). In accordance with the tariff, minor abuse consisting of isolated or intermittent assault(s) beyond ordinary chastisement resulting in bruising, weals, hair pulled from scalp etc would attract an award of £1,000, whereas a persistent pattern of repetitive violence resulting in severe multiple injuries would attract an award of £13,500. In cases of sexual abuse, awards range from £1,000 for minor isolated incidents of non-penetrative indecent acts to £22,000 for repeated non-consensual vaginal and/or anal intercourse over a period exceeding 3 years.

CHAPTER 10

CONTACT

'The companionship of a parent is in any ordinary circumstances of such immense value to the child that there is a basic right in him to such companionship. I, for my part would prefer to call it the basic right in the child rather than a basic right in the parent. That only means this, that no court should deprive a child of access to either parent unless it is wholly satisfied that it is in the interest of that child that [contact] should cease, and that is a conclusion at which a Court should be extremely slow to arrive' (*per* Wrangham J in *M v M* [1973] 2 All ER 81).

'Broken homes abused by parents and family, poor and disadvantaged, deprived upbringing, never been to school. To be honest nobody cares a toss about them. Very few get visited regularly by parents and they've been in care for the best part of their lives. There is a girl in here now, she's just 14 and she has had 53 different placements' (Secure Unit Residential Social Worker talking to Goldson in *Vulnerable Inside* (Goldson (2002), at p 96).

'The primary piece of welfare legislation – the Children Act 1989 – much to the dismay of Her Majesty's Inspectorate of Prisons, does not even apply to the prison estate. . . . The picture for young prisoners on remand is extreme. Many of them have experienced significant trauma and are without the personal and social support they need to overcome their difficulties. Before any work can be done to sensitise them to the needs of others and the impact of their offending on victims, their own needs as maturing adolescents for care, support and direction have to be met' (*Young Prisoners: A Thematic Review by HM Inspector of Prisons for England and Wales* (HMSO) 1997, at p 8 and 2000, at p 25).

'States Parties shall respect the right of the child who is separated from one or both parents to maintain personal relations and direct contact with those parents on a regular basis, except if it is contrary to the child's best interests' (UNCRC, 1989, Art 9(3)).

'It is the right of a child to have a relationship with both parents wherever possible. This principle has been stated again and again in the appellate courts. It is underlined in the United Nations Convention on the Rights of the Child (UNCRC) and endorsed in the Children Act 1989' (*per* Butler-Sloss LJ in *Re R (A Minor) (Contact)* [1993] 2 FLR 762, at p 767).

Introduction

10.1 All of the above quotations illustrate the fact that workers, Chief Inspectors of Prisons as well as the courts in England and Wales accept and fully endorse the provisions contained in Article 9 of the UNCRC that it is the right of the child to have contact with both parents, where he or she may be living away from them, except where this is contrary to the child's best interests. Butler-Sloss LJ also made the point that this right in the child to have contact is 'endorsed in the Children Act 1989'. This endorsement is contained in a number of different provisions scattered throughout the Act which apply to different groups of children. Thus ss 9 and 10 of the CA 1989 give various important people in the child's life the right to apply for s 8 contact orders usually in private law proceedings arising out of the breakdown of the parent's relationship. For those children who are 'looked after' by the local authority, which includes those who are accommodated under ss 20 and 21 of the CA 1989, those who are the subject of care orders under s 31, as well as those who are placed in secure accommodation under s 25 whilst being accommodated or on care orders, there are a number of provisions designed to review, encourage, support and facilitate contact contained in s 26(2), and Sch 2, Part II, paras 15 and 16 of the CA 1989. In addition, for these children, where no member of their family is visiting them, then the local authority is placed under a duty to appoint an independent visitor (Sch 2, Part II, para 17). Further endorsement of the principle of the presumption of the right to beneficial contact applicable to children, who may have been made the subject of a court order under s 31 of the CA 1989 arising out of child protection concerns, is to be found in the CA 1989, s 34. This provides a statutory presumption that where a child is in the care of a local authority, the authority shall allow the child reasonable contact with his parents; any guardian of his; any person in whose favour a residence order had been enforced immediately before the making of a care order; and in favour of any person who had the care of the child by virtue of an order made in the exercise of the High Court's inherent jurisdiction with respect to children. This presumption permeates throughout the whole of s 34 and receives further endorsement through the provisions in s 34(11), which provide that before making a care order with respect to any child, the court shall consider the arrangements which the authority has made, or proposes to make, for affording any personal contact with the child and invite parties to the proceedings to comment on those arrangements. It should also be noted that in those circumstances where emergency protective measures are taken under the CA 1989, similar statutory presumptions in favour of contact also operate, thus s 44(13)) provides for contact while a child is on an emergency protection order, s 46(10) provides for contact where a child has been taken into police protection, and in those circumstances where an interim care order is made then the principles laid down in s 34 will govern the situation. In addition, where a child assessment order is made under s 43, which provides for the child to be kept away from home, then s 43(10) provides that the order should contain such directions as to contact which the court thinks fit. The presumption in favour of contact running through all of these provisions in the CA 1989 is now further reinforced by the provisions of Article 8(1) of the ECHR, as enacted in Sch 1 to the Human Rights Act 1998, which guarantee the child's right to private and family life, although, of course, Article 8(2) allows for interference with this right where to do so is necessary to protect the child (see further, Chapter 1). The importance of providing a statutory means through the courts of challenging decisions made by local authorities with regard to children, who are the subject of orders removing them from their families, was emphasised by the European Court in *Scott v UK* [2000] 1 FLR 958. Thus, the Court stated (at p 969) that:

'local authorities enjoy a wide margin of appreciation in assessing the necessity of taking a child into care. However, stricter scrutiny is called for any further limitations, such as restrictions placed by those authorities on parental rights and access, or on the legal safeguards designed to secure the effective protection of the right of parents and children to respect for their family life, where such further limitations might entail the danger that the family relations between the parents and a young child are effectively curtailed.'

In addition to the provision of a right to apply to the courts for contact orders, any contact arrangements made or refused pursuant to the local authority s 31A or s 26(2)(f)(i) care plan, can also be monitored and if the prescribed person referred to in s 26(2)(k) of the CA 1989 is unhappy about them, then the prescribed person can refer these concerns to an officer of CAFCASS. It can be seen, therefore, that those children who, in particular, fall within the category of 'looked after' children benefit from a whole raft of measures intended to promote contact between them and their families.

10.2 As is so graphically pointed up, however, by the quotations from the Chief Inspector of Prisons and the Secure Unit Residential worker cited above, the provisions with regard to the review of contact arrangements, the promotion of contact, the appointment of an Independent Visitor, and the rights to apply for orders or variation of orders conferred by the CA 1989, which are the subject of detailed analysis in this chapter, are not necessarily applied energetically to children in secure units and they do not apply at all to the children and young people locked up in penal institutions. As Her Majesty's Chief Inspector points out, 'In recent years the massively increased numbers of children sent to custody have been dumped on prison service establishments in a prison system that has not, traditionally, recognised that it has a role in caring for children in need of care, development and control. Within this system children are quite frankly lost' (Her Majesty's Chief Inspector of Prisons Report, *Young Prisoners: A Thematic Review* (HMSO, 1997) at p 63). Without a properly promoted, supported, regulated and reviewable regime of contact, which might be afforded to these children and young people by extending to them the measures provided in s 26(2), Sch 2, Part II and the presumptions and regime laid down in Part IV of the CA 1989, the system is clearly failing them. As such, it is in clear breach of Art 9 of the UNCRC and Articles 8 and 9 of the ECHR (see further, para **10.60**).

Contact under the CA 1989

10.3   For those children who are being offered accommodation under s 20 of the CA 1989, as a result of the decision of a child protection conference that accommodation be offered as part of the child protection package, then it should be noted that there is far less rigorous statutory control of contact in those circumstances. The explanation for this apparent lack of statutory protection is that it is assumed that the local authority, parents and others, who might wish to have contact with the child, would be able to reach an amicable agreement on the basis of working in partnership together as to the levels of contact which would be deemed to be appropriate with the child in each particular case. Detailed guidance on issues of contact with children, who are being accommodated under the provisions of s 20 or with those who are being accommodated subject to care orders, can be found in the various documents of guidance issued by the DOH. Thus detailed discussion of the issues relating to contact can be found in *Children Act 1989: Guidance and Regulations*, vol 3: 'Family Placements', at chapter 6; vol 4: 'Residential Care', at chapter 4 (DOH, 1991), *Standards for Residential Child Care Services: A Handbook for Social Services Managers and Inspectors, Users of Services and their Families* (DOH, 1994) and also in Standard 4 of the *National Minimum Standards* (DOH, 2002) and in Standard 10 of *Fostering Services – National Minimum Standards* (DOH, 2002) for those in children's homes, which include secure units. Where the local authority and the child's parents or other family members cannot agree on contact arrangements with the child who is being accommodated, or where the parents together with the local authority might be blocking contact with a particular family member, then application may be made under the provisions of s 8 of the CA 1989 for a contact order. The ultimate remedy, of course, for parents who remain dissatisfied with arrangements for contact to an accommodated child is to remove the child from local authority accommodation.

10.4   The importance of the principle of the promotion and maintenance of contact between the child and his family where the child is being looked after by a local authority, is further emphasised in CA 1989, Sch 2, Pt II, para 15. Thus para 15 provides that where a child is being looked after by a local authority, unless it is not reasonably practicable or consistent with his welfare, the authority shall endeavour to promote contact between the child and his parents, anyone who has parental responsibility for him, and any relative, friend or other person connected with him. This provision can be seen to go somewhat further than the statutory presumptions which operate in favour of children who are made the subject of care orders, but it should be noted that they extend to all 'looked after children', a term which encompasses children who have been made the subject of care orders (see CA 1989, s 22(1)). Very importantly, para 16 goes on to provide that where it appears to the authority that any visits to the child could not be made without undue financial hardship and the circumstances of those wishing to visit the child warrant the making of payments, then the local authority may make payments to a parent, any person with parental responsibility, or any relative, friend or other person connected with the child in respect of the travelling, subsistence or other expenses incurred by that person in visiting the child. Although these provisions with regard to the promotion of contact and the payment of expenses are not couched in terms of duties, they are, nevertheless, extremely important in underlining the general principle that the local authority must promote contact between the 'looked after' child, the parents, relatives and friends. The discretionary power conferred upon the local authority to pay expenses is often overlooked by social workers and by those advising families as to how they may meet the expectation of visiting children who are being looked after by the local authority (see further, para **10.61**).

10.5 The critical importance to the child in having contact with members of his family or friends is also emphasised by the provisions, which may come into operation where it appears to the local authority that there has been infrequent communication between the child and his parent, or anyone else with parental responsibility, or where the child has not been visited by any such person during the preceding 12 months. Paragraph 17, Sch 2, Part II, goes on to provide that the local authority is then under a duty to appoint an independent person to be the 'child's visitor'. Most of the evidence available suggests that local authorities are not fulfilling the duty laid down in CA 1989, Sch 2, Pt 2, para 17 to appoint independent visitors (see *People Like Us: The Report of the Review of The Safeguards for Children Living Away From Home* (DOH/Welsh Office, 1997), at paras 10.13–10.16; *Children Looked After by Local Authorities* Cm 4175 (DOH, 1998), at para 80; *Safeguarding Children* (SSI et al) (2002); and Oakley (1999)). Placement at a distance from the child's family home or in circumstances where the care authority has failed to use its powers under paras 15–17 can mean that some children may be cut off from the critical support they might derive from visits by parents, relatives or friends. This was particularly pointed up in the North Wales Children Enquiry (the Waterhouse Report) and the importance of contact in terms of eventual rehabilitation of the child within the family was also recognised throughout the DOH *Guidance on Family Placements* (HMSO, 1991), at chapter 6 (and in *Guidance on Residential Care* (HMSO, 1991), at chapter 4) as well as now in Standard 4 of *Children's Homes – National Minimum Standards – Children's Homes Regulations* (DOH, 2002). Where a local authority is looking after a child then it has responsibilities itself to keep in contact with the child as a result of s 22(3), otherwise how can it be said to be 'safeguarding and promoting the child's welfare' as required by that section? (see Chapter **4**). A number of Reports have revealed that young people in residential and foster care were often unhappy about the lack of contact from their social worker, particularly those in out-of-authority placements (see Phase 3 of *Children's Services Inspections 2000–2002* (DOH/SSI, 2002) and *Fostering for the Future: Inspection of Foster Care Services* (DOH/SSI, 2002)). The first Joint Inspectorate's Report *Safeguarding Children* (DOH/SSI et al, 2002) notes that some councils are still not meeting the minimum requirements for visits by social workers of looked after children, although many had set up independent visitor and advocate schemes and one council had arranged for an independent visitor to undertake monthly well-being interviews with each child in residential care (at p 63).

10.6   Whether a child is being accommodated pursuant to the provisions of CA 1989, s 20 or is in the care of the local authority under a care order, then the law requires that the child's case is reviewed once within the first 3 months of placement and thereafter at 6-monthly intervals. The purpose of such reviews is not only to provide a forum for discussion as to the child's progress and a review of any plans in relation to the child, but also to provide the child with relevant information. This should include explaining to the child any action which he may take under CA 1989 including, where appropriate, his right to apply with leave for a s 8 order (which includes a contact order in those situations where the child is being accommodated) or to make an application for contact or for definition of contact under the provisions of s 34 (where the child is subject to a care order). See Review of Children's Cases Regulations 1991, SI 1991/895, Sch 1 (see further, para **10.12** *et seq* and para **10.27** *et seq*). When the Adoption and Children Act 2002 amendments to the CA 1989 are implemented the reviews will also be attended by a prescribed person whose function is to participate in the review, to monitor the performance of the authority's functions in respect of that review, and to refer the case to an officer of CAFCASS where he considers it appropriate to do so (s 26(2A)(a), (b), (c)). Thus, under these provisions, the prescribed person may, if unhappy about any aspect of contact with the child, choose to refer the matter to a CAFCASS officer (s 26(2A)(c) of the CA 1989, as amended). Doubtless, the enactment of these provisions is in direct response to long-standing and still widely found dissatisfaction with the performance of local authority social services in reviews held on children being looked after. (See, for example, *Someone Else's Children* (SSI, 1998), *Developing Quality to Protect Children: SSI Inspection of Children's Services: August 1999–July 2000* (SSI/DOH, 2001), at p 403, and Phase 3 of *Children's Services Inspections 2000–2002* (SSI/DOH, 2002).) In the most recent report to highlight children's dissatisfaction with reviews, *Safeguarding Children* (DOH/SSI, October 2002), the Inspectors noted that a number of service users reported difficulties in making their views known in reviews and finding them uncomfortable and intimidating. The report points up that practice is variable across councils in relation to the efforts and mechanisms used to enable children and parents to participate effectively in these processes (*Safeguarding Children*, p 63).

10.7 The term 'contact' as used in the CA 1989 is now recognised as being a very wide concept, and far wider than the older notion of 'access'. 'Access' was usually taken to connote physical contact with the child, whereas 'contact', which certainly includes physically visiting the child or having the child to visit or to stay for short or long periods (s 8(1)), also encompasses contact by letter, telephone, e-mail or fax (see *Children Act 1989: Guidance and Regulations* (HMSO, 1991), vol 1: 'Court Orders', para 2.29 and Standard 4.2 of the *Children's Homes – National Minimum Standards* (DOH, 2002) and in Standard 10 of *Fostering Services – National Minimum Standards* (DOH, 2002)). Both general and detailed guidance on issues of contact with children being looked after by the local authority, including those who have been made the subject of care or interim care orders can be found in the *Children Act 1989: Guidance and Regulations* (HMSO, 1991), vol 3: 'Family Placements', chapter 6; in vol 4: 'Residential Care', chapter 4, and at Standard 4 of the *Children's Homes – National Minimum Standards*. In this chapter, therefore, attention will focus primarily on provisions relating to contact with children who are deemed to have suffered or who are likely to suffer from significant harm. As discussed in Chapter 5, a decision on contact with a child suffering or likely to suffer significant harm will have to be made at a very early stage, but such decisions are now subject to the statutory presumptions and also to directions given by the court pursuant to the CA 1989, most particularly where the child is being made subject to any of the orders under Parts IV and V of the Act.

10.8 Where, as a result of the recommendation of the initial child protection conference or in response to an emergency, resort has to be made to the seeking of court orders in respect of the child in need of protection, then at every stage in the legal process consideration is given to the issue of contact. The provisions contained in the CA 1989 dealing specifically with contact issues when the court makes each of the relevant orders are, in large part, as a result of the *Report of the Inquiry into Child Abuse in Cleveland 1987* (The Cleveland Report) (HMSO, 1988) which highlighted serious gaps in the then existing legislation which gave too much discretion to local authorities to restrict contact, without any recourse to the courts being available (see Cleveland Report, Recommendation 4(d)). Depending on the order being sought, therefore, consideration will have to be given to the issue of contact and decisions made about what directions will be sought from the courts (see Chapter 5 and paras **10.18**, **10.19** and **10.22**). The importance of the child having contact with family members receives further support from Article 8 of the ECHR and relevant case-law such as *Marckx v Belgium* 2 EHRR 330 and *Boyle v UK* (1990) 19 EHRR 181.

10.9 In those circumstances where the local authority or the NSPCC is considering making an application for a child assessment order, and the child is to be kept away from home, the order must contain such direction as the court thinks fit with regard to the contact that the child must be allowed to have with persons whilst away from home (CA 1989, s 43(10) and see para **10.18**). Advance consideration must therefore be given to the issue of the nature of the harm from which the child is believed to be suffering, and to the person deemed responsible for that harm. Clearly, however, a child assessment order is very different from the emergency and other orders and powers, which are made or exercised with regard to the protection of children, since it is intended to be a means by which confirmation may be sought on whether a child is suffering from significant harm or not. It may, therefore, be entirely inappropriate to take steps to terminate contact for all or any part of the duration of the order, since at the end of the day it may be established that no responsibility lies with the parents or existing carers. Where an initial child protection conference has been held to discuss the application for a child assessment order, serious consideration must be given to the issue of whether the court should be requested to make such contact directions, and a recommendation concerning this must also be passed on to the local authority making the application for the order.

10.10 By contrast, where it is believed necessary to apply for an emergency protection order, the applicant may feel that it is in the best interests of the child to seek a direction that contact not be allowed between the child and any named person, which can include adults and children depending on the age of the abuser or potential abusers (CA 1989, s 44(6)(a), and see para **10.19**). Where no such direction is sought from the court, contact between the child and other persons connected with him will be presumed to be reasonable (s 44(13)). As far as other emergency situations are concerned, where the police exercise their powers of protection under the CA 1989, s 46, the designated officer is required to allow a wide range of people to have such contact (if any) with the child as, in the opinion of the designated officer, is both reasonable and in the child's best interests (see para **10.21**). The clear difference between the emergency protection order and the police powers of protection is that whilst issues of contact can be challenged in relation to the emergency protection order as provided by s 44(9)(b), there is no provision actually in the statute to challenge the exercise by the police of their discretion under s 46(10). This may, however, be another area where Art 8 of the ECHR may be of relevance since a decision to refuse contact between the child and members of his family may well constitute a violation of the Art 8(1) rights to a private home and family life. Again, it must be emphasised that in reaching a decision to refuse contact the police must be able to show that they have not acted disproportionately in the situation in question (see *Core Guidance: Human Rights Comes to Life* (Home Office, 1999), at para 73).

10.11 As pointed out above, where an interim care order is made, this is treated for the purposes of contact as being the equivalent of the making of a full care order (CA 1989, s 31(11)), and thus before the making of any interim care order the court will be required to consider any proposed contact arrangement and to invite the parties to the proceedings to comment upon them in the same way as they would when making a full order (s 34(11)). Where any party is dissatisfied with the proposed contact arrangement under an interim order they may also seek a contact order using s 34 (see *Oldham Metropolitan Borough Council v D* [2000] 2 FLR 382) as can the child if he becomes unhappy about current contact arrangements (s 34(2)) (see *A v M and Walsall Metropolitan Borough Council* [1993] 2 FLR 244). The children's guardian, who would have been appointed from the ranks of the officers of CAFCASS, would be expected to advise the court in such situations and, if necessary, make a further report relating to problems over contact. The impact of Article 8 of the ECHR and the interpretation given to the law on contact between children in care and their parents and families, particularly by the appellate courts, would suggest that there is now a greater possibility of challenging the local authority's determination on contact with the child and other members of his family than was previously the case (see especially *Re M (Care Contact: Grandmother's Application for Leave)* [1995] 2 FLR 86). It should also be pointed out, however, that the local authority in seeking to terminate contact as part of its plans for the child must be able to show that it is doing so in order to protect the best interests of the child, and must also be able to show that such action is not in breach of Article 8 of the ECHR (see *Re F (Care Proceedings: Contact)*, (2000) *The Times*, June 22 and see *Re C and B* [2001] 1 FLR 611).

Contact with accommodated children

10.12 Where, as a result of the assessment of the child's needs, the child protection conference recommends to the local authority, or the local authority social services themselves, make an offer to accommodate the child with the agreement of the parents, instead of resorting to compulsory removal, it is presumed that the local authority and the child's parents (or anyone else who might be relevant) will reach agreement with the local authority on the appropriate level of contact with the child (CA 1989, Sch 2, Pt 2, para 15). It is, however, provided in para 15 that the local authority is able to exercise its discretion as to whether or not it is reasonably practicable or consistent with the child's welfare to endeavour to promote such contact. In *L v London Borough of Bromley* [1998] 1 FLR 709, Wilson J emphasised that whilst such contact is at the discretion of the local authority, the local authority generally should endeavour to promote it unless it could be demonstrated not to be practicable or consistent with the welfare of the children. In that case, the court had to decide whether there should be contact between children who had been taken into care and one of their siblings who had remained in the home with the mother and her cohabitant and also whether there should be contact with the mother's cohabitant.

10.13 Wilson J pointed out in the *Bromley* case that the mother's cohabitant and the sibling did not come within the statutory framework encompassed in s 34(1) but rather within the provisions of Sch 2, Pt 2, para 15(c) so that any arrangements were at the discretion of the local authority. Wilson J stated that the order for contact between the mother's cohabitant and the children, whilst made of the court's own motion under CA 1989, s 34(5) was itself, nevertheless, subject to the discretion granted to the local authority by virtue of Sch 2, Pt 2, para 15. He stated that the discretion exercised by the local authority in this sort of situation was to weigh the benefits of contact between the children and the cohabitant and that if the local authority determined that it was inconsistent with the children's welfare to have such contact, then it would be under no obligation to endeavour to promote it. In an order made in such circumstances, therefore, Wilson J emphasised that the order can do no more than to point up the limited duty cast upon the local authority under Sch 2, Pt 2, para 15. The local authority was in a similar situation with regard to the discretion allowed to them as a result of the making of the order in respect of the sibling, still living at home with the mother and the mother's cohabitant. In the particular case, Wilson J's view of the contact between the siblings was that it was unsettling the children and he suggested that the local authority might have to review the appropriateness of the sibling's participation in the contact sessions.

10.14 As pointed out above, the local authority is also empowered by Sch 2, Pt 2, para 16 to make payments to parents, anyone with parental responsibility, and any relative, friend or other person connected with the child in order to enable such persons to maintain contact with the child. The *Children Act 1989: Guidance and Regulations* (HMSO, 1991), vol 3: 'Family Placements', indicates that for the majority of children, there is no doubt that their interests will be best served by efforts to sustain or create links with their natural families. It is suggested that contact with families by way of personal meeting and visits is generally the most common and, for both families and children, the most satisfactory way of maintaining their relationship. Other means of keeping family bonds alive are suggested in the guidance such as letters, telephone calls and exchange of photographs, and Standard 4 of the *Children's Homes – National Minimum Standards* and Standard 10 of *Fostering Services – National Minimum Standards* add contact by email if available. The guidance states that the first few weeks in which a child is looked after by the local authority are likely to be particularly crucial for the success of the relationship between the parent, the social worker and the child's carers and to the level of future contact between parent and child. *The Framework for the Assessment of Children in Need and their Families* (DOH, 2000) also emphasises that the quality of the early or initial contact will affect later working relationships and the ability of professionals to secure an agreed under-standing of what is happening and to provide help (at para 1.43). The guidance also advises that it is at this time (ie the early period) that patterns are set which may be difficult to change, whether the child is looked after by a voluntary arrangement or as a result of a care order (see para 6.10).

10.15 The reason for the emphasis on the importance of reaching agreements between the child and the child's family, where the child is to be accommodated, is not simply that this will contribute to a better working partnership between social services and the child's family, but also because the evidence shows that most children who are accommodated under s 20 of the CA 1989, will usually return home to live with their families (see House of Commons, Health Committee, *Children Looked After by Local Authority: Minutes of Evidence 13 November 1997* (HMSO, 1997)). Similar advice is also given in relation to children who are placed in residential care (see Standard 4 of *Children's Homes – National Minimum Standards* and the *Children Act 1989: Guidance and Regulations* (HMSO, 1991), vol 4: 'Residential Care', at para 4.10). *Child Protection: Messages from Research* (DOH, 1995) also emphasises the importance of the continuity of contact with the child's family and other significant persons in the child's life. It recognises that in most cases this will be agreed by local authority social workers, parents and other relatives negotiating on a relatively informal basis where the child has not yet been made the subject of any formal court order but has merely been offered accommodation (see p 56 and see also *The Last Resort: Child Protection, the Courts and the Children Act 1989* (The Stationery Office, 1999), at p 341).

10.16 It should be noted that before making any decision regarding contact, whether it is in respect of accommodated children or other children subject to various orders, the local authority is required to give due consideration to the child's wishes and feelings, having regard to his age and understanding (CA 1989, s 22(4)(a) and (5)(a)). The National Foster Care Association has recommended that the child's views should, wherever possible, be given priority in reaching decisions about any contact arrangements (see *UK National Standards for Foster Care* (National Foster Care Association, 1989), Standard 19.3). The local authority may be concerned about the effect which contact may be having on a child, but should it seek to restrict contact with the child's parent or anyone with parental responsibility, that person has the ultimate sanction against the local authority which is removal of the child. Clearly, in those situations in which a child has suffered or is at risk of suffering significant harm, has been accommodated by the local authority, and would be deemed to be at risk if a move to return the child to his own home was undertaken by the parents, local social services must be prepared to take emergency action, if necessary, to prevent removal, which may well involve the initiation of proceedings (eg for an emergency protection order) in which the court will have to give specific directions with regard to contact (CA 1989, s 44(6)(a)).

10.17 Where the child has been having ongoing contact with parents, relatives and other friends, there would not usually be any necessity to advise the child in the course of any reviews of the child's case (see CA 1989, s 26(2)) of his right to apply for orders under the provisions of CA 1989, s 8. On occasions, however, the parents and the local authority may agree that some particular person is felt to have an undesirable influence on the child and may, thus, determine that contact between the child and that person should be ended. In such circumstances, the child would be able to challenge such a decision by applying for contact to be ordered under the provision of s 8, although the child would first have to seek leave to make an application under the provisions of s 10(8). The person with whom the child wishes to have contact could also seek leave to make an application for a contact order with the child concerned using the provisions of the CA 1989, s 10(9) and, if given, such leave would be able to apply for a contact order as provided for in s 8.

Contact under a child assessment order

10.18 As was pointed out above (see Chapter **5** and para **10.9**) where the court makes a child assessment order providing for the child to be kept away from home for any length of time, it must also consider giving such directions as it thinks fit concerning contact with the child and other persons during the period of the order. Whilst it is appreciated that a temporary overnight stay cannot be equated with being placed in care, the court must be guided on issues of contact by the circumstances of the case, the age of the child and the presumption of reasonable contact between a child in care and its family, which is established by other provisions such as CA 1989, ss 34 and 44. When giving a direction with regard to contact with a child, subject to a child assessment order, the court is required to regard the child's welfare as its paramount consideration (s 1) but, since a child assessment order is an order under CA 1989, Part V, the court is not required to apply the welfare checklist (see s 1(3)), although many courts will seek to apply the principles laid down in the checklist.

Contact under an emergency protection order

10.19 The CA 1989 provides that where the court has made an emergency protection order with respect to any child, then the applicant must allow the child reasonable contact with his parents, anyone who has parental responsibility, anyone with whom he was living immediately before the making of the order and any person in whose favour contact orders (whether under s 8 or s 34) are enforced or with anyone acting on behalf of any of those persons (s 44(13)). The operation of this statutory presumption in favour of reasonable contact, however, is subject to any direction which might have been given by the court under s 44(6) and thus where the applicant believes that there may be risks to the child from having such contact, then the applicant should apply to the court to exercise its discretion to give such directions as it deems appropriate with regard to contact between the child and any person (s 44(6)(a)). Any directions given by the court may further impose conditions with regard to the exercise of an individual's rights to contact; thus, where it is felt that any person constitutes a threat to the child but the threat is not of such a nature as to merit a direction for no contact, a direction may be sought as to the supervision of such contact. Where the applicant, local authority, NSPCC, the police or any other person have not sought or obtained any such directions from the court, then the general statutory presumption in favour of reasonable contact will operate. Such reasonable contact is not, however, the same as contact at the discretion of the local authority. The courts have held (see *Re P (Minors) (Contact with Children in Care)* [1993] 2 FLR 156) that 'reasonable' implies contact which is agreed between the local authority and the parents or, in the absence of such an agreement, contact which can be regarded as objectively reasonable.

10.20 As indicated above, the *Children's Homes – National Minimum Standards* and *Fostering Services – National Minimum Standards* both emphasise that emergency admissions require special care if parents are to be reassured from the outset that they have a continuing role in their child's life and also to minimise distress for the child. Early visits and meetings should be encouraged, even though parents may need help to cope with the child's stress as well as with their own. Where contact between a child and any of the other persons referred to in CA 1989, s 44(13) is thought to be causing the child undue distress or is posing a risk to the child, or, alternatively, where a parent, other person entitled, or the child is dissatisfied with the proposed levels of contact, then an application to the court may be made at any time during the emergency protection order for the court to issue new directions (s 44(9)).

Contact with the child in police protection

10.21 In those circumstances where the police have exercised their powers of protection pursuant to s 46 of the CA 1989, either to remove a child from the care of particular persons or to authorise the child's retention in a particular place, it is for the designated officer to decide on the extent of contact which he feels is both reasonable and in the child's best interests (s 46(10)). The police must allow contact between the child and the same range of people who are allowed contact under an emergency protection order (see para **10.19**). In those cases where social services and the police are conducting a joint investigation of a serious allegation, it is interesting to note that if it is deemed necessary to exercise police powers rather than resorting to an emergency protection order, then the police would have the right to refuse contact between the child and the alleged perpetrators of any abuse, without the need to resort to court for an order of any description. Nevertheless, any disproportionate restriction of contact by the police between a parent and his or her child could result in a challenge using Article 8(1) of the ECHR.

Contact under an interim care order

10.22 Where a child is made the subject of an interim care order, then the court must treat the issue of contact in exactly the same way as it would if it was making a full care order. It must, therefore, consider any proposed contact arrangements being put forward by the local authority and invite the parties to the proceedings to comment upon them (CA 1989, ss 31(11), 34(11) as seen in *Oldham Metropolitan Borough Council v D* [2000] 2 FLR 382). Where a parent, a child or anyone else who desires contact is dissatisfied with any of the proposed contact arrangements put before the court, then they are able to seek a contact order under the provisions of s 34. Where a children's guardian has been appointed, he would be expected to provide a report to the court in such circumstances.

10.23 The way in which a court might deal with the issue of preventing contact between a child and alleged abusers in the context of an interim care order was considered by the court in *Croydon London Borough Council v A* [1992] 2 FLR 341. In that case, a 2-year-old child had been the victim of repeated physical abuse by his father who had been convicted of the offence. The child, who had originally been placed under a place of safety order and on a local authority Child Protection Register, was allowed staying access with his mother who, unbeknown to social services and the guardian, was still seeing the child's father. A number of further incidents followed and a supervision order was made, although the child was returned to live with the mother. Following the birth of another child, a violent incident occurred in the premises below the mother's flat, during which the father received stab wounds. The father and mother were clearly in contact with each other, which constituted a considerable risk to the children. Emergency protection orders were made and the children placed in foster care. An application was then made for an interim care order, under which the children were to be placed with the mother in a charitable home with a view to rehabilitation, to assess her with the children and to protect them from their father. The court, instead of making the interim care order requested and dealing with contact via a s 34 order, made a prohibited steps order under s 8 forbidding the parents having any contact with each other. The justices gave as their reasons that the order was to ensure the bonding of the children with their mother for their long-term benefit. The local authority appealed, contending that the justices were wrong to make the prohibited steps order and should, instead, have dealt with the matter by means of an interim care order together with an order for no contact under s 34, which could then have been disputed by either of the parents.

10.24 In the appeal, Hollins J stated that the appellate court would not normally interfere with the discretion of a court below unless it considered that that court was plainly wrong or had erred in principle or had taken into account something which it should not have done or failed to take into account something that it should have done. On this occasion, however, he stated that the justices were plainly wrong to refuse to make an interim care order which would give more flexibility to the local authority. He indicated that where justices were of a mind to make such an order, rather than the interim care order sought by an applicant, they should give the parties an opportunity to address them on the question as to whether such an order should or could be made. He further emphasised that a failure to allow the applicants such a hearing might constitute a defect in the proceedings. As far as the issue of contact was concerned, the justices were also wrong in making a prohibited steps order since contact between adults was not a step which could be taken by a parent in meeting a parent's responsibility for the child and therefore fell outside the terms of the CA 1989, s 8(1). The issue of contact could either be dealt with, as should have been the case here, under the flexibility and discretion afforded to the local authority by the making of an interim care order, or by the local authority seeking an order for no, or restricted, contact under s 34.

10.25 The question of whether a local authority should seek an order under s 34 for no contact before the final hearing in the care proceedings came up for consideration in *A v M and Walsall Metropolitan Borough Council* [1993] 2 FLR 244. In that case, an interim care order had been made but before the final care order hearing the local authority successfully applied to the family proceedings court for contact between the mother and baby to be terminated, and the mother appealed. Ewbank J stated that the justices were plainly wrong in coming to a premature decision and he allowed the appeal. He emphasised that this was not a case where matters were so exceptional and the risks so severe that contact between a mother and baby should be stopped. The problem was that the justices had come to such a firm decision in their judgment, ie that the mother was unable to provide the baby with the level of care that could reasonably be expected from a parent, that they had precluded a reassessment of the provision at the final hearing. They had made findings of fact and gone into details of evidence which were more appropriate for a final hearing and thus the order could not be allowed to stand.

10.26 Where the local authority wishes to be able to continue to assess a difficult situation and where it also wishes to be able to respond flexibly to contact arrangements, then the making of an interim care order, which carries with it the operation of the statutory presumption of reasonable contact and allows alternative orders to be sought from the court, might be considered the best way of proceeding (see *Re G (Minors) (Interim Care Orders)* [1993] 2 FLR 839).

Contact with children subject to care orders

10.27 Where the court is considering whether or not the making of a care order would be in the paramount interest of the child (the 'welfare stage'), the court will need to have before it the local authority's s 31A care plan and, as part of that care plan, the local authority should have included arrangements about contact with the child who is to be made the subject of the order. Pursuant to the CA 1989, s 34(11) the court will consider those contact arrangements and invite the parties to the proceedings to comment upon them. Arrangements as to contact will be particularly important in situations where the local authority is adopting a twin-track planning approach (see *Re D and K (Children) (Care Plan: Twin Track Planning)* [1999] 2 FLR 872). As noted earlier with regard to contact orders made pursuant to interim care orders (see para **10.22**), there is a statutory presumption of reasonable contact and, as was seen in the case of *Re P (Minors) (Contact with Children in Care)* [1993] 2 FLR 156, this has been held to mean 'objectively reasonable'. Further definition as to what is meant by 'reasonable' in this context was provided in the *Children Act 1989: Guidance and Regulations* (DOH, 1991), vol 3: 'Family Placements' and vol 4: 'Residential Care', as well as in the *Standards for Residential Child Care Services: A Handbook for Social Services Managers and Inspectors, Users of Services and their Families* (DOH, 1994) but it was not replicated in the new National Standards documents. Where it is proposed that children are to be swiftly rehabilitated with their parents, it is stated that contact should be in the family home at the earliest possible stage. Such visits have the advantage of maintaining links with the neighbourhood to which the child will be returning (vol 3, 'Family Placements', para 6.18). The guidance goes on to state in the same paragraph that: 'If possible, parents should be encouraged to participate in some way in the child's daily life, by preparing tea, for example, or by shopping for clothes, or putting the young child to bed'.

10.28 This marks a considerable departure from previously accepted local authority social services practice in relation to contact with children subject to care orders, and many such orders are now open to challenge not only using the procedures laid down under the CA 1989, s 34, but also pursuant to implementation of the ECHR by the HRA 1998 (see para **1.19** *et seq*). (For an example of the former approach using the CA 1989, see *H v West Sussex County Council* [1998] 1 FLR 862; and for a successful challenge using Article 8 of the ECHR where a social services authority had denied the parents contact with two of their children, see *S and G v Italy* [2000] 2 FLR 771 and see also *Hokkanen v Finland* [1996] 1 FLR 289.) The courts have also been considerably influenced by the messages about the benefits which may accrue to the child from the maintenance of contact with the child's family, even where long-term fostering or adoption may be being contemplated by the local authority. Thus in *Re E (A Minor) (Care Order: Contact)* [1994] 1 FLR 146, the President of the Family Division stated (at p 154) that:

'although the value of contact may be limited by the parents' inadequacy, it may still be of fundamental importance to the long-term welfare of the child, unless of course it can be seen that in a given case it will inevitably disturb the child's care. In short, even when the s 31 criteria are satisfied, contact may well be of singular importance to the long-term welfare of the child; first in giving the child the security of knowing that his parents love him and are interested in his welfare; secondly by avoiding any damaging sense of loss to the child in seeing himself as abandoned by his parents; thirdly, by enabling the child to commit himself to the substitute family with a seal of approval of the natural parents; and fourthly, by giving the child the necessary sense of family and personal identity. Contact if maintained is capable of reinforcing and increasing the chances of success of a permanent placement, whether on a long-term fostering basis or by adoption.'

10.29 Where, however, any party to care proceedings is dissatisfied with the proposed contact arrangements as set out in the s 31A care plan, then they may seek a contact order under s 34 and this includes the child who is unhappy about any contact proposals. Where this occurs, the guardian would be expected to give further advice to the court and, if necessary, furnish a further report or an addendum to the original, which will have dealt with contact issues in the care proceedings (s 41). Similarly, where contact arrangements had been agreed at the time of the making of the care order pursuant to the consideration of the care plan and then subsequently a party or some other person becomes dissatisfied with the arrangement for contact, an application can be made for a contact order under s 34(3). Where any authority feels that contact with the child would be positively detrimental in the light of the child protection issues involved in the case, an application may also be made by the local authority to terminate or reduce contact with a named individual or individuals (s 34(2) and (4)).

10.30 Whether or not any application for the making, variation, definition or termination of contact is successful will be determined by a number of issues and the court's decision whether or not to make any order requested will be determined by consideration of the paramountcy principle in s 1 of the CA 1989. All the various constituent parts of s 1 come into play, and it could be argued that the court retains control not only over the relationship between the child and his family, but also over the authority's plans for the child by virtue of any orders which it may make in relation to contact (see *Re B (Minors) (Care: Contact: Local Authority's Plans)* [1993] 1 FLR 543; *Re E (A Minor) (Care Order: Contact)* [1994] 1 FLR 146; *Re J (Minors) (Care: Care Plan)* [1994] 1 FLR 253 and most particularly *Berkshire County Council v B* [1997] 1 FLR 171 and *L v London Borough of Bromley* [1998] 1 FLR 709).

10.31 The problem of determining whether or not the making of an order in relation to contact will be in the child's paramount interests, especially where the parent herself may also be a child, came up for consideration in *Birmingham City Council v H* [1993] 1 FLR 883. In this case the local authority decided to apply for termination of contact between a 16-year-old disruptive mother living in secure accommodation and her baby son who was to be placed with long-term foster parents with a view to adoption. The judge in this case made a finding that contact with the mother was contrary to the son's best interests as the mother's volatile behaviour pattern could cause unacceptable risks to the son. He took the view that since contact was the right of the child and not the right of the parent, in a case where conflict arose between a mother and son who were both minors, the son's welfare took priority over that of the mother. Accordingly, he terminated contact between mother and son under the provisions of s 34(4) save for an exchange of information on a twice yearly basis. The mother appealed to the Court of Appeal which allowed her appeal but then the local authority appealed to the House of Lords.

10.32 The House of Lords confirmed the orders of the first instance judge: applying the principle that the baby's interests were the court's paramount consideration and given that the making of the order under s 34(4) allowed the local authority to refuse contact between the parent and the child, this meant that the court was bound to refuse any application by the mother under s 34(3) when any question arose as to the child's upbringing. As the making of the order under s 34(4) in favour of the local authority meant that they could then refuse all contact between the child and the mother, there was no point at all in making any order under s 34(2) for the mother to have contact with the child. Where the court has been requested, on an application made by the authority or the child, to exercise its powers under s 34(2), to make such order as it considers appropriate with respect to the contact to be allowed between the child and any named person, then the case-law suggests that careful consideration must be given by the court to the s 31A care plan (see *Re D and H (Care: Termination of Contact)* [1997] 1 FLR 841).

10.33 In circumstances where the court is considering making an order refusing contact and this is inconsistent with the proposals made by the local authority under the s 31A care plan, then the court may use its powers in s 34 to authorise, but not to require, the local authority to refuse contact. This approach was confirmed by the Court of Appeal in *Re W (Section 34(2) Orders)* [2000] 1 FLR 502. As the Court of Appeal emphasised, on its true construction, s 34 did not create a prohibitory jurisdiction. There was no intention when the legislation was framed to create a jurisdiction under s 34 to inhibit the local authority in the performance of its statutory duty by preventing contact which the local authority might consider advantageous to the welfare of the child. The court in this case also emphasised that the Contact with Children Regulations 1991, SI 1991/891, provided a useful means of enlarging pre-existing positive orders without unnecessary returns to the court in circumstances where the relationship between the child in care and significant adults was thriving. The court pointed out that there was no valid distinction to be drawn in reg 3 between departure from the order and departure from 'the terms of the order' and the local authority was entitled both to alter details such as place and time of collection or date of commencement or termination, and to change the nature of the contact, for example by allowing staying contact rather than visiting contact.

10.34 The CA 1989 provides in s 34(2) that the child may make an application with regard to contact and that the court may make such order as it thinks appropriate (s 34(3)). Although there are no provisions in s 34(2) that the child should satisfy the court that he or she possesses sufficient understanding to make the application, it is nevertheless not unreasonable to expect that the court would apply the criteria laid down in CA 1989, s 10(8) that the child should establish that he has sufficient understanding to make the application. In the case of *Re F (Contact: Child in Care)* [1995] 1 FLR 510, the child concerned was 16 years old and in the care of the local authority and had applied for contact with her siblings. Despite the fact that behavioural problems had led to her being in care, there was no question of her not being able to seek an application for contact with her siblings under s 34(2) despite her parents' objections. In the event, however, her application was unsuccessful as a result of opposition from both the parents and the siblings. Parents, guardians, the holders of prior residence orders or any person who has previously had the care of the child, may also make an application for a contact order, as may any person who has obtained leave of the court (s 34(3)). Thus, whilst parents may be excluded in a case involving serious child abuse from having contact with the child, either at the instigation of the child or the local authority (under the provisions of s 34(4)), grandparents, aunts, uncles, godparents or any other significant person in the child's life, including a brother or sister, could seek leave of the court to make an application under s 34. Although no criteria have been laid down within the provisions of s 34 to assist the court, the Court of Appeal in *Re M (Care: Contact: Grandmother's Application for Leave)* [1995] 2 FLR 86, stated that the criteria laid down in s 10(9) which govern the position with regard to such people seeking leave to make an application for s 8 orders should be considered apposite for the purposes of s 34(3). Therefore, the court should have regard to the following factors:

(a) the nature of the contact sought, whether frequent, infrequent, direct or indirect;

(b) the applicant's connection to the child: the more important and meaningful the connection, the greater the weight to be given to the application;

(c) any disruption: the need for stability and security is vital and any foster placement should not be put at risk; the risk must arise from the proposed application (see the comparable provision in CA 1989, s 10(9), risk of 'disrupting a child's life to such an extent that he would be harmed by it', although knowledge of pending litigation can be sufficiently disruptive);

(d) the wishes of the parents and the local authority (these are very material but not determinative).

10.35 When looking at the wishes of the local authority under para (d) (above), the exercise of the local authority's duty under s 22(3) of the CA 1989 is to 'safeguard and promote the child's welfare'. The court emphasised that in weighing up the factors which might influence the granting of leave, the following tests should be applied:

(1) if the application is frivolous, vexatious or an abuse of process it must fail;

(2) if the applicant fails to show that there is any real prospect of eventual success, or the prospect is so remote as to make the application unsustainable, then the application for leave should be dismissed;

(3) the applicant must satisfy the court that there is a serious issue to try, ie they must present a good arguable case.

In that particular case, therefore, the Court of Appeal allowed the grandmother's appeal against the refusal by the first instance judge of leave for her to seek contact with the children, where the current plan was the children's adoption.

10.36 Where an application is made under the provisions of s 34(3), the local authority may still seek to oppose such contact where it views with suspicion the ability of the person having the benefit of a contact order to restrain visits by the child's parents while the other person is having contact. Where the local authority or the child makes an application to the court for an order, the court may make an order authorising the authority to refuse to allow contact between the child, any parent or guardian, any holder of a prior residence order or any person who has care of the child under an order made pursuant to the exercise of the High Court inherent jurisdiction (s 34(4)).

10.37 Where an application for a contact order has been made, the court must appoint a guardian for the child concerned unless it is satisfied that it is not necessary to do so in order to safeguard the child's interests (CA 1989, s 41(1)). The role of the guardian in such proceedings came up for detailed consideration by the Court of Appeal in *Re S (A Minor) (Guardian ad Litem: Welfare Officer)* [1993] 1 FLR 110. In the course of a father's application for contact with a child who had been placed for adoption following the making of a care order, the local authority had issued a counter-application for contact to be terminated and the court appointed the guardian ad litem who had acted in the earlier care proceedings. The guardian ad litem's report supported the local authority's view; responding to the father's concern that the guardian might be considered to be partisan because his views coincided with those of the local authority, the judge directed that a welfare officer's report be obtained in order to alleviate the father's anxiety. The guardian ad litem appealed against that direction on the grounds that the welfare officer's report was superfluous and unnecessary and the Court of Appeal allowed his appeal. The Court of Appeal stated that since the role of the guardian ad litem is to represent the child and to advise as to her best interests, that could not be regarded as partisan. It was, therefore, not appropriate to accommodate the father's natural but unjustified perception by allowing the introduction of yet another reporting officer, which would mean a duplication of efforts.

10.38 The guardian may play a crucial role in contact order proceedings. In *Kent County Council v C* [1993] 1 FLR 308, the guardian ad litem took a very strong line in opposing the local authority's proposals for contact between a mother and child in order to assess the possibilities of rehabilitation. The guardian ad litem took the view that rehabilitation would be unsuccessful and would merely prolong the child's sense of impermanence, and advised instead that the child be placed with long-term foster parents. The justices were extremely concerned about the guardian ad litem's views, however, and although they had power under s 34(2) to order that there be no contact between mother and child, which would effectively prevent the local authority from carrying out the rehabilitation plan, they determined not to exercise that power in the circumstances. Instead, in making a care order, they added a direction that the local authority should allow the guardian to have continued involvement with the child for 3 months to enable him to investigate the rehabilitation process so that, if appropriate, he could apply on behalf of the child to have contact with the mother terminated under s 34(2). The local authority appealed, querying whether, in an inappropriate case, the family proceedings court had power to order that no contact take place and, further, whether the court had power to add a direction as to the involvement of a guardian when making a care order under the CA 1989. In this particular case, Ewbank J, in the High Court held that:

> 'Whilst it was open to the Family Proceedings Court to make orders under s 34(2) that no contact take place between the child and the parent, in most cases it would be ill advised to do so and the preferable course would simply be to make no order for contact, thus allowing the local authority room to exercise its discretion.'

10.39 It was further held that there was no power under the CA 1989 to make directions in relation to care orders since, once a care order has been made, and subject to any subsequent orders as to contact under s 34, sole responsibility for the care of the child fell on the local authority, and the addition of a direction of any sort to a care order would be a fetter on the local authority's plans, authority and responsibility. Accordingly, Ewbank J stated:

'Since the pace and success of any rehabilitation programme entered into after the care order was made was a matter which could only be decided by the local authority, the appeal would be allowed and the direction deleted from the order.'

10.40 According to statistics released in the *Children Act Report 1995–1999* (DOH, 1999) in the *Supplement to the Children Act Report 1995–1999* (DOH, 2000) at chapter 10, and in *Children Act Report 2001* (DOH, 2002), guardians ad litem have been appointed in the majority of applications for contact orders. The duties of the newly named children's guardian will be the same as those which he performs in proceedings for a care and supervision order (see Chapter 7). The focus of the guardian's work in contact cases will, however, be on whether there should or should not be contact with a specific named individual, and whether or not this is in the paramount interests of the child. The guardian will often be assisted in this assessment by an expert, usually a child psychologist or child psychiatrist, and the court has indicated that in cases involving complex and delicate issues of psychological harm it was appropriate that such applications should be heard by a higher court than the magistrates (see *Berkshire County Council v B* [1997] 1 FLR 171).

10.41 Where the local authority is of the view that it is desirable in the child's interests to refuse to allow contact with a person to whom the presumption of contact applies, then except in urgent cases such a decision must be referred to the court in order for it to make an order under the CA 1989, s 34(4) after the court has had the opportunity of considering all the evidence. It should be noted, however, that s 34(6) authorises the local authority to refuse contact which would otherwise be required under the presumption set out in s 34(1) or pursuant to any order which has been made by the court under s 34 if:

(1)   it is satisfied that it is necessary to do so in order to safeguard or promote the child's welfare; and
(2)   the refusal:
    (a)   is decided upon as a matter of urgency and;
    (b)   does not last for more than 7 days.

10.42 To succeed in continuing to refuse contact, therefore, the local authority would have to ensure that its application for authority to refuse to allow contact would be heard in that 7-day period, as otherwise it would be obliged to continue to allow contact between the child and the person in respect of whom it is seeking to terminate contact. There could in such circumstances be an interim application to deal with the position until such time as the court is able to have a full hearing on the matter. This was confirmed in *West Glamorgan County Council v P* [1992] 2 FLR 369. The court emphasised in that case that s 34(4) gave the court complete discretion, exercisable within the general principles of the CA 1989, to authorise such refusal of contact for as short or as long a period as it considered necessary for the child's welfare.

10.43 The Court of Appeal's judgment in the case of *Re B (Minors) (Contact: Local Authority's Plans)* [1993] 1 FLR 543 gives clear guidance on the approach to be taken in applications under s 34, emphasising that a key factor in all such decisions would be the welfare principle contained within the CA 1989, s 1. In *Re B*, two girls, aged 2, and 4 were the subject of care orders and the local authority's plans for adoption of the girls had been approved by the Adoption Panel. The children's mother had had a third child, her parenting skills were much improved and she had had regular and frequent contact with the two older children. Despite these improvements, the local authority applied for an order under s 34(4) to terminate contact and the mother applied for the discharge of the care order or an increase in contact, supported by the guardian ad litem, with the ultimate view of rehabilitation of the children with her. The judge in the first instance said that it would not be right to attempt directly or indirectly to force the local authority's hand and put pressure on it towards rehabilitation because he had to consider the application for contact in the context of the plan for adoption and, thus, whether the welfare of the children required that contact be refused. He therefore allowed the authority's application. On the guardian ad litem's appeal, supported by the mother, the local authority relied upon the principle established in *A v Liverpool City Council* [1981] 2 All ER 385, that courts would not generally interfere with a local authority's decision to refuse access by a parent of a child in its care under a care order where the appeal was based solely on the merits of the decision.

10.44 On appeal to the Court of Appeal, Butler-Sloss LJ, in her judgment, declared:

> 'I do not, however, believe that the important principle set out in *A v Liverpool City Council* … applies to the intervention of the court in response to an application which is properly made, or fetters the exercise of the judicial discretion in an application under the Children Act 1989' (at p 549).

The Court of Appeal went on to elaborate in considerable detail the approach which should now be taken to obligations under s 34 and stated that this guidance should be followed carefully. Thus, the court directed that, when an application for contact comes before the court, at whichever tier, the court has a duty to apply s 1 of the CA 1989, which states that when a court determines any question with respect to the upbringing of a child, the child's welfare shall be the court's paramount consideration. The court must have regard to the prejudicial effect of delay, to the checklist including the range of orders available to the court and to the important issue of whether to make an order. On hearing a s 34 application, therefore, the Court of Appeal emphasised that the court has a duty to consider and apply the welfare provisions.

10.45 The Court of Appeal went on to point out that contact applications generally fall into two main categories: those which asked for contact as such and those which are attempts to set aside the care order itself (this analysis has subsequently been adopted by the court in *H v West Sussex County Council* [1998] 1 FLR 862). In the first category, the court stated that there is no suggestion that the applicant wishes to take over the care of the child and the issue of contact often depends upon whether contact would frustrate long-term plans for the child in a substitute home, such as adoption, where continuing contact may not be for the long-term welfare of the child (this was the case in *Re F (Care Proceedings: Contact)* (2000) *The Times*, June 22). The presumption of contact, which has to be for the benefit of the child, has always to be balanced against the long-term welfare of the child and, in particular, where he will live in the future. The court emphasised that contact must not be allowed to destabilise or endanger the arrangements for the child and that, in many cases, the plans for the child will be decisive for the contact application. The court also stated that there may be cases where the parent is having satisfactory contact with the child and there are no long-term plans or those plans do not appear to the court to preclude some future contact. The proposals of the local authority, based on its appreciation of the best interests of the child, must command the greatest respect and consideration from the court, but Parliament have given to the court, and not the local authority, the duty to decide on contact between the child and those named in s 34(1). Consequently, the court has the task of requiring the local authority to justify its long-term plans to the extent only that those plans exclude contact between the parent and the child.

10.46 The court went on to state that, in the second category, contact applications may be made by parents by way of another attempt to obtain the return of the children. In such a case, the court is obviously allowed to take into account the failure to apply to discharge the care order and, in the majority of cases, the court will have little difficulty in coming to the conclusion that the applicant cannot demonstrate that contact with a view to rehabilitation with the parent is a viable proposition at that stage, particularly if it has already been rejected at the earlier hearing when the child was placed in care. The Court of Appeal suggested that the task for the parents would be too great and the court would be entitled to assume that the plans for the local authority to terminate contact were for the welfare of the child and were not to be frustrated by inappropriate contact with a view to the remote possibility, at some future date, of rehabilitation. In all cases, however, the Court of Appeal emphasised that the principles laid out in the CA 1989, s 1 have to be considered, and the local authority has the task of justifying the cessation of contact to the court.

10.47 The court also stated that there may be unusual cases where the local authority has not made effective plans or there has been considerable delay in implementing them and a parent, who had previously been found by the court unable or unwilling to care for the child so that a care order had been made, reappears on the scene as a future possible primary care-taker. If the local authority with a care order decides not to consider that parent on the new facts, it is for the court, under the jurisdiction of the CA 1989, to consider whether, even at this late stage, there should be some investigation of the proposals of the parent and the possibility of reconsidering the local authority's plans. The Court of Appeal made it plain that it totally rejected the argument that the court could not go behind the long-term plans of the local authority unless the local authority could have been shown to be acting capriciously or was otherwise open to scrutiny by way of judicial review. Butler-Sloss LJ, quite uncompromisingly, stated that she 'unhesitatingly rejected the local authority's argument'. She did, however, state that the local authority's plan has to be given the greatest possible consideration by the courts and it is only in the unusual case that a parent will be able to convince the court, the onus being firmly on the parent, that there has been such a change of circumstances as to require further investigation and reconsideration of the local authority plan. She went on to state that:

> 'If, however, a court was unable to intervene, it would make a nonsense of the paramountcy of the welfare of the child, which is the bedrock of the Act, and would subordinate it to the administrative decision of the local authority in a situation where the court is seized on the contact issue.'

That, she declared, 'could not be right'. The court went on to allow the mother's appeal.

10.48 Butler-Sloss LJ did, however, go on to emphasise, at the end of her deliberations, that she did not wish her judgment to be seen as constituting an open door to court to challenge the plans of local authorities. She stated that, generally, where parties choose not to pursue applications they are well advised not to do so. But, she added, there is now a flexibility in the approach of the court to the problem of the child before it and, occasionally, the court may wish to invoke the CA 1989, s 10(1)(b) which provides that a court may, in any family proceedings, which include care proceedings, make a s 8 order with respect to a child if the court considers that the order should be made, even if no application has been made. A court, she suggested, may also make a contact or an interim contact order under s 34 and impose such conditions as it considers appropriate (s 34(7)).

10.49 Another example of a case in which the local authority's plans for the child were being frustrated by the child's condition, and which necessitated the court re-evaluating a proposed reduction in contact by the mother to her child, was *Berkshire County Council v B* [1997] 1 FLR 171. The child in this case had lived with his mother for some 6 years when at the mother's request he was accommodated by the local authority and placed with foster parents. The mother had severe personality problems and a psychologist described the child's relationship with his mother as an 'anxious avoidant attachment'. The local authority had obtained a care order on the child when it was feared that the mother might remove the child from foster parents with whom he was beginning to improve. The local authority's long-term plan for the child was that adoption was in his best interests and that the twice-weekly contact meetings with the mother should be reduced to two meetings a year with letterbox contact. The child psychiatrist and the guardian ad litem were both of the view that it would be difficult to place the child for adoption as he was an emotionally damaged child and they believed that the child should have regular contact with his mother. The magistrates agreed and ordered that the child should continue to have contact with the mother for 2 hours twice a week whereupon the local authority appealed. Hale J dismissed the local authority's appeal, holding that on considering an application under the CA 1989, s 34 to authorise refusal of contact, the welfare of the child was the paramount consideration and the court could order parental contact if such contact was in the child's best interests even if the long-term care plan of the local authority envisaged that parental contact would eventually be terminated. In the circumstances of the present case, therefore, the magistrates had exercised their discretion properly on the evidence before them and the court would not interfere with their decision.

10.50 *Berkshire County Council v B* (above) was an example of the first type of application referred to by Butler-Sloss LJ, namely those who are simply asking for contact as such with no suggestion that the applicant wishes to take over the care of the child him- or herself. The case of *Re E (A Minor) (Care Order: Contact)* [1994] 1 FLR 146 is another example. In this case the local authority had made an application to refuse contact between the children and the parents as they were of the opinion that continued face-to-face contact would conflict with the local authority's plans for closed adoption. The judge at the first instance had approached the issue of contact upon the basis that the court would not make an order which was incompatible with the local authority's plans unless the children's welfare dictated otherwise. The guardian ad litem and the psychiatrist believed that the children would benefit from contact with their parents because the parents were unlikely to undermine an alternative permanent placement. The local authority believed that contact should be refused between the parents and the children because there was no prospect of rehabilitation between the parents and the level and quality of the contact was low. The judge at first instance granted the local authority's application, but the guardian and the parents appealed.

10.51 The Court of Appeal allowed the appeal stating that the judge at first instance had placed too great an emphasis on the care plan of the local authority which was not the appropriate test to be applied having regard to the Court of Appeal's decision in *Re B* (see para **10.43**). The Court of Appeal further emphasised that *Re B* was the authority for the proposition that where the judge had concluded that the benefits of contact outweighed the disadvantages of disrupting any of the local authority's long-term plans, which were inconsistent with such contact, then the judge had to refuse the local authority's application to terminate contact. These principles derived from *Re B* were also applied in the case of *Re T (Termination of Contact: Discharge of Order)* [1997] 1 FLR 517. Here the four boys, three of whom were very disturbed, and their parents were described as a problem family, and the judge made care orders relating to the children and authorised the local authority to terminate contact between the parents and the three elder boys under s 34(4) of the CA 1989. The father separated from the mother and took the view that the children should have no further contact with him or their mother. The second boy had been in three successive foster placements with a view to adoption but a therapeutic residential placement was now being considered, and there were plans to place the third boy, who was very disturbed and was currently in a small special residential school, for adoption. The mother applied to discharge the orders made under s 34(4) and the judge refused her application. The mother appealed and the Court of Appeal allowed her appeal in relation to the second boy affirming that: on considering whether to discharge an order under s 34(4), the welfare of the child was paramount; that it had to be shown that there had been some material change in the circumstances since the making of the order; and that the court had to look closely at the extent of the change and then consider whether it was appropriate to discharge the order. In this case the circumstances had changed since the making of the order in relation to the second boy since adoption was no longer being considered by the local authority and so the order under s 34(4) would be discharged. The Court of Appeal emphasised, again, that it is not appropriate on an application to discharge to reinvestigate whether the original order was made appropriately. The courts must be astute to see that the application to discharge is bona fide and not a disguised attempt to appeal the original order. The court said, however, that a s 34(4) order should not be made: (a) whilst there remains a realistic possibility of rehabilitation of the child with the person in question; or (b) merely against the possibility that circumstances may change in such a way as to make termination of contact desirable. For an order to be justified, a probable need to terminate contact must be foreseeable and not too remote and Holman J stated that if on an application to discharge a s 34(4) order the court exceptionally concludes that the factors are so evenly balanced as not to come down on one side or the other on the question of discharge, then the order should be discharged. He stressed that if an order under s 34(4) cannot be justified then it should not remain in force. In cases similar to those just considered here it is of course possible that in future the difficult issues over contact may be referred by the prescribed person appointed under the amended provisions of s 26(2)(k) of the CA 1989 to a CAFCASS officer for further consideration, again under the amended provisions of s 26(2A)(c) of the CA 1989.

10.52 An example of a case in which there was absolutely no hope of rehabilitation, and which was treated by the court as robustly as Butler-Sloss LJ wished such cases to be treated, was that of *Re F (Care Proceedings: Contact)* (2000) *The Times*, June 22. The local authority in this case sought an order under s 34(4) giving it permission to terminate contact with the mother when prospective adopters had been found and were to be introduced to the children. The mother appealed against the making of this order arguing that such an order breached her rights under Articles 6 and 8 of the ECHR. Wall J dismissed the mother's appeal emphasising that the mother's opportunity to be heard in the s 34(4) proceeding meant that it could not be said in any way that her Article 6 rights to a fair hearing had been breached. In Wall J's view, the length of the hearing in the particular case and the involvement of several expert witnesses reflected the fairness of the hearing in that due consideration had been given to every aspect of the matter, considering that the interests of the child were paramount. Insofar as the decision affected the mother's right to family life under Article 8, the court held that the removal of the children on a care order and the subsequent authorisation of a refusal of contact under s 34(4) were not in breach of such rights as the decision was clearly based on the paramount interests of the children with regard to their future health and welfare. Such a decision came within the framework for intervention envisaged by Article 8(2) of the ECHR.

10.53 Where a contact order is made under s 34, a local authority cannot depart from the terms of that order except by agreement with the person in relation to whom the order was made and in accordance with regulations made by the Secretary of State (s 34(8) and see the Contact with Children Regulations 1991) or in an emergency, where the situation does not last more than 7 days (s 34(6)). Before the expiry of 7 days, the authority, if it wishes to stop contact permanently or to reduce contact to a considerable degree, must make an application to the court to this effect. Notice must be given to all the relevant parties and a guardian ad litem will again be appointed. It is unlikely that in such circumstances the court will be ready to proceed immediately, but at what will effectively be an interim hearing on contact, the court has complete discretion under s 34(4) to make a temporary order pending a full hearing (this was then decided by the High Court in *West Glamorgan County Council v P* [1992] 2 FLR 369). Where an application for an order authorising contact to be refused is made at an interim hearing, except in exceptional circumstances, contact should be maintained pending a final hearing (see *A v M and Walsall Metropolitan Borough Council* [1993] 2 FLR 244, at p 246). In circumstances where the issue for consideration at the interim hearing is renewal of contact, then it may be in the child's best interests for the decision on such renewal to be deferred until the final hearing, for example where re-introduction of contact with the possibility of further termination of contact at the final hearing might cause even greater distress to the child (see *Greenwich London Borough Council v H* [1998] 2 FLR 736).

10.54 In *Hampshire County Council v S* [1993] 1 FLR 559, the local authority had become concerned as to the effects of staying contact on the child, and had refused contact for 7 days using s 34(6) and had applied to the court for an order reducing the contact between the child and the parent. It had been agreed at the directions hearing that only the issues relating to the reduction of contact would be considered at the interim hearing. At that interim hearing the magistrates made an order substantially reducing the parents' contact on the basis of the parties' submissions only and without reading the statement of the local authority or the guardian ad litem's report. No proper reasons were given by the magistrates prior to the order being made and a final hearing was not to take place for a further 5 months. In allowing the parents' appeal against the making of an interim order, Cazalet J stressed that magistrates should bear in mind that they are not required to make a final conclusion at any interim hearing. On the particular facts of this case, an early hearing date was imperative, the magistrates should have considered transferring laterally to obtain an earlier date, and where the interim order would lead to a substantial change in the child's position they should have permitted all evidence to be led and challenged at cross-examination.

10.55 Where the court is concerned about repeated or vexatious applications for contact with a child subject to a care order, it may take the step of issuing a direction under CA 1989, s 91(14) that no further application for contact be made with respect to the child by a named person without the leave of the court. In the case of *F v Kent County Council* [1993] 1 FLR 432, the President of the Family Division held that the power under s 91(14) should be used sparingly and only after hearing representations. In this case, a father had applied for contact with his children who were in care. The justices made a consent order granting him contact but went on to make an order under s 91(14) restricting his right to apply again, although they acknowledged that his application had been proper. The President upheld the father's appeal, finding that the justices had acted improperly in making such an order against a father who had not been vexatious, frivolous or unreasonable in making his application. The President stated that the power to make such a direction should be exercised where applications were being made too often and the other party and the child were suffering from them.

10.56 Neither of these conditions were actually fulfilled in the case of *Re Y (Child Orders: Restricting Application)* [1994] 2 FLR 699. In this case the mother had died as a result of a violent assault by the father witnessed by the three young children who had been made the subject of a local authority care order.

After his release from custody, the father instituted proceedings for a residence order, which was later withdrawn, and then applied for contact. His application was heard together with applications by the local authority:

(1) for an order prohibiting contact under s 34(4); and
(2) for an order under s 91(14) that the father should make no further application for contact without the leave of the court.

At the hearing, the court heard reports by the guardian ad litem, by a psychiatrist instructed by the local authority, by the social worker in the case and by the psychiatrist selected on the father's behalf. All, including the expert instructed by the father, were emphatic in their opinion that the children would suffer intense psychological distress if they had contact with the father. The father, in his oral evidence, by presenting himself as a victim of conspiracy and injustice, showed that he was incapable of making any change in his attitudes and behaviour and Thorpe J dismissed the father's application for contact, holding that it was a hopeless one, blind to reality and blind to the children's needs. As well as discussing the application, Thorpe J ordered that there should be no contact between the father and the children without leave of the court. Having refused the father's application, there was no need for the court to consider the local authority's application under s 34. With regard to the second application by the local authority, notwithstanding that there was no history of repeated or vexatious applications by the father, the court would, in the extreme circumstances of the case, make an order under s 91(14) that no application be made by the father either for contact or for discharge of the care order without leave.

Communicating decisions about contact

10.57 All decisions made either by local authorities or the courts should be carefully explained to the parents and children and discussed with them. The *Children Act 1989: Guidance and Regulations* (DOH, 1991) states that local authorities should also confirm in writing to the parents and other relevant persons all decisions and agreements about contact arrangements and any changes to the arrangements and also the outcome of all formal and informal reviews of contact. Issues concerning contact should be fully discussed at a child's review where the child has been looked after by the local authority and the child should also be informed, where appropriate, of his right to apply for any order under the CA 1989 (see the Review of Children's Cases Regulations 1991, Sch 1, para 5). The guidance further suggests that contact arrangements should be monitored to check whether the arrangements are working as intended and this is particularly important in cases which involve significant harm to the child. Steps should be taken to identify any problems which have arisen and any changes which are needed, and difficulties should be discussed openly with the parents and the child's carers so that solutions can be explored and help given. The guidance further emphasises that:

> 'it cannot be in the interest of the child and is no service to parents to allow them to drift to the periphery of a child's life, without reminding them of the possible implications of this course to the plan for their child and his/her relationship with them' (*Children Act 1989: Guidance and Regulations*, vol 3: 'Family Placements', at para 6.38, and vol 4: 'Residential Care', at para 4.38).

10.58 Where there is any disagreement between those desiring to have contact with the child and the local authority, the local authority should ensure that it has clear arrangements to inform parents and others about how to deal with complaints about contact and how to ask for decisions to be reviewed. Responsible authorities should ensure that the representations procedure recognises the need to accept complaints from people, above all parents, who have contact with children who are being looked after (see Chapter **11**). As the guidance points out, 'arrangements should be made for families to discuss their anxieties and dissatisfaction with senior officers if they feel they have reached an impasse with a social worker'. It was further pointed out that those arrangements should not be used to prevent or hinder use of the representations procedure provided in the CA 1989 and that all parents and, where appropriate according to the child's understanding, the child, should be informed of those proceedings (see *Children Act 1989: Guidance and Regulations*, vol 3: 'Family Placements', at para 4.3, and vol 4: 'Residential Care', at para 6.37 (see further, Chapter **12**)).

Appeals

10.59 As must be apparent from the number of cases described, there has been no shortage of appeals being taken in relation to orders made for determination, definition, reduction or expansion of contact. It should be noted that the same appeals procedure which applies to decisions regarding contact with the child in care applies equally on the making of or refusal to make an order in care or supervision order proceedings. Reference, therefore, should be made back to the description of the appeals process in Chapter **7**.

Contact with children in secure units and penal establishments

10.60 It has already been noted at para **10.2** that children held in penal establishments are not covered by the provisions on contact contained in Part IV of the CA 1989. They are thus subject to the regimes on contact determined by the authorities in those establishments. Whilst the *Children's Homes – National Minimum Standards* (DOH, 2002) (Standard 36) emphasise that secure units are to be seen as children's homes in the same way as other children's residential homes, the likelihood of a particular establishment being close to a child's home is not great (see Chapter **4**). According to interviews carried out by Goldson, placements of children in secure units and penal establishments, in some cases over 200 miles from their family home, means that families often cannot afford to visit the children. This is in clear breach of Article 9 of the UNCRC but critically it is also in breach of Article 8 of the ECHR. Despite the fact that all the children in secure units qualify as 'looked after', there is no evidence whatsoever that their families are informed of the local authority's powers under Sch 2, Part 2, para 16 of the CA 1989 to make payments in respect of travelling, subsistence or other expenses incurred, to any of the members of a child's family or even to the child's friends or other persons connected with him or her to enable such persons to visit the child. Such payments are subject to the conditions that the visits could not otherwise be made without those persons experiencing undue financial hardship and the circumstances warrant the making of such payments. Therefore, particularly for those 'looked after children' who are placed in secure units at considerable distances from their families, friends, and support networks, the availability of financial assistance and a far wider use of these empowering provisions by local authorities could lead to a dramatic improvement in the experiences of such places by children and young people and immeasurably improve their life chances on release. The evidence, however, would tend to suggest for these groups of children, as much as for 'looked after children' generally, that these powers are little if ever used. For those children in penal establishments who do not qualify as 'looked after children', the prospect of support from the local authority where the child had his home before placement is even bleaker. Potential support for these children and young people has to be derived instead from more restricted empowering provisions in Sch 2, Part 2, para 10 aimed at 'promoting contact between the child living apart from his family'. The provision in para 10 applies to children in need *within the local authority's area* whom the authority is not 'looking after', but who are living apart from their family. The key restricting words here are *within the local authority's area* since, for so many children placed in penal establishments, their placement is not in the locality and so they will not be *within the local authority area*. From discussions with Goldson it is apparent that local authorities are making little or no effort to use the powers given to them in para 10 of Sch 2, Part 2 to the CA 1989 promoting contact with these vulnerable children and young people and their families and friends, and certainly the families who might benefit from such assistance are not even aware that the powers exist. Thus, little real consideration has been given to the welfare needs in relation to contact for those children in secure units and penal establishments.

10.61 An additional element of protection which could be extended to children and young people in penal establishments is the appointment of the independent visitor as provided for looked after children under para 17 of Sch 2, Part 2 to the CA 1989. The Joint Inspectorate's report *Safeguarding Children* (DOH/SSI, 2002) noted that many councils had set up independent visitor and advocate schemes and further that one council had arranged for an independent visitor to undertake monthly well-being interviews with each child in residential care (at p 63). This could beneficially be extended to children in penal establishments

Conclusion

10.62 It is undoubtedly the case now that both local authorities and the courts have been forced into recognising the messages from research given by children themselves: that there is a great need in children to keep in contact with their own families even where such families prove to be incapable of looking after them on a full-time basis. This need has been very apparent at the time when young people might be leaving care or some form of penal setting (see *Caring for Children Away from Home – Messages from Research* (DOH, 1998), at p 59 and Goldson (2002), at p 91). Maintaining close relationships with family members other than parents has also been recognised to be of importance in children's lives and, crucially, the European Court has played its part in acknowledging the critical part which such relatives can play in contributing to the child's sense of his or her own worth (see eg *Boyle v UK* 19 EHRR 179). The provisions of the CA 1989 with regard to contact with children who are being 'accommodated' or 'looked after' by the local authority are, as was acknowledged by the European Court, an important part of the checks and balances on the powers of the local authorities with regard to the lives of such vulnerable children in their care. Local authorities looking after such children are in a position of trust in terms of the execution of their plans for the children, but they can be supervised to a degree by the courts hearing appeals from parents and children as well as other relatives against the making of contact orders or hearing applications to vary or discharge such orders. It will be interesting to see, in due course, whether the requirement to submit to the court the new s 31A care plans will lead parents and other relatives to be more aware of the local authority's responsibilities to carry out their plans. It remains to be seen whether this will mean that parents as well as the prescribed persons will subject them to greater scrutiny and be prepared to challenge the authorities more, if and when they move to terminate or dramatically vary contact arrangements with family members. Where the prescribed person appointed to oversee and monitor reviews and the care plans (see s 26(2)(k) of the CA 1989, as amended) is unhappy with levels of contact or proposed changes to contact, then they can refer the case to a CAFCASS officer to consider the position on behalf of the child (see s 26(2A) as inserted by the Adoption and Children Act 2002). This will be even more important if the new drive to place older children in the care of local authorities for adoption comes to fruition after implementation of the Adoption and Children Act 2002 and following on from the recommendations of the Prime Minister's Review on Adoption, and if insufficient attention is given to the needs and wants of the children and young people both in the short and long term.

10.63 Critically, despite the concerns of secure unit workers and Her Majesty's Inspector of Prisons voiced in successive reports, the welfare provisions of the CA 1989 and, more particularly, the provisions relating to the existence, promotion, support and review of rights to contact still are not interpreted expansively and have not been applied energetically or comprehensively to children in secure units and, it has been argued, do not apply at all to the most vulnerable groups of children and young people, those placed in penal establishments. It is quite apparent that a directive is needed from central government that local authorities must interpret their duties under Sch 2, Part 2, para 10 much more expansively and seriously and that the CA 1989 should be amended to require local authorities to take proper steps to use their powers to promote contact between the child, whether or not he is a 'looked after' child and wherever he is accommodated, and his family and others, as provided for in paras 15–17 of Sch 2, Part 2 to the CA 1989. How many more of these children must take their own lives or engage in serious self-harm before we extend to them the same concern and rights which we would give them if they were in the childcare system protected by the provisions of the CA 1989, as so many Chief Inspectors' of Prisons reports have urged?

10.64 The decision of the High Court in R *(on the application of the Howard League for Penal Reform) v Secretary of State for the Home Department* was issued on 29 November 2002 after very late minor amendments were completed on the text. This is a brief note to report that the League brought the case in order to determine the responsibility of the authorities towards children in penal establishments. Mr Justice Munby in the High Court ruled that whilst the CA 1989 does not confer any duties or powers upon the Home Secretary or the Prison Department, the functions, powers and duties imposed upon local authorities by the CA 1989, particulary ss 17 and 47, do apply to all children in prison service establishments including Young Offender institutions, subject to the necessary requirements of imprisonment. The judge ruled therefore that the statement in para 3.14 of *Prison Service Order 4950: Regimes for prisoners under the age of 18 years old in Prison Establishments* that 'the Children Act 1989 does not apply to under 18-year-olds in prison establishments' is wrong in law. In the judge's view there was no need to grant any further relief as he was sure that the Prison Service could be relied upon to make the necessary amendments to guidance and practice to ensure that effect was given to his judgment. This judgment, taken together with the recommendations of the Joint Inspectorates Report *Safeguarding Children* (see Chapter **12**) in relation to the responsibilities of social services and ACPCs to children in penal establishments, have the potential to work a very radical change in the lives of all the children in such institutions. As with so much else, it remains to be seen whether practitioners in the field can transform this potentiality into reality.

CHAPTER 11

REPRESENTATIONS PROCEDURES AND JUDICIAL REVIEW

'"Safeguards" and "promote" are equal partners in an overall concept of welfare. Safeguards are an indispensable component to the child's security, and should be the first consideration for any body providing or arranging accommodation for children. Safeguards form the basis for ensuring physical and emotional health, good education and sound social development. These are the proper objectives of all institutions providing care and education for children. I cannot emphasise too strongly the importance of these objectives for all children living away from home, the difficulty of achieving them for children in the public care, and the need for renewed and sustained effort in accomplishing them' (Sir William Utting, *People Like Us: The Report of the Review of the Safeguards for Children Living Away from Home* (DOH/Welsh Office, 1997), at para 1.23).

'No-one who has read *Lost in Care* could fail to be shocked by the catalogue of abuse it records of children in care in the former County Council area of Clwyd and Gwynedd. That abuse destroyed young lives over a period of more than twenty years. The Government is determined to learn the lessons contained in *Lost In Care*. We must use this as a catalyst for meaningful and radical change in children's services. It should serve as a warning of the constant need for vigilance, of the need to ensure that children being looked-after can also talk freely about their concerns and worries and of our duty to listen and treat them as we would our own children. Safeguarding children is an absolute priority for this Government' (*Report of the Ministerial Task Force on Children's Safeguards* (DOH/Welsh Office, 2000), chapter 5, at p 61).

Introduction

11.1　The provisions in the CA 1989, s 26(3), as amended and s 24D, providing that every local authority should establish procedures to enable them to consider representations (including any complaints) made to them by: children who are being 'looked after' or who are in need; any child 'qualifying for advice and assistance'; 'eligible' or 'relevant' children and by 'former relevant' children (see Chapter **4**); any parent or person with responsibility; any local authority foster parent; or any such other person as might be considered to have a sufficient interest in the child to warrant his representation being considered by the local authority, were supposed to provide a proper safeguard for all children who are being provided with services by the local authority, but most particularly those who are 'looked after' by the local authority (see s 26(3)). Thus the Minister of State responsible for the implementation of the CA 1989, Virginia Bottomley MP, when pressed to answer questions about whether children who had suffered in the same way as those children who had experienced the 'Pin Down Regime' would feel able to make complaints about their care or treatment after the implementation of the Act, declared that the representations procedure would 'ensure that children are protected in the future and will safeguard their position whenever they are being looked after away from home' (see *Newsnight*, BBC 2, 14 October 1991). The reason why Mrs Bottomley was being so closely questioned with regard to the 'Pin Down Regime' was that the report of that enquiry had only recently been published and the issues regarding children not feeling safe in complaining to those who were providing their care had been highlighted.

11.2 The difficulty is, however, that the provisions in s 26(3) even as amended by the Children (Leaving Care) Act 2000 and by the Adoption and Children Act 2002 do not provide for children to be able to make such representations to a totally independent person. Sir William Utting has constantly returned to this theme of the failure of the legislation even from a very early stage to provide children with adequate safeguards. Thus, as he reminded the government in 1997, he had recommended back in 1991, just after the coming into force of the CA 1989, that the DOH should 'review with other interested groups, the legislation safeguarding the welfare of children across the full range of residential settings' (*Children in the Public Care: A Review of Residential Child Care* (DOH, 1991), at p 28). Sir William Utting returned to these comments and to his concern about the lack of appropriate legal rights and procedures which he urged should apply to all children living away from home in chapter 10 of *People Like Us* (DOH, 1997) at paras 10.5 and 10.6. He also stressed, however, that children in foster care are at similar risk of their rights not being adequately protected and emphasised in chapter 3 of *People Like Us* that:

> 'it is also accepted that children are at risk of abuse in foster care. Its isolation and private nature does make them more vulnerable. Some of the safeguards available in residential care are not suitable for care which is provided in a family home, such as unannounced visits from social workers and those from elected members. Another factor is that many of the children are very young, over 13,000 are under 10 and many (1,200) pre-school age. That renders some other safeguards such as complaints procedures ineffective' (at para 3.8).

11.3 It is quite clear, therefore, that despite the hopes which government ministers had at the time of the implementation of the CA 1989, even at its inception the provisions on complaint or representations procedure were felt to be inadequate to safeguard the position of children being looked after away from their parents' homes.

11.4 The government's response to *Lost In Care* (DOH/Welsh Office, 2000) through the *Report of the Ministerial Task Force on Children's Safeguards* (DOH/Welsh Office, 2000) has been to re-emphasise that safeguarding children is a top priority for the government and that the approach taken by the government has involved major reforms of the public care system as well as the criminal law in order to provide better protection for children from those who would harm them. The government has also been keen to stress that when they talk about children they mean all children, including disabled children, in recognition of the fact that disabled children are particularly vulnerable to abuse of all kinds and that high priority needs to be given to protecting them and ensuring that safeguards are rigorously applied (at p 5). The government nevertheless emphasises that safeguarding children can never be the sole preserve of any one organisation and that it intends to work with everyone who shares the ambition to create a safer and more secure environment in which children can thrive and prosper. The government points out (at p 6) that many of the recommendations in *Lost in Care* echo those made by Sir William Utting in his report *People Like Us* on the review of safeguards for children living away from home. The government published its response to *People Like Us* in November 1998 setting out a comprehensive programme of policy and management changes to deliver the safe environment that children living away from home deserve (see *The Government's Response to the Children's Safeguards Review* (The Stationery Office, 1998)) and is continuing to pursue this programme of action and is addressing many of the recommendations made in both *People Like Us* and *Lost in Care* through current policy and legislative initiatives.

11.5 The *Quality Protects* programme is intended to focus on working with some of the most disadvantaged and vulnerable children in society, namely those children looked after by local authorities, those children in the child protection system, and other children in need. The main elements of the *Quality Protects* programme are:

- new national government objectives for children's services which for the first time set out clear outcomes for children, and in some instances give precise targets which local authorities are expected to achieve;
- an important role for local councillors in delivering the programme, which has been formalised in new guidance issued by the government to all councillors;

–   evaluation of each local authority's progress and plans through annual
     Quality Protects management action plans (MAPs);
–   a new children's service grant of £375 million.

11.6   On the legislative front, the Protection of Children Act 1999 places the
DOH's Consultancy Index (the list of individuals deemed unsuitable to work
with children) on a statutory footing. Regulated childcare providers will be
required to check the name of anyone they propose to employ in any post
involving regular contact with children against the Index and the DfEE's
equivalent 'List 99' (already on a statutory footing). The DOH was working
towards implementation of the Protection of Children Act 1999 by the end of
2000, but progress has been slower than expected (see, for much further detail
on this, Chapter **9**).

11.7   The CSA 2000 has also now been passed by Parliament. It sets out
widescale reforms of the system to protect vulnerable people being looked
after by or on behalf of local authorities and thus does not just apply to
children. It is intended, however, to regulate and improve standards in
children's homes, care homes, private and voluntary health-care and other care
services. The CSA 2000 also established the National Care Standards
Commission (NCSC) for England. This new independent national body has
powers to inspect all children's homes (including those with fewer than four
children), fostering agencies, voluntary adoption agencies, local authority
voluntary and adoption services, residential family centres and welfare
arrangements in boarding schools and further education colleges with
boarding provision. The CSA 2000 also establishes the post of a new
Children's Rights Director, a senior post within the NCSC, with a remit across
all children in receipt of services regulated by the NCSC. The services for
which the Children's Rights Director is to have oversight are all 'regulated'
services for children as defined in the National Care Standards Commission
(Children's Rights Director) Regulations 2001. The creation of this post and
the attendant regulations have already been dealt with in Chapter **4**, as have
the new *Children's Homes – National Minimum Standards* (DOH, 2002) and
Fostering Services – National Minimum Standards (DOH, 2002). Since the new
Children's Rights Director has a critical role in relation to the supervision of
complaints procedures across all regulated children's services (see reg 3(1)(i)),
these responsibilities will be referred to again in paras **11.32–11.36**).

11.8   As has been pointed out earlier (see Chapter **4**), whilst it is to be hoped
that the new framework of independent inspections introduced by the
CSA 2000 will improve the position of children, nothing has been done to
respond to the demands of *People Like Us* and *Lost In Care* to provide children
with a means of access to an easily accessible, locally based, and properly
independent complaints and representations process. The position offered by
the CA 1989, s 26(3) as amended, thus remains relatively untouched and as

inadequate as it has been in the past to remedy the serious issues which may confront children living away from home, who may be the subject of abuse and wish to voice complaints or make representations about their treatment. (See, eg, the comments of the first Joint Inspectorate Report *Safeguarding Children* (DOH/SSI, 2002), at p 65.) Thus, *Safeguarding Children* notes that 'young people still experience serious barriers to making complaints about services'. Despite these limitations, it is nevertheless the case that s 26(3) as amended, provides for the establishment of representations procedures by local authorities for making complaints about, or taking up issues relating to, the handling by the local authority of child protection issues. This may arise in a number of different ways and it is also possible that events may give rise to the consideration of taking action against the local authority using judicial review. In *R v Birmingham City Council ex parte A* [1997] 2 FLR 841, a challenge was made by way of judicial review to a local authority's inability speedily to place a child who had special needs with an appropriate foster parent. Stephen Brown P stated that, in cases such as these, where neither fact nor law was in dispute but instead the ground of complaint was the way the authority was carrying out or failing to carry out its duties, the appropriate response was a complaint under s 26(3) and not by way of judicial review. A similar stance was taken by the court in *R v East Sussex County Council ex parte W* [1998] 2 FLR 1082, where the court stated that the complaints procedure under s 26(3) would in ordinary circumstances provide an appropriate alternative remedy to judicial review to question a local authority decision not to apply for a care order (see per Scott Baker J, at p 1084).

11.9 Whilst it should be noted that the representations procedure is available in relation to the discharge by a local authority of any of its functions under Part III of the CA 1989 in relation to children, nevertheless, as had been seen in Chapters **4** and **5**, the duties under that Part extend to taking reasonable steps to prevent children suffering ill-treatment and neglect, and taking steps to reduce the need to bring care or supervision order proceedings in respect of children. In addition, where child protection conferences come to the conclusion that no formal legal action is required under Parts IV and V of the CA 1989, they may conclude that recommendations be made to social services concerning the delivery of services to a child in need of protection in the family, and this may form part of the child protection plan. Where services are being provided in relation to a family in pursuance of such a child protection plan or, indeed, in situations where a decision has been reached that no services should be provided, the representations procedure gives parents, children and others concerned with the child, the ability to make representations about the delivery of services or, indeed, to make representations objecting to the delivery of such services. Other child protection arenas in which the representations procedure has already been employed relate to treatment in children's homes, foster homes and other residential settings, where either the children themselves, independent advocates acting on their behalf or parents have made representations to local authorities using a procedure available under Part 3 of the CA 1989. Thus Standard 16 of the *Children's Homes National Minimum Standards* (DOH, 2002) provides that children should know how, and feel able, to complain if they are unhappy with any aspect of living in children's home and states that any complaint must be addressed seriously and without delay and that a complaint will be fully responded to within a maximum of 28 days and children are kept informed of the progress (see paras 16.1–16.7). It is anticipated that when the DOH issues *National Minimum Standards for Foster Care* these will make identical provisions for children in foster-care placements.

11.10 Voluntary organisations, including private organisations running residential establishments, are also required to provide representations procedures for the parents and others with parental responsibility as well as for children who are being looked after in such homes (CA 1989, s 59(4)(b), Sch 6, para 10(2), Sch 7, para 6 and note that the National Minimum Standards apply to all residential children's homes (see the *Children's Homes – National Minimum Standards – Children's Homes Regulations* (DOH, 2002), at p viii).

11.11 As well as the concerns voiced by Sir William Utting in his *Children in the Public Care* review and *People Like Us* review, a number of concerns have been raised about the operation of the representations process both in relation to the framing of legislation and the consequent regulations (see the Representations Procedure (Children) Regulations 1991, SI 1991/894) and also in relation to the way in which local authorities have actually conducted the procedures (see the Social Services Inspectorate's Reports for 1993, 1994, 1996, 1997, 1998 and, more latterly, in *Phase 3 Children's Services Inspections 2000–2002* (DOH/SSI, 2002), *Fostering for the Future: Inspection of Foster Care Services* (DOH/SSI, 2002) and *Safeguarding Children* (DOH/SSI, 2002), at para 7.31). Nevertheless, it remains important to realise that using a representations procedure established under the CA 1989 offers the potential to be a fruitful and productive way of encouraging local authorities to take their duties seriously, and if this can now be backed up by a complaint being referred to the Children's Rights Director at the NCSC (see Chapter **4**) then it is to be hoped that the process will become much more responsive. The greater involvement of councillors in the representations process may also have a more direct political effect in raising the profile of concerns voiced by children, parents and others, in that the elective members will be more fully involved in such cases. Such action is also generally a much speedier and cheaper process than seeking to resort to the more complex, lengthier and expensive process of judicial review (see para **11.48** *et seq*). Both procedures have an important role to play, and there will obviously be occasions when it will be necessary to resort to court rather than, or after, seeking to use the local authority representations procedure taken together with the possibility of procedural issues being referred on to the Children's Rights Director. In the course of this chapter, both processes will be examined and concerns raised about the possible failure of the processes to respond to the needs of children and others who feel let down by the legal framework of child protection.

Accessing the representations procedure

11.12   The CA 1989 provided, for the first time, a means whereby children, parents, anyone with parental responsibility, any local authority foster parent and any such person as the authority considers to have sufficient interest in the child's welfare, might exercise the right to make representations (including any complaints) to a local authority about the provision of any services, including the provision of accommodation under the CA 1989, s 20, or the failure to provide any such services as are envisaged under Part III of the CA 1989 (s 26(3)). In addition, those persons having such an interest may also make representations, where relevant, to a voluntary organisation or to a registered children's home using these procedures (see CA 1989, s 59(4), Sch 6, para 10(2)(l)). The rights to make representations or complaints have now been extended by the Children (Leaving Care) Act 2000 and by the Adoption and Children Act 2002. Thus, in addition to the children and others who can make representations as set out above, these Acts extend the rights to make such representations to any child qualifying for 'advice and assistance', any 'eligible' or 'relevant' child, any 'former relevant child' (for an explanation of these terms see Chapter **4**), such persons with parental responsibility, any foster carers, any person for whose needs provision is to be made by the adoption service, anyone in need of adoption support services and any other such person as the authority considers has a sufficient interest in any of these children, who may be provided with any services under these provisions. By a very late amendment to s 26(3) under the provisions of the Adoption and Children Act 2002, children must also now be given access to advocates, although there is no provision that such advocacy services should be independent.

11.13 As the *Children Act 1989: Guidance and Regulations*, vol 3: 'Family Placements' points out, the authority, voluntary organisation or home (generally referred to as the 'Responsible Authority') must consider what type of support and encouragement it can offer to its clients, both to make use of the system and to pursue their representations or complaints through the procedure (para 10.28). The guidance goes on to suggest that information leaflets and open letters to children and parents being provided with services will help to make clients aware of the procedure, and a large number of authorities now attempt to ensure that such information is made available to children and parents as soon as the service is being provided. Children admitted to residential homes run by local authorities, voluntary organisations or private individuals must be given, upon admission, clear information about procedures for making representations. It is apparent from *Lost in Care*, *People Like Us* and from *Safeguarding Children*, that there are still major difficulties about making such processes accessible to children and being clear that they have really understood their rights to make such complaints or representations. Where child protection procedures are concerned, since many services are being provided pursuant to prevention or protection packages, local authority child protection procedures and ACPC guidelines also point out that families and children should be given information about the representations procedure to enable them to follow through any concerns which they may have which cannot be addressed by any other means. The guidance points out, however, that 'some parents and most children will need advice and confidential support to make their representation or complaint, to pursue it, to understand the administrative process and to cope with the outcome' (at para 10.28). The amendments to s 26(3) providing that all children must have access to assistance, advocacy and representation services in order to enable them to make such representations or complaints should help to ensure the provision of such advice and support even though there are no guarantees in the provision that such services will be independent.

11.14 *Working Together to Safeguard Children* (DOH, 1999) suggests that any complaints about the functioning of child protection conferences should be addressed to the conference Chair and they will then be passed on to the social services department which, since they relate to Part V of the CA 1989, should be responded to in accordance with the Complaints Directions 1990 (see para **11.40**). In considering and responding to complaints, *Working Together to Safeguard Children* advises that the local authority should form an inter-agency panel made up of senior representatives from the ACPC member agencies. The panel should consider whether the relevant inter-agency protocols and procedures have been observed correctly and whether the decision that is being complained about follows reasonably from the proper observation of the protocols (para 5.72).

11.15 Where parents and/or children wish to make complaints or representations in response to concerns which they may have about a child protection conference including the process of the conference, its outcome in terms of initial or continuing registration and any decision not to register or to de-register, these may be referred to the appropriate responsible authority. Complaints about individual agencies, their performance and provision or non-provision of services should be responded to in accordance with the relevant agency's complaints handling process. In the case of social services this is as laid down under the CA 1989, s 26(3) (see *Working Together to Safeguard Children*, at para 5.71).

11.16 Whilst it is appropriate that the responsible authorities should seek to make access to the representations procedure clear and well understood (including, where necessary, the translation of information documents into other languages), it may be possible to resolve many issues which have arisen before any formal step is taken of referring the matter to the complaints procedures. Efforts should be made, especially in child protection situations, to resolve any issues which may be causing a parent, child or other person to consider using the representations procedure. The aim should be to resolve any issue satisfactorily as near to the point at which it arises as possible, and since a number of local authorities have now appointed specialist children's rights officers or representations officers (or even in conjunction with voluntary agencies a children's commissioner, as in Oxford and London) it may be extremely advantageous to involve such a person in providing independent advice and assistance in solving problems. This should not be seen as a means of preventing the person who wishes to make a more formal complaint from using the representations procedure. As the guidance issued to social services points out:

'A well publicised statement of commitment to the representations procedures should encourage the identification and speedy resolution of representations and complaint as they arise. A secondary benefit of the system will be to illustrate for the responsible authority how policies translate into practice and to highlight areas where the responsible authority should be more responsive to the needs of individual clients and the community' (*The Right to Complain: Practice Guidance on Complaints Procedures in Social Services Departments* (HMSO, 1991), at para 11).

11.17   The guidance also makes it clear that statutory requirements and the associated guidance seek to achieve an accessible and effective means of making complaints close to the point at which the problem arose, but with an independent element which is meant to inspire confidence in the procedure. The inspiring of confidence was obviously a necessary and desirable end, but not one which everyone involved in the system has necessarily felt was possible to achieve, even with relatively newly introduced provisions (see Utting, *Children in the Public Care* (DOH, 1991), at paras 3.47–3.50; the Waterhouse Report, *Lost in Care* (DOH/Welsh Office, 2000), and also the comments of the Joint Inspectorates, *Safeguarding Children* (DOH/SSI, 2002), at para 7.31). A similar sceptical view is taken of the late amendments made by the Adoption and Children Act 2002 to the provision of s 26(3).

11.18 In order to achieve the objectives of accessibility and efficiency, but also to inspire confidence, it is necessary that any complaints are acted upon in the shortest possible time and an early opportunity provided to challenge the outcome of the considerations when these are known. As is the case under the regulations, the new National Minimum Standards emphasise that the complaint must be fully responded to within a maximum of 28 days (*Children's Homes – National Minimum Standards* (DOH, 2002), Standard 16.1). As has been indicated, it is not intended that all problems which arise in the day-to-day handling of childcare services in the child protection arena should automatically be elevated to the status of a complaint or representation. It is understood that when operating in the child protection arena, everyone will be working under considerable pressure and a matter which is promptly resolved to everyone's satisfaction when drawn to the attention of an officer of the responsible authority should not then require referral to the representations procedure. It is important, therefore, that everyone involved in the child protection process and the provision of services on behalf of the local authority should understand the role and nature of representations procedures, and that these are not confused with any sort of disciplinary proceedings. It has become apparent from the first 11 years of operation of the CA 1989 that there is still considerable concern and ambivalence, especially in the residential childcare sector as well as amongst children and young people, as to the role and function of the representations process, all the more so because the process is not fully independent. (See especially, for example, Growney (1998).) The process is a peculiarly hybrid one and as both Utting and Waterhouse have identified not one which is likely to inspire confidence in any of those involved in it.

The representations procedure

11.19   Under the provisions of the CA 1989, s 26(3), as amended, s 59(4) and Sch 6, para 10(2)(l), local authorities, voluntary organisations or registered children's homes must establish a procedure for considering any representations (including any complaints) made to it by children, their carers or other persons with sufficient interests, about the discharge of any functions under Part III of the CA 1989. 'Representations' are said to include inquiries and statements about such matters as the availability, delivery and nature of services and will not necessarily be critical. A complaint is said to be a written or oral expression of dissatisfaction or disquiet in relation to the individual child about the local authority's exercise of its functions under the CA 1989, and about matters in relation to children accommodated by voluntary organisations in children's homes. *The Children Act 1989: Guidance and Regulations*, vol 3: 'Family Placements' states that 'a complaint may arise as a result of an unwelcome or disputed decision, concern about the quality or appropriateness of services, delay and decision making about services or about their delivery or non delivery' (at para 10.5). Again, as indicated earlier, in the child protection arena complaints could include those made by children about their treatment in a variety of residential establishments or in foster care, or complaints made by children, carers or parents in relation to the outcome of recommendations made in the child protection conference or the delivery of any services in respect of a local authority's performance of duties to prevent children in its area suffering ill-treatment or neglect, or to prevent the taking of care or supervision order proceedings in respect of them.

11.20 *Working Together to Safeguard Children* and the *National Minimum Standards* (Standard 16) state that complaints procedures should be clear, effective, user friendly and readily accessible to children and young people, including those with disabilities and those for whom English is not a first language. Procedures, according to *Working Together to Safeguard Children*, should address informal as well as formal complaints and it notes that systems that do not promote open communication about 'minor' complaints will not be responsive to major ones, and a pattern of 'minor' complaints may indicate more deeply seated problems in management and culture which need to be addressed. It goes on to advise that there should be a complaints register in every children's home which records all representations or complaints, the action taken to address them and the outcomes (at para 6.5). These points are reiterated in the *Children's Homes National Minimum Standards* (DOH, 2002) but both the *Standards* and *Working Together to Safeguard Children* seem to be entirely missing the point that children who feel extremely vulnerable and who need to complain about the behaviour or action of the staff are scarcely likely to do so where the requirement is to make a complaint in the first instance to those against whom they may be making an allegation. The inadequacies of the then complaints procedures, their lack of independence and the lack of anyone independent to whom children could complain was voiced by Sir William Utting in his report *People Like Us* but has also been pointed up most markedly by Ernest Ryder QC, one of the counsel to the North Wales Children enquiry. He commented that:

> 'children should be given choices about their external contacts and these choices should include the right to speak to accredited lay advocates of their choice and be assisted by lay advocates in expressing their views and wishes. There should be total independence in the complaints process matched by effective rights of representation for the child, which will need to be mirrored by independent scrutiny of the effect upon the child, regardless of the result of the complaints determination.' ('Lost and Found: Looking to the Future after North Wales' [2000] Fam Law 406, at p 408).

11.21 Whilst the introduction of the *National Minimum Standards for Children in Residential Care* (DOH, 2002) and the improved Children's Homes Regulations 2002 and recent developments such as the *Quality Protects* programme, including the wider provision of access to independent advocacy services for looked after children generally, the establishment of independent regional inspection units and the provision of a Commissioner for Wales (but not for England) and limited amendments to s 26(3) of the CA 1989, may be seen as welcome steps, these are by no means sufficient to address the very real concern as to independence which many children who have been made the subject of care orders actually voice. If the Joint Inspectors are concerned that children cannot gain access to advocacy services then the system is still failing (see *Safeguarding Children* (DOH/SSI, 2002)). Yet other concerns are raised by

Working Together to Safeguard Children itself in relation to foster care. Thus para 6.9 of *Working Together to Safeguard Children* states that foster care is undertaken in the private domain of carers' own homes, which may make it more difficult to identify abusive situations and for children to find a voice outside the family. In order to try to ensure that the case social worker really does give the child adequate opportunity to be able to voice any concerns or complaints, *Working Together to Safeguard Children* now recommends that social workers are required to see the children in foster care on their own for a proportion of visits, and that evidence of this must now actually be recorded. The new *Fostering Services – National Minimum Standards* (DOH, 2002) expand upon these duties for the greater protection of the children.

11.22 Thus, all local authorities, voluntary authorities and those providing care for children in registered children's homes must have a formal representations and complaints process. Failure to have such a process or having one which fails to comply with the regulations (see the Representations Procedure (Children) Regulations 1991) can be remedied by invoking the default powers of the Secretary of State under s 84 of the CA 1989. This was indeed emphasised by Auld J in *R v London Borough of Barnet ex parte B* [1994] 1 FLR 592, at p 598. Under Standard 16.2 of the *Children's Homes – National Minimum Standards* (DOH, 2002), which now must be taken to be the standard to be applied to all representations and complaints, children (and where appropriate) their families, significant others, and independent visitors must be provided with information on how to complain, including how they can secure access to an advocate. Where necessary, the Standards provide that this access must be to an advocate who is suitably skilled, for example in signing or in speaking the complainant's preferred language. The procedure is formally a two-stage process, but three stages can in fact be identified within the structure laid down in the Representations Procedure (Children) Regulations 1991 (RP(C)R 1991, SI 1991/894), as amended. What must be called into question now, however, in the light of the decision of the Administrative Court in *R on the application of the personal representative of Christopher Beeson v Dorset County Council and the Secretary of State for Health* [2001] EWHC Admin 986, unreported (discussed at para **11.65**) is whether any local authority complaints procedure which is not completely independent of the authority is lawful under Article 6 of the ECHR. This provides that 'in the determination of his civil rights and obligation ... everyone is entitled to a fair and public hearing ... by an independent and impartial tribunal'. Much may, however, turn on the extent to which dealing with a particular child's complaint or representation, or one made by a parent or other interested individual, can be said to be 'determinative' of an individual's 'civil rights and obligations'. Where it is, or may be, then the lack of total independence and impartiality within the present process must in, human rights terms, be fatal and thus capable of being challenged in the same way as in the *Beeson* decision (see Article 6 of the ECHR). It also remains to be seen whether this decision is upheld on appeal. The three stages laid down under the RP(C)R 1991 are:

(1) preliminaries;
(2) consideration by the local authority together with an independent person and notification of decision to complainant;
(3) notification of dissatisfaction from complainant and reference on to the representations panel.

Each of these stages will be discussed below.

Preliminaries

11.23 Where a local authority, voluntary organisation or listed children's home receives representations from any complainant, it must forward to that complainant an explanation of the procedure set out in the RP(C)R 1991 as amended and must offer advice, assistance and guidance on the use of the procedure or, alternatively, provide the complainant with advice as to where he may seek such assistance (see *The Right to Complain: Practice Guidance on Complaint Procedures in Social Services Departments*, at p 9). Pursuant to Standard 16 of the *Children's Homes – National Minimum Standards*, information must also be provided on how to access an advocate (see Standard 16.2 (DOH, 2002)). Where any representation is made orally, the responsible authority must cause such representation to be recorded in writing and forwarded to the complainant, who is then given an opportunity to agree that it has been properly recorded in writing. Once a representation has been properly received by the responsible authority, the authority must decide whether it has received a representation from someone 'having a sufficient interest in the child', which under the *Children's Homes – National Minimum Standards* (DOH, 2002) now clearly includes an independent visitor (see Standard 16.2). Where that person has such an interest, the authority must cause the information which would be sent to the child, the child's parents or the child's carer, also to be sent to that person (see RP(C)R 1991, reg 4).

Consideration by authority with independent person

11.24 Where an authority receives representations, it must then appoint an independent person, who must not be an employee or officer of the authority, to join with it in consideration of the representations being made. The authority, together with the independent person, must then consider the representations and formulate a response within 28 days of receipt. The independent person must take part in any discussions which are held by the authority about the action (if any) to be taken in relation to the child in the light of the consideration of the representations (RP(C)R 1991, reg 6). The first stage is very much a paper consideration of the representations and once this stage has been completed the local authority must send a written notification of the formal response, determined by the authority with the independent person, to the person making the representations (or, if different, the person on whose behalf the representations were made, unless the authority considers that person is not of sufficient understanding or it would be likely to cause serious harm to his health or emotional condition), to the independent person, and to any other person whom the local authority considers has sufficient interest in the case. In addition to notifying such persons of the result of the consideration of the representations, the authority must inform the person making the representations of his right to have the matter referred to a panel. When such notification is made to the person making the representations, that person then has the right to inform the authority, in writing, within 28 days of the date upon which notice has been given to him, that he is dissatisfied with the proposed results and wishes the matter to be referred to a representations panel appointed by the authority for that purpose (RP(C)R 1991, reg 8(2)).

Consideration of representations by the panel

11.25 The representation panel must include at least one independent person and must meet within 28 days of the receipt by the authority of the complainant's request that the matter be referred to a panel (RP(C)R 1991, reg 8(4)). Where the person making a representation before the panel wishes to be accompanied by another person of his or her choice to speak on his or her behalf, the regulations permit this (reg 8(6)). It may be that the child cannot face making a complaint about the way he or she has been treated in a particular children's home without the support of an advocate to act on his or her behalf. The guidance (see para **11.19**) recognises this at various stages, and the importance of access to such an independent advocate if children are to have any confidence in the system has been pointed up not only by Sir William Utting (see *People Like Us*, paras 7.7 and 10.3) but also by other research studies (see Williams (2002) and Williams and Jordan (1996)). The right to the services of such an advocate is now provided for in the *Children's Homes – National Minimum Standards* (at Standard 16.2) but lack of accessibility to any, or suitably qualified, advocates was a cause for concern in the first Joint Inspector's Report, *Safeguarding Children* (DOH, 2002) at para 1.22. Some children will have received such support from an independent advocate at the very first stages of the process and later at the formal stage of the panel procedure. Other authorities have not, however, been so generous and some children have been overwhelmed by the reaction of local authorities to children's efforts to instigate the complaints procedures (see Williams (2002) and Williams and Jordan (1996), and see also Lyon (1997), at pp 126–146).

11.26 Where it is felt necessary that a lawyer accompanies parent, child or other with sufficient interest then, in certain circumstances, by analogy to a decision to allow public funding (legal aid) to be used to finance a lawyer accompanying parents or children into child protection conferences, the Legal Services Commission may, where satisfied that it is an appropriate case to be supported by legal representative, sanction the provision of services by a lawyer to assist the child or parents in the hearing before the panel. It could be argued that this stage could prevent the bringing of possible actions for judicial review or breach of statutory duty, the possible taking of care-linked proceedings, or a challenge under the HRA 1998, Sch 1, Part I, art 6 in that the right to a fair trial was prejudiced by the lack of legal representation (see para **11.24**).

11.27 At the meeting of the panel, it must consider any oral or written submissions the complainant or the local authority wish to make and, where the independent person appointed to the panel is different from the person who considered the original complaint, the panel must also consider any oral or written submissions from the previous independent person (RP(C)R 1991, reg 8(5)). When a panel has heard the representations, it must determine on its own recommendations and record them with its reasons in writing within 24 hours of the end of the meeting (RP(C)R 1991, reg 9(1)). The panel must give notice of its recommendations to the local authority, the complainant, the independent person first involved in its considerations (if different from the independent person on the representations panel), and any other person whom a local authority considers has sufficient interest in the case (reg 9(2)). This may include a children's guardian who has been appointed in the early stages of child protection meetings where the child protection conference subsequently decided that no further formal legal action was to be considered for the time being. Once in receipt of the panel decision, the local authority must, together with the independent person on the panel, consider what action, if any, should be taken in relation to the child in the light of the representations, and the independent person must take part in any discussions about any such action (reg 9(3)).

11.28 Whilst a panel decision is not strictly binding upon the local authority given that the CA 1989, s 26(7) only requires the authority to take such steps as are 'reasonably practicable' having had due regard to the findings of the panel, it would be unusual for a local authority to act otherwise than in accordance with the panel's recommendations and the independent person's views (see Peter Gibson LJ in *R v London Borough of Brent ex parte S* [1994] 1 FLR 203, at p 211). Were a local authority simply to ignore or fail to consider the recommendations then this would almost certainly lay the authority open to judicial review (see Ward J in *R v Royal Borough of Kingston Upon Thames ex parte T* [1994] 1 FLR 798, at p 814). Ward J in the *Kingston* case specifically rejected arguments that because the panel was dominated by local authority membership it was likely to be biased and ineffective. As far as the likelihood of bias was concerned, he stated that he was satisfied that professional integrity would ensure fairness and, in relation to the charge of ineffectiveness, he emphasised that judicial review would be available in any case where any recommendation of the panel was simply ignored. This case was, of course, decided before the implementation of the HRA 1998 giving effect to Article 6 of the ECHR. Given the decision of Richard J in R *on the application of the personal representative of Christopher Beeson v Dorset County Council* (discussed in detail at para **11.65**), that local authority representation procedures which are not totally independent are in breach of Article 6, a challenge to the legality of all other types of representation procedures, particularly those for children, which may be considered to be determinative of civil rights and obligations, must be imminent.

11.29 Where any person making a representation, including a child, remains dissatisfied with the results of the determination of the panel, that person must consider if there is evidence of maladministration which would justify the making of a complaint to the local government ombudsman, the Commissioner for Local Administration, under Part III of the Local Government Act 1974, or taking an action against the local authority, possibly for breach of statutory duty or for judicial review.

11.30 The responsible authority must then give written notice to the complainant, the child if considered to be of sufficient understanding, and any such other persons as are affected, of its decision and its reasons and of any action which has been taken or it proposes to take as a result. Once the panel has made its recommendations then notification should take place within 28 days (see the CA 1989, s 26(7)(b)). The authority should implement any further necessary action without delay and any failure to implement the panel's recommendations is likely to provide further grounds for complaint and give rise to an action for judicial review.

11.31 It should be emphasised that the courts have been extremely reluctant to intervene in those cases in which they believe the complaints procedure should have been used rather than resorting to the use of judicial review. This was emphasised very clearly by the court in R *v Royal Borough of Kingston upon Thames ex parte T* [1994] 1 FLR 798 where the mother was seeking accommodation of her daughter in a particular project and the local authority had failed to respond to this specific request. It was also emphasised in R *v Birmingham City Council ex parte A* [1997] 2 FLR 841 where there was a complaint that a child had not been placed with specialist foster parents after a period of treatment in a clinic and the delay was such that the child was not placed until 18 months after she first went to the specialist clinic. In this case, the child and her mother, as next friend, applied for judicial review seeking a declaration that the local authority had erred in law in not acting with reasonable diligence and expedition to ensure that the child was placed in appropriate accommodation. Sir Stephen Brown, then President of the Family Division, held that the declaration sought was not appropriate in the context of judicial review. It was far more appropriate for there to be a complaints investigation under the CA 1989, s 26, which provided, as he put it, for a wide range of procedures to investigate cases where there was an allegation of neglect on the part of the local authority.

11.32 A similar stance, although for different reasons, was also adopted in *R v East Sussex County Council ex parte W* [1998] 2 FLR 1082, where a 13-year-old boy sought to challenge the decision of the local authority not to apply for a care order in respect of him. The child sought judicial review of that decision, arguing that the authority had not taken his wishes and feelings into account in that he wanted to have nothing more to do with his parents, and had not had proper regard taken of his emotional need for security and stability. At the time of the application for judicial review the child was in an open unit where he was progressing well. Scott Baker J took the view that although a care order might have been justified on the basis that it gave the child a greater sense of security, it was difficult to see how the authority could have justified applying for an order in this case, even if it had given greater weight to the child's views, when such an order would not have resulted in the provision of different services, and where his parents were co-operating fully. Again, Scott Baker J in this case emphasised that in deciding not to apply for a care order, the local authority was exercising a function under Part III of the CA 1989 and therefore the complaints procedure under s 26 was applicable. In his view, where someone was aggrieved at the failure of a local authority to apply for a care order, the complaints procedure established under that section would, in ordinary circumstances, provide a suitable alternative remedy to judicial review.

11.33 As a result of the new provisions of the Care Standards Act 2000 establishing the Children's Rights Commissioner for Wales and the office of the Children's Rights Director for England, it is likely that both the Local Government Ombudsmen as well as the courts would have to be satisfied either that these procedures had been used, if applicable to the particular case in question, or that they were inappropriate to deal with the specific issues raised in the case, before they would accept a reference to their jurisdictions. Given the very narrow remit of the Children's Rights Director for England which does not envisage the Director dealing with complaints in individual cases, judicial review in England, at least, looks like remaining as popular as it has recently become as a means of challenging local authorities.

The Care Standards Act 2000, the Children's Rights Commissioner for Wales and the office of the Children's Rights Director for England

11.34 Whilst the improvements to the system of reviews under the CA 1989, s 26(2), as amended, the widening of access to the representation procedures in s 26(3), as amended, the *Quality Protects* programme, and the introduction of the CSA 2000 are intended to improve the ability of children to make their voices heard, very considerable doubts have remained. The new independent Regional Inspection Units established under the CSA 2000 should have as one of their priorities the duty to ensure that all children, wherever they are being looked after pursuant to a care order, can easily obtain access to a fully independent body to whom they can safely raise concerns or complaints. The first set of *National Minimum Standards for Children in Residential Care* issued by the National Care Standards Commission established under the CSA 2000 does not, however, guarantee to advance in any sense the position of children or others, who might wish to refer their position to an independent body, more especially when even access to independent advocacy services is proving problematical (see *Safeguarding Children* (DOH/SSI, 2002), at para 1.22). Whilst the CSA 2000 does provide for the establishment of the office of a Children's Rights Director in England, this position also appears to have very restricted powers of operation and does not provide for individual children to be able to refer complaints to the Director. The rather different position of the office of the Children's Commissioner for Wales, and his attendant powers and functions, are provided for by ss 72–78 of the CSA 2000. The case for an independent Children's Commissioner for Wales was first recommended by the Welsh Social Services White Paper, *Building for the Future* (1998) then taken up by the Waterhouse Report, *Lost in Care* (2000) (see Chapter 4); Children in Wales, the Welsh Local Government Association and the Welsh Affairs Committee also all made the case for such a post. The powers and functions provided for in the statute include: the monitoring and oversight of the operation of complaints and whistle-blowing procedures (s 73(2) and (3)); the monitoring of arrangements for children's advocacy (s 73(4)); examining the handling of individual cases brought to the Commissioner's attention, including making recommendations on their merit when he considers it necessary or appropriate (s 74) (although the Assembly has to enact further regulations to allow for this to happen); and publishing reports, including an annual report to the Welsh Assembly. The task of the Commissioner is thus to review and monitor the operation of all these arrangements for the purpose specifically of ascertaining whether and to what extent the arrangements are effective in safeguarding and promoting the welfare of children being provided with regulated children's services (s 73(1)). These provisions are effective for the full range of children's services, ie not just children looked after by local authorities but also those being provided with domiciliary care, those in private hospitals or clinics, those being provided with care in day care or child-minding services and also to cover all children living away from home in boarding schools.

11.35 As noted above (and see para **4.76**), there is no comparable provision in England to the Children's Commissioner for Wales, but the legislation does establish the new Office of the Children's Rights Director to be located within the National Care Standards Commission (CSA 2000, Sch 1, para 10). The establishment of such an office is an honouring of a commitment made in *Learning the Lessons: the Government's Response to Lost in Care*, Cm 4776, chapter 4, at para 2, but many are very unhappy about the differences in the powers and responsibilities of the new positions and this was a target for criticism by the UN Monitoring Committee (see further, Chapter **12**). The office of Children's Rights Director within the National Care Standards Commission is not defined in the legislation and regulations therefore had to be issued to provide for the further detail of the position (see CSA 2000, Sch 1, para 10.2). These regulations, The National Care Standards Commission (Children's Rights Director) Regulations 2001, came into force on 1 April 2002, and provide for the Children's Rights Director to have duties to monitor the work of the National Care Standards Commission in relation to the provision of 'regulated' children's services, which are defined to include the provision of all services to children whether provided by social services or any other agencies, a provision similar to that in Wales. It is obvious from the regulations that it is no part of the director's role to hear complaints or concerns directly from individual children, but rather to: generally safeguard and promote the rights and welfare of children who are provided with regulated children's services; monitor and review the effectiveness of the National Care Standards Commission in its regulation of children's services; and to monitor and review the effectiveness of the arrangements made by the providers of regulated children's services in relation to dealing with complaints and representations made by or on behalf of children about such services. Thus, rather than having any powers and responsibility in relation to individual children, the Director is only to be concerned with the overall operation of regulated children's services, and if individual concerns are raised in relation to the operation of a particular service the Director must inform the police or social services for the area in which the service is provided or situated (National Care Standards Commission (Children's Rights Director) Regulations 2001, reg 3(a)–(p)).

11.36 Whilst much has been expected from the appointment of Peter Clarke, the new Welsh Children's Commissioner, the potential impact of the Commissioner and his powers and duties set out in the CSA 2000, ss 72–78 may be very limited if confined to those provided under the statute. Thus, whilst s 73 provides for the Commissioner to be able to review and monitor certain arrangements made by providers of services in Wales or by the Welsh Assembly in respect of services for children regulated under the CSA 2000, the government has stated that it 'is not the Assembly's intention that the Commissioner should routinely take the place of existing complaints procedures but that he or she should investigate the situation in which a matter of principle is involved or in which there is evidence of a systematic breach of children's rights' (see Baroness Farrington, *Hansard*, HL, vol 615, col 960). Such a restriction may be viewed with concern by the UN Monitoring Committee.

11.37 It remains to be seen whether the operation of the regulations governing the office of the Children's Rights Director in England and the performance of the Director in office, as compared to that of the Commissioner for Wales, lead to parity as between the two jurisdictions. One is forced to ask why the same office, with much more extensive powers to respond to the individual serious complaints of children, could not have been created for both jurisdictions and the UN Monitoring Committee have raised serious questions about the UK government's commitment to observing the principles of Article 3 of the UNCRC, specifically Article 3(2) in respect of this. The UN Monitoring Committee did not see either the appointment of a Children's Commissioner or the appointment of a Children's Rights Director with such limited rights and powers and lack of accessibility to individual children as fulfilling the obligation to take *all* appropriate legal and administrative measures to ensure the child's care and protection as required by Article 3 of the Convention.

Representations or complaints outside the CA 1989, Part III

11.38 In some circumstances there may be representations or complaints about childcare matters which fall outside the expanded scope of the CA 1989, Pt III which, as has been seen, includes the right of children to make complaints about their treatment where they are being 'looked after' by a local authority, and the ability of children and others to make representations about services or the failure to provide services including the taking of care proceedings, in the child protection arena (see *R v East Sussex County Council ex parte W* (see para **11.32**)). Such concerns which cannot be covered by the representations procedure fall under the Complaints Procedure Directions 1990, which are being reconsidered in the light of the CSA 2000. These directions direct the local authority on the way it should establish a procedure for dealing with a whole variety of representations and complaints made by, or on behalf of, individuals qualifying for services from a local authority under a range of statutory provisions. The guidelines are described in detail in *Community Care: Guidance for Managers* (DOH, 1991), at chapter 9, 'Complaints Procedures'. The procedure set out there differs, however, from that laid down under the CA 1989, s 26 in that there is no involvement of an independent person until the review stage and those working with children have had real concerns about personnel who administer such procedures having the relevant childcare expertise (see, eg, *Children Act 1989: Guidance and Regulations*, vol 3: 'Family Placements', at para 10.19). Concerns about such procedures insofar as they might be being used in relation to children's services could now legitimately be referred to either the Welsh Commissioner, in the case of Wales, or the Children's Rights Director in the case of England. It is quite clear, however, that where such procedures are not wholly independent of the local authority they might now be seen as being in breach of Article 6 of the ECHR. This is the only conclusion which can be drawn from a reading of Article 6 and was the approach adopted by the Court in *R on the application of the Personal Representative of Christopher Beeson v Dorset County Council and the Secretary of State for Health* [2001] EWHC Admin 986, unreported, the implications of which are discussed fully at para **11.22**).

Other types of representations procedures

11.39 As was noted above, complaints about the functioning of child protection conferences must be passed on to the social services department which, since they relate to Part V of the CA 1989, should be responded to in accordance with the Complaints Direction 1990. Where there are any complaints about the functioning of the children's guardian it should be noted that there was a separate representations system in relation to the guardian ad litem service (see the Guardian ad Litem and Reporting Officers (Panels) Regulations 1991, SI 1991/2051, and similar provisions have been implemented in relation to the performance of children's guardian duties by CAFCASS).

Other avenues for complaint

The Secretary of State's default powers

11.40 Provision is made in the CA 1989 to enable the Secretary of State to declare a local authority in default where he is satisfied that it has, without reasonable cause, failed to comply with a duty under the Act. The Secretary of State may then give the necessary directions to the authority to ensure that it complies with the duty within a specified period. If it becomes necessary, the Secretary of State may enforce a direction issued by him by applying to the court for judicial review under Ord 53 of the Rules of the Supreme Court 1965 (see para **11.48** *et seq*). The Secretary of State's default powers contained in the CA 1989, s 84, appear therefore to offer those seeking to complain about a local authority decision, or lack of it, the opportunity for taking their grievance to the Secretary of State, usually following the use of the complaints procedure established under s 26(3). As the court emphasised in *R v London Borough of Barnet ex parte B* [1994] 1 FLR 592, where a local authority failed to provide a child in need with appropriate day care, the proper remedy first was to apply under s 26(3) and, in the event of failure by the local authority to follow the statutory procedure in that section, then to apply to the Secretary of State to exercise his default powers under s 84. The court in *R v London Borough of Brent ex parte S* [1994] 1 FLR 203, at p 204, stated that the existence of a default power such as s 84 could properly be taken into consideration by the court as an avenue of redress, or alternative to judicial review. The court, however, emphasised (*per* Peter Gibson LJ) that s 84 does not give the aggrieved person a right of appeal from a local authority's decision. It was suggested by the Solicitor-General in debates upon this particular provision that it was not expected that such powers would be exercised often, still less that they would assist individuals, as it was considered more likely that the Secretary of State would exercise his powers, if at all, where an authority's failure to discharge its statutory duties affected a class as opposed to individual children (see HC Official Report (Six Series) SC, col 493, 13 June 1989).

Commissioner for local administration

11.41 Guidance issued by the DOH and by the Social Services Inspectorate (see para **11.23**) emphasises that the existence of a second stage panel within the complaints procedure established under the CA 1989 does not affect any rights which a particular individual might have under Pt III of the Local Government Act 1974 (LGA 1974) (a free booklet explaining the procedure to be adopted before the local government ombudsman is available from the offices of the Commissioner for Local Administration). The LGA 1974 provides individuals with a right to make a complaint about local authority maladministration, which includes such maladministration by social services departments or others acting on behalf of social services and the individual's right is not excluded by virtue of the representations process, because the second stage panel consideration is not a decision-making process. Complaints may only be made after the local authority has first been given an opportunity to address any concerns being raised on an individual's behalf (see the LGA 1974, s 26(5)). It is, therefore, entirely appropriate that the Commissioner for Local Administration may then investigate a complaint where the complainant has not been satisfied with the conduct or outcome of the authority's own investigation or with the outcome of the complaints or representations process. A complaint can be made either directly to the Commissioner or through a local councillor, but the Commissioner will generally only consider complaints concerning decision-making processes or events which have occurred within the previous 12 months (LGA 1974, s 26(4)).

11.42 Those who seek to make a complaint to the Commissioner should appreciate that the best sources of advice as to how to proceed would be Citizens' Advice Bureaux, Neighbourhood Law Centres and individual solicitors listed as having an expertise in public law areas. It should be noted that the complainant is asking the Commissioner to investigate whether an authority has been guilty of 'maladministration' leading to the particular injustice of which the individual is complaining, although it is sufficient if an individual merely states clearly the actions taken by the local authority which he is alleging are wrong, but it should be noted that the basis of the complaint should relate to the process by which a decision has been made or translated into actions rather than a complaint as to the rights or wrongs of a decision in itself (see *R v Local Commissioner for Administration for the North and East Area of England ex parte Bradford Metropolitan City Council* [1979] 2 All ER 881). It should therefore be emphasised that the work of the Commissioner is focused on the process by which decisions are reached rather than on the merits of a particular decision. There is thus a tendency to concentrate on matters of due process and procedural propriety, rather than on the concept of what is in the child's best interests. It should also be noted that the investigation can take quite some considerable time and could potentially delay the local authority's plans for a particular child. The Commissioner's powers are laid down in the relevant sections of the LGA 1974 and s 29 provides that for the purposes of any investigation a Local Commissioner may require any member or officer of the authority concerned, or any other person who in his opinion is able to furnish information or produce documents relevant to the investigation, to furnish any such information or produce any such documents. This was held by Carnwath J in the case of *Re A Subpoena (Adoption: Commissioner for Local Administration)* [1996] 2 FLR 629 to include confidential documents relating to the adoption of children within the area of responsibility of a particular social services department.

11.43 Once the Commissioner has concluded his investigation he then issues a report and, in those cases where he has found maladministration leading to injustice, may recommend that the local authority concerned should take specific action or in some cases may recommend financial compensation. Specific action will usually be the recommendation where the injustice has arisen from the failure to take action, for example, where the local authority has failed to issue a statement of special educational needs in relation to a child, has failed to assess entitlement to benefits for children in need, or has failed to make the necessary repairs to local authority housing. Sometimes the action recommended may be an amelioration of the injustice, for example the provision of specialist services where a child's education has been adversely affected by the local authority's inaction. Financial compensation is recommended where there has been financial loss, or where there is no other action which would provide an appropriate remedy, for example where there has been undue delay. Financial compensation may also be appropriate where the complainant has incurred costs which would not have been necessary but for the maladministration. Clearly, where the complainant is owed money, for example where a grant or housing benefit has not been paid, the remedy will involve payment of the money due and interest may also be added to this sum. The Local Commissioner will also have to consider cases where the injustice has involved a loss of opportunity, for example the loss of a right of appeal because the local authority failed to inform him of his right. Where it is reasonably certain that the outcome would otherwise have been beneficial to the complainant, the compensation will reflect this. In other cases, where the outcome was uncertain, only a small sum will be recommended. If, as is sometimes the case, it is reasonably certain that there would not have been a beneficial outcome for the complainant, there would be no compensation payable as there would have been no injustice found.

11.44 It should also be noted that the Commissioner may allow recovery of legal or other professional costs incurred whilst a complainant is taking up his case with the local authority where this is felt to be justifiable, although fees paid out to lawyers to pursue a case with the Commissioner will only be recommended for reimbursement in exceptional circumstances. The Commissioner can also award sums by way of compensation for 'distress' or for 'time and trouble' experienced by the complainant as a result of taking the complaint forward. Before the Commissioner makes such a recommendation it would be usual to find that the distress or 'time and trouble' is rather more than would be routinely expected in pursuing a complaint. The sums awarded have generally been quite small, varying between £25 and £250. The Commissioner would also expect, as a matter of routine, that the local authority will make an apology where appropriate and in some cases an apology is the only remedy which the Commissioner requires. The Commissioner may also recommend that the particular local authority reviews its practices, procedures or policies and where the authority has already undertaken to review a situation that fact will often be mentioned in the Local Commissioner's report.

11.45 A constant theme for 3 years' worth of reports issued by the three local government ombudsmen for England of recent times has been the inadequacies of the local authority complaints procedures. In the reports issued to the year ending 31 March 1999, social services complaints accounted for 7 per cent of all complaints to the Commissioner and 8 per cent of issued reports. Of the 1,132 social services complaints, about one-third (382) concerned services for children. The Commissioner identified weaknesses in the operation of the statutory social services complaints system by authorities and found that some local authorities were not implementing in full the recommendations of the review panels which their Directors of Social Services have accepted. In addition, the reports identified that some local authorities have not kept complainants properly informed about progress in implementing recommended changes and some review panels had not adequately analysed what harm the complainants had suffered as a result of the fault and recommended an appropriate remedy. The Commissioner emphasised that since the government was considering preparing new guidance on social services complaints generally, pursuant to the Care Standards Act 2000, the view was expressed that specific advice on the response to complaints panels should be included. The Commissioner also noted in the report to 31 March 1999 that there were a number of cases where the local authority had exceeded the statutory time-limit for each stage of the representations/complaints procedure. He did, however, note that these time-limits were at times unrealistic for complex cases, acknowledging that there was no benefit in local authorities having to face a choice between complying with the time-limits, and acting fairly and thoroughly (see *The Local Government Ombudsman Annual Report 1998–1999* (The Stationery Office, 1999)). The criticisms contained in the report for the period ending 31 March 1999 echo those expressed in the previous report for the period ending 31 March 1998, which again had serious criticism of the statutory social services complaints systems. Again the Commissioner for that year had noted that local authorities were not implementing in full the recommendations of the review panels which their Directors of Social Services had accepted. The local authorities were urged to identify those responsible for implementing agreed panel recommendations and then urged to monitor outcomes in a way which could be formally reported to senior management or members. It is clear from the report of 31 March 1999 that there had been continued failure to monitor such outcomes. It was further noted by the Commissioner that some complainants were having to approach the Commissioner because, although their complaints had been upheld by the review panel, they had been offered no remedy or one which was inadequate and accordingly the Commissioner was urging Directors of Social Services to ensure that panels do propose suitable remedies.

11.46 There is thus a considerable degree of overlap between the complaints/representations procedures and the work of the Commissioners for Local Administration. Those working in social services, particularly in the child protection arena, should be very much aware of those cases where there has been a referral to the Commissioner and to the types of remedies which may have been proposed by the Commissioner. It should be noted that awards of £1,000 have been recommended where a local authority failed to follow a case conference's recommendation, and of £2,000 where children were inappropriately interviewed about allegations of sexual abuse (see Commissioner for Local Administration, *Digest of Cases* (HMSO, 1999)). If there is overlap between the work of the Commissioners for Local Administration and the representation procedures, there is also overlap as between the Commissioners for Local Administration and the newly established Children's Commissioner for Wales and the Children's Rights Director in England. The Local Government Ombudsmen in England have detected problems within the current system in relation to children and have commented in the past that they would be better placed to assist in child abuse cases 'if they had the power to investigate on their own initiative, without receiving a complaint, or at the request of the local authority' (*Commission for Local Administration Annual Report*, 1986, at p 34). A power in the Local Commissioners to investigate on their own initiative would provide enhanced protection for children who, as has been seen repeatedly, do not feel able to complain easily. In evidence in 2000 to the Health and Social Services Committee considering the position of a Children's Commissioner for Wales, the local Government Commissioner for Wales and the Welsh Administration Ombudsman stated that although children could complain to them, they rarely did so. They pointed out that their role and function in investigating complaints of injustice caused by maladministration was different to that of a

Children's Commissioner. They stressed that they were not policy advisers or advocates, that they had to remain impartial and thus saw neither a conflict of interest nor an overlap with their jurisdiction if the new Children's Commissioner investigated complaints that did not fall within the ambit of their duties.

Elected members

11.47 It should be noted that the complaints and representations procedures should not, in any way, affect the right of an individual, be they a child, parent, carer or any child protection professional or organisation, to approach a local councillor for advice or assistance or to voice their particular concerns. Indeed, where an individual has indicated that he is not satisfied with the panel's decision (see para **11.22**) in many local authority areas the complaints procedure goes beyond the second stage to a third, informal stage set up by individual local authorities, and which includes the involvement of more elected members. The Ministerial Task Force for Children's Safeguards has also indicated that more detailed guidance will be given to local councillors concerning their roles in ensuring appropriate standards of local authority work in childcare cases and also concerning their involvement in the complaints/representations process (see *Report of the Ministerial Task Force on Safeguards for Children* (DOH/Welsh Office, 2000)). It is clear from the above discussion that not every child, parent, carer or other person with sufficient interest in a child will necessarily be satisfied with the results of representations which they may wish to make. Wherever there is such dissatisfaction, and provided that in appropriate cases they have first of all exhausted the representations process, consideration can then be given to the possibility of taking an action for breach of statutory duty or lodging an application for judicial review of administrative action.

Judicial review and child protection

The scope and meaning of judicial review

11.48 Judicial review is the standard administrative law remedy available to individuals or groups, by which the legality of a decision taken by an inferior court, tribunal or a public body, such as a local authority, may be challenged on the grounds that it has acted illegally, irrationally or with procedural impropriety. A challenge by way of judicial review must, since 2 October 2000, be taken in the newly named Administrative Court. The court may quash the decision taken (a quashing order, formerly known as an order of certiorari); or order the respondent to do something such as reconsideration of the matter (a mandatory order, formerly known as an order of mandamus), or order the respondent to refrain from doing something (a prohibiting order, formerly known as an order of prohibition); or the Administrative Court may issue a declaration or injunction. The court may also issue an order for damages but only if damages have been sought in conjunction with one of the three prerogative orders, ie the quashing order, the mandatory order or the prohibiting order (see CPR 1998, r 54). It should be noted that a separate Administrative Court has been established in Wales so that a claim for judicial review involving a Welsh public body may be brought in the Administrative Court in Wales, but may also be brought in the Administrative Court in London if the applicant prefers. The Administrative Court may direct that the hearing is to take place otherwise than in either Cardiff or London. The crucial point about judicial review is that it is primarily a decision based on an assessment of the procedural propriety of the case in question, and not on the merits of the case, because the Administrative Court's jurisdiction is said to be supervisory and not appellate. The legality of the decision-making process is the only matter under review (*R v Cornwall County Council ex parte LH* [2000] 1 FLR 236; *R v Tameside Metropolitan Borough Council ex parte J* [2000] 1 FLR 947).

11.49 In this area of the law, concerned as it is with all aspects of decision-making related to child protection, applicants for judicial review may be seeking to establish whether a whole range of local authority personnel or differently constituted bodies such as, for example, the Director of Social Services or the local authority complaints panel have correctly carried out their decision-making functions. Hence, the Administrative Court can only be asked to rule on whether the decision-making process of the individual or body was correctly carried out, not on the rightness or wrongness of the decision (*Re T (Accommodation by Local Authority)* [1995] 1 FLR 159).

Leave from the administrative court must first be obtained

11.50 The person wishing to apply for judicial review must first of all apply to the Administrative Court for leave to make a judicial review application (CPR 1998, r 54.4). The Administrative Court will grant leave to apply for judicial review to anyone who has sufficient interest in the subject matter. The test of sufficient interest has been established through case-law and the new rules appear to make little difference to that law (*IRC v National Federation of Self Employed and Small Business Limited* [1981] 2 All ER 93 and *Council of Civil Services Unions v Minister for the Civil Service* [1985] AC 374, at p 408). A child, anyone with parental responsibility, any significant other including the children's guardian, advocate or independent person, would almost certainly be deemed to have a 'sufficient interest'. Once sufficient interest is established, a claim for judicial review of a decision made by an inferior court or, in this area of the law, a body charged with a public duty, such as a local authority or child protection conference, will then lie. On the application for leave to apply for judicial review, case-law backed up by the new rules provides that claimants must show that they have sufficient ground for bringing a case. Thus the claim form must include, or be accompanied by, a detailed statement of the claimant's grounds for bringing the claim for judicial review, a statement of facts relied on, a time estimate for the main hearing, any written evidence in support of the claim, copies of any document on which the claimant proposes to rely and a list of essential documents for advance reading by the court (CPR 1998, r 54.6(2) and Practice Direction 54, paras 5.6 and 5.7).

11.51 In *R v Secretary of State for the Home Department ex parte Swati* [1986] 1 All ER 717, the court stated that:

> 'an applicant must show more than that it is not impossible that grounds for judicial review exist. To say that he must show a prima facie case that such grounds do in fact exist may be putting it too high, but he must at least show that it is a real, as opposed to a theoretical possibility. In other words, he must have an arguable case' (at p 723H).

Unfortunately, therefore, the court may not necessarily grant leave at this preliminary application stage unless it is convinced that there is enough evidence to pursue the remedy of judicial review. The application must, therefore, contain sufficiently cogent grounds for judicial review, which may be very difficult if the applicant does not possess sufficient information to justify the application for review. Hence, the giving of reasons and the general openness of the local authority may be critical factors in many cases. In *R v Lancashire County Council ex parte M* [1992] 1 FLR 109, the Court of Appeal refused to grant leave to apply for judicial review, on a renewed application, where the complaint was that the local authority had wrongly concluded that a child should be moved from his foster home to prospective adopters, and had refused to approve the foster parents as adoptive parents. The Court of Appeal held that it could not be said that no local authority could have come to this decision and, therefore, the application should fail.

Procedural limitations of judicial review

11.52 The use of judicial review in the family law and child law arena has had a relatively short history but as Robin Spon-Smith points out 'its use is growing, in the family law field as in other fields' (see Spon-Smith (2000), at p 564). Spon-Smith also predicted that the coming into force of the HRA 1998 on 2 October 2000 would also lead to a significant increase in the number of judicial review applications in the family law field, as well as in other areas of law, and such has indeed been the case. As well as its relatively short history, however, indications from case-law suggest that the judiciary appear to adopt a different attitude towards judicial review of decisions taken in these areas (see *R v East Sussex County Council ex parte R* [1991] 2 FLR 358). Apart from the need to obtain leave, judicial review itself is not as effective as other ordinary actions in private law, for a number of reasons:

(1) the judicial review procedure is not conducive to the determination of factual disputes (discovery and cross-examination, for example, are not available as a matter of course as in private law proceedings);

(2) even if the court decides that, in law, the local authority acted improperly, it cannot substitute its decision for that of the local authority, thus the authority may make the same decision as before, provided the correct procedures are followed the second time around;

(3) damages will not be available where applicants have shown that the local authority acted contrary to the principles of fairness, legality or propriety, thus litigants would have to prove, in addition, that there had been a tortious wrong, a breach of contract or a breach of statutory duty (see, eg, *R v Lancashire County Council ex parte M* [1992] 1 FLR 109) before damages may be awarded (Supreme Court Act 1981, s 31(4)); and

(4) the Administrative Court also expects persons to exhaust all other available remedies before applying for judicial review and may exercise its discretion to refuse judicial review if this has not been done (*R v Birmingham City Council ex parte A* [1997] 2 FLR 841 and *R v East Sussex County Council ex parte W* [1998] 2 FLR 1082).

Reasons for using judicial review in child protection cases

11.53 Prior to the implementation of the CA 1989 on 14 October 1991 the challenging of the exercise of local authority decision-making in relation to children was mainly effected through the use of a wardship application to the High Court Family Division. There may, therefore, be said to be at least three reasons for using judicial review in cases involving local authority decision-making powers in relation to children and their parents in the child protection arena.

11.54 First, the use of wardship to review the decisions of local authorities was severely circumscribed and effectively ended by the courts in a series of cases, the most important being the House of Lords' decisions in *A v Liverpool City Council* (1981) FLR 222 and *Re W (A Minor) (Care Proceedings: Wardship)* [1985] FLR 879. The restrictions on the use of wardship established by *A v Liverpool City Council* and the other cases which followed it have been the subject of judicial regret on a number of occasions, as more importantly has been the restriction on the power of the High Court to ensure that the local authority's care plan was properly implemented after a care order was made (see Sir Stephen Brown P in *Nottinghamshire County Council v P* [1994] Fam 18, at p 43, and also *Re MD and TD* [1994] Fam Law 489), although potentially this is now remedied by the right of the prescribed person to refer a child's case to a CAFCASS officer under s 26(2A) of the CA 1989, as amended. The CAFCASS officer is then given the opportunity to refer the matter on to the courts (s 26(A)(c) of the CA 1989, as amended). Secondly, wardship is not generally available to individuals whose child is in care because a child in care cannot be made a ward of court (CA 1989, s 100(2)). Thus, the aggrieved parties cannot invoke wardship to review the exercise of local authority's powers and duties in relation to children in their care. Thirdly, experience has shown that it is not any easier to invoke the inherent jurisdiction of the High Court (see CA 1989, s 100) in order to review the merits of any local authority decisions. Interestingly enough, however, the inherent jurisdiction has regularly been invoked by local authorities in order to enable them to achieve results which are not provided to them under the CA 1989 (see *South Glamorgan County Council v W and B* [1993] 1 FLR 574).

11.55 Thus, while the inherent jurisdiction of the High Court remains in being, its operation is severely restricted by the interpretation given to different parts of the CA 1989 (see further on this, Chapter **8**). Although the CA 1989 provides that the court has power to regulate parental contact with children in care (see s 34(2)), the court has no powers to direct the local authority to take any particular course of action with regard to the future placement of a child who is the subject of a full care order. Although the Court of Appeal, in its decision in *Re W and B; Re W (Care Plan)* [2001] EWCA Civ 757, [2001] 2 FLR 582 indicated that in order to avoid breaching ECHR rights when applying the CA 1989, the courts must be given the power to intervene wherever there is a failure to achieve a 'starred milestone' within a care plan which had been put before the court before the making of a care order, their decision was, of course, overturned in the House of Lords (see *Re S (Minors); Re W (Minors)* [2002] UKHL 10, [2002] 1 FLR 815). The Adoption and Children Act 2002 has amended the CA 1989 now to provide that after a s 26(2) review on any child being looked after by the local authority, where the prescribed person considers it appropriate to do so he may refer the case to a CAFCASS officer. The CAFCASS officer will then have to determine whether to take the case back to court in family proceedings, in which he will have the functions provided for in yet-to-be-made Rules of court (see 26(2C) of the CA 1989, as amended). (These provisions are also considered in detail in Chapters **4** and **10**.)

11.56 Aside from this new development with regard to the ability of the prescribed person to be able to refer a child's case to a CAFCASS officer, in order to provide for the possibility of referring the matter back to the court to review the local authority's actions under the s 31A or s 26(2)(f)(i) care plan, the family court has generally only been able to consider issues affecting contact with regard to the child in care under the CA 1989, s 34(2) and before making a care order they are now required to consider the local authority's s 31A care plan for the child. One of the intentions of the legislature in enacting the CA 1989 was to remove the notion that judges could exercise some degree of supervision over the life of a child in care in the way in which they had done when children were committed into the care of the local authority under wardship prior to the implementation of the Act. Thus, apart from the recent amendments to s 26 of the CA 1989 (effected by the Adoption and Children Act 2002, in an attempt to meet acute judicial concern over the decision of the House of Lords in *Re S (Minors); Re W (Minors)* [2002] UKHL 10, [2002] 1 FLR 815 and also in response to concerns voiced in judicial review cases such as *F v Lambeth London Borough Council* [2002] 1 FLR 217, see para **11.101**), and it remains to be seen how effective these will be in practice, and the court's powers to regulate contact and now also to consider a s 31A care plan, the only other means open to anyone to challenge the decision-making process of the local authority or any of its personnel is by way of judicial review. As Lord Scarman stated in *Re W (A Minor) (Care Proceedings: Wardship)* [1985] FLR 879:

> 'The ground of decision in [the Liverpool case] was an application ... of the profoundly important rule that where Parliament has by statute entrusted to a public authority an administrative power subject to safeguards which ... contain no provision that the High Court is to be required to review the merits of decisions taken pursuant to the power, the High Court has no right to intervene. If there is abuse of power, there can, of course, be judicial review.'

The CA 1989 and judicial review

In general

11.57 It has already been pointed out that some commentators have noted the exponential growth in the use of judicial review in the field of family and child law. Spon-Smith (see para **11.52**) commented in mid-2000 that when he had reviewed the index for the Family Law Reports he had counted some 148 cases involving judicial review in the family law and child law field in the period 1980–1999. The author of this book, when considering specifically the cases involving judicial review of local authority decision-making under the CA 1989, has counted some 56 cases of the use of judicial review to question the propriety or legality of such decisions. This particular count covers the period since publication of the previous edition of this book and thus runs from 1992 to mid-2002. What is very noticeable about this case count is the very considerable rise in the use of judicial review from late 1999 to the present.

11.58 Judicial review has been used most imaginatively by lawyers concerned with either the propriety or validity of certain local authority decisions with regard to the interpretation of the CA 1989. There have thus been challenges to local authority decisions made under each of the Parts of the CA 1989 with which this work is closely concerned, namely Parts III, IV and V, but there have also been challenges in relation to the interpretation by local authorities of their duties under government guidance issued pursuant to the CA 1989.

11.59 There have been successful and unsuccessful challenges with regard to the interpretation of local authority duties under the CA 1989, s 17. Thus in *R on the application of S v Wandsworth, Hammersmith and Lambeth London Borough Council* [2002] 1 FLR 469 judicial review was granted in respect of two of the three London boroughs' refusal to carry out assessments of children in need within their area. By contrast, in *R on the application of A v London Borough of Lambeth* [2002] 1 FLR 353, judicial review of a decision not to supply a mother and her three children with alternative accommodation was refused because of the court's view that s 17 did not create an enforceable duty in respect of any individual child, and the decision of the first instance judge was upheld by the Court of Appeal. Some flexibilty in the use of powers under s 17 has, however, been restored by the decision of the Court of Appeal in another judicial review case, that of *R on the application of W v Lambeth LBC* [2002] 2 FLR 327, where the Court of Appeal ruled that Parliament had not intended so rigid a demarcation of powers as between social services and housing departments and thus this case constitutes a reversal of that aspect of its earlier decision. In *R on the application of AB and SB v Nottingham City Council* [2001] 3 FCR 350 the failure by the local authority to carry out a core assessment under the government's *Framework for the Assessment of Children in Need and their Families* (DOH, 2000), where the local authority had accepted that the child was a 'child in need' under s 17, led to the court's granting judicial review and ordering that the core assessment be completed within the 35 days laid down in the *Framework for Assessment*. There are a number of other cases with regard to the interpretation of s 17 which will be considered in detail below.

11.60 Judicial review has also been used to challenge the provision of day care under CA 1989, s 18. Thus in *R v London Borough of Barnett ex parte B* [1994] 1 FLR 592, judicial review was used by children in need to complain about the local authority's closure of a day nursery. In the circumstances of this case judicial review was in fact refused because the court held that there had been sufficient consultation with the families concerned which could lead the court to conclude that the decision to close the nursery was a reasonable one and one which had been fully considered.

11.61 The provisions of the CA 1989, s 20 have also been productive of a number of recent cases concerning the interpretation of local authority duties under that section. Judicial review was used in *R on the application of A v Lambeth London Borough Council* [2002] 1 FLR 353, where the court determined that judicial review would not be granted as its view was that the generalised s 17 duty could not be engaged to secure the provision of accommodation to a child, although as noted above this has now been in part reversed by the decision of the Court of Appeal in *R on application of W v Lambeth LBC* [2002] 2 FLR 327. In that case, the Court of Appeal held that the local authority did indeed have the power under s 17 of the CA 1989 to accommodate a family with dependent children where they were not entitled to housing under the housing legislation. The authority, however, had a discretion with regard to the exercise of that power and in the particular instance had given sufficient and intelligible reasons for the decision not to accommodate the family so that judicail review would not be exercised to quash the decision of the local authority. Judicial review was also successfully used in *R v Tameside Metropolitan Borough Council ex parte J* [2000] 1 FLR 942 where judicial review was granted and the local authority's decision to move a s 20 'accommodated' child from residential care to foster care without parental permission was declared invalid.

11.62 The interpretation by local authorities of their duties to provide accommodation for children under s 23 has also been considered by the Administrative Court recently in a case which was unreported at the time of writing. Thus in *R on the application of L and Others* and *R and Others v Manchester City Council* [2002] 1 FLR 43, issues were raised by foster families who had been drawn from within the children's extended families with regard to the payment of differential fostering rates as between stranger foster parents and extended family foster parents. The policy of the city council was to pay lower rates to foster parents drawn from within the child's extended family than those which they would have paid had the foster parents been strangers. The Administrative Court held that such a policy was unlawful and did not represent a proper interpretation of both ss 22 and 23 of the CA 1989. The duty of the local authority was to safeguard and promote the children's welfare and discouragement of extended family placements by the paying of lower fostering allowances was not a decision which could be held to be an exercise of the duty to safeguard and promote the children's interests. The Administrative Court in this case made a very detailed examination of the different responsibilities of the local authority under the provisions of ss 20, 22 and 23, and this is discussed in more detail below.

11.63 Judicial review has also successfully been used by a young adult to challenge the refusal by two different local authorities to provide him with after-care and subsistence under the old unamended provisions of s 24. These provisions have now been overtaken by the amendments made by the Children (Leaving Care) Act 2000, ss 23A–24D (see Chapter 4) but the use of judicial review by the young man in this case was very interesting (see *R v Lambeth London Borough Council ex parte Cadell* [1998] 1 FLR 253).

11.64 Another decision made by the Administrative Court, which was not within the field of children and families may, however, have far-reaching repercussions in relation to the complaints procedures under the CA 1989, s 26(3) and (4). Thus the representations (complaints) procedures required to be established by that section provide, in common with all other statutory local authority representations procedures, that:

'at least one person who is not a member or officer of the authority should take part in the consideration and any discussions which are held by the authority about the action to be taken in relation to the child in the light of the consideration of the representation or complaint.'

11.65 Regulations have been provided with regard to the way in which the local authority carries out the consideration of representations and these were dealt with in detail above (see para **11.28**). In the recent case of *R on the application of the personal representative of Christopher Beeson v Dorset County Council and the Secretary of State for Health* [2001] EWHC Admin 986, unreported, Richards J held that the Complaints Procedure Directions 1990 made under the Local Authority Social Services Act 1970, s 7B(3), laid down procedures which are in direct breach of Article 6 of the ECHR as contained in the HRA 1998, Sch 1. Richards J in this case found that judicial review could not compensate for the lack of an independent element in the complaints process so as to ensure compliance with Article 6. On the current rules, which are common to those provided for children and their families under the CA 1989, s 26(3) and (4), only one member of the complaints panel has to be an independent member. Richards J ruled that in order to be Article 6 compliant, all panel members must be entirely independent of the local authority and that therefore simply substituting two independent panel members for two council members and still retaining one council member would not be sufficient to render the process Article 6 compliant. He therefore concluded that in order to achieve compliance with Article 6, all members of the complaints panel must be independent of the local authority in every way. Thus, by means of the interpretation of the court in a judicial review case, the process on complaints and representations made by children and their families may finally become truly independent of the local authority and be seen by children, young people and their families as properly safeguarding their interests.

11.66 The local authority's interpretation of its duty to investigate the situation of children in respect of whom there is reasonable cause to suspect that they might be suffering significant harm was called into question by the use of judicial review in *Re S (Sexual Abuse Allegations: Local Authority Response)* [2001] 2 FLR 776. In that case, judicial review was unsuccessful and the court ruled that the need to establish facts on the balance of probability had no place in the exercise by a local authority of its various protective responsibilities under the CA 1989 and, in particular, with regard to its investigation of information tending to suggest that children were likely to suffer significant harm. The court thus ruled that the threshold for having 'reasonable cause to suspect' that a child was likely to suffer significant harm was really quite low and if the court were to set the threshold any higher, the result would then be to prevent local authorities from carrying out effective and timely risk assessment. In addition, the court feared that local authorities would be forced to take care proceedings to identify whether grounds for intervention were present, and that, in the opinion of the court, would be completely contrary to the principle established by the CA 1989 of non-intervention in children cases.

11.67 Perhaps not surprisingly, the area of the greatest number of challenges to the interpretation by local authorities of their duties in the child protection field is the area of case conferences and actions following upon them. The areas most productive of claims for judicial review have concerned the operation of local authority policies in relation to the running of conferences and decisions flowing therefrom, but the issue of the making of disclosures by various of the agencies involved in child protection conferences has also been productive with a very considerable number of cases appearing in the law reports. As far as local authority policies are concerned (but also linked with the issue of local authority interpretation of government guidance), the case of *R v Cornwall County Council ex parte LH* [2000] 1 FLR 236 is illustrative of the problems which may be engendered. Thus, in this case the local authority, in clear breach of the guidance laid down in *Working Together to Safeguard Children* (DOH, 1999), had a policy that:

(1) solicitors were not to be permitted to attend child protection conferences; and
(2) parents attending such conferences were not to be given minutes of the conference. The claim for judicial review was successful and the court held that the actions of the local authority were illegal as being contrary to the specific guidelines laid down in *Working Together to Safeguard Children*.

11.68 Local authority policy was also under review in *R v Local Authority and a Police Authority in the Midlands ex parte LM* [2000] 1 FLR 612, where the local authority's blanket policy that disclosures should be made where concerns have been raised about adults in a child protection conference was ruled to be again unlawful. The issue of disclosure of information about adults who have been discussed at child protection conferences or in other inter-agency strategy discussions is a very vexed one and has produced a number of challenges using judicial review since the 1980s. Despite a now very considerable body of case-law, those individuals affected by decisions to make disclosures about them have continually challenged such decisions by local authorities (for a recent example see *Re S (Sexual Abuse Allegations: Local Authority Response)* (at para **11.66**) and *R v Chief Constables of C and D ex parte A* [2001] 2 FCR 431) (see further, Chapter **3**).

Grounds for judicial review

11.69 The leading case dealing with the grounds for judicial review is that of *Council of Civil Service Unions v Minister for the Civil Service* [1984] 3 All ER 935, where both Lord Diplock and Lord Roskill separately examined the grounds for judicial review. Lord Roskill's speech (at p 953J) examined the grounds in some detail, whereas Lord Diplock (at p 942C) classified the grounds much more simply as being: illegality, irrationality and procedural impropriety.

Illegality or error of law

11.70 Lord Roskill (at p 953J) characterised this first ground as being 'where the authority concerned has been guilty of an error of law in its action, as for example, purporting to exercise a power which in law it does not possess'. Other examples of such an error of law will include those situations where the local authority or other public body has wrongly interpreted its duties under the law or has simply acted unlawfully. Illegality may also arise where a local authority abuses its jurisdiction or power. Examples of the use of judicial review in which review has been granted on the basis of illegality include *R v Cornwall County Council ex parte LH* [2000] 1 FLR 236, where the local authority was held to have acted illegally in not permitting solicitors to attend child protection conferences on behalf of parents save to read out prepared statements and in not giving parents attending such conferences copies of the conference minutes. In this case the mother of three children had a history of mental instability. Private care proceedings had been commenced in respect of two of the children and interim care orders had been made. The local authority had a policy which did not permit the attendance of a solicitor to represent parents at child protection conferences, and in consequence the mother's solicitor wrote to the local authority asking, in the specific context of this case, for their permission to allow him to attend with the mother. The local authority refused that request on the basis that there were no exceptional circumstances persuading them to depart from their usual policy. Nevertheless, the solicitor attended the conference and was permitted to make representations on behalf of the mother. When he was asked to leave, he cited the committee guidelines that permitted the presence of a friend or relative, but upon being told that solicitors could not be regarded as friends, he left. Thereafter the solicitor tried to obtain a copy of the minutes of the meeting, but since the local authority's policy was that, as a matter of course, neither a parent nor his solicitor were permitted a copy of the minutes other than through an order of the court, he only obtained disclosure by order of the court. The mother therefore applied for judicial review of the decision of the local authority: (i) not to allow the presence of her solicitor at the conference; and (ii) not to provide her with a copy of the minutes of the conference, contending that their policies were contrary to the statutory guidance of the Secretary of State contained in *Working Together to Safeguard Children*, seeking declarations that their conduct was unlawful.

11.71 Scott Baker J allowed the application for judicial review and granted the declarations holding that: (1) a blanket ban on solicitors of the kind operated by the local authority was contrary to the statutory guidance and thus unlawful. He emphasised that, in general, solicitors ought to be allowed to attend and participate unless and until it was felt that they undermined the purpose of the conference by, for example, making it unnecessarily confrontational. He also stressed that any experienced Chair of the conference who had a discretion under the guidance as to who should be permitted to attend and for what purpose, should be more than able to assess the situation; (2) the local authority's position with regard to the minutes of the meeting was ludicrous and blatantly contravened paras 6.19 and 6.35 of the statutory guidance, which requires that a parent and/or his solicitor should be provided with a copy of the minutes of that part of the meeting that he attended so that, apart from anything else, if a parent or solicitor disagreed with the accuracy of anything that was minuted, he could say so at an early stage. The minutes were not more or less than a record of what occurred at the meeting and it could reasonably be assumed that most people who were furnished with the minutes would behave responsibly. Scott Baker J indicated that where there were reasons in a particular case to suppose that minutes would be misused, then it would be open to the Chair of the conference to withhold them for specific reasons. He therefore held that the local authority's refusal, as a matter of course, to permit those present to have a copy of the minutes was also unlawful. The version of *Working Together* to which reference was made in this case was that produced in 1991. In *Working Together to Safeguard Children* (DOH, 1999), at para 5.57 it is stated that 'the parents should normally be invited to attend the conference and helped fully to participate. Social Services should give parents information about local advice and advocacy agencies, and explain that they may bring an advocate, friend or supporter'. As far as guidance on the provision of minutes of the conference is concerned, the new guidance indicates at para 5.74 that:

'The written record of the conference is a crucial working document for all relevant professionals and the family. It should include the essential facts of the case; a summary of discussion at the conference which accurately reflects the contributions made; all decisions reached, with information outlining the reasons for decisions; and a translation of decisions into an outline or revised child protection plan enabling everyone to be clear about their tasks. A copy should be sent as soon as possible after the conference to all those who attended or who were invited to attend, including family members, except for any part of the conference from which they were excluded.'

11.72 In the case of *R v Tameside Metropolitan Borough Council ex parte J* [2000] 1 FLR 942, the local authority's decision to move a child accommodated under s 20 from residential care to foster care without parental permission was declared unlawful. The particular facts of this case were that the child, who was at the date of the hearing 13 years old, had severe physical and learning disabilities. She lived at home with her parents until she was accommodated by the local authority under a voluntary agreement pursuant to s 20 rather than under a care order. In September 1997 she was placed in a residential home for disabled children but the following year the local authority suggested that the child should be moved to live with foster parents. The parents, however, who both had parental responsibility for the child, profoundly disagreed with this move. They wished her to remain in the children's home and were of the view that great care and research would be required before suitable foster parents could be identified. Despite the parents' objections, the local authority commenced contact between the child and a particular family. The child, through her mother and litigation friend, applied for permission to apply for judicial review of the local authority's decision to move her.

11.73 Scott Baker J again in this case held that the local authority had acted illegally and could not make the decision to move the child. He held that a local authority accommodating a child in need under s 20, rather than under a care order pursuant to the CA 1989, was only able to exercise mundane day-to-day powers of management as to provision of that accommodation. He stressed that a mere power of management could not override the wishes of a parent with parental responsibility. The decision to place a child with foster parents went beyond the exercise of day-to-day management powers and trespassed into the kind of decision-making that was ultimately exercised by those with parental responsibility. Accordingly, he held that the general duty of the local authority to safeguard and promote the welfare of children in its area who were in need contained in s 17(1) and the duties of the local authority under s 22(3), (4) and (5) did not entitle the local authority to place a child who was voluntarily in their care with foster parents against the express wishes of the parents.

11.74 In the case of R *on the application of* L *and Others and* R *and Others v* Manchester City Council [2002] 1 FLR 43, the local authority was held to have acted illegally in seeking to pay lower rates of fostering allowances to extended family members acting as foster parents. Munby J in this case had before him two separate applications by two different families for judicial review of the legality of Manchester City Council's policy under which it paid those of its short-term foster carers who were friends or relatives of the child at a different and very significantly lower rate than it paid to other foster carers. The children involved in both cases were placed with members of their own families following their removal via care proceedings from their immediate families. In the case of L *and Others* the children had been placed with their maternal grandparents who became long-term foster parents for the children, and in the case of R *and Others* the children were placed with their elder half-sister.

11.75 Munby J referred to the duties and powers of Manchester in relation to the children as set out in ss 22 and 23 of the CA 1989. He noted that the statutory framework envisages that all appropriate steps are taken to ensure that children are placed with their families so far as possible (s 23(6)). In this way, he emphasised that the Act promotes the aim of implementing the right to respect for family life enshrined in Article 8 of the ECHR as contained in the HRA 1998, Sch 1. The main point being raised by the families in each of these cases was that when they were acting as short-term foster parents the amounts of allowances paid to them did not fulfil Manchester's obligations under the provisions of the CA 1989 since its policy in making payments to members of the child's family might operate as a disincentive to achieving the objective laid down in s 23(6), now as strongly supported by Article 8. As Munby J emphasised (at para 90) it followed that the obligation of Manchester under both the Act and the ECHR is to take all appropriate *positive* steps (subject to contrary welfare considerations as set out in s 23(6) and Article 8(2)) to ensure that the children should live with their families.

11.76   Munby J accepted that Manchester's policy made it more difficult for family members to foster children than non-family members, that the setting of low fostering rates for relative foster carers will inevitably tend to discourage such persons from applying and thus be likely to diminish the child's opportunity to participate in family life within its own family, and that Manchester failed to observe its positive obligations under the CA 1989 or the ECHR to allow relatives to have children in care living with them. In addition, in the case of the *R and Others*, family children who had been placed with their elder half-sister, the authorities had continually failed to approve her as a long-term foster parent and thus she had remained on the short-term lower fostering rate paid to relatives. In doing so, Munby J found that Manchester appeared to have breached its own policy with regard to ensuring the children's welfare and best placement. Munby J went on not only to declare that the practices of the Manchester City Council were unlawful in each of the cases concerned, but also to order that the defendant's decision to pay the lower rates of fostering allowances were to be quashed and redetermined in accordance with the findings of the court and that in consequence of the finding that the fostering allowances should be recalculated, the claim for damages in both the cases would be stayed.

11.77   In *R on the application of AB and SB v Nottingham City Council* [2001] 3 FCR 350, the failure by Nottingham City Council to conduct core assessments on children whom they had accepted were 'children in need', was also held to be illegal. In this case the first claimant AB was the mother of the second claimant SB. SB had challenging behaviour, emotional problems and profound learning difficulties. His behaviour had brought him into regular contact with the police and he was the subject of a supervision order. The police referred SB's case to the defendant local authority's social services department. The defendant accepted that SB was 'a child in need' within the meaning of the CA 1989, s 17 so that an assessment of his needs was required. *Working*

Together to Safeguard Children and *Framework for Assessment* laid down a framework for first an initial and then a core assessment of the child's needs in the context of the family and wider community. Child protection conferences were convened and short reports were prepared by a social worker, a child psychologist and a community paediatrician. The social worker's report also referred to housing problems. The social worker prepared an assessment described as being based on *Framework for Assessment*. He recommended that SB remain a child in need, that there be a review in 6 months, that SB be given appropriate educational provision and that appropriate housing should be accessed. The claimants applied for judicial review; they contended that the defendant had failed to carry out a proper core assessment of need in accordance with *Framework for Assessment* which was in breach of the Local Authorities Social Services Act 1970, s 7 and was unlawful and that they had failed to prepare a plan and provide the services to meet those needs.

11.78 Richards J in the Administrative Court held that where a local authority followed a path that did not involve the preparation of a core assessment as such, it had nevertheless to adopt a similarly systematic approach with a view to achievement of the same objectives. That, he stated, involved an assessment of needs which took into account the three domains: the child's development needs, parenting capacity, and family and environmental facts. Such an assessment involved a collaboration between all relevant agencies so as to achieve a full understanding of the child in his or her family and community context. The authority then had to complete a three-stage process: first to identify the child's needs, second to produce a care plan, and third to provide the identified services. Failure to do so without cause would constitute an impermissible departure from the guidance. In the instant case, Richards J found that there was nothing in the documentation which even approached an assessment capable of meeting the requirements set out in *Framework for Assessment*. As to housing, he found that it was common ground that accommodation could be provided under the CA 1989, s 17 and that the assessment of a child's needs had to encompass the question of his housing needs. That assessment had to take into account the position of the child and the position of the carer with whom he lived. Richards J found that in the circumstances, there had been no proper assessment of housing need. Further, he found that even if there had been an assessment there had been no proper provision of services to meet that need. He found that it was the responsibility of the social services to meet the identified housing need and although it could seek the assistance of the housing authority, it could not simply wash its hands of the matter by referring those in need to the housing authority.

11.79 Richards J therefore reached the view that the claim for judicial review should succeed on the basis that the authority had not acted lawfully and he issued a mandatory order requiring the defendant local authority to carry out a full assessment of SB's needs under s 17. The judge also imposed a time limit on the performance of such an assessment, and although it was suggested to him that a shorter period might be appropriate, he decided to allow the defendant local authority the maximum period specified in *Framework for Assessment* for a core assessment, namely 35 days.

11.80 Finally, another example of a local authority acting illegally in clear breach of a statutory duty imposed under the CA 1989, s 17 can be found in the case of R *v Hammersmith and Fulham London Borough Council ex parte D* [1999] 1 FLR 642. In this case, the applicant, a mother of two children sought judicial review of a decision of the local authority acting under Part III of the CA 1989:

(a) to offer her financial assistance to enable her and her children to return to Sweden; and

(b) to terminate the provision of accommodation and a financial allowance for her children from the following day were the applicant to decline the local authority's offer to fund the family's return to Sweden.

Kay J held that in deciding to limit its use of its statutory powers under the CA 1989, the respondent authority was in breach of its duties. He indicated that a local authority might, in the discharge of its duties under Part III of the Act, make an offer to a parent of a child it had determined to be in need of financial assistance, for the family to return to another country where it is believed that the needs of the child would be best met. It had, however, been wrong for the authority in this case to decide to withdraw all further assistance for the child in the event that the parents declined to accept what was offered, and the judge further held that it was wrong for the local authority to have threatened such a course of action even if it had made no decision.

11.81 It can be seen, therefore, that there have been a number of cases in which judicial review has been successfully used to challenge the legality of local authority decision-making, the proper exercise of its discretion, the lack of independence in its complaints procedures, the failure to comply with the requirements of government guidance which has the status of law, the failure to make a decision when one is required, the making of a decision without the relevant facts to back it up, or the authority acting where it has no power so to act.

11.82 As Wade and Forsyth point out, a lack of resources, usually financial, often constrains public authorities in deciding how to exercise their duties and powers lawfully. They note that, as a general rule, impoverishment may not be treated as a relevant reason for failing to perform a statutory duty expressed in objective terms which allows for the exercise of no discretion (see Wade and Forsyth (2000), at p 82). Wade and Forsyth go on to indicate that the House of Lords made this principle very clear in a case where the statutory duty of a local authority was to arrange for 'suitable full time or part time education' defined as 'efficient education' suitable to the pupil's age, ability, aptitude and any special educational needs. When a cut in government funding compelled the local authority to economise, they reduced the home tuition for a handicapped girl from 5 to 3 hours per week. It was clear from the CA 1989 that the standard of suitability was to be determined purely by educational considerations, so that shortage of funds was irrelevant and a matter for Parliament only; otherwise the court would have 'to downgrade a statutory duty to a discretionary power' (see *R v East Sussex County Court ex parte Tandy* [1998] AC 714). In addition, in *R v Gloucestershire County Council ex parte Mahfood* [1995] 8 Admin LR 180, it was emphasised that a decision of a local authority that arrangements in accordance with its statutory duty were necessary but would not be implemented because of a lack of funds, was illegal. It was emphasised in that case that it is right for a local authority to consider resources when assessing needs, but where a decision has been made that there is a need to be met, it is no answer to refuse to meet that need by reason of a lack of resources. In looking at provisions under the CA 1989, however, the issue of funding may be more relevant to determining the priorities as between different groups of children in need and their families rather than those who might try to assert a 'right' to resources and thus it is unlikely that there could be much scope for an application for judicial review in these sorts of situations.

Irrationality or unreasonableness

11.83 Lord Diplock in *Council of Civil Service Unions v Minister for the Civil Service* (see para **11.69**) identified this ground simply as irrationality but administrative lawyers tend to refer to it also as 'unreasonableness'. Thus, in the same case, Lord Roskill described the second ground for judicial review as being 'where a body exercises a power in so unreasonable a manner that the exercise becomes open to review on what are called in lawyer's shorthand the *Wednesbury* principles' (see *Associated Provincial Picture Houses Ltd v Wednesbury Corporation* [1948] 1 KB 223). As to precisely what the *Wednesbury* principles involve, Lord Green, another of the judges in *Council of Civil Service Unions*, stated (at p 685C) that:

'the court is entitled to investigate the action of the local authority with a view to seeing whether it has taken into account matters which it ought not to take into account, or conversely, has refused to take into account or neglected to take into account matters which it ought to take into account. Once that question is answered in favour of the local authority, it may still be possible to say that the local authority, nevertheless, has come to a conclusion so unreasonable, that no local authority could ever have come to it. In such a case, again, I think the court can interfere.'

11.84 For an example of the local authority making a decision without taking into account matters which it ought to have taken into account, reference should be made to the case of *R v Devon County Council ex parte O* [1997] 2 FLR 388. In this case the child, who was the subject of a care order, was placed with the applicants as approved prospective adopters. Some 2 years later the placement was assessed by the local authority and a strategy meeting was held following concerns about the child's welfare. The decision was made to remove the child from the applicants and place him with foster parents who had previously cared for the child some 2 years earlier in 1994. The approved prospective adopters, who had not been present at the strategy meeting, sought judicial review of the decision on the following grounds:

(1) the failure by the local authority to consult the prospective adoptive applicants;
(2) the failure to take account of relevant matters and taking into account irrelevant ones;
(3) the decision was *Wednesbury* unreasonable;
(4) the refusal of the local authority to review the decision.

11.85 Scott Baker J allowed the application for judicial review, quashed the decision to remove the child from the prospective adoptive applicants and ordered that the child should stay with the applicants whilst the authority reconsidered its decision. He found as a matter of course that the applicants should have been consulted when the possibility of the child's removal arose even though in this particular case the requirements of the Adoption Act 1976, s 30 did not in fact apply. He found that in the light of the considerable period that the child had lived with the applicants, and where there was no urgent need for the child's removal, the applicants should have been given an opportunity to meet the local authority's concerns at the strategy meeting. A careful evaluation of the advantages and disadvantages of a move away from the applicants was vital. The child's wishes and feelings had not been ascertained when they should have been, in the light of evidence available at the strategy meeting that the child wanted to be adopted by the prospective adoptive applicants. The right of the local authority to remove the child from the placement was not an unfettered one. He found that the failure by the local authority to engage in full consultation not only with the applicants but also with the child, and the authority's failure to take account of relevant matters and taking into account irrelevant ones, meant that its decision was flawed and thus that the decision to remove the child from the applicants should be quashed.

11.86 As regards the unreasonableness of a local authority's decision, judicial review was granted and the local authority's decision deemed *Wednesbury* unreasonable in the case of *R v Cornwall County Council ex parte G* [1992] 1 FLR 270. In this case the local guardians ad litem in Cornwall made complaints about the Director of Social Services' decision to put limits on the number of hours which they could spend on any one case, alleging that his decision was *Wednesbury* unreasonable. The court upheld this approach.

11.87 In the case of *Re T (Accommodation by Local Authority)* [1995] 1 FLR 159, a 17-year-old girl used judicial review to oppose the decision of the Director of Social Services that she should not be provided with accommodation under the provisions of the CA 1989, s 20(3). In this case, the girl had taken her complaint that she was not to be provided with ongoing support in her placement with foster carers to the local authority complaints review panel which had upheld her complaint. The Director of Social Services in this case nevertheless concluded that the girl's welfare was not likely to be seriously prejudiced if the authority did not provide her with accommodation and the application was for judicial review of his decision. It was found in this case that the Director of Social Services had not acted reasonably in considering the obligations arising under s 17 of the CA 1989. He had erred when he decided that the past provision of support under s 17 made it unlikely that the girl's welfare would be seriously prejudiced if she were not provided with accommodation.

11.88 By contrast, in *R v London Borough of Brent ex parte S* [1994] 1 FLR 203, the Court of Appeal found that the provision of accommodation for a child with autism and limited means of communication who was hyperactive and had to be constantly supervised to protect himself was adequate. The housing accommodation provided to the child's grandparents who were looking after him met all the requirements with regard to those needs, with the possible exception of the accommodation not offering sufficient space for the child. Under the provisions of the CA 1989, s 23(8) the council owed a duty to provide accommodation, as far as was reasonably practicable, to secure that the accommodation was not *unsuitable to the child's particular needs*. In the circumstances the Court of Appeal found that the accommodation was not unsuitable to the child's particular needs, although it was not perhaps as suitable as it might have been. Accordingly, the court refused to issue any of the orders with regard to judicial review and held that the claim failed. As Peter Gibson LJ put it (at p 215):

'the wording of the duty in s 23(8) of the CA 1989 seems to me designed to avoid placing an unrealistically heavy burden on local authorities. The accommodation to be secured is not required to be suitable to the particular needs of the child, but only to be not unsuitable, and the duty to secure even that is qualified by what is reasonably practicable. Accordingly, it may not be reasonably practicable to secure accommodation which is not unsuitable, but so long as the council is doing the best it can, within the bounds of what is reasonably practicable, to secure not unsuitable accommodation, I do not think it is in breach of its statutory duty.'

11.89 Peter Gibson LJ went on to emphasise that the accommodation offered certainly failed to meet all of the special requirements of the child but that he had no reason to doubt that it was the best available that the council could offer from its housing stock. He therefore concluded that it had not been shown to his satisfaction that it was irrational of the council to seek to meet its duty to rehouse the child without recourse to the private sector.

Judicial review of decisions to disclose made by various agencies involved in child protection

11.90 Within this area of the unreasonableness of local authority decision-making or the decision-making of others involved in child protection processes, it is now necessary to look at the cases involving judicial review of decisions to make disclosures of information usually gained either in child protection conferences or in the processes leading up to those conferences. There is a very considerable body of case-law stretching back to the late 1980s which provides guidance not only to social services but also to health and education services and the police with regard to the steps which should be taken in reaching a decision to disclose information to other bodies or even individuals on a 'need to know' basis.

11.91 It should be recognised that judicial review of the decisions made by a variety of agencies to disclose information with regard to persons who may constitute a risk to children are not always based on the grounds of unreasonableness; therefore, whilst such decisions are being considered under this heading, they may also be brought based on an allegation that the authority has proceeded illegally or on the basis of procedural impropriety and thus challenges may be brought against such decisions on any one or more of the grounds for judicial review.

11.92 The leading case in this area of disclosures as acknowledged by the courts in subsequent decisions is that of *R v Chief Constable of North Wales Police ex parte Thorpe* [1998] 2 FLR 571. In this case, the complainants making the application for judicial review had served a sentence of 11 years' imprisonment for rape, indecent assault and gross indecency. On their release and following the usual strategic discussions between probation, police and social services, a flat had been made available for them but they had had to leave that accommodation because of fear of reprisals from the local community in which the flat was situated. After a number of moves they purchased a caravan and moved to a site. Shortly before the release of the applicants from prison, the local police force in the area of the caravan site had received a copy of a report prepared by another police force, indicating that the applicants posed a considerable risk to children and vulnerable adults in any community where they settled. It had, however, been agreed at a meeting between the police, social services and the probation service that it was preferable for all agencies to know where the applicants were living and to monitor their activity. It was agreed that the owner of the caravan site should be made aware of the applicants' background but that before this happened the applicants should be informed and allowed a period of time to find alternative accommodation. The applicants were then visited by a police officer and they told him that they wanted to avoid their identities being disclosed and that they would move from the site to prevent this happening. The applicants, however, remained at the caravan site and the police officer visited the site owner and showed him the material which had appeared in the press. This resulted in the applicants being told that they had to move on, which they duly did.

11.93 Applications for judicial review of the decision of the police to reveal the applicants' identity were made on the basis that disclosure should only have been made by the police where there was a pressing need for it, that the decision of the police to disclose was unreasonable, and that the policy of the police and their actions in relation to disclosure of such information was not lawful. All of these applications for judicial review were dismissed but because of the importance of the issues at stake the applicants were given leave to appeal from the Divisional Court (this was before the institution of the Administrative Court). Since the first hearing there were two new factors before the court, namely: (a) the applicants had gone to ground and their whereabouts were not known to the authorities; they were not co-operating with the authorities as they had in the past and they had not received treatment that a forensic psychologist might have been able to provide; it was the applicants' case that they refuted the critical comments contained in the police report; and (b) the policy which was the subject of the applicants' application had been overtaken by publication of a new policy issued by the Home Office.

11.94 The Court of Appeal dismissed the applicants' appeal. In doing so, the Court of Appeal held the following:

(1)   Disclosure should only be made where there was a pressing need for it. The subject of the possible disclosure would often be in the best position to provide information which would be valuable when assessing the risk. Consideration should have been given as to whether the report from the police should have been disclosed to the applicants. However, the probation officers were aware of the inaccuracies in the information which had been provided by the police report but were still of the opinion that the applicants created a high degree of risk, and therefore any information which the applicants could have given would not have altered the outcome.

(2)   The fact that the convictions of the applicants had been in the public domain did not mean that the police or a public authority were free to

publish information about their previous offending in the absence of any public interest that this be done. This was not a situation where the disclosure could amount to an infringement of any right of the applicants in private law. Nonetheless the Court of Appeal stressed that the information, having come into the possession of the police to enable them to perform their function as a public body, only entitled them to use that information when this was reasonably required to enable them properly to carry out their functions. In this case, the Court of Appeal determined that the use of the information which the police had obtained was indeed reasonably required to enable them to carry out their functions properly. The Court of Appeal went on to stress, however, that it was as impossible as it was undesirable to lay down anything like a lexicon of the circumstances that would amount to reasonable use. Where the use in question was decided upon as a result of the exercise of an honest judgment by professional police officers, that would of itself go a long way to establishing its reasonableness.

(3)   The policy of the police in determining that they should share the information in the circumstances of this case was not unlawful nor was the action of the police in giving effect to that policy. The Court of Appeal noted, however (see Lord Woolf at p 582), that the authority should have made the policy which it was applying available to the public, as to do so would provide a safeguard against arbitrary action.

11.95 The Court of Appeal in this case also went on to endorse the approach taken by the judge in the court below as well as taking into account the demands of Article 8 of the ECHR. The Court of Appeal noted (at p 582) that both under the ECHR and as a matter of English administrative law, the police are entitled to use information when they reasonably conclude this is what is required (after taking into account the interests of the applicants) in order to protect the public and in particular children.

11.96 On the specific issue of whether the actions of the police could be held to be unreasonable in any way, the comments of the Court of Appeal in relation to the exercise of an honest judgment by professional police officers going a long way to establish its reasonableness has already been noted, but the Court of Appeal also dealt with the allegation that the decision to disclose was irrational on the basis that it might result in an offender 'going underground'. Lord Woolf stressed that the actions of the North Wales police were supported by other agencies and that it was quite impossible to categorise the action of the police as irrational. There was no doubt in the court's mind that the police officer who had approached the caravan site owner was seeking to do the best he could in a very difficult situation. The court held that the actions of the North Wales police gave effect to Home Office policy. By the time of the hearing in the Court of Appeal more recent policy guidelines had been issued which meant that agencies should always try to obtain the offender's version of events where this is practical. The guidance had also highlighted the significance of trying to find appropriate accommodation for offenders when they are released from prison. The Court of Appeal, however, noted that:

> 'determining what is the right action to take to protect children from risk will still remain an immensely difficult problem, but if previous sexual offenders know that help with safe accommodation will be available, they are less likely to go to ground' (at p 583).

11.97 Finally, the Court of Appeal commented that:

> 'the advantage which has flowed from the unfortunate occurrences which have from time to time occurred is that it is now recognised that what is required above all is a proactive rather than a reactive policy for dealing with offenders who have committed offences against children in the past.'

11.98 In the next case to come before the courts, Dyson J in *R v Local Authority and Police Authority in the Midlands ex parte LM* [2000] 1 FLR 612 carefully applied the principles in *R v Chief Constable of North Wales Police ex parte Thorpe* (above). This particular case involved the court examining issues with regard to unsubstantiated allegations of child sexual abuse and whether in the circumstances of the applicant's running of his business, it was really necessary to disclose such information as the police had discovered. It must be recognised that this case should be considered with particular regard to the facts of the case. Here LM owned a bus company which had a contract with the local education department to transport school children. After LM had filled in a form entitling the local authority to run a police check, his contract was terminated. He discovered that this was because information disclosed by the police and social services raised concerns with regard to his having contact with children. The information related to a police investigation into indecent assault on his daughter 7 years previously, where there had been insufficient evidence to prosecute, and the fact that 10 years earlier, while employed by the social services, an allegation of abuse had been made against LM, although no action was taken after investigation. As a result of the disclosures made between the various agencies, ie police, social services and education, LM suffered some persecution after the termination of the bus contract, and this was almost certainly due to rumours as to why the termination had occurred. LM's company then entered into a contract with another local authority for the provision of school bus services and LM also wished to take up a voluntary teaching post with the youth service. He requested assurances from the police and social services that when the council checked, the allegations would not again be disclosed. These assurances were refused, and thus LM sought judicial review of those decisions.

11.99 His claim for judicial review was upheld and quashing orders were made. Dyson J reiterated the principles in the *Thorpe* case. Thus in quashing the decision of the authorities to disclose the information between the different agencies, Dyson J confirmed that both the police and the social services have the power to disclose to a third party allegations of sexual abuse of children if they genuinely and reasonably believe that it is desirable to do so to protect children. The judge confirmed that the principles for the exercise of the power to disclose are those set out in *Thorpe*. The judge stressed, however, that the authorities must consider each case on its own facts and that a blanket approach is impermissible. Disclosure, he stressed, should only be made if there is a 'pressing need' and should be the exception rather than the rule. In the exercise of balancing the public interest in the need to protect children against the need to safeguard the right of the individual to a private life (see Article 8 of the ECHR) factors that will usually have to be considered include the authority's belief as to the truth of the allegations and the interest of the third party in obtaining the information, and here Dyson J emphasised that some assessment should, therefore, be made of the level and quality of access to children that is likely to be available to the person about whom the information is held. The judge noted that para 15 of Home Office Circular 47/93 (*Protection of Children: Disclosure of Criminal Background of those with Access to Children*) provides valuable guidance as to the factors which should be taken into account in deciding whether to seek or undertake a police check. He stated that these are:

– Does the position involve one to one contact?
– Is the position unsupervised?
– Is the situation an isolated one?
– Is there regular contact?
– Are the children particularly vulnerable?

The final factor which has to be considered by any agency determining issues relating to disclosure was said by the judge to be 'the degree of risk posed by the person if disclosure is not made'.

11.100 In this case, Dyson J went on to hold that although both authorities had already made the decision that they would disclose the allegation to the council with whom LM's company was seeking a school bus contract and to the youth service with whom he was intending to seek employment in a voluntary teaching post, the authorities had not adopted the correct approach in doing so. Dyson J held that the police had not applied the pressing need test nor had they considered the particular facts of the case, but had applied a blanket approach. In addition, the social services department had also not applied the pressing need test. The judge, however, also went on to hold that even if the correct tests had been applied, the decisions by the different authorities to disclose would have been unlawful. He held that disclosures of allegations of child sex abuse can have grave consequences and so there must be real and cogent evidence of a pressing need for disclosure and there was no such evidence here and therefore to have disclosed the allegations to the other council would have been irrational and unreasonable.

11.101 It is quite clear, therefore, from both the *Thorpe* and *LM* cases that the authorities must make a decision on the particular facts of each case, that a decision to disclose must be made on the clear basis that there is a risk to children or other vulnerable individuals if such disclosures are not made, and thus there is a pressing need to make such disclosures.

11.102 This approach received considerable support in the following year in the case of *R v Hertfordshire County Council ex parte A* [2001] ELR 239 (referred to by Scott Baker J in *Re S* [2001] 2 FLR 776, at p 787), where at first instance Kay J heard arguments that disclosure of information from one agency to another should be bound by the same principles at work in a criminal trial and thus if someone had been acquitted in the course of a criminal trial of the allegations which formed the basis of suspicion that the individual constituted a danger to children, then such allegations could not be passed on to the other agencies because of the acquittal in the criminal trial. Kay J rejected these suggestions and pointed out that different considerations apply and that a local authority is not constrained by the rules of evidence which obtain at a criminal trial. In the case with which he was concerned, R was a headteacher of a secondary school for boys excluded from mainstream education because of emotional and behavioural problems. The local authority became concerned about the circumstances in which he took boys from the school on his barge. He was prosecuted for indecent assault, but acquitted. A multi-disciplinary strategy meeting, however, concluded that he still posed a risk to children. R applied for judicial review of the recommendations of the disciplinary panel of the school governors recommending his dismissal and also the strategy meeting's decision that he posed a risk of significant harm to children in his care.

11.103 Kay J dismissed his claims for judicial review except for one issue on which leave to appeal to the Court of Appeal was given, namely whether there was power to communicate to others that he posed a risk. R's counsel argued before the Court of Appeal that an authority making enquiries in performance of its duties under the CA 1989, s 47(1) was not entitled to form a view that a particular individual poses a risk to children in its area. Keene LJ, with whom other members of the court agreed, said that the point was entirely without merit but said about s 47 (at para 16) that:

'it is implicit in s 47 that the local authority must seek to form a view as a result of its enquiries as to whether a child or group of children in its area is suffering or is likely to suffer significant harm. That is a necessary part of the process of deciding whether to seek one of the statutory orders, such as a care order, or to take any other action. Frequently, the conclusion reached on that matter will embrace the view that the harm is coming or is likely to come from a particular individual. In many situations, that individual may be the partner of the child's mother or it may be the child's step-father. The courts are familiar with such situations. There is nothing unlawful or ultra vires about the local authority reaching, as a result of its s 47 enquiries, such a view about the risk to certain children that that individual poses. It may be a necessary step in their process of making decisions about what action to take and may indeed be a particularly important step if there are other children potentially at risk from that individual, beyond the child whose welfare gave rise to the enquiries in the first place. I conclude that a local authority has a power by necessary implication to form such a view.'

11.104   It is thus open to a local authority having made such enquiries to pass on the relevant information to another agency where the 'pressing need' test is satisfied and it is clear that children are at risk. The local authority in *R v Hertfordshire County Council* were clearly of that view.

11.105   In the case of *R v Chief Constables of C and D ex parte A*, Turner J in the Administrative Court had to consider a further case concerning disclosure of information from one police authority to another and then onwards to an education authority. This case was heard by Turner J in September and October 2000. The case concerned an applicant who applied for a job with D county education authority for the headship of an infant school, and who was interviewed and offered the post. The application form gave permission for a police check to be made for the existence and content of any criminal record of convictions or cautions. The form included a request to the relevant police authority, stating that the applicant would have substantial access to young persons under the provisions of Joint Circular 9/93. That Joint Circular provided guidance about criminal background checks on persons appointed to work with children and allowed for the provision of information about decisions not to prosecute where the circumstances of the case gave cause for continuing concern. The enquiries made by D constabulary revealed that an investigation had been carried out by C constabulary following allegations of inappropriate behaviour with children at a school where the applicant was head teacher and a second and independent investigation by B police into similar allegations while he had been employed at a different school. There had been no charges because the CPS had been of the opinion that there was insufficient evidence. C constabulary, however, had disclosed the information to D constabulary who then conveyed it on to the education authority. The applicant was then informed that the offer of employment was withdrawn due to an incorrect date on his application form. He was also advised that the authority had received a negative police check and he suspected that it was the police check rather than the inaccurate information that had led to the withdrawal of the offer. The applicant applied for judicial review, arguing in this case that the decision to pass on the information was not in accordance with the principles of procedural fairness; that there had been a failure to comply with the provisions of the Joint Circular which made the decisions unlawful; and that the disclosure contravened provisions of the Data Protection Acts of 1984 and 1998 and the Data Protection (Processing of Sensitive Personal Data) Order 2000.

11.106 Turner J held that the passing of information between one police force and another did not amount to a decision which attracts an obligation which was to be judged according to the principles of procedural fairness. He stated that a police force was merely a local division of an agency with national responsibilities and therefore the transfer of sensitive personal information, namely non-conviction material, as the result of a child access vetting enquiry from one police force to another had no immediate or even indirect consequence for the individual concerned. Moreover, no procedural impropriety would arise where a police force communicated that information to a local education authority since that authority would have a lawful interest and a pressing need to receive it.

11.107 Turner J went on to hold that the purpose behind Joint Circular 9/93 issued by the Home Office, the DOH and the Welsh Office was to ensure that confidential information about an individual would be kept out of the public domain and would only be made available to those working in a limited range of positions in a public body *who had a real need to receive it*. Similarly, Turner J held that those who were required to obtain such information in order to pass it on to an appropriate authority, were required to give consideration to the need to pass it on. He stated that the legal significance of the Circular was limited – it set out a code prescribing a means of limiting the opportunity for sensitive personal data to reach the public domain. He emphasised that that was a matter of administrative best practice and thus did not impose fetters on the obligations of police authorities to pass information between each other.

11.108 In addition, Turner J held that disclosure of non-conviction material between police forces or by a police force to an education authority did not contravene the Data Protection Act 1984 because the Act did not apply to information which was manually processed, as was the present case. Further, he held that the disclosure was not contrary to the Data Protection Act 1998 as the information fell within the category of 'sensitive personal data' which was exempt by virtue of the first 'data protection principle', namely that data was being processed for the prevention and detection of crime. He also stressed that disclosure of non-conviction material between police forces or by a police force to an education authority did not fall foul of the provision of the Data Protection (Processing of Sensitive Personal Data) Order 2000 since that Order exempted data where the processing was necessary for the exercise of any functions conferred on a constable by any rule of law.

11.109 In the course of giving judgment Turner J again extensively relied on the case of *Thorpe* and also on the case of *LM* (see above) and it is clear that the principles of these cases were influential in enabling Turner J to reach the decision which he did.

11.110 A recent decision in this area, heard before Scott Baker J on 4 May 2001 is that of *Re S (Sexual Abuse Allegation: Local Authority Response)* [2001] 2 FLR 776. This case relied heavily on the cases already discussed and raised similar issues to those discussed in relation to the actions of child protection conferences (para **11.70**). In this case, the claimant, a consultant gynaecologist, whose second marriage had ended in 1994, formed a relationship with the mother of a 12-year-old girl. A couple of years later in January 1999, he was arrested and charged with having indecently assaulted the girl over the previous 18 months. He was tried and acquitted of four charges and formally found not guilty of three more charges when the jury was unable to reach agreement. In the meantime, the claimant had moved on to form a relationship with a former patient who had daughters aged 11 and 7, and the couple wished to set up house together with their respective children. This was hindered by the need to await the outcome of the deliberations of the first defendant local authority and the second defendant authority, into whose area the claimant and his new partner and children intended to move, in relation to their statutory duties under the CA 1989, s 47. The first defendant's decision letter of 26 April 2000 asserted that the girl's allegations had been highly credible and that there was a need to deal with the prospect of the claimant interfering with other children, with steps only being taken if really necessary. The second defendant's decision letter of 5 May 2000 concerning the new partner's children, concluded that on the balance of probability the girl's allegations of abuse had been true and that the claimant was likely to present a medium to high risk of sexual abuse to children unrelated to him and who lived in the same house. The new partner's former husband was to be informed of the risk analysis and he was already seeking a residence order to prevent contact. The claimant sought judicial review of the respective decisions of the first and second defendants on the basis that they had not applied their statutory duties correctly.

11.111 Scott Baker J, in dismissing the claim for judicial review, determined that each of the defendants had acted lawfully in the assessment of risk. He held that they were not required to make a finding on the balance of probabilities as to past conduct before assessing risk and taking any necessary protective steps. The risk conclusion set out in the respective decision letters were not perverse and all the defendants' actions fell within a range of responses open to a reasonable decision-maker. The judge therefore held that these actions were reasonable in all the circumstances of the case. The judge also held that the ECHR added nothing to the balancing exercise that had previously been carried out in domestic law. He stressed that the defendants had not exceeded the discretion that had been given to them and there was no material difference in exercising that discretion between, on the one hand, complying with the provisions of the CA 1989 and, on the other, balancing the competing obligations under the ECHR. The judge also held that given that the decision on risk would be justified, he found that there was a need to make disclosure by the various local authorities and that they should enter into discussions with those responsible for children who could potentially come under the claimant's control. In reaching his decision, Scott Baker J drew attention to the government guidance issued in *Working Together to Safeguard Children* (1999) which refers at para 7.27 and in paragraphs following to the importance of sharing information between professionals and others where it will help to protect children. In addition, in looking at the demands of the ECHR and in conducting the balancing exercise between intervening too much and too little in child protection matters, the courts have repeatedly recognised that the interest of persons in a similar position to the claimant in this case may have to come second to the interests of the protection of children.

11.112 Lawyers on behalf of the claimant had in addition sought to place reliance on a Family Court decision in *Re V (Sexual Abuse: Disclosure); Re L (Sexual Abuse: Disclosure)* [1999] 1 FLR 267. The issue in *Re V* and *Re L* had been whether the local authority should be granted leave to disclose to third parties findings of sexual impropriety made in family proceedings. Although in the case of *Re V* and *Re L* a decision was made that there should be non-disclosure since the interests of specific children were not at stake, Butler-Sloss LJ, having referred to the CA 1989, s 47 said:

> 'There will be occasions when one local authority will have the duty to pass on information about abuse and abusers to other local authorities. An example would be when children from one area who are at risk move to another local authority area. The local authority may also need to respond to enquiries from another authority who are conducting enquiries about a possible abuser. Nothing in this judgment is intended to inhibit the necessary exchange of relevant information between agencies.'

11.113 Again, Scott Baker J was able to distinguish the case before him from that set out in *Re V* and *Re L*. In *Re V* and *Re L* Butler-Sloss LJ had emphasised that disclosure of information must, in accordance with the principles of the *Thorpe* case (above), be regarded as exceptional and only occur where there is a pressing need for that disclosure. In the case of *Re S*, Scott Baker J found that there was indeed a pressing need for disclosure in a situation where the claimant had been assessed as posing a medium to high risk of sexual abuse to any children unrelated to him who might live in the same house. The authorities had before them sufficient information to suggest that they could have reasonable cause to suspect (as set out in CA 1989, s 47) that children might be likely to suffer significant harm if living in the same household as the complainant. As the judge put it, 'Were the defendants justified in concluding that they had reasonable cause to suspect a child in their area was likely to suffer significant harm? Were the decisions unreasonable in the *Wednesbury* sense?' (at p 789). Scott Baker J stressed that 'in my judgment there was little if any room for either defendants concluding other than that there was reasonable cause to suspect the likelihood of harm' (at p 789). The judge went on to state that:

> 'given my conclusion that the decision on risk was justified and bearing in mind the obligations both in domestic law and under the European Convention, there was in my judgment a need to make disclosure and to enter into discussions with those responsible for children who could potentially come under the claimant's control and I accept the defendants' submission that they were scrupulous in their approach to the issues and to the decisions that had to be taken.'

11.114 Finally, it should be noted in this case that applications were made at the time of the hearing for permission to appeal to the Court of Appeal, which Scott Baker J refused. He determined that if there was to be an appeal in the case it should be one authorised by the Court of Appeal, rather than by the trial judge (at p 798). At the time of writing, it is not known whether the Court of Appeal has given leave to appeal against Scott Baker J's decision. Given that his decision is entirely within the principles set out by the Court of Appeal in the *Thorpe* case, it is unlikely that such permission to appeal will be given.

Procedural impropriety

11.115 This ground was referred to by Lord Diplock in *Council of Civil Service Unions v Minister for the Civil Service* (see para **11.69**) as being that of 'procedural impropriety', but Lord Roskill in the same case put it in a more comprehensible fashion. Thus he stated that the third ground for judicial review is where the body or in some cases the court has acted:

> 'contrary to what are often called principles of natural justice ... better replaced by speaking of a duty to act fairly. But that latter phrase must not in its turn be misunderstood or misused. It is not for the courts to determine whether a particular policy or particular decisions taken in fulfilment of that policy are fair. They are only concerned with the manner in which those decisions have been taken and the extent of that duty to act fairly will vary greatly from case to case' (see [1984] All ER 935, at p 953J).

11.116 The rules of natural justice embody a duty to act fairly and impartially. This notion receives further reinforcement from Article 6 of the ECHR. In *O'Reilly and Others v Mackman and Others* [1983] 2 AC 237, Lord Diplock stated that:

'Wherever any person or body of persons has authority conferred by legislation to make decisions of a kind I have described, it is amenable to the remedy of an order to quash its decision, either for error of law in reaching it or for failure to act fairly towards the person who will be adversely affected by the decision by failure to observe either one or other of the two fundamental rights afforded to him, the rules of natural justice or fairness, viz to have afforded to him a reasonable opportunity of learning what is alleged against him and of putting forward his own case to answer it, and to the absence of personal bias against him on the part of the person by whom the decision falls to be made' (at p 279F).

11.117   In the pre-CA 1989 case of *R v Norfolk County Council ex parte X* [1989] 2 FLR 120, a 13-year-old girl alleged that the applicant, a plumber working in her parents' house, had indecently assaulted her. The local authority social services department convened two case conferences which heard that the girl had previously been registered twice as an abused child (involving other men), that after the child's allegation against the plumber she had made a complaint against a van driver, that she went to school dressed in tight jeans and high heels and that she was living an unsettled home life between the mother and other relatives and friends. Without reference to the plumber and without giving him any opportunity to hear about the allegations, the case conference decided that it was persuaded that the applicant had committed sexual abuse of the child and that both the mother's name and his should be entered on the child protection register. The applicant was sent a letter informing him of this decision and his solicitor wrote complaining about the registration and the conduct of the case conference. The applicant applied for judicial review and was then offered the opportunity to attend a reconvened case conference at which he would be allowed to make representations in person or through his solicitor.

11.118   Waite J held that the applicant had every reason for refusing to attend the reconvened case conference. Waite J found that that was an offer from a body which had already condemned him in his absence and he described the consequences of registration as having been sufficiently serious to impose on the local authority a legal duty to act fairly. He gave his view that:

'It is a particularly troubling feature of the present case that the possibility does not appear even to have occurred to either case conference – or for that matter to any level of the county council's social services – that [the girl's] accusations might be a fantasy or fabrication proceeding directly from her own very evident emotional problems; and that if there was the slightest possibility that such might be the case, they were at risk of stigmatising an innocent man as an abuser. That is a risk to which their minds could, of course, have been immediately opened if [the plumber] and his professional advisers had been allowed, before the registration was effected, an opportunity of informed comment on the material considered by the two case conferences.'

11.119   Although he acknowledged that registration of suspected abusers was useful, he stated that 'a child abuse register, nevertheless, remains (at all events as regards the abuser's named on it) in essence a black list, and as such it also has dangerous potential as an instrument of injustice and oppression'. Since the local authority had, without warning, applied a procedure which had denied the applicant the opportunity of prior consultation or objection to its decision to place him on the register, the local authority's conduct was unfair and so unreasonable as to come within the *Wednesbury* unreasonableness definition and its decision was, accordingly, quashed.

11.120   Waite J did, however, stress that judicial review would not be granted if the particular procedure followed by a local authority represented a genuine attempt to reconcile the duty of child protection on the one hand and the duty of fairness to the alleged abuser on the other.

11.121   Similarly, when purporting to engage in procedures laid down in government guidance such as that contained in *Working Together to Safeguard Children* (1999), the local authority must ensure that it follows guidance which is issued specifically to ensure that parties before the case conference receive a fair hearing (see *R v Cornwall County Council ex parte LH* [2000] 1 FLR 236 discussed in detail at para **11.70**).

11.122   Another example of an allegation of unfairness but where on this occasion the court found that there was no unfairness, is the case of *R v Secretary of State for Health ex parte C* [1999] 1 FLR 1071. In this case, the applicant worked for the social services department of a county council as a childcare worker from 1981 but was dismissed in 1985 after allegations that he had sexually assaulted a foster child in his care. It was also alleged that he had abused his own and his partner's children. His claim for unfair dismissal had been rejected by the Employment Appeal Tribunal, confirming a decision of the Industrial Tribunal. In February 1997 the DOH wrote to inform the applicant that his name had been placed on the Consultancy Service Index, a document designed to assist prospective employers in childcare to decide on a person's suitability to work with children. After making representations to the DOH which were not successful, the applicant applied for judicial review of the DOH's decision, questioning:

(1)   whether the operation of the Index was ultra vires;

(2)   whether the inclusion of the applicant on the Index was in breach of the ECHR; and

(3)   whether it was unfair to include the applicant's name on it having regard to the standard of proof and the procedure adopted.

11.123   In this case, Richards J held that the DOH had not acted unfairly in adding the name of the person to the Consultancy Service Index. The applicant had submitted that the DOH had not acted on sufficient information, ie a conviction or a finding to an equivalent standard of proof, and had failed to constitute itself as a tribunal of fact before deciding whether the applicant should be included on the Index. The court concluded, however, that the lawful operation of the Index could not be dependent on the adoption of that approach. Richards J confirmed that when acting to protect the welfare of children the Secretary of State had to strike a balance between the interests of the individual concerned and the interests of the children whom the Index was designed to protect. The precise approach to be adopted was a matter for him provided he acted within the limits of rationality. The court confirmed that in this case the DOH had acted fairly and that the matter had been approached lawfully and that the Minister had reached a conclusion reasonably open to him. The other grounds for the applicant's claim for judicial review were also dismissed with the court finding that the operation of the Consultancy Service Index was entirely lawful; and with regard to the ECHR point, the court held that a decision to include the applicant on the Index could not be said to be directly decisive of his right to work in his chosen profession, given that the Index was simply to enable a prospective employer to be put in touch with a previous employer for the purpose of obtaining a reference. The court therefore confirmed that this was not a determination of the applicant's civil rights and obligations within Article 6(1).

11.124 Again, in the case of *R v Wokingham District Council ex parte J* [1999] 2 FLR 1136, an adoption panel had refused the natural mother the opportunity to appear before it or to make written representations. After considering the information before it the panel recommended that the agency applied for dispensing with the mother's agreement to an application for freeing for adoption on the ground that she was withholding her agreement unreasonably. The mother sought judicial review of the panel's decision to make the recommendation arguing that the rules of natural justice and fairness required that natural parents be allowed to make written representations in such cases. Collins J, however, dismissing the application held that whilst it might be desirable that an adoption panel should allow short written representations from parents, such an approach was not essential to the fairness of the entire adoption procedure. He determined that the panel was not deciding final questions affecting the natural mother's rights but merely taking a decision as one step in a sequence of measures and thus there was no obligation to hear representations. He stated that fairness required that the mother should have the opportunity to present her case before a final decision was made, but that that would happen in the course of the adoption proceedings which had yet to follow.

11.125 Many of the cases alleging unfairness tend to date back to the late 1980s and early 1990s and thus it would appear that since the implementation of the CA 1989 and, in particular, the issuing of detailed guidance to local authorities by the DOH examples of such procedural unfairness in the operation of local authority processes are comparatively rare. (See further, *R v London Borough of Wandsworth ex parte P* [1989] 1 FLR 387, where unfairness was found in the circumstances of a local authority removing a person's name from the list of approved foster parents without giving that person an opportunity to answer the allegations made against him; *R v Hampshire County Council ex parte K and Another* [1990] 2 ELR 129, where judicial review on the grounds of unfairness was again successful in circumstances where a local authority failed to disclose details of medical examinations carried out on a child before the commencement of care proceedings, and then refused to consent to examination of that child by a doctor instructed by the child's parents.)

11.126 The court also seems to have improved practices in terms of giving reasons for refusing to discharge a care order; see *R v Worcester City Juvenile Court ex parte F* [1989] 1 FLR 230 and *R v Pontlottyn Juvenile Court ex parte R* [1991] 2 FLR 86, where the court clerk told the natural mother that her attendance at access proceedings was unnecessary and where he further failed, when the application was opposed at the directions hearing, to raise the question of the absence of the mother and the reason for her absence. In this case the High Court held that there was both a denial of natural justice and also evidence of unreasonableness in the local authority's opposition to the appointment of a guardian ad litem in contact proceedings. It should be noted that in care proceedings, where substantial evidence is adduced before juvenile justices who, nevertheless, refuse to state their reasons for dismissing an application to discharge a care order, and there is conflict between the parties, then judicial review may be granted in the form of a mandatory order (see para **11.148**) requiring justices to state a case, ie give reasons for the consideration of the High Court (see Chapter **8**).

Judicial review in cases involving registration on Child Protection Registers and procedures followed in child protection conferences

11.127 There have now been several cases in this area, a number of which have already been examined. However, some of the leading cases again date back to the period immediately preceding the implementation of the CA 1989 and the early days of implementation. It is proposed to highlight here some of the issues raised in those early cases which are still relevant today, but also to consider some more recent cases involving decisions about registration, and procedures at child protection conferences which have not so far been discussed. Two of the critically influential cases in this area are those of *R v Harrow London Borough ex parte D* [1989] 2 FLR 51, and *R v Norfolk County Council ex parte X* (sometimes referred to as *ex parte M*) [1989] 2 FLR 120. Both of these cases are pre-CA 1989 cases, but they still remain important as they have been cited in more recent cases concerning the conduct of child protection conferences and consequent steps such as the placing of an adult's name on the Child Protection Register. These two cases highlighted the issue of the reasonableness of the actions of a child protection conference in placing an adult suspect's name on a Child Protection Register as well as a child's. Both cases were referred to in the 1991 version of *Working Together*; significantly there is no reference to any decided case-law in the new version *Working Together to Safeguard Children* (1999) (see further the guidance in *Working Together* and at para **11.138**). The pivotal issue in both of these cases was: if a child's name is placed on a Child Protection Register, what are the legal rights of the person suspected of having abused him? Has such a person the right to be treated 'fairly and reasonably'?

11.128   In the *Harrow* case, a mother of three children whose names had been placed on the Child Protection Register, sought judicial review on the grounds that failure to invite her to a case conference concerning the abuse of her children was unfair or unreasonable. She was the alleged abuser of her children, who had suffered bruising. The conference had before it the evidence of two paediatricians who had found physical injuries on all three children and believed them to be non-accidental, and the evidence of the social worker, who claimed to have heard an account from one of the children accusing the mother of causing bodily harm. The children had been removed under a place of safety order (the precursor of the current emergency protection order) obtained by the social worker but were returned to the mother after 24 hours. She had asked, through her solicitor, to attend the case conference (now referred to in *Working Together to Safeguard Children* as the child protection conference), but was informed that she could not, although she was allowed to make written submissions, which she did.

11.129   The mother's appeal failed in both the lower court and the Court of Appeal. Anthony Lincoln J, at first instance, said that he could not accept that the failure to invite the mother to the conference was unfair or unreasonable. Two reasons were given:

(1)   the DOH guidelines in *Working Together* (DOH, 1988, original version) omitted parents from the categories of person to be invited and to make submissions to the conference;
(2)   the facts of the case failed to establish any unfairness as the case conference had the mother's written submissions before it. Furthermore, the children were not, in fact, removed from the mother's care at the conclusion of the conference. The purpose of the conference was not to reach a verdict on the mother's guilt or innocence; it was simply to decide the next step. This step was to place their names on the Child Protection Register. Anthony Lincoln J could not see how the mother's presence and advocacy at the conference could have affected this result.

11.130 In the Court of Appeal, his decision was upheld. *Working Together* (1988) was again considered, the child protection conference and the Register were both confirmed as non-statutory in status, but, nevertheless, were part of good social work practice and necessary for the protection of children. In the course of her judgment, Butler-Sloss LJ made several important observations, pointing out that, 'Although the contents of the register are confidential, a significant number of people inevitably have to be aware of the information contained in it'. She concluded that the 'level of fairness … was amply met by the procedure followed', since the mother had been allowed to make written representations to the case conference although she had been excluded from it and the council's decision to place the children's names on the Register was not unfair, unreasonable nor contrary to natural justice. Butler-Sloss LJ went on to emphasise that 'it would also seem that recourse to judicial review is likely to be, and undoubtedly ought to be, rare. Local authorities have laid on them by Parliament the specific duty of protection of children in their area'.

11.131 She also made a number of other important points.

(1) If the decision to register can be shown to be utterly unreasonable, in principle there is no reason why an application to review the decision cannot lie. In coming to its decision, the local authority is exercising a most important public function which can have serious consequences for the child and the alleged abuser.

(2) The case conference has a duty to make an assessment as to abuse and the abuser if sufficient information is available. Of its nature, the mechanism of the case conference leading to the decision to place names on the Register and the decision-making process, is unstructured and informal. It is accepted that it is not a judicial process. It is part of a protection package for a child believed to have been the victim of abuse.

(3) In this field, there is a third component not present in other judicial review cases (which usually involve only the individual who may have been prejudiced and the organisation that might have been criticised) which is the welfare of the child, who is the purpose of the entry in the Register. In proceedings in which the child is the subject, his or her welfare is paramount. In balancing adequate protection to the child and fairness to the adults, the interests of any adults may have to be placed second to the needs of the child.

11.132 Butler-Sloss LJ went on to emphasise a critically important point. She commented that:

'All concerned in this difficult and delicate area should be allowed to perform their task without looking over their shoulder all the time for the possible intervention of the court. The important power of the court to intervene should be kept very much in reserve, perhaps confined to the exceptional case which involves a point of principle which needs to be resolved, not only for the individual case but in general, so as to establish that registration is not being conducted in an unsatisfactory manner. In the normal case where criticism is being made of some individual aspect of the procedure which does not raise any point of principle, leave should be refused. The decision of Waite J, right though it was in that case, should not be the excuse for over-formalising the procedure which is not intended to be confined within a rigid legal structure. In this area, unbridled resort to judicial review would frustrate the ability of those involved in their efforts to protect the victims of child abuse.'

11.133 In the *Harrow* case, Butler Sloss LJ was giving a clear indication that successful judicial review applications in relation to the procedures adopted at child protection conferences would be rare but was nevertheless emphasising that where points of principle are involved judicial review may well be granted. The case of *R v Norfolk County Council ex parte X* [1989] 2 FLR 120, was decided only a little while later. It too is frequently cited in much more recent decisions. (See the discussion of this case at para **11.127**.)

11.134 Both the cases of *Harrow* and *R v Norfolk County Council* were extensively relied upon by the Court of Appeal in their judgment in *R v Hampshire County Council ex parte H* [1999] 2 FLR 359. In this case a child had complained at school that his step-father, a senior education welfare officer with the council, had physically abused him causing facial bruising. The step-father offered to leave the family home, but because the pregnant mother clearly needed his support in the home, it was considered more appropriate to place the three step-children outside the home; P and S with foster parents and R with grandparents. At the case conference all three children were placed on the Child Protection Register, P in the category of physical and emotional abuse and the other two in the category of emotional abuse. The step-father's job required him to attend child protection conferences and as a result of the registration he was suspended. Both mother and step-father appealed, but before the appeal was heard P and S were removed from the Register, with only R's name remaining on it. The appeal panel made various criticisms of the original conference, in particular of R's placement on the Register in the category of emotional abuse, but made no recommendation, being under the misapprehension that all three children had been de-registered. Shortly afterwards, P retracted the allegation that the step-father had caused the facial bruising and the step-father was reinstated at work. R had already returned home, P returned home some months later but S remained with foster parents. The mother and step-father sought judicial review of the original decision to register R under the heading of emotional abuse, the appeal process, and the decision to continue R's registration.

11.135 The Court of Appeal, which included Lord Wolf, Butler-Sloss and Auld LJJ, granted a declaration in the judicial review proceedings that there was insufficient material to justify the registration of R in the case of emotional abuse and that the decision to continue R's registration was void – unlike P and S, whose relationship with the step-father was clearly unhappy, whatever the truth of the allegations there was no evidence before the original conference that R was subject to emotional abuse. The Court of Appeal found that no medical or psychological evidence had been presented, neither the school nor the GP attended, and no information had been specifically presented about R. Evidence which supported her registration in one category, such as her position as a sibling of a child alleging physical abuse, could not justify registration in another category. The court emphasised that before a child could be registered under any category there had to be evidence of, or a likelihood of, significant harm to the individual child, and to register a child under the category of emotional harm such significant harm had to be in the form of persistent or severe emotional ill-treatment or rejection which was likely to have had a severe adverse effect on her emotional and behavioural development (see *Working Together* (1991)). The court found that there was evidence of stress within the family, but that that could not, on its own, demonstrate significant harm. The court emphasised that a medical or psychological assessment or report was not a prerequisite for placing a child's name on the Register; an assessment of the child by some professional with actual knowledge relating to the child would probably be sufficient, but in this case there was no relevant evidence.

11.136 The court determined that there would be no relief by way of judicial review in relation to the original decision and the appeal process because the appeal procedure, not judicial review, was the appropriate remedy, and the appeal panel had performed its review function effectively, despite the unfortunate misunderstanding about de-registration. The Court of Appeal determined that relief would, however, be granted in relation to the decision by the review case conference to continue R's registration despite the appeal panel's criticism of the original decision. The Court of Appeal further stressed that it was to be hoped that in future, decisions and recommendations of an appeal panel in similar circumstances would be properly respected. In this case the Court of Appeal quoted extensively from both the *Harrow and Norfolk County Council* cases, as both determined important matters of principle.

11.137 Similarly, in R *v Cornwall County Council ex parte LH* [2000] 1 FLR 236 (examined more fully at para **11.70**) the local authority policy of not allowing solicitors to attend child protection case conferences on behalf of parents save to read out a prepared statement, and secondly not giving parents attending such conferences a copy of the conference minutes, were both declared to be unlawful and the claims for judicial review were again successful. This case established an important matter of principle that local authorities must follow the guidance issued by government in relation to the interpretation of their duties in an administrative process such as a child protection conference. The guidance in *Working Together to Safeguard Children* (1999) is not as strong as that which appeared in the 1991 version (see below).

Working Together to Safeguard Children: parental involvement in child protection and review conferences

11.138   The rules of natural justice require both the absence of bias or partiality in the hearing of the case and the opportunity for both sides to present their views. *Working Together to Safeguard Children* (1999) contains advice on the involvement of children, parents and carers and their advocates or representatives in child protection conferences (see paras 5.57 and 5.74 and see Chapters **5** and **6** of this book). It must be said, however, that the guidance issued in 1999 is considerably weaker and less detailed than that which was issued in 1991, particularly with regard to the issue of legal representation.

11.139   As to the presence of parents or involved family members, para 5.57 states that before a conference is held, the purpose of the conference, who will attend and the way in which it will operate should always be explained to a child of sufficient age and understanding, and to the parents and involved family members. The guidance goes on to emphasise that:

> 'the parents should normally be invited to attend the conference and helped fully to participate. Social services should give parents information about local advice and advocacy agencies, and explain that they may bring an advocate, friend or supporter. The child, subject to consideration about age and understanding, should be given the opportunity to attend if he or she wishes, and also to bring an advocate, friend or supporter.'

11.140   As to the fairness of the procedure at the conference, para 5.62 of *Working Together* (1991) emphasises that:

> 'children and family members should be helped in advance to think about what they want to convey to the conference and how best to get their points across on the day. Some may find it helpful to provide their own written report, which they may be assisted to prepare by their adviser/advocate.'

11.141   It is significant that the 1999 version omits any reference at all to the presence of a legal representative, preferring instead at both paras 5.57 and 5.62 the use of the terms 'advocate', 'friend', 'supporter' or 'adviser'.

11.142   Since various of the judicial review cases discussed above have considered the issue of the fairness or otherwise of excluding a parent from a child protection conference, para 5.58 of *Working Together to Safeguard Children* emphasises that 'exceptionally, it may be necessary to exclude one or more family members from a conference, in whole or in part'. The guidance goes on to stress that local ACPC procedures should set out criteria for excluding a parent or carer, including the evidence required. It further states that 'a strong risk of violence or intimidation by a family member at or subsequent to the conference towards a child or anybody else, might be one reason for exclusion'.

11.143 The guidance does, however, state that:

> 'the possibility that a parent or carer may be prosecuted for an offence against a child is not in itself a reason for exclusion although in these circumstances the chair should take advice from the police about any implications arising from an alleged perpetrator's attendance.'

The guidance goes on to suggest that where criminal proceedings have been instigated, the view of the CPS should be taken into account.

11.144 *Working Together to Safeguard Children* also caters for the situation which arose in cases such as the *Harrow* case (see para **11.127**). Paragraph 5.58 further emphasises that if parents are excluded, or are unable or unwilling to attend the child protection conference, they should be enabled to communicate their views to the conference by another means. This might be through a letter or tape-recording. It also allows for the possibility of the social worker and/or another professional agreeing with the parents that they should represent the parents' views and wishes.

11.145 Thus, even the 1999 version of *Working Together* does not say that parents or carers may not be excluded from such conferences, but only suggest that local ACPC procedures should set out criteria for excluding a parent or carer, including the evidence required. This again is in marked contrast to the 1991 version of *Working Together* which suggested that individual ACPCs should 'formally agree the principle of including parents and children in all conferences and that guidance on their inclusion should be contained in the ACPC guidelines and all child protection procedures' (see *Working Together* (1991), at para 6.14).

Information about abusers

11.146 *Working Together to Safeguard Children* does not specifically deal with any aspects of the Child Protection Register being maintained for the purposes of inserting names of adult abusers. Instead, para 6.23 of *Working Together to Safeguard Children* refers to the PCA 1999 which requires childcare organisations to refer to names of individuals considered unsuitable to work with children, on the DOH list (previously referred to as the Consultancy Index) and List 99 maintained by the DfES. The PCA 1999 requires childcare organisations not to offer work to anyone so listed for any post involving regular contact with children in a childcare capacity. (For a more detailed discussion on this Act see Chapter **9**.) The PCA 1999 provides for rights of appeal to an independent tribunal against inclusion on either list. The Care Standards Act 2000 which was passed after the introduction of *Working Together to Safeguard Children* in 1999, came into force on 1 April 2002. It contains further provisions with regard to placing on a register those deemed unsuitable to work with vulnerable adults by reason of past conduct. Neither of these pieces of legislation seem to deal entirely with the issue of the more general registration of adults deemed to be a risk to children as was envisaged in the *Norfolk* case. Instead, as has been seen from the discussion above, greater attention now appears to be focused by local authorities on taking steps to disclose relevant information across agencies on a 'need to know' basis where there is a likelihood that particular individuals might come into contact with children. See, for a particular example of this, the discussion relating to *R v A Local Authority and Police Authority in the Midlands ex parte LM* [2000] 1 FLR 612.

Remedies under judicial review

11.147 When an application for judicial review succeeds, the Administrative Court has the power to make the following orders ((a)–(c) previously known as the prerogative orders since their names came from the prerogative writs used by the common law courts):

(a) a mandatory order (previously referred to as an order of mandamus);
(b) a prohibiting order (previously referred to as an order of prohibition);
(c) a quashing order (previously referred to as an order of certiorari);
(d) a declaration;
(e) an injunction; and
(f) the court can also make an order for damages but only if damages have been sought in conjunction with mandatory, prohibitory or quashing orders.

11.148 A mandatory order is an order requiring the body concerned to perform a specified duty. Thus in *R on the application of S v Hammersmith, Wandsworth and Lambeth Borough Council*, a mandatory order was issued requiring Wandsworth and Lambeth to carry out assessments under the CA 1989, s 17. A prohibiting order prevents the organisation concerned from acting or continuing to act in excess of jurisdiction or contrary to the rules of natural justice. Such an order, for example, was made in the case of *R v Cornwall County Council ex parte LH* [2000] 1 FLR 236, where in addition a declaration was issued. A quashing order quashes a decision made by a local authority, social services committee or sub-committee of social services and such an order may then remit the matter back to the organisation concerned with a direction to reconsider it and arrive at a decision in accordance with the findings made by the court. Such an order was issued in the case of *Re T (Accommodation by a Local Authority)* [1995] 1 FLR 159. A declaration or injunction can also be issued where the court considers it just and convenient to do so and declarations were issued in both *R v Hampshire County Council ex parte H* [1999] 2 FLR 359 and *R v Birmingham City Council ex parte A* [1997] 2 FLR 841. In the *Hampshire* case, the Court of Appeal granted a declaration that there had been insufficient material against a step-father to justify the continuation of one child's registration on the Child Protection Register.

11.149 In all of the proceedings for judicial review and the issuing of the various forms of relief, the Administrative Court is concerned only with the decision-making process and not with the merits of individual decisions. Moreover, it is quite apparent from the case-law that the court can refuse judicial review where:

(1) there was an unreasonable lapse of time between the incident and the application;

(2) even if the local authority had acted correctly, the decision would have been the same;

(3) the procedural irregularity is only a technicality;

(4) the issue is academic because, for example, the decision has already been carried out and the applicant has not suffered any real detriment; or

(5) the paramount welfare of the child overrides all other considerations.

11.150 It is worth bearing in mind that although the High Court can no longer ward a child who is in local authority care because of the CA 1989, s 100(2), the inherent jurisdiction of the High Court, from which wardship may be distinguished, may still be invoked, although it has to be said that it has never been used in the sorts of situations where wardship would previously have been allowed to challenge the actions of local authorities in relation to children (see on this Chapter **8**).

Use of judicial review by a guardian

11.151 The case of *Re C (Adoption: Religious Observance)* [2002] 1 FLR 1119 illustrates a case in which the court viewed the guardian's legal initiative in issuing proceedings for judicial review whilst care proceedings were ongoing, precisely to challenge the actions contained in the care plan, as misguided. In this case the local authority had placed a child with mixed Jewish, Irish Roman Catholic and Turkish-Cypriot Muslim elements with a Jewish couple with a view to adoption. Although the parents had originally objected they were not doing so now, but the guardian issued proceedings for judicial review of the authority's decision to place the child with the Jewish couple arguing that they were unsuitable on the basis that they were too Jewish and would not properly serve the needs of the child with such a complex ethnic and cultural background. The guardian also objected on the ground that the parents' views had not been sufficiently considered. Wilson J dismissed the guardian's application approving the plan and making the care order, holding that where a child's heritage was very mixed, it would rarely be possible for it all to be reflected in the identity of the adoptive home. In addition to describing the guardian's action as misguided, Wilson also observed that the proper forum for a challenge to the care plan was the care proceedings in which the full merits rather than the bare lawfulness of the decision fell for debate. Judicial review had led to the decision in the care proceedings being delayed for over 6 months, and Wilson J stressed that it was to be hoped that no court would again be required to consider so painstakingly the lawfulness of a decision when the real issue was as to whether it best served the child's best interests. He observed that it should only be in the event of a failure by a local authority to amend its proposals for the child so as to accord with the court's determination of the child's best interests that it would be proper for a guardian to consider taking proceedings for judicial review.

Conclusion

11.152 It is obvious that there remains considerable dissatisfaction about the lack of independence with regard to local authority complaints procedures and it remains to be seen what will happen more widely as a result of the *Beeson* case (see para **11.65**). The fact that such procedures are only available to children in local authority placements or in receipt of local authority services again means that we should be very concerned that there is no comparable avenue to make representations for those children and young people in penal establishments, who are without the benefit of most of the support measures provided by Part III of the CA 1989 (see Chapter **4** but see also para **10.64**). Those in local authority secure units benefit from the availability of such procedures as further guaranteed by Standard 16 of the National Minimum Standards, because they are being 'looked after' by a local authority. It is quite apparent from the very considerable number of cases in which judicial review has been used to challenge the decisions of local authorities that Butler-Sloss LJ's warning in the *Harrow* case that local authorities should not be having to look over their shoulders at the courts has not been strictly adhered to. Nevertheless, it is also apparent that the considerable body of case-law which has now developed is a recognition of the importance of having such a process as that of judicial review to call into question the legality and reasonableness of local authority actions and decision-making processes. The upsurge in the use of judicial review in the 4 years from 1998 to 2002 is noteworthy for the variety of circumstances in which judicial review has been successfully deployed. As has been noted above, virtually no area of Part III of the CA 1989 has been untouched by challenges made by way of judicial review, nor have many of the child protection procedures referred to in *Working Together*. Even s 47 has been the subject of interpretation by the Administrative Court in *R on the application of S v Swindon Borough Council* [2001] 3 FCR 702 (see the discussion in Chapter **5**). Whilst Butler-Sloss LJ, President of the Family Division in 2002, might have expressed concern in the *Harrow* case in 1989 at there being quite so many cases going to judicial review, nevertheless she was concerned in that case with the paramountcy of the welfare interests of the child and it is beyond doubt that the burgeoning case-law on judicial review is testament to the fact that lawyers have employed the judicial review procedure most imaginatively to try to protect the paramount interest of the welfare of the child.

CHAPTER 12

CHILD ABUSE AND CHILD PROTECTION: INTO THE NEXT MILLENNIUM

'While the English do not wish ill of their children, their society is not child-friendly. While the depth of inquiry and compassion is impressive, the children would probably get just as much attention if they were going to be hung!' (Southern European respondent (now working in England) response to the team preparing the *Learning from Past Experience – A Review of Serious Case Reviews* Report, (DOH, 2002) at p 1).

'How can the system be designed so that it feels fair to the participants in it, and so that the professionals in it are motivated to act carefully and diligently on children's behalf ? How can the law be structured so that it "demands" the protection of children in their everyday lives in homes, schools, recreation centres and other neighbourhood settings? Can the law and the legal system be used to stimulate family and community responsibility for such activity and to ensure that children, no matter how vulnerable, always have effective watchdogs on their behalf' (Melton (1996), at p 50).

'We can only succeed in our campaign to end cruelty to children if every person in a local community takes responsibility for that community's children. That is why initiatives aimed at strengthening communities so that they can support children – particularly those who are vulnerable – are an integral part of our strategy. Government policy has recently recognised that the strengthening of communities provides other, more general benefits, such as improved public health, a reduced crime rate and economic regeneration' (from Part IV of the *NSPCC Vision for Children pack, the Child Friendly Communities Programme* (NSPCC, 1998)).

Introduction

12.1 It is clear from the three quotations above, and from issues identified in all of the chapters in this book, that whilst the roles of the various agencies involved in child protection are critical, little will improve for our children unless there is some recognition that people living in the communities in which our children live and grow and live their lives also have a responsibility to protect the children. Interfering in other people's family lives is not something which comes easily to those living in the UK, perhaps because there has always been a reluctance to see our children as having rights to anything let alone a right to protection. We are seen by outsiders as not being a child-friendly society and we have been repeatedly criticised by the UN Monitoring Committee for legitimising assault upon our children and for failing to take other measures to properly protect them (see para **12.41**). The government has demonstrated that it is frightened of taking the political and moral lead on outlawing assault on children and, thus, we have to ask what hope there is for the population as a whole when that is the message given to them by central government. Perhaps campaigns such as those run by the NSPCC and an increasing awareness of the potentially beneficial impact of the ECHR as implemented by the HRA 1998 will begin the process of making us aware of the critical nature of the responsibility which we all have to protect our children. But what is the contribution of the law and the legal system to making us all aware of our responsibilities. The judiciary have at last begun to make their position really felt in the law relating to child protection. Without the decision in the Court of Appeal in *Re W and B; Re W (Care Plan)* [2001] [2001] EWCA Civ 757, [2001] 2 FLR 582 and the disappointed reaction of children's lawyers and judges alike to its overruling in the House of Lords (*Re S (Minors); Re W (Minors)* [2002] UKHL 10, [2002] 1 FLR 815), the government would never have moved to put in place the new amendments to the CA 1989. We need the judiciary in this country to speak out more on behalf of the most vulnerable in our society where the legal system is manifestly failing to protect their interests, and this was what was happening to a number of children in care for whom no plans were being made or where they were being poorly executed. The result was a significant number of children drifting in care. This is not to urge the judges to make political points, it is to ask them to ensure that the basic principles of justice are upheld, and one of the most fundamental principles must be that the legal system protects those who are the weakest and who would otherwise have their rights trampled upon or disregarded by the more powerful in society.

The impact of the HRA 1998

12.2 Work was originally started on this book in the summer of 2000; however, production of the final version was delayed until late 2002 in order to incorporate a huge number of both legislative and policy changes in relation to child protection. When writing the very first chapter of this book, the author predicted that there would be very many changes to the system of child protection as a result of the impact of the HRA 1998, the changes to the criminal justice system, and also as a result of the introduction of the Care Standards Act 2000 and the Children (Leaving Care) Act 2000. Even the author, however, could not predict the very radical changes which have occurred to the system of child protection in the UK as a result of additional legislative changes introduced by the Adoption and Children Act 2002, the huge range of government initiatives, and the issuing of new guidance in so many areas, as well as the impact of such decisions as *A v UK* [1998] 2 FLR 959, *Z v UK* [2001] 2 FLR 612, *TP and KM v UK* [2001] 2 FLR 549 and the decision of the Court of Appeal, influenced by the demands of the HRA 1998, in the case of *Re W and B; Re W* [2001] EWCA Civ 757, [2001] 2 FLR 582. The House of Lords has of course since issued judgment on the appeal in the case of *Re W and B; Re W*, now reported as *Re S (Minors); Re W (Minors)* [2002] UKHL 10, [2002] 1 FLR 815, and as discussed in detail in Chapter 7 confirmed what many had anticipated, that it could not uphold the approach of the Court of Appeal on the basis that such a considerable change as 'starring' a care plan could not be effected by a process of creative judicial interpretation such as had been engaged in by the Court of Appeal. The decision of the House of Lords in *Re S (Minors); Re W (Minors)* [2002] UKHL 10, [2002] 1 FLR 815 was described by one Family Division judge as clearly 'intellectually pure' but as 'extremely disappointing'.

12.3   Lord Nicholls of Birkenhead, who gave the main judgment in the case, emphasised that the Court of Appeal had exceeded the bounds of its jurisdiction under s 3 of the HRA 1998 by interpreting the CA 1989 in such a way as to introduce a system whereby the essential milestone of a care plan had to be identified and 'starred' when a care order was made, with the effect that action had to be taken by the local authority if those milestones were not achieved within a reasonable time after the date set by the court. Lord Nicholls emphasised that the HRA 1998 sought to preserve parliamentary sovereignty and maintain the constitutional boundary. He emphasised that:

> 'Interpretation of statutes was a matter for the courts; the enactment and amendment of statutes were matters for Parliament. A cardinal principle of the Children Act was that the courts were not empowered to intervene in the way local authorities discharged their parental responsibilities and final care orders. Parliament entrusted to local authorities, not the courts, the responsibility for looking after children who were the subject of care orders. The new "starring" system would depart substantially from that principle. That judicial innovation passed well beyond the boundary of interpretation. There was no provision in the Children Act which lent itself to the interpretation that Parliament was thereby conferring that supervisory function on the court. On the contrary, the "starring" system was inconsistent in an important respect with the scheme of the Children Act. It would have far reaching practical ramifications for local authorities and their care of children. It would not come free from additional administrative work and expense and would be likely to have a material effect on authorities' allocation of scarce financial and other resources. That in turn would affect local authorities' discharge of their responsibilities to other children. Those were matters for decision by Parliament, not the courts. It was impossible for a court to attempt to evaluate those ramifications. However, rejection of "starred milestones" on legal grounds could not obscure the pressing need for the Government to attend to the serious practical and legal problems identified by the Court of Appeal. One question needing urgent consideration was whether some degree of court supervision of local authorities' discharge of their parental responsibilities would

bring about an overall improvement in the quality of child care provided by local authorities. Answering that question called for a wider examination than could be undertaken by a court. The judgment of the Court of Appeal had performed a valuable service in highlighting the need for such an examination to be conducted without delay.'

12.4 Whilst many felt huge disappointment that the House of Lords decided that they could not interpret the CA 1989 in the light of the demands of the ECHR, it was certainly 'legally correct' for Lord Nicholls to emphasise that the enactment and amendment of statutes were matters for Parliament, and his stinging comments as to the necessity for the government to urgently consider the question certainly had its effect. The response of government to the House of Lords' decision has been that amending legislation has been included in the Adoption and Children Act 2002 still going through Parliament at the time of proofreading this work. Currently, as indicated in Chapters **4** and **7**, the Adoption and Children Act 2002 provides for the amendment of s 31 of the CA 1989 by including in the statute what had previously been settled good practice of the courts to refuse to make a care order until they had considered a plan for the future care of the child prepared by the local authority. The Act thus provides a new s 31A of the CA 1989 which provides as follows.

'Section 31A   Care Orders: Care Plans

(1) Where an application is made on which a care order might be made with respect to a child, the appropriate local authority must, within such time as the court may direct, prepare a plan ("a care plan") for the future care of the child.

(2) While the application is pending, the authority must keep any care plan prepared by them under review and, if they are of the opinion some change is required, revise the plan, or make a new plan, accordingly.

(3) A care plan must give any prescribed information and do so in the prescribed manner.

(4) For the purposes of this section, the appropriate local authority, in relation to a child in respect of whom a care order might be made, is the local authority proposed to be designated in the order.

(5) In s 31(A) and this section, references to a care order do not include an interim care order.

(6) A plan prepared, or treated as prepared, under this section is referred to in this Act as a "section 31A plan".'

12.5 It can be seen that this provision by itself would not clearly provide the courts with any role in reviewing the local authority's care plans for a particular child. But this is not the sum total of the amendments provided in this critical area of the law by the amending legislation. Thus, as was discussed in detail in Chapters **4** and **7**, s 26(2) of the CA 1989 has been amended to provide for: s 31A care plans to be considered at the reviews held on all children looked after by the local authority (s 26(2)(e)); that where there is no such plan for the future care of the child for one to be made and for it to be reviewed (s 26(2)(f)(i) and (ii)), thus extending the benefit of s 31A care plans to all 'looked after' children; for a prescribed person referred to by the Minister as the 'independent reviewing officer' to be appointed to participate in the review, to monitor the performance of the authority's functions in respect of that review, and to refer the case to a CAFCASS officer where he considers it appropriate to do so. It would appear to be the case that it is then intended that the CAFCASS officer would be able to take action in the courts in relation to the authority's plans for the child (see Minister's statement introducing clause 116, 20 May, 2002 and see Explanatory Note to the Adoption and Children Bill 2001, clause 116). One cause for concern must be voiced and that is that the Minister seemed to imply that the reviewing officer might not be totally independent. Thus, she stated that 'the regulations would require the reviewing officer to be a senior professional with expertise in children's cases who will have the status to ensure that the care plan is implemented. The reviewer will be independent of the line management of the child's case but not necessarily independent of the local authority itself'. This should sound grave warning bells in a system which has already been shown to inspire little confidence in the children who attend their own reviews, and where reviews are a purely perfunctory exercise or have not been properly held at all (see Chapter **4** and *Safeguarding Children* (DOH/SSI, 2002) at para **7.22**). Whilst there is still time to influence those who are drawing up the regulations, lawyers and all who work in the child protection system should exert pressure on the DOH to learn the lessons from the past to ensure that the reviewing officer is truly independent. So much will rest upon their shoulders for it is they who will determine whether or not to refer the case on to a CAFCASS officer. Perhaps the best idea would be for the court approving the care plan also to have the power to appoint the independent reviewing officer and to hear evidence of this person's independence before confirming his appointment. The Minister confirmed that the effect of the new s 26(2C) of the CA 1989, as amended, would be to empower CAFCASS officers to take proceedings on behalf of the child. She stated that she envisaged that the CAFCASS officer might seek orders preventing the local authority from removing the child from an established placement or declarations that the child's human rights were being breached. As is apparent from the Minister's statement, much that is needed to give these provisions real bite is left to be drawn up in the relevant rules of court and regulations, and these will have to be very clear and rigorous as to the bases upon which CAFCASS officers will be able to initiate proceedings. Again, one would hope that subject to personnel changes some attempt will be made to provide in the regulations for the reviewing officer to approach the guardian originally involved in the case where there was one, although such will not be the case for accommodated children. This would seem to be an attempt to stem any further potential growth of actions by way of judicial review (see Chapter **11**) in that it imposes clear duties on the local authority: to keep care plans under review; where it is of the opinion that a change is required, to revise the plan or to make a new plan; and it gives considerable power to the prescribed persons and the CAFCASS officers to engage in a process which has the potential to end up before the courts. Given the burgeoning case-law identified in Chapter **11** with regard to the use of judicial review in relation to the CA 1989, it would appear that no further encouragement is to be given to a considerably developing role for family judges sitting in the Administrative Court in relation to the interpretation of duties laid down in the CA 1989 (see Chapter **11** and the recommendations of Butler-Sloss P in the case of *C v Bury Metropolitan Borough Council* [2002] 2 FLR 868). These rights provided now by the amended s 26(2) and the additional s 26(2A–C) and s 31A are, of course, similar in potential impact to the proposed rights of review laid down by the 'starring milestones' approach of the Court of Appeal in the case of *Re W and B; Re W* [2001] EWCA Civ 757, [2001] 2 FLR 582. In the context of human rights applications before our courts, however, it was very interesting to note the comments of the Minister in relation to potential remedies available to children pursuant to ss 7 and 8 of the HRA 1998.

12.6   As has been seen from earlier chapters, the impact of the HRA 1998 has been felt across the board in all areas relating to child protection. Thus far, by mid-2002, this has manifested itself in decisions ranging from the meaning of 'reasonable cause to suspect' when local authorities are conducting child protection investigations under s 47 of the CA 1989 (see *Re S* [2001] 3 FCR 1131), a case where the actions taken by the local authority were not held to have breached the step-father's Article 8 rights (see Chapter **6**) through to the decision in *L and P v Reading Borough Council and Chief Constable of Thames Valley Police* [2001] 2 FLR 50, where it was held that both the father's and daughter's rights to private and family life had been contravened by the way in which the local authority social services and the police had conducted the child protection conference and their subsequent actions. In the latter case, both the father and daughter were given leave to sue the local authority social services department and the police in negligence, a step which in 1995 would have been unthinkable. The previous immunity from suit conferred by such decisions as *X v Bedfordshire County Council* had by the date of the passing of the HRA 1998 already been seen to be vulnerable. Thus the decision of the House of Lords in *Barrett v Enfield London Borough Council* [1999] 2 FLR 426, HL and the decision in *W v Essex County Council* [2000] 1 FLR 657, HL had revealed chinks in the armour of the protection previously conferred on all the so-called 'helping' professions by the court's view that it was against public policy to allow actions to be taken against statutory agencies in the performance of their statutory duties. The HRA 1998 and the ever-increasing trail of cases being taken to the European Court in Strasbourg had, however, worked a sea change and with the European Court's decision in *Z v UK* [2001] 2 FLR 612 that the children had been subject to inhuman and degrading treatment or punishment by their parents from which social services ought to have protected them in breach of Article 3, and that the children had been denied their right to an effective remedy before the courts of this country by a rule of public policy which conferred such immunity from suit, the doors had finally been opened to allow those so adversely affected by an authority's failure to act to receive compensation for such failure. A further decision to the same effect was published by the European Court of Human Rights on 23 October 2002. Thus, in *DP and JC v UK* (2002) *The Times*, October 23, the European Court again found that the UK had failed to guarantee two children who had been sexually abused by their step-father relevant access to the courts in order to be able to benefit from a thorough and effective investigation capable of leading to the identification and punishment of those responsible for the failure to act in response to the children's complaints and consideration of their rights to compensation.

12.7 The voice of the child has also not been absent from decisions of the courts considering the child's position in proceedings affecting them. Whilst it has long been the case that children in public law proceedings have been entitled to the dual system of representation guaranteed them by the provisions of the CA 1989, those children equally at risk in private proceedings had been denied the right to separate representation except where the children could successfully negotiate a veritable obstacle course of hurdles put in their way to prevent them exercising rights given to them by the CA 1989. Thus, in *Re A (Contact) (Separate Representation)* [2001] 1 FLR 464, a boy aged 14 who had alleged sexual abuse of both himself and his 4½-year-old sister, claimed the right to be separately heard in residence and contact order proceedings between his mother and his father. His plea was not one based on a desire to make an application himself for an order since his mother was indeed making such an application, but rather arose out of a concern that no one appeared to be 'listening' and 'hearing' what he was saying. He had transmitted his views that he did not wish to see his father to the court welfare officer. The officer had determined that it was in the best interests of both the boy and his sister to see their father. The boy claimed, not surprisingly, that his views were not being heard and thus, through the National Youth Advocacy Service, his position that he was being denied his rights to a fair trial in the determination of his civil rights and obligations was put before the President of the Family Division. Dame Elizabeth Butler-Sloss P found that indeed there was a breach of the boy's human rights under Article 6 and thus an important step has been taken in the area of private law proceedings where such proceedings may raise issues of child protection. The lack of representation as of right to children in private law proceedings where there are child protection concerns, as well as more generally in an effort to hear the voice of the child as required by Article 12, has also been the subject of criticism by the UN Monitoring Committee in its latest observations on the rights of children in the UK (see the *Concluding Observations* (noted at para **12.40**), at para 29).

The impact of the Victoria Climbie enquiry

12.8 At the time of writing, Part II of the enquiry into the death of Victoria Climbie was still continuing in London under the Chairmanship of Lord Laming, and the details of the death of 2-year-old Ainlee Labonte (also known as Walker) at the hands of both her parents were emerging in the press. Ainlee died whilst Newham Council was under special measures, and the Council is due to publish its Part 8 report as to how Ainlee could have died in such circumstances. Similar horrified reactions had been displayed at the revelations of the details of the progressively torturing treatment meted out to 7-year-old Lauren Wright at the hands of her step-mother but with the willing connivance of her own father. The horrific details of Victoria's death had led all those concerned with the child protection system to question how, again, it could happen that the systems in place relating to child protection could so badly fail a little girl. Time after time, as revealed in Chapters **1**, **3**, **5** and **6**, enquiries have been held into the tragic deaths of children whose plight has been missed by the very people charged with protecting them. The appalling statistics on child deaths every week in the UK revealed by the NSPCC report *Out of Sight* (NSPCC, 2001) and confirmed in *Safeguarding Children* (Joint Chief Inspectors of Social Services, 14 October 2002), are to many scarcely credible: that at least two children die every week at the hands of their parents is a damning statistic. It is, as was seen in Chapter **2**, unlikely to be the case that these figures reveal the whole story. Thus, as many paediatricians point out, the real statistics on child deaths every week are probably closer to four or five per week at a minimum.

12.9 What was again so horrific to those watching the unfolding story of Victoria and her suffering at the hands of her great-aunt and her partner, was that there had been such a massive failure by all the relevant statutory agencies concerned to exercise their very considerable powers of protection over such a child. The catalogue of failure by health, social services, education and the police is one which led all of those agencies publicly to apologise and has also led to a very public examination of their conduct through the enquiry. Alan Milburn, the Secretary of State for Health, has in consequence of the initial findings of the Climbie enquiry, already announced a review of the child protection system in England. He promised reform of the law if it proved to be necessary in order to ensure that such a case could not occur again. However, Lord Laming reported that the law was sound but that the gap was in its implementation. Thus it emerged from the Report of the Climbie Inquiry (28 January 2003) (*www.victoria-climbie-inquiry.org.uk/report*) that it is not the system as such which is at fault but rather the human beings who are called upon to administer that system. Human beings are not infallible and mistakes will always be made, but what must occur as a result of the Climbie enquiry should be a very careful examination of the stresses and strains currently experienced within the child protection system. The father of Victoria Climbie at one point during the enquiry commented that he found it difficult to believe that 'social workers in England could not read' (in Broadcasting House, BBC Radio 4, Sunday, 2 March 2002). It had transpired during the enquiry that both the key social worker for Victoria and the senior supervising social worker had not read *Working Together to Safeguard Children* (DOH, 1999). They had been forced to admit this in the course of the enquiry; if they had tried to say that they were familiar with the document the lawyers in the enquiry would have easily demonstrated otherwise. Within the system, therefore, both a key social worker working in the child protection arena with children and a senior supervising social worker had been employed by Harringey Social Services when they were clearly not competent to do the job.

12.10 Certainly, the new Codes of Practice for Social Care Workers issued in draft form on 8 January 2002, and in final form in September 2002, by the General Social Care Council under the provisions of the Care Standards Act 2000 demand that social care workers are familiar with all the legislation and guidance which governs their areas of practice. But the Code of Practice for Employers also requires that they take steps to ensure that those whom they employ are competent to do the job and have the necessary knowledge and skills base with which to do so. If those selecting social workers for employment are forced because of a shortage of qualified personnel with the relevant skills to employ those who do not possess the relevant knowledge and skills, then to whom should we look for responsibility for that situation?

The position of social services in the child protection arena

12.11 If social workers, their managers and ultimately their employers are put into a position where they have been employed to engage in a particular type of work in which they have no skills or knowledge, then it is hardly surprising that the systems imposed by central government break down. Social services have, however, been extremely hard pressed by all governments from the Thatcher government through to the present. The de-professionalisation of social work started by the Thatcher government's determination that the social work qualifying degree should be eliminated to be replaced with a 2-year qualification, was the first step in a catastrophic central government approach to social services and social work.

12.12 The picture from social workers across the country is one which has been considered very recently by Chris Jones who explores the condition of State social work in England today (Jones 2001)). He conducted a series of interviews with experienced social workers employed by local authority social services departments across the North of England. These front line State social workers provided a penetrating insight into the diverse ways in which their work has been transformed and degraded and the manner in which the needs of clients have been largely ignored. From their perspective, the election of a Labour government in 1997 proved in due course to be a massive disappointment and many social workers reported that this government has further undermined State social work practice, workers and clients.

12.13 Jones's article above all seeks to provide an opportunity for the views of front line state social workers to be heard in their pleas for time to do their work and more resources to be devoted to their profession. In many departments, child protection is seen as 'fire fighting' principally because the necessary social work personnel are not available to do the essential preventative work with children and families so well espoused in the provisions of the CA 1989. Those involved in child protection are suffering huge amounts of stress – partly imposed as a result of ever-increasing numbers of government initiatives such as the *Quality Protects* programme, but also as a result of sheer pressure caused by the lack of sufficient numbers of social workers. Jones comments that 'for the first time in my experience I was listening to social workers describe their work as if they were in a factory'. This was how one social worker described the experience:

'I now work much harder than I have ever worked in my life. You are expected to work at a much faster rate with no breaks. It is no wonder that so many social workers are off with stress and on long-term sick. It is appalling and it is going to get worse now we have all these league tables that are beginning to drive things.'

12.14 These are the words of a child protection worker and Jones comments that it 'captured some of the bewilderment felt by State social workers – a sort of madness in the system'. The social worker went on to explain aspects of the duty system in her agency: 'everyone closes things as soon as they possibly can, but you know that 3 weeks later it is going to come back again. It's a complete nonsense'.

12.15 Many of the social workers interviewed by Jones pointed to the veritable onslaught of regulatory intrusion in their work which they felt had dramatically accelerated since 1997 with the election of the Labour government. One children's worker commented:

'I don't have a problem with the LAC [looked after children] forms but then we also have to fill in initial assessment forms, comprehensive assessment forms and lots of other forms, many of which don't make any sense to me. I don't know what happens to all these forms, but I think they are government driven and it is considered to be proof of what we are doing.'

12.16 Again, many of the social workers interviewed by Jones could cite at least some of the many critical comments which Paul Boateng, a senior government minister, had made over the years with respect to State social workers' record with children in the childcare system. Jones comments that: 'what troubled the social workers was that Boateng had not identified a woeful lack of investment over the years as the principal cause and in his focus on the frailties of social workers and their local authority agency was just like his Conservative predecessors'. The view that the failing social workers must be completely regulated also meant, as Jones identified, that the form-filling required by central government today seems to reflect a concern to regulate the 'ordinary' and everyday professional conduct of social workers. Jones interprets these latest developments as further evidence that traditional, mainstream, client-focused social work has little place in current State social work agencies. He reports that a particular family social worker captured the feelings of many of his respondents thus:

'I used to enjoy the freedom of being a social worker, to develop relationships with clients, to take a few risks, but now everything is controlled and other people make the key decisions and feed it back to you to implement. It all seems to be about covering people's backs and saving money.'

12.17 Jones comments on this, that, in so doing 'the heart has been ripped out of social work'. The growth of management notions in social work was further identified by Jones as contributing to the utterly demoralised state of our social workers in England and Wales. Jones notes that in many of the agencies he visited the depth of the division between the front line practitioners and their managers surprised him. He comments that:

'if a "them and us" culture is a measure of proletarianization then I have no hesitation in describing State social workers as being thoroughly proletarianized. I heard no positive word about managers. I did hear some sympathy: "The first line manager's job is a horrible job. It's a shit of a job. I wouldn't want to do it. It is an incredibly pressuring job but so many of them behave like bastards, even I can see why, but oh some are so horrible".'

12.18 Jones indicates (at p 559) that he had been told that social work managers had lost touch with the welfare ideals of social work. Thus, one social worker stated:

'It seems to me that many of the senior managers have no feel for social work any more. They are managers, professional managers, who have little feeling for the clients.'

12.19 Of even greater concern, when considering the issues which may face those working in child protection, were those comments which revealed very real fear of managers. Thus, Jones reports the statement of another social worker:

'Much of the stress at work is fear; social workers are scared of their managers, scared of all the monitoring stuff. We get no help and if we can't manage our work then we are told that we are poor time managers. There is no solution offered. Most managers now are only interested in allocating work irrespective of the pressure on us, the social workers. We will be blamed for the problems which are due to lack of resources. This is the attitude of quite a few of the managers who are also being pressed by the senior management group to take more and more work. The pressure is always downwards.'

12.20 It is hardly surprising, therefore, that serious and, for the children, catastrophic mistakes of the type made in Victoria Climbie's case are made by such a hard-pressed, fearful and stressed workforce. That employers themselves are so under pressure that they should employ key workers and senior supervising child protection workers without the necessary knowledge and skills to deal with cases such as Victoria's, points to a system as a whole which is under-resourced and over-stressed. In the same way as the Labour government has now realised, the dangers of demoralising the teaching workforce and the health workforce, urgent attention should be given to the state of social services in this country if we are really concerned about the need to protect our society's children both now and in the future. The CA 1989 and the various administrative procedures and policies which are laid down to implement it, is in reality only one very small part of the bigger picture in child protection. The key people in child protection are the child's family, who when under stress for a variety of different reasons may feel the need to turn to the support of social services. We need an extremely dedicated and skilled workforce to respond to the sorts of issues raised in the Victoria Climbie case. Jones in his 2001 article identified (at p 560) how hard local authorities are finding it to recruit new staff, especially in the south-east of England. As with other areas of work such as nursing, Jones comments that there is 'an extraordinary movement of social workers into agency work which needs some investigation'. He points out that many social services departments only manage to get by with high numbers of such temporary workers. Indeed, he comments that Harringey in London, the area serving Victoria Climbie's family, had somewhere in the region of 40 per cent of agency staff. In addition, as the author is aware as a result of her work in evaluating the Children's Fund in Liverpool and Knowsley in the North West of England, new government initiatives such as the *Children's Fund*, and *Sure Start* are creaming off social workers, who once again want to be part of teams experiencing the warmth of appreciation and respect, which comes from being engaged in the best sort of preventative projects and assistance, which used to be part and parcel of everyday social work.

12.21 Jones concludes his article with an examination of the notion of 'winners and losers'. He comments that New Labour is undoubtedly more prepared than were the previous Conservative administration to talk of giving the losers a chance or two – a 'new deal' – but if they cannot manage it, or if they are such losers that they cannot even obtain a 'new deal', then there is very little on offer. Except, perhaps, he suggests, 'a visit from a State social worker'. Jones concludes by stating that:

> 'as long as we have societies which are prepared to treat some of its most vulnerable people in this way then State social work will continue to be a grim occupation – something increasingly akin to the Poor Law of 1834 – and no amount of spin and repackaging will make any difference.'

Safeguarding Children – the Joint Chief Inspectors' Report on Arrangements to Safeguard Children

12.22 All of those who work within the child protection system, but especially those who are familiar with the work done by social services, should be extremely concerned that this is the state of the service upon which children in need of protection must primarily depend. What does it say about our attitude as a society that we should have let this group of professionals slip into such a state that we are prepared to countenance employing those who do not possess the necessary skills because we simply have not expended enough resources on ensuring that we have the right calibre of people necessary to do this most critical work? At the time of going to press, many of the criticisms set out in this book have been found to be justified by the first report from the Joint Inspectors of eight different government bodies. This is the first of the three yearly reports by all the relevant government Inspectorates having responsibilities in some way for children and young people, which Sir William Utting initially recommended should be done in *People Like Us* in 1997 (see *The Report of the Review of Safeguards of Children Living Away from Home* (The Stationery Office, 1997)). The government made a commitment in *Modernising Social Services (Promoting Independence, Improving Protection, Raising Standards* (The Stationery Office, 1998) that the Chief Inspector of the Social Services would, with all the relevant government Inspectorates, conduct such a review and report on a 3-yearly basis as to how well children are being safeguarded from harm. The Report, *Safeguarding Children on the Joint Chief Inspectors' Report on Arrangements to Safeguard Children*, Chief of the SSI and seven other Chief Inspectors (DOH, 14 October 2002) and available on the internet at www.doh.gov.uk/ssi/childrensafeguardsjoint.htm is, as noted above, the result of the first such review and includes a collation of relevant inspection findings over the last 3 years as well as the findings of a joint inspection of eight ACPC areas.

12.23 This Report contains stark warnings (although, interestingly, not generally to be found in the chapter presenting the main findings, see Chapter 1, about professional staff, particularly social workers, muddling through in chaotic conditions in a line of work that attracts minimal recognition or praise, and warns that many social services departments are so under-resourced that they struggle to keep abreast of even the most serious cases (see paras 4.49, 5.33, 5.34, 6.8). The report further states that Child and Adolescent Mental Health Services almost everywhere are short of money and staff, and have long waiting lists, another example of the clear breaches of Article 19 of the UNCRC in terms of the provision of necessary therapeutic support for those children and young people who have suffered from the most horrific experiences as children and young people at the hands of those who are supposed to care for them (see for more detail on this Chapter 1). The inquiry team also encountered complaints that social workers intervened only when faced with solid evidence of abuse or neglect, leaving alone situations where abuse was not proved (paras 6.10, 6.15). In one area visited by the inquiry team, teachers admitted that they had given up reporting suspected cases of child abuse or neglect to the social services department because they had lost confidence that anything would be done (para 6.9). Police in another area reported a loss of confidence in the response of social services (para 6.9). Other agencies reported to the team that the response of social services to child welfare concerns operated with too strong a distinction between children perceived to be at risk of significant harm, and other children deemed only to be in need. For children considered to be at risk of significant harm, the response of the majority of social services assessment focused almost exclusively on an assessment of the risk of harm and social workers failed to consider the wider needs of the child within the family. Given the 'fire-fighting' approach identified by Jones (2001), the necessarily selective approaches identified in the various chapters of this book (see Chapters 1, 2, 3 and 4) as a result of the massive starvation of resources experienced by social services, as well as past SSI Reports (see, eg, *Developing Quality to Protect Children – SSI Inspection of Children's Services: August 1999–July 2000* (DOH, 2001)), these results should come as no surprise. The question which has to be asked is, 'What is the government proposing to do in response to this report?'.

12.24 The report also warns of shortages of psychiatrists specialising in the treatment of children, shortages of paediatricians, health visitors and midwives, and criticises the police for treating child protection work as beneath them. The team praises the work of specialist child protection teams set up by the police, adding a complaint that they are undervalued by their fellow police officer's, who seem to take the view that preventing child abuse is not part of a police officer's job. The question must be asked that if police officers cannot see the prevention of the crimes of child abuse and neglect as part of their job of fighting crime and the work of their specialist units as crime prevention, then there can be little hope that the public will see it as any part of their role to engage in the protection of such vulnerable children in our midst. What then is the role of the community in the UK today – do we simply close our eyes to what is happening as so many people did who saw two children dragging another distressed child along behind them for several hours on the streets of Liverpool before he was then brutally assaulted and murdered? Do people in the UK really care deeply about the plight of children throughout our society who are in need of protection? It is perhaps significant that the media's assessment of what people in the UK would be more interested in reading about on the day before the report was issued, even though the media knew about the report's disturbing findings, was the sex life of the England football manager as revealed by his some-time girlfriend, the presenter Ulrika Jonnson, or the alleged sexual assault of a woman in South Africa by the Manchester United football manager. Only one newspaper, the *Independent on Sunday*, had the news about the report and it placed it prominently on the front page as its main Sunday news headline – 'Scandal of Britain's Neglected Children'. The remaining newspapers did not report the Enquiry Team's findings at all that day and the Bali bombing in the early hours of the Monday morning meant that other newspapers which might have given the report greater focus generally ignored it on the day it was actually published as well as in succeeding days.

Messages from *Safeguarding Children*

Areas of concern and findings

12.25 The official areas of concern and findings from this 118-page report are again a confirmation of some of the many of the criticisms which have been made throughout this book. Other areas which have been the focus of criticism in this book were not picked up by the report at all. Various areas of concern and findings are summarised and highlighted in the first chapter of the report, although interestingly to find the really critical findings, which cry out for immediate government intervention, one has to dig deeper into the report, as was done in the previous paragraphs. The findings and main areas for concern as set out in the first chapter of the report are presented here as clustered under the relevant headings in the report.

12.26 *Arrangements by agencies for safeguarding children* – Thus, as was identified in Chapters **2**, **3**, **4** and **6** of this book, the report notes at para 1.11 that local agencies across the board tend to interpret their safeguarding responsibilities in different ways or with different emphases and the priority given to safeguarding children in recent legislation and guidance has not been reflected firmly, coherently or consistently enough in service planning and resource allocation nationally or locally across all agencies. It was clear to the team that other priorities have competed for attention with action on safeguarding, and the priority which senior staff said was given to safeguarding children was not reflected in many agencies' business plans (see chapter 6 of the report). The team inspected safeguarding arrangements in eight local authority areas and drew additionally on evidence from a range of inspection work conducted by the different Inspectorates involved. The team observed that in those areas where they were most confident of the safeguarding arrangements, they found senior managers who were committed to protecting children, who communicated their commitment through their organisations, and who ensured their staff were child-focused and kept the safeguarding of children high on the agenda at all times. In those areas there was apparently an open culture between local agencies and good lines of communication between senior managers, who had sufficient trust and confidence in each other to accept and address concerns brought to their attention. What should be noted here about the team's comments about managers is that they state that these comments relate to 'those areas where they were most confident', they say nothing in this main findings chapter about those areas where they were not confident; this is left to the interstices of chapter 6 of the report, where one can find deeply worrying concerns about areas like the ones in which Jones did his interviewing.

12.27 *Responding to welfare concerns* – Whilst the team was satisfied that in the vast majority of cases children were protected from risk of further harm and all children on child protection registers were allocated to social work staff, and that there were good working relationships between almost all local agencies at various levels in most of the areas inspected, it did find that many services were under the pressures identified earlier in this book in Chapters **1**, **2**, **3**, **4**, **5** and **6**, and also by Chris Jones (see Jones (2001)). Thus, the team comments at para 1.15 that many services were under pressure and experiencing major difficulties in recruiting and retaining key skilled and experienced staff, which was having a major impact upon safeguarding arrangements for children and young people. Should one be surprised after reading the interviews with Jones set out above? The team observed that in most areas there was a high level of understanding, sympathy and support for those services under pressure provided that senior managers were open with other agencies about their difficulties and entered into discussion and dialogue with them about how they were managing the services, which promoted flexible working together to maintain crucial service to safeguard children. However, it was noted that in those areas where there were long-standing tensions between agencies and less co-operation, it was difficult to achieve the necessary level of inter-agency commitment to ensure that arrangements to safeguard children were effective. The team was also concerned to find, what is noted in Chapters **5** and **6** of this book, that many staff from all agencies were confused about their responsibilities and duties to share information about child welfare concerns with other agencies, they were not confident about whether other agencies shared information with them, and that despite consistency in the findings of inquiries over past years about weaknesses and failings in information sharing, there were few formal agreements between agencies about how and when information should be shared.

12.28 *Thresholds for responding to child welfare concerns* – The team also found that there were serious concerns amongst staff of all agencies about the thresholds which social services were applying in their children's services. Thus, the report notes (at para 1.19) that professional staff from other agencies considered that social services were not providing an adequate response when they judged that a situation did not involve a high risk of serious harm to children and young people. Equally, they considered that social services did not provide adequate guidance, advice and support when they raised concerns about the welfare of children and young people. Many of these difficulties were explained by staff shortages within children's teams in social services, exactly as was found by Jones in his work. In some areas the team found that there was reluctance by some agencies to refer child welfare concerns to other agencies: teachers to social services, and social services and others to the police. Where this occurred, the local ACPC had not actively addressed these concerns. The team were advised that some specific services did not appear to be well integrated into the local safeguarding arrangements and these included GPs, child and adolescent mental health services, adult mental health services, some independent schools, NHS Direct and walk-in health centres. The report notes at para 1.22 that the quality of care and responses to safeguarding issues for many children living away from home varied very considerably in different parts of the country. This applied to children in family placements, children's homes and residential schools. As has been noted in Chapters **4** and **11** of this book, the participation of children and parents in reviews, the frequency of social worker visits to looked after children, and the availability of and access to independent visitors and advocates were not of a consistent quality. The care and protection of children and young people placed in secure accommodation was generally found to be of a good standard, a finding curiously at odds with the findings of Goldson (see Goldson (2002), generally and specifically at pp 157 and 159 and of the UN Monitoring Committee, *Concluding Observation* 57).

12.29 *The leadership of the Area Child Protection Committee* – The report notes (at paras 1.23–1.27) that there were many factors which contributed to there being few ACPCs equipped and able to exercise their key responsibilities to promote and ensure safeguards for children and young people. ACPCs needed strong leadership as well as a commitment of all local agencies to support its work through joint funding arrangements. Local agencies did not generally accept that they were accountable to the ACPC for safeguarding arrangements. ACPCs, the report notes, did not command the authority to require local agencies to report on how they undertook their safeguarding duties, were not required to account for their work and although they are expected to produce a business plan (see chapter 6), some did not and those that did rarely specified their objectives or provided evidence of local activities and the standards they set for their work.

12.30 *Young people who commit offences* – The report, like Chapters **1**, **2** and **6** of this book, highlights the fact that HM Prisons Inspectors have stressed the very serious risks to the welfare of young people held in Young Offender Institutions (YOIs), commenting that although young people in YOIs are amongst those at highest risk of serious harm, their safeguarding had not been addressed in most areas. The team note the fact that few ACPCs had representatives from YOTs on them and therefore were not actively addressing the needs of these particularly vulnerable young people and comment that the YOTs are working in relative isolation from other services, were not demonstrating a commitment to risk assessment of these young people, and focused upon offending behaviour at the expense of considering welfare needs. Since this is what the current youth justice legislation focuses upon, it is somewhat unfair that the YOTs are targeted for this criticism when it should instead be directed at the government.

12.31 *Potentially dangerous persons* – The final area for the team's concerns related to measures in relation to potentially dangerous persons. The team found that all areas had developed Multi-Agency Public Protection Arrangements (MAPPA) and Panels (MAPPPs), but that in the absence of detailed national guidance, these had been developed in different ways. Confusion about the terminology used to describe the different categories of offenders who present a high risk of harm to the public including children was identified, and although there were good working relationships between the police and probation services who took the lead for MAPPA there was no consistency in how they addressed their tasks. The team also noted that MAPPPs and ACPCs had no formal links addressing their common concerns in safeguarding children and, as identified in Chapter **9** of this book, that all areas were struggling to respond to unconvicted people who present a high risk of harm to the public including children.

The report's recommendations

12.32 The report makes some 30 recommendations for the government to address, nearly all of which have been identified in other reports before. Some will clearly take some time and a very considerable injection of resources to achieve, and it remains to be seen whether the government has the political will to take some of the quite radical steps urged by this book as well as to implement the recommendations of its own body of Inspectorates. The recommendations are grouped under headings directed to be attended to by the various government departments with particular responsibilities and they are set out here in that way.

The Department of Health, Home Office, Department for Education and Skills, and the Lord Chancellor's Department should:

1. Ensure the safeguarding of children is firmly and consistently reflected in national and local service planning.

2. Support and facilitate national and local agencies to recruit and retain sufficient levels of appropriately qualified staff, paying particular regard to the image, status, morale, remuneration and working conditions of specialist child protection staff.

3. Establish minimum expectations, standards and curriculum for child protection training as part of the core professional training of all professionals working with children and young people (eg teacher training, medical and health staff training, police training etc).

The DOH should:

4. Review the current arrangements for ACPCs to determine whether they should be established on a statutory basis to ensure adequate accountability, authority and funding.

5. Review the purpose of child protection registers and issue guidance to local authorities.

The Lord Chancellor's Department, the Home Office and the DOH should:

6. Ensure that there is clear guidance provided to all agencies under their respective responsibilities on the implications of the Data Protection Act 1998 and the Human Rights Act 1998 and other relevant law, in respect of sharing information about children where there are welfare concerns.

The DOH and the Home Office with the Youth Justice Board, should:

7. Issue immediate guidance to ensure that local YOTs and the CPS are invited to become full members of all ACPCs.

The Home Office and the Youth Justice Board should:

8. Issue revised guidance to the Prison Service and the ACPC member organisations on the requirements and arrangements to safeguard children in prisons and YOIs.

The Home Office should:

9. Ensure that children and young people are a national priority for police services and the National Probation Services as part of their public protection arrangements, and ensure that this priority is reflected in local service plans.

10. Review the current arrangements for MAPPPs to identify whether they should be established on a statutory basis to ensure adequate accountability, authority, funding and consistency of practice.

11. Ensure that the relationship between MAPPPs and ACPCs is clarified.

12. Implement a national policy framework for public protection, including

MAPPPs and wider children's safeguarding issues as a matter of priority in order to develop a more consistent approach to the assessment and management of potentially dangerous people.

13. Issue a set of national standards and performance measures for police and probation services' joint management of potentially dangerous offenders.

All relevant Inspectorates should:

14. Review their inspection activity to ensure there is sufficient emphasis on examining arrangements to safeguard children.

15. Ensure that prior to the next report appropriate inspection activity has been undertaken on the following safeguarding areas:

    – YOIs;
    – Residential Independent Schools;
    – the impact of domestic violence on children;
    – children looked after outside of their home authority;
    – unaccompanied asylum-seeking children and the children of refugees and asylum seekers;
    – children with disabilities;
    – the work of YOTs;
    – children living in all forms of residential care.

16. Ensure that the finding of the National Care Standards Commission in relation to arrangements for safeguarding the children in residential and boarding schools and residential care for children and young people are included in future joint Chief Inspector's reports.

ACPCs with their constituent agencies should:

17. Develop integrated planning processes in partnership with MAPPPs to ensure that the safeguarding of children is an individual agency and inter-agency priority.

18. Review their constitution, membership, level of representation and funding arrangements to ensure that the committee is adequately resourced and fit to lead the children's safeguarding agenda across the area and in all relevant settings.

19. Ensure that there is an appropriate range and quantity of joint and single agency training to meet the needs of the workforce of constituent agencies (including non-specialist staff), relevant voluntary and independent organisations in their locality, and agree minimum expectations in terms of attendance and content of training.

20. Ensure that there are robust management information processes to support the monitoring, evaluation and auditing of local child protection procedures and practice.

21. Ensure that reviews of serious cases are undertaken on all appropriate

cases within the timescales and expectations of chapter 8 of *Working Together to Safeguard Children*, that reports are circulated appropriately and action plan recommendations are implemented.

22. Develop explicit arrangements for sharing information within a framework of joint protocols in order to strengthen the safeguarding of children.

23. Ensure that concerns about the safety of young offenders are identified and addressed in partnership with the local YOT, YOIs and prisons.

24. Review the local arrangements for maintaining and accessing the child protection register to ensure that relevant information is captured and used to maximise the safeguarding of children.

Social Services Departments should:

25. Review the thresholds for providing services, instigating child protection inquiries and convening initial child protection conferences in order to ensure that children are protected from harm, and ensure that there is a shared understanding of these thresholds across all agencies.

Police services should:

26. Review and clarify the role, remit, location and status of forced child protection units to ensure that all abuse of children is dealt with to a consistently high standard.

Health services should:

27. Ensure that pre- and post-recruitment checks are undertaken for all appropriate people working with children in the NHS.

28. Ensure that workforce plans adequately reflect the workload of child and adolescent mental health services and community paediatric services.

29. Establish clear lines of responsibility to ensure:

    – there is appropriate provision of and support for 'designated' and 'named' doctors and nurses;
    – there is appropriate senior representation on ACPCs;
    – the active involvement in and contribution of Primary Care Trusts (PCTs) including GPs in the local arrangements to safeguard children;
    – attendance by general and other medical practitioners at initial child protection conferences or the advance provision of written reports;
    – adequate provision of specialist nurses and doctors to provide services to looked after children.

Local Education Authorities should:

30. Monitor the efficiency of arrangements in maintained schools to safeguard children, including the effectiveness of child protection procedures and training.

12.33 These then are the recommendations and targets for change over the next 3 years to 2005. As identified above almost none are new, the major exception to this being the recognition in Recommendation 2 that government departments must support and facilitate national and local agencies to recruit and retain staff, paying particular regard to the image, status, morale, remuneration and working conditions of specialist child protection staff. Given the findings of Jones, many would argue that this is long overdue, but should we not be saying, as he certainly would, that this should apply across all services to all of the most vulnerable in our society and not just to those involved in child protection. To single out such staff, or the vulnerable whom they serve, is to create gradations of response to need, a criticism which the team itself makes of social workers prioritising as between children in need and children who are at risk of significant harm (see chapter 6 of the report). Other new demands which are of a more managerial type include 3, 4, 7, 10, 11, 12, 13. It remains to be seen whether over the next 3 years there is the sort of radical change which is required or whether no real change will be masked by the production of masses of management information directives on processes. Since so many of the recommendations have been in previous Chief Inspectors' reports as well as in Part 8 Reviews or major government inquiries, we will have to see if real, properly resourced change can and does occur.

The impact of new legislation

12.34 Several chapters of this book have been concerned with the impact of new legislation in relation to the child protection system. The demands of the new provisions of the criminal law and the HRA 1998, in particular, have already been noted, but increasing concern about the state of health, education, and life experience of children leaving care and the appalling catalogue of abuse revealed by the Waterhouse Enquiry, *Lost in Care* (DOH/Welsh Office, 2000) pointed up the necessity for the imposition of new statutory duties upon local authorities towards this most vulnerable group. In addition, the Prime Minister himself became concerned about the issue of children in local authority care and determined that placements should be found more quickly for children in the care of local authorities.

12.35 In terms of the improvement of the health, education and life experiences of children in care, the Children (Leaving Care) Act 2000 and the Care Standards Act 2000, which was implemented in April 2002 and has introduced National Minimum Standards for the provision of care for children in residential homes and substitute families, together with other government health initiatives for children in care (see Chapter 1) have meant that, increasingly, onerous duties are now placed on local authorities in an attempt to ensure that children leaving care should not be in so disadvantaged a position as was identified in earlier chapters of this book (see Chapters **1**, **2**, **3** and **4**).

12.36 It is hoped by central government that the Adoption and Children Act 2002, when implemented together with its own set of National Minimum Standards, will also improve the chances of children in care being placed for adoption with a wider range of families. Nevertheless, there should be concern about a system which imposes the notion of targets in such a delicate area as adoption of children, more particularly where it has been shown so often to be the case that even children adopted in their babyhood feel a need to get back in touch with their own birth families. (For further discussion of the issue of contact, especially as it might affect older children, see Chapter **10**.) Given the demands of the HRA 1998 that we should ensure the protection of each individual's right to private and family life, the government should be even more wary of the risks to children which might be engendered.

Quality Protects and other government initiatives

12.37 In addition to legislation, the important programme *Quality Protects* has undoubtedly raised the profile of the needs of all children whose lives may be touched by service provision from social services. However, the government has also introduced a whole range of other initiatives concerned with a preventive strategy being adopted towards children and their families. The initiative of *Sure Start*, designed to meet the needs of 0–4-year-olds, the *Children's Fund*, designed to meet the needs of children aged 5–13, and the *Connexions Service* designed to meet the needs of children aged 13–19 all focus on the importance of preventative strategy, as was identified particularly in Chapter **4**. *Sure Start* and the Early Years Development and Childcare Partnerships which have sprung up across local authorities in England and Wales all have as their focus the importance of a good start for children at a very early stage in their lives. The importance of early years education, not only in terms of the more traditional aspects of education but also in terms of preventative strategies and socialisation, are key critical aspects of this new initiative.

12.38 The *Children's Fund* which focuses on children aged 5–13 is a relatively recent initiative commenced in 2001 (see also Chapters **1** and **4**). Grants are made from the fund to partnerships based in particular areas in respect to plans put forward by the areas for ways in which a range of needs might be met. The two chief objectives of the *Children's Fund* are, first, to ensure that in each area there is an agreed programme of effective intervention that picks up early signs of difficulties, identifies needs and introduces children and young people and their families to appropriate services, and secondly to ensure that children and young people exhibiting early signs of difficulty receive appropriate services in order to gain maximum life-chance benefits from

Child Abuse

educational opportunities, health care and social care and to ensure good outcomes (see *Children's Fund Part 1 Guidance* (Children and Young People's Unit at the DOH, 2001, Annex D). In order to gain money from the *Children's Fund*, partnerships have to demonstrate that they have applied the two principal objectives identified above to the specific services they wish to develop in their area, and the seven *Children's Fund* sub-objectives should also have been addressed in their plans. These sub-objectives are:

- to promote attendance in schools attended by the majority of 5–13-year-olds living in the area;
- to achieve overall improved educational performance among children and young people aged 5–13;
- to ensure that fewer young people aged between 10 and 13 commit crime and fewer children aged between 5 and 13 are victims of crime;
- to reduce child health inequalities among those children and young people aged 5–13 who live within the area;
- to ensure that children, young people and their families and local people feel that the preventive services being developed through the partnerships are accessible;
- to develop services which are experienced as effective by individuals and clusters of children, young people and families commonly excluded from gaining the benefits of public services that are intended to support children and young people at risk of social exclusion from achieving their potential;
- to involve families in building the community's capacity to sustain the programme and thereby create pathways out of poverty.

12.39 The aims and objectives of the *Children's Fund* echo closely those already developed with the *Connexions Service* established for the 13–19 age group and which are beginning to evaluate the success of these strategies for the older age group. The emphasis on preventative work in all these initiatives is noteworthy. What should also now be focused upon is the necessity of ensuring that when these short-term funding arrangements cease, what is left is not a population of children and young people who feel abandoned, deskilled and demotivated by the whole experience. One of the key features of the *Children's Fund* and one of its most encouraging features is that of the identification of the need to build capacity within our children and young people so that they may rise above the problems that they may have to face both now and in the future.

United Nations Convention on the Rights of the Child and the UN Monitoring Committee on the Rights of the Child

The parental right of corporal punishment of children

12.40 As was discussed in Chapter **1**, the UK has submitted two reports to the United Nations Monitoring Committee on the Rights of the Child. The *Second Report*, together with a 106-page document (submitted 30 August, 2002) provided answers to questions raised by the UN Monitoring Committee (14 June 2002), and had just been discussed by the UN Monitoring Committee at the time of checking the proofs of this book (31st Session, CRC/C/15/Add.188, 4 October 2002); see www/unhchr/ch/reports). As it turned out, the main targets for criticism of the UK's record between 1995 and 1999 echo many of those made by the Committee previously in 1995. Many areas that might have been the subject of concern for the Committee were identified in Chapter **1** and, indeed, throughout this book where children's rights to protection are inadequately protected by the UK this has been demonstrated and suggestions made for possible improvement. The issue of the corporal punishment of children is one which still offends against the principal provisions of the UNCRC in relation to the protection of children. Thus, the decision by the government in England that no legislation would be taken forward in response to the European Court's decision in *A v UK* is quite incredible. Scotland, by contrast, had indicated (see the proposals of the Scottish Executive, 6 September 2001) that it would introduce legislation to ban the use of any implement in relation to corporal punishment of children, to ban hitting any child under the age of 3, and to ban the shaking of any child at any age (*Press Statement Scottish Executive*, 6 September 2001). By September 2002, however, the Scottish First Minister was going back on this undertaking indicating that he did not think that the proposals had the support of the majority of people in Scotland. Wales and Northern Ireland are still in the process of consultation, but in England reliance has to be placed instead on the decision of the Court of Appeal (Criminal Division) in the case of *R v Hills* (reported as *R v H* [2001] 2 FLR 431 and see Chapter **1** for a fuller discussion of this case.) What that case did was to provide that, at a minimum, the English courts must follow the guidance laid down in *A v UK*, but in discussions with parents and children's groups in the period which has elapsed since then, none of them had the slightest idea of the major change which this decision made in English law. Therefore, the position remains in England that parents receive little if any guidance on how they should bring up their children, nor on what is deemed to be acceptable behaviour within families. The fact that the UK has the highest record of domestic violence within Europe cannot be divorced from the experience of children in families within the UK of legitimisation of violence within the family setting embodied in the parental right physically to chastise children.

12.41 When the UN Monitoring Committee considered the *First Report of the United Kingdom*, it severely criticised our adherence to the notion that parents ought still to be allowed to hit children. It questioned how parents could come to realise when they were perpetrating 'significant harm' upon their children when by the law of this country we allow parents to hit children and leave it up to juries to determine whether such punishment is 'reasonable'. (As the result of the decision in *R v H* [2001] 2 FLR 431, juries in cases of assault where the defence of reasonable chastisement is raised, must now be directed to take sufficiently into account the age, sex and characteristics of the child being punished, the nature of the offence for which the child is being punished and the need to ensure that such punishment is not excessive.) Quite why any government cannot make the connection between the huge levels of domestic violence in this country and the legitimisation of violence within the family, embedded in the notion of the parental right physically to chastise children, can only be a matter of speculation. There could be no doubt, however, that the UN Monitoring Committee would criticise England, in particular, for adhering to this last vestige of the notion that children are the property of their parents, and indeed this is precisely what occurred (see *UN Monitoring Committee on the Rights of the Child – 31st Session – Concluding Observations of the Committee on the Rights of the Child* (CRC/C/15/Add.188, 4 October 2002) on the internet at *www.unhcrh.ch/reports*).

12.42 The UN Monitoring Committee expressed specific concern that legislation prohibiting all corporal punishment in all forms of day care, whilst in place in Wales, is not in place for England, Scotland and Northern Ireland. Referring back to the last occasion on which it issued recommendations on this issue back in 1995, the Committee stated that it deeply regretted that the UK persists in retaining the defence of reasonable chastisement and has taken no significant action towards prohibiting all corporal punishment of children in the family. It also stated that the Committee 'is of the opinion that governmental proposals to limit rather than to remove the reasonable chastisement defence do not comply with the principles and provisions of the Convention, particularly since they constitute a serious violation of the dignity of the child. Moreover, they suggest that some forms of corporal punishment are acceptable and therefore undermine educational measures to promote positive and non-violent discipline' (*Concluding Observations* no 35, at p 8). It is very apparent that the Committee is extremely disappointed that so little progress has been made in this area by the UK. Its reference to the governmental proposals limiting the defence are either a reference to the proposals of the Scottish Executive from September 2001 and the Committee does not seem to have been made aware that the Scots are now back-tracking on even these limited proposals, or given that there is no reference to the issue of the defence of reasonable chastisement in the list of further questions asked by the Committee on 14 June 2002 or in the 106-page document of answers provided by the UK on 30 August 2002, this may be a reference to the Consultation Paper, issued by the government in England in January 2000, to which it only published the public's responses finally in November 2001, and which has been matched by total silence on the subject from the government in England ever since. Reference was made to the plan to issue a Consultation Paper on the subject in the UK's original *Second Report* of August 1999, so perhaps the Committee were thinking instead of this. Neither, however, constitute anything approaching a government proposal to limit the defence, and the Committee rather surprisingly does not seem to have been referred to the decision in *R v H* [2001] 1 FLR 431 (discussed at length in Chapter 1) which has incorporated the guidelines laid down by the European Court in the full text of their judgment in *A v UK* [1998] 2 FLR 959. No proposals have, of course, been made for other areas of the UK. The Committee therefore recommended (at para 36) that the UK:

(a) adopt with urgency legislation throughout the State Party to remove the defence of reasonable chastisement and prohibit all corporal punishment in the family and in any other contexts not covered by existing legislation;

(b) promotes positive, participatory and non-violent forms of discipline and respect for children's equal right to human dignity and physical integrity, engaging with children and parents and all who work with and for them, and carry out public education programmes on the negative consequences of corporal punishment (see, for further discussion on this, Lyon (2000a)).

Other child protection concerns of the UN Monitoring Committee on the Rights of the Child

12.43 The UN Monitoring Committee made a number of other findings and expressed a number of concerns about a number of child protection issues identified throughout this book. Whilst the Committee noted a number of initiatives which have been taken for the greater protection of children in different settings, including Circular 10/95 *Protecting Children from Abuse – the Role of the Education Service* (see Chapter 6), the Committee was deeply concerned that between one and two children die every week as a result of violence and neglect in the home (see Chapters 1 and 2). It was also concerned at the high prevalence of violence, including sexual violence, throughout the UK against children within families, in schools, in institutions, in the care system and in detention. It also noted with deep concern growing levels of child neglect (see Chapters 2 and 6). The Committee was alarmed at the lack of coordinated strategy to reduce the rate of these phenomena. It particularly noted the absence of an adequate systematic follow up of child deaths and that crimes committed against children below the age of 16 years are not recorded. In the care system, the Committee noted a lack of consistent safeguards for children who are privately fostered. The Committee welcomed the steps taken by the government to support child witnesses in court (see

Chapter **9**), but noted the lack of public education on the role of the child protection system (see Chapters **1** (at paras **1.12–1.13**) and **2**). The Committee therefore recommended that the UK should:

(a) introduce a system of statutory child death inquiries;

(b) develop a coordinated strategy for the reduction of child deaths as a result of violence and the reduction of all forms of violence against children;

(c) ensure consistent legislative safeguards for all children in alternative care, including those who are privately fostered;

(d) carry out large-scale public education campaigns and programmes (including through schools) on reducing child death and child abuse with information on the role of statutory and other services in protecting children;

(e) establish effective procedures and mechanisms to receive, monitor, investigate and prosecute instances of abuses, ill-treatment and neglect, ensuring the abused child is not victimised in legal proceedings and that his privacy is protected;

(f) record in the British Crime Survey all crimes committed against children;

(g) provide for the care, recovery and integration for victims; and

(h) strengthen the reporting system, through full support of the confidential centres for abused children, and train teachers, law enforcement officials, care workers, judges and health professionals in the identification, reporting and management of cases of ill-treatment.

The protection of children from abuse in the criminal justice system

12.44 The UN Monitoring Committee remained extremely concerned at a number of abuses being perpetrated within the juvenile justice system upon children and young people. The Committee was strongly of the view, which it had also expressed in 1995, that:

(a) the ages in the UK of criminal responsibility remain far too low, especially in Scotland where the age of criminal responsibility is 8;

(b) that we incarcerate far too many children and young people;

(c) that children and young people should never be tried or accommodated together with adults (see Chapter **9**);

(d) that children under 18 involved in proceedings in which anti-social behaviour orders had been made were having their privacy breached by processes such as naming and shaming in the media on the making of such orders;

(e) that children accommodated in penal settings, including those in secure units, lack access to appropriate and effective advocacy services and complaints procedures (see Chapter **11**).

As a result of those concerns the Committee recommended that the UK should:

(a) raise considerably the age for criminal responsibility;

(b) review the new orders introduced by the Crime and Disorder Act 1998 and make them compatible with the principles and provisions of the Convention;

(c) ensure that no child can be tried with an adult irrespective of the circumstances or the gravity of his/her offence;

(d) ensure that the privacy of all children in conflict with the law is protected fully;

(e) ensure that the detention of children is used as a measure of last resort and for the shortest period of time and that children are separated from adults in detention, and encourage the use of alternative measures to the deprivation of liberty;

(f) ensure that every child deprived of liberty has access to independent advocacy services and an independent, child-sensitive and accessible complaint procedure;

(g) take all necessary measures, as a matter of urgency, to review the conditions of detention and ensure that all children deprived of their liberty have an equal statutory right to education, health *and child protection* as other children;

(h) review the status of young people of 17 years of age for the purpose of remand with a view to giving special protection to all children under the age of 18 years;

(i) allocate appropriate resources to Children's Hearings in Scotland to substantively increase disposals to allow young offenders of 16–18 years of age to be included within the Children's Hearings system (Recommendations, para 58, pp 15–16).

Access to an effective Children's Rights Commissioner

12.45 The UN Monitoring Committee also welcomed the establishment of an independent Children's Commissioner in Wales but, as was highlighted in Chapter **11**, the Committee too was concerned at the limited powers of this Commissioner, in particular, in relation to non-devolved matters. The Committee welcomed the plans for the establishment of an independent human rights institution for children in Northern Ireland and in Scotland. The Committee was, however, deeply concerned that there were no plans for an independent human rights institution (as was the author of this book (see Chapter **11**)) for children in England. The Committee was clearly singularly unimpressed with the establishment of the office of the Children's Rights Director for England and his even more limited powers as provided for in the CSA 2000 (para 16).

Participation of children and young people in the framing of policies directly affecting them

12.46 The UN Monitoring Committee welcomed the increasing encouragement of participation of and consultation with children in government, local authorities and civil society through the establishment of Youth Advisory fora in the Children and Young People's Unit together with other platforms for children and young people, such as the Scottish Youth Parliament. Concerns were expressed that there had been no consistent incorporation, however, of the obligations of Art 12 in legislation, for example in private law procedures involving divorce, in adoption, in education and in protection throughout the UK. The Committee was also concerned that, in education, school children were not systematically consulted on matters that affect them. The Committee recommended that the UK take further steps to promote and monitor systematic and effective participation of all groups of children in society, including in schools. The Committee also recommended changes to ensure that a child capable of forming his/her own views has the right to express those views and that they are given due weight in courts and administrative proceedings. The Committee further recommended that procedures be formed to acknowledge publicly the views expressed by children and the impact they have on developing programmes and policies and reflect how they were taken into consideration.

The incorporation of the UNCRC into UK law in order to better protect our children

12.47 Whilst commending the incorporation of the ECHR into domestic law through the HRA 1998, the UN Monitoring Committee on the Rights of the Child encouraged the UK to incorporate into domestic law the rights, principles and provisions of the UNCRC to ensure compliance of all legislation with the Convention, a more widespread application of the provisions and principles in legal and administrative proceedings, and better dissemination and training on the Convention. This, it argued incontrovertibly, would lead to the better protection of all our children (para 9).

12.48 It was also of concern to the UN Monitoring Committee on the Rights of the Child that the UK has, over the years, had a succession of public enquiries into the abuse of children in the care of the State. The catalogue of enquiries over the period since the last edition of this book has been highlighted in Chapter **3** as well as discussed in other chapters (see Chapters **2**, **4**, **5** and **6**). It is to be hoped, with the introduction of the CSA 2000 and a far more rigorous system of training and qualification of social care workers as urged in *Safeguarding Children* (DOH/SSI 2002) and of the inspection and registration by an independent body of homes provided for children, that abuse on such a scale will never again be seen. Equally, careful consideration needs to be given to the training and qualifications of staff as well as to the position of children in secure accommodation and other penal settings in the light of findings by the Chief Inspectors of Prisons, the evidence provided by writers such as Goldson and the concerns of the UN Monitoring Committee (see Chapters **1**, **4** and **10**). However, as has been identified in this book, abuse does not only occur in institutional settings and thus we have to adopt the same rigorous standards with regard to the recruitment of foster parents and the approval of adoption placements for children, more particularly if such placement is to be subject to the sort of management targets more commonly the feature of the factory workplace.

12.49 In government circles, most particularly through the work of the CYPU, it is now fashionable to talk about hearing the voices of children and young people (see further on this, Chapters **1** and **4**). It is particularly important that those children and young people who enter the care system as a result of well-meaning protective measures should themselves also feel that they have been listened to and heard. Some older children and young people, although by no means all, do indicate that they would not wish to be placed in substitute families but would prefer instead the opportunity to live in a setting in which they are protected but, nevertheless, in which they can freely associate with their own families. Their view is that they have a family and do not need another one, nor is a family setting necessarily always the best for children and young people for whom families have been a disaster and a totally abusive experience. The massive closure of children's homes throughout England and Wales may yet prove to be a very dubious step in the advancement of children's welfare. The mixed approach of the past may be lamented. The government's report to the UN Monitoring Committee also focused on major improvements to children and young people's lives particularly in the educational setting, and the UN Monitoring Committee recognised in 2002 that there had been improvements in this area (see *Concluding Observations*, at para 37). Considerable advances have been made in the field of anti-bullying policies within schools and children's settings and thus one aspect of child protection, that of bullying in school, which was identified by the National Commission of Enquiry into Child Abuse and Neglect back in 1996 as being a major source of concern for all children and young people, has immeasurably improved. The prevalence of endemic bullying within the penal settings accommodating children remains, however, a cause for deep concern (see Goldson (2002), at pp 143–148). As Her Majesty's Chief Inspector of Prisons has commented:

'Children are made worse by the experience of imprisonment and the bullying and harassment they inflict on each other ... The emphasis on Child Protection procedures should not be so much on children being molested by staff, although this must, of course, be guarded against, but on protecting them from bullying and intimidation by their peers when staff are not present. The worst examples of this are reflected in establishments where verbal intimidation is practised by shouting from cells, and physical bullying takes place in unsupervised places such as showers and recesses on landings. It is essential that all parts of establishments holding children and young adults are made safe, so that the ravages of bullying and intimidation cannot be wrought' (*Report of Her Majesty's Chief Inspector of Prisons December 1999–2000* (Home Office, 2001), at p 9).

It remains to be seen whether the concerns expressed and the recommendations made in *Safeguarding Children* (DOH/SSI, 14 October 2002) together with the decision in R *(on the application of the Howard League for Penal Reform) v The Secretary of State for the Home Department* (29 November 2002) will lead to a real improvement in the welfare of children and young people in our secure and penal institutions and to their greater protection.

12.50 The depressing statistics on levels of violence within the family within England and Wales must, however, be a continuing cause for concern. Here, again, the UK government was subject to considerable censure by the UN Monitoring Committee.

The introduction of CAFCASS

12.51 The introduction of CAFCASS in April 2001 can now be seen with hindsight as having been both badly planned and badly executed. This service, which very importantly supplies the personnel who should safeguard the position of children in legal proceedings being taken to protect them under the CA 1989, has still not at the time of writing been able to deliver the service which had been anticipated. The amalgamation into one service of the former guardians ad litem, court welfare officers, and personnel from the Official Solicitor's office should have meant a vastly improved, better co-ordinated and better targeted service provision. Instead, as one High Court Family Division judge has put it, the introduction of CAFCASS was under-resourced and, in consequence, some 10 months after its institution is still in disarray. What was a 'Rolls Royce' system for children is no longer that (see the comments of Sir Nicholas Wall in *The Times*, 19 March 2002). The judge in his article comments that when asked for an urgent report he is told that it cannot be provided and that if he asks that a child be urgently seen, again, this cannot be done. To have taken such a step as to write such an article in *The Times* clearly reveals that Sir Nicholas Wall, in common with many other Family Division judges, is in despair at the collapse of a service intended to protect and safeguard the paramountcy of the welfare of children caught up in the child protection system.

12.52 It is to be hoped that by the time practitioners are reading this work the service provided by CAFCASS will have improved dramatically, for the sake of the children. If it has not, then the government again has to ask itself whether it has demanded a new service intended to cut costs and has thereby put at risk the future lives of children whose interests the system is supposed to protect.

Conclusion

12.53 As the author hopes she and her collaborators have identified throughout the course of this book, the law now contains a much wider range of powers and responsibilities providing for the protection of children and for the investigation of situations in which children may be said to be at risk than was previously the case. The CA 1989 is about to enter its adolescent phase. We all of us know through our own experiences and those of our own adolescent children that this is a particularly difficult age for children and young people, usually made the more so by adults who appear to have totally forgotten their own adolescence. The next few years may well prove to be a very challenging and testing period for the operation not only of the CA 1989, but also of the Children (Leaving Care) Act 2000, the CSA 2000, and the Adoption and Children Act 2002, as well as many of the new and recent provisions of the criminal law such as the SOA 1997, the CDA 1998, the PCA 1999, and the CJCSA 2000, in terms of improving child protection within our society. In addition to, and in support of, the legislation there have been a whole series of policy initiatives which have been examined in detail throughout this book. The responses of the judiciary, the lawyers, all of those who work within the child protection system and, most of all, the government will be key to identifying whether we have produced a programme of policies and legislation which truly promote the protection of all our children. As the Laming Report of the Inquiry into the death of Victoria Climbie (28 January 2003, accessible at *www.victoria-climbie-inquiry.org.uk*) has demonstrated yet again, there still remains huge scope for improvement in the field of child protection, but we must recognise that the law is only one part of the framework which is needed to channel the energies and commitment of all those who are concerned with the protection of children from abuse. Were the aims set by the legislators of the CA 1989, and succeeding pieces of legislation in both the civil and criminal fields, and all the different policy initiatives to be pursued to their logical conclusion, using to their fullest extent and properly resourced, all the various powers and duties set out therein, we would be much further down the road to eradicating child abuse altogether. The fact that 11 years on from implementation of the CA 1989 we have still to fulfil most of the aims of that Act, let alone later ones, with regard to the protection of our children means that so much more remains to be done as we move on through the new millennium.

12.54 As United Nations Secretary-General Kofi Annan has put it in answer to the question of 'why make a special case for children?':

'To look into some aspects of the future, we do not need projections by supercomputers. Much of the next millennium can be seen in how we care for our children today. Tomorrow's world may be influenced by science and technology, but more than anything it is already taking shape in the bodies and minds of our children.'

So how much do we care for our children in the UK today?

BIBLIOGRAPHY

Adcock, M and White, R (eds) (1998) *Significant Harm: Its Management and Outcome* (Significant Publications, 2nd edn).

Aldgate, J and Tunstill, J (1996) *Making Sense of Section 17* (HMSO).

Araji, S and Finkelhor, D (1986) 'Abusers: A Review of the Research' in Finkelhor, D et al *A Sourcebook on Child Sexual Abuse* (Sage).

Aries, P (1962) *Centuries of Childhood* (Penguin).

Arora, CMT and Thompson, DA (1987) 'Defining Bullying for a Secondary School' 4(3) *Education and Child Psychology* 110–120.

Asher, R (1951) 'Munchausen Syndrome' 1 *Lancet* 339–341.

Balding, J (1998) *Young People in 1977: The Health-Related Behaviour Questionnaire Results for 37,538 Pupils Between the Ages of 9 and 16* (Schools Health Education Unit).

Beaumont, B (1999) 'Risk Assessment and Prediction Research' in P Parsloe (ed) *Risk Assessment in Social Care and Social Work* (Aldgate).

Bell, M (2002) 'Case Conferences in Child Protection' in K Wilson and A James (eds) *The Child Protection Handbook* (Balliere Tindall, 2nd edn).

Besag, VE (1989) *Bullies and Victims in Schools* (OUP).

Bevan, L and Lidstone, K (1985) *A Guide to the Police and Criminal Evidence Act 1984* (Butterworths).

Bifulco, A and Moran, A (1998) *Wednesday's Child: Research into Women's Experience of Neglect and Abuse in Childhood, and Adult Depression* (Routledge).

Bluglass, K (1997) 'Munchausen Syndrome by Proxy' in EV Welldon and C Van Velson (eds) *A Practical Guide to Forensic Psychotherapy* (Jessica Kingsley Publishers).

BMA (2001) *Consent Rights and Choices in Health Care for Children and Young People* (BMJ Books).

Bools (1996) *Factitious Illness by Proxy*.

Bowlby, J (1951) *Maternal Care and Mental Health*, World Health Organization Monograph (Serial No 2) (WHO).

Bracewell, Hon Mrs Justice, 'Best Practice Guidance June 1997' (Jordans), Part IV.

Brassard, MR, Germain, R and Hart, SN (eds) (1987) *Psychological Maltreatment of Children and Youth* (Pergamon).

Brasse (1996) 'The Duty of Disclosure in Children's Cases' [1996] *Fam Law* 358.

Bridge Child Care Consultancy Service (1991) *Sukina: An Evaluation Report of the Circumstances Leading to her Death*.

Bridge Child Care Consultancy Service (1995) *Paul – Death Through Neglect*.

Broad, B (ed) (2001) *Kinship Care* (Russell House Publishing).

Browne, K (2002) 'Child Abuse: Defining, Understanding and Intervening' in K Wilson and A James (eds) *The Child Protection Handbook* (Balliere Tindall).

Bullock, R (1988) 'Secure Provision Ten Years On' in *Secure Units: The Way Ahead* (Orchard Lodge Regional Resource Centre).

Burden, T, Cooper, C, Petrie, S (2000) *Modernising Social Policy: Unravelling New Labour's Welfare Reforms* (Ashgate).

Burrows, D (1996) 'Disclosure on Children's Cases' [1996] Fam Law 566.

Burrows, D (1999) *Evidence in Family Proceedings* (Family Law).

Butler, I (2002) 'Abuse in Institutional Settings' in K Wilson and A James (eds) *The Child Protection Handbook* (Balliere Tindall, 2nd edn).

Caffey, D and Silverman, R (1953) 'The Roentgen Manifestations of Unrecognised Skeletal Trauma in Infants' 69 *American Journal of Roentgenology, Radiumtherapy, Nuclear Medicine* 413.

Calder, M 'Young People who Sexually Abuse: Towards an International Consensus' 4(1) *Social Work in Europe*.

Campbell, B (1988) *Unofficial Secrets: Child Sexual Abuse – The Cleveland Case* (Virago).

Card, R and Ward, R (1996) *The Criminal Procedure and Investigations Act 1996* (Jordans).

Central Statistical Office (1994) *Social Focus on Children* (HMSO).

Children's Society (1999) *One Way Street*.

Children's Society (2002) *Vulnerable Inside – Children in Secure and Penal Settings*.

Christenson, E (1996) *Definition, Measuring and Prevalence of Child Neglect: A Study of Children aged 0–1 year* (Danish National Institute of Social Research).

Clausen, AH and Crittenden, PM (1991) 'Physical and Psychological Maltreatment: Relations among Types of Maltreatment' 15 *Child Abuse and Neglect* Nos 1/2.

Cleaver, H, Wattam, C and Cawson, P (1998) *Assessing Risk in Child Protection* (NSPCC).

Cobley, C (1991) 'Child Victims of Sexual Abuse and the Criminal Justice System in England and Wales' 5 *Journal of Social Welfare and Family Law* 362.

Cobley, C (1998) 'Financial Compensation for Victims of Child Abuse' 20(3) *Journal of Social Welfare and Family Law* 221.

Cobley, C (2000) *Sex Offenders: Law, Policy and Practice* (Jordans).

Corby, B (2000) *Child Abuse: Towards a Knowledge Base* (OUP, 2nd edn).

Corby, B, Doig, A and Roberts, V (1998) 'Inquiries into Child Abuse' 20 *Journal of Social Welfare and Family Law* 377–396.

Corby, B, Doig, A and Roberts, V (2001) *Public Inquiries into Abuse of Children in Residential Care* (Jessica Kingsley Publishers).

Craig, G, Elliott-White, M, Kelsey, S and Petrie, S (1999) *An Audit of Children's Needs* (Policy Studies Research Centre, ULH).

CRDU (Children's Rights Development Unit) (1994) *UK Agenda for Children*.

Creighton, S and Russell, N (1995) *Voices from Childhood: A Survey of Childhood Experiences and Attitudes to Child Rearing Among Adults in the UK* (NSPCC).

Crosse, SB, Kaye, E and Ratnofsky, AC (1993) *A Report on the Maltreatment of Children with Disabilities* (National Centre on Child Abuse and Neglect, Washington).

Dale, P et al (1986) *Dangerous Families* (Tavistock).

David, M and Appell, G (2001) *Loczy. An Unusual Approach to Mothering* (Association Pikler-Loczy for Young Children).

David, TJ (2001) 'Munchausen Syndrome by Proxy' Fam Law 445.

Dawkins, J (1995) 'Bullying in Schools: Doctors' Responsibilities' 310 *British Medical Journal* 274–275.

Dawkins, J and Hill, P (1995) 'Bullying: Another Form of Abuse' in TJ David (ed) *Recent Advances in Paediatrics* (Livingstone).

Deardon, C and Becker, S (2000) *Growing Up Caring: Vulnerability and Transition to Adulthood – Young Carers' Experiences* (Youth Work Press).

Dingwall et al (1983) *Protecting Children, Controlling Parents: State Intervention in Family Law* (Blackwell).

Dixon, J (2001) 'Children and the Statutory Restraints on Publicity' *Fam Law* 757.

Dominelli, L (1997) *Sociology for Social Work* (Macmillan).

Doyle, C (1997) 'Emotional Abuse of Children: Issues for Intervention' 6(5) *Child Abuse Review*.

Eminson, M and Postlewaite, RJ (eds) (2000) *Munchausen Syndrome by Proxy: A Practical Approach* (Arnold).

Fahlberg, MD (1994) *A Child's Journey through Placement* (British Association for Adoption and Fostering (BAFF)).

Family Law Service *The Human Rights Act (1998) – A Special Bulletin for Family Lawyers* (Butterworths).

Farmer, E and Bushel, M (1999) 'Child Protection Policy and Practice: Woman in the Front Line' in S Watson and L Doyal (eds) *Engendering Social Policy* (OUP).

Farmer and Pollock (1998) *Sexually Abused and Abusing Children in Substitute Care* (Wiley).

Finkelhor, D et al (1986) *A Sourcebook on Child Sexual Abuse* (Sage).

Fitzgerald, J (2000) 'Lessons from the Past – Experiences of Inquiries and Reviews' in *Out of Sight. Report on Child Deaths from Abuse 1973 to 2000* (NSPCC).

Flynn, N and Hurley, D (1993) *The Market For Care* (London School of Economics and Political Science).

Ford, R and Millar, J (1997) *Private Lives and Public Responses: Lone Parenthood and Future Policy* Foundations 4 (Joseph Rowntree Foundation) (www.jrf.org.uk/knowledge/findings/foundations/4.asp.

Freeman, R (1999) 'Recursive Politics: Prevention, Modernity and Social Systems' 13 *Children and Society* 232–241.

Freeman, M (2001) *Child Abuse: the Search for a Solution in Overcoming Child Abuse: a Window on a World Problem* (Ashgate).

Freeman, MDA (1992) *Children, their Families and the Law* (Macmillan).

Frosh, S (2002) 'Characteristics of Sexual Abusers' in K Wilson and A James (eds), *The Child Protection Handbook* (Balliere Tindall).

Furniss, T (1991) *The Multi-professional Handbook of Child Sexual Abuse: Integrated Management, Therapy and Legal Intervention* (Routledge).

Garbarina, C, Guttman, JW and Seeley, JW (1986) *Psychologically Battered Child: Strategies for Identification, Assessment and Intervention* (Jossey-Bass).

Ghate, D and Daniels, A (1997) *Talking About my Generation* (NSPCC).

Gibbons, J, Conroy, S and Bell, C (1995) *Operating the Child Protection System: A Study of Child Protection Practices in English Local Authorities* (HMSO).

Gil, DG (1970) *Violence Against Children* (Harvard University Press).

Gil, DG (1975) 'Unravelling Child Abuse' *American Journal of Orthopsychiatry* 346–354.

Gilbert, P (1995) 'Male Violence: Towards an Integration' in J Archer, *Male Violence* (Routledge).

Gillespie, R (1998) 'Victims and Sentencing' *NLJ* 1263.

Gilmour, A (1988) *Innocent Victims: Questions of Child Abuse* (Michael Joseph).

Glass, N (1999) 'Sure Start: The Development of an Early Intervention Programme for Young Children in the United Kingdom' 13 *Children and Society* 257–264.

Gordon, Parker and Loughram (1992) *Children with Disabilities in Communal Establishments: A Further Analysis of the OPCS Investigations* (University of Bristol).

Gordon, Parker and Loughram (1996) *Children with Disabilities in Private Households: a Reanalysis of the OPCS Investigation* (University of Bristol).

Goldson, B (1999) *Youth Justice: Contemporary Policy and Practice* (Ashgate).

Goldson, B (2002) *Vulnerable Inside – Children in Secure and Penal Settings* (Children's Society).

Gordon et al, (1999) *Introduction to Youth Justice* (Waterside Press).

Gray, C et al (1995) *Illness Induction Syndrome*.

Gregg, P, Harkness, S and Machin, S (2000) *Child Development and Family Income* (JRT/YPS).

Growney, T (1998) *Sometimes You've Got to Shout to be Heard: Stories from Young People in Care about Getting Heard, using Advocates and making Complaints* (Voice for the Child in Care).

Gutch, R (1992) *Contracting Lessons from the US* (NCVO).

Hanks, H and Stratton, P (2002) 'Consequences and Indicators of Child Abuse' in K Wilson and A James (eds), *The Child Protection Handbook* (Balliere Tindall, 2nd edn).

Hardiker, P (1994) 'Thinking and Practising Otherwise: Disability and Child Abuse' 9(2) *Disability and Society* 257–264.

Harding, T (1992) *Great Expectations and Spending on Social Services* (NISW).

Harris, D and Timms, N (1993) 'Between Hospital and Prison – Or Thereabouts, Secure Accommodation in the Child Care System', in J Timms *Children's Representation* (Sweet & Maxwell).

Harris-Hendricks, J and Newman, M (1998) *Key Messages from the Research Literature* in R Dent (ed) (The Bridge Child Development Service).

Haugaard, J and Reppucci, N (1988) *The Sexual Abuse of Children: A Comprehensive Guide to Current Knowledge and Intervention Strategies* (Jossey-Bass).

Head, A (2002) 'The Work of the *Guardian ad Litem*' in K Wilson and A James *The Child Protection Handbook* (Bailliere Tindall, 2nd edn).

Hedley, R and Davis Smith, J (1994) *Volunteers and the Contract Culture* (Volunteer Centre, UK).

Hershman, D and McFarlane, A *Children Law and Practice* (Family Law), looseleaf, at para C1171.

Hester, M and Pearson, C (1999) *From Periphery to Centre: Domestic Violence in Work with Abused Children* (The Policy Press).

Hoggett, B, Pearl, D, Cooke, E, Bates (1996) *The Family, Law and Society* (Butterworths)

Holman, J 'Allowing Children into Court' in *Representing Children* vol 12, at p 336.

Howe, D, Brandon, M, Hinings, D and Schofield, G (1999) *Attachment Theory, Child Maltreatment and Family Support: A Practice and Assessment Model* (Macmillan).

Hunt et al (1999) *The Last Resort: Child Protection, the Courts and the Children Act 1989* (The Stationery Office).

Iwaniec, D (1997) 'An Overview of Emotional Maltreatment and Failure to Thrive' 6(5) *Child Abuse Review* 370–388.

James, LJ and Wilson, K (1986) *Couples, Conflict and Change* (Tavistock Publications).

Jones, C and Novak, T (1999) *Poverty, Welfare and the Disciplinary State* (Routledge).

Jones, C (2001) 'Voices from the Front Line: State Social Workers and New Labour' 31 *British Journal of Social Work* 547–562.

Jones, D and Ramchandanai, P (1999) *Child Sexual Abuse – Informing Practice from Research* (Radcliffe Medical Press).

Katz, A (1999) *Leading Lads* (Young Voices).

Kempe, RS and Kempe, H (1978) *Child Abuse, the Developing Child* (Fontana).

Kempe, RS and Kempe, H (1984) *The Common Secret: Sexually Abused Children and Adolescents* (WH Freeman).

Kempe, Silverman, Steele, Drogemuller and Silver (1962) 'The Battered Child Syndrome' *Journal of American Medical Association*.

Kennedy, M 'The Abuse of Deaf Children' 3(1) *Child Abuse Review* 3–7.

King, P and Young, I (1992) *The Child as Client: A Handbook for Solicitors who Represent Children* (Family Law).

Kingham (1991) 'Medical Confidentiality' *Fam Law* 506.

Kirkwood Report, The (1993) (Leicestershire Social Services).

Kumpulainen, K, Rasanen R and Henttonen, I (1999) 'Children Involved in Bullying: Psychological Disturbance and the Persistence of the Involvement' 23 *Child Abuse and Neglect*.

Lamb, S and Coakley, M (1993) 'Normal Childhood Sexual Playground Games – Differentiating Play from Abuse' *Child Abuse and Neglect*, pp 515–526.

Lane, M and Walsh, T (2002) 'Court Proceedings and Courtcraft' in A James and K Wilson (eds) *The Child Protection Handbook* (Bailliere Tindall).

Langan, M (1995) 'Who Cares? Women in the Mixed Economy of Care' in M Langan and L Day (eds) *Women, Oppression and Social Work: Issues in Anti-Discriminatory Practice* (Routledge).

Lau, A (1998) 'Cultural and Ethnic Perspectives on Significant Harm, its Assessment and Treatment' in M Adcock and R White (eds) *Significant Harm* (Significant Publications, 2nd edn.

Leach, P (1999) *The Physical Punishment of Children: Some Input from Recent Research* (NSPCC).

Lee, M and O'Brien, R (1995) *The Game's Up – Redefining Child Prostitution*.

Le Grand, J (1990) *Quasi-Markets and Social Policy* (SAUS).

Lyon, CM (1994) *Legal Issues Arising from the Care and Control of Children with Severe Learning Disabilities and Severely Challenging Behaviour* (Mental Health Foundation).

Lyon, CM (1997) 'Children Abused within the Care System: Do Current Representation Procedures Offer the Child Protection and the Family Support?', in N Parton ed, *Child Protection and Family Support* (Routledge).

Lyon, CM (2000a) *Loving Smack – Lawful Assault – A Contradiction in Human Rights and Law* (IPPR).

Lyon, CM (2000b) 'Children's Participation in Proceedings with Particular Emphasis on the Question of Meetings between the Judge and the Child in Family Proceedings' in *No Fault or Flaw* (Family Law).

Mackay, R (1993) 'The Consequences of Killing Very Young Children' *Criminal Law Review* 21.

Maclure RJ, Davis PM, Meadow SR and Sibert JR (1996) 'Epidemiology of Munchausen Syndrome by proxy: non-accidental poisoning and non-accidental suffocation', 75 *Archives of Diseases in Childhood* 57–61.

Manocha, K and Mezey, G (1998) 'British Adolescents who Sexually Abuse: A Descriptive Study' 9 *Journal of Forensic Psychiatry* 588–608.

Marsh, P and Crow, G (1998) *Family Group Conferences in Child Welfare* (Blackwell).

Masson, J (2002) 'Police Protection – Protecting Whom?' *JSWFL* 157–173.

McKewan J (1988) 'Child Evidence: More Proposals for Reform' *Criminal Law Review* 813.

Meadow, R (1997) 'Munchausen Syndrome by Proxy: the Hinterland of Child Abuse' 2 *Lancet* 343–345.

Meadow, R (1984) 'Factitious Epilepsy' 2 *Lancet* 25–28.

Meadow, R (1992) 'Factitious Kidney Disease' in CM Edelmann et al (eds), *Paediatric Kidney Disease* (Little, Brown and Co).

Meadow, R (1993) 'False Allegations of Abuse and Munchausen Syndrome by Proxy' 68 *Archives of Disease in Childhood* 444–447.

Meadow, R (1999) 'Meetings of Expert Witnesses' *Fam Law* 29.

Melton, GB et al (1996) 'Empirical Research on Child Mal-treatment and the Law' *Journal of Child Psychology*.

Mitchell, J (2000) 'Family Law and the Single Joint Expert' [2000] *Fam Law* 815.

Mitchell, J (2001a) 'Whatever Happened to Wardship': Part 1, [2001] *Fam Law* 130.

Mitchell, J (2001b) 'Whatever Happened to Wardship': Part 2, [2001] *Fam Law* 212.

Morrison, T (1991a) 'Change, Control and the Legal Framework' in M Adcock, R White and R Hollows (eds) *Significant Harm* (Significant Publications).

Morrison, T (1991b) 'Partnership, Collaboration and Change under the Children Act' also in *Significant Harm: Its Management and Outcome* (Significant Publications).

Newell, P (2001) *Children's Rights to Life: UK Obligations under Human Rights Standards in Out of Sight: NSPCC Report on Child Deaths from Abuse (1973–2000)* (NSPCC).

Newman, J (1989) *Young Runaways: Findings from Britain's First Safe House* (Children's Society).

Newman, J and Clarke, J (1995) 'Going About Our Business? The Managerialization of Public Services' in J Clarke, A Cochrane and E McLaughlin (eds) *Managing Social Policy* (Sage).

Newson, J and Newson, E (1970) *Four Years Old in an Urban Community* (Pelican).

Novak, T, Owen, S, Petrie, S and Sennett, H (1997) *Children's Day Care and Welfare Markets – Research Study Funded by NHS Executive (Northern and Yorkshire)* (University of Lincolnshire and Humberside).

NSPCC (1997) *A Case for Balance – Demonstrating Good Practice when Children are Witnesses – a Video aimed at Judges and Lawyers.*

NSPCC (1998) *Vision for Children Pack, the Child Friendly Communities Programme.*

NSPCC (2000) *Child Maltreatment in the United Kingdom – A Study of the Prevalence of Child Abuse and Neglect.*

NSPCC (2001a) *Out of Sight NSPCC Report on Child Deaths from Abuse 1973 to 2000* (NSPCC, 2nd edn).

NSPCC (2001b) *Reporting Child Deaths: the Role of the Media.*

Oakley, W (1999) 'Official Friends and Friendly Officials: Independent Visitor Services for Looked After Children' 159 *Childright* 16.

Owers, M, Brandon, M and Black, J (1999) *Learning How to Make Children Safer: An Analysis for the Welsh Office of Serious Child Abuse Cases in Wales*, University of East Anglia/Welsh Office.

Parton, N (1991) *Governing the Family* (Macmillan).

Parton, N (ed) (1997) *Child Protection and Family Support: Tensions, Contradictions and Possibilities* (Routledge).

Parton, N (2002) 'Protecting Children: A Socio-Historical Analysis' in K Wilson and A James (eds) *The Child Protection Handbook* (Balliere Tindall, 2nd edn).

Parton, N, Thorpe, D and Wattan, C (1997) *Child Protection – Risk and the Moral Order* (Macmillan).

Pears, D (1999) 'Confidentiality and the Celebrity Client' [1999] *Fam Law* 779.

Petrie, S (1995) *Day Care Regulation and Support: Local Authorities and Day Care under the Children Act 1989* (Save the Children).

Petrie, S and Corby, B (2002) 'Partnership with Parents' in K Wilson and A James (eds), *The Child Protection Handbook* (Balliere Tindall, 2nd edn).

Petrie, S and James, A (1995) 'Partnership with Parents' in K Wilson and A James (eds), *The Child Protection Handbook* (Balliere Tindall, 1st edn).

Petrie, S and Wilson, K (1999) 'Towards the Disintegration of Child Welfare Services' 33(2) *Social Policy and Administration* 181–196.

Philimore, S (2001) '*Re B* – Disclosure After the Human Rights Act 1998', [2001] *Fam Law* 905.

Pratt, A (1997) 'Universalism or Selectivism? The Provision of Services in the Modern Welfare State' in M Lavalette and A Pratt, *Social Policy: A Conceptual and Theoretical Introduction* (Sage).

Reder, P and Duncan, S (1999) *Lost Innocence: A Follow up Study of Fatal Child Abuse* (Routledge).

Rodger, B and Pryor, J (1998) *Divorce and Separation: the Outcomes for Children* (Joseph Rowntree Foundation).

Rogers, D et al, (1976) 'Non-accidental Poisoning: An Extended Syndrome of Child Abuse' 1 *British Medical Journal* 793–796).

Rouse, S (2002) 'Protecting Children: The Role of the Health Visitor' in K Wilson and A James (eds), *The Child Protection Handbook* (Balliere Tindall, 2nd edn).

Russell, P (1996) 'Children with Disabilities and Special Needs: Current Issues and Concerns for Child Protection Procedures' in D Platt and D Shemmings (eds) *Making Enquiries into Alleged Child Abuse and Neglect – A Partnership with Families* (Wiley).

Ryder, E QC (2000) 'Lost and Found: Looking to the Future after North Wales' *Fam Law* 406.

Sas, LD, Wolfe, DA and Gowdey, K (1996) 'Children and Courts in Canada' in BL Bottoms and GS Goodman (eds) *International Perspectives on Child Abuse and Children's Testimony* (Sage).

Schorr, (1992) A *Social Services: An Outsider's View* (Joseph Rowntree Foundation).

Sidebotham, P (2001) 'An Ecological Approach to Child Abuse: A Creative Use of Scientific Models in Research and Practice' 10 *Child Abuse Review* 97–112.

Smart, C (1997) 'Wishful Thinking and Harmful Tinkering? Sociological Reflections on Family Policy' in 26(3) *Journal of Social Policy*.

Smith, G (1996) 'Reassessing Protectiveness' in D Batty and D Cullen (eds), *Child Protection: The Therapeutic Option* (British Agencies for Adoption and Fostering).

Smith, M and Grocke, M (1995) *Normal Family Sexuality and Sexual Knowledge in Children* (London Royal College of Psychology/Gorkill Press).

Smith, V (1999) 'Passing on Child Abuse Findings' [1999] *Fam Law* 249.

Smith, V (2000) 'Disclosing Child Abuse Suspicions – A Public Authority Dilemma' [2000] *Fam Law* 910.

Somerset, C (2001) *What the Professionals Know: The Trafficking of Children Into, and Through, the UK for Sexual Purposes* (ECPAT, UK).

Song, M and Edwards, R (1997) 'Comment: Raising Questions about Perspectives on Black Lone Motherhood' 26 *Journal of Social Policy*.

Spon-Smith, R (2000) *Family Practice and Judicial Review* (Family Law).

Stace, S and Tunstill, J (1990) *On Different Tracks: Inconsistencies between the Children Act and the Community Care Act* (VOPSS).

Statham, J (1994) *Child Care in the Community* (Save the Children).

Statham, J, Dillon, J and Moss, P (2001) *Placed and Paid For: Supporting Families through Sponsored Day Care* (The Stationery Office).

Stevenson, O (1988) *Neglected Children: Issues and Dilemmas* (Blackwell).

Swindells, H, Neaves, H, Kushner M and Skilbeck, R (1999) *Family Law and the Human Rights Act 1998* (Family Law).

Temple-Bone, G (2002) 'Experts, Witnesses and Procedures in Non-Accidental Injury' [2002] *Fam Law* 223.

Timms, J (1995) *Representing Children* (Sweet & Maxwell).

Tolson, R, QC (2002) *Care Plans and the Human Rights Act* (Family Law).

Tomison, AM and Tucci, J (1997) 'Emotional Abuse, the Hidden Form of Maltreatment', 8 *Issues in Child Prevention* (Australian Institute of Family Studies).

Townley, B (2001) 'The Cult Of Modernity' 17(4) *Financial Accountability & Management* 303–310.

Tunstill, J (1997) 'Family Support Clauses of the 1989 Children Act' in N Parton (ed), *Child Protection and Family Support* (Routledge).

Van Beuren, G (1995) *The International Law on the Rights of the Child* (Martinus Nijhoff).

Wade, HWR and Forsyth, CF (2000) *Administrative Law* (OUP).

Wall N and Hamilton, I (2000) *A Handbook for Expert Witnessesn in Children Act Cases* (Family Law).

Wall, Hon Mr Justice (1997) *Rooted Sorrows* First Plenary Session (Family Law).

Wattam, C and Woodward, C (1996) 'And do I abuse my Children? No! Learning about prevention from people who have experienced child abuse', in *Childhood Matters, Report of the National Commission of Inquiry into the Prevention of Child Abuse* (The Stationery Office).

Wilczynski, A (1994) 'The Incidence of Child Homicide: How Accurate are the Official Statistics?' *Journal of Clinical Forensic Medicine* 1, at pp 61–66.

Wilczynski and Morris (1993) 'Parents who Kill their Children' *Criminal Law Review* 31.

Williams, C (2000) 'A Controversial Expert Witness' [2000] *Fam Law* 175.

Williams, C (2002) 'The Practical Operation of the Children Act Complaints Procedure' [2002] *Child and Family Law Quarterly* 25.

Williams, F (1992) 'Women with Learning Difficulties are Women Too' in M Langan and L Day (eds) *Women, Oppression and Social Work: Issues in Anti-Discriminatory Practice* (Routledge).

Williams, F (1995) *Social Policy. A Critical Introduction* (Polity Press).

Williams, C and Jordan, H (1996) *The Children Act 1989 Complaints Procedures: A Study of Six Local Authority Areas* (University of Sheffield).

Wilson, K and Petrie, S (1998) 'No Place Like Home: Lessons Learned and Lessons Forgotten – The Children Act 1948' in 3 *Child and Family Social Work* 183–188.

Winter, D (2001) 'A Practical Guide to Chairing an Experts' Meeting' [2000] *Fam Law* 771.

Woolley, R and Evans, A (1955) 'Significance of Skeletal Lesions in Infants Resembling those of Traumatic Origin' *Journal of the American Medical Association*, at pp 158 and 539.

INDEX

References are to paragraph numbers.

Child Abuse